Signature THE OF GOD

Handwriting THE OF GOD

THE *Signature* OF GOD

THE *Handwriting* OF GOD

The Two Bestselling Works
Complete in One Volume

GRANT R. JEFFREY

INSPIRATIONAL PRESS

NEW YORK

First Inspirational Press edition published in 1999.

Inspirational Press
A division of BBS Publishing Corporation
386 Park Avenue South
New York, NY 10016

Inspirational Press is a registered trademark of
BBS Publishing Corporation.

This edition published by arrangement with
Frontier Research Publications, Inc.

Library of Congress Catalog Card Number: 99-71868

ISBN: 0-88486-255-0

Printed in the United States of America.

CONTENTS

THE
Signature
OF GOD

THE
Handwriting
OF GOD

The Signature of God

Astonishing Biblical Discoveries

Grant R. Jeffrey

Acknowledgement

The Signature of God is affectionately dedicated to my lovely wife Kaye, who is my partner in ministry and the joy of my life. She accompanies me in my research tours around the world, and shares my love of the Scriptures.

Many of the greatest scholars in the last two thousand years have explored the Scriptures and concluded that they are truly inspired by God. During the last few decades, I completed many research trips and communicated with bookstores throughout the world acquiring numerous old and often rare books written by these great men of God from past generations. These volumes contain tremendous archeological, historical and scientific evidence that confirms the inspiration and authority of the Word of God. I am greatly indebted to the work of countless Bible scholars who have labored to find the wealth of evidence that proves the inspiration of the Scriptures.

I have truly enjoyed completing the research and writing *The Signature of God*. My hope is that every reader will be as thrilled by this evidence proving the inspiration of the Bible as I was to uncover it as a researcher. Finally, if my book renews in the hearts of my readers a new love and appreciation for the Word of God, I will be well rewarded.

Table of Contents

"The Bible is the greatest of all the books ever penned by men; to study it diligently is the most worthy of all possible pursuits; to clearly understand what the Lord is saying to us through its pages is truly the most noble and the highest of my goals. The application to my heart, mind and spirit of the truths of the Word of God through the Holy Spirit's gift of understanding and my subsequent obedience to that revelation is my supreme purpose and duty."

Found in an old Bible in England

Introduction

Is there a God? Does my life have any meaning or does everything happen solely by chance? How can I find the truth about life and death? What will happen when I die? Is the Bible truly the "inspired" Word of God or is it just the philosophical writings of a group of ancient men? These questions occur to all of us at some point in our life. Our answers to these questions are vitally important because they affect our goals, our relationships, our peace of mind and, ultimately, our eternal destiny. The Bible claims to be the inspired Word of God and declares that its message is absolutely true. Therefore, it is of utmost importance that each of us determine for ourselves whether the Bible is truly the Word of God or not.

If the Bible is literally true and God does exist, then everyone of us will someday stand before God to be judged by Him as to our eternal destiny — heaven or hell. The Scriptures tell us that, following our death, we will give an account to God about how we have responded to Jesus Christ and His offer of personal salvation. On the other hand, if the Bible is untrue and God does not exist, then men are free to live as they please and experience the consequences of their choices only in this world. The philosophy of "Eat, drink and be merry for tomorrow we die" is one logical response if man lives in a universe that has no God and no purpose. The answer to this question, "Is the Bible truly the Word of God?" is of the greatest possible importance to every human being whether we admit it or not.

Our beliefs are the most important thing in our life because they determine the decisions and the course of our life. If we change our deeply held beliefs we will change our actions, our decisions, and the direction of our life.

Is there some way to determine the truth about God and the Bible? This book, *The Signature of God,* will examine incredible scientific discoveries that prove that the Bible is authoritative and inspired by God. Some people are content to follow a blind faith based on the religious convictions of their forefathers. However, many of us want to examine these matters for ourselves to determine the answer to these vital questions.

How Would God Reveal Himself to Mankind?

Let's conduct an experiment to examine the question of how God would reveal Himself to mankind if He truly exists. After creating this universe and mankind, how would God reveal Himself and His instructions to His creatures? He could choose to speak to every single one of the billions of humans in every generation, but that would be somewhat impractical. On the other hand, God could choose a number of men over a period of years and inspire them to faithfully record in writing His instructions for the rest of mankind. Obviously, the second option is the most practical.

However, there is another problem that God would face in revealing His will to mankind. How would God prove that the Bible was His legitimate revelation to mankind? The challenge would be how best to differentiate the true inspired Scriptures of God from the many other religious books produced by religious philosophers over the centuries. I believe the solution is quite obvious: God would authenticate His own true revelation by writing His signature on the pages of His Scriptures. This signature of God would consist of evidence, knowledge and phenomenon in the text of the Bible that no unaided human could possibly have written. In other words, the genuine Scriptures should contain supernatural evidence within its text that no one apart from a divine intelligence could create. Interestingly, the Scriptures do contain a direct statement from God that He had provided precisely this type of supernatural evidence as unmistakable proof of the Bible's inspiration and His divine powers to foretell future events through His prophets. Twenty-five centuries ago the prophet Isaiah recorded this amazing declaration from God: "Remember the former things of old: for I am God, and there is none else; I am God, and there is none like me, Declaring the end from the beginning, and from ancient times the things that are not yet done, saying, My counsel shall stand, and I will do all my pleasure" (Isaiah 46:9,10). In this passage God declared that fulfilled prophecy is an absolute proof that the Scriptures are inspired by the Lord because no one but God, whether human or Satan, can possibly predict precise events in the future. It is significant that not one of the hundreds of religious books outside of the Bible contain detailed predictions about future events. The reason is simple. Any attempt by humans to precisely predict the future always ends in abject failure. The writers of other religious books knew that they did not know what would occur in the future. They wisely refrained from exposing themselves to ridicule by creating what would have inevitably proved to be false predictions. God is the only one who knows the future as well as the past.

My thesis in *The Signature of God*, is that the Bible contains a number of fascinating proofs that absolutely authenticate the Scriptures as the inspired and authoritative Word of God. The evidence from hundreds of fulfilled prophecies form one of the strongest and most obvious proofs of divine inspiration. However, there are a number of other intriguing and undeniable proofs that only God could have inspired the ancient writers to record His message in the Scriptures.

The Bible Contains the Characteristics of a Genuine Revelation from God

How would God authenticate His message so that naturally skeptical men and women could be assured that the Scriptures were truly from God and not simply the speculations of religious philosophers? How would the Lord identify His presence, His divine nature and His commands to mankind and provide proof that this communication was truly from God?

1. The written revelation of God's nature and commands was progressively revealed step-by-step to a series of carefully chosen men over a period of sixteen centuries. The recipients were closely connected by race and faith to facilitate their gathering, assembling, preserving, and distributing God's written revelation throughout this time. The Lord chose the Jewish people, a small defined race that has maintained its identity over the centuries, as the faithful guardian of His written revelations.

9

2. Although His divine communications were transmitted by inspiration to individual Jews, it was recorded in a permanent written form capable of being examined and read by the writer's contemporaries as well as generations to follow.

3. These divine communications were sometimes accompanied by supernatural miracles to prove its origin from God.

4. This revelation contains internal evidence that proves that God is the ultimate author. The Bible includes information that could not have been written by men without divine inspiration.

5. The Bible contains thousands of detailed prophecies concerning events that were precisely fulfilled many years after the predictions were made. Their fulfillment proves that God inspired the Bible. No one but God can prophesy accurately.

6. God inspired biblical writers to record His profound wisdom and truth that transcend all of man's wisdom.

7. God's Holy Spirit supernaturally transforms the lives of millions who commit themselves to the Bible's revelation.

8. The primary purpose of the Bible is to reveal God's plan of salvation. However, whenever the Scriptures deals with history, archeology, nature, or science, it reveals advanced knowledge that is true and verifiable. Such biblical statements are far in advance of the knowledge of the time of the original human writer.

9. The Bible's wisdom, knowledge, and ethics clearly proclaim its supernatural origin to anyone who is truly seeking answers to life's profound questions. The wisest people of all cultures and times are committed to its truths.

10. The Scriptures contain advanced medical and sanitation knowledge that was thousands of years ahead of its time. This medical knowledge from the Bible has saved countless millions of lives of those who followed its divine precepts over the centuries since the Bible was written. In addition, its lifesaving commands still prove their worth in this century.

11. A careful examination of the names and numbers in the Bible's text reveals special mathematical designs and codes that are so complex that no human or super-computer could have produced these features. Many of these designs are not obvious and occur throughout a series of biblical books written by different biblical authors over several centuries. There is no human explanation for this phenomenon except for divine inspiration.

12. Recently, Jewish computer scientists discovered a series of incredible messages encoded at equally spaced intervals hidden beneath the Hebrew text of the first five books of the Bible, the Torah. God inspired the writers to unknowingly use specific words and letters to produce the most astonishing and incredibly complicated mathematical and letter codes ever produced. These features were carefully hidden from the eyes of everyone until this century and the development of mathematical and super-computer analysis. The discovery of these complex patterns of wheels within wheels provides compelling evidence that constitutes an unanswerable argument for the divine inspiration of the Bible. The scientists declared that these patterns are so complex that they could not have been produced by humans. Furthermore, while these incredible patterns exist in the Hebrew text of the Torah, no other apocryphal texts display this pattern, nor can they find it in any other Hebrew religious or secular texts. This incredible phenomenon provides overwhelming evidence that there is one inspired author of the Scriptures.

13. In normal human literature, authors naturally try to present themselves in the best light possible. However, the Bible presents these men "warts and all" revealing them often as weak, afraid, and lacking in wisdom. It runs contrary to human experience to find authors revealing themselves with such candor. Additionally, biblical revelation contains many intricate details and unintended coincidences in its stories that, while easily overlooked, prove the overall truthfulness of the historical accounts.

14. Although written by forty-four men over sixteen centuries, the complete text of the Bible reveals a coherent unity and progressive revelation from Genesis to Revelation that develops God's plan of redemption for mankind. The books of the Old Testament continuously point to the coming of a Messiah-King to redeem His people. The New Testament displays the fulfillment of these divine prophecies in the life, death, and resurrection of Jesus the Messiah. The unity of theology and the focus on the message of redemption throughout the Bible argues strongly that a single author created this text. The combined evidence presented in this book reveals that the single author who inspired the writers of the Bible was God.

Three thousand years ago King David, the great king of Israel, wrote these words revealing the nature of God's inspired Word:

"The law of the Lord is perfect, converting the soul: the testimony of the Lord is sure, making wise the simple. The statutes of the Lord are right, rejoicing the heart: the commandment of the Lord is pure, enlightening the eyes. The fear of the Lord is clean, enduring for ever: the judgments of the Lord are true and righteous altogether. More to be desired are they than gold, yea, than much fine gold: sweeter also than honey and the honeycomb. Moreover by them is thy servant warned: and in keeping of them there is great reward" (Psalm 19: 7–11).

The Inspiration of Scripture

The early Christians, Jewish scribes, and generations of Christian believers shared an unshakable conviction that the Scriptures contain the infallible, inspired, and authoritative words of God. The Bible itself claims that "All scripture is given by inspiration of God, and is profitable for doctrine, for reproof, for correction, for instruction in righteousness" (2 Timothy 3:16). The Greek word translated "inspired" literally means "God breathed" indicating the Lord's direct supervision of the writing by the biblical writer. The Bible claims that its words were not written by men in an ordinary manner but that God actually inspired men to record His direct words as His revelation to mankind for all time. Just as God created only one sun to provide light to our planet, He gave us only one book, the Bible, to enlighten our world spiritually.

Tragically, during this century many pastors, professors, and laymen have lost their faith and confidence that the Bible is truly the inspired and reliable Word of God. Dr. Kennedy, a Regius Professor of Classics at Cambridge University in the early decades of this century, warned of the relentless battle that was about to begin over the authority of the Bible. "The inspiration of Scriptures will be the last battle ground between the Church and the world." Unfortunately, many in our churches and seminaries today have abandoned this battlefield too easily and accepted defeat at the hands of skeptics that hate the authority of the Word of God. This widespread rejection of the truthfulness of the Scriptures reveals the folly of men who "have forsaken me the fountain of living waters, and hewed them out cisterns, broken cisterns" of vain philosophy (see Jeremiah 2:13). Jeremiah the prophet spoke these words twenty-five centuries ago.

The Bible itself declares in numerous passages that it is the inspired Word of God. The prophet Jeremiah declared, "Then the Lord put forth His hand and touched my mouth, and the Lord said to me: 'Behold, I have put My words in your mouth'" (Jeremiah 1:9). God confirmed that He directly inspired His servants, the prophets, to record His words and instructions "word for word." In the New Testament the apostle Peter declared that "Knowing this first, that no prophecy of Scripture is of any private interpretation, for prophecy never came by the will of man, but holy men of God spoke as they were moved by the Holy Spirit" (2 Peter 1:20,21). One of the strongest statements found in the Bible records the inspired words of Jesus Himself who declared, "The Scripture cannot be broken" (John 10:35).

We will examine the overwhelming scientific evidence that proves the inspiration and authenticity of the Bible as the Word of God. The evidence provided in *The Signature of God* will establish the credibility and authority of the Scriptures for both non-believers and Christians as a credible foundation for faith in God's inspired revelation. The book is divided into sections that will examine the various areas in which the Scriptures can be tested as to their authenticity and authority. The evidence we will explore includes the following areas:

1. Fascinating ancient inscriptions and manuscripts that prove the historical accuracy of the Scriptures.

2. Little known archeological discoveries that provide overwhelming confirmation of the biblical accounts, including the Tower of Babel and the Exodus.

3. The tremendously accurate scientific statements in the Bible that cannot be explained apart from God's inspiration.

4. The incredible fulfillment of prophecies in our generation that authenticate the Scriptures.

5. The staggering phenomenon of hidden codes and mathematical patterns found in the text of the Bible that could not have been produced by human intelligence.

6. Scriptural "coincidences" that confirm the divine inspiration of the Scriptures.

7. The phenomenon of the transformed character and lives of the writers of the Bible.

8. The unprecedented influence of the Bible on the lives of individuals, the culture, and history of the Western world.

While many of the topics we will explore in this book are fascinating in and of themselves, their true value for a Christian lies in their ability to confirm and illustrate the events, personalities, and statements of the Word of God. Alexander Knox once wrote about the relationship between human and sacred knowledge as follows: "If in the rills which trickle down amidst these intellectual Alps and Apennines, I could discern no connection with that river which maketh glad the city of God, I own that I should look upon them with as little interest as upon the rocky fragments through which they passed" (Quoted by Rev. Charles Forster in *Sinai Photographed*, London: Richard Bentley, 1862). As a researcher and writer I feel a tremendous responsibility to carefully check the accuracy of every statement because of the incredible importance of prophecy and scriptural truths. Those who write about the truths of the Scriptures are like the scribes of ancient Israel. The Scriptures declare that, "every scribe which is instructed unto the kingdom of heaven is like unto a man that is an householder, which bringeth forth out of his treasure things new and old" (Matthew 13:52). When we seek as writers to explore the wonderful truths of the Bible we also "bring forth out of his treasure things new and old" in our attempt to reveal the deeper truths of the Word of God.

The Accuracy of the Bible Manuscripts

Over the last four thousand years, Jewish scribes, and later, Christian scribes, were very careful to correctly copy and transmit the original manuscripts of sacred Scriptures without any significant error. The Jewish scribes who carefully copied out by hand the manuscripts of the Old Testament were called "Masoretic" from the Hebrew word for "wall" or "fence." Their extreme care in meticulously counting the letters of the Bible created a "fence around the Law" to defend its absolute accuracy. For example out of the 78,064 Hebrew letters in the Book of Genesis, they counted precisely 4,152 ה letters and 8,448 י letters. These sages were so precise in counting the exact number of letters in the Scriptures, that they were able to pinpoint the middle verse of Genesis which is: "And by thy sword shalt thou live, and shalt serve thy brother; and it shall come to pass when thou shalt have the dominion, that thou shalt break his yoke from off thy neck" (Genesis 27:40). When a scribe completed his copy, a master examiner would painstakingly count every individual letter to confirm that there were no errors in the newly copied manuscript. If an error was found, the mistaken copy was destroyed to prevent it ever being used as a master copy in the future.

As a proof of the incredible accuracy of this transmission through the centuries, consider the Masoretic and Yemenite translations of the Torah. Over a millennium ago, Yemenite Jews were separated from their brother Jews in the Middle East and Europe. Despite separate transmissions and copying of their Torah manuscripts, a thousand years later only nine Hebrew letters, out of some 304,805 letters in the Yemenite Torah manuscript, differ from the accepted Hebrew Masoretic text of the Torah. Not one of these nine variant letters in the Yemenite Torah changes the meaning of a significant word. This astonishing fact proves how exceptionally careful, over a thousand year period, Jewish scribes were in copying their original Torah manuscripts. God has carefully preserved the original text of His sacred Scriptures throughout the last three and a half thousand years, enabling us to have confidence that we still possess the inspired Word of God. The prophet Isaiah declared that the Word of God is eternal: "The grass withereth, the flower fadeth: but the word of our God shall stand for ever" (Isaiah 40:8). In the New Testament, Jesus Himself confirmed the indestructibility of His Holy Word. "For verily I say unto you, Till heaven and earth pass, one jot or one tittle shall in no wise pass from the law, till all be fulfilled" (Matthew 5:18).

Dr. Samuel Johnson's suggestion, "Keep your friendships in repair," was excellent advice regarding our relationship to our Bible as well as for our human relationships. Our relationship with the Word of God needs to be cared for just as much as our friendships. We need to respect God's Holy Word and handle it with care and love. We can enjoy the unchanging companionship of God expressed through His divine Word even when we are separated from human friends by distance or death. Our Bibles that show signs of wear and tear reveal our love and use of them. While our experiences, our possessions, and our relationships constantly undergo change throughout the years we can return again and again to the unchanging Word of God as a solid foundation for our faith that will never change. Unlike human friends who sometimes misunderstand or fail to communicate when we need them, our Bible will always be there to speak to our heart with God's words of wisdom, comfort, and love.

The Oldest Biblical Inscription Ever Found

Several years ago archeologists found more than one thousand items of jewelry and pottery in nine burial caves across the Hinnom Valley opposite the southern walls of the Old City of Jerusalem. The treasures from the past included two silver charms with remarkable biblical inscriptions. The cave where these charms were found was about nine hundred yards south of where Solomon's Temple stood three thousand years ago. While most of the burial caves had previously been cleaned out by grave robbers, these fascinating silver inscriptions were still there in 1979, as confirmed to the *Associated Press* by Tel Aviv archeologist Gabriel Barkay. The items of jewelry were composed of thin pieces of pure silver that were rolled up like tiny scrolls to be worn as charms around the neck. While part of the text was lost, the remaining portion revealed that these silver charms contained the oldest biblical inscription ever found. The remaining text recorded the priestly blessing from the Book of Numbers. It reads, "The Lord bless thee, and keep thee: The Lord make his face shine upon thee, and be gracious unto thee: The Lord lift up his countenance upon thee, and give thee peace" (Numbers 6:24–26). I had the privilege of examining this inscription in the Israel Museum. Incredibly, the archeologists found that this ancient biblical text was inscribed by some Jewish craftsman over 2,600 years ago in the seventh century before Christ, over four hundred years before the writing of most of the Dead Sea Scrolls.

It is fascinating to note that the Bible records only one statement made by God to the atheist or agnostic who declares, "There is no God." This sole declaration and verdict of God in response to those who deny His existence is, "The fool hath said in his heart, There is no God." (Psalm 14:1). When I attended school I used to engage in debates with atheists and agnostics about the existence of God. However, as I began to analyze the underlying attitude of those I debated I began to realize that debates of this kind were futile. Now when I get into a discussion with an atheist or agnostic I simply respond as follows: I will not debate you about whether or not God exists for the same reason that I would not debate someone about whether or not the world was round. I believe that those who claim

"There is no God," in the face of overwhelming evidence of design found throughout nature, are either fools or liars. Any person who honestly believes that all of the marvelous complexity of this universe simply happened by chance is a fool. If he is not a fool, yet still claims to believe that this incredibly complex universe is a result of random chance, then I must conclude that he is not being honest. In either case it is clearly a waste of time to argue the obvious.

The wonders of creation reveal God's awesome creative power to anyone whose eyes are open to see the truth. God's marvelous providence reveals His wisdom; God's Law revealed in the Old Testament shows us His great justice; the Gospels reveal His overwhelming love for mankind through the person of Jesus Christ.

The Supreme Value of the Bible

Sir Walter Scott, the brilliant author of more than sixty popular books, was finally approaching his moment of death. As he lay on his deathbed, Scott asked his son-in-law, Lockhart, to bring him "the book" from his huge library. When Lockhart naturally asked, "Which book, Sir Walter?" Scott answered, "There is only one book," pointing to the Holy Bible. In this final deathbed conversation, Sir Walter Scott, one of the greatest writers of his day, correctly assessed the supreme value of the Holy Scriptures far above the other great books in his large library, including his own classics.

The most important event in the history of man is the life, death, and resurrection of Jesus Christ. The most important fact in the life of mankind is the reality of God and His divine revelation to us through His Holy Word. The most important decision in the life of any human is the choice they must make in regard to their personal faith in Jesus Christ. Another great man, Abraham Lincoln, wrote: "I believe that the Bible is the best gift God has ever given to man. All the good from the Savior of the world is communicated to us through the book."

The Pony Express Bible

The history of the Pony Express forms a fascinating part of the history of the American West. These dedicated and resourceful riders carried the mail from St. Joseph, Missouri, over nineteen hundred miles through dangerous Indian country, to Sacramento, California. The Pony Express acquired five hundred of the strongest and fastest horses the company could find. Incredibly, forty brave men rode these magnificent horses in relays with each man riding fifty miles to the next station. Using four relays per day, the Pony Express riders travelled up to two hundred miles a day. A letter could be delivered in relays covering the complete nineteen hundred miles in only ten days.

In order to cut down on any unnecessary weight the riders would use the lightest saddles made, with very small, flat leather bags holding the mail. Amazingly, to cut down on the weight the riders carried no rifles. Mail carried by the Pony Express was written on very thin paper. However, the postage rate was $5 an ounce (equal to $200 per letter in today's currency). The managers of the Pony Express believed that the Holy Scriptures were so important that they presented a special full size Pony Express Bible to each rider when they signed up to join this unusual company. Surprisingly, despite their overwhelming concern for reducing the weight of their rider's equipment, every one of the riders carried a full size Pony Express Bible as part of his regular gear.

Stanley and Livingstone

The famous Christian missionary and explorer David Livingstone had disappeared without a trace on a trip into the unknown regions of central Africa. The last reliable news of his expedition reported that Livingstone was sick, without supplies and deserted by his guides. Many in Europe gave him up as lost forever after more than a year with no news from Africa. However, a small group of supporters in London believed that they must launch a rescue mission in an attempt to save Scotland's finest son. This group outfitted the brilliant explorer, Henry M. Stanley, to mount an expedition to find Livingstone. Stanley embarked on an arduous journey across the jungles and rivers of the unknown continent of Africa in his valiant attempt to locate David Livingstone. When he commenced his journey Stanley carried extensive baggage that included several cases containing seventy-three of his favorite hard-bound books weighing one hundred and eighty pounds. As he and his group of African carriers began to succumb to fatigue after three hundred miles of arduous travel through the jungle, Stanley reluctantly began to abandon or burn his precious books to light fires each night. As they continued through the jungle, Stanley's library dwindled in size until there was only one book left, his precious Bible. With God's supernatural assistance Stanley finally found the great man of God and greeted him with the famous words, "Dr. Livingstone, I presume?" The two explorers shared their deep personal faith in Jesus Christ. Livingstone told Stanley about the wonderful conversions of many tribes to faith in Christ although they had previously engaged in cannibalism. When he returned from his incredible journey Stanley reported that he had read his beloved Bible through from Genesis to Revelation three times during his long journey.

As you read *The Signature of God* I hope you will experience the same thrill of discovery and wonder that I have felt as the Lord led me to research the incredible evidence for the inspiration of the Scriptures that I share in this book. I hope this book will be a great resource for pastors and families to help them provide those who are seeking the truth about the Bible with the latest exciting research proving the authority of the Word of God. My prayer is that the information I share in these chapters will enable many readers to restore their confidence in the Bible as God's inspired Word. Then, they can confidently study the Scriptures knowing that God has provided the proof that the Bible is truly the Word of God because the evidence of His signature appears throughout its pages. The apostle Paul wrote to all Christians as follows, "All scripture is given by inspiration of God, and is profitable for doctrine, for reproof, for correction, for instruction in righteousness" (2 Timothy 3:16).

1

The Battle for the Bible

Our modern world has departed so far from the religious faith that governed the founding fathers of both the United States and Canada that it is almost impossible for the average citizen to recognize the vast gulf that exists between the beliefs of our modern world and the beliefs of those who founded our nations. The colonists who came to North America centuries ago were determined to escape the religious oppression of Europe. They wanted to create a free nation on this continent where men and women could worship God freely without restriction. The founders of the United States of America determined to create an educational system based on Christianity and the inspired Word of God. A close examination of the lives and the writings of the framers of the American Constitution clearly reveals that their intent was to create in America a "freedom for religious expression; not a freedom from religious expression."

The writer Frederick Rudolph wrote in his book, *The American College and University,* that within a generation of their landing on Plymouth Rock the original Puritan settlers laid the foundations of an educational system dedicated to training "a learned clergy and a lettered people." These Christians created Harvard College in 1636 as a Christian college dedicated to upholding the truths of the Bible. In fact, during the first century of Harvard University's existence, every single one of its professors was a minister of the Gospel. The initial Charter of Harvard College declares unashamedly, "Everyone shall consider the main end of his life and studies to know Jesus Christ which is eternal life." It has been calculated that 87 percent of the first one hundred and nineteen colleges built in America were established by Christians to educate young people in their faith. Most major universities in the eastern United States were created as Christian institutions of learning — including Harvard, Princeton, Yale, and Columbia. More than twenty-five percent of the 1855 graduating class of these universities became ministers of the Gospel.

Although our society is increasingly agnostic, millions still seek the truth by studying the Word of God. The *Dallas Times Herald* in October 24, 1983, found in one study that over forty-three million Americans are involved in regular Bible study groups (Roy Abraham Varghese, *The Intellectuals Speak Out About God,* [Chicago: Regenery Gateway, Inc., 1984], p.xxii–xxiii).

The Attempt to Destroy the Bible

Throughout history there has been a continual and relentless conflict between acceptance of God and an open rebellion against His rule. This continuing struggle can be correctly described as a tale of two cities: the ongoing war between the City of God and the City of Man. For two thousand years the battleground has revolved around the Bible. Satan hates the Word of God because it reveals the truth about Jesus Christ, our hope of salvation and the eternal destiny facing each of us between heaven and hell. A close examination of the history of Christianity over the last two thousand years reveals that the greatest attacks that occurred during the first centuries following Christ came from the pagans outside the Church. However, during the last one hundred and fifty years, the most effective enemies of the Cross arose from those false Christians who profess to follow Christ while denying the authority of the Bible and His identity as the Son of God.

The Roman emperors did everything in their power to destroy the new faith of Christianity by burning both Christians and the manuscripts of the Bible throughout their vast empire. As an example, in A.D. 303, the Emperor Diocletian issued an official command to kill Christians and burn their sacred books. Professor S. L. Greenslade, the editor of the *Cambridge History of the Bible,* recorded the history of this persecution: "an imperial letter was everywhere promulgated, ordering the razing of the churches to the ground and the destruction by fire of the Scriptures, and proclaiming that those who held high positions would lose all civil rights, while those in households, if they persisted in their profession of Christianity, would be deprived of their liberty" (Professor Stanley L. Greenslade, *Cambridge History of the Bible*, [Cambridge University Press, 1963]).

However, the Christian's enthusiasm and dedication to the Scriptures in those first centuries following Christ motivated them to produce numerous manuscripts that were widely copied, distributed, and translated throughout the empire. The New Testament is the most widely quoted book in history from the moment of its writing by the apostles until today. Ignatius, the Bishop of Antioch in A.D. 70, the minister responsible for several churches in Syria, quoted extensively from the New Testament in his writings. Clement, the Bishop of Rome in A.D. 70 (mentioned by Paul in Philippians 4:3) also quoted extensively from the New Testament only forty years after Christ's resurrection. Historians have recovered almost one hundred thousand manuscripts and letters from the first few centuries of this era that were composed by Christian writers. Their love and devotion to the inspired Scriptures was so overwhelming that these letters contain an enormous number of direct quotations from the New Testament. This was the primary way that the truths of Scripture were transmitted throughout the Roman Empire, despite the rampant persecution and burning of Bibles by the Roman emperors. If the Roman government had been successful in totally destroying every New Testament throughout the Roman Empire, the survival of these one hundred thousand letters from early Christians guaranteed the survival of the Word of God. These numerous letters by the early Christians contain an astonishing 98 percent of the New Testament. In other words, even if the Romans had succeeded in destroying the New Testament, we could still reliably reconstruct 98 percent of the New Testament text from these numerous quotations. This fact shows the absolute integrity of the text of the New Testament as it exists today as well as demonstrating the passion the early Christians possessed for the Holy Word of God.

Despite the efforts of the pagan emperors to burn every copy of the Bible during the first three centuries after Christ, Christianity became the official state religion of the Roman Empire following the conversion of the Emperor Constantine in A.D. 325. Eventually, however, the medieval church fell into apostasy from biblical truth and compromised with the kings and aristocracy of Europe. Over the centuries, laws were issued that made possession of the Bible illegal for any Christian layman. During those centuries of the Inquisition in Europe there were appalling penalties, including burning at the stake, for anyone found to possess a copy of the Scriptures. During the Dark Ages even priests in the medieval church of Rome were usually unable to read the Latin manuscripts of the Bible for themselves. As a result of their ignorance of the Bible they were unable to compare the false doctrines that were widespread in the medieval Roman church against the doctrines of the Word of God. Few Christians today realize that, in Italy, it was illegal to possess a Bible until 1870 due to the hatred of apostate church officials for the truth of the Scriptures.

John Lea reported in his book, *The Greatest Book in the World*, that a French king once proposed to his court that they should launch a new wave of persecution against the Christians within his realm. However, a wise counselor and general replied to the king's proposal in these words, "Sire, the Church of God is an anvil that has worn out many hammers." (John Lea, *The Greatest Book in the World*, [Philadelphia: 1929]). The enemies of the Bible have attacked the Scriptures without respite for almost two thousand years. However, the Bible still stands unshaken as the most widely read and published book in history, while the philosophies of the enemies of the Scriptures are buried with their spokesmen. The survival of the Scriptures against these unrelenting attacks by Satan provides irrefutable evidence that it is truly inspired by God.

Finally, after almost a thousand years of virtual spiritual darkness, the Protestant Reformation under the leadership of Martin Luther opened the floodgates of biblical truth to the European population through the translation and printing of the Bible in contemporary languages such as German, French, and English. The revolution in religion and spiritual freedom surpassed anything ever seen in the history of mankind. The spiritual rallying cry of the Reformation was *Sola Scripture* meaning "solely Scripture." In opposition to the medieval Roman church's position that church councils, tradition and papal decrees could supersede the teaching of Scripture, the Reformers insisted that every doctrine taught in the Church must be drawn from the clear teaching of the Bible. This absolute reliance on the actual words of the inspired Word of God placed the Reformation on the strongest possible spiritual foundation. The stronghold of Scripture motivated the Reformers to preach the Gospel of Jesus Christ everywhere, leading to the greatest influx of souls into the Kingdom of God in the history of the Church.

While most people in our Western culture in past centuries accepted the truth of God's existence and His creation of the universe, a growing number of people in our modern world deny the existence of God and His creative role. Those who accept evolution as the answer to how human life was formed have rejected the concept of a divine creator who created this earth in all of its awesome complexity. In addition, large numbers of people today totally reject the inspiration and authority of the Scriptures in the false belief that the Bible has somehow been proven to be "full of errors and contradictions." The unrelenting attack by agnostic scholars and the media on the authority of the Bible during the last century is unprecedented in Western history. The attack launched on the accuracy and reliability of the Scriptures and the resurrection of Jesus Christ has come not only from academics outside the Church but also from countless pastors and theologians who have lost their personal confidence and faith in the authority of the Word of God.

Professor E. B. Pusey, in his brilliant defense of the authenticity of the Book of Daniel against the higher critics of his day, wrote about the continual attacks on the inspiration of Scripture from those who claimed to be ministers of the Gospel: "The faith can receive no real injury except from its defenders. Against its assailants, those who wish to be safe, God protects. If the faith shall be (God forbid!) destroyed in England, it will not be by open assailants, but by those who think that they defend it, while they have themselves lost it. So it was in Germany. Rationalism was the product, not of the attacks on the Gospel but of its weak defenders. Each generation, in its controversies with unbelief, conceded more of the faith, until at last it was difficult to see what difference there was between assailants and defenders. Theology was one great graveyard; and men were disputing over a corpse, as if it had life. The salt had 'lost its savour.' The life was fled" (Dr. E. B. Pusey, *The Prophet Daniel*, [Plymouth: Devonport Society, 1864], p. xxv, xxvi).

There are few things in life so spiritually ineffective or ridiculous as a preacher or seminary professor who has lost his faith in the authority and inspiration of the Scriptures, yet continues to preach or teach about the Bible. People who refuse to accept the authority of the Word of God will never learn the truths of life and death from such unbelieving teachers. Jesus Christ Himself declared: "If they hear not Moses and the prophets, neither will they be persuaded, though one rose from the dead" (Luke 16:31).

The Loss of Faith by Religious Leaders

After a century and a half of continuous assault on the authority and reliability of the Scriptures many pastors and seminary professors have lost their confidence in the inspiration of the Word of God. The sociologist Jeffrey Hadden completed a survey of the beliefs of over ten thousand Protestant ministers in 1965 for the Danforth Foundation. These ten thousand mainline Protestant pastors from six major denominations were asked these questions:

1. Was Jesus born of a virgin?
2. Was Jesus the Son of God?
3. Is the Bible the Inspired Word of God?

More than half of these pastors could not answer "Totally Agree" to these questions. A majority of the pastors surveyed qualified their answers to these questions indicating either partial agreement or disagreement. Significantly, a century ago, the vast majority of pastors would have answered "Totally Agree" to these questions.

Is there any doubt as to why many church leaders and denominations are spiritually weak and without conviction? When pastors and teachers lose their faith in the Word of God, they would be more honest if they openly left the ministry rather than lead a whole generation of laymen in their congregations to an eternity without Christ and without hope of salvation based on the Word of God.

The widespread agnosticism and atheism in our modern government, media, universities, and seminaries has resulted in the moral collapse of our society. The philosopher Thomas Hobbes wisely described the inevitable effects on our society of the growing agnosticism and the gradual abandonment of the authority of Scriptures in the life of our nations. Hobbes described the terrible results that would follow the loss of a national religious faith in Christ in these insightful words. "No arts, no letters, no society, and which is worst of all, continual fear and danger of violent death, and the life of man solitary, poor, nasty, brutish and short." Tragically, the results of our national apostasy were accurately predicted in his writings. In 1830 the government of France sent a well respected judge, Alexis de Tocqueville, to study the society, the beliefs, and the prisons of the

United States of America to find out why there was so little crime and so few prisons. After several years of study he wrote a celebrated book called *The Democracy of the United States* in 1840. Alexis de Tocqueville wrote about the reason for America's greatness as a nation and the real reason for her low crime rate at that time. "I sought for the greatness of the United States in her commodious harbors, her ample rivers, her fertile fields, and boundless forests — and it was not there. I sought for it in her rich mines, her vast world commerce, her public schools system and in her institutions of higher learning — and it was not there. I looked for it in her democratic Congress and her matchless Constitution — and it was not there. Not until I went into the churches of America and heard her pulpits flame with righteousness did I understand the secret of her genius and power. America is great because America is good, and if America ever ceases to be good, America will cease to be great!"

A century and a half later, America has publicly abandoned the Bible as the moral anchor of our society and education. It should surprise no one that, after decades of teaching our children that there are no absolute rights and wrongs, we face an appalling breakdown in public morality and rising levels of crime. President Andrew Jackson shared the same opinion as Alexis de Tocqueville about the central position of the Scriptures to the life of his nation. As he lay on his deathbed President Jackson pointed to the Bible on the table by his bed and said to his companion, "That Book, Sir, is the rock on which our Republic rests."

The Authenticity of the Old Testament

Dr. Robert Dick Wilson was the professor of Semitic Philology at Princeton Seminary for many decades. He was an expert in forty-five languages and dialects. He was considered the greatest expert alive in the Hebrew Old Testament. Dr. Wilson contributed numerous scholarly works confirming the accuracy of the Old Testament throughout his career of fifty years. His brilliant criticism of errors and weaknesses in the positions of the higher critical school were so powerful they were never answered. The liberal critics simply ignored his devastating arguments against their dismissal of the Bible's accuracy. Over the years a series of authorities, including R. D. Wilson, James Orr, Oswald Allis, and Edward J. Young, thoroughly refuted the anti-Bible claims of the higher critics. Dr. Wilson summarizes the situation as follows: "In conclusion, we claim that the assaults upon the integrity and trustworthiness of the Old Testament along the line of language have utterly failed. The critics have not succeeded in a single line of attack in showing that the diction and style of any part. of the Old Testament are not in harmony with the ideas and aims of writers who lived at, or near, the time when the events occurred that are recorded in the various documents. . . . We boldly challenge these Goliaths of ex-cathedra theories to come down into the field of ordinary concordances, dictionaries, and literature, and fight a fight to the finish on the level ground of the facts and the evidence" (Dr. Robert Dick Wilson, *A Scientific Investigation of the Old Testament*, [Chicago: Moody Press, 1959], p. 130).

Old Testament Statements Regarding its Inspiration

The Scriptures themselves clearly and repeatedly declare that the Bible is inspired by God. Moses closed his ministry with this command to the Children of Israel affirming inspiration: "Set your hearts unto all the words which I testify among you this day, which ye shall command your children to observe to do, all the words of this law" (Deuteronomy 32:46). The Book of Proverbs also states: "Every word of God is pure: he is a shield unto them that put their trust in him. Add thou not unto his words, lest he reprove thee, and thou be found a liar" (Proverbs 30:5,6).

The Authority of the Old Testament Confirmed by Jesus Christ

One of the most important evidences regarding the accuracy and inspiration of the Old Testament Scriptures is that both Jesus Christ and the apostles absolutely confirm the authority of these writings as being inspired directly by God. Jesus Christ declared that "the scripture cannot be broken" (John 10:35). In another passage Jesus stated, "And it is easier for heaven and earth to pass, than one tittle of the law to fail" (Luke 16:17). In addition, the Lord confirmed that Moses was the writer of the first five books of the Law (Luke 24:27; John 5:46,47). Christ also stated that Isaiah was the author of the Book of Isaiah (Matthew 13:14, citing Isaiah 6:9,10). One of Jesus' most significant statements was His declaration that Daniel had written the Book of Daniel (Matthew 24:15) thereby contradicting those critics who claim that Daniel was written by someone pretending to prophecy in 165 B.C. Jesus spoke of Adam, Eve and their son Abel as real personalities (Matthew 19:4,5; 23:35). In Luke

17:26,28, Jesus referred to both Noah and Lot. According to John 8:56–58, the Lord confirmed the Bible's narrative about Abraham. Perhaps, most importantly, Jesus confirmed the accuracy of the Genesis account about the creation (Mark 10:6–9) and the worldwide flood (Matthew 24:37–39).

Christ affirmed his belief in the Old Testament miracles when He talked about the supernatural judgment on Sodom and Gomorrah (Luke 17:29) including the death of Lot's wife (v. 32). In other passages Jesus described the feeding of manna to the Israelites during the Exodus (John 6:32), and the miraculous healing of the serpent's bites (John 3:14). The Gospels record Christ's confirmation of the miraculous events in the life of Elijah and Elisha (Luke 4:25–27), and the supernatural swallowing of Jonah by a great fish (Matthew 12:39,40). Jesus settled all doubts of Christians in His declaration: "For verily I say unto you, Till heaven and earth pass, one jot or one tittle shall in no wise pass from the law, till all be fulfilled" (Matthew 5:18). Jesus Christ rebuked Satan by quoting Deuteronomy 8:3: "Man doth not live by bread only, but by every word that proceedeth out of the mouth of the Lord doth man live" (Matthew 4:4; also Luke 4:4). In His discussion with the Pharisees, Jesus won His argument based on the presence of a single word in the Scriptures. The Lord asked the Jewish scholars, "If David then call him Lord, how is he his son?" (Matthew 22:45).

In light of these absolute confirmations by Jesus Christ of historical events and miraculous occurrences in the Old Testament, it is astonishing that some preachers and Christians dare to deny the truthfulness of these biblical events. Those who accept Jesus Christ as truly God should find it quite easy to accept His divine verdict that the Old Testament is absolutely truthful and inspired directly by God. If I accept Jesus as my God and Savior; then I will accept His confirmation that I can safely trust in the authority of the Old Testament.

Statements from the Apostles

The apostles constantly affirmed verbal inspiration. The apostle Paul described the Scriptures as the very "oracles of God" (Romans 3:2; Hebrews 5:12). Later, in Galatians 3:16, Paul said: "Now to Abraham and his seed were the promises made. He saith not, And to seeds, as of many; but as of one, And to thy seed, which is Christ." Notice that in this passage, Paul based his entire argument to his readers on the presence of a single word and noted the fact that the word was the singular word "seed" and not the plural word "seeds." Paul's doctrine regarding the inspiration of Scripture is absolutely clear: "All scripture is given by inspiration of God, and is profitable for doctrine, for reproof, for correction, for instruction in righteousness: That the man of God may be perfect, thoroughly furnished unto all good works" (2 Timothy 3:16,17).

The Early Date of the Writing of the New Testament

It is now acknowledged, even by many liberal scholars, that the New Testament Gospels and Epistles were written and widely circulated throughout the Christian communities of the Roman Empire within forty or fifty years of the events they describe. This fact is of overwhelming importance in verifying the absolute historical accuracy of these documents. Thousands of people who witnessed the events of Jesus Christ's life, teaching, death, and resurrection were still alive when the disciples composed and distributed the Gospels and Paul's Epistles to the various churches. These carefully copied manuscripts were read in hundreds of Christian assemblies every Sunday, by millions of Gentile and Jewish believers, from the cold northern shores of Britain to the hot deserts of Syria and North Africa. In addition to Christian testimony about the enormous number of new believers, even the enemies of Christ, such as the Roman historians Tacitus and Pliny, acknowledged that there were vast multitudes of Christians throughout the Roman Empire.

If the New Testament actually contained factual errors regarding the events of Christ's life, His teaching, or the miracles He performed, there would have been an enormous split within the early Church as witnesses to these historical events would have debated and contested any inaccurate historical records. Although the Christians were subject to the most terrifying tortures and martyrdom conceivable, not one of them ever declared that the Gospel account of Jesus Christ was in error. If they had denied the reality of the life, death, and resurrection of Jesus, the Roman judges would have been delighted to set them free. Rome would have widely published such a denial of the Gospels' statements about Jesus Christ's death and resurrection. However, despite the fact that a large number of Roman official records and a much larger number of Christian writings have survived till today, we cannot find evidence of a single eyewitness to these Gospel events ever denying their truthfulness. This fact is of outstanding importance in assessing the reliability and truth-fulness of the Gospel records as any judge or lawyer would confirm.

The early Church had many enemies among the pagans. During the second and third century of this era some pagans and gnostics infiltrated the Church. In response to the warnings of our Lord and the apostle Paul about false teachers and "teachers having itching ears," the Church leadership was vigilant in detecting and rejecting any spurious writings that counterfeited the genuine New Testament inspired writings. As an example, two important early Church writers, Tertullian and Jerome, tell us that a presbyter from Asia [Turkey] published a counterfeit epistle that he claimed the apostle Paul had written. Church leaders instantly instigated an ecclesiastical trial to examine this claim. They subsequently convicted this counterfeiter and repudiated his spurious forgery. Their rejection of this forgery was widely published to other churches throughout the empire. Is it probable that people who were so vigilant to establish the truth of the Gospel and to preserve the genuine Scriptures would blindly accept the New Testament record of Christ's miracles and resurrection unless they had overwhelming proof of its truthfulness? When you consider that millions of these converts died horribly as martyrs rather than deny their Lord it stands to reason that they were convinced with all their mind, soul, and spirit that the Gospels spoke the truth about Jesus Christ as the Son of God.

The Universal Distribution of the New Testament

All scholars acknowledge that the New Testament was widely copied and translated into many other languages during the first few decades following the resurrection of Christ. Numerous ancient manuscripts of the New Testament have survived in different languages. These manuscripts confirm that there were no differences in the text regarding doctrine or factual matters. The libraries of Europe and North America contain many ancient copies and translations of the Greek New Testament, including the Syriac, Egyptian, Arabic, Ethiopian, Armenian, Persian, Gothic, Slavonic, and Latin translations. This widespread publication assisted greatly in the effective distribution of the Gospels and Epistles into "Judea, and Samaria and the uttermost parts of the earth." In addition, the widespread copying and translation of the Scriptures made it absolutely impossible for anyone to corrupt the legitimate text of the New Testament by introducing an invented story of a miracle or a false doctrine into a counterfeit copy. Due to their overwhelming love of the Scriptures, the early Christians constantly quoted from these texts.

If anyone was so foolish as to attempt to introduce a spurious text with an invented story, miracle, or doctrine, this counterfeit alteration would have been instantly detected and denounced throughout the hundreds of churches. Once the original Greek manuscript of the New Testament was translated faithfully into Hebrew, Syriac, Egyptian, Coptic, Latin, and other languages between A.D. 60–70, it would have been impossible for anyone, even a corrupt high Church official, to impose a counterfeit text on the Christians. A counterfeit text's alterations would be compared against the countless other widely available genuine Greek manuscripts and the additional translations in other languages. Any textual differences would instantly identify a counterfeit text as a forgery. The profound love of the saints for the New Testament during the first centuries of the Church age assure us that they were vigilant in their defense and preservation of the integrity of the Scriptures. This fact allows us to have total confidence that we possess today the same New Testament that was given to the Church by the inspired writers.

The Survival of the Bible

The famous French writer Voltaire, a skeptic, often wrote expressing his contempt for the Bible and Christianity. He had an intense hatred of the Word of God because it reminded him that he would someday stand before the Great White Throne to be judged by Almighty God. His sinful arrogance expressed itself in his utter contempt for the Scriptures and Christians who followed the words of Jesus Christ. Voltaire wrote a prediction about the future of the Bible more than two centuries ago from his library in Paris: "I will go through the forest of the Scriptures and girdle all the trees, so that in one hundred years Christianity will be but a vanishing memory." Despite Voltaire's prediction, there are more Christians alive today than any other time in history. Those who study the statistics have found that more than 85,000 people accept Jesus Christ as their personal Savior every day around the world. Ironically, despite Voltaire's confident prediction about the imminent death of Christianity, his library, in which he wrote his false prediction, was acquired years later by the British and Foreign Bible Society. His library was soon filled from floor to ceiling with thousands of copies of the Bible he hated, but could not destroy (David John Donnan, *Treasury of the Christian World*, [New York: Harper Brothers, 1953]).

Despite the opposition of Satan and his followers to the Scriptures the Bible remains triumphant as the most widely read, published, and influential book in the history of man. The truths found in its pages have changed the lives and destiny of untold billions. The Scriptures have profoundly influenced the course of history for nations and empires. When an ambassador of an African prince was introduced to Queen Victoria, the greatest queen of England, he asked her the question his monarch had requested he present to her. "What is the secret of your country's power and success throughout the world?" Queen Victoria picked up the Bible on her table and answered, "Tell your prince that this book is the secret of England's greatness."

2

Incredible Evidence From Historical Documents

The Incredible Accuracy of the Old Testament

Although the Bible has been relentlessly attacked by unbelieving scholars for more than a century it still stands as the most accurate and authoritative book ever written, Despite the continuing media assaults on the Bible's claim to be a supernatural revelation from God, evidence from historical inscriptions and manuscripts discovered in the last century proves that the Word of God is inspired. Although we will never be able to verify every one of the thousands of historical personalities, events, and places recorded in the Bible, the overwhelming evidence presented in this chapter will provide any intelligent reader with the confidence that we have established the credibility of the greatest book ever written.

My library has hundreds of books containing accounts from numerous historians of the ancient world including Herodotus, the so-called "Father of History." However, a Roman historian titled Herodotus "the Father of Lies" in recognition of the factual inaccuracy of his fanciful accounts of the past. Any examination of these secular histories reveals a multitude of gross errors regarding details such as dates, locations, people, sequence and duration of events. To state that ancient secular historians were casual in their approach to accuracy is an understatement. An example of this casual attitude regarding factual accuracy is revealed in Herodotus's own history where he wrote, "My business is to record what people say. But I am by no means bound to believe it — and that may be taken to apply to this book as a whole" (*Mysteries of the Bible*, New York: The Reader's Digest Association, Inc. 1988, p. 107). However, when we closely examine the evidence found in the Bible we discover that the writers are extremely careful and accurate in their recording of historical facts. The writers of the Bible were contemporaries of the times and events they recorded. A comparison of the discoveries during the last century of historical and archeological research with the statements of the Bible reveals forty-one different kings of Israel and surrounding nations that are confirmed by contemporary inscriptions and documents. The whole body of ancient literature does not reveal a single report from secular historians that can be confirmed by archeology with the same degree of confidence by which we can prove thousands of biblical statements, personalities, and events.

In the last one-hundred-and-fifty years many critics of the Bible upheld the so-called Documentary Hypothesis that denied the biblical claim that Moses was the author of Genesis and the rest of the first five books of the Bible. They claimed that the different names for God that appeared in Genesis (Elohim, Jehovah, Adonai, etc.) indicated that five different authors composed portions of this book. They believed that an editor later recompiled the five records into one book approximately six hundred years before Christ. However, this widely taught theory is absurd when you carefully consider the history of the Jewish people. Remember that in a court of law a judge and jury place great weight on evidence that is acknowledged to be factual by both sides, the prosecutor and the defense, for the simple reason that if both sides agree, it is extremely likely that it is true.

The Jewish people are known for their brilliance and their willingness to debate at great length any issue involving their religion and history. Ask yourself if it is credible that the Jews would universally adopt the complicated and onerous religious regulations of Passover, Pentecost, and the Feast of Tabernacles unless their forefathers had begun celebrating these feasts to commemorate the miraculous events of the Exodus. Obviously, such national festivals were transmitted from generation to generation through the ages. How could this happen if the original miraculous deliverance from

Egypt had never occurred? Moses, the great Lawgiver of Israel, reminded the Jews that they had personally witnessed with their own
eyes these miracles and supernatural acts by God to deliver them
from the bondage of Egypt. "Know today that I do not speak with
your children, who have not known and who have not seen the chas-
tening of the Lord your God, His greatness and His mighty hand
and His outstretched arm — His signs and His acts which He did in
the midst of Egypt, to Pharaoh king of Egypt, and to all his land;
what He did to the army of Egypt, to their horses and their chariots:
how He made the waters of the Red Sea overflow them as they pursued you, and how the Lord has destroyed them to this day; what
He did for you in the wilderness until you came to this place; . . .
but your eyes have seen every great act of the Lord which He did"
(Deuteronomy 11:2–7).

If an unknown editor had created the five books of the Torah a
thousand years later and tried to get the Jewish people, scattered in
diverse communities from Iran to Spain, to universally adopt these
festivals of Passover, etc., when no one had ever celebrated them before, he would have been denounced as an impostor. At the very
least, Jewish rabbis and sages would have conducted strong debates
opposing the introduction of such a book that no one had ever seen
before. However, there is no record whatsoever that such debates or
discussions ever occurred. The critics' theory of an unknown editor
creating the Torah is absurd. The Samaritans were a group of
colonists imported into the West Bank of Israel around 700 B.C., by
the Assyrians to repopulate the area after they took the Israelite population of the ten northern tribes in chains back to Assyria (modern
Iraq-Iran). One of the oldest manuscripts in the world is the Samaritan Pentateuch, an ancient copy of the first five books of the Law,
which contained virtually every single word found in the Hebrew
text of the Torah. From the moment the Samaritan colonists moved
into the center of Israel, they found themselves in opposition to the
Jewish people who returned from the Babylonian Captivity, which
continued into the time of Christ's ministry. Although the Samaritans accepted the five books of the Torah as genuine, their own version was jealously guarded and preserved for thousands of years
until today. Why would the Samaritans, who hated the Jews, accept
the historical accuracy and authority of the Torah of the Jews if they
knew these books were not authoritative and true? The fact that the
Samaritans, the enemies of the Jews, agree with them in accepting

An illustration of the Israelites Leaving Egypt

the genuineness of the five Books of Moses should prove to any unbiased mind that we have the original unaltered writings of Moses,
the great Lawgiver of Israel.

In addition, critics denied that Moses could have written his account in the fifteenth century before Christ because they claimed
that writing was not yet invented. However, the discovery by archeologists of numerous ancient written inscriptions, including the famous black stele containing the Laws of Hammurabi written before
2000 B.C., have conclusively proven that writing was widespread for
many centuries before the time of Moses.

The Greek historian Herodotus discussed the Exodus in his
book *Polymnia*, section c. 89: "This people [the Israelites], by their
own account, inhabited the coasts of the Red Sea, but migrated
thence to the maritime parts of Syria, all which district, as far as
Egypt, is denominated Palestine." It is interesting to note that
Strabo, a pagan historian and geographer who was born in 54 B.C.,
also confirmed the history of the Jews and their escape from Egypt
under the leadership of Moses. He wrote, "Among many things believed respecting the temple and inhabitants of Jerusalem, the report most credited is that the Egyptians were the ancestors of the
present Jews. An Egyptian priest named Moses, who possessed a
portion of the country called lower Egypt, being dissatisfied with

the institutions there, left it and came to Judea with a large body of people who worshipped the Divinity" (Strabo, *Geography*, lib. xvi., c.2).

Food and Water in Sinai

Many critics have suggested that such a dry desert area as Sinai could never have supported the huge flocks of sheep of the Israelites as recorded in Exodus. In 1860, W. Holland explored most of the Sinai Peninsula, Despite the present desolate and dry condition of the barren land, he found that some areas would still support large flocks of sheep. If the temperature or level of rainfall was only slightly changed, the amount of available pasturage would have been much greater than today's conditions would indicate. In his book Holland wrote, "Large tracts of the northern portion of the plateau of the Tih, which are now desert, were evidently formerly under cultivation. The Gulf of Suez (probably by means of an artificial canal connecting it with the Bitter Lakes) once extended nearly fifty miles further north than it does at present, and the mountains of Palestine were well clothed with trees. Thus there formerly existed a rain-making area of considerable extent, which must have added largely to the dews and rains of Sinai. Probably, also, the peninsula itself was formerly much more thickly wooded. The amount of vegetation and herbage in the Peninsula, even at the present time, has been very much underrated; and a slight increase in the present rainfall would produce an enormous addition to the amount of pasturage. I have several times seen the whole face of the country, especially the wadies, marvelously changed in appearance by a single shower" (W. Holland, *Recent Explorations in the Peninsula of Sinai*, 1869).

It is fascinating to note that numerous biblical personalities (including Nebuchadnezzar, Belshazzar, and Darius), who were totally repudiated by higher critics in past decades, have now been reliably verified by recent historical and archeological discoveries, In the past, critics of the Bible's accuracy contemptuously rejected the story of the defeat of the confederation of five kings from the East by the small army of Abraham as found in Genesis 14. These critics claimed that there was no evidence to support this biblical account, and therefore denied the story. However, the continuing archeological research in the Middle East has found ample evidence proving that the story is credible in all its particular details.

Dr. Nelson Glueck, considered by many to be the leading Palestinian archeologist in this century, was the president of the Hebrew Union College. Reporting on the newly discovered evidence about this invasion, Glueck wrote the following report: "Centuries earlier, another civilization of high achievement had flourished between the 21st and 19th centuries B.C., till it was savagely liquidated by the Kings of the East. According to the Biblical statements, which have been borne out by the archaeological evidence, they gutted every city and village at the end of that period from Ashtaroth Karnaim, in southern Syria through all of Trans-Jordan and the Negev to Kadesh-Barnea in Sinai (Genesis 14:1–7)" (Nelson Glueck, *Rivers in the Desert*, [New York: Farrar, Straus and Cudahy, 1959], p. 11).

Dr. Glueck spent many years of his life exploring the land of Israel in his search for archeological records. As a result of his many discoveries he concluded that the Bible was totally reliable in every area where he could examine the evidence. Summarizing the results of the numerous archeological discoveries during the last century, Dr. Glueck concluded: "As a matter of fact, however, it may be stated categorically that no archeological discovery has ever controverted a Biblical reference. Scores of archaeological findings have been made which confirm in clear outline or in exact detail historical statements in the Bible. And, by the same token, proper evaluation of Biblical descriptions has often led to amazing discoveries. They form tesserae in the vast mosaic of the Bible's almost incredible correct historical memory" (Nelson Glueck, *Rivers in the Desert*, [New York: Farrar, Straus and Cudahy, 1959], p. 31).

The explorations and excavations in the Middle East during the last century and a half have thrown remarkable light on the accuracy and reliability of the words of the Holy Scriptures. With each additional discovery we find new exciting confirmations of the most remarkable statements from the Word of God. In this chapter I will share some of the most fascinating of these discoveries and their implications for the authority of the Bible.

King Nebuchadnezzar's Inscription About the Tower of Babel

From the time of Adam and Eve, "The whole earth had one language and one speech" (Genesis 11:1), before the dispersion of the population following God's supernatural act causing the confusion of their languages at the Tower of Babel. God purposely confounded

Illustration of the Tower of Babel

the language of all the people on the earth (Genesis 11:9) so they could not understand the speech of their neighbors to force them to disperse throughout the earth. The people had gathered together in sinful pride against God in their attempt to build a tower that would reach to the heavens. Moses recorded God's subsequent judgment and destruction of the Tower of Babel and the city of Babylon. The remains of the Tower of Babel are vitrified (melted to form a kind of rough glass) which indicates that God used a huge amount of heat to destroy this tower that was erected at the dawn of time by men in their sinful pride to reach up to the heavens in defiance of God. Scientists who study the origin of languages, known as philologists, have concluded that it is probable that the thousands of dialects and languages throughout the planet can be traced back to an original language in man's ancient past. Professor Alfredo Trombetti claims that he can prove the common origin of all languages. Max Mueller, one of the greatest oriental language scholars, declared that all human languages can be traced back to one single original language. Professor Otto Jespersen stated that the first language was given to man by God (Joseph Free, *Archeology and Bible History,* [Wheaton: Scripture Press Publications, 1969]).

The French government sent Professor Oppert to report on the cuneiform inscriptions discovered in the ruins of Babylon. Oppert translated a long inscription by King Nebuchadnezzar in which the king referred to the tower in the Chaldean language as *Barzippa,* which means *Tongue-tower.* The Greeks used the word *Borsippa,* with the same meaning of *tongue-tower,* to describe the ruins of the Tower of Babel. This inscription of Nebuchadnezzar clearly identified the original tower of Borsippa with the Tower of Babel described by Moses in Genesis. King Nebuchadnezzar decided to rebuild the base of the ancient Tower of Babel, built over sixteen centuries earlier by Nimrod, the first King of Babylon. He also called it the Temple of the Spheres. During the millennium since God destroyed it, the tower was reduced from its original height and magnificence until only the huge base of the tower (four hundred and sixty feet by six hundred and ninety feet) standing some two hundred and seventy-five feet high remained within the outskirts of the city of Babylon. Today the ruins have been reduced to about one hundred and fifty feet above the plain with a circumference of 2,300 feet. Nebuchadnezzar rebuilt the city of Babylon in great magnificence with gold and silver, and then decided to rebuild the lowest platform of the Tower of Babel in honor of the Chaldean gods. King Nebuchadnezzar resurfaced the base of the Tower of Babel with gold, silver, cedar, and fir, at great cost on top of a hard surface of baked clay bricks. These bricks were engraved with the seal of Nebuchadnezzar. (A photograph of one of these Babylonian bricks created by Nebuchadnezzar is included in the photo section.) In this inscription found on the base of the ruins of the Tower of Babel, King Nebuchadnezzar speaks in his own words from thousands of years ago confirming one of the most interesting events of the ancient past.

King Nebuchadnezzar's Inscription Found on the Tower of Babel

The tower, the eternal house, which I founded and built.
I have completed its magnificence with silver, gold, other
metals, stone, enamelled bricks, fir and pine.
The first which is the house of the earth's base,

the most ancient monument of Babylon; I built and
finished it.

I have highly exalted its head with bricks covered with
copper.

We say for the other, that is, this edifice, the house of the
seven lights of the earth,

the most ancient monument of Borsippa.

A former king built it, (they reckon 42 ages) *but he did not
complete its head.*

*Since a remote time, people had abandoned it, without
order expressing their words.*

Since that time the earthquake and the thunder had
dispersed the sun-dried clay.

The bricks of the casing had been split, and the earth of the
interior had been scattered in heaps. Merodach, the
great god, excited my mind to repair this building.

I did not change the site nor did I take away the
foundation.

In a fortunate month, in an auspicious day,

I undertook to build porticoes around the crude brick
masses, and the casing of burnt bricks.

I adapted the circuits, I put the inscription of my name in
the Kitir of the portico.

I set my hand to finish it. And to exalt its head.

As it had been in ancient days, so I exalted its summit.

(Italics added)

This inscription was translated by Professor Oppert. In addition, Mr. William Loftus translated this fascinating inscription in his book, *Travels and Researches in Chaldea and Sinai* (William Kennett Loftus, *Travels and Researches in Chaldea and Sinai*, [London: James Nisbet, 1857), p. 29). This incredible inscription confirms the biblical accuracy of one of the most fascinating stories in the Book of Genesis. The pagan king Nebuchadnezzar confirms in his own words the incredible details that "a former king built it, but he did not complete its head," confirming the truthfulness of the Genesis account that God stopped the original builders from completing the top of the Tower of Babel. Most significantly, King Nebuchadnezzar's inscription declares that the reason the original king could not complete the tower was because, "Since a remote time, people had abandoned it, without order expressing their words." In other words, they lost the ability to control their language and communication!

The Bible's Account of the Tower of Babel

"And it came to pass, as they journeyed from the east, that they found a plain in the land of Shinar, and they dwelt there. Then they said to one another, 'Come, let us make bricks and bake them thoroughly.' They had brick for stone, and they had asphalt for mortar. And they said, 'Come, let us build ourselves a city, and a tower whose top is in the heavens; let us make a name for ourselves, lest we be scattered abroad over the face of the whole earth.' But the Lord came down to see the city and the tower which the sons of men had built. And the Lord said, 'Indeed the people are one and they all have one language, and this is what they begin to do; now nothing that they propose to do will be withheld from them. Come, let Us go down and there confuse their language, that they may not understand one another's speech.' So the Lord scattered them abroad from there over the face of all the earth, and they ceased building the city. Therefore its name is called Babel, because there the Lord confused the language of all the earth; and from there the Lord scattered them abroad over the face of all the earth" (Genesis 11:2–8).

Compare the statement of Nebuchadnezzar, "A former king built it, but he did not complete its head. Since a remote time, people had abandoned it," with the words of Moses in Genesis 11:7; "So the Lord scattered them abroad from there over the face of all the earth, and they ceased building the city." Even more startling is the phrase of the pagan king where he declared that the reason they could not complete the top of the "tongue-tower" was that the "people abandoned it, without order expressing their words." This expression by Nebuchadnezzar clearly confirms the historical event recorded in Genesis that God supernaturally "confused the language of all the earth" and He "scattered them abroad over the face of all the earth" (Genesis 11:2–8). This inscription by King Nebuchadnezzar is one of the strongest proofs possible that the Bible is an accurate record of the events it describes.

Joseph and the Seven Years of Famine

A fascinating inscription confirming the Bible's account of the "seven years of great plenty" followed by the "seven years of famine" (Genesis 41:29,30) was discovered during the nineteenth century in southern Saudi Arabia. This inscription was found on a marble tablet in a ruined fortress on the seashore of Hadramaut in present-day Democratic Yemen. An examination of the writing suggests that it was written approximately eighteen hundred years before the birth of Christ, a time that corresponds with the biblical narrative about Jacob and his twelve sons. This inscription was rendered in Arabic by Professor Schultens and was later translated into English by Rev. Charles Forster.

This is his translation of this ancient inscription:

We dwelt at ease in this castle a long tract of time;
nor had we a desire but for the region-lord of the vineyard.
Hundreds of camels returned to us each day at evening,
their eye pleasant to behold in their resting-places.
And twice the number of our camels were our sheep,
in comeliness like white does, and also the slow moving
    kine.
We dwelt in this castle *seven years of good life*
— how difficult for memory its description!
Then came years barren and burnt up:
when one evil year had passed away,
Then came another to succeed it.
And we became as though we had never seen a glimpse of
    good.
They died and neither foot nor hoof remained.
Thus fares it with him who renders not thanks to God:
His footsteps fail not to be blotted out from his dwelling.

This ancient poem records the devastation of the years of famine and barrenness that followed the seven years of plenty. The language of the poem implies that the famine also lasted seven years. This account from ancient Arabia provides independent evidence confirming the accuracy of the biblical account of the seven years of plenty in the Middle East followed by seven years of famine that occurred during the rule of Joseph as prime minister of Egypt.

Moses recorded the history of the Egyptian famine and the wise preparations that Joseph made to gather up the surplus grain during the seven years of plenty to provide against the coming years of famine. "So he gathered up all the food of the seven years which were in the land of Egypt, and laid up the food in the cities; he laid up in every city the food of the fields which surrounded them" (Genesis 41:48). Again, Moses recorded: "Then the seven years of plenty which were in the land of Egypt ended, and the seven years of famine began to come, as Joseph had said. The famine was in all lands, but in all the land of Egypt there was bread. . . . The famine was over all the face of the earth, and Joseph opened all the storehouses and sold to the Egyptians. And the famine became severe in the land of Egypt. So all countries came to Joseph in Egypt to buy grain, because the famine was severe in all lands" (Genesis 41: 53–57). As the Book of Genesis recorded, the seven-year famine was so severe in Egypt that Joseph, as the chief administrator, had to be very careful in selling food from the precious grain reserves to satisfy the hunger of all the inhabitants of the surrounding countries. Joseph could not sell the grain reserves of Egypt for gold and silver to everyone because of the danger that the grain would run out. When the famine was at its peak, grain was much more valuable than gold or money.

Explorers during the last century discovered a number of other fascinating ancient inscriptions in the Middle East that provided confirmation of facts recorded in the sacred Scriptures. Ebn Hesham, an Arab from Yemen, showed the English explorer, Mr. Cruttenden, a rich tomb of a wealthy Yemenite woman who had died during the time of the Egyptian famine recorded in Genesis 41. This Yemenite tomb was fortunately discovered around 1850 after being exposed following a flood that uncovered the grave site.

The tomb contained the body of a rich noblewoman who was covered in beautiful jewels. Seven collars of pearls surrounded her neck; her hands and feet were covered with seven bracelets, armlets, rings, and ankle-rings displaying costly jewels. In addition, her tomb contained a coffer filled with rich treasure.

However, the greatest treasure of all was a fascinating engraved stone tablet bearing her final inscription which confirmed the biblical account of Joseph's careful management of the remaining food reserves during the seven years of famine in Egypt.

A Yemenite Inscription About a Famine During the Time of Joseph

In thy name O God, the God of Hamyar,
I Tajah, the daughter of Dzu Shefar, *sent my steward to Joseph,*

And he delaying to return to me, I sent my hand maid
With a measure of silver, to bring me back a measure of
    flour:
And not being able to procure it, I sent her with a measure
    of gold:
And not being able to procure it, I sent her with a measure
    of pearls:
And not being able to procure it, I commanded them to be
    ground:
And finding no profit in them, I am shut up here.
Whosoever may hear of it, let him commiserate me;
And should any woman adorn herself with an ornament
From my ornaments, may she die with no other than my
    death.

(Italics added)
(reported in Niebuhr's *Voyage en Arabie*, PL. LIX.
Translation by Rev. Charles Forster).

This ancient inscription reveals a Yemenite Arab noble woman's sincere complaint that she could not purchase Egypt's grain with her gold. It also reveals Joseph's determination to resist any appeal from a stranger offering gold in return for Egypt's precious grain reserves. This determination reminds us of Joseph's similar resolve earlier in his life when he resisted the attempt of Potiphar's wife to destroy his virtue. The tragic history of famines often recorded the bartering of the most precious of metals and luxuries in trade for the smallest amount of food available.

Ancient Histories Confirm the Exodus

The biblical record in the Book of Exodus about the supernatural deliverance of the Jews from their bondage in Egypt is one of the most miraculous and fascinating accounts in the Bible. Very few Christian pastors or laymen are aware that we have numerous historical records and ancient inscriptions that provide evidence and confirmation for these key events that resulted in the creation of the Jewish people as a distinct nation. Moses recorded the following statement: "And the children of Israel journeyed from Rameses to Succoth, about six hundred thousand on foot that were men, beside children. And a mixed multitude went up also with them; and flocks, and herds, even very much cattle" (Exodus 12:37,38).

It is fascinating that the Jewish historian Flavius Josephus reported that two ancient Egyptian priest-scholars, Manetho and Cheremon, specifically named both Joseph and Moses in their history of Egypt as leaders of the Jews (Flavius *Josephus, Josephus Against Apion.* I., 26, 27, 32). Josephus recorded that the Egyptians remembered a tradition of an Exodus from their country by the Jews whom they hated because they believed the Israelites were unclean. It is interesting to note that Manetho and Cheremon stated that the Jews rejected Egyptian customs, including the national worship of Egyptian gods. Most importantly, these pagan historians acknowledged that the Jews killed the animals which they held as sacred, indicating the Israelite's practice of sacrificing lambs on that first Passover. These historians also confirmed that the Israelites immigrated into the area of "southern Syria" which was the Egyptian name for ancient Palestine. Perhaps the most important confirmation is found in the statement by Manetho that the sudden Exodus from Egypt occurred in the reign of "Amenophis, son of Rameses, and father of Sethos, who reigned toward the close of the 18th dynasty" which places this event between 1500 and 1400 B.C. This evidence confirms the chronological data found in the Old Testament that suggests the Exodus occurred approximately 1491 B.C.

A few years ago, after much searching, I was able to locate a set of volumes containing the forty books in the *Library of Diodorus Siculus*, a Greek historian from Agyrium in Sicily who lived from 80 B.C., until his death approximately twenty years before the birth of Jesus. Diodorus traveled extensively throughout the Middle East acquiring a vast knowledge of ancient events. He compiled records from various peoples which are quite valuable because they often recorded fascinating historical details that would otherwise have been lost forever. In his book, Diodorus reported: "In ancient times there happened a great plague in Egypt, and many ascribed the cause of it to God, who was offended with them because there were many strangers in the land, by whom foreign rites and ceremonies were employed in their worship of the deity. The Egyptians concluded; therefore, that unless all strangers were driven out of the country, they should never be freed from their miseries. Upon this, as some writers tell us, the most eminent and enterprising of those foreigners who were in Egypt, and obliged to leave the country . . . who retired into the province now called Judea, which was not far from Egypt, and in those times uninhabited. These emigrants were led by Moses, who was superior to all in wisdom and prowess. He gave them laws, and ordained that they should have no images of the gods, because there was only one deity, the heaven, which surrounds all things, and is Lord of the whole" (Diodorus *Siculus, Library of History,* lib. 1., ap Phot.).

The historical records and inscriptions I have included in this chapter are only a small sample of the evidence confirming the historical accuracy of the Old Testament. However, these discoveries provide ample evidence that we can trust the Old Testament writers as accurate historians, even when they describe miraculous events such as the Tower of Babel and the seven-year famine in Egypt.

3

Ancient Sinai Inscriptions and the Exodus

During the last century a number of explorers rediscovered a group of ancient inscriptions in the Wadi Mukatteb (the Valley of the Writing) in the Sinai Peninsula. When they were deciphered the researchers concluded that they contained detailed descriptions of the events of the Exodus from Egypt by the Children of Israel under the leadership of Moses. Naturally, the finding of these inscriptions attracted a great deal of attention and led to serious debate between scholars regarding their origin and meaning. Most of the scholars immediately rejected any possibility that these inscriptions could be an independent record of the events of the Exodus made by the ancient Israelites. Significantly, many of those who automatically rejected the authenticity of these inscriptions also rejected the literal interpretation of the Exodus biblical record altogether. However, a number of biblical scholars concluded that these mysterious inscriptions may actually have been written in the distant past by Jews who either took part in these momentous events or by people who were alive at the time of the Exodus.

We know these inscriptions are truly ancient because they were first described by the historian Diodorus Siculus before the birth of Christ (10 B.C.) in his *Library of History*. In describing the Sinai Peninsula, Diodorus wrote: "Moreover, an altar is there built of hard stone and very old in years, bearing an inscription in ancient letters of an unknown tongue. The oversight of the sacred precinct is in the care of a man and a woman who hold the sacred office for life" (Diodorus Siculus, *Library of History,* bk. 3, sect. 42, Loeb Classical Library, C. H. Oldfather, trans. [Cambridge: Harvard University Press, 1993], p. 211). This passage by Diodorus and a parallel description by the Greek writer Strabo (A.D. 24) in his seventeen volume *Geography* confirm that these inscriptions were so ancient in their own day that the language was unknown to those living at the time of Christ.

Cosmas Indicopleustes, a Byzantine Christian writer, also reported that the inscriptions were ancient in his day, almost 1,400 years ago. In A.D. 518, Cosmas wrote that the engravings appeared "at all halting places, all the stones in that region which were broken off from the mountains, written with carved Hebrew characters." It is fascinating that his Jewish companions confirmed the Hebrew nature of the script that he translated as follows: "The departure of such and such a man of such a tribe, in such a year, in such a month" (Arthur Penrhyn Stanley, *Sinai and Palestine* [London: John Murray, 1905], p. 57). Cosmas concluded that the strange inscriptions carved in the rocks were made by the ancient Israelites fleeing their Egyptian captivity. The native Arabs claimed these inscriptions were written in a language that was lost to them and of very great antiquity. Since the Arabs of the Sinai Peninsula had not suffered under foreign conquest during the five centuries between the time of Christ and A.D. 518 when Cosmas visited the site, it is safe to conclude that these inscriptions must have been written long before the time of Christ. Otherwise, the Arab natives would not have described them as written in a lost language and unknown character. The fact that these inscriptions survived in the hot dry climate of Sinai from the time of Diodorus (10 B.C.) until today, gives us ample evidence that they could have survived intact a further fifteen hundred years back in time to the era of Moses.

The Language of the Inscriptions

In the last few centuries numerous explorers have noted these unusual inscriptions on the rocks and cliffs of Sinai, including Bishop Robert Clayton of Ireland (1753). He wrote a report about his discovery in the *Journal of the Franciscans of Cairo* (1753), concluding that the inscriptions were of ancient Hebrew origin. However, the most interesting exploration of these inscriptions was completed by the Rev. Charles Forster in his book published in 1862. He concluded that these writings were original records of an ancient Hebrew-Egyptian alphabet describing the Israelites' exodus from Egypt. Professor Arthur Penrhyn Stanley, in his *Sinai and Palestine*, explained that Rev. Forster and Dr. Stewart concluded that "a Sinaitic inscription has been found contemporaneous with a tablet of Egyptian hieroglyphics." Dr. Stanley and other explorers recorded that numerous graffiti and Christian crosses located near the sites of these ancient inscriptions indicate that Christian pilgrims in subsequent ages also visited and left a record of their pilgrimage as they have in other locations in the Middle East. Professor Stanley described these ancient inscriptions in numerous locations in the Sinai in Wadi Sidri, Mugharah, Mukatteb, Feirah, Aleyat, Abu-Hamad and in great numbers in Wadi Nukb-Hawy. However, a detailed examination of seven hundred of the genuine Sinai inscriptions revealed that there were only ten cross-forms found in the whole group of ancient writings. The Egyptian cross-form is their form of the letter *T* or *Tau* that appears in most languages. To put this in context, another well-known Egyptian inscription, the Rosetta Stone, contained seventy cross-forms of Ts and no one would ever suggest that these cross marks on the Rosetta Stone were placed there by Christian pilgrims.

One of the strongest reasons for believing that some of these inscriptions may have been composed by Israelites in the time of the Exodus is that the language appears to be an original account of the Exodus events rather than an attempt to copy Exodus passages from the inspired pages of the Torah. Although these incredible rock inscriptions describe in great detail many of the supernatural events that occurred during the Exodus from Egypt, the writers did not use any of the words or characteristic language of Moses as recorded in the Torah. In other words, there is no indication that the writers of these Sinai inscriptions derived their information about the Exodus from reading Moses' words in the Torah. An examination of the evidence suggests that the writers may have been independent witnesses who described these supernatural events in their own original language. If this conclusion is correct, then these inscriptions would be an important independent confirmation of the truth of the biblical account.

Although numerous additional inscriptions were obviously created by medieval Christian pilgrims, experts were able to distinguish the genuine ancient writings from the medieval writings. Professor Stanley rejected an Israelite origin for the inscriptions because the ones he saw personally, were obviously written by pilgrims in Greek, Arabic, or Latin. The presence of casually etched crosses proved that this group of inscriptions was put there by Christian visitors to Sinai over the centuries. However, Dr. Stanley confessed that he did not have the training in ancient languages to interpret these inscriptions. Other scholars, such as Niebuhr and Forster, concluded that the graffiti and crosses were made by pilgrims much later than the original Sinai inscriptions. Scholars who examined the older Sinai inscriptions concluded that they may have been recorded by the Israelites who participated in the Exodus. All of the sites where these original inscriptions are located are on the western side of the Sinai closest to Egypt, suggesting that the writers came from that direction. Since none of these older inscriptions contain Christian or Jewish names it is unlikely that pilgrims created them. No Christian populations ever lived in the western part of the Sinai, where these inscriptions were found, in the early centuries of our era.

One of the interesting aspects of these ancient inscriptions is that Rev. Forster notes that they were written in a twenty-three letter combination Egyptian-Hebrew alphabet that included twelve Hebrew letters. The other eleven letters are similar to those found in the alphabets of the Phoenicians, the Greeks, Ethiopians and Hamyarites (ancient Arabs living before the time of Mohammed). While the letters in the Sinai inscriptions are primarily Hebrew, the language pattern is clearly Egyptian. Forster found that five out of every six words used in these inscriptions are related to the Hamyarite (ancient Arabic) language, the vernacular language of Egypt and Yemen. He claimed that the Sinai inscriptions cannot be deciphered from the Hebrew lexicon. After several centuries of captivity as slaves in Egypt, the Israelites would naturally speak and write a language that, while containing the initial evidence of Hebrew, would be heavily influenced by the Egyptian language. It is probable that God inspired Moses to modify, expand and purify the Hebrew language when he wrote the first five books of the Bible, the Torah. These Sinai inscriptions and the Torah are the earliest known examples of the use of Hebrew in writing.

One of the fascinating features of these inscriptions is that the writer would draw a picture of a quail side by side with the inscription describing God's miraculous provision of the quails to feed the Israelites (as shown in the photo section). Another curious feature is that numerous images of animals appear in the writing but only of animals that live in the Sinai Peninsula, not those that live only in Egypt. If a native Egyptian wrote these inscriptions you would expect to find Egyptian animals, also images of pagan gods. However, although numerous Sinai inscriptions contain Egyptian hieroglyphics as well as the Sinai writings, we find no evidence of pagan gods or symbols. This provides very strong evidence that these were created by Jews.

We know from Stephen's sermon in the Book of Acts that Moses and his followers were perfectly capable of producing written inscriptions in the style of the Egyptians. "Moses was learned in all the wisdom of the Egyptians, and was mighty in words and deeds" (Acts 7:22). Clement of Alexandria confirms this in his book *The Stromata*, as follows: "Having reached the proper age, he [Moses] was taught arithmetic, geometry, poetry, harmony, and besides, medicine and music, by those that excelled in these arts among the Egyptians; and besides the philosophy which is conveyed by symbols, which they point out in the hieroglyphical inscriptions. The rest of the usual course of instructions, Greeks taught him in Egypt as a royal child, as Philo says in his life of Moses. He learned, besides, the literature of the Egyptians, and the knowledge of the heavenly bodies from the Chaldeans and the Egyptians; whence in the Acts he is said 'to have been instructed in all the wisdom of the Egyptians.' And Eupolemus, in his book *On the Kings in Judea*, says that 'Moses was the first man, and the first that imparted grammar to the Jews'" (Clement of Alexandria, *The Stromata*, bk. 1, chap. XXIII).

The writings in Sinai are of two distinct kinds. One is enchorial or common writing while the other is in the hieroglyphic style of Egypt as used by the priests and royalty. The fact that several inscriptions contain lines that alternate from the enchorial writing to hieroglyphic style is the strongest evidence that the people who created these inscriptions spent time in Egypt. However, we have no historical evidence of any group of Egyptians living in Sinai at any time. On the other hand, the Bible tells us that the Israelites did live in the Sinai for forty years. The Bible reveals that the Israelites had the necessary skills to create such inscriptions with metal tools because they created the golden calf, the metal work in the Tabernacle, and their weapons. A historical precedent exists for such inscriptions at that time. The Book of Deuteronomy declares the command of God to record His Law on stone: "And it shall be, on the day when you cross over the Jordan to the land which the Lord your God is giving you, that you shall set up for yourselves large stones, and whitewash them with lime. You shall write on them all the words of this law, when you have crossed over, that you may enter the land which the Lord your God is giving you, 'a land flowing with milk and honey,' just as the Lord God of your fathers has promised you. . . . And you shall write very plainly on the stones all the words of this law" (Deuteronomy 27:2,3,8). The Children of Israel fulfilled this command according to Joshua 8:30.

The Sinai Inscriptions Describe the Exodus

The Minister of Public Instruction and Worship of France sent one of their top scholars, Professor Lottin de Laval, in February 1851, to examine these inscriptions to determine whether or not they were genuine descriptions of the Exodus. After crossing the Gulf of Suez from Egypt to land on the shore of the Sinai where Moses had crossed thousands of years ago, Professor de Laval discovered the first of these incredible inscriptions near the place the Arabs call "the wells of Moses." His extensive experience in examining ancient inscriptions enabled Professor de Laval to distinguish the original ancient inscriptions from the later medieval graffiti written by Armenian Christian pilgrims. He was able to make three hundred plaster casts or squeezes of the most important of these ancient inscriptions. He recorded his discoveries in his book *Voyage dans la Peninsule Arabique du Sinai et l'Egypt emoyenne.* (Lottin de Laval, *Voyage dans la Peninsule Arabique du Sinai et l'Egypt emoyenne* [Paris: S.E.M. le Ministre de l'Instruction publique et des Cultes, 1855–1859]).

Rev. Charles Forster translated and recorded photographs of these inscriptions from the distant past in his 1862 book *Sinai Photographed*. This book is quite rare, but fortunately, I was able to obtain from England the only copy still available. As a language expert, Rev. Forster translated these ancient engravings and found they described many of the events of the Jews' Exodus from Egypt under Moses' leadership. While these accounts confirm the accuracy of the biblical account of the miraculous passage of the Israelites through the Red Sea, the inscriptions describe these Exodus events in original language. This fact suggests that the inscribers were not copying from the biblical account of the Exodus from Egypt as found in the Book of

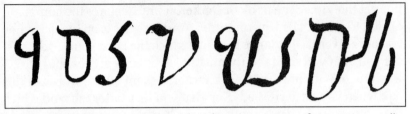

"The wind blowing, the sea dividing into parts, they pass over."
Sinai Inscription No. 1
Translated by Charles Forster

Exodus; rather, they were describing the events from their own experience or from the eyewitness descriptions of others. One of the most fascinating of these inscriptions was described in Rev. D. A. Randall's book *The Handwriting of God in Egypt and Sinai* (Rev. D. A. Randall, *The Handwriting of God in Egypt and Sinai,* [Philadelphia: John E. Potter, 1862], p. 264). This long inscription was one hundred feet high and contained forty-one successive lines in hieroglyphic characters beneath the title that was engraved in letters six feet high.

Inscriptions Describing The Red Sea Crossing

Consider the words of this ancient inscription about the Israelites' escape from Egypt. Six ancient inscriptions were found on different cliffs in the Wadi Sidri, located on one of the natural routes the Jews would have chosen when entering the interior of the Sinai Peninsula from Egypt. In his book, *Sinai and Palestine,* Dr. A. P. Stanley wrote about his 1853 visit to Wadi Sidri as the natural place leading up from the Red Sea: "A stair of rock, the Nukb Badera, brought us into a glorious Wadi (Sidri) enclosed between red granite mountains. . . . In the midst of the Wadi Sidri, just where the granite was exchanged for sandstone, I caught sight of the first inscription" (A. P. Stanley, *Sinai and Palestine,* London: John Murray, 1905, p. 70). Another writer, Golius, revealed that the Arabic word *Sidri* can be interpreted as "a way that leads up from the water as at a landing place." Consider the message found in the following eight separate inscriptions about the Israelites' crossing of the Red Sea. (Moses described the events of their escape from Egypt in Exodus, chapter 14). The numbers in brackets following the translated inscription refer to their original numbering identification as recorded in Rev. Forster's book, *Sinai Photographed.* Rare photographs of several of these precious inscriptions are located in the photo section in the center of this book, *The Signature of God.* Note that the inscription, Number 41, actually names Moses as the leader of the Israelites.

The Sinai Inscriptions

The wind blowing, the sea dividing into parts, they pass
over.   (1)
The Hebrews flee through the sea; the sea is turned into
dry land.   (4)

The waters permitted and dismissed to flow,
burst rushing unawares upon the astonished men,
congregated from all quarters banded together
to slay treacherously being lifted up with pride.   (5)

The leader divideth asunder the sea, its waves roaring.
The people enter, and pass through the midst of the
waters.   (10)

Moses causeth the people to haste like a fleet-winged she-
ostrich crying aloud;
the cloud shining bright,
a mighty army propelled into the Red sea is gathered into
one;
they go jumping and skipping.
Journeying through the open channel,
taking flight from the face of the enemy.
The surge of the sea is divided.   (41)

The people flee, the tribes descend into the deep.
The people enter the waters.
The people enter and penetrate through the midst.
The people are filled with stupor and perturbation.
Jehovah is their keeper and companion.   (23)

Their enemies weep for the dead, the virgins are wailing.
The sea flowing down overwhelmed them.
The waters were let loose to flow again.   (8)

The people depart fugitive.
A mighty army is submerged in the deep sea,
the only way of escape for the congregated people.   (21)

The Bible's Account of the Red Sea Crossing

Contrast the wording and details of the Sinai inscriptions and Moses' words as recorded in Exodus 14:21–29. "And Moses stretched out his hand over the sea; and the Lord caused the sea to go back by a strong east wind all that night, and made the sea dry land, and the waters were divided. And the children of Israel went into the midst of the sea upon the dry ground: and the waters were a wall unto them on their right hand, and on their left. And the Egyptians pursued, and went in after them to the midst of the sea, even all Pharaoh's horses, his chariots, and his horsemen. And it came to pass, that in the morning watch the Lord looked unto the host of the Egyptians through the pillar of fire and of the cloud, and troubled the host of the Egyptians, And took off their chariot wheels, that they drove them heavily: so that the Egyptians said, 'Let us flee from the face of Israel; for the Lord fighteth for them against the Egyptians.' And the Lord said unto Moses, 'Stretch out thine hand over the sea, that the waters may come again upon the Egyptians, upon their chariots, and upon their horsemen.' And Moses stretched forth his hand over the sea, and the sea returned to his strength when the morning appeared; and the Egyptians fled against it; and the Lord overthrew the Egyptians in the midst of the sea. And the waters returned, and covered the chariots, and the horsemen, and all the host of Pharaoh that came into the sea after them; there remained not so much as one of them. But the children of Israel walked upon dry land in the midst of the sea; and the waters were a wall unto them on their right hand, and on their left" (Exodus 14:21–29).

The ancient inscriptions precisely describe the Exodus, the role of Moses, and the Jews' miraculous crossing of the Red Sea. The obvious questions are: Who inscribed these messages? And when? Another obvious question is: What could have motivated someone in the past to inscribe this record with such enormous effort when the desolate nature of the terrain would guarantee that very few people would ever see and admire the writer's handiwork? A close examination of the inscriptions reveals that the manner and style of expression is quite different from the language Moses used in the Book of Exodus. If a religious pilgrim or traveler in the distant past wanted to inscribe the biblical story from the Book of Exodus in stone, we would expect him to either quote Exodus exactly or at least use many of the same words as written by Moses. In addition,

Illustration of the Israelites Coming Out of the Red Sea

we would expect such a person to follow the biblical narrative quite closely. However, the inscriptions are quite different from the biblical text of Exodus. While the Sinai inscriptions detail many of the key events described in Exodus, the original language suggests that the writer was either an independent observer of these events or was recording events told to him by someone who had personally observed the Exodus.

The ancient Greek historian Diodorus Siculus wrote an extraordinary ancient report about the tribes in Egypt and the miraculous drying up of the Red Sea: "It is an ancient report among the Ichtheophagi, who inhabit the shores of the Red Sea, that by a mighty reflux of the sea which happened in former days, the whole gulf became dry land, and appeared green all over; and that the water overflowed the opposite shore, and that all the ground continued bare to the very lowest depth of the gulf, until the water, by an extraordinary high tide, returned to its former channel." (Diodorus Siculus, *Library of History,* lib. iii., c. 40). The parallels between Diodorus' report and the Exodus account of the Red Sea crossing are fascinating.

The Murmuring Against Moses

The explorers found two inscriptions in Wadi Sidri that referred to the murmuring of the Jewish people against Moses about their great thirst, hunger and the terror they experienced during their flight from the Egyptians as they entered the great desert of the Sinai Peninsula.

> Pilgrims fugitive through the sea find a place of refuge at Sidri.
> Lighting upon plain ground they proceed on their pilgrimage full of terror. (77)

> The Hebrews pass over the sea into the wide waterless desert,
> famishing with hunger and thirst. (17)

The prophet Moses recorded the experience in the wilderness when the Israelites complained bitterly against God and their leader because they were hungry and thirsty. It is interesting to note that while it took only one day for God to get Israel out of Egypt, it took forty years in the desert to get Egypt out of Israel. Consider how closely the Sinai inscriptions parallel the biblical account as recorded by Moses: "And all the congregation of the children of Israel journeyed from the wilderness of Sin, after their journeys, according to the commandment of the Lord, and pitched in Rephidim: and there was no water for the people to drink. Wherefore the people did chide with Moses, and said, 'Give us water that we may drink.' And Moses said unto them, 'Why chide ye with me? Wherefore do ye tempt the Lord?' And the people thirsted there for water; and the people murmured against Moses, and said, 'Wherefore is this that thou hast brought us up out of Egypt, to kill us and our children and our cattle with thirst?'" (Exodus 17:1–3).

The Miraculous Provision of Water

Another Sinai inscription describes God's miraculous provision of water to the Children of Israel through God commanding Moses to miraculously cause the pure water to flow from the rock. It is worth noting that, only seventy-two hours after the Israelites miraculously escaped from Egypt through the Red Sea, they came to the bitter waters of Marah. God often tested Israel just as He tests us as individuals by bringing us to a difficult experience shortly after a great spiritual victory. The Lord wants to teach us to always rely upon His leading and deliverance instead of our natural tendency to trust in ourselves and our own resources and gifts.

> The people clamour vociferously. The people anger Moses.
> Swerving from the right way, they thirst for water
>   insatiably.
> The water flows, gently gushing out of the stony rock.
> Out of the rock a murmur of abundant waters.
> Out of the hard stone a springing well.
> Like the wild asses braying,
> the Hebrews swallow down enormously and greedily.
> Greedy of food like infants,
> they plunge into sin against Jehovah.   (46)

> The people drink, winding on their way,
> drinking with prone mouth,
> Jehovah gives them drink again and again.   (39)

The people sore athirst, drink vehemently.
They quaff the water-spring without pause, ever drinking.
Reprobate beside the gushing well-spring.   (58)

The Book of Exodus also records that God supernaturally provided water in the desert for His Chosen People: "Behold, I will
stand before thee there upon the rock in Horeb; and thou shalt smite
the rock, and there shall come water out of it, that the people may
drink. And Moses did so in the sight of the elders of Israel" (Exodus
17:6). Despite God's ample and miraculous provision for the Israelites, the Jews remained reprobate in their attitude, drinking the
water but refusing either to thank God for His provision of water or
trust in His continuing provision for their daily needs. Moses described their thanklessness: "And he called the name of the place
Massah, and Meribah, because of the chiding of the children of Israel, and because they tempted the Lord, saying, 'Is the Lord among
us, or not?' " (Exodus 17:7).

God's Judgment on Israel's Gluttony

The inscriptions in Sinai record that the Israelites' succumbed to
gluttony in eating the quails which God miraculously provided at a
place called Kibroth-hattaavah. Despite God's daily provision of
manna, the Israelites rebelled against the Lord and against Moses by
complaining about the sameness of food. This rebellion unleashed
the wrath of God on their sinfulness. He sent a massive flock of quail
to provide meat for the Israelites. Rather than gratefully accepting
this quail meat as a gift from God, the Israelites greedily stuffed
their mouths with the quail. Many of the Israelites died in the plague
of gluttony at Kibroth-hattaavah.

The people have drink to satiety. In crowds they swill.
Flesh they strip from the bone, mangling it.
Replete with food, they are obstreperous.
Surfeited, they cram themselves; clamouring, they vomit.
The people are drinking water to repletion.
The tribes, weeping for the dead, cry aloud with downcast
     eyes.
The dove mourns, devoured by grief.
The hungry ass kicketh: the tempted men, brought to
     destruction, perish.
Apostasy from the faith leads them to the tomb.   (28)

Devouring flesh ravenously, drinking wine greedily,
Dancing, shouting, they play.   (34)

Congregating on all sides to ensnare them,
the people voraciously devour the quails.
Binding the bow against them, bringing them down.
Eagerly and enormously eating the half raw flesh,
the pilgrims become plague-stricken.

Compare the message of the inscriptions with Moses' account in the Book of Numbers: "And say thou unto the people, 'Sanctify yourselves against to morrow, and ye shall eat flesh: for ye have wept in the ears of the Lord, saying, "Who shall give us flesh to eat? For it was well with us in Egypt:" therefore the Lord will give you flesh, and ye shall eat. Ye shall not eat one day, nor two days, nor five days, neither ten days, nor twenty days; But even a whole month, until it come out at your nostrils, and it be loathsome unto you: because that ye have despised the Lord which is among you, and have wept before him, saying, 'Why came we forth out of Egypt?'" (Numbers 11:18–20), In the balance of the chapter, Moses describes God's supernatural provision of meat: "And there went forth a wind from the Lord, and brought quails from the sea, and let them fall by the camp, as it were a day's journey on this side, and as it were a day's journey on the other side, round about the camp, and as it were two cubits high upon the face of the earth. And the people stood up all that day, and all that night, and all the next day, and they gathered the quails: he that gathered least gathered ten homers: and they spread them all abroad for themselves round about the camp. And while the flesh was yet between their teeth, ere it was chewed, the wrath of the Lord was kindled against the people, and the Lord smote the people with a very great plague" (Numbers 11:31–33). The next statement by Moses records the location where this event occurred: the very same place where this Sinai inscription was discovered over fifteen centuries later. "And he called the name of that place Kibroth-hattaavah: because there they buried the people that lusted" (Numbers 11:34).

In a confirmation of Exodus 32:6 where Moses declares that "the people sat down to eat and drink and rose up to play," the Sinai inscription Number 34 describes the activities of the Israelites as, "Dancing, shouting, they play." Moses records that God destroyed the ungrateful Israelites who indulged in this sinful gluttony: "And there went forth a wind from the Lord, and brought quails from the sea, let them fall by the camp, as it were a day's journey on this side, and as it were a day's journey on the other side, round about the camp, and as it were two cubits high upon the face of the earth" (Numbers 11:3).

William Houghton described the abundance of quails in the Middle East in an article in *Smith's Dictionary of the Bible:* "The quail migrates in immense numbers. (See Pliny, H. N. X. 23). Tourneyfort says that all the islands of the Archipelago at certain seasons of the year are covered with these birds. Col: Sykes states . . . 'that 160,000 quails have been netted in one season on this little island; according to Temminck, 100,000 have been taken near Nettuno in one day.' The Israelites would have had little difficulty in capturing large quantities of these birds, as they are known to arrive at places sometimes so completely exhausted by their flight as to be readily taken, not in nets only, but by the hand. Sykes says, 'They arrive in spring on the shores of Provence so fatigued that for the first few days they allow themselves to be taken by the hand.' It is interesting to note the time specified by Moses; 'it was at even' that they began to arrive, and they no doubt continued to come all the night." (William Houghton, *Smith's Dictionary of the Bible* [Boston: D. Lothrop & Co., 1878] p. 2,650).

Another authority on the wildlife in the Sinai, Professor H. B. Tristram, reported in his book, *Natural History of the Bible:* "The quail migrates in vast flocks and regularly crosses the Arabian desert, flying for the most part at night; and when the birds settle they are so utterly exhausted that they may be captured in any numbers by the hand. . . . Thus in spring and autumn they are slaughtered in numbers on Malta and many of the Greek islands. . . . The period when they were brought to the camp of Israel was in spring, when on their northward migration from Africa . . . they would follow up the coast of the Red Sea till . . . they fell, thick as rain, about the camp in month of April, according to our calculation. Thus the miracle consisted in the supply being brought to the tents of Israel by the special guidance of the Lord, in exact harmony with the known habits of the bird. . . . I have myself found the ground in Algeria, in the month of April, covered with quails for an extent of many acres at daybreak, where on the preceding afternoon there had not been one. They were so fatigued that they scarcely moved till almost trodden upon; and although hundreds were slaughtered, for two days they did not leave the district" (Professor H. B. Tristram, *Natural History of the Bible*, p. 231, 232).

Sarbut-el-Khadem – An Ancient Mountain Graveyard at Kibroth-hattaavah

One of the most remarkable of the discoveries found in the Sinai in recent centuries was that of the graves of those Jews who had died from a supernatural plague. The Book of Numbers records: "And the Lord smote the people with a very great plague. And he called the name of that place Kibroth-hattaavah: because there they buried the people that lusted" (Numbers 11:34,35).

In 1761, the German explorer Barthold Niebuhr discovered an extensive ruined cemetery with carved inscriptions on the tombs and within a sepulcher on top of an inaccessible mountain in Sinai called Sarbut-el-Khadem *(Voyage en Arabie,* tom. i, p. 191). Niebuhr noted that these inscriptions could not have been made by native Egyptians because there, are no carved stone inscriptions found in Egypt; rather the Egyptians painted their inscriptions on plaster surfaces. He found numerous gravestones with legible inscriptions in addition to a small temple carved out of the rock which also contained numerous inscriptions in the same language as appeared at other Exodus sites. Niebuhr remarked on "the wonderful preservation of the inscriptions upon this soft sandstone, exposed as they have been to the air and weather during the lapse of so many ages. On some of the stones they are quite perfect" (Niebuhr, *Biblical Researches,* vol. i, pp. 113, 114), The Byzantine monk Cosmas Indicopleustes had previously recorded his discovery of these graves in A.D. 535.

Niebuhr also found numerous engravings of quails in the cemetery. The tombstones actually depict these birds "standing, flying and apparently, even trussed and cooked" (Rev. Charles Forster, *Sinai Photographed* [London: Richard Bentley, 1862], p. 62). Niebuhr noted that the native Bedouin Arabs from the deserts of Sinai call these tombs "the Jews' graves." He said that these hieroglyphics on the tombstones were quite different than the inscriptions he had found in Egyptian tombs. The Sinai tomb inscriptions contained no mention of any of the Egyptian gods that are found in virtually all Egyptian tombs. When Dr. Stewart visited the site he described the tombs as follows: "The whole of this part of the Wadi seems to have

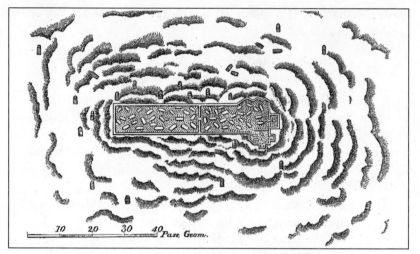

Turbet es Yahoud — "the Graves of the Jews"
Illustration of Graveyard at Kibroth-hattaavah

been covered with graves, the stones of which are scattered abroad in all directions. . . . The Bedouins still maintain that they are the *Turbet es Yahoud* (the graves of the Jews)." Another graveyard at the mouth of the Wadi is called *Bounli Abou Israel* by the Arabs indicating their belief that it contains the bones of the ancient Israelites. Significantly, there is no evidence of any other human settlement in the Sinai area, either modern or ancient. While the Egyptians always buried their dead in the plain or in a valley, this extensive graveyard sits on the top of a seven-hundred-foot-high mountain. The work involved in bringing the bodies here for burial would have been immense. However, this practice of mountain burial is normal for the Jews. Both Moses and Aaron were buried in the mountains by God. Even today, Jews in Israel often choose to be buried on the Mount of Olives and other mountains surrounding Jerusalem. Who else would be buried here on a desolate mountain in Sinai except for those ancient Israelites killed by the wrath of God?

Tombstone Inscriptions in the Sinai

The detailed molds and photographs which Dr. Stewart made when he explored this huge graveyard were translated by Rev. Charles Forster and appeared in his, Forster's, 1862 book *Sinai Photographed* (p. 84).

The apostates smitten with disease by God,
by means of feathered fowls.
Smitten by God with disease in the sandy plain,
(when) exceeding the bounds of moderation.
Sickening, smitten by God with disease;
their marrow corrupted by God by means of the feathered
    fowls.
The people, given over to destruction, cry aloud.
God pours down deep sleep,
messenger of death, upon the pilgrims.
The tomb is the end of life to the sick,
smitten with disease by God.

Moses described the Jews' constant rebellion against his leader-ship. Despite repeated miracles that proved God's support, the Bible described the Israelites' failure to trust in His power to protect them from hunger and thirst.

Miriam's Rebellion Against Moses

One of the most interesting stories recorded in the Torah is that of Miriam's attack on Moses' leadership because she rejected his Ethiopian wife. Among the inscriptions discovered in Sinai was one that may have been engraved on the rocks of Sinai even before Moses recorded the event in the Book of Numbers. A translation of this inscription from Rev. Forster reads as follows:

Miriam, Prophetess of lying lips and deceitful tongue.
She causes the tribes to conspire against the pillar and
    prince of the people.
Convoked for tumult, perverted, full of strife,
the people revile the meek and generous man.
They lead with reproaches the blessed one of God.   (48)

Moses also recorded the tragic history of his family's rebellion against his leadership: "And Miriam and Aaron spake against Moses because of the Ethiopian woman whom he had married: for he had married an Ethiopian woman. And they said, 'Hath the Lord indeed spoken only by Moses? Hath he not spoken also by us?' And the Lord heard it. Now the man Moses was very meek, above all the men which were upon the face of the earth" (Numbers 12:1–3). The parallels between the biblical record and the Sinai inscriptions are remarkable. The Bible records that God judged Miriam's sinful challenge to Moses' leadership by causing her to succumb to the dreaded disease of leprosy. However, when Moses appealed to God that she would be healed, the Lord graciously healed her after an imposed period of seven days isolation from the camp of the Israelites.

The Plague of Fiery Serpents

The final Sinai inscription that we will examine is one that deals with the incident of the fiery serpents recorded in the Book of Numbers.

Bitten and destroyed by fiery, hissing serpents,
the Hebrews are wounded for their crimes.
Jehovah makes a stream flow from the stony rock. (47)

In Numbers 21, Moses described the Israelites' ungrateful rebellion when they complained against God's supernatural provision of manna and water in the desert: "And the people spake against God, and against Moses, 'Wherefore have ye brought us up out of Egypt to die in the wilderness? For there is no bread, neither is there any water; and our soul loatheth this light bread.' And the Lord sent fiery serpents among the people, and they bit the people; and much people of Israel died" (Numbers 21:5–6).

The profound silence of the deserts of the Sinai Peninsula have hidden and preserved these fascinating inscriptions for three and a half thousand years. These ancient monuments and inscriptions have been inaccessible to mankind for three millennia, but they were preserved by the providence of God. A careful comparison of these ancient inscriptions from the deserts of Sinai reveal an astonishing degree of confirmation of the facts recorded in the original accounts in Genesis, Exodus and Numbers.

The French government commissioned Professor Lottin de Laval to explore the Sinai in 1851 and to create plaster casts of the inscriptions directly from the rocks. Later, the government of England instructed its agents to take exact photographs of these inscriptions to enable scientists to examine them. Following the publication of Rev. Charles Forster's photographs of these engravings, Professor A. P. Stanley, who had disputed their antiquity in his earlier editions of his book, suggested in the fourth edition of his book, *Sinai and*

Palestine (1857) that language experts should carefully reconsider the evidence of their antiquity.

An Astonishing Discovery–A Trilingual Inscription

Some critics naturally reject out of hand the possibility that these Sinai inscriptions could actually be genuine contemporary records of the Exodus. They finally challenged Rev. Forster by stating that they would not be convinced of the accuracy and authenticity of his detailed translations unless someone discovered a bilingual inscription containing the Sinai inscriptions on one side and another known language on the other side for comparison. In other words, they demanded that someone find another inscription similar to the marvelous trilingual inscription known as the Rosetta Stone, which was found in 1799 near Rosetta, Egypt, that enabled the scholars Young and Champollion to finally decipher the Egyptian hieroglyphics. Incredibly, another Sinai explorer, Pierce Butler, made a phenomenal discovery in 1860 of a trilingual inscription in a cave on the Djebel Maghara mountain. This incredible inscription contained three descriptions of the same event engraved in three languages including the alphabet used in the Sinai inscriptions. (A photograph of this incredible trilingual inscription appears in the photo section.) The importance of this final trilingual inscription discovery cannot be overestimated because it confirmed that Rev. Forster's translation of the Exodus inscriptions was accurate.

Professor Lottin de Laval declared in his 1859 book, *Voyage dans la Peninsule Arabique du Sinai et l'Egypt emoyenne,* that the miscellaneous graffiti were obviously quite different from the ancient inscriptions because the graffiti were scratched with sword points or similar rough tools on the soft rocks, often only four feet from the ground. (M. Lottin de Laval, *Voyage dans la Peninsule Arabique du Sinai et l'Egypt emoyenne* [S.E.M. le Ministre de l'Instruction publique et des Cultes, 1859]). He noted that the older Sinai inscriptions were carefully engraved in the granite with proper tools after the rock surface was prepared by hard labor due to the great height and difficulty of access for the engraver. Laval reported that Christian crosses appear infrequently and bear no connection to the original older inscriptions. Precise impressions from plaster castings of these Sinai engravings created by Professor de Laval were brought to Paris for detailed examination and verification. Most importantly, Rev. Charles Forster published his photographs for the examination of other scientists in his 1862 book, *Sinai Photographed*, which made it possible for other scholars and lay people to examine these marvelous inscriptions for themselves.

Professor de Laval wrote, "As for the connection existing between the Sinaitic writing and that of Egypt, we are perfectly of Mr. Forster's opinion, and shall support him with proofs. Twenty-two letters of the demotic Egyptian alphabet are constantly found in the Sinaitic inscriptions. With the exception of two or three variants, it is the same alphabet." Professor de Laval ended his remarks by concluding that it was virtually impossible that ". . . a people so intelligent, so persevering as the Hebrew people, have not left in the indelible granite of the Peninsula of Sinai a single monument of their Exode, to thank God for being able, in the midst of so much misery and danger, to recover safety and liberty."

Three scholars, Professor de Laval, Niebuhr and Forster, have independently translated these fascinating rock inscriptions. Each of them concluded that the inscriptions were made by the ancient Israelites during the Exodus. While other scholars have dismissed their conclusion, to my knowledge, no one has produced any alternative translation of the inscriptions as evidence that anyone else produced them. The weight of the evidence supports the conclusion that these ancient inscriptions proclaim a message from the distant past confirming the accuracy of the account of the Exodus recorded in the Word of God.

4

Startling Archeological Discoveries

Can we trust the Bible? The answer is an overwhelming *YES!* The reason for this confident statement is that for the past one hundred and fifty years many brilliant scholars have conducted detailed archeological examinations at thousands of sites throughout the Middle East. The results of their discoveries have proven that the Bible is reliable and accurate in every single area where its statements could be tested. In the balance of this chapter I will share some of the wonderful archeological discoveries that provide tremendous proof that the Bible is a true and accurate record of past events in ancient Israel.

Throughout most of the last two thousand years, the majority of men living in the western world have accepted the statements of the Scriptures as genuine. Respected biblical scholars including Brown, Adam Clarke, and Faussett, among others, wrote numerous Bible commentaries in the early part of the 1800s. However, despite their best efforts, their knowledge of the history and archeology of the ancient world was limited solely to the Bible and excerpts from classical writings from Greek and Latin writers. Unfortunately, most writers of the classics either exaggerated or failed to differentiate between mythology and historical events. As a result, most Bible commentators in past centuries were unable to add much additional knowledge to confirm the Bible's accounts of events. Fortunately, the field of biblical archeology has exploded in the past century and a half. The discoveries have provided tremendous insight into the life, culture and history of the ancient biblical world. Most importantly, these discoveries have confirmed thousands of biblical statements as true.

Beginning with the higher critical school of biblical critics in Germany and England in the nineteenth century we have witnessed a progressive abandonment of the historic faith in the Word of God. While European seminaries gradually abandoned the authority of the Scriptures, North American seminaries and Bible colleges still upheld the accuracy of the Bible to some degree. In the 1960s most North American seminaries still accepted the basic records of the Old and New Testaments as being historically true. However, in the following decades there occurred a wholesale abandonment of belief in the historical accuracy of the Bible. The attitudes behind these attacks on biblical accuracy and authority were those of complete rejection of God's inspiration of the Scriptures. In addition, many critics approach the Bible with an attitude of outright denial of supernatural events, such as miracles, and biblical prophecy. To these unbelieving critics, the presence of a miracle or prophecy in a biblical text was absolute proof that it was not genuine. Critics rejected the possibility of inspiration, miracles, and prophecy before they began their examination of the evidence.

Despite the overwhelming success unbelieving critics have had in establishing their unbelieving attitudes within the seminaries, textbooks, and popular media, something strange began to occur. The new discoveries by archeologists digging at sites in the Middle East continued to produce fascinating finds that contradicted their attitudes. Every new discovery in Israel and the surrounding nations provided tremendous confirmation of the accuracy of the Word of God in incredible ways. As a result of these continuing discoveries, Dr. Nelson Glueck, the most outstanding Jewish archeologist of this century, wrote in his book, *Rivers in the Desert*, this fascinating statement. "It may be stated categorically that no archaeological discovery has ever controverted a Biblical reference. Scores of archaeological findings have been made which confirm in clear outline or in exact detail historical statements in the Bible. And by the same token, proper evaluation of Biblical descriptions has often led to amazing discoveries. They form tesserae in the vast mosaic of the Bible's almost incredibly correct historical memory" (Dr. Nelson Glueck, *Rivers in the Desert* [New York, Grove, 1960], p. 31).

In confirmation of Dr. Glueck's statement, another respected scholar, Dr. J. O. Kinnaman, declared: "Of the hundreds of thousands of artifacts found by the archeologists, not one has ever been discovered that contradicts or denies one word, phrase, clause, or sentence of the Bible, but always confirms and verifies the facts of the biblical record." The well-known language scholar, Dr. Robert Dick Wilson, formerly professor of Semitic philology at Princeton Theological Seminary, made the following comment, "After forty-five years of scholarly research in biblical textual studies and in language study, I have come now to the conviction that no man knows enough to assail the truthfulness of the Old Testament. When there is sufficient documentary evidence to make an investigation, the statement of the Bible, in the original text, has stood the test" (Dr. Robert Dick Wilson, *Speaker's Source Book*, p. 391).

The Bible claims that it is the inspired and accurate Word of God. Therefore, it is vital that we compare the Scriptural records against the archeological discoveries uncovered at actual sites where many of the thrilling events of the Bible actually occurred. The results of these detailed investigations are available for anyone to examine. The archeological record provides overwhelming confirmation of thousands of detailed statements and facts recorded in the sacred Scriptures. Scholars have not found one single confirmed archeological discovery that absolutely disproves a statement of the Scriptures. To the contrary, as the evidence in *The Signature of God* reveals, the scholars have discovered literally hundreds of objects, inscriptions, and sites that confirm the accuracy of biblical statements in even unimportant areas. The most important thing for believers in God is that these archeological proofs of scriptural accuracy confirm the accuracy, the inspiration, and the authority of the Word of God. No one should expect that archeology will be able to provide detailed proof of such personal events like the sacrifice of Isaac by Abraham. By their nature, it is unlikely that such events in the lives of private individuals would ever leave any archeological evidence. Most personal events recorded in the Bible would never have left evidence that could be discovered thousands of years later. However, whenever the Bible dealt with the rise and fall of kingdoms, cities, buildings, etc., the spade of the archeologist has been able to discover wonderful confirmation of the truth of Holy Scripture.

Only fifty years ago many disbelieving scholars totally rejected the historical accuracy of the Bible because they claimed that the Scriptures talked about numerous kings and individuals that could not be confirmed from any other historical or archeological records. Recent discoveries, however, have shown that they should not have abandoned their faith in the Word of God so easily. If they had only trusted in the truthfulness of the Bible or waited a little longer they would have been rewarded with the recent archeological discoveries that confirm many biblical details, events, and personalities. For example, many scholars contemptuously reject the Bible's statements about King David. Many textbooks used in universities and seminaries openly reject any historical statements in the Scriptures about King David or Solomon. They believe that David is a myth or literary fiction. Examples of this approach include the books *In Search of Ancient Israel,* by Philip R. Davis, and the *Early History of the Israelite People,* by Thomas L. Thompson. He wrote, "The existence of the Bible's 'United Monarchy' during the tenthcentury [B.C.] is . . . impossible" (Thomas L. Thompson, *Early History of The Israelite People,* [Brill: 1992]). These so-called "minimalist" scholars accept only the minimum about the Bible, rejecting every biblical statement unless it can be established by other non-biblical evidence.

This is a totally biased position and would be ridiculed in any other area of study. Imagine a student of Plato's Greek philosophy who rejected outright any statement by Plato himself, his followers, or any Greek philosophical writer in later years who quoted him favorably. This is an absurd way to approach the study of any subject. Yet many biblical scholars in the secular universities take this "minimalist" approach today. The rational way to study ancient history is to carefully examine every bit of evidence regarding a personality or event from both those who support and those who oppose the particular subject. The true scholar will then carefully weigh the evidence of all sources and come to a balanced conclusion based on the facts.

The House of David

Recent archeological investigations have demolished the position of those who rejected the biblical account of Israel's kings such as King David. In 1993, archeologists digging at Tel Dan in the

Galilee in northern Israel found a fragment of a stone inscription that clearly refers to the "house of David" and identifies David as the "king of Israel." This is the first inscription outside the Bible that confirms the Bible's statement that David was the king of Israel in the ninth century before Christ. Many Bible critics who had rejected King David as a myth were upset to discover their position could no longer be defended. Some critics suggested that the fragment was a "fake." The following summer, two additional fragments of the original inscription were found that provided scholars with the whole inscription, confirming that it referred to David as king of Israel. Furthermore, another scholar, Andre Lemaire from the College de France, discovered another ninth century B.C. stone inscription created by King Mesha of Moab that also referred to "the House of David." These incredible inscriptions, recorded a century after David's death, confirm that David was king of Israel at the time the Bible stated and that he established a dynasty, the "House of David" as the Scriptures said.

A stone inscription from Egypt confirms that Israel was established as a nation in Canaan centuries before the reign of King David, just as the Bible claims. The Merneptah Stela is a seven-and-a-half-foot-high stone inscription discovered in the temple of Pharaoh Merneptah at Thebes in Egypt. Scholars determined that Pharaoh Merneptah ruled Egypt from 1213 to 1203 B.C. and confirmed that he launched an invasion into the area of the modern-day West Bank in Canaan, defeating the Jewish inhabitants of the land. The second line from the bottom of this inscriptions boasts, "Israel is laid waste; his seed is not."

Critics of the Bible have claimed for decades that the Bible's statements in Joshua about the conquest of the Promised Land in the centuries before the monarchy of King David were pure fiction. Obviously, the king of Egypt would not need to invade Canaan with an army unless the Jews had established a significant presence on the frontiers of the Egyptian Empire. In light of this new archeological evidence critics will be forced to relinquish their rejection of the Bible's record of Israel's conquest as stated by Joshua. Critics claimed that the books of Samuel, Kings, and Chronicles were recorded by Jews living in Persia centuries after the events occurred. They suggest that such records contain numerous errors and myths. However, the Bible claims these books were written at the time of the events and that God's Holy Spirit inspired the writers to correctly record the events. When you compare the Word of God to the accuracy of the ancient historians such as Herodotus, you can quickly see that most ancient histories were nothing more than creative fiction and records of hearsay evidence without careful research or checking of facts. In stark contrast, the Bible is extremely careful and accurate as to events, chronology, sequence, and personalities.

In addition to the archeological evidence for King David, we now have confirmation of other kings of Israel. The name of Omri, king of Israel, is recorded on an inscription known as the Stela of King Mesha of Moab. In addition, Omri's name appears on the rock inscriptions of three kings of Assyria, the annals of both Tiglath-Pileser III and Sargon II, and the Black Obelisk of King Shalmaneser III, who wrote, "I conquered . . . all of the Land of Omri (Israel)." Other Assyrian inscriptions found in Nineveh confirm the Bible's records about these kings of Israel: Ahab, Jehu, Joash, Menehem, Pekah, and Hoshea. In addition, the names of many of the kings of the southern kingdom of Judah are also recorded on inscriptions of the nations that fought against the Jews. The inscriptions found by archeologists also confirm the names of these kings of Judah: Ahaziah, Uzziah, Ahaz, Hezekiah, Manasseh, and Jehoiachin. Scholars found ration records of the army of Nebuchadnezzar, king of Babylon (606 to 562 B.C.) that state, "ten sila of oil to Jehoiachin, king of Judah. . . . Obviously, the fact that these foreign nations listed the kings of Israel and Judah provides the strongest evidence confirming the accuracy of the Word of God.

In 1846, the explorer Austen Henry Layard discovered an incredible Black Obelisk in the ruins of Nimrud *(present-day Iraq),* the ancient capital of the great Assyrian Empire that conquered the northern kingdom of Israel. This six-and-a-half-foot-high Black Obelisk, a four-sided stone inscription, recorded the conquest of the Assyrian King Shalmaneser Il over numerous foreign kingdoms including King Jehu of Israel (approximately 841 to 814 B.C.). A detailed examination of the obelisk reveals King Jehu bowing down in obedience to the Assyrian king. The obelisk refers to Jehu as the "son of Omri" indicating their awareness that his dynasty traced back to Omri in confirmation of the Book of Kings.

The Walls of Jericho

During excavations of Jericho between 1930 and 1936, Professor John Garstang found one of the most incredible confirmations of the biblical record about the conquest of the Promised Land. The results were so amazing that he took the precaution of preparing a written declaration of the archeological discovery, signed by himself and two other members of his team. "As to the main fact, then, there remains no doubt: the walls fell outwards so completely that the attackers would be able to clamber up and over their ruins into the city." This fact is important because the evidence from all other archeological digs around ancient cities in the Middle East reveal that walls of cities always fall inwards as invading armies push their way into a city. However, in the account in Joshua 6:20, we read, "the wall fell down flat, so that the people went up into the city every man straight ahead, and they took the city." Only the supernatural power of God could have caused the walls to fall outward as described in Joshua's account of the conquest of Jericho (John Garstang, *Joshua Judges*, [London: Constable, 1931]).

Following the fall of East Jerusalem to the Jordanians in the 1948 War of Independence, the Jordanian army dynamited Jewish synagogues and other buildings in the Jewish Quarter of Jerusalem in the years following their conquering of the Old City. Nevertheless, this wanton destruction over a twenty-year period, until Jerusalem was liberated during the 1967 Six Day War, created a unique archeological opportunity. When the Jews recaptured the Jewish Quarter in 1967 they had to rebuild every building because of the Jordanian destruction. However, this made it possible for Israeli archeologists to remove the rubble built up over the last two thousand years and explore the bedrock of this fascinating biblical city. This was a unique opportunity because the existing modern buildings in most ancient cities prevent large archeological exploration. In addition to numerous discoveries confirming the accuracy of many passages in the Bible, the scholars, under the leadership of the archeologist Nahman Avigad of Hebrew University, found the remains of the wall of King Hezekiah built when the Assyrian army attacked Israel in 701 B.C. The Bible tells us that King Hezekiah built the walls of Jerusalem to resist the Assyrian armies: "And when Hezekiah saw that Sennacherib was come, and that he was purposed to fight against Jerusalem, He took counsel with his princes . . . they did help him. Also he strengthened himself, and built up all the wall that was broken, and raised it up to the towers, and another wall without" (2 Chronicles 32:2–5). The archeologists found that portions of the wall actually cut through walls of recently built houses, indicating the urgency of the defensive actions and the authority of the king. This is confirmed in the Bible's own account, "And ye have numbered the houses of Jerusalem, and the houses have ye broken down to fortify the wall" (Isaiah 22:10).

Dr. Millar Burrows, a professor at Yale University, studied the evidence that indicates the historicity of Abraham and the other patriarchs of Israel as recorded in Genesis. "Everything indicates that here we have an historical individual. As noted above, he is not mentioned in any known archaeological source, but his name appears in Babylonia as a personal name in the very period to which he belongs" (Millar Burrows, *What Mean These Stones?*, [New York: Meridian Books, 1956], pp. 258–259). Burrows wrote about the underlying reason most scholars reject the authority of the Bible, "The excessive skepticism of many liberal theologians stems not from a careful evaluation of the available data, but from an enormous predisposition against the supernatural. . . . On the whole, however, archaeological work has unquestionably strengthened confidence in the reliability of the scriptural record."

The Discovery of the Seals of Biblical Personalities

One of the most interesting discoveries in recent years was the finding of two bullæ, or clay seals, that bear the impression of the actual seal used by Baruch, the scribe of Jeremiah the prophet who transcribed the Book of Jeremiah. Both bullæ bear the inscription, "Belonging to Berekhyahu, son of Neriyahu, the Scribe." One of these clay seals is on view in the Israel Museum in Jerusalem. However, the second bullæ was found in Jerusalem earlier in this century and purchased by collector Shlomo Moussaieff of London who owns the greatest private collection of ancient Jewish inscriptions in the world. This second clay seal, bearing the same inscription, also reveals a fingerprint that probably belonged to Baruch.

At the beginning of this century a fascinating seal was discovered in Israel that bore an inscription of a beautiful lion and the words, "Belonging to Shema servant of Jeroboam." This amazing find indicates that it belonged to an official of King Jeroboam of Israel. Other seals have been discovered confirming the biblical records about King Uzziah (777 to 736 B.C.) and King Hezekiah (726 to 697 B.C.).

Another important seal found in Jerusalem dates from the seventh century before Christ and is inscribed as follows: "Belonging to

Abdi Servant of Hoshea." This seal made of orange chalcedony, used to authenticate royal documents for security, belonged to Abdi, a high official of King Hosea, the last king of the northern kingdom of Israel before it was conquered by the Assyrian Empire in 721 B.C. Another large seal on red limestone was found bearing the inscription "Belonging to Asayahu, servant of the king" together with a galloping horse. The name "Asaiah" is a short form of the name "Asayahu." This name occurs twice in the Old Testament in connection with the title "servant of the king." In 2 Chronicles 34:20 we find the name, "Asaiah a servant of the king's" and again in 2 Kings 22:12, "Asahiah a servant of the king's." It is possible that this seal was owned by "Asaiah, the servant of the king" a high court official who was sent by King Josiah to carefully examine the scroll of the lost Book of Deuteronomy that was found in the Temple by the High Priest Hilkiah in approximately 622 B.C.

Dr. Henry M. Morris concluded his in-depth study of the archeological evidence concerning the Bible with these words. "Problems still exist, of course, in the complete harmonization of archaeological material with the Bible, but none so serious as not to bear real promise of imminent solution through further investigation. It must be extremely significant that, in view of the great mass of corroborative evidence regarding the Biblical history of these periods, there exists today not one unquestionable find of archaeology that proves the Bible to be in error at any point" (Henry M. Morris, *The Bible and Modern Science*, [Chicago: Moody Press, 1956]).

Explorers in Iraq in the last century found the ancient inscribed clay cylinder bearing the actual decree of King Cyrus of Persia allowing the various captured natives of many different nations to return freely to their ancient homelands. It was the government policy of the preceding Babylonian Empire of King Nebuchadnezzar to displace whole peoples such as the Jews and resettle them in the far reaches of their empire. However, King Cyrus of Persia, a moderate and God-fearing monarch, reversed the cruel Babylonian policy. Immediately after conquering the Babylonian Empire, King Cyrus issued a decree allowing the Jews to freely return to their homeland in Israel ending the seventy-year-long captivity. The decree of King Cyrus began with these words, "I am Cyrus, king of the world, great king." After describing his conquests and deeds, the cylinder inscription reads, "I gathered all their former inhabitants and returned to them their habitations." In this incredible discovery we find the confirmation of one of the most astonishing events in the pages of Scripture. "Now in the first year of Cyrus king of Persia, that the word of the Lord by the mouth of Jeremiah might be fulfilled, the Lord stirred up the spirit of Cyrus king of Persia, that he made a proclamation throughout all his kingdom, and put it also in writing, saying, Thus saith Cyrus king of Persia, The Lord God of heaven hath given me all the kingdoms of the earth; and he hath charged me to build him an house at Jerusalem, which is in Judah. Who is there among you of all his people? his God be with him, and let him go up to Jerusalem, which is in Judah, and build the house of the Lord God of Israel, he is the God, which is in Jerusalem" (Ezra 1:1–3).

The Archeological Evidence of the New Testament

Obviously, the entire basis for the faith and hope of Christians depends on the truthfulness of the historical records of the New Testament. Our hope for heaven and salvation itself depends on the accuracy of the words of Jesus of Nazareth and the apostles as recorded in the pages of the New Testament manuscripts. It is significant that there is a relentless attack on the reliability of the Gospels and the Epistles because those who hate the Bible understand that if they can cause men to doubt the New Testament, then their faith will be immeasurably weakened. Fortunately, the continued archeological discoveries during the last century have provided an awesome amount of further evidence that confirms the total reliability of the written documents that form the foundation of the Christian faith.

The English scholar, William Ramsay, traveled as a young man to Asia Minor over a century ago for the sole purpose of disproving the Bible's history as described by Luke in his Gospel and in the Book of Acts. Ramsay and his professors were convinced that the New Testament record must be terribly inaccurate. He believed that Luke could not be correct in his history of Christ or in his account about the growth of the Church during the first decades following Christ. Dr. Ramsay began to dig in the ancient ruins of sites throughout Greece and Asia Minor, searching for ancient names, boundary markers, and other archeological finds that would conclusively prove that Luke had invented his history of Christ and His Church. To his amazement and dismay, William Ramsay discovered that the statements of the New Testament Scriptures were accurate in the smallest detail. Finally, Dr. Ramsay was convinced by the over-whelming evidence proving the Bible's accuracy. As a result, he accepted Jesus Christ as His personal Savior. He became both a Christian and a great biblical scholar. As a result of his conversion to belief in Jesus Christ, Sir William Ramsay's books became classics in the study of the history of the New Testament. Another great scholar, A. N. Sherwin-White, was a great classical historical scholar at Oxford University who studied the extensive evidence for and against the historical accuracy of the Book of Acts. Sherwin-White wrote his conclusion after studying the evidence, "For Acts the confirmation of historicity is overwhelming . . . any attempt to reject its basic historicity even in matters of detail must now appear absurd" (Quoted by Rubel Shelley, *Prepare To Answer* [Grand Rapids: Baker Book House, 1990]).

Dr. William F. Albright was unquestionably one of the world's most brilliant biblical archeologists. In 1955 he wrote: "We can already say emphatically that there is no longer any solid basis for dating any book of the New Testament after circa A.D. 80." However, additional discoveries over the next decade convinced him that all the books in the New Testament were written "probably sometime between circa A.D. 50 and 75." Significantly, Albright concluded that the writing of the New Testament within a few years of the events it described made it almost impossible that errors or exaggeration could have entered the text. He wrote that the duration between the events of Christ's life and the writing was "too slight to permit any appreciable corruption of the essential center and even of the specific wording of the sayings of Jesus." In other words, Professor Albright, one of the greatest minds in the field of archeology and ancient texts, concluded that the New Testament records the truth about Jesus Christ and his statements.

Dr. John A. T. Robinson was a distinguished lecturer at Trinity College, Cambridge and developed a reputation as a great scholar. Naturally, he accepted the academic consensus universally held since 1900, that denied the disciples and Paul wrote the New Testament and concluded that it was written up to a hundred years after Christ. However, an article in *Time* magazine, March 21, 1977, reported that Robinson decided to personally investigate for himself the arguments behind this scholarly consensus against the New Testament's reliability because he realized that very little original research had been completed in this field in this century. He was shocked to discover that much of past scholarship against the New Testament was untenable because it was based on a "tyranny of unexamined assumptions" and what he felt must have been an "almost willful blindness." To the amazement of his university colleagues, Robinson concluded that the apostles must have been the genuine writers of the New Testament books in the years prior to A.D. 64. He challenged other scholars to complete original research necessary to truly examine the question fairly. As a result of such a new analysis Robinson believed that it would necessitate "the rewriting of many introductions to — and ultimately, theologies of — the New Testament." Robinson's book, *Redating the New Testament*, published in 1976, suggests that Matthew's Gospel was written as early as A.D. 40, within eight years of Christ.

5

The Historical Evidence About Jesus Christ

Many modern scholars dispute the historical accuracy of the Bible. They especially reject the Gospel accounts of the life, death and resurrection of Jesus Christ. As an example of this rejection of biblical authority, the Jesus Seminar, a group of seventy-five New Testament liberal scholars, meet semi-annually to determine whether or not any of the Gospel quotations of Jesus' words meet with their scholarly approval. Incredibly, these liberal scholars examine individual "sayings" of Jesus recorded by the four Gospels and each academic votes to accept or reject these statements of Christ. The Jesus Seminar is sponsored by the Westor Institute, a private California study center, founded by Robert Funk, a liberal New Testament scholar. This group arrogantly pretends to sit in judgment of whether or not a particular biblical statement meets with their approval and is "genuine."

One indication of the underlying attitudes of these seminarians regarding the authenticity of Jesus' words, is found in the comments of Arthur Dewey of Xavier University, a member of the infamous Jesus Seminar. As reported in an article in *Time* magazine in April 1994, he stated that, while rejecting most of Christ's words, they believed Jesus was occasionally humorous. "There is more of David

Letterman in the historical Jesus than Pat Robertson." These particular liberal scholars are openly contemptuous in their rejection of the authority of the Bible based on their own exalted opinions. However, they merely represent the tip of the iceberg of academic scholarship that rejects, in whole or in part, most of Scripture as being the genuine inspired Word of God. These agnostic and unbelieving attitudes have permeated not only the academic world but also modern media. It is virtually the universal opinion today among secular academics that the Bible is without historical accuracy and cannot be relied upon by serious students.

Beginning in 1985, the Jesus Seminar has used a system of colored beads to indicate their vote or determination of the validity of particular statements which Jesus made. If, in their exalted opinion, these scholars think that Jesus would "certainly" have made such a statement, they vote by dropping a red bead in the box. If they believe that Jesus "might" have made a statement close to what the Gospel writer recorded, then they vote by dropping a pink bead. When they believe that the statement may be close to what Jesus thought, but not what He actually stated, they drop a grey bead in the box. Finally, when they reject a given statement in the Gospels as something they believe that Jesus would never have said, the scholars drop a black bead into the box showing that they totally reject the authenticity of the Gospel's statement.

During their last meeting in Santa Rosa, California, *Time* magazine reported in their April 6, 1996 issue that the scholars had decided that the Gospels of Matthew, Mark, Luke and John were "notoriously unreliable: the judges . . . had to throw out the Evangelists' testimony on the Nativity, the Resurrection, the Sermon on the Mount." The article in *Time* repeats "the assertion, published by the 75-person, self-appointed Seminar three years ago, that close historical analysis of the Gospels exposes most of them as inauthentic." The criteria used by these liberal scholars to judge the Gospel records, reveals clearly why they reject almost everything that Christians have believed during the last two thousand years. Among the criteria used to reject statements included: any prophetic statements, statements by Jesus on the cross, descriptions of His trial, the Resurrection, and any claims to be the Messiah or the Son of God. Their bottom line rule: "When in sufficient doubt, leave it out." However, if the view of the Jesus Seminar is correct — that almost nothing definite can be known about the life of Jesus of Nazareth — the basis for all Christian belief is destroyed.

Incredibly, this group has chosen to publish a new version of the Gospels which display the "words of Jesus" in various colors of ink reflecting their verdicts on the validity of His words. Not surprisingly, very little of their final Gospel text reveals Christ's words printed in red, indicating that these scholars reject many of Christ's statements. The arrogance of these self-appointed guardians of the validity of the words of Jesus Christ is almost unbelievable. As an example, when these academics examined the text containing the Lord's Prayer, they rejected every word in this prayer as spurious except for two single words, "Our Father." In reality, these liberal scholars declare by their votes whether or not they would have made these Gospel statements if they were Jesus! The cable channel Cinemax 2, ran a program in April of 1996, called *The Gospel According to Jesus*, that records people reading from a new version of the Bible created by the author Stephen Mitchell. In this astonishing version, Mitchell eliminated almost all of the statements and most of the miracles by Jesus as recorded in the Gospels.

The brilliant conservative evangelical scholar, Professor Michael Green, of Regent College, rejects the analysis of the Jesus Seminar. Professor Green stated that the Gospels are the best authenticated of all ancient documents from that period some two thousand years ago. Green declared, "We have copies of them going back to well within the century of their composition, which is fantastic compared with the classic authors of the period. And in striking contrast to the two or three manuscripts we have attesting the text of these secular writers, we have hundreds of the New Testament. They give us the text of the New Testament with astonishing uniformity." In addition, Professor Green noted the remarkable harmony found in the Gospel records: "The artless, unplanned harmony in their accounts is impressive and convincing."

Many people see Jesus as a wonderful moral teacher, but reject the Bible's claims for His deity and that He died on the cross for our salvation. However, this opinion is totally contradicted by historical evidence and logic. The famous English theologian C. S. Lewis presented his famous trilemma argument which makes the following statements. Any person who did the miracles and spoke the messages ascribed to Jesus could not be a mere human teacher or an uninspired prophet, no matter how enlightened or exalted they might be. Anyone who performed the miracles ascribed to Jesus and made the statements Jesus made about His nature and powers must be the Son of God as He claimed, or a liar, or a lunatic. Anyone who claimed the things that Jesus said must be either insane, a demon from hell, or the true Son of God. As you examine the evidence in this chapter and the overwhelming evidence found in the Gospel records, I believe that every reader will conclude that Jesus Christ could not possibly have been a liar or a lunatic. This analysis leaves us with the final remaining possibility: that Jesus of Nazareth was precisely who He claimed He was, namely, the Son of God.

Historical Documents About Jesus

In this chapter I will share a number of fascinating documents and ancient inscriptions that confirm the historical accuracy of the Gospel accounts about Jesus of Nazareth. Obviously, I can only touch on the highlights in this chapter, but the evidence shared will provide ample proof that the Gospel statements can be relied upon to stand the test of historical scrutiny. The evidence presented will prove conclusively that tremendous historical evidence exists both within and outside of the Bible that confirms the details of the life, death, and resurrection of Jesus Christ. Many skeptics contemptuously reject the Bible's claims that Jesus Christ is the Messiah. They reject out of hand the historical evidence that has survived from the first century which confirms many facts about Jesus that are recounted in the Gospel records. One of the strongest pieces of evidence about Jesus comes from the well-known Jewish historian Flavius Josephus who lived at the time of the apostle Paul. Josephus mentions Jesus twice in his exhaustive history, *The Antiquities of the Jews.* One of these references, known as the Testimonium Flavianum Passage, confirms a number of historical facts regarding the life, death and resurrection of Jesus of Nazareth. This testimony will be examined later in this chapter.

After a detailed analysis of the historical evidence for the life and resurrection of Jesus of Nazareth, Professor Simon Greenleaf, the greatest authority in the Western world on the matter of legal evidence and the author of the authoritative work, *The Testimony of the Evangelists,* concluded that the evidence for Jesus was overwhelming.

Sir William Ramsay began his scholarly career as a complete

skeptic regarding the historical evidence about Jesus of Nazareth. William Ramsay, possibly the greatest of all New Testament archeologists, completed the most in-depth studies ever completed on the Book of Acts. He wrote, "Luke is a historian of the first rank; not merely are his statements of fact trustworthy; he is possessed of the true historic sense, . . . In short this author should be placed along with the very greatest of historians" (William Ramsay, *The Bearing of Recent Discovery on the Trustworthiness of the New Testament*, [Grand Rapids: Baker Book House, 1953], p. 80). Professor Ramsay's comment on Luke's reliability as a historian is of tremendous importance in that not only was Luke the author of the Gospel account that bears his name, he also records the greatest number of details about Christ's virgin birth, career, death and resurrection. If Luke's writing is reliable regarding the Book of Acts, then he is also a worthy historian regarding the details of Christ's life and resurrection.

President Abraham Lincoln was an agnostic until he reached the age of forty. Then he read Dr. James Smith's brilliant examination called *The Christian's Defence* that proved the historical reality of the events in Christ's life. The overwhelming evidence from this book convinced Lincoln with the result that he became a genuine Christian for the rest of his life. "My doubts scattered to the winds and my reason became convinced by the arguments in support of the inspired and infallible authority of the Old and New Testaments." (Quoted in Sir Lionel Luckhoo's book, *Evidence Irrefutable Which Can Change Your Lives*." Daniel Webster, one of the greatest lawyers of his age, declared that "I believe the Scriptures of the Old and New Testaments to be the will and word of God, and I believe Jesus Christ to be the son of God."

Throughout history many men have examined the evidence regarding the life of Jesus of Nazareth. To any unbiased observer who is willing to evaluate it without prejudice, the accumulated evidence proving the Gospel record is truly overwhelming. Otto Betz, a respected scholar, stated in his book, *What Do We Know About Jesus?* that "No serious scholar has ventured to postulate the non-historicity of Jesus."

Some writers have suggested that there is little historical evidence regarding the life of Jesus. For example, the writer Solomon Zeitlin wrote, "Even Paul's epistles have awakened the question, Does he speak of a real historical personage or of an ideal? The main sources for the historicity of Jesus, therefore, are the Gospels." However, Zeitlin dismisses the Gospel historical accounts and concluded: "So we are right to assume that even the Gospels have no value as witnesses of the historicity of Jesus. The question therefore remains: Are there any historical proofs that Jesus of Nazareth ever existed?" Scholars such as Zeitlin casually dismiss the strong historical evidence that validates the Gospel accounts about Jesus because it contradicts the opinion they tenaciously hold on to that rejects the Bible's accuracy. If liberal scholars applied the same arbitrary rejection of historical evidence to other historical personages, such as Julius Caesar or Alexander the Great, they would be forced to reject all history as myth.

However, a careful unbiased analysis of the historical sources available will convince most fair-minded readers that Jesus of Nazareth is the Messiah of both history and prophecy. In his book, *The New Testament Documents: Are They Reliable?* the brilliant historian F. F. Bruce wrote, "The historicity of Christ is as axiomatic for an unbiased historian as the historicity of Julius Caesar."

The Reliability of the New Testament Confirmed by Scholars

During the earlier years of this century many liberal scholars concluded that the Gospels were unreliable as historical evidence, because they believed that they were written almost one hundred years after the events described. They concluded that the Gospel documents were based on hearsay and oral traditions rather than on eyewitness accounts. This prejudice led a whole generation of liberal scholars to reject the Gospels as competent eyewitness history.

The average Christian, believing the Bible to be the inspired Word of God, rejected the liberal argument because the Gospels and the Epistles declare that they are direct eyewitness accounts of the life of Christ. For example, Luke declared that he wrote these truths, "Even as they delivered them unto us, which from the beginning were eyewitnesses, and ministers of the word" (Luke 1:2). Later, in the Book of Acts, Luke confirmed that his reports as written to the Roman officer Theophilus, contained "many infallible proofs," the strongest historical and legal proofs possible. Luke stated that Jesus "showed Himself alive after His passion by many infallible proofs, being seen of them forty days" (Acts 1:3).

Fortunately, the tremendous advances in historical research and biblical archeology in the last century have convinced most scholars in the last two decades that the Gospels and Epistles were written within thirty-five years or less of the events which they describe. The late William F. Albright, the greatest biblical archeologist of his day, declared, "We can already say emphatically that there is no longer any solid basis for dating any book of the New Testament after about A.D. 80." In an article for *Christianity Today*, January 18, 1963, W. F. Albright wrote: "In my opinion, every book of the New Testament was written by a baptized Jew between the forties and eighties of the first century A.D."

Sir Frederic G. Kenyon, the director of the British Museum, was possibly the most respected New Testament textual scholar in our century. He commented on the significance of the fact that the evidence is overwhelming that the Gospels were composed shortly after the events of Christ's life and that the early church widely distributed them within its congregations within a relatively short period of time. Kenyon wrote: "The interval, then, between the dates of original composition and the earliest extant evidence becomes so small as to be in fact negligible, and the last foundation for any doubt that the Scriptures have come down to us substantially as they were written has now been removed. Both the authenticity and the general integrity of the books of the New Testament may be regarded as finally established."

After a professional lifetime of in-depth review of the New Testament manuscripts, Kenyon concluded that the present text in our Bible is absolutely reliable. He wrote: "It is reassuring at the end to find that the general result of all these discoveries and all this study is to strengthen the proof of the authenticity of the Scriptures, and our conviction that we have in our hands, in substantial integrity, the veritable Word of God" (Frederic G. Kenyon, *The Story of the Bible*, Special U.S. Edition [Grand Rapids: Eerdmans Co. 1967], p. 133).

Luke's reliability as a historian is unquestionable. Professor Merrill F. Unger declares forthrightly that the recent discoveries of archeology have proven the accuracy and authority of the Gospel accounts as reliable eyewitness accounts. Unger wrote, "The Acts of the Apostles is now generally agreed in scholarly circles to be the work of Luke, to belong to the first century and to involve the labors of a careful historian who was substantially accurate in his use of sources." (*Archeology and the New Testament* [Grand Rapids: Zondervan Publishing House, 1962]).

Modern scholars now possess more than five thousand manuscript copies of portions of the New Testament in the Greek language. In addition, there are an additional fifteen thousand manuscripts in other languages from the first few centuries of this era. No other important text, whether historical or religious, has more than a few dozen copies that have survived until our generation. The twenty thousand surviving manuscripts of the New Testament reveal numerous individual differences of spelling, et cetera. However, this huge number of manuscripts provides the strongest evidence possible, allowing scholars to check and trace the origin of the various readings to ascertain with certainty the original text. Most importantly, these discrepancies, mostly caused by careless copying, are usually trivial. Not one of these small differences affect a single important fact or doctrine of the Bible.

It is virtually impossible that anyone could have created and introduced significant changes into the authenticated New Testament manuscripts during the few years that elapsed between their original recording by the apostles, and the time they were widely distributed among the early churches in the final four decades of the first century. In addition, any significant changes would have been instantly detected and corrected. Many Christians who had personally known and listened to the words of the apostles were still alive at the time these New Testament manuscripts were being read in churches every Sunday. One of the chief followers of Christ, John the Apostle, was still the bishop in charge of seven churches in Turkey until the first few years of the second century. He would obviously have instantly detected and denounced any counterfeit passages that anyone might have attempted to insert into genuine biblical manuscripts.

The significance of these scholars' conclusion about an early date for the Gospels is overwhelming. It was impossible to widely distribute a blatantly false story about Christ while thousands of followers and observers were still alive to dispute it. Furthermore, the Greek originals of the Gospels and Epistles were widely copied, distributed and translated immediately into Hebrew, Syriac, Latin, Coptic and other languages. These documents were treasured by the churches and read in their Sunday services. If anyone had wanted to introduce a false miracle, event, or doctrine into the Gospels, they would have faced an impossible task. In order to introduce a false statement, the forger would have to simultaneously forge this counterfeit passage into every single copy of the Gospels in every country and language without being detected or challenged by any Christian. This would have been absolutely impossible. It is significant that the Gospel's historical account about Christ's life, death and resurrection was not denied by the Jews or the Romans who lived in the first century. This fact provides strong evidence that the Gospel account is historically true.

To put this in proper perspective, imagine that some writer wanted to create a false story in the 1990s about President Kennedy performing miracles and being raised from the dead for forty days after his tragic assassination in November, 1963. To succeed with his plan the writer would have to accomplish two impossible things: (1) He would have to simultaneously acquire every one of the millions of books and newspaper reports about the president and insert his counterfeit passages in this material without being detected by a single reader. (2) He would have to simultaneously convince millions of people around the world to accept his forgery as true, despite the fact that these people who were alive when Kennedy lived have independent recollections that contradict his invented story. It is obvious to anyone who considers the problem carefully that it is impossible for anyone to successfully produce such a forgery about President Kennedy's life that would convince anyone, let alone the whole population of the world. However, the liberal scholars who suggest that the Gospel records were altered to introduce new doctrines and statements about Christ's virgin birth and resurrection are proposing something that is just as ridiculous as the above example. The only reason these scholars have been able to convince many people is that there is a great desire in the minds of many to reject the truth of the Bible. If they accept the reality of the Bible's accuracy they must admit in their own mind that they will someday have to give an account of their life to God. Their inability to accept this reality forces them to reject out of hand the possibility that the Gospel records are true.

However, the evidence proving the historical reality about Jesus is powerful and convincing for anyone who will openly examine the evidence. One of the most convincing proofs of the supernatural nature of Christ's life is found in His absolutely unprecedented influence on the subsequent history and books that have reflected western philosophy, theology and ideas. The brilliant biblical scholar Bernard Ramm described this incredible influence on western literature as a result of the life, death and resurrection of Jesus Christ: "From the Apostolic Fathers dating from A.D. 95 to the modern times is one great literary river inspired by the Bible — Bible dictionaries,

Bible encyclopedias, Bible lexicons, Bible atlases, and Bible geographies. These may be taken as a starter. Then at random, we may mention the vast bibliographies around theology, religious education, hymnology, missions, the biblical languages, church history, religious biography, devotional works, commentaries, philosophy of religion, evidences, apologetics, and on and on. There seems to be an endless number" (Bernard Ramm, *Protestant Christian Evidences* [Moody Press, 1957], p. 239). In his comment on the sustained and overwhelming attacks on the authority of the Bible from the academic community, Bernard Ramm wrote about the total failure of these attacks to make a serious dent in the popularity and influence of the Scriptures. "A thousand times over, the death knell of the Bible has been sounded, the funeral procession formed, the inscription cut on the tombstone, and committal read. But somehow the corpse never stays put."

Confirmation From Non-Christian Sources

Following is an overview of several Roman and pagan historical manuscript records from the early centuries of this era about the life and influence of Jesus Christ which have survived for almost two thousand years.

Cornelius Tacitus – Governor of Asia

Cornelius Tacitus was a Roman historian and governor of Asia [Turkey] in A.D. 112. He referred to the persecution of the Christians caused by Emperor Nero's false accusation that the Christians had burned Rome. "Christus [Christ], the founder of the name, was put to death by Pontius Pilate, procurator of Judea in the reign of Tiberius: but the pernicious superstition, repressed for a time broke out again, not only through Judea, where the mischief originated, but through the city of Rome also" (Annals XV 44). Tacitus, as a careful historian with access to the government archives of Rome, confirmed many details in the Gospels, Acts, and Romans.

Suetonius – Roman Historian

Suetonius was the official historian of Rome in A.D. 125. In his *Life of Claudius* (25.4) he referred to the Christians causing disturbances in Rome which led to their being banished from the city. He identifies the sect of Christians as being derived from "the instigation of Chrestus" which was his spelling of the name Christ.

Pliny the Younger

Plinius Secundus, known as Pliny the Younger, declared that the Christians were "in the habit of meeting on a certain fixed day before it was light, when they sang in alternate verse a hymn to Christ as to a god, and bound themselves to a solemn oath, not to any wicked deeds, but never to commit any fraud, theft, adultery, never to falsify their word, not to deny a trust when they should be called upon to deliver it up."

Pliny was governor of the Roman province of Bithynia [Turkey] in A.D. 112. He wrote to the emperor requesting instructions about the interrogation of the Christians whom he was persecuting. In his *Epistles X 96*, he states that these believers would not worship Emperor Trajan and would not curse their leader, Jesus Christ, even under extreme torture. Pliny described the Christians as people who loved the truth at any cost. It is impossible to believe that these people would willingly die for something they knew was a lie. Their martyrdom was based on the fact that they knew the truth of the statements in the Gospels about Jesus.

Lucian of Samosata

Lucian lived in Samosata a century after Christ. In his book, *The Passing Peregrinus*, he declared that Jesus was worshiped by his followers and was "the man who was crucified in Palestine because he introduced this new cult into the world."

Evidence About Jesus from Flavius Josephus

"Now there was about this time Jesus, a wise man, if it be lawful to call him a man, for he was a doer of wonderful works, a teacher of such men as receive the truth with pleasure. He drew over to him both many of the Jews, and many of the Gentiles. He was [the] Christ, and when Pilate, at the suggestion of the principal men among us, had condemned him to the cross, those that loved him at the first did not forsake him: for he appeared to them alive again the third day: as the divine prophets had foretold these and ten thousand other wonderful things concerning him. And the tribe of Christians so named from him are not extinct at this day" (Flavius Josephus, *Antiquities of the Jews*, bk. XVIII, chap. III, Section 3).

Flavius Josephus was a Pharisee and priest living in Jerusalem. Born in A.D. 37, following the death of Christ, he witnessed firsthand The events leading up to the destruction of Jerusalem and the

Temple. He fought as a general of the Jewish rebel forces in Galilee in the war against Rome. Josephus was captured by the Romans at the fall of the city of Jotapata and became friends with the Roman general Vespasian. As a historian, with access to both Roman and Jewish governmental records, he described the events in Israel during the turbulent decades of the first century. In A.D. 94, Josephus published in Rome his definitive study of the history of the Jewish people called *Antiquities of the Jews*. One of the most fascinating passages in his important history concerned the events in the life, death and resurrection of Jesus Christ.

Numerous liberal scholars have declared that this reference to Jesus Christ and another reference to James and John the Baptist must be interpolations or forgeries by later Christian editors. In other words they have concluded that Josephus's reference to Jesus could not possibly be genuine. However, such an assertion of forgery requires significant proof. Yet none of these scholars can produce a single ancient copy of Josephus's *Antiquities of the Jews*, that does not contain this passage on Jesus. If they had found dozens of ancient copies of Josephus's book that failed to contain this passage they would have some "evidence" that this was not an original passage by the Jewish historian. However, Phillip Schaff declared in his book, *History of the Christian Church*, that all ancient copies of Josephus's book, including the early Slavonic [Russian] and Arabic language versions, contain the disputed passage about the life of Christ. Every one of the ancient copies from the fourth and fifth centuries in several different languages contains these passages. No one has ever explained how an editor could have altered each of these widely distributed versions during the centuries following their publication. The real reason why these liberal scholars reject the Josephus passage out of hand is their deeply ingrained prejudice that it could not be genuine because it confirms the historicity of the claims about Jesus Christ. If the events recorded in the Gospels actually occurred, it is only natural that Josephus would mention them at the appropriate place in his narrative of that turbulent century. In fact, it would be astonishing if Josephus had failed to mention anything about the ministry and resurrection of Jesus.

The biblical scholar Craig Blomberg wrote in his 1987 book, *The Historical Reliability of the Gospels*, that "many recent studies of Josephus however, agree that much of the passage closely resembles Josephus' style of writing elsewhere.... But most of the passage seems to be authentic and is certainly the most important ancient non-Christian testimony to the life of Jesus which has been preserved." Blomberg concluded his lengthy analysis of the historical evidence for and against Jesus, with this statement; "The gospels may therefore be trusted as historically reliable." In addition, R. C. Stone, in his article titled "Josephus" wrote the following: "The passage concerning Jesus has been regarded by some as a Christian interpolation; but the bulk of the evidence, both external and internal, marks it as genuine. Josephus must have known the main facts about the life and death of Jesus, and his historian's curiosity certainly would lead him to investigate the movement which was gaining adherents even in high circles. Arnold Toynbee rates him among the five greatest Hellenic historians" (ZPEG, vol. 3:697).

Evidence About James, the Brother of Jesus

In another passage in Josephus's book, *Antiquities of the Jews* (bk. XX, chap. IX, sect. 1) he described the death of James, the brother of Jesus. "As therefore Ananus (the High Priest) was of such a disposition, he thought he had now a good opportunity, as Festus (the Roman Procurator) was now dead, and Albinus (the new Procurator) was still on the road; so he assembled a council of judges, and brought before it the brother of Jesus the so-called Christ, whose name was James, together with some others, and having accused them as law-breakers, he delivered them over to be stoned." While many liberal scholars reject the historicity of the first passage about Jesus Christ, most modern scholars accept the authenticity of this second passage about James "the brother of Jesus the so-called Christ."

Evidence About John the Baptist

Josephus described the death of John the Baptist as follows: "Now, some of the Jews thought that the destruction of Herod's army came from God, and that very justly, as a punishment of what he did against John, that was called the Baptist; for Herod slew him, who was a good man, and commanded the Jews to exercise virtue, both as to righteousness towards one another, and piety towards God, and so to come to baptism; for that the washing [with water] would be acceptable to him, if they made use of it, not in order to the putting away, [or the remission] of some sins [only] but for the purification of the body: supposing still that the soul was thoroughly purified beforehand by righteousness. Now, when [many] there came to crowd about him, for they were greatly moved [or pleased] by hearing his words, Herod, who feared lest the great influence John had over the people might put it into his power and inclination to raise a rebellion [for they seemed ready to do anything he should advise], thought it best, by putting him to death, to prevent any mischief he might cause, and not bring himself into difficulties, by sparing a man who might make him repent of it when it should be too hate. Accordingly he was sent a prisoner, out of Herod's suspicious temper, to Macherus (Masada), the castle I before mentioned, and was there put to death" (*Antiquities of the Jews*, bk. XVIII, chap. V, sect. 2). These historical descriptions by Josephus, together with the other sources mentioned above, provide ample evidence that Jesus of Nazareth lived in the first century of this era.

Further Confirmation – Julius Africanus and Thallus

Julius Africanus was a North African Christian teacher writing in A.D. 215. He recorded the writing of a pagan historian by the name Thallus who lived in A.D. 52 shortly after the resurrection of Christ. Thallus recorded in his history that there was a miraculous darkness covering the face of the earth at the Passover in A.D. 32. Julius Africanus records, "Thallus, in the third book of his histories, explains away this darkness as an eclipse of the sun — unreasonably, as it seems to me." Julius explained that Thallus's theory was unreasonable because a solar eclipse could not occur at the same time as the full moon and it was at the season of the Paschal full moon that Christ died.

This historical reference by the pagan historian Thallus confirmed the Gospel account regarding the darkness that covered the earth when Jesus was dying on the cross. There are other ancient historical references to this supernatural darkness at the death of Christ. Modern astronomers confirm that Julius Africanus was right in his conclusion that a normal eclipse could not possibly occur at the time of a full moon, which was the time of the Passover. The high priest carefully calculated the position of the full moon to the smallest degree because their whole Jewish liturgical calendar, especially Passover, depended on following the lunar position exactly.

It is interesting to note that the ancient Jewish Targums, or paraphrases of the Old Testament, contain additional evidence that the Jews expected the Messiah to be born in Bethlehem as prophesied in

Micah 5:2. Charles R. Condor discovered that seventy-two of the Targums on various passages of the Old Testament contain information about the coming Messiah although the biblical passage itself did not contain the name Messiah. It is fascinating to note that two of these well respected Targums indicated clearly that the Messiah would be born at or near Bethlehem. For example, the Targum on Genesis 35:21 talks about Israel pitching its tents "beyond the tower of Eder." The Targum of Jonathan adds this comment identifying this location, "which is the place where shall be revealed the King Messias in the end of days." Charles R. Condor noted in his submission to *the Palestine Exploration Fund Report* (Quarterly Report, April 1875), that "Migdol Eder, or 'the Tower of the Flock' was known in A.D. 700 as about 1,000 paces from Bethlehem," which is the location of the ruins of the Monastery of the Holy Shepherds. Another Targum, commenting on the passage Exodus 12:42, makes a fascinating reference to the area of Nazareth where Jesus was raised by His parents in His father's carpentry shop. This Targum states that "Moses cometh forth from the desert and Messias goeth forth from Roma." This "Roma" was a village located near to the town of Nazareth (Charles R. Condor, *Palestine Exploration Fund* [Quarterly Report, January 1876], p. 98).

Following an exhaustive study of the literature regarding the archeological and historical controversies about the accuracy of the New Testament, the researcher and scientist Henry M. Morris, Ph.D., concluded that we can totally trust the manuscripts as correct records of the events described. Morris wrote, "no statement in the New Testament has to this date been refuted by an unquestioned find of science or history. This in itself is a unique testimony to the amazing accuracy and authenticity of the New Testament records."

The historian Philip Schaff outlined the overwhelming influence which the life of Jesus of Nazareth had on subsequent history and culture of the western world. "This Jesus of Nazareth, without money and arms, conquered more millions than Alexander, Caesar, Mohammed, and Napoleon; without science and learning, He shed more light on things human and divine than all philosophers and scholars combined; without the eloquence of schools, He spoke such words of life as were never spoken before or since, and produced effects which lie beyond the reach of orator or poet; without writing a single line, He set more pens in motion, and furnished themes for more sermons, orations, discussions, learned volumes, works of art, and songs of praise than the whole army of great men of ancient and modern times" (Philip Schaff, *The Person of Christ* [American Tract Society, 1913]).

While the historical records provide overwhelming evidence to prove the absolute reliability of the Gospel records about Jesus Christ, the statements of the disciples can only reveal His earthly existence as the Messiah. We have not yet witnessed the reality of His awesome glory that will be revealed when we see Him returning in His glory to take His church home to heaven nor when He will reveal Himself to the population of earth at the Second Coming. The Puritan writer John Owen discussed the glory of Jesus Christ in these words. "Should the Lord Jesus appear now to any of us in His majesty and glory, it would not be to our edification nor consolation. For we are not meet nor able, by the power of any light or grace that we have received, or can receive, to bear the immediate appearance and representation of them. His beloved apostle John had leaned on His bosom probably many a time in His life, in the intimate familiarities of love; but when He afterward appeared to Him in His glory, 'he fell at His feet as dead.'" The men and women living in the first century of this era, who heard the words of Jesus of Nazareth, were amazed at the tremendous wisdom shown by His words. When Jesus Christ finally appears in His revealed glory as Almighty God at the Great Day of the Lord, Matthew prophesied that "then shall all the tribes of the earth mourn, and they shall see the Son of Man coming in the clouds of heaven with power and great glory" (Matthew 24:30).

Extraordinary Evidence About Jesus in the Dead Sea Scrolls

If someone had asked a minister in 1947 to prove that the original Hebrew Scriptures from the Old Testament were reliably copied without error throughout the last two thousand years, he might have had some difficulty in providing an answer. The oldest Old Testament manuscript used by the King James translators was dated approximately A.D. 1100. Obviously, that old manuscript from A.D. 1100 was a copy of a copy of a copy, etc., for over two thousand years. How could we be sure that the text in the A.D. 1100 copy of the Scriptures was identical with the original text as given to the writers by God and inspired by Him? However, an extraordinary discovery occurred in the turbulent year before Israel became a nation. A Bedouin Arab found a cave in Qumran near the Dead Sea which ultimately yielded over a thousand priceless manuscripts dating back before A.D. 68, when the Roman legions destroyed the Qumran village during the Jewish war against Rome.

An Arab shepherd boy discovered the greatest archeological find in history in 1947. When the ancient Hebrew scrolls from these caves were examined by scholars they found that this Qumran site contained a library with hundreds of precious texts of both biblical and secular manuscripts that dated back before the destruction of the Second Temple and the death of Jesus Christ. Once the Bedouins recognized the value of the scrolls they began searching for additional documents in every valley and cave near the Dead Sea. The most incredible discovery was the immense library of biblical manuscripts in Cave Four at Qumran that contained every single book of the Old Testament with the exception of the Book of Esther. Multiple copies of several biblical texts such as Genesis, Deuteronomy and Isaiah were found in Cave Four. Scholars were able to reach back a further two thousand years in time to examine biblical texts that had lain undisturbed in the desert caves during all of the intervening centuries. The scholars discovered that the manuscript copies of the most authoritative Hebrew text, the received text, used by the King James translators in 1611, were virtually identical to these ancient Dead Sea Scrolls. After carefully comparing the manuscripts they discovered that, aside from a tiny number of spelling variations, not a single word was altered from the original scrolls in the caves from the much copied A.D. 1100 manuscripts used by the Authorized King James Version translators in 1611. How could the Bible have been copied so accurately and faithfully over the many centuries without human error entering into the text? The answer is found in the overwhelming respect and fear of God that motivated Jewish and Christian scholars whose job was to faithfully copy the text of the Bible. In a later chapter dealing with the Hebrew Codes beneath the text of the Bible, I will share how the Masoretic scribes meticulously copied the text of the Scriptures over the centuries.

The Essenes were a Jewish community of ascetics that lived primarily in three communities: Qumran at the Dead Sea, the Essene Quarter of Jerusalem (Mount Zion), and Damascus. They appear to have existed from approximately 200 B.C., until the destruction of their communities in Jerusalem and Qumran by the Roman armies in A.D. 68. During the first century there were three significant Jewish religious communities: the Pharisees, the Sadducees, and the Essenes. The Essenes established their religious community near the shores of the Dead Sea. In their love for the Word of God they faithfully copied each Old Testament scroll in their Scriptorium in the village of Qumran. New evidence indicates that these men of God were aware of the new religious leader in Israel known as Jesus of Nazareth and the group of writings about Him known as the New Testament. The Christian historian Eusebius, who wrote around A.D. 300, believed that the Essenes were influenced in their beliefs by Christianity.

When the scrolls were first discovered, many Christian scholars naturally wondered if they might contain evidence about the new faith of Christianity. Despite overwhelming interest, the vast majority of scrolls were not translated for publication in the intervening forty-nine years. For almost fifty years, the hopes of Christian scholars were frustrated by the decision of the small group of original scroll scholars to withhold publication and release of a significant number of these precious scrolls. Some scholars speculated publicly that there might be evidence about Christ in the unpublished scrolls but the original scroll scholars vehemently denied these claims. While some scroll scholars had published part of their assigned texts, after forty-five years the team responsible for the huge number of scrolls discovered in Cave Four had published only twenty percent of the five hundred Dead Sea Scrolls in their possession.

Quotes from the New Testament in the Dead Sea Scrolls

Finally, after a public relations campaign led by the Biblical Archeology Review magazine demanded the release of the unpublished scrolls to other scholars, the last of the unpublished scrolls were released to the academic world. To the great joy and surprise of many scholars, the scrolls contain definite references to the New Testament and, most importantly, to Jesus of Nazareth. In the last few years several significant scrolls were released that shed new light on the New Testament and the life of Jesus. One of the most extraordinary of these scrolls released in 1991 actually referred directly to the crucifixion of Jesus Christ.

The Crucified Messiah Scroll

In 1991 the world was astonished to hear that one of the unpublished scrolls included incredible references to a "Messiah" who suffered crucifixion for the sins of men. The scroll was translated by Dr. Robert Eisenman, Professor of Middle East Religions of California State University. He declared, "The text is of the most far-reaching significance because it shows that whatever group was responsible for these writings was operating in the same general scriptural and Messianic framework of early Christianity." Although the original scroll team still claimed that there was no evidence about early Christianity in the unpublished scrolls, this new scroll totally contradicted their statements. This single scroll is earth-shaking in its importance. As Dr. Norman Golb, Professor of Jewish History at the University of Chicago said, "It shows that contrary to what some of the editors said, there are lots of surprises in the scrolls, and this is one of them."

This remarkable five-line scroll contained fascinating information about the death of the Messiah. It referred to "the Prophet Isaiah" and his Messianic prophecy (Chapter 53) that identified the Messiah as one who will suffer for the sins of his people. This scroll provides an amazing parallel to the New Testament revelation that the Messiah would first suffer death before He would ultimately return to rule the nations. Many scholars believed that the Jews during the first century of our era believed that, when he finally came, the Messiah would rule forever without dying. The exciting discovery of this scroll reveals that the Essene writer of this scroll understood the dual role of the Messiah as Christians did. This scroll identified the Messiah as the "Shoot of Jesse" (King David's father) the "Branch of David," and declared that he was "pierced" and "wounded." The word "pierced" remind us of the Messianic prophecy in Psalm 22: 16: "They pierced my hands and feet." The prophet Jeremiah (23:5) said, "I will raise unto David a righteous branch."

The scroll also describes the Messiah as a "leader of the community" who was "put to death." This reference pointing clearly to the historical Jesus of Nazareth is creating shock waves for liberal scholarship that previously assumed that the Gospel account about Jesus was a myth. Jesus is the only one who ever claimed to be the Messiah who was crucified. The genealogies recorded in both Matthew and Luke's Gospels, reveal that Jesus was the only one who could prove by the genealogical records kept in the Temple that He was the lineage of King David as the "Son of Jesse." Since the tragic destruction of the Temple and its records in A.D. 70, it would be impossible for anyone else to ever prove their claim to be the Messiah based on their genealogical descent from King David. Additionally, the scroll identified the Messiah as "the sceptre" which probably refers to the Genesis 49:10 prophecy: "The sceptre shall not depart from Judah, nor a lawgiver from between his feet, until Shiloh come; and unto him shall the gathering of the people be." This scroll confirms the historical truthfulness of the New Testament record about Jesus and His crucifixion. The evidence from the scroll suggests that the Jewish Essene writer acknowledged that Jesus of Nazareth was the "suffering Messiah" who died for the sins of His people.

The "Son of God" Scroll

Another fascinating scroll discovered in Cave Four known as 4Q246 refers to the hope of a future Messiah figure. This is another of the scrolls that was unpublished until recently. Amazingly, the text in this scroll refers to the Messiah as "the son of God" and the "son of the Most High." These words are the exact wording recorded in the Gospel of Luke.

The Text of Scroll 4Q246 – the Son of God Scroll

"He shall be called the son of God,
and they shall designate [call] him son of the Most High.
Like the appearance of comets, so shall be their kingdom.
For brief years they shall reign over the earth and shall
    trample on all;
one people shall trample on another and
one province on another until the people of God shall rise
    and all shall rest from the sword."

Compare the words in the scroll 4Q246 text to the inspired words found in Luke 1:32 and 35: "He shall be great, and shall be called the Son of the Highest: and the Lord God shall give unto him the throne of his father David. . . . And the angel answered and said unto her, The Holy Ghost shall come upon thee, and the power of the Highest shall overshadow thee: therefore also that holy thing which shall be born of thee shall be called the Son of God" (Luke 1:32–35).

Anyone comparing these two first century texts will be startled by the amazing similarity of concept and wording describing the Messianic leader. One of the great differences between Christian and Jewish conceptions of the promised Messiah revolves around His relationship to God. While the Jews believe the Messiah will be a great man, such as Moses, with a divine mission, the Christians believe that the Bible teaches that the Messiah would be uniquely "the Son of God." The Jewish view usually held that the concept of a "son of God" violated the primary truth of monotheism found in Deuteronomy 6:4, "Hear, O Israel: The Lord our God is one Lord." The Christians believed that Jesus' claim to be the Son of God was not a violation of Deuteronomy 6:4. Rather, Christians believe in the Trinity, the doctrine that the Father, the Son and the Holy Spirit are revealed in the Bible to be One God, revealed in three personalities. As Christians, we do not believe in three separate gods. Therefore, Christians understand the statements about Jesus as the Son of God to be in complete conformity to the truth of monotheism — there is only one God. It is fascinating in this regard to consider the presence of these statements in this first century Jewish text: "He shall be called the son of God, and they shall designate [call] him son of the Most High."

The presence of these statements in the Dead Sea Scrolls suggests that some of the Essenes either accepted the Messianic claims of Jesus to be the Son of God or anticipated this concept. Either possibility opens up new areas for exploration. Another possibility that must be considered is this: Is it possible that this scroll 4Q246 is a direct quote from the writer hearing the words of the Gospel of Luke that was now widely circulating according to early Christian witnesses? Luke, the physician, claimed that he wrote the Gospel of Luke as an eyewitness of the events he personally observed. In Luke 1:1–3, he says: "Forasmuch as many have taken in hand to set forth in order a declaration of those things which are most surely believed among us, Even as they delivered them unto us, which from the beginning were eyewitnesses, and ministers of the word; It seemed good to me also, having had perfect understanding of all things from the very first, to write unto thee in order, most excellent Theophilus."

The discovery of the virtually identical wording "the Son of God" from Luke 1:32 and 35 with the scroll found buried in a cave in A.D. 68, stands as a tremendous witness to the early existence and transmission of the Gospel records within thirty-five years of Christ. If the Gospels were written and distributed within thirty-five years of the events of the life of Jesus (as the Gospels claim) then they stand as the best eyewitness historical records we could ever hope to possess. In fact, all of these ancient historical records confirm the truth of the Gospels.

Other New Testament Quotes Identified in the Scrolls

In 1971, a Spanish biblical scholar named Jose O'Callaghan studied some of the small fragments of scrolls discovered in Cave Seven at Qumran. He was looking for correspondences between these fragments of Greek scrolls and the Septuagint, the Greek translation of the Hebrew Old Testament that was widely used by Jesus and the apostles.

These fragments are quite small, containing only small portions of each verse. After almost two thousand years, the elements and insects have significantly damaged these manuscripts. In some cases only small fragments containing parts of a verse on three or four lines remain from an original scroll. It required considerable detective work to determine the precise text in these tiny fragments.

One day he carefully examined several small scroll fragments located in a photo page in *The Discoveries of the Judean Desert of Jordan*. To his great surprise O'Callaghan noticed that several did not fit any Old Testament text. These fragments were listed as "Fragments not identified." To his amazement, Dr. O'Callaghan found that these Greek language fragments bore an uncanny resemblance to several verses in the New Testament. He read the Greek words "beget" and a word that could be "Gennesaret," a word for the Sea of Galilee. The fragment containing "Gennesaret" appears to be a quotation of the passage referring to the feeding of the five thousand found in Mark 6:52,53, which states: "For they considered not the miracle of the loaves: for their heart was hardened. And when they had passed over, they came into the land of Gennesaret, and drew to the shore."

If these texts are actually portions of these Christian writings they would be the earliest New Testament texts ever discovered. The *New York Times* responded, "If O'Callaghan's theory is accepted, it would prove that at least one of the Gospels, that of St. Mark, was written only a few years after the death of Jesus." The *Los Angeles Times* headlined, "Nine New Testament fragments dated A.D. 50 to A.D. 100 have been discovered in a Dead Sea Cave." It stated that "if validated, [they] constitute the most sensational biblical trove uncovered in recent times."

Other Scroll Fragments and the New Testament

Dr. Jose O'Callaghan ultimately identified eight different scroll fragments from Cave Seven that appear to be quotes from New Testament passages. The scholarly magazine *Bible Review* ran a fascinating article on Dr. O'Callaghan, these scrolls, and their possible connection with the New Testament in an article in December, 1995.

The fragments appeared to O'Callaghan to be portions of the following verses from the Gospels and Paul's Epistles:

"For the earth bringeth forth fruit of herself . . . "
(Mark 4:28).
"And he saw them toiling in rowing; . . . "(Mark 6:48).
"And Jesus answering said unto them, Render to Caesar . . .
(Mark 12:17).
"And when they had eaten enough, they lightened the
ship . . . " (Acts 27:38).
"And not only so, but we also joy in God through our Lord
Jesus Christ . . ."(Romans 5:11–12).
"And without controversy great is the mystery of
godliness: . . . "(1 Timothy 3:16).
"For if any be a hearer of the word, and not a
doer . . ."(James 1:23–24).

As one example of Dr. O'Callaghan's study, he examined a small scroll fragment known as 7Q5 that contained only twenty Greek letters on five lines of text. Many of the thousands of scroll fragments that were successfully identified from the Qumran site are equally small. Another scroll scholar, Carsten Thiede, agrees with O'Callaghan that portions of the Mark 6:52,53 passage appears in this scroll fragment. While other scroll scholars disagree with the identification of this fragment as a verse from the New Testament they do admit that almost *all* of the scrolls found in Cave Seven were written in the period between 50 B.C. and A.D. 50, which is consistent with the time of the writing of the Gospel of Mark.

Naturally, as with other matters connected with the controversial Dead Sea Scrolls, many scholars disagreed with the conclusions of Dr. O'Callaghan. The debate still continues twenty years later. At this stage we cannot be certain that O'Callaghan's conclusion is correct. More work needs to be done. However, the recent publication of the discovery of Scroll 4Q246 and its identical reference to "the Son of God" as found in Luke 1:32 and 35, provide strong support for the possibility that these fragments are related to these New Testament passages. In addition, I have great hopes that the new archeological exploration of recently detected caves at Qumran by my friend Gary Collett may provide new evidence including New Testament references. Many of these mysteries will be solved when the final four hundred unpublished scrolls are finally published in the next few years. The new dig at Qumran may also uncover additional scrolls that will help us understand more clearly the Messianic beliefs of this group of religious men and women who lived at this desert site during the time when Jesus walked the earth.

When we consider the total amount of evidence that confirms the biblical record about Jesus of Nazareth we can have confidence that we know more about the life and resurrection of Christ than we know about any other person in the ancient world. God has not left us in darkness concerning the truthfulness of the miracles, prophecies and teaching of His Son, Jesus Christ.

6

Scientific Proof that the Bible is Accurate

One of the greatest proofs that the Scriptures are inspired by God is that they reveal a staggering amount of advanced scientific knowledge. The Bible is not a scientific book; however, when it does make scientific statements, they are stunning in their accuracy. These biblical statements are thousands of years in advance of the scientific knowledge present in the day when the writers penned the words of the Holy Scriptures. The psalmist David wrote, "That I may publish with the voice of thanksgiving, and tell of all thy wondrous works" (Psalm 26:7). As you consider God's "wondrous works" and the astonishing level of scientific knowledge from the Bible presented in this chapter, ask yourself a question: How could the writers of the Scriptures possibly know these facts unless they were supernaturally inspired by God?

Throughout the Word of God are statements which can now be tested as to their accuracy due to the incredible advances in scientific knowledge in the last few decades. The Book of Genesis describes the supernatural creation of man in these words, "And the Lord God formed man of the dust of the ground, and breathed into his nostrils the breath of life; and man became a living being" (Genesis 2:7). For many years scientists laughed at the apparent simplicity of the scriptural account that God used "the dust of the ground" to construct the complex elements and molecules that make up a human being. However, after a century of scientific examination of the elements within the human body, scientists have been startled to discover that clay and earth contain every single element found in the human body. *A Reader's Digest* article in November 1982, described a fascinating discovery by the researchers at NASA's Ames Research Center which confirmed the Bible's account that every single element found in the human body exists within the soil. The scientists concluded, "We are just beginning to learn. The biblical scenario for the creation of life turns out to be not far off the mark."

It might surprise you to know that many of the greatest scientific minds of the last several centuries were Bible-believing Christians who totally accepted the scientific accuracy of the Word of God. For example, Isaac Newton, perhaps the greatest scientific mind in history, firmly accepted the Word of God and creation. Other strong believers in God who changed the face of scientific knowledge included: Lord Kelvin, the creator of the science of thermodynamics; Louis Pasteur, the discover of pasteurization; Johann Kepler, the brilliant astronomer who created modern astronomy; and Robert Boyle, the greatest chemist of his age. With every new scientific discovery we find additional proof of the complexity of the great design that God used to create our universe.

The Creation of The Universe

The Book of Genesis begins with the words, "God created the heaven and the earth." Until 1950, most scientists believed in some variation of the "steady state theory," which suggested that the universe had always existed as we observe it today. This theory was in total contradiction to the Word of God which, as recorded in its opening pages, affirms that God had created the entire universe at a definite point of time in the past. New discoveries in astronomy and astrophysics then forced the scientific world to change their theory. Today, virtually all scientists accept some variation of the "Big Bang Theory" which suggest the whole universe came into existence at a particular point of time, when an incredibly dense mass of matter exploded, forming all of the stars, galaxies and planets we witness today. Dr. P. Dirac, a Nobel Prize winner from Cambridge University, wrote: "It seems certain that there was a definite time of creation." Until quite recently, the word *creation* was never written or spoken by scientists with approval. Then, a scientific article in the 1982 issue of *Physics Letters*, an international journal of physics, contained an article by Dr. A. Vilenkin which was entitled "Creation of the Universe From Nothing." While scientists claim the creation of the universe is "outside the scope of presently known laws of physics" (S. Hawking and G. Ellis, *The Large Scale Structure of Space-Time*, [Cambridge: At the University Press, 1973], p. 364) the Word of God clearly tells us that "God created the heaven and the earth" (Genesis 1:1). However, in opposition to theoretical explosion of the Big Bang Theory, the Bible affirms that God created everything in the universe with absolute purpose and intelligence. The evidence from nature and the incredible scientific discoveries pointed out in this book reveal the meticulous design of the supernatural intelligence and power of God in that initial moment of creation when "God created the heaven and the earth."

The Lord challenged Abraham to count the stars to demonstrate the awesome number that He had created by His supernatural power. "Then He brought him outside and said, 'Look now toward heaven, and count the stars if you are able to number them.' And He said to him, 'So shall your descendants be'" (Genesis 15:5). The unaided human eye can see and count about 1,029 stars. With a pair of binoculars or an inexpensive telescope you can see over 3,300 stars. In the last few years modern telescopes have allowed us to view over two hundred million stars in our own galaxy called the Milky Way. As late as 1915 astronomers believed that our galaxy composed the entire universe. Then in 1925, the great astronomer Edwin Hubble used his new one-hundred-inch mirror telescope on Mount Wilson, the largest in the world at that time, to view whole new galaxies of stars that were more than six million trillion miles away from earth. Professor Hubble proved that the universe contained as many galaxies outside our galaxy as there were stars inside our home galaxy, the Milky Way. During the last century very powerful telescopes of astronomers revealed the known universe contains over ten billion galaxies like our Milky Way. However, in the last few months, scientists have used the Hubble Telescope to focus on a tiny point in space so small that it is equal to focusing your eye on an area the size of a grain of sand held at arm's length.

After intensely examining this very small area of space the astronomers determined that it contained an additional fifteen hundred galaxies, each the size of our Milky Way. They were astonished to discover that the universe is more than five times larger than we previously believed. They now know that the known universe contains more than fifty billion galaxies with each galaxy containing more than two hundred million stars. The mind of man can scarcely conceive of such a vast universe in which stars extend out from our solar system for millions of trillions of miles in every direction. To obtain a sense of the vastness of our universe, try this exercise. Take a piece of paper and draw two circles with one small circle representing our sun at the top of the page. Using the scale of one inch to represent ten million miles, draw a much smaller circle nine inches lower at the bottom of the page to represent our earth. Now let's draw another small circle to represent our nearest neighboring star, Alpha Centauri. You would need to draw the circle representing the star Alpha Centauri over forty miles away from your piece of paper to correctly represent the vast distance between the earth and the closest star. Light travels through space at an amazing speed of 187,000 miles every second or six trillion miles every year. A ray of light leaving our closest neighbor, Alpha Centauri, would take four years to reach our planet as it crosses an astonishing twenty-four trillion miles of empty space.

The psalmist David wrote, "By the word of the Lord the heavens were made, And all the host of them by the breath of His mouth. . . . For He spoke, and it was done; He commanded, and it stood fast" (Psalm 33:6,9). Despite all of the billions spent on astronomy, scientists have failed to come up with a credible theory to account for the existence of either the universe or even our own earth. In 1980, the astronomer Professor Herman Bondi declared the total failure of modern science to account for the universe: "As an erstwhile cosmologist, I speak with feeling of the fact that theories of the origin of the universe have been disproved by present day empirical evidence as have various theories of the origin of the solar system" (Herman Bondi, *New Scientist*, Nov. 21, 1980, Letters Section: Reference to quote by Karl Popperp, p. 611). Another great astronomer, Sir Harold Jeffreys, wrote, "To sum up, I think that all suggested accounts of the origin of the solar system are subject to serious objections. The conclusion in the present state of the subject would be that the system cannot exist" (Harold Jeffreys, *The Earth: Its Origin, History, and Physical Constitution* [Cambridge: England: University Press, 1970], p. 359). In other words, Professor Jeffreys admitted that none of the atheistic theories can account for the universe as it exists.

Perhaps they should return to the first words in Genesis as recorded by Moses, "In the beginning God created the heaven and the earth" (Genesis 1:1).

The Bible declares that God separated the waters below from the waters that were above (in the heavens): "And God said, Let there be a firmament in the midst of the waters, and let it divide the waters from the waters. And God made the firmament, and divided the waters which were under the firmament from the waters which were above the firmament: and it was so" (Genesis 1:6,7). This biblical statement declares that God created a large amount of water which He placed in the heavens or outer space. Does any evidence exist to prove the accuracy of this statement from the Bible? The existence of water in space seemed improbable, to say the least, to scientists until quite recently. However, further astronomical discoveries have proven conclusively that massive amounts of water do exist in space, just as the Bible claimed. Naturally, because of extreme temperatures, the waters in space are frozen into permanent ice. Recently our satellites discovered large quantities of ice in the ice caps of Mars as well as in the rings of Saturn. In addition, we now know that the huge comets that travel through our solar system are composed of massive amounts of ice.

A massive block of ice from space collided with the earth at the beginning of this century at a point in northern Russia: "In the morning of 30 June 1908, a fantastic explosion occurred in central Siberia. . . . Witnesses described an enormous meteoric bolide visible in the sky for a few seconds. Other witnesses from a distance of 60 kilometers (36 miles) from the point of impact were knocked over . . . Seismic shocks were registered over the whole world . . . this event was due to the collision with the earth of a block of ice weighing 30,000 tons which . . . released energy equivalent to that of a thermonuclear bomb of 12 megatons." (J. Audouzze, *The Cambridge Atlas of Astronomy*, [Cambridge: At the University Press, 1985], p. 219). Researchers found that this Siberian explosion was caused by a small fragment of the comet Encke that broke away during its passage through our solar system. The latest scientific research has revealed that massive amounts of ice also exist at the outer edge of our solar system. The Ort Cloud at the edge of our solar system is a vast region of space that is estimated to hold as many as a trillion large comets composed of ice and rock. Each large comet is calculated to contain as much as one trillion tons of ice. The vast amount of water in our oceans is less than a fraction of the quantities of water that exist in the "firmament above" in the heavens as reported in the Book of Genesis. A passage in Job also refers to the ice and frost in the heavens: "Hath the rain a father? or who hath begotten the drops of dew? Out of whose womb came the ice? and the hoary frost of heaven, who hath gendered it? The waters are hid as with a stone, and the face of the deep is frozen. Canst thou bind the sweet influences of Pleiades, or loose the bands of Orion?" (Job 38:28–31).

The Law of Conservation of Energy

After exhaustive experiments, modern scientists have developed two fundamental laws of the science of thermodynamics that describe the nature of our known universe. The first law is the Law of Conservation of Energy which reveals that "energy can be neither created nor destroyed." The Law of Conservation of Energy was explained by the science writer Isaac Asimov as follows: "Energy can be transferred from one place to another, or transformed from one form to another, but it can be neither created nor destroyed." In other words, this law states that the whole amount of energy that exists throughout our universe remains constant and can never change. For example, when they explode a nuclear device, the uranium 235 and plutonium within the warhead are not annihilated. The matter is simply transformed into a staggering release of heat and light energy. Every experiment has confirmed this Law of Conservation of Energy as the most basic fundamental understanding of the way the universe works. This law describes the present state of the universe after its initial creation by God.

Although this fundamental law of the universe was only discovered and proven scientifically during the last century, the Word of God recorded this principle thousands of years ago. Moses wrote in Genesis: "And on the seventh day God ended his work which he had made; and he rested on the seventh day from all his work which he had made. And God blessed the seventh day, and sanctified it: because that in it he had rested from all his work which God created and made" (Genesis 2:2,3). This inspired passage clearly declares that when God completed the creation of man on the sixth day, "He rested from all His work which He had made." After He created man on the sixth day, His work was complete: this accounts for the First Law of Conservation of Energy. In addition, the Scriptures reveal why nothing can now be either totally destroyed or annihilated because Jesus Christ, who created all things, is "upholding all things by the word of His power" (Hebrews 1:3). In another passage the writer of the Book of Hebrews declared that Jesus, the Creator of the universe, had finished His acts of creation: "For he that is entered into his rest, he also hath ceased from his own works, as God did from his" (Hebrews 4:10).

The Law of Entropy

The second law of science is the Law of Entropy. This second Law of Thermodynamics describes the fact that all systems and elements of the universe tend to disintegrate to a lower order of available energy or organization. Another way of expressing this universal fact of entropy is to note that, over time, all things, whether a house or a sword, will tend to disintegrate to dust or rust, a lower order of organization than the original house or sword. Throughout history mankind has observed that everything, from a human body to a castle, begins to decay from the moment of maximum amount of order or organized information at the beginning until, years later, the object ceases to function. When you think seriously about this universal principle you can immediately see that this principle proves that it is absolutely impossible for the theory of evolution to be true. Evolution suggests that all simple systems and elements become increasingly more organized and complicated by random chance. However, common sense and scientific observation have proven that all systems and elements over time tend to disintegrate to something less organized and less useful. In fact, the second Law of Thermodynamics, the Law of Entropy, absolutely proves the theory of evolution is nonsense.

Consider the implications. The Law of Conservation of Energy proves that the universe could not have created itself. It had to be created by a supernatural force outside the universe. "In the beginning God created the heaven and the earth" (Genesis 1:1). However, the Law of Entropy shows that the whole universe is running down as it decays to a lower order of available energy. This fact reveals that the universe must have been created at some point in the past and has been running down like a clock ever since that initial moment of creation. The current evolutionary theory that postulates a universe that was created from nothing by itself is totally contradicted by all the known laws of science. In addition, the Law of Entropy reveals that the universe must have been created at some definite point in the past to account for the fact that all scientific observation confirms that everything continues to decay. As an example, the fact that the sun burns up its nuclear fuel, at the rate of 200,000 nuclear explosions every second, provides the enormous radiation that floods our solar system. However, since it is burning up its store of fuel, logic declares that there must have been a point in time somewhere in the distant past when the sun was created and began this process.

The Gospel writer Luke described the coming of Christ in the daytime as follows: "Even thus shall it be in the day when the Son of man is revealed." However, several verses later, Luke described the same event by declaring that Christ will come in the night: "I tell you, in that night there shall be two men in one bed; the one shall be taken, and the other shall be left" (Luke 17:34). To the natural mind of his day, Luke's words must have sounded like a contradiction. How could a single event, the coming of the Messiah, occur simultaneously "in the day" and "in the night"? This statement by Luke must have appeared impossible and contradictory at any time from the first century until recently. However, we can now understand that, on whatever day Christ returns, it will be a daytime event for those on one side of the globe while the event will occur during the night for those living on the other side of the planet. How could Luke have known this scientific fact two thousand years ago?

The psalmist David wrote a wonderful song of praise to God in recognition of the awesome glory of the heavens that he could witness from the roof of his palace in Jerusalem: "Their line has gone out through all the earth, And their words to the end of the world. In them He has set a tabernacle for the sun, Which is like a bridegroom coming out of his chamber, And rejoices like a strong man to run its race. Its rising is from one end of heaven, And its circuit to the other end; And there is nothing hidden from its heat" (Psalm 19:4–6). In his song of praise King David declared that the sun traveled in "his circuit unto the ends of it [the heavens]." During the last few centuries many Bible critics denounced this statement as inaccurate because they falsely claimed the Bible's statement declared that the sun moved in an orbit around the earth. However, the Bible never made that claim. The Scriptures declare that the sun moved "in his circuit unto the ends of it [the heavens]." Recent discoveries by the Hubble Telescope confirmed the accuracy of the Scriptures when they proved that the sun actually moves through space in a circuit covering an enormous orbit that lasts over two hundred and sixty million years.

One of the most curious scientific revelations in the Bible regarding astronomy was pointed out by my friend David Harris, an astronomer from Toronto, Canada. This statement is found in the Book of Amos where we read about the seven stars in the constellation known as Pleiades. The King James Version translators set out the verse Amos 5:8 as: "Seek him that maketh the seven stars and Orion" (Amos 5:8 [KJV]). The King James Version translators confirmed that Amos' original Hebrew statement about "the seven stars" referred to the constellation Pleiades. However, modern translators render this verse as, "He made the Pleiades and Orion" (Amos 5:8 [NKJV]). Early translators were puzzled by this verse because there were only six stars that could be seen by the naked eye in the constellation Pleiades. Now, however, modern telescopes have revealed the existence of a seventh star in Pleiades; it is so dim that only a telescope can detect it. How else did Amos know that there were "seven stars" in the constellation unless God told him? The Bible was correct all along in its description of "seven stars" as recorded by the prophet Amos over twenty-five centuries ago.

The Earth – Created by God For Humans

Critics of the Bible have often falsely suggested that the Bible stated the earth was flat because of the biblical expression, "the four corners of the earth" (Isaiah 11:12; Revelation 7:1), as if the writers actually believed in a flat earth. However, this phrase was simply a colloquial expression. It is still used by educated individuals to indicate either the whole earth or the four extremities of the globe from a central position. God inspired the prophet Isaiah to reveal that our planet was a globe, knowledge that was far in advance of what the men in that day knew. "It is he that sitteth upon the circle of the earth, and the inhabitants thereof are as grasshoppers; that stretcheth out the heavens as a curtain, and spreadeth them out as a tent to dwell in" (Isaiah 40:22). This expression "the circle of the earth" clearly describes the earth as a sphere or globe.

The Book of Job tells us that, "He stretcheth out the north over empty space; he hangs the earth on nothing" (Job 26:7). This was an astonishingly advanced and accurate scientific statement. The ancient pagans, who were contemporary with Job, believed that the earth was balanced on the back of an elephant that rested on the back of a turtle. Other pagans believed that the mythological hero Atlas carried the earth on his shoulders. However, four thousand years ago, Job was inspired by God to correctly declare that God "hangs the earth on nothing." Only a century ago scientists believed that the earth and stars were supported by some kind of ether. Yet Job accurately stated that our planet moves in its orbit through empty outer space. An astonishing discovery by astronomers recently revealed that the area to the north of the axis of our earth toward the polar star is almost empty of stars in contrast to the other directions. There are far more distant stars in every other direction from our earth than in the area to the far north of our planet. As Job reported, "He stretches out the north over empty space" (Job 26:7). Mitchell Waldrop wrote the following statement in an article in *Science* magazine. "The recently announced 'hole in space,' a 300 million-light-year gap in the distribution of galaxies, has taken cosmologists by surprise. . . . But three very deep core samples in the Northern Hemisphere, lying in the general direction of the constellation Bootes, showed striking gaps in the red shift distribution." (Mitchell Waldrop, "Delving the Hole in Space," *Science* magazine, Nov. 27, 1981). This relative emptiness in the direction to the North of our solar system is not visible by the naked eye. It is only as the result of very careful observation by telescopes that scientists have recently proven that Job was correct.

Jewish scholars in Israel have calculated that the Torah describes the exact duration of the time that passes between the appearance of new moons as precisely 29 days, 12 hours, 44 minutes and 5 seconds or 29.53059 days. With billions of dollars of research and sophisticated observation through telescopes NASA has only recently calculated that a new moon appears every 29.530588 days! The Scriptures declare, "In the beginning God created the heaven and the earth" (Genesis 1:1). This statement revealed that God created our earth and the universe in a single moment of time. However, Genesis also reveals God's purpose: "Then God blessed them, and God said to them, 'Be fruitful and multiply; fill the earth and subdue it; have dominion over the fish of the sea, over the birds of the air, and over every living thing that moves on the earth'"(Genesis 1:28).

After examining the complexity of the variables that govern this solar system and our planet earth many scientists have declared that this solar system is "anthropic." This word simply means that this earth bears evidence that it was designed by a superior intelligence to allow human life to exist. The scientists use this word "anthropic" to indicate that they have discovered an astonishing number of scientific variables that fit within a very narrow range that allows human life to exist on this planet. Let me explain. If our earth were located much farther away from our sun we would freeze like the planet Mars. If it were much closer to the sun then we would be burned up like the hot surface of Mercury or the 860-degree temperature on Venus. If the magnetic forces within our planet were stronger or weaker, life could not exist. If our earth did not revolve every twenty-four hours then one-half of the planet would be in permanent darkness without vegetation. Meanwhile, if the earth did not revolve, the other side of the planet would be an uninhabitable desert as it suffered from the overwhelming heat of permanent exposure to the sun. If our earth were not tilted at twenty-three degrees, we would not have the seasonal variation that produces the incredible abundance of crops that feed our planet's huge population. Without the twenty-three degree tilt, less than half of the present land used for cultivation of crops would grow vegetables. The moon produces the tides that continually replenish the oceans with oxygen allowing the fish to breathe. If the earth were significantly smaller, the lessened gravity would be incapable of holding the atmosphere that is essential for breathing. A much thinner atmosphere would provide no protection from the 25,000 meteors that burn up in the atmosphere over the earth every day. In addition, a thinner atmosphere would be incapable of retaining the higher temperatures required for human and animal life to exist. If our planet earth were twice as large, the effect of increased gravity would make everything on the planet's surface weigh eight times what it weighs today. This increased weight would destroy many forms of animal and human life.

Professor Robert Jastrow has stated that "the smallest change in any of the circumstances of the natural world, such as the relative strengths of the forces of nature, or the properties of the elementary particles, would have led to a universe in which there could be no life and no man. For example, if nuclear forces were decreased by a few percent, the particles of the universe would not have come together in nuclear reactions to make the ingredients, such as carbon atoms, of which life must be constructed" (Dr. Robert Jastrow, *The Intellectuals Speak Out About God* [Regnery Gateway, 1984] p. 21). The professor noted, the same argument can be made about the strength of the electromagnetic force and the strength of the gravitational force. In other words, if the universe was changed in the slightest way, no human life could exist. The ultimate conclusion of these scientists is that our universe, solar system and, especially, our earth was purposely constructed by a very powerful intelligence within very narrow scientific parameters to allow human life to flourish. The prophet Nehemiah wrote the following declaration centuries before the birth of Jesus Christ: "You alone are the Lord; you have made heaven, the heaven of heavens, with all their host, The earth and everything on it, The Seas and all that is in them. And You preserve them all. The host of heaven worships You" (Nehemiah 9:6).

The Hydrological Cycle of Weather

People living in past centuries did not have a clear understanding about the weather and climatic patterns that controlled our planet's environment. However, the books of Job, Ecclesiastes, Isaiah and Jeremiah all describe details about the complexity of the weather system far beyond the knowledge of the inhabitants living at that time. The complete hydrological cycle governing evaporation, cloud formation, thunder, lightning and rain is explained in surprising detail in the words of the Old Testament. For example, Ecclesiastes states, "If the clouds be full of rain, they empty themselves upon the earth" (Ecclesiastes 11:3). Throughout history most people assumed evaporation of water from lakes and rivers was responsible for the clouds. However, Ecclesiastes confirms that most clouds are formed by evaporation from the oceans: "All the rivers run into the sea, yet the sea is not full; to the place from which the rivers come, there they return again" (Ecclesiastes 1:7). Incredibly, a recent study by the United States Department of Agriculture proved that most of the water that forms into the clouds worldwide comes from the evaporation of the waters found in the oceans that cover over seventy percent of the planet's surface.

The Book of Job asked the question, "Do you know how the clouds are balanced, Those wondrous works of Him who is perfect in knowledge?" (Job 37:16). When you consider the weight of water compared to air it is astonishing that enormous quantities of water are raised from the oceans and lakes every hour by evaporation and lifted thousands of feet in the air where they remain suspended for long periods. Air rises upward as it cools supporting the water vapor in the clouds until the drops become large and heavy enough to fall to earth as rain. The answer is also found in Job, "For He draws up drops of water, which distil as rain from the mist, Which the clouds drop down and pour abundantly on man. Indeed, can anyone understand the spreading of clouds, the thunders from His canopy?" (Job 36:27–29). This incredible biblical passage reveals the complete hydrological cycle of evaporation, cloud formation, and precipitation.

The Complexity of Weather Patterns

King Solomon described the complex climatic circular wind patterns that determine the weather throughout the globe. "The wind goes toward the south, and turns around to the north; the wind whirls about continually, and comes again on its circuit" (Ecclesiastes 1:6). How could Solomon have known three thousand years ago that the planetary winds followed a circular pattern from south to north and south again? Job speaks of God controlling the weather: "For He looketh to the ends of the earth, and seeth under the whole heaven; To establish a weight for the wind, and apportion the waters by measure. When He made a law for the rain and a path for the thunderbolt" (Job 28:24–26). In this intriguing statement the Bible reveals that the winds are governed by their weight, a fact that scientists have only determined in the last century. How could Job have known that the air and the wind patterns are governed by their actual weight? Meteorologists have found that the relative weights of the wind and water greatly determine the weather patterns.

This passage also reveals a profound appreciation of the fact that there is a scientific connection between lightning, thunder, and the triggering of rainfall. Apparently, a slight change in the electrical charge within a cloud is one of the key factors that causes microscopic water droplets in the clouds to join with other droplets until they are heavy enough to fall to earth. In addition, we now know that a powerful electrical charge as high as 300 million volts in a cloud sends a leader stroke down through the air to the ground. Instantaneously, only one-fiftieth of a second later, a second more powerful return stroke travels back up to the cloud following the path through the air opened by the leader stroke. The thunder occurs because the air within this channel or path has been vaporized by superheating it to fifty thousand degrees by the lightning. The superheated air expands outward at supersonic speed creating the noise of thunder. Job's description, "He made a law for the rain and a path for the thunderbolt" (Job 28:26) is startling in its accuracy. No human could have known this in ancient times without the divine revelation of God.

King David, the writer of Psalms, refers mysteriously to "the paths of the seas." He wrote, "The fowl of the air, and the fish of the sea, and whatsoever passeth through the paths of the seas" (Psalm 8:8). It wasn't till 1786 that Benjamin Franklin published the information he gleaned from conversations with ocean-going captains that huge currents such as the Gulf Stream ran like deep rivers far beneath the surface of the Atlantic Ocean. The massive Gulf Stream carries more than five thousand times as much water as the great Mississippi River. This awesome current that warms the climate of the U.K. and Western Europe, carries more than twenty-five times as much water as all the rivers on the planet. Scientists have discovered that the Gulf Stream is only a small part of an enormous "gyre," a huge thirteen-thousand-mile current of water circling the Atlantic Ocean. They have recently discovered that the Pacific Ocean has its own "Black Current" gyre as well.

CNN ran a news report in May 1996, of marine scientists' discovery of a massive river of water flowing north beneath the Pacific Ocean, parallel to the coast of the western United States. However, they also found that another huge current ran under the surface of the ocean above the first current, only this higher current flowed south at a very fast flow rate. The turbulence produced by these opposing currents passing each other at different depths in the Pacific produced massive storms beneath the surface of the ocean. These massive currents not only warm the north of the planet but they are also essential to refreshing the otherwise stagnant waters of the ocean and constitute an essential part of the life system of the planet. How could King David have known thousands of years ago that there were huge currents or rivers that existed in the depths of the boundless oceans?

In another passage Job referred to deep springs of water at the bottom of the ocean. "Have you entered the springs of the sea? Or have you walked in search of the depths?" (Job 38:16). In this verse the Bible refers to the existence of springs of water flowing beneath the depths of the sea. It is only in the last thirty years that underwater exploration of the ocean depths has revealed a remarkable phenomenon of numerous huge springs of fresh water pouring out of the ocean floor. The Book of Job also contains questions that suggest a level of knowledge that would be impossible for a human writer living in the Middle East during ancient times. For example, Job refers to deep oceans whose surface waters are frozen hard like a stone: "From whose womb comes the ice? And the frost of heaven, who gives it birth? The waters harden like a stone, And the surface of the deep is frozen" (Job 38:29,30). How could someone like Job, living in the area of Saudi Arabia in ancient times, have known about Arctic ice caps?

Evolution or Creation?

Billions of people have been taught throughout their life that science has proved that evolution is true and that the Bible is scientifically wrong about creation. As a result of this virtually universal acceptance, evolution has destroyed the faith of countless people during the past one hundred and fifty years. This false theory of evolution has caused untold numbers of people to refuse to seriously consider the claims of the Bible regarding personal salvation because they wrongly believed the Bible was full of errors. The theory of evolution holds that there is no God and that everything in the whole universe, including the complexities of biological life, has developed by random chance over billions of years.

However, the theory of evolution is falling apart today in the face of the total lack of evidence to support its hypothesis. Very few scientists still subscribe to the original theory of evolution as proposed by Charles Darwin over a century ago. Many of them accept that the mathematical odds against life forming by random chance is impossible. As one example, Dr. Harold Urey, a Nobel Prize winner for his research in chemistry wrote about the impossibility of evolution, but still admitted he believed in the theory! "All of us who study the origin of life find that the more we look into it, the more we feel that it is too complex to have evolved anywhere." Incredibly, Dr. Urey then added these words, *"We believe as an article of faith that life evolved from dead matter on this planet. It is just that its complexity is so great, it is hard for us to imagine that it did."* (Italics added). His admission proved that his acceptance of evolution was not based on logic or evidence, but on blind faith. He found the alternative to evolution, a divine Creator, totally unacceptable. At the Alpach Symposium conference which dealt with the growing problems with the theory of evolution, one of the speakers admitted that the reason evolution was still supported by intellectuals, the education establishment, and the media had nothing to do with whether it was true or false. "I think that the fact that a theory so vague, so insufficiently verifiable and so far from the criteria otherwise applied in 'hard' science has become a dogma can be explained only on sociological grounds." (Gershon Robinson, Mordechai Steinman, *The Obvious Proof* [New York: CIS Publishers, 1993], p. 87). In other words, evolution survived despite the lack of evidence because they wanted to believe it was true.

Darwin admitted that millions of "missing links," transitional life forms, would have to be discovered in the fossil record to prove the accuracy of his theory that all species had gradually evolved by chance mutation into new species. Unfortunately for his theory, despite hundreds of millions spent on searching for fossils worldwide for more than a century, the scientists have failed to locate a single missing link out of the millions that must exist if their theory of evolution is to be vindicated. It is significant that the various educational groups supporting evolutionary teaching have encouraged their members to refuse to enter debates about evolution with creation science supporters at high schools and colleges. The evolution supporters found to their dismay that the audiences almost always believed in evolution before the debate began but that they accepted the evidence for divine creation by the end of the debate.

It is not my purpose to fully explore the errors of evolution, nor to fully present the overwhelming evidence for the creation of the universe by God. Many excellent scholars have written books that demolish the theory of evolution in defense of the Bible's account of creation. In the Appendix at the end of this book I list several excellent books that I strongly recommend to anyone who wishes to study this subject in depth. However, I will outline in this chapter some of the astonishing evidence that proves that evolution is simply impossible and supports creation as outlined in the Bible. As we explore this topic we will also encounter overwhelming evidence proving the inspiration of the Scriptures.

When you understand the incredible number of problems with the theory of evolution you are immediately struck with the thought that there is something very strange about the continuing universal acceptance of this theory. However, the answer is clear. If the theory of evolution is rejected, then people have no other credible alternative than the Bible's account of creation by a personal God. This alternative is unacceptable to many people in modern society because they dread the thought of facing their God. They would like to evade this issue by firmly avoiding examining the overwhelming evidence against evolution through the use of ridicule and rejection. In the final analysis the greatest obstacle to seeing the truth about God's role in creation is often our own attitudes and prejudices. If we will lay aside our former attitudes and carefully examine the evidence, the truth about creation as well as our relationship with God will become evident through the Word of God.

The odds against life evolving by chance on earth are absolutely staggering. It is impossible to believe that the awesome complexity involved in the simplest living cell could have occurred as a result of chance even if this process had occurred over billions of years. Scientists found that over twenty different amino acids are required to produce the proteins that exist in the smallest living cell. Despite scientific experiments where they tried to create these twenty amino acids in the laboratory, they failed every time. The proteins that make up living cells are composed of long thin lines of amino acids only one-millionth the size of a human hair. The smallest living thing contains more than five hundred amino acids. All amino acids have side groups of atoms. Scientists found that 50 percent of the side groups of atoms that are attached to non-living amino acids are on the left side and another 50 percent are on the right side. When biologists examined proteins within living cells they discovered that all proteins are "left handed." In other words, all living cells contain amino acids with their side group of atoms on the left side only. Amino acids produced in a laboratory are exactly like those found in non-living matter with 50 percent "left-handed" and 50 percent "right-handed." Yet, living cells can only exist when the atoms are solely "left-handed." To calculate the likelihood of life occurring by chance, the scientists calculated the probability that amino acids would form chains of atoms solely on the "left-hand." The odds against this happening by chance are one chance in 10^{123}. In other words, it is absolutely impossible that even a single protein could have been formed by chance alone, let alone the staggering number of awesomely complex proteins that make up the multitude of living creatures in our world. The only logical explanation for this situation is the instantaneous creation by God.

The proteins in living creatures are composed of long chains of different amino acids that must be linked together in a precise sequence to allow the protein to live. The evolutionary scientist believes that these complex amino acids simply came together by chance in the exact necessary sequence to allow life to exist. This is mathematically impossible. Mathematicians have calculated that the odds against these five hundred amino acids lining up in the correct order to produce one single living cell is equal to one chance in 10^{200} which is ten followed by two hundred zeros. Even if the amino acids and chemicals could combine together a trillion times faster than they do in the laboratory, and the experiment used every single atom on the planet, the odds against a single living protein forming by chance would be less than one chance in ten followed by one hundred and sixty-six zeros. This incredible number vastly exceeds the total number of atoms within the known universe. The odds against a single living protein being formed by chance alone is equal to the chance that a blind-folded man could locate a single grain of sand painted gold within a universe composed of fifty billion galaxies of two hundred million stars apiece composed of nothing but sand.

However, the formation of life requires far more complex structures than simple amino acids and proteins. DNA (Deoxyribo-Nucleic Acid) creates the genetic code that commands the various elements in the cell to form the building blocks of life itself. Mathematicians have calculated that the odds against a single DNA gene forming by chance is equal to one chance in ten followed by one hundred and fifty-five zeros, a number that staggers the mind. Anyone who can believe that life on earth evolved by random chance without the presence of a supernatural intelligence designer must do so on absolute blind faith. Their decision to accept evolution reflects a deep need to evade the overwhelming evidence and logic that proves the universe was created by God.

The Genetic Code Governing Life

The incredibly intricate genetic DNA code controls every element and cell in the body of any biological creature. The genetic code contains a staggering amount of information. Professor Leslie Orgel, a scientist working in this area wrote: "The origin of the genetic code is the most baffling aspect of the origins of life" (Leslie Orgel, "Darwinism at the Very Beginning of Life," *New Scientist* [April, 1982], p. 151). Scientists who study genetics realize that the amount of genetic information encoded in the DNA of the most simple form of life, contains a staggering amount of information that is far more complicated than the computer software that runs the complete accounting program controlling the inventory, costs, sales and financial records of hundreds of General Motors plants throughout the world. Sir Fred Hoyle, one of the greatest biologists in this century wrote: "Precious little in the way of biochemical evolution could have happened on the earth. If one counts the number of trial assemblies of amino acids that are needed to give rise to the enzymes, the probability of their discovery by random shufflings turn out to be less than one in 10^{400000}. (Fred Hoyle, *New Scientist*, Where Microbes Boldly Went, p. 412–415). As a result of his findings, Hoyle eventually abandoned his agnosticism and became a believer in a special creation of life. Several top scientists have concluded that life must have been brought from outer space to the earth due to the impossible mathematical odds against the spontaneous development of life on earth. Some of these scientists, such as Sir Fred Hoyle and Dr. Frances Crick arrived at the theory that life originated in some far part of the universe and was later imported to earth by some extraterrestrial intelligence. However, this novel solution does not solve their problem at all. This solution only pushes the problem away from the earth to some unknown place in space. How could life have been created by random chance in some far part of the universe? Obviously, only God could have created life with all of its incredible complexity and order.

The Book of Proverbs declares that, "A merry heart does good, like medicine, but a broken spirit dries the bones" (Proverbs 17:22). While many Bible readers accepted this advice from Proverbs as a general statement, they would be surprised to learn that modern psychiatry has discovered that good humor and laughter truly improves our overall health. An article in the *Birmingham News* entitled "Laughter: Prescription for Health," confirms the statement found in Proverbs. "At some point during laughter, your body issues a prescription from the pharmacy in your brain." The article revealed that scientists discovered that the emotion of humor triggers the release of certain hormones and endorphins that greatly improve our overall sense of well-being.

Moses, in Leviticus 17:11, declared, "For the life of the flesh is in the blood." This statement revealed advanced scientific knowledge at a time when the level of pagan medical knowledge was abysmal. This statement by Moses was incredibly astute because doctors have discovered that our blood is essential to many of our body's life processes. The blood carries nutrients and material that produce growth, healing, store energy as fat, and support every organ in our body. When the blood supply is restricted to any part of the body, that part begins immediately to die. Blood is essential to fighting disease, clotting wounds and growing new skin and cells. For centuries ignorant doctors used to "bleed" their patients by draining large amounts of blood from their bodies in a vain attempt to defeat disease. They did not realize that our blood is the key to our flesh. Truly, as the Bible declares, "the life of the flesh is in the blood."

The Population of the Earth

Those who reject the Bible's account of divine creation believe the evolutionary argument that mankind evolved by chance from lower life forms over billions of years. One of their conclusions is that mankind has existed on this earth for more than a million years. In contradiction to this evolutionary position, the Bible declares that mankind was created approximately six thousand years ago according to the chronological data presented in the Old Testament. The Bible clearly declares, through a detailed list of the generations from Adam to Christ, that mankind was created on the earth approximately four thousand years before the birth of Jesus Christ. Obviously, a huge discrepancy exists between the evolutionists' suggestion of man's origin approximately one million years ago compared to the Bible's declaration of man's creation by God approximately six thousand years ago.

Let us consider the growth rate of our human population to determine whether the Bible's account of man's creation only six thousand years ago, or the evolutionary scientists' account of man's evolution over one million years is consistent with known scientific data. According to the Scriptures, eight people comprising four couples survived the great Flood approximately forty-three hundred years ago as described in biblical chronology. To be conservative, we will make these calculations assuming that mankind started forty-three hundred years ago with only one surviving couple and that all families produced only 2.5 children on average over the following centuries. This rate of population growth is much slower than we are experiencing in this century. If families produce only two children on average then the population would remain static without any growth. This conservative assumption of an average of

2.5 children per family will account for the natural depletion caused by war, famine and disease. Throughout history the average lifespan has lasted only forty-three years per generation. Using these assumptions, during the last forty-three hundred years, there would have been one hundred generations lasting forty-three years each. The calculations reveal that our population would have grown from the time of the Flood till today to reach approximately five billion people. It is fascinating to note that the earth's population today (5.5 billion worldwide) is almost identical with what we would expect if mankind began repopulating the earth after the Flood forty-three hundred years ago. I am indebted to Professor Henry M. Morris for his brilliant work on this topic in his excellent book, *The Biblical Basis For Modern Science*, which I highly recommend for any reader who wishes to explore this topic in greater depth. (Henry M. Morris, *The Biblical Basis For Modern Science* [Baker House: Grand Rapids, 1984], pp. 414–426). In this chapter I am simplifying the calculations but the results are the same.

Now let us consider what the earth's population would be if the evolutionary theory were correct. The evolutionary scientists who believe that man has existed for over a million years have an almost insurmountable problem. Using the same assumption of forty-three years for an average human generation, the population growth over a million years would produce 23,256 consecutive generations. We calculate the expected population by starting with one couple one million years ago and use the same assumptions of a forty-three year generation and 2.5 children per family. The calculations reveal that we should have a total human population on earth today of 10^{2091} people. The evolutionary theory of a million years of growth would produce trillions × trillions × trillions × trillions of people that should be alive today on our planet. To put this in perspective, this number is vastly greater than the total number of atoms in our vast universe. If mankind had lived on earth for a million years we would all be standing on enormously high mountains of bones from the trillions of skeletons of those who had died in past generations. However, despite the tremendous archeological and scientific investigation in the last two centuries, the scientists have not found a fraction of the trillions of skeletons predicted by the theory of the evolutionary scientists. The conclusion is obvious. The Bible's account of Noah's family repopulating the earth following the Flood approximately forty-three hundred years ago is in agreement with the current population of the earth.

The Wonders of Creation

The Bible claims that God created all of the living creatures on earth. When we examine these creatures we discover an awesome degree of complexity that simply defies the evolutionary theory that claims these animals and their behavior have occurred by chance alone. One of the most amazing examples of God's design is found in the fact that birds have hollow bones. This makes them much lighter than they would be with normal solid bones and facilitates aerial flight. As an example of God's providential design, consider the woodpecker that is so familiar to North Americans. As I write this chapter, a beautiful woodpecker is standing on a branch of the tree only five feet beyond my library window, pecking away in diligent search for an insect beneath the bark of the tree. The woodpecker has two toes in front and two toes in the rear allowing it to grip the trunk of a tree firmly while pecking for insects. While all other birds have their bill connected directly to their skull, only the woodpecker has an unusual spongy tissue between its bill and skull that acts as a shock absorber while it pecks forcefully at the trunk of a tree for hours at a time seeking to locate insects. Some woodpeckers have actually pecked through solid concrete in their quest for insects or to bury seeds for future food. The woodpecker's short tail feathers act as support to brace its body against the trunk of the tree while it pecks searching for food. When it locates a tunnel bored through the tree by an insect the woodpecker inserts its extremely long tongue into the narrow tunnel until it reaches its prey. Unlike other birds, the tongue of a woodpecker is not attached to the rear of its mouth. Incredibly, the woodpecker's tongue is five inches long coiled within its skull, allowing the bird to locate its insect prey deep within the tree trunk.

Those who reject divine creation believe that the awesome complexities of biological life have occurred by simple chance through evolution without intelligent design. This argument appears ridiculous to people who examine the awesome complexity of animal and human life. Those who honestly and carefully consider the evidence must conclude that God has created this incredible design. As an example of this design we should consider the migratory pattern of birds. The Manx shearwater birds that live in Wales migrate from

America to home every year flying approximately 250 miles every day. A Manx shearwater captured in Wales was transferred by plane in a crate to America. Then scientists released the bird in Boston. Incredibly, the bird flew home across the trackless expanse of the Atlantic Ocean to its home in Wales, more than 3,100 miles away, in only twelve days despite the fact that the bird had never flown over the ocean before. How could this occur unless God planted within the bird the knowledge of where its home was located thousands of miles away? Another example of God's creative design is found in the ability of the rattlesnake to detect its prey. This ability depends on a small sense organ found between the nostril and the eyes of the snake, that is so sensitive it can detect a difference of temperature of only one thirty-third of a degree. This ability to detect the precise temperature of an object in front of the snake enables it to precisely measure the distance and direction to its prey. This ability to detect such a small temperature variation is so difficult that only a computerized thermometer device can detect so small a difference. How could such a sensitive awareness of temperatures have evolved in the rattlesnake by chance?

Evolutionists believe that the complex systems found in living creatures have been formed as a result of random chance. However, King David declared: "You [God] formed my inward parts; You covered me in my mother's womb. I will praise You, for I am fearfully and wonderfully made" (Psalm 139:13,14). Consider the case of the human eye and ask yourself whether or not such an astonishingly complex system could have occurred by chance alone. When a baby is conceived in its mother's womb the genetic code governing the eye programs the baby's body to begin growing optic nerves from both the brain as well as from the eye. Each eye will have a million nerve endings that begin growing through the flesh toward the baby's brain. Simultaneously, a million optic nerves will begin growing through the flesh towards the baby's eye. Each of the million optic nerves must find and match up to its mate to enable sight to exist. We are impressed when highway engineers are able to correctly align two thirty-foot wide tunnels dug from opposite sides of the mountain to meet somewhere precisely in the middle of the mountain. However, every day hundreds of thousands of children are born with the ability to see; their bodies have precisely aligned a million separate optic nerves from each eye to meet matching optic nerve endings growing out from the baby's brain. If you think this miracle of design has happened by random chance, you probably still believe in the Tooth Fairy.

The human eye has the ability to transmit to the brain over one and a half million messages simultaneously. The retina at the back of the eye contains a dense area of rods and cones that gather and interpret information presented to the eye. The retina contains over one hundred and thirty-seven million nerve connections which the brain uses to evaluate data in its attempt to interpret the scene in front of your eyes. One hundred and thirty million of these special cells are rods that enable us to have black and white vision. However, about seven million eye cells are cone-shaped cells that allow us to see color. Each of these one hundred and thirty-seven million cells communicates directly with the brain, allowing us to interpret the visual image in front of us. Amazingly, scientists have discovered that while the image we receive in our eye is "upside-down" the cellular structure in our eye actually reverses the image to "right-side up" within the eye before sending it to the mind. The eye then transmits the corrected image at three hundred miles an hour to the brain where we "see" the image that is before us.

The human brain is the most complex organ in the known universe. While it weighs less than three pounds, it contains an amazingly intricate connection of nerves with more than thirty billion special cells known as neurons. In addition, there are another two hundred and fifty billion glial cells that facilitate communication between neurons. Incredibly, every one of the thirty billion neurons is connected to other neurons in a staggering degree of complicated connections. Every neuron is connected directly with more than fifty thousand other neurons allowing instantaneous transfers of messages across your brain. In less than a second your brain can calculate the trajectory of a football thrown at thirty miles an hour toward you without warning, In a moment your brain calculates your position, the ball's ultimate trajectory, and sends detailed electronic messages to the muscles in your arms and legs at more than three hundred miles a second to move you into position to catch the ball. Despite hundreds of billions of dollars and fifty years of advanced research by computer scientists, there are no computer systems on the planet that can equal this marvelous instantaneous computing that is required to allow a ten-year-old boy to catch a football! When

The Tomb of Cyrus

Grant and Kaye Jeffrey in front of the Western Wall

*A Clay Brick from Babylon Inscribed
with the Name of King Nebuchadnezzar*

*Wadi Mukatteb.
The Valley of the Inscriptions in the Sinai*

ΚΑΤΑ ΙΩΑΝΝΗΝ

ΕΝΑΡΧΗΗΝΟΛΟΓͦ
ΚΑΙΟΛΟΓΟϹΗΝ
ΠΡΟϹΤΟΝΘΝΚΑΙ
ΘϹΗΝΟΛΟΓΟϹΟΥ
ΤΟϹΗΝΕΝΑΡΧΗ
ΠΡΟϹΤΟΝΘΝΠΑ
ΤΑΔΙΑΥΤΟΥΕΓΕΝ
ΤΟΚΑΙΧΩΡΙϹΑΥΤΟΥ
ΕΓΕΝΕΤΟΟΥΔΕΝ
ΟΓΕΓΟΝΕΝΕΝΑΥ
ΤΩΖΩΗΕϹΤΙΝ
ΚΑΙΗΖΩΗΗΝΤͦ
ΦΩϹΤΩΝΑΝΘΡΩ
ΠΩΝΚΑΙΤΟΦΩϹ
ΕΝΤΗϹΚΟΤΙΑΦΑΙ
ΝΕΙΚΑΙΗϹΚΟΤΙ
ΛΑΥΤΟΟΥΚΑΤΕ
ΛΑΒΕΝ·
ΕΓΕΝΕΤΟΑΝΘΡΩ
ΠΟϹΑΠΕϹΤΑΛΜε

A New Testament Greek Manuscript

131

The Trilingual Inscription in a mountain cave on Djebel Maghara.
Two Columns are Hieroglyphics; one Column in the Sinaitic Alphabet

The Mountains and Valleys of Sinai

Example of Sinai Inscription

No. XL.

Causes to descend into the deep valley [1] Moses the tribes.

Leader of the way he causes to descend into the deep the young ostrich [2]
the sea foaming.

Divides it asunder power given him by GOD.

[1] "That led them through the deep, as an horse in the wilderness, that they should not stumble : As *a beast goeth down into the valley*, the Spirit of the Lord caused him to rest : so didst thou lead thy people, to make thyself a glorious name.'—*Isaiah* lxiii. 13, 14.

[2] "The daughter of my people is become cruel, like *ostriches* in the *wilderness.*'—*Lam.* iv. 3.

Reproduced from
Sinai Photographed *by Rev. Charles Forster*
A.D. 1862

134

No. XLI.

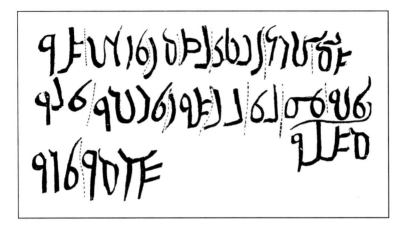

The People like a she-ostrich fleet-winged crying aloud causeth to haste
  Moses, the Cloud bright shining. [3]
A mighty army propelled into the Red Sea [4] gathered into one by GOD, they
  go jumping and skipping [5] journeying through the fissure taking flight
  from the face of the enemy.
The flux of the sea divided.[6]

[3] Exod. xiv. 20.
[4] Hab. iii. 15.
[5] Wisdom xix. 9.
[6] Exod. xiv. 21.

Reproduced from
Sinai Photographed *by Rev. Charles Forster*
A.D. 1862

Example of Sinai Inscription with Hieroglyphs

Sinai Inscription with Girl Praying.
Found in Tomb at Turbet es Yahoud
– "the Graves of the Jews"

Close-up of Girl
Praying

we carefully consider the evidence, I believe that any fair-minded observer will conclude that our universe and all of life was designed by God exactly as revealed in the Bible.

The Bible reveals that a supernatural God designed and created our extremely complicated universe. Any person with an unbiased mind who examines the evidence must conclude that only a designer with miraculous powers could possibly account for the marvelously designed universe. The many scientific statements found throughout the Bible are perhaps the greatest proof of God's inspiration. There are no scientific errors or mistakes found in its thousands of passages. These conclusive evidences provide overwhelming proof that God exists, and that He inspired the writers of Scripture to record His message to all of mankind. The incredible scientific insights and revelations found throughout the Bible from Genesis to Revelation, act as God's genuine signature on the pages of the Scriptures authenticating the Word of God.

7

Advanced Medical Knowledge in the Bible

Keep in mind as you read this chapter that man's medical knowledge was virtually abysmal until the beginning of the twentieth century. Even the existence of germs was unknown until around A.D. 1890. Yet, the first five books of the Bible, known as the Torah, or the Law, recorded by Moses approximately 1491–1451 B.C., reveal surprising advanced scientific principles. In addition, the Bible contains advanced medical and scientific knowledge about hygiene and sanitation. As you will discover, the Scriptures contain God's medical instructions for Israel that far exceeded the level of knowledge possessed by the Egyptians and other ancient societies of that day. This advanced information in the Bible, written over three and a half millennia ago, is strong proof that a divine creator inspired it. What other rational explanation is there for this precise medical knowledge in the five books of the Law recorded while Moses led the Israelites through the wilderness of Sinai? God inspired Moses to record these medical commandments to protect the health of His chosen people. The Book of Exodus reveals one of the most astonishing promises which God ever made to mankind.

God's Promise: "the Lord will take away from you all sickness"

God promised that, if they obeyed all of His commandments and statutes which He gave to Moses, the Lord would protect them from the plagues and sicknesses that afflicted the ancient Egyptians. This incredible promise is found in Exodus 15:26, "If you diligently heed the voice of the Lord your God and do what is right in His sight, give ear to His commandments and keep all His statutes, I will put none of the diseases on you which I have brought on the Egyptians. For I am the Lord who heals you." Throughout the Bible, especially the first five books of Moses from Genesis to Deuteronomy, we discover incredibly advanced medical laws and principles that are designed to protect us from the devastating diseases that have afflicted mankind throughout history.

For centuries the Jews had lived as slaves among the pagan Egyptians. Obviously they learned and adopted the traditional folk medicine and remedies of their Egyptian masters. As a result the Israelites would have been afflicted during their long captivity by the same terrible diseases and plagues that repeatedly devastated the people of ancient Egypt. The Book of Deuteronomy 28:27,28 records a number of these terrible diseases of the Egyptians. "The Lord will strike you with the boils of Egypt, with tumors, with the scab, and with the itch, from which you cannot be healed. The Lord will strike you with madness and blindness and confusion of heart." However, if the Israelites would turn from their sins and follow the commandments of God, the Lord promised that "none of the terrible diseases of Egypt which you have known" would afflict the Jews from that moment on. "And the Lord will take away from you all sickness, and will afflict you with none of the terrible diseases of Egypt which you have known, but will lay them on all those who hate you" (Deuteronomy 7:15).

When the children of Israel left Egypt through the miraculous intervention of God, the Lord demanded that they obey His commandments against sinning. God's specific medical laws and sanitation commandments that were given to Moses, would protect the Jews from the most terrible diseases of the Egyptians and their attendant high mortality rates. An examination of the medical remedies of the ancient Egyptians and other pagan cultures of the Middle East reveals an appalling ignorance of even the most rudimentary medical knowledge as we know it today. However, the laws of Moses contained specific laws and sanitation procedures that, if faithfully followed, would eliminate the dreadful diseases that afflicted the Egyptians of that day and still afflict most of mankind in the Third World today.

The Medical Knowledge of Ancient Egypt

It is fascinating to study the several hundred prescriptions in the *Papyrus Ebers* to gain an understanding of the level of medical and sanitary knowledge possessed by the Egyptians, the most advanced society on earth in the days of Moses. Despite their advanced astronomical and engineering knowledge, as evidenced by their great temples at Karnak and the three great pyramids at Giza, the Egyptian's level of medical knowledge was extremely primitive and dangerous. Yet, they prided themselves on their great medical knowledge as revealed in various medical manuscripts that have survived the ravages of time, including the *Papyrus Ebers*, written about the time of Moses.

As an example of the medical ignorance and primitive state of their medical know ledge, consider the Egyptian doctor's suggestion for healing an infected splinter wound. The prescription involves the application of an ointment mixture composed of the blood of worms mixed with the dung of a donkey. The various germs, including tetanus, contained in donkey's dung must have assured that the patient would rapidly forget the pain of his splinter as he died from an assortment of other diseases produced by his doctor's contaminated medicine. The medical solution for a patient's hair loss involved the application to his scalp of a solution composed of various fats from a horse, a crocodile, a cat, a snake, and a donkey's tooth crushed in honey. The Egyptian doctors had an equally wondrous cure for a poisonous snake bite. They poured "magical water" over a pagan idol and then gave it to the victim for what probably turned out to be his last drink on earth.

According to these ancient documents, the pharmacies of ancient Egypt provided popular prescriptions including "lizards' blood, swines' teeth, putrid meat, stinking fat, moisture from pigs' ears, milk, goose grease, asses' hoofs, animal fats from various sources, excreta from animals, including human beings, donkeys, antelopes, dogs, cats, and even flies." Believe it or not, this list is quoted from pages of the *Papyrus Ebers* manuscript as translated in

S. E. Massengill's *A Sketch of Medicine and Pharmacy.* During my last research trip to the Middle East I located a fascinating book about ancient Egyptian medical knowledge. This book, An *Ancient Egyptian Herbal,* by Lise Manniche (London: British Museum Press, 1989) describes a number of Egyptian cures that use ingredients such as "cat's dung," "hippopotamus dung," "donkey's hoof," "gazelle dung," "snakeskins" and of course, the ever popular "fly dung" that appears in numerous prescriptions. The Egyptian's remedy for "constipation: zizyphus bread, gurma, cat's dung, sweet beer, wine." In another passage we read, "a painful tumour was treated with fly dung mixed with sycamore juice applied to the tumour so that it goes down by itself." Among these amazingly dangerous medicines we find an incredible suggestion for curing a baby of excessive crying: "A remedy for too much crying in a child: spn-seeds; fly dung from the wall; is made to a paste, strained and drunk for four days. The crying will cease instantly." No doubt the crying would cease with the death of the poor child receiving this deadly potion. As the author noted, "In general, Coptic medicine is not held in very high esteem." A majority of the medicines described in documents from ancient Egypt included dung from either humans or animals. The mortality rate from infection must have been dreadful with such unhelpful and deadly advice from doctors. Due to the total lack of knowledge of germs and infection, almost any serious illness or injury treated by the medical system of pagan Egypt would result in a painful and virtually certain death.

The Bible records that Moses was adopted and grew up as the son of "Pharaoh's daughter." Moses would have had access to the knowledge of the royal and priestly colleges of Egypt. The Jewish historian Flavius Josephus tells us in his *Antiquities of the Jews,* that Moses, as a prince of Egypt, became a great general in his successful war against the Ethiopian Empire. As a royal prince he was taught all that Egypt, as the most advanced culture of the day, could transmit to his genius. The Book of Acts (7:22) tells us that; "And Moses was learned in all the wisdom of the Egyptians, and was mighty in words and deeds." Therefore, as a royal heir, he would have been educated in all of these amazing medical cures. Both the writer of the Torah and the millions of ancient Israelite slaves would have absorbed the medical knowledge and traditional treatments of the Egyptians during the centuries of Israel's captivity. However, a close examination of the first five books of the Bible written by Moses does not include a single reference to these "deadly" medical cures of the pagan Egyptian society in which Moses and the Israelites were raised. Rather, we discover in the pages of ancient Scriptures the most advanced sanitation instructions and the most sophisticated medical knowledge that the world has ever known, until the explosion of medical research in this century following World War I. Despite the natural human tendency to add our own natural education and knowledge to what God tells us, Moses resisted such temptations in writing exactly what God inspired him to write as he composed the Torah. There are no references to the disgusting and dangerous ancient Egyptian medical practices in the five books of Moses.

Any intelligent reader must ask this question: Where did Moses obtain his incredibly advanced medical knowledge? Obviously he did not receive this accurate medical knowledge from the Egyptians or any other pagan culture of that time. This advanced and accurate knowledge reveals a profound understanding of germs, infectious transmission routes, human sanitation needs and many other medical advances unknown outside the Bible during the last thirty-five centuries. Moses abandoned the medical ignorance of the Egyptians when he left the palace in Egypt and spent the next eighty years of his life in the wilderness. The first five books of the Bible contain detailed medical laws regarding the careful kosher inspection of meat and exacting sanitation regulations regarding the burial of bodies. How could Moses have acquired such a profound and medically advanced knowledge without help from some outside force? The only answer that makes sense is that found in the first five of the books of the Bible as written by Moses. Moses declared that he received this knowledge from God by direct and supernatural inspiration. A careful examination of the medical treatises from the Egyptians and the comprehensive Babylonian Code of Hammurabi reveals absolutely nothing about preventative medicine to enable people to avoid these deadly diseases that devastated ancient societies. However, the presence of incredibly advanced and accurate knowledge of diseases, sanitation and preventative medicine in the ancient Scriptures is one more incontrovertible proof that the Bible is truly the inspired Word of God. It is fascinating to note that a total of two hundred and thirteen out of the six hundred and thirteen biblical commandments found in the Torah were detailed medical regulations that insured the good health of the children of Israel if they would obediently follow the laws of God.

God's Ancient Laws of Hygiene and Sanitation

Medical science did not know of the existence of germs and their methods of transmission of infection until the end of the last century. Doctors until this century believed that the presence and transmission of disease was entirely haphazard and governed by simple chance or bad luck. Those who were sick with deadly diseases were cared for in the home without any awareness of the contagious transmission of disease from one sick individual to others around them. People had no idea that invisible and deadly microscopic germs could exist on eating and cooking utensils. However, Leviticus 6:28, written over thirty-five hundred years ago, reveals a clear commandment to discard broken pottery (because the cracks could contain harmful germs): "But the earthen vessel in which it is boiled shall be broken. And if it is boiled in a bronze pot, it shall be both scoured and rinsed in water." In other words, a cracked vessel should not be used for cooking or eating but should be discarded. The Bible tells us further that "if it be sodden in a brazen pot, it shall be both scoured, and rinsed in water" indicating that a metal pot should be disinfected by scouring and rinsing in water. These instructions certainly saved hundreds of thousands of Jews from infections over the centuries at a time when the rest of the world didn't even know that germs existed. How could Moses have known of the dangers of infectious germs in cooking and eating utensils thousands of years ago unless God actually inspired him to write these words?

Moses' writing also reveals an astonishing knowledge of deadly germs associated with dead animal bodies and anything they touch. Throughout history people stored and cooked their meat with ample spices to delay the rotting and to disguise the smell of decay. Without refrigeration, the eating of meat was often hazardous because of the great danger of infection. In Leviticus 11:35, Moses revealed his knowledge of the danger of germs from animal carcasses when he wrote, "And everything on which a part of any such carcass falls shall be unclean; whether it is an oven or cooking stove, it shall be broken down; for they are unclean, and shall be unclean to you." God inspired Moses to record these medical and sanitation instructions in the Bible to protect the Israelites from invisible, but deadly infectious germs, found in dead animal bodies that would kill them. It is important to remember that, until this century, even medical researchers and doctors denied that disease could be transmitted by invisible germs or viruses.

The Book of Leviticus 7:24 forbids the people to eat of the flesh of any animal that has died naturally of disease or by wild animals: "And the fat of a beast that dies naturally, and the fat of what is torn by wild animals, may be used in any other way; but you shall by no means eat it." Any animal carcass found after natural death would be dangerous to eat because it would likely contain the germs that caused its premature death or the infectious germs that would develop within hours of an animal's violent death following an attack by another animal. The children of Israel were saved from countless invisible germs and diseases by following these religious laws and prohibitions given by their God through their prophet Moses.

Laws Designed to Prevent Infectious Disease

God provided the Israelites with wise and beneficial laws to protect their health including advanced sanitation laws to prevent the spread of infections. "This is the law when a man dies in a tent: All who come into the tent and all who are in the tent shall be unclean seven days; and every open vessel, which has no cover fastened on it, is unclean. Whoever in the open field touches one who is slain by a sword or who has died, or a bone of a man, or a grave, shall be unclean seven days. And for an unclean person they shall take some of the ashes of the heifer burnt for purification from sin, and running water shall be put on them in a vessel" (Numbers 19:14–17).

Throughout history mankind has suffered billions of untold deaths due to infections from microscopic germs. Germs from a dead human body are more dangerous to another human than germs from an animal's body because of the greater likelihood of transmission of infection. These deadly germs are everywhere, but especially within the bodies of those who are already sick or those who have died due to some disease. Mankind's ignorance of these deadly microscopic germs has exposed countless humans to premature death. However, thirty-five centuries ago the Bible clearly gave instructions that would protect us from many of these infectious diseases.

A brilliant Hungarian doctor of the last century, Dr. Ignaz Semmelweis, created a tremendous improvement in practical medical treatment and the control of deadly infectious diseases. I am indebted to the fascinating book, *None Of These Diseases* by S. I. McMillen, M.D., for making me aware of the importance of the medical contributions of Dr. Semmelweis. An article in the *Encyclopædia Britannica* documents that, as a young doctor in Vienna in 1845, Semmelweis was appalled by the staggering rate of death by infection of women who gave birth in hospitals. While most children were born at home at that time, a number of women, usually the homeless or sick, gave birth to their children in the local hospitals. The level of infectious puerperal (child-bed) fever was horrendous with between 15 and 30 percent of such mothers dying in hospital. This tragic situation was considered normal at that time. Dr. Semmelweis noted that every morning the young interns examined the bodies of the mothers who had died and then immediately, without washing their hands, went to the next ward where they would examine the expectant mothers. This astonishing behavior was considered normal medical practice in the last century because the existence of microscopic infectious germs was unknown and unsuspected.

However, the young doctor insisted that the doctors under his supervision follow his new orders to wash their hands vigorously in water and chlorinated lime prior to examining living patients. Immediately, the mortality rate caused by infection among the expectant mothers fell to less than 2 percent dying due to these infections. Despite these fantastic improvements the senior hospital staff despised Dr. Semmelweis's medical innovations and eventually fired him. Most of his medical colleagues rejected his new techniques and ridiculed his demands that they wash their hands because they could not believe infections could be caused by something invisible to the naked eye. Later he took a position with another hospital in Pest, Hungary [Budapest], the St. Rochus Hospital, which was experiencing an epidemic of puerperal fever in the ward where mothers were giving birth. Immediately, his new sanitary procedures had a positive effect, with the mortality rate dropping to less than 1 percent instead of the 15 percent that was normal in other hospitals in the area. During the following six years, he received the approval of the Hungarian government which sent medical advisory letters to all district authorities demanding that all medical staff follow Dr. Semmelweis's instructions for washing hands and general hospital sanitation. Although the beneficial results of washing hands were obvious, the medical establishments of Europe and North America continued to ignore his techniques. Patients continued to die needlessly of infectious diseases while they were in the hospital. Decades of rejection by his colleagues finally drove Dr. Semmelweis to a nervous breakdown that placed him in a mental institution. Tragically, due to an infection he received through a cut on his hand during an operation in 1865, Dr. Semmelweis succumbed to the same disease he spent his life trying to alleviate. Dr. Joseph Lister, the father of modern antisepsis (the science of fighting infection), said of him, "I think with the greatest admiration of him and his achievement."

Thousands of years ago, God commanded the Israelites to wash their hands in "running water" when dealing with those afflicted with infectious diseases. "And when he who has a discharge is cleansed of his discharge, then he shall count for himself seven days for his cleansing, wash his clothes, and bathe his body in running water; then he shall be clean" (Leviticus 15:13). Until this century most doctors who did choose to wash their hands, did so in a bowl of water which obviously would allow the germs to remain on their hands. However, Moses instructed the Israelites to wash in "running water" which is the only way to effectively remove these infectious germs.

Laws to Prevent Plague and Leprosy

Throughout history the scourge of leprosy has killed untold millions of people and afflicted many more with misery. There is some debate among medical scholars about whether the Hebrew word translated "leprosy" in the Bible is exactly the same disease as the modern variant. It may have been another deadly infectious disease that differs from modern forms of leprosy. Amazingly, an examination of the detailed laws of Numbers and Leviticus reveals an advanced system for the control of infectious diseases at a time when ancient pagan nations did not understand the dangers of infections. For example, the Bible commands that the priests act as medical control officers, examining all sick individuals and take action to protect them and the community. "Then the priest shall look at it; and indeed if the swelling of the sore is reddish-white on his bald head or on his bald forehead, as the appearance of leprosy on the skin of the body, he is a leprous man. He is unclean. The priest shall surely pronounce him unclean; his sore is on his head" (Leviticus 13:43,44). In addition to identifying the diseased individual the priest was responsible for the isolation of those afflicted with leprosy. "He shall be unclean. All the days he has the sore he shall be unclean. He is unclean, and he shall dwell alone; his habitation shall be outside the camp" (Leviticus 13:46).

The Lord's concern to protect His children from infectious disease was manifested in His command to forbid those who were still infected with disease from participating in the three great annual festivals of the Jews, lest they infect others. "But the man who is unclean and does not purify himself, that person shall be cut off from among the congregation, because he has defiled the sanctuary of the Lord. The water of purification has not been sprinkled on him; he is unclean" (Numbers 19:20). Even after a man recovered from his disease and returned from medical isolation, the individual was subject to strict medical supervision for seven days under the medical orders of the priest to ascertain that he was truly healed. "He who is to be cleansed shall wash his clothes, shave off all his hair, and wash himself in water, that he may be clean. After that he shall come into the camp, and shall stay outside his tent seven days" (Leviticus 14:8). After this period of quarantine the individual must submit to a careful medical by the priests to ascertain that he was truly free of disease and able to resume his position in society. "But on the seventh day he shall shave all the hair off his head and his beard and his eyebrows; all his hair he shall shave off. He shall wash his clothes and wash his body in water, and he shall be clean" (Leviticus 14:9). When you consider these ancient medical instructions, you can see that they are amazingly similar to the medical quarantine orders a modern public health official would follow to absolutely determine that someone was cured of his disease and able to safely reenter society.

The continents of Europe and Asia have been periodically engulfed by epidemics of leprosy and plague, such as those in the medieval period, especially A.D. 1200 to A.D. 1400. This dreaded disease terrified the populations of Europe and appeared unbeatable. Over sixty million people, almost one-third of the population of Europe in the fourteenth century are estimated to have died by the Black Death (bubonic plague). Entire counties and towns were devastated with no known survivors. Those who survived portray scenes that sounded like the haunting visions of Dante's descriptions of hell. Renowned doctors of the time were unable to respond adequately because of their lack of knowledge. They were reduced to offering medical advice to prevent the plague such as, "Stop eating pepper or garlic." Some suggested the plague was caused by the position of the planets and stars. Mostly, the doctors helplessly comforted their dying patients and finally succumbed to the disease themselves.

How was this dreaded plague finally stopped before it killed everyone in Europe? As ministers prayed and held their Bibles in their hands, little did they realize that God had already provided the divine solution in the pages of Holy Scripture. While doctors failed the people totally, some church leaders wisely looked to God and the Bible for a divine medical solution to the apparently hopeless situation. During my last trip to Vienna, I examined a strange-looking statue in the center of the city dedicated to the Black Death's countless victims and the actions of the church fathers, in accordance with Scripture, to abolish the curse of that disease. The history of that time reveals that the doctors could do nothing. It was only after the people began to follow the ancient biblical laws of sanitation and disease control that the epidemic was broken. In the midst of fear and panic, several church leaders in Vienna began to search the Bible to discover whether or not there was a practical biblical solution to this plague. They discovered in Leviticus 13:46 that Moses laid down strict regulations from God regarding the medical treatment of those afflicted with leprosy or plague: "He shall be unclean. All the days he has the sore he shall be unclean. He is unclean, and he shall dwell alone; his habitation shall be outside the camp." God answered their prayers for deliverance when they finally began to obey His declared commands. Both the scourge of leprosy and the Black Death were eliminated by following God's inspired commands given to Moses in the ancient past.

The Divine Laws of Quarantine

This divine medical rule demanded that a person who contracted leprosy or the plague must be isolated and segregated from the general population during his infectious period, until he was healed or died. God's commands included detailed instructions regarding protection from infection for those who treated the segregated patient. After feeding and caring for the plague sufferer, the care givers must change their clothes, wash in running water, and expose both themselves and their clothing to sunlight. Doctors today know that sunlight and vigorous washing in running water are among the most effective preventative steps to minimize infectious transmission between patients. Moses' instruction to segregate infected patients from their families and other people was one of the most important medical advances in human history. The biblical instructions reveal a profoundly advanced scientific understanding that invisible germs can be transmitted to others unless preventative sanitary steps are taken. Until this century, all previous societies, except for the Israelites who followed God's medical laws regarding quarantine, kept infected patients in their homes — even after death, exposing family members and others to deadly disease. During the devastating Black Death of the fourteenth century, patients who were sick or dead were kept in the same rooms as the rest of the family. People often wondered why the disease was affecting so many people at one time. They attributed these epidemics to "bad air" or "evil spirits." However, careful attention to the medical commands of God as revealed in Leviticus would have saved untold millions of lives. Arturo Castiglione wrote about the overwhelming importance of this biblical medical law, "The laws against leprosy in Leviticus 13 may be regarded as the first model of a sanitary legislation" (Arturo Castiglione, *A History of Medicine* [New York: Alfred A. Knopf, Inc., 1941], p. 71).

Fortunately, the church fathers of Vienna finally took the biblical injunctions to heart and commanded that those infected with the plague must be placed outside the city in special medical quarantine compounds. Care givers fed them there until they either died or survived the passage of the disease. Those who died in homes or streets were instantly removed and buried outside the city limits. These biblical sanitary measures quickly brought the dreaded epidemic under control for the first time. Other cities and countries rapidly followed the medical practices of Vienna until the Black Death was finally halted.

Laws of Cleanliness – Next to Godliness

While people repeat the phrase, "Cleanliness is next to godliness" they often forget that God has actually provided stringent laws of cleanliness that, if followed, would immeasurably prevent disease and premature death. Throughout the Scriptures we find God commanding His people to follow laws of hygiene and cleanliness. To put these laws and instructions in perspective, we need to understand that cleanliness and bathing were almost unknown through much of human history. Most people lived from the cradle to grave in past centuries without ever having a bath. In fact, most Europeans until the 1840s believed that taking a bath was the most dangerous thing you could do to your health. Most Europeans, until the end of the last century, experienced a bath less than once a year. King James I of England, who ordered the translation of the Bible, known as the King James Bible, never bathed once. He kept a bowl of talc beside him that he applied to his fingers and hands to keep them soft. When Kaye and I visited the thousand-room Hampton Palace several years ago, the guide pointed out that King James' numerous guests did not have access to a single bathtub in the whole castle. One of the reasons they loved snuff and perfume so much in those days was to mask dreadful body odors.

However, thousands of years ago God commanded the Israelites to deal with their uncleanliness by following His specific instructions to avoid infection and death. For example, even before God gave Moses the Ten Commandments at Mount Sinai, He told the Israelites to sanctify themselves by washing their clothes: "And the Lord said unto Moses, Go unto the people, and sanctify them to day and to morrow, and let them wash their clothes" (Exodus 19:10). Preparations for ministering in the Tabernacle required that Aaron and his sons wash their bodies before putting on their priestly garments: "And Aaron and his sons thou shalt bring unto the door of the tabernacle of the congregation, and shalt wash them with water" (Exodus 29:4) prior to giving them their priestly garments. "Moses, Aaron, and Aaron's sons would wash their hands and their feet with water whenever, they entered the tabernacle of meeting, and approached the altar, just as the Lord had commanded Moses" (Exodus 40:31,32). This rule still applied years later when the priests ministered in the Temple.

When you consider that the priests were responsible for preparing and sacrificing animals on the altar, the need for strict rules of washing are obvious in light of our present knowledge of the dangers from infectious germs. The Bible also contains detailed sanitation instructions concerning the purification following the birth of a child, and very detailed instructions were laid out regarding hygiene for women.

Incineration of Animal Waste to Prevent Disease

One of the most astonishing of the sanitation commandments found in the Bible is the demand that the internal organs and waste of the animals to be sacrificed were to be carefully burned "without the camp" to prevent the possibility of transmitting infection to the Israelites from the germ-filled waste of the sacrificed animals. Incredibly, the Israelites were commanded to create, in effect, an incinerator "outside the camp" to safely dispose of the dangerous infectious materials produced by their sacrifices. "But the bull's hide and all its flesh, with its head and legs, its entrails and offal; the whole bull he shall carry outside the camp to a clean place, where the ashes are poured out, and burn it on wood with fire; where the ashes are poured out it shall be burned" (Leviticus 4:11,12). At a time when no one knew that animal waste and decaying organs would be dangerous because of the microscopic germs, the Bible commands the Israelites to destroy these infectious agents in the most sanitary method available to an ancient culture — burning outside the camp.

The Medical Importance of the Red Heifer Sacrifice

In Numbers 19, Moses wrote these inspired instructions regarding the mysterious sacrifice of the Red Heifer: "Then the heifer shall be burned in his sight: its hide, its flesh, its blood, and its offal shall be burned. And the priest shall take cedar wood and hyssop and scarlet, and cast them into the midst of the fire burning the heifer. Then the priest shall wash his clothes, he shall bathe in water, and afterward he shall come into the camp; the priest shall be unclean until evening. And the one who burns it shall wash his clothes in water, bathe in water, and shall be unclean until evening. Then a man who is clean shall gather up the ashes of the heifer, and store them outside the camp in a clean place; and they shall be kept for the congregation of the children of Israel for the water of purification; it is for purifying from sin. And the one who gathers the ashes of the heifer shall wash his clothes, and be unclean until evening. It shall be a statute forever to the children of Israel and to the stranger who sojourns among them. He who touches the dead body of anyone shall be unclean seven days. He shall purify himself with the water on the third day and on the seventh day; then he will be clean. But if he does not purify himself on the third day and on the seventh day, he will not be clean. Whoever touches the body of anyone who has died, and does not purify himself, defiles the tabernacle of the Lord. That person shall be cut off from Israel. He shall be unclean, because the water of purification was not sprinkled on him; his uncleanness is still on him" (Numbers 19:5–13).

The primary spiritual significance of the Sacrifice of the Red Heifer is the fact that it symbolically points to the ultimate sacrifice of Jesus Christ as our only hope of being cleansed from the uncleanliness of our sins. The Talmud claims that the Red Heifer sacrifice was the only one of God's commands that King Solomon, the wisest man who ever lived, claimed he did not understand. Although the priest obediently offered the sacrifice as demanded by God, Solomon apparently did not understand why Numbers 19 declared that the priest would be "unclean until evening." This unusual sacrifice symbolically pointed to Jesus Christ and His sacrifice because our Lord, who was perfectly sinless, judicially took upon Himself the sins of the world so that we who are sinful could become righteous before God. Christ paid the price for our sins. Just as the Red Heifer was sacrificed "outside the camp" in contrast to all other sacrifices that took place in the Tabernacle or Temple, Jesus was sacrificed outside the city of Jerusalem. In contrast to the normal male animals sacrificed, the Red Heifer was one of the few female animals the Law commanded to be sacrificed. Significantly, our Lord was betrayed for thirty pieces of silver, the price of a female slave.

In addition to the obvious spiritual significance of the law of the Sacrifice of the Red Heifer we now understand that the water of purification described in Numbers 19 actually had the ability to destroy germs and infection. The resulting water of purification solution contained ashes from the Red Heifer sacrifice combined with cedar, hyssop and scarlet thread. This water of purification contained "cedar" oil that came from a kind of juniper tree that grew in both Israel and in the Sinai. This cedar oil would irritate the skin, encouraging the person to vigorously rub the solution into their hands. Most importantly, the hyssop tree — associated with mint, possibly marjoram — would produce hyssop oil. This hyssop oil is actually a very effective antiseptic and antibacterial agent. Hyssop oil contains 50 percent carvacrol which is an antifungal and antibacterial agent still used in medicine, according to the book *None Of*

These Diseases. When we note that the waters of purification from the Red Heifer Sacrifice were to be used to cleanse someone who had become defiled and unclean due to touching a dead body, we begin to understand that this law was an incredibly effective medical law as well as a spiritual law. The Book of Hebrews reveals that Paul, an educated rabbi, understood that the Red Heifer sacrifice had a practical medical effect as well as its more obvious spiritual element. Paul declared that "the blood of bulls and goats and the ashes of a heifer, sprinkling the unclean, sanctifies for the purifying' of the flesh" (Hebrews 9:13). The Jews stood apart from the pagan nations in their attention to sanitation and personal cleanliness as a result of the commands of God revealed in the Old Testament.

Another of the medical commands that is simply astonishing in its understanding of the need for disinfecting items is found in the command of God regarding all captured material from an enemy's camp. This command of the Lord stated that, "whoever has killed any person, and whoever has touched any slain, purify yourselves and your captives on the third day and on the seventh day. Purify every garment, everything made of leather, everything woven of goats' hair, and everything made of wood" (Numbers 31:19,20). The clear instructions for disinfecting these items was as follows: "Everything that can endure fire, you shall put through the fire, and it shall be clean; and it shall be purified with the water of purification. But all that cannot endure fire you shall put through water. And you shall wash your clothes on the seventh day and be clean, and afterward you may come into the camp" (Numbers 31:23,24). These instructions would purify any materials captured from pagans that might carry dangerous germs.

Life Is in The Blood

Moses makes a fascinating statement in the Book of Leviticus about the importance of blood. "For the life of the flesh is in the blood" (Leviticus 17:11). Incredibly, Moses reveals that our blood is the essence of life. Our blood is one of the most amazing features in our wonderful body. We have over seventy-five thousand miles of blood vessels in our body, enough to circle the world three times! These incredibly tiny veins, arteries, and capillary vessels carry blood cells with nutrients to feed every one of the sixty trillion cells in our bodies. The sixty trillion amazingly complex cells that make up a human body are produced from a single microscopic cell formed when a father's sperm is joined to a mother's egg. This complex system of interconnected blood vessels must bring the needed nutrients to the particular cells that require these chemicals. This is the equivalent of a courier company delivering trillions of packages daily to sixty trillion business customers over a route covering seventy-five thousand miles of territory. Each of our cells requires a number of different nutrients and chemicals. Special chemical sensors detect the nutrient needed as the blood passes through the bloodstream and allow that cell to connect with the necessary substance. In addition, we have over a million special types of white cells, antibodies specially designed to fight one particular disease. As soon as the body detects that it has been invaded by a particular germ or virus the whole blood system goes on special alert to produce an explosive increase in whatever antibody is required to fight the disease.

The Hebrew word for the heart is *lev*. This word and variations of it appear at least eight hundred and twenty-five times in the Old Testament and another one hundred and sixty times in the New Testament. Our enormously complex blood system that allows life to exist is pumped by our heart, the most powerful muscle in our body. Though it is only the size of your clenched fist it. is far stronger than our legs or arms. However, while the heart works non-stop for eighty years or more, the muscles of our legs or arms are exhausted after only a short time of exertion. Weighing less than a pound, this fantastically reliable organ pumps over one and a half million gallons of blood every year of our life, In the course of a normal lifespan the average human heart will pump forty million times pushing almost one million pounds of blood through the seventy-five thousand miles of blood vessels that make up our body. How could Moses have understood thirty-five centuries ago, that "the life of the flesh is in the blood" unless God revealed it to him by inspiration?

God's Command Concerning Circumcision

One of the most interesting of the medical details in the Bible is found in the specific instructions regarding the process of circumcising every Hebrew male child at the age of eight days as a sign of their obedience to the Covenant of God. Abraham was commanded specifically that, "He who is eight days old among you shall be circumcised, every male child in your generations" (Genesis 17:12). For thousands of years righteous Jews have faithfully obeyed this commandment. Why would God demand that Moses command the Israelites to circumcise their male children on the eighth day of life rather than any other day? The Arabs, for example, circumcise their male children on their thirteenth birthday. Medical scientists have been examining the biological processes that lead to blood clotting. The rapid healing of a wound begins with clotting of the blood. Any wound that continues to bleed, especially in a primitive environment, will provide a tremendous likelihood of infection. Recently they discovered that two specific factors in our blood are closely related to the ability of our blood to quickly and safely clot to facilitate healing and resistance to infection. These medical researchers found that two different blood clotting factors, Vitamin K and prothrombin, are at the highest level of your life (110 percent of normal) on the eighth day of life. In addition, they discovered that the blood clotting factor, Vitamin K, is formed in the blood of a baby between day five to day seven of the baby's life. Therefore, of all the days of the baby's life, the eighth day of life is the optimum day for an operation because of the high level of Vitamin K and the prothrombin which will clot the blood and facilitate wound healing. How would Moses have known that the eighth day of life was the ideal time to circumcise the Israelite male children unless God inspired him to write this command?

The Bible's Laws on Sanitation

Since the beginning of human civilization mankind has suffered from the many diseases that are carried in human waste. When men lived primarily in widely distributed rural areas there was little danger of infection. However, as men began to move into villages, towns and cities, the danger of contamination grew geometrically. Throughout the Medieval and Renaissance periods, and in many societies of the Third World today, waste is thrown into the gutter in the street and allowed to be flushed through the drains by occasional rains or floods. The stench from such a primitive system is beyond imagination. During the days of Shakespeare, the River Thames in London was an open sewer containing untreated human waste. Even then, four hundred years ago, salmon could not survive in the river because of toxic poisons. People could not bear to walk near the River Thames because of the stench from the open cesspool. It is interesting to note that modern pollution treatment has now succeeded in reclaiming the Thames to the point where fishermen are actually catching edible salmon from the bridges of London. According to an article in the *Encyclopædia Britannica,* the foul smells arising from the River Thames in London in past centuries was so terrible that they hung burlap sacks saturated in chloride of lime in the windows of Parliament in an ineffective attempt to kill the odors.

The smells in cities and towns were as indescribable and deadly as the comparable odors in Calcutta today. The result of this deplorable condition is that humans died in huge numbers every year as they succumbed to a variety of germ-related diseases including typhoid, dysentery and cholera. As difficult as it might be to believe, even the educated people of the day ignored the appalling threat to their health represented by the lack of any sanitation whatsoever. It is not an exaggeration to claim that hundreds of millions of people have died throughout history due to infectious disease produced by the absence of even the most elementary sanitation regarding human waste. Yet obedience to God's law of sanitation, proclaimed thousands of years ago in the pages of Scripture, would have saved countless millions of lives from needless death caused by germs spread through untreated and unburied sewage.

My reason for dwelling on this unpleasant subject is an attempt to emphasize the extraordinary nature of the advanced sanitation commands issued by God over three and a half thousand years ago. At a time when no one humanly understood anything about the true deadly nature of microscopic germs and infections, God instructed Moses about how he could insure adequate sanitation for his huge Jewish refugee population. As the history of refugee situations reveals, they almost inevitably lead to terrible infections, such as cholera and typhoid, due to the lack of adequate sanitation facilities. The germs from untreated human waste, produced in such unorganized refugee groups, contaminate the ground water and lead to horrendous epidemics.

God's basic sanitation order regarding human waste for the children of Israel was recorded in the Book of Deuteronomy: "Also you shall have a place outside the camp, where you may go out; and you shall have an implement among your equipment, and when you sit down outside, you shall dig with it and turn and cover your refuse" (Deuteronomy 23:12). While such a basic sanitation law concerning latrines may seem very normal and obvious to us today, it is an extraordinary instruction when you consider that it was made thirty-five centuries before the existence of invisible germs was discovered.

As a student of biblical and military history I have long noted the historical truth that the vast majority of soldiers who have been killed during the countless wars have succumbed to infectious disease rather than bullets or other weapons of war. The history of war until A.D. 1900, reveals that five times as many soldiers usually died due to disease than to wounds inflicted by enemy weapons. Sickness and plague often determined the outcome of a battle. Often the army that suffered the greatest diseases lost the war. A huge percentage of the diseases of mankind, especially in war or refugee situations, developed due to the lack of sanitation regarding waste disposal. Even as late as the Boer War in South Africa (1899–1902), an analysis of military casualties indicates that five times as many soldiers died or were incapacitated due to infections, often caused by exposure to germs generated from waste. When armies marched across a country and besieged a city, tens of thousands of soldiers were forced to encamp in the open for months. Without obedience to the strict sanitation rules found in the Bible, the unburied waste from these soldiers inevitably ended up in the ground water system and ultimately infected the rest of the army.

It is certain that the strict obedience to the Law of God by the soldiers of Israel allowed them to escape many of the terrible diseases that would have afflicted their pagan enemies. It is likely that Israel was assisted in winning many of its ancient battles against the pagan troops of Syria and Moab because Jewish soldiers were not exposed to the tremendous infections that would afflict their enemies who did not know God's rules of sanitation. Consider the logistic problems of trying to meet the human needs of hundreds of thousands of Jews during the forty years in the wilderness. Most Israelites would have died due to infectious diseases during those years if God had not instructed Moses to teach His chosen people these advanced laws of sanitation. In his book, *A History of Medicine*, the medical historian Arturo Castiglione declared that Moses' sanitation commands to his army were, "certainly a primitive measure, but an effective one, which indicates advanced ideas of sanitation" (p. 70).

These simple but profoundly important instructions from God told the Israelites that each soldier must carry a shovel and bury his waste. Such instructions would assure that there would be no risk of infection to himself and his fellow soldiers from the waste. This command on latrines is so obvious to us today that it is easy to overlook its importance as a proof of the divine inspiration of the Scriptures. Before the recent medical advances during the last one hundred and thirty years, medical doctors did not know that microscopic infections from human and animal waste were among the deadliest dangers to mankind. Yet, here we find this advanced sanitation and medical knowledge clearly expressed in the Bible written thousands of years ago. Where could Moses have learned this incredibly important and life saving medical knowledge about the dangers of human waste unless he received a divine revelation as he recorded? Moses could not possibly have learned this knowledge from his schooling in the medicine of Egypt. Remember that one of the favorite ingredients found in the traditional medicines of ancient Egypt as described in the Egyptian *Ebers Papyrus*, was manure from insects, animals and humans. How could Moses have written these incredibly accurate and advanced medical instructions unless God inspired him?

8

Precise Fulfillment of Bible Prophecy – The Signature of God

"From all the angelic ranks goes forth a groan,
'How long, O Lord, how long?'
The still small voice makes answer 'Wait and see,
O sons of glory, what the end shall be.'"
Thomas Macaulay—*Marriage of Tirzah and Ahirad.*

This study of the fulfillment of biblical prophecy provides over-whelming proof that God is controlling human history. Despite the apparent anarchy of daily events, the hand of God is still moving behind the scenes of current history to bring about His divine will. The details in the history of God's chosen people was precisely prophesied throughout the Bible. Each of the three long captivities of Israel were prophesied: their first exile in Egypt, which lasted four hundred and thirty years; the seventy years of captivity in Babylon; the final worldwide dispersion of the Jewish people for the last two thousand years. Every time Israel was out of the Promised Land, the duration of the captivity was foretold regarding how long God would keep the Jews in exile. Incredibly, the actual time of the miraculous rebirth of Israel on May 15, 1948, was foretold by the prophet Ezekiel over twenty-five centuries before it occurred. It is obvious to any who will examine this evidence that history is following a purposeful pattern, a design laid down centuries ago in the Word of God. The question we must ask is this, "Who is the designer?" And, "What is His purpose in history and in our own lives?"

The Bible itself declares that the evidence of fulfilled prophecy is the unmistakable proof of God's inspiration of Scripture. It is clear from the words of the prophet Isaiah that God Himself declared that the phenomenon of correctly and precisely prophesying future events is the absolute proof that the Lord inspired biblical writers to write the Scriptures. The prophet Isaiah recorded God's declaration: "Behold, the former things have come to pass, and new things I declare; before they spring forth I tell you of them" (Isaiah 42:9).

No one except God can accurately predict future events in detail. Neither Satan nor his demons can predict the future. Twenty-five centuries ago the prophet Isaiah recorded these powerful words directly from God Almighty. "Remember the former things of old, for I am God, and there is none else; I am God, and there is none like Me, Declaring the end from the beginning, and from ancient times the things that are not yet done, saying, 'My counsel shall stand, and I will do all My pleasure'" (Isaiah 46:9,10). The Bible contains 1,817 individual predictions concerning 737 separate subjects found in 8,352 verses. These numerous predictions comprise 27 percent of the 31,124 verses in the whole of the Scriptures. Multitudes of biblical scholars over the last two thousand years have explored many of these prophecies and their detailed fulfillments as proven by ample historical evidence.

Only God Can Correctly Prophesy the Future

Despite the fact that the world is full of spiritual texts by multitudes of religious writers, a close examination of this literature reveals that not one of these texts contains detailed prophecies that have been fulfilled. The reason is quite simple: Since no one but God can know the future accurately, religious philosophers who wrote other texts were wise enough to refrain from attempting detailed prophecies which would quickly prove their authors to be in error. "Thus says the Lord, the King of Israel, and his Redeemer, the Lord of hosts: I am the First and I am the Last; besides Me there is no God. And who can proclaim as I do? Then let him declare it and set it in order for Me, since I appointed the ancient people. And the things that are coming and shall come, let them show these to them'" (Isaiah 44:6–7). The classical and religious literature of the Greeks, Romans, and other Middle Eastern cultures contains no specific, detailed prophecies regarding future events, people, or trends. There were no prophecies concerning the coming of Buddha, Mohammed, or any other religious leader. Only Old Testament prophecies predicted numerous precise details about the life, death, and resurrection of Jesus of Nazareth.

Despite the impossible odds against correctly guessing future events, multitudes of false prophets have attempted to make predictions in the past and continue to do so in our generation. However, these human predictions are almost always wrong with the exception of very few lucky guesses. As I noted in my first book, *Armageddon — Appointment With Destiny* (pp. 14,15), a fascinating study of the predictive claims of New Age psychics called *The Shattered Crystal Ball* proved that these modern psychics are hopelessly wrong in their predictions. "The study analyzed the accuracy of the ten top psychics whose prophecies were published over a three-year period, 1976 to 1979. The study compared all of the published predictions with their subsequent success or failure rate. The results are certainly intriguing: 98 percent of their predictions were totally incorrect! Only 2 percent of their predictions were fulfilled ... six out of the ten psychics were wrong 100 percent of the time."

Some New Age writers have claimed that several non-biblical prophets such as Nostradamus (A.D. 1555) were able to correctly predict the future. Many modern New Age writers have claimed that Nostradamus actually predicted that Adolph Hitler would be the future leader of Germany in his hundreds of predictions called "centuries." This claim is totally false! In fact, Nostradamus never mentioned Adolph Hitler by name in any of his predictions. The closest he came to "Hitler" was his mention of the word "Ister" in several predictions that the majority of interpreters admit refers clearly to a European river called the Ister River, a tributary of the River Danube. However, some writers who wrote their analysis after World War II have falsely claimed that Nostradamus actually predicted the history of Hitler, the German dictator. Incredibly, they claim that the name "Hitler" is quite close to the word "Histler" which is not all that different than the actual word "Ister" that appeared in Nostradamus's prediction! The New Age writer Erika Cheetham, who wrote *The Final Prophecies of Nostradamus* in 1989, admitted in her book that, "until 1936, approximately, all commentators on the Centuries thought that the word referred to the River Danube, the Ister." Even strong supporters of Nostradamus, such as Henry C. Roberts, the editor of *The Complete Prophecies of Nostradamus*, (Jericho, N.Y.: Nostradamus, Inc. 1976) admitted in his Introduction that these prophetic writings of Nostradamus are "unintelligible." He wrote that these predictions are "unintelligible and garbled to the uninitiate. The strange, broken, and often incoherent nature of the quatrains, both in French and English, is the hallmark of prophetic media."

Other New Age writers have made great claims for the accuracy of the predictions of Edgar Cayce, the so-called American "sleeping prophet" who lived in the early part of this century. I had the experience of interviewing both Hugh Lynn Cayce, the son of Edgar Cayce, and his grandson in the early 1970s at their research center in Virginia Beach, Virginia. It was fascinating to hear them describe the research they had completed on a manuscript revealing numerous mistaken predictions Edgar Cayce made during his career. Some of these false predictions were prophecies Cayce made about where they could locate oil wells or mineral deposits. Not surprisingly, they indicated that they did not intend to publish the manuscript.

No One But God Knows the Future

The ability of humans to correctly predict future events or trends is virtually non-existent outside of lucky guesses. Despite the great knowledge and genius of mankind we are unable to correctly predict future events and trends. As examples of this blindness as to the future, consider the following statements. The director of the U.S. Patent Office resigned his high position in 1875. He complained in his letter to the government that there was no point in continuing the Patent Office because "there's nothing left to invent." Since his resignation we have witnessed an astonishing number of brilliant inventions and developments every year in all areas of knowledge and science. Only a few years later, in 1887, the brilliant French chemist Marcellin Berthelot wrote, "From now on there is no mystery about the universe." In the years that followed we have seen the mysteries of the atomic structure of matter unfold, the creation of a hundred new sciences including biophysics, astrophysics and molecular biology. Another great scientist at that time, Professor Simon Newcomb, wrote a highly acclaimed manuscript that proved that it was mathematically impossible for any machine that was heavier than a balloon to fly in the air. Every day thousands of large airplanes take off from thousands of airports carrying a staggering number of passengers throughout the world. An equally brilliant French philosopher by the name of Poincare ridiculed a scientist's speculations about unleashing the power of the atom through chain reactions in uranium. "Common sense alone is enough to tell us that the destruction of a town by a pound of metal is an evident impossibility." Tragically, the discoveries of awesome nuclear energies locked within the metal uranium allowed scientists to create atomic weapons of staggering power that annihilated two Japanese cities, Hiroshima and Nagasaki, in only seconds with only a few pounds of metal (*Morning of the Magicians*, Louis Pauwels and Jacques Bergier, [New York: Stein and Day, 1964], pp. 9,10,14).

More recently, in 1943, Thomas Watson, the chairman of IBM, declared, "I think there is a world market for maybe five computers." Today, the world contains over a billion computer devices, In the 1940s the first generation of computers were so large that they filled a whole room and weighed several tons. The magazine *Popular Mechanics* examined the state of scientific knowledge in 1949 and made this forecast about the future of computer development. "Computers in the future may weigh no more than 1.5 tons." Today we have sophisticated computers capable of billions of calculations per second that weigh less than five pounds and are much smaller than a TV set. In 1981, Bill Gates, the brilliant creator of Microsoft, the largest computer software company in history, declared, "640K (640,000 bytes of memory) should be enough for anybody." Little did he realize that in less than fifteen years the average personal desktop computer, such as the Macintosh system Power Tower 180MHz I use, would contain as much as 48MB (48 million bytes) of RAM (Random Access Memory) and 2 billion bytes of fast computer memory on its hard drive. These inaccurate predictions reveal the profound limitations of man's intelligence and his inability to correctly forecast future events.

However, when we turn to the pages of the Holy Scriptures we discover a staggering number of precise predictions that were made thousands of years ago concerning the future of nations and individuals. A careful analysis of these predictions reveals that every one has been fulfilled with an awesome precision that can only be explained by divine knowledge predicting the event, and the hand of God bringing the event to pass. Let's examine one of the most incredible of the thousands of Old Testament prophecies that actually predicted that rebirth of Israel in the spring of 1948.

Ezekiel Prophesied Israel's 1948 Rebirth

Several years ago I discovered that God had hidden in the pages of Scripture a precise prophecy about the exact time when He would miraculously restore His chosen people to their ancient Holy Land. While everyone knew that the Scriptures contained numerous prophecies that the Jews would return to Israel in the last days, God's prediction about the exact time of Israel's return to the Promised Land was not revealed until after the fulfillment of the prophecy. In God's divine purpose, many details about the prophecies concerning the last days were sealed in biblical visions in such a way that they could not be clearly discerned prior to their accomplishment. Then, when the prophecy was fulfilled, this confirmed the inspiration of the Scriptures and glorified God. An examination of the prophecies reveals that God often specified in great detail the exact duration of time involved in various predictions concerning Israel. However, times were never given in prophecies that deal with the Church. There are no prophecies that reveal the time of. the Rapture. The Lord has specifically hidden the time of the future resurrection of the saints from all but Himself. The Lord Himself told us, "But of that day and hour knoweth no man, no, not the angels of heaven, but My Father only" (Matthew 24:36). The failure to appreciate this fact has led to many errors in prophetic interpretation. The interpretation of Ezekiel's prediction about the time of Israel's rebirth appeared in my book *Armageddon — Appointment With Destiny* in 1988. Despite the fact that over five hundred thousand people have read this material in various editions and languages of *Armageddon,* no one has been able to refute the accuracy of this incredible biblical prophecy that was given to the prophet Ezekiel when he was taken captive to Babylon twenty-five centuries ago.

Israel's Return to the Land

Israel's relationship to the Holy Land is a major focus of biblical prophecy, both fulfilled and unfulfilled. God prophesied precisely when Israel would return to the Promised Land after her citizens went into exile in the first two captivities, the Egyptian and Babylonian. The Egyptian captivity was prophesied to last exactly 430 years and it is significant that it ended precisely to the day when the 430-year captivity ended. "And it came to pass at the end of the four hundred and thirty years; even the self-same day; it came to pass, that all the hosts of the Lord went out from the land of Egypt" (Exodus 12:41). The prophet Jeremiah predicted the exact duration of the captivity of the Jewish exiles in Babylon would last 70 years. "And this whole land shall be a desolation and an astonishment, and these nations shall serve the king of Babylon seventy years" (Jeremiah 25:11). The Babylonian army conquered Israel in the spring of 606 B.C. Both secular history and the Bible reveal that, as predicted, the Babylonian Captivity ended exactly 70 years later in the spring of 536 B.C., in the Jewish month Nisan, when the Persian King Cyrus freed the Jews to return to their land (Ezra 1:3).

The three major Jewish prophets, Daniel, Jeremiah and Ezekiel, were all alive at this time. Naturally, the prophet Ezekiel was aware of the prophet Jeremiah's prophecy that the Jews could return from Babylon after 70 years in 536 B.C. However, God gave him a new revelation that looked much farther into the future revealing how long it would be until the Jewish people would finally re-establish their nation in the last days. The prediction began with God's declaration that "this shall be a sign to the house of Israel" (Ezekiel 4:3). The full prediction is found in Ezekiel 4:3–6: "This will be a sign to the house of Israel. Lie also on your left side, and lay the iniquity of the house of Israel upon it. According to the number of the days that you lie on it, you shall bear their iniquity. For I have laid on you the years of their iniquity, according to the number of the days, three hundred and ninety days; so you shall bear the iniquity of the house of Israel. And when you have completed them, lie again on your right side; then you shall bear the iniquity of the house of Judah forty days. I have laid on you a day for each year" (Ezekiel 4:3–6).

In this passage the prophet Ezekiel clearly declares that this prophecy would be "a sign to the house of Israel" and that each day represents one biblical year. The prediction revealed that Israel would be punished for a combined period of 430 years (390 years plus another 40 years). The beginning point for this worldwide captivity occurred in the spring of 536 B.C., at the end of the seventy years of predicted captivity in Babylon (Jeremiah 25:11). However, in the month Nisan, 536 B.C., only a small remnant of the Jews from the nation of Judah chose to leave their homes in Babylon and return to Jerusalem. The Jewish exiles who remembered their former homes in Israel were now over 70 years old. Their children who had been born in Babylon naturally had little connection or attachment to the former home of their parents. The vast majority were quite happy to remain in the pagan Persian Empire as colonists rather than immigrate six hundred miles to rebuild the devastated colony of Israel. God decreed to Ezekiel a period of punishment of 430 years for Israel's and Judah's sin (390 years + 40 years = 430 years). However, when we deduct the 70 years of punishment the Jews had endured during the 70-year Babylonian captivity, which ended in 536 B.C. there still remained a total of 360 years of further punishment beyond the year 536 B.C. When we examine the history of that period we note that the Jews did not return to establish an independent country at the end of either 360 or of 430 years of additional punishment. In light of the precision of Ezekiel's prophecy, it was difficult to understand why nothing occurred at that time to fulfill the detailed prediction.

Both the Bible and history reveal that Israel did not repent of its sins at the end of the seventy-year captivity in Babylon. In fact, the Scriptures record in the books of Ezra and Nehemiah that the minority of fifty thousand who chose to return with Ezra to the Promised Land did so with little faith. The vast majority of the Jews remained in pagan Babylon. They failed to repent of their disobedience, which was the reason God sent them into captivity in the first place. This majority who refused to immigrate home to Israel, composing over 95 percent of the Jewish captives, simply settled down as colonists in what is now Iraq-Iran. Over the centuries that followed, travelers such as Benjamin of Tuldela reported that thousands of Jews still lived in several of the cities of present-day Iraq, Iran, and Afghanistan.

I discovered the solution to the mystery of the duration of Israel's worldwide dispersion and return in a divine principle that God revealed to Moses in Leviticus 26. In this chapter the Lord established promises and punishments for Israel based on her obedience and her disobedience to His commands. God declared to Israel four times in this passage that if, after being punished for her sins, she still did not repent, the punishments previously specified would be multiplied by seven (the number of completion). "And after all this, if you do not obey Me, then I will punish you seven times more for your sins" (Leviticus 26:18; see also Leviticus 26:21, 23–24, 27–28). In other words, if Israel failed to repent of her disobedience, the punishments already decreed by God would be multiplied or extended seven times. Since the majority of Israel refused to repent of her sin after the Babylonian Captivity ended, the period of 360 years of further punishment declared by Ezekiel 4:3–6 was multiplied by seven times. This meant that the Jews would remain without an independent nation for another 2,520 biblical years from 536 B.C., the beginning point of the prediction (360 years × 7 = 2,520 years biblical years).

The Biblical Year of 360 Days

The period of punishment was to last 2,520 biblical years rather than 2,520 calendar years. The reason is that the Bible always used the ancient Jewish calendar composed of 360 days, making up a biblical year, in both the historical and prophetic passages. The true length of the Jewish, biblical prophetic year was only 360 days because it was a lunar-solar year composed of twelve months of 30 days each. The modern solar year of 365.25 days was unknown to the ancient nations in the Old Testament. According to articles on Chronology in the *Encyclopædia Britannica* and *Smith's Bible Dictionary*, Abraham used a 360-day year. The Genesis' record of Noah's flood confirms that the ancient year consisted of twelve months of thirty days each. Moses declared in Genesis that the period of 150 days when the flood waters were at their height lasted precisely five months from the seventeenth day of the second month to the seventeenth day of the seventh month, proving that each month consisted of thirty days. Sir Isaac Newton relates that "all nations, before the just length of the solar year was known, reckoned months by the course of the moon, and years by the return of winter and summer, spring and autumn; and in making calendars for their festivals, they reckoned thirty days to a lunar month, and twelve lunar months to a year, taking the nearest round numbers, whence came the division of the ecliptic into 360 degrees."

Therefore, if we wish to understand the precise times involved in the fulfillment of prophecy, we need to calculate using the same biblical lunar-solar year of 360 days which the prophets used. Both the prophet Daniel and John, in the Book of Revelation, clearly used a year of 360 days. The failure to understand the true length of the biblical year as 360 days has prevented some prophecy students from clearly understanding many prophecies which contain a precise time element. This 360-day prophetic year is also borne out in the Book of Revelation where John's vision refers to the future Great Tribulation period. He describes the Great Tribulation of three and one-half years as lasting precisely 1,260 days (Revelation 12:6), "a time, times and half a time" where a "time" in Hebrew stands for a year of 360 days (verse 14), and "forty-two months" of thirty days each (13:5). All of these biblical references confirm that the 360-day biblical year is the one we must use to correctly understand biblical prophecy and chronology.

Therefore, Ezekiel's prophecy of the 430 years declared that the end of Israel's punishment and her final restoration to the land would be accomplished in 2,520 biblical years of 360 days each which totals precisely 907,200 days. To convert this period into our calendar year of 365.25 days we simply divide the period of 907,200 days by 365.25 days to reach a total of 2,483.8 of our modern calendar years. Therefore, Ezekiel prophesied that the end of Israel's worldwide captivity would occur precisely 2,483.8 years after the end of the Babylonian Captivity which occurred in the spring of 536 B.C. In these calculations we must keep in mind that there was only one year between 1 B.C. and A.D. 1. There was no year Zero. As an illustration, there were only twelve months between the Feast of Passover on 14th of Nisan in the spring of 1 B.C. and the next annual Feast of Passover in the spring of A.D. 1.

To Calculate When Ezekiel Prophesied the Jews Would Become a Nation Again

The Babylonian captivity ended in the Spring of 536 B.C.	536.4 B.C *MINUS*
The duration of Israel's captivity (from Ezekiel 4:3–6)	2,483.8 calendar years
	1,947.4
To adjust for the fact there was no year zero between 1 B.C. and A.D. 1, we adjust one year	1
Therefore; the end of Israel's captivity would occur:	_____
The Rebirth of Israel	**1948–May 15**

On the afternoon of May 14, 1948, the Jews proclaimed the independence of the reborn state of Israel. As an old rabbi blew on the traditional shofar, a ram's horn, the Jewish people celebrated the end of their tragic worldwide dispersion and captivity in precise fulfillment of the prophecy made thousands of years earlier by the prophet Ezekiel. At midnight, as May 15, 1948, began, the British Mandate officially ended and Israel became an independent nation. This great day marked the first time since the days of Solomon that a united Israel took its place as a sovereign, independent state among the nations of the world.

In Ezekiel's amazing prophecy we are witnessing a fulfillment of prophecy in our generation of such incredible precision, that one is forced to marvel at the power of God to foresee and control all of man's plans and their outcomes. Despite the apparent anarchy of the events of our time, God is still on the throne of this universe and remains in full control of events. The universe is unfolding precisely as our Lord ordained and foresaw millenniums ago. In addition, this amazingly accurate fulfillment of prophecy in our lifetime should focus our attention on the prophecy of Jesus Christ about the budding of the fig tree. The Bible used the symbol of the fig tree or figs in six different passages as an exclusive symbol of the nation Israel (Judges 9:8–15; Hosea 9:10; Jeremiah 24:1–10; Matthew 21:18–20, etc.). "Now learn this parable from the fig tree: When its branch has already become tender and puts forth leaves, you know that summer is near. So you also, when you see all these things, know that it is near, at the very doors. Assuredly, I say to you, this generation will by no means pass away till all these things are fulfilled" (Matthew 24:32–34). In light of the startling precision of the fulfillment of Ezekiel's prophecy about Israel's rebirth and the prophecy of Jesus that the generation who witnessed this rebirth "will by no means pass away till all these things are fulfilled" everyone of us should realize that we are living in the generation when Christ indicated He will return to judge mankind.

Predictions About Jesus Christ the Messiah

The Old Testament contains over three hundred passages that refer to the first coming of the Messiah. Within these hundreds of prophecies, Bible scholars have found forty-eight specific details about the life, death and resurrection of Jesus. These Scriptural prophecies were published over five centuries before Christ was born in Bethlehem. In this chapter we will discuss seventeen of these prophecies, examine the evidence for their fulfillment, and prove that Jesus of Nazareth fulfilled them, showing that He is the promised Messiah, the Son of God.

The Laws of Probability

The study of statistics includes the theory and Laws of Mathematical Probability. The Laws of Probability are not abstract. They are so dependable that huge insurance companies write policies promising to pay a million dollars to the family of a thirty-year-old male in return for a small premium of only $30 per month. How can they take on such a huge risk in return for only $30 in monthly premiums? The answer is found in the Laws of Probability. After careful analysis of the mortality tables, insurance companies know that only a tiny fraction of the thirty-year-old clients they insure will actually die within the next year. Every day insurance companies risk billions of dollars on similar well established calculations of mathematical probability.

The Laws of Probability reveal that if the probability of a single event occurring randomly is one chance in five, and the probability of another event occurring is one chance in ten, then the combined probability that both events will occur together in sequence is five multiplied by ten. Thus, the combined chance of both events occurring in sequence is one chance in fifty. To put this in a perspective we can appreciate, consider the odds when we toss a coin in the air. Since a coin has two sides, the odds are 50 percent or one chance in two that you will get "heads" when you toss a dime. However, suppose that you toss two dimes in a row. What are the odds against getting "heads" twice in a row? The answer is four. The combined odds are $2 \times 2 = 4$. The odds of tossing ten coins in a row and getting ten "heads" one after another are quite staggering. According to the laws of probability, the odds against getting ten "heads" are one chance in 1,024. Don't bet your salary that you can beat such odds. However, when you consider the odds against these seventeen prophecies about the life and death of Jesus Christ happening by chance, you will realize that the evidence proves that Jesus was the promised Messiah and the Savior of all who will believe in Him.

To further prove the inspiration and authority of the Bible, let us examine only one area of specific prophecy, out of literally hundreds, that has to do with the life and death of the coming Messiah who will save humanity from their sins. In this chapter we will examine a series of specific predictions that were made by different Jewish prophets who lived in widely separated communities over a period of a thousand years. These predictions were fulfilled over five hundred years after they were recorded.

We will also examine the possibility that these individual predictions could have occurred by random chance alone. After considering the evidence presented in this chapter, you will understand that the precise fulfillment of these different predictions in the life of one man was so improbable, that any unbiased observer must accept that the Bible was truly inspired by God and that Jesus Christ is the promised Messiah.

Seventeen Incredible Prophecies about the Messiah

In this chapter we will examine seventeen specific prophecies in this analysis of Old Testament predictions that were fulfilled in the life of Jesus of Nazareth. As you consider the likelihood that any one of these particular prophecies could have occurred by chance, ask yourself if it was possible that all seventeen of these predictions could have been fulfilled by random chance in the life of one man, Jesus Christ.

The Old Testament Predictions About the Coming Messiah

The odds against these events occurring by chance

The First Prediction:
His birth in Bethlehem from the tribe of Judah

Probability: 1 chance in 2,400

The Old Testament prediction:

"But you, Bethlehem Ephrathah, though you are little among the thousands of Judah, yet out of you shall come forth to Me the One to be ruler in Israel, Whose goings forth have been from of old, from everlasting" (Micah 5:2).

"The scepter shall not depart from Judah, nor a lawgiver from between his feet, until Shiloh comes; and to Him shall be the obedience of the people" (Genesis 49:10).

The New Testament Fulfillment:

"Now after Jesus was born in Bethlehem of Jude a in the days of Herod the king, behold, wise men from the East came to Jerusalem" (Matthew 2:1).

There were twelve tribes in ancient Israel from which the Messiah could have been born. Yet He was born from the tribe of Judah as Moses predicted fifteen hundred years earlier. Since there were twelve tribes, the odds were 12 to 1 against Moses guessing correctly the tribe of Christ's birth. In addition, there were over two thousand villages and towns in the densely populated area allotted to the tribe of Judah during the first century of this era. However, to be conservative I used the figure of 1 chance in 2,400 to estimate the odds against anyone guessing that He would be born in Bethlehem and that He would descend from the tribe Judah centuries before Jesus was born.

The Second Prediction:
He would be preceded by a messenger

Probability: 1 chance in 20

The Old Testament Prediction:

"The voice of one crying in the wilderness: 'Prepare the way of the Lord; make straight in the desert a highway for our God'" (Isaiah 40:3).

The New Testament Fulfillment:

"In those days John the Baptist came preaching in the wilderness of Judea, and saying, 'Repent, for the kingdom of heaven is at hand!'" (Matthew 3:1,2).

I estimated the odds as 1 in 20, but historical records do not reveal any other king to my knowledge who was preceded by a messenger such as John the Baptist. To calculate the combined probability of these two predictions we must multiply 2,400 times 20 which equals only one chance in 48,000 that Jesus would fulfill both predictions by chance.

The Third Prediction:
He would enter Jerusalem on a colt

Probability: 1 chance in 50

The Old Testament Prediction:

"Rejoice greatly, O daughter of Zion! Shout, O daughter of Jerusalem! Behold, your King is coming to you; He is just and having salvation, lowly and riding on a donkey, a colt, the foal of a donkey" (Zechariah 9:9).

The New Testament Fulfillment:

"Then they brought him to Jesus. And they threw their own garments on the colt, and they set Jesus on him. And as He went, they spread their clothes on the road. Then, as He was now drawing near the descent of the Mount of Olives, the whole multitude of the disciples began to rejoice and praise God with a loud voice for all the mighty works they had seen" (Luke 19:35–37).

Of all the kings of history I do not know of a single king who ever entered his capital on a colt, as Jesus did on Palm Sunday, A.D. 32, in fulfillment of this prophecy. The combined odds of the three predictions occurring by chance are $50 \times 48,000$ which equals one chance in 2,400,000. With the addition of every subsequent prediction the laws of probability reveal that the combined odds against anyone fulfilling these multiple prophecies are simply astronomical.

The Fourth Prediction:
He would be betrayed by a friend

Probability: 1 chance in 10

The Old Testament Prediction:

"Even my own familiar friend in whom I trusted, Who ate my bread, Has lifted up his heel against me" (Psalm 41:9).

The New Testament Fulfillment:

"And while He was still speaking, behold, Judas, one of the twelve, with a great multitude with swords and clubs, came from the chief priests and elders of the people. Now His betrayer had given them a sign, saying, 'Whomever I kiss, He is the One; seize Him' "(Matthew 26:47,48).

Although it is not that unusual for a secular king to be betrayed by a close associate the betrayal of a religious leader is quite unusual historically. However, to be conservative, I have assigned the odds of this occurring by chance as only one chance in ten. The combined probability for these four predictions (10 × 2,400,000) is now only one chance in 24 million.

The Fifth Prediction:
His hands and feet would be pierced

Probability: 1 chance in 100

The Old Testament Prediction:

"For dogs have surrounded Me; The assembly of the wicked has enclosed Me. They pierced My hands and My feet" (Psalm 22:16).

The New Testament Fulfillment:

"And when they had come to the place called Calvary, there they crucified Him, and the criminals, one on the right hand and the other on the left" (Luke 23:3 3).

The combined probability of these five predictions (10 X 24 million) has now reached an astonishing one chance in 2.4 billion.

The Sixth Prediction:
He would be wounded by His enemies

Probability: 1 chance in 10

The Old Testament Prediction:

"But he was wounded for our transgressions, he was bruised for our iniquities: the chastisement of our peace was upon him; and with his stripes we are healed" (Isaiah 53:5).

The New Testament Fulfillment:

"Then he released Barabbas to them; and when he had scourged Jesus, he delivered [Him] to be crucified" (Matthew 27:26).

Throughout history most kings who were killed were murdered suddenly. Very few were ever subjected to torture as was inflicted on our Lord Jesus Christ. The odds against this occurring by chance were less than one chance in ten. The combined odds for the six predictions (10 × 2.4 billion) now rises to one chance in 24 billion.

The Seventh Prediction:
His betrayal for 30 pieces of silver

Probability: 1 chance in 50

The Old Testament Prediction:

"Then I said to them, 'If it is agreeable to you, give me my wages; and if not, refrain.' So they weighed out for my wages thirty pieces of silver'" (Zechariah 11:12).

The New Testament Fulfillment:

"What are you willing to give me if I deliver Him to you? And they counted out to him thirty pieces of silver" (Matthew 26:15).

Consider how impossible it would be to correctly predict five hundred years in advance the exact price of betrayal that would be paid for the death of a future king. The odds (50 × 24 billion) now rise to one chance in one trillion, two hundred billion.

The Eight Prediction:
He will be spit upon and beaten

Probability: 1 chance in 10

The Old Testament Prediction:

"I gave My back to those who struck Me, and My cheeks to those who plucked out the beard; I did not hide My face from shame and spitting" (Isaiah 50:6).

The New Testament Fulfillment:

"Then they spat in His face and beat Him; and others struck Him with the palms of their hands" (Matthew 26:67).

Although many kings throughout history were killed, very few were tormented, beaten and ridiculed. However, Jesus Christ bore those stripes for our healing and salvation. The odds of these eight predictions (10 × one trillion, two hundred billion) occurring by chance are now one chance in 12 trillion.

The Ninth Prediction:
His betrayal money would be thrown in the Temple and then given to buy a potter's field

Probability: 1 chance in 200

The Old Testament Prediction:

"And the Lord said to me, 'Throw it to the potter'; that princely price they set on me. So I took the thirty pieces of silver and threw them into the house of the Lord for the potter" (Zechariah 11:13).

The New Testament Fulfillment:

"Then he threw down the pieces of silver in the temple and departed, and went and hanged himself. But the chief priests took the silver pieces and said, 'It is not lawful to put them into the treasury, because they are the price of blood.' And they took counsel and bought with them the potter's field, to bury strangers in" (Matthew 27:5–7).

This complicated prophecy actually seems contradictory on its surface. However, despite its apparent impossibility every detail of this prophecy was fulfilled in precise detail. Judas threw the thirty pieces of betrayal money into the Temple. Later the priests used this money to purchase a potter's field to bury strangers including Judas who, overcome with guilt, hanged himself. I calculated the odds extremely conservatively as one chance in 200. However, the combined odds (200 × 12 trillion) against these nine predictions occurring have risen to one chance in 2,400 trillion.

The Tenth Prediction:
He would be silent before His accusers

Probability: 1 chance in 100

The Old Testament Prediction:

"He was oppressed and He was afflicted, yet He opened not His mouth; He was led as a lamb to the slaughter, and as a sheep before its shearers is silent, so He opened not his mouth" (Isaiah 53:7).

The New Testament Fulfillment:

"And while He was being accused by the chief priests and elders, He answered nothing. Then Pilate said to Him, 'Do You not hear how many things they testify against You?' And He answered him not one word, so that the governor marveled greatly" (Matthew 27:12–14).

When we are accused of a crime we naturally defend ourselves, even when we are guilty. Consider how unlikely this prediction was that a totally innocent man would stand before His accusers in absolute silence without speaking to defend himself. While I assigned the odds as one chance in one hundred the realistic chances against this event occurring are much higher. The odds against these ten predictions occurring (100 × 2,400 trillion) is now one chance in 24,000 trillion.

The Eleventh Prediction:
He would be crucified with thieves

Probability: 1 chance in 100

The Old Testament Prediction:
"Therefore I will divide Him a portion with the great, and He shall divide the spoil with the strong, because He poured out His soul unto death, and He was numbered with the transgressors, and He bore the sin of many, and made intercession for the transgressors" (Isaiah 53:12).

The New Testament Fulfillment:
"Then two robbers were crucified with Him, one on the right and another on the left" (Matthew 27:38).

The continued multiplication of these odds reaches a truly staggering number when we examine the chances that all seventeen prophecies occurred by chance. At the end of this analysis I will give the final calculation of these incredible odds.

The Twelfth Prediction:
People would gamble for His garments

Probability: 1 chance in 100

The Old Testament Prediction:
"They divide My garments among them, And for My clothing they cast lots" (Psalm 22:18).

The New Testament Fulfillment:
"Then the soldiers, when they had crucified Jesus, took His garments and made four parts, to each soldier a part, and also the tunic. Now the tunic was without seam, woven from the top in one piece. They said therefore among themselves, 'Let us not tear it, but cast lots for it, whose it shall be,' that the Scripture might be fulfilled which says: 'They divided My garments among them, and for My clothing they cast lots.'" (John 19:23,24).

Think of how unlikely it was that Roman soldiers would bother to gamble to see who would win the right to claim the garments of a crucified prisoner. Yet, the prophecy was fulfilled precisely.

The Thirteenth Prediction:
His side would be pierced

Probability: 1 chance in 100

The Old Testament Prediction:

"And I will pour on the house of David and on the inhabitants of Jerusalem the Spirit of grace and supplication; then they will look on Me whom they have pierced; they will mourn for Him as one mourns for his only son, and grieve for Him as one grieves for a firstborn" (Zechariah 12:10).

The New Testament Fulfillment:

"But one of the soldiers pierced His side with a spear, and immediately blood and water came out" (John 19:34).

The cruelty of the Romans was expressed in the unspeakable pain inflicted on prisoners in their lengthy death on the cross. However, despite their orders to produce a drawn-out death, the Roman centurion was motivated by God to pierce Christ's side with his spear. The blood and water flowing out of Christ's side proved that He had already died before the spear entered His side. The odds against anyone plunging a spear into the side of a man being crucified on a cross is estimated conservatively as one chance in 100.

The Fourteenth Prediction:
None of His bones would be broken

Probability: 1 chance in 20

The Old Testament Prediction:

"He guards all his bones; Not one of them is broken" (Psalm 34:20).

The New Testament Fulfillment:

"But when they came to Jesus and saw that He was already dead, they did not break His legs" (John 19:33).

When a prisoner of Rome was crucified, his body was placed on the cross in such a manner that the only way he could breathe was by painfully lifting his upper body, using the strength of his legs, to expand his diaphragm. When the Roman soldiers wished to speed up the death of the condemned prisoner they would break his legs with a club and thus prevent him from lifting himself up to breathe. Within minutes the prisoner would die due to oxygen deprivation and fluid accumulating in his lungs. To avoid desecrating the Sabbath, which was about to begin, the soldiers broke the legs of the prisoners on either side of Jesus to assure their quick death. However, in fulfillment of the ancient prophecy, Jesus had already "given up the ghost" and died by His own will. Therefore, they did not break Christ's legs and thus fulfilled the prophecy.

The Fifteenth Prediction:
His body would not decay

Probability: 1 chance in 10,000

The Old Testament Prediction:

"For You will not leave my soul in Sheol, Nor will You allow Your Holy One to see corruption" (Psalm 16:10).

The New Testament Fulfillment:

"He, foreseeing this, spoke concerning the resurrection of the Christ, that His soul was not left in Hades, nor did His flesh see corruption" (Acts 2:31).

Obviously, the odds against anyone dying and their body not decaying, but later rising from the dead, are obviously astronomical. However, I have estimated the odds as only one chance in 10,000 because several individuals were resurrected in the Old Testament, such as the Shunammite widow's son who was raised from the dead by Elisha (2 Kings 4:28–37).

The Sixteenth Prediction:
His burial in a rich man's tomb

Probability: 1 chance in 100

The Old Testament Prediction:

"And they made His grave with the wicked; but with the rich at His death, because He had done no violence, nor was any deceit in His mouth" (Isaiah 53:9).

The New Testament Fulfillment:

"Now when evening had come, there came a rich man from Arimathaea, named Joseph, who himself had also become a disciple of Jesus. This man went to Pilate and asked for the body of Jesus. Then Pilate commanded the body to be given to him. And when Joseph had taken the body, he wrapped it in a clean linen cloth, and laid it in his new tomb which he had hewn out of the rock; and he rolled a large stone against the door of the tomb, and departed" (Matthew 27:57–60).

The probable site of the tomb of Christ is located just north of the Damascus Gate of the old walled city of Jerusalem, only a few hundred yards from the probable site of Golgotha. When the tomb was discovered in the last century, archeologists found that only one body depression was ever used. The owner did not complete the stone carving work to bury a second body. In addition, they found a huge cistern capable of holding 200,000 gallons of water beneath the garden, indicating that it was a rich man's garden tomb. Furthermore, they found the remains of an ancient wine press in the garden.

The Seventeenth Prediction:
The darkness covering the earth

Probability: 1 chance in 1,000

The Old Testament Prediction:

"'And it shall come to pass in that day,' says the Lord God, That I will make the sun go down at noon, and I will darken the earth in broad daylight' "(Amos 8:9).

The New Testament Fulfillment:

"Now from the sixth hour until the ninth hour there was darkness over all the land" (Matthew 27:45).

Although this prophecy is one of the most incredible of the seventeen, the *Third History of Thallus,* a pagan historian of the third century, reported that there was an unusual darkness that blotted out the sun for a number of hours at the time of Passover in the year A.D. 32, the year of Christ's crucifixion. Although Thallus speculated that this darkness was the result of an eclipse, any astronomer can tell you that it is absolutely impossible that an eclipse could have occurred at that time, because Passover was carefully calculated to occur at the time of the full moon. The position of the sun, moon, and earth at the time of the full moon makes it impossible that this darkness recorded by the historian Thallus could have been the result of a natural eclipse. However, his report does confirm that the Bible's prophecy and the New Testament record of its fulfillment is accurate.

This analysis has shown that seventeen detailed prophecies, made five centuries before the birth of Jesus of Nazareth, were fulfilled with absolute precision in the life, death, and resurrection of Jesus Christ. The question to consider is this: What are the chances that all seventeen of these predictions occurred by chance rather than by the divine plan of God? Either these seventeen predictions are simply the result of chance or this evidence provides overwhelming proof that God inspired the Bible and is in control of history.

The combined probability AGAINST these 17 predictions occurring is equal to
1 chance in 480,000,000,000,000,000,000,000,000,000,000

or

1 chance in 480 Billion × 1 Billion × 1 Trillion

In other words, there is only one chance in 480 billion × 1 Billion 1 ×Trillion that these Old Testament prophets could have accurately predicted these seventeen specific prophecies about the life, death, and resurrection of Jesus Christ by chance alone. The odds are equally impossible that any man could have fulfilled these detailed prophecies by chance alone. Let any reader assign any other estimates they might choose for these probabilities that these predictions occurred. Regardless of the size of the estimates for probability you assign to these individual predictions, you will still be confronted with a combined probability so staggering in its magnitude that it will be impossible to honestly convince yourself that these things occurred by chance. In the unlikely event that you still are not convinced, consider the fact that we have examined only seventeen of the forty-eight major prophecies given in the Old Testament about the promised Messiah. If we were to calculate the odds against all forty-eight predictions occurring by chance we would arrive at a number so large that it would exceed our capacity to comprehend it.

Some Bible critics have suggested that Jesus of Nazareth, as a rabbi, knew about these predictions and simply arranged the events of His life to fulfill them. However, consider the impossibility of any normal human arranging the fulfillment of these specific predictions. How would you arrange to be born in Bethlehem and manage to be descended from the tribe of Judah? How would you arrange the price of your betrayal to be precisely thirty pieces of silver? How would you arrange to be crucified with thieves and then, to be buried in a rich man's grave? Obviously, only God could either foresee these events in advance or fulfill these precise predictions in the life of Jesus Christ.

These Prophecies Prove the Bible Is Inspired By God

When we consider these seventeen specific Messianic prophecies, the odds against any one person fulfilling these predictions by chance alone are absolutely astronomical. To fully grasp the reality that these fulfilled prophecies prove that Jesus Christ is the promised Messiah and Son of God, consider the following illustration:

First, the odds against the prophets correctly guessing all seventeen prophecies are:

1 chance in 480 Billion × Billion × 1 Trillion!

Next, to fully grasp these incredible odds we must try to get a picture of these odds in our minds. Imagine that every one of these chances was represented by a small grain of sand. Furthermore, imagine that a single grain of sand is painted gold and represents the one chance out of this astronomical number that Christ fulfilled these predictions by chance. We are going to blindfold you and ask you to search for the single gold-painted grain of sand. Imagine that the entire galaxy known as the Milky Way, encompassing two hundred million stars like our sun plus millions of planets, moons, and asteroids is composed only of these 480 Billion × 1 Billion × 1 Trillion grains of sand. In a galaxy filled with this incredible number of grains of sand, your target is the only grain of sand that is painted gold. Remember the galaxy is so vast that if you could travel in the Star Trek Enterprise at the speed of light, 187,000 miles per second, it would still take you a hundred thousand years to cross the galaxy. If we were to blindfold you and send you blindly searching through our entire galaxy to find a single gold-painted grain of sand, you would face the same impossible odds in finding the gold grain of sand as the odds against these seventeen prophecies occurring by chance alone.

With such odds against you, would you bet a thousand dollars that you would find a single grain in a whole galaxy filled with sand? I doubt that you would risk your money on such impossible odds. Yet, tragically, every year millions will die who have bet their lives and their eternal souls on the "chance" that these fulfilled prophecies about Jesus Christ are not reliable. They believe they can safely ignore the claims of Christ upon their lives. However, in light of the overwhelming evidence for the authority of the Bible and the reality of Jesus Christ as God's Messiah, each of us needs to personally consider the decision we must make about our response to Christ's life, death and resurrection.

In light of the Bible's own declaration that fulfilled prophecy is the absolute proof that it was written under the direct inspiration of God, I believe the evidence in this chapter provides a staggering level of proof for the authority of the Scriptures.

9

Evidence From Prophecies Fulfilled In Our Generation

"Now as He sat on the Mount of Olives, the disciples came to Him privately, saying, 'Tell us, when will these things be? And what will be the sign of Your coming, and of the end of the age?'"

(Matthew 24:3).

One of the greatest proofs that the Bible is inspired is the evidence of thousands of detailed prophecies that were fulfilled to the smallest particular throughout history. Centuries before the events occurred the ancient prophets foretold the rise and fall of empires and cities including Babylon, Tyre, and Nineveh. However, in the balance of this chapter I would like to examine several astonishing prophecies that were fulfilled in our lifetime that prove the Bible's inspiration and also point to the nearness of Christ's return.

For thousands of years men have studied the Bible's ancient prophecies and wondered if they would live to witness the return of Christ to redeem the earth. Many today are longing for the return of Jesus Christ. Naturally, skeptics remind us that past generations also looked for the Second Coming but never saw the promise fulfilled. Why should we believe our generation will witness the return of Christ when other generations were disappointed? Thirty years of study of Bible prophecies have convinced me of the overwhelming evidence that Christ will likely return in our lifetime. Jesus and the other prophets described numerous prophecies that would occur in the lifetime of those who would see Him return with their own eyes. Is ours the generation that will see Christ coming for His Church? The answer to this question will have profound implications for our life, our witnessing, and our priorities.

In this chapter we will examine numerous prophecies relating to the last days and the biblical passages where the original prophecies were announced over two thousand years ago. Each of these prophecies is a unique event that was never fulfilled in any other generation. By their very nature many of these predictions could not be fulfilled again in another generation. Our Lord Jesus Christ warned, "Now when these things begin to happen, look up and lift up your heads, because your redemption draws near" (Luke 21:28). Let's examine in detail several of these fascinating predictions to illustrate the tremendous precision of biblical prophecies as proof that God inspired the writers of the Bible.

The Rebirth of Israel

The rebirth of Israel is one of the most extraordinary and unlikely of all the prophecies in the Bible. In an earlier portion of this book we examined the marvelous precision of the prophecy in which Ezekiel predicted that Israel would be reborn in the spring of 1948.

Jesus Christ foretold the rebirth of Israel in his famous prophecy of the "fig tree" budding that was recorded in Matthew's Gospel. Our Lord declared in Matthew 24:32–35: "Now learn a parable of the fig tree; When his branch is yet tender, and putteth forth leaves, ye know that summer is nigh: So likewise ye, when ye shall see all these things, know that it is near, even at the doors. Verily I say unto you, This generation shall not pass, till all these things be fulfilled. Heaven and earth shall pass away, but my words shall not pass away." No other ancient nation ever ceased to exist for a period of centuries and then returned to take its place on the stage of world history. "Who hath heard such a thing? Who hath seen such things? Shall the earth be made to bring forth in one day? or shall a nation be born at once? For as soon as Zion travailed, she brought forth her children" (Isaiah 66:8).

Most nations evolved gradually over the centuries, such as Egypt or France. In the time of the ancient prophecies, no one had ever witnessed a nation being created "in one day." Yet, in his prediction, Isaiah prophesied that Israel would come into existence in "one day." The prophecies of Isaiah and Ezekiel were fulfilled precisely as predicted on May 15, 1948.

Predictions About the Present Arab – Israeli Conflict

However, the prophecies surrounding the rebirth of Israel did not stop with the declaration of Israel's independence in 1948. Three thousand years ago God inspired King David to predict that the reborn nation of Israel would be immediately surrounded by enemies, including the Arab nations of Jordan, Egypt, Saudi Arabia and Syria. "For, lo, thine enemies make a tumult: and they that hate thee have lifted up the head. They have taken crafty counsel against thy people, and consulted against thy hidden ones. They have said, Come, and let us cut them off from being a nation; that the name of Israel may be no more in remembrance. For they have consulted together with one consent: they are confederate against thee: The tabernacles of Edom, and the Ishmaelites; of Moab, and the Hagarenes; Gebal, and Ammon, and Amalek; the Philistines with the inhabitants of Tyre; Assur also is joined with them: they have helped the children of Lot. Selah" (Psalm 83:2–8). In this incredible prophecy, David described the modern states of the Middle East by naming the ancient nations that have now joined with the Palestinians in their attempt to destroy the Jewish state in the last days.

The Miraculous Restoration of the Hebrew Language

The prophet Zephaniah had predicted something equally impossible as the rebirth of Israel. God predicted through His prophet Zephaniah that He would restore the ancient dead language of Hebrew as the living, spoken language of Israel. Hebrew ceased to be the common language of the Jews long before the life of Christ. "For then will I turn to the people a pure language, that they may all call upon the name of the Lord, to serve him with one consent" (Zephaniah 3:9). No other nation has ever lost its language and later recovered it. No one is speaking ancient Egyptian or Chaldee today. A Jewish scholar by the name of Eliazar ben Yehuda began working earlier in this century in Israel, in his attempt to revive the dead language of Hebrew with its original seven thousand words related to Temple worship as used by the priests. He invented thousands of new words for fountain pen, air plane, etc. Ultimately, Eliazar created modern Hebrew as the living language of five million Israelis. As the Jews began to return from seventy different nations to their Promised Land in 1948 after two thousand years of exile, the government and army began to unify these widely divergent peoples into a united people through teaching them the revived Hebrew language. The Jews of Israel will someday fulfill the prophecy of Zephaniah by calling "upon the name of the Lord, to serve him with one consent."

The Return of the Ethiopian Jews to Israel

The prophet Zephaniah predicted another seemingly impossible prophecy when he declared that God would return the Ethiopian Jews to the land of Israel after they were separated from their Jewish brethren for almost three thousand years. In the days of King Solomon a group of Jews from each of the twelve tribes immigrated to Ethiopia with Prince Menelik, the son of King Solomon and the Queen of Sheba, as detailed in my book *Armageddon*. The prophet foretold their return to their homeland in the last days in these words, "From beyond the rivers of Ethiopia my suppliants, even the daughter of my dispersed, shall bring mine offering" (Zephaniah 3:10). Another prophet, Isaiah, also confirmed this prediction. "I will say to the north, Give up; and to the south, Keep not back: bring my sons from far, and my daughters from the ends of the earth" (Isaiah 43:6). Isaiah predicted the miraculous return of the Jews from both Russia (the north) and from Ethiopia (the south). In the later part of the 1980s and especially in 1991 over eighty-five thousand black Jews returned home to Israel from Ethiopia in fulfillment of Zephaniah's ancient prophecy. Ezekiel 3 7:21 and numerous other prophecies foretold of the return of the exiles to the Holy Land.

The Astonishing Fertility of Israel

In addition to recovering their homeland, their lost language and their exiles, the prophet Isaiah predicted that Israel would become fertile again. "He shall cause them that come of Jacob to take root: Israel shall blossom and bud, and fill the face of the world with fruit" (Isaiah 27:6). The returning Jews have transformed the previously deserted and desolate land into the most agriculturally efficient land on earth according to the United Nations. Israel now supplies over 90 percent of the citrus fruit consumed by hundreds of millions of Europeans. Another prophecy connected with Israel's return was made by the prophet Joel who declared that the desert nation of Israel would experience tremendous increases of rain in the last days. "Be glad then, ye children of Zion, and rejoice in the Lord your God: for he hath given you the former rain moderately, and he will cause to come down for you the rain, the former rain, and the latter rain in the first month" (Joel 2:23). As the rainfall increased dramatically by over 10 percent every decade for the last century the returning Jewish exiles planted over two hundred million trees and transformed the complete environment of the Promised Land. "And the parched ground shall become a pool, and the thirsty land springs of water: in the habitation of dragons, where each lay, shall be grass with reeds and rushes" (Isaiah 35:7).

Another curious prediction was found in Ezekiel 38 which claimed that Israel would dwell "without walls or gates" in the last days. In the ancient past even small villages as well as cities depended on walls for defense against invading armies. Yet God inspired Ezekiel to record the following verse in his prophecy about the coming Russian — Arab invasion of Israel. "And thou shalt say, I will go up to the land of unwalled villages; I will go to them that are at rest, that dwell safely, all of them dwelling without walls, and having neither bars nor gates" (Ezekiel 38:11). How could Ezekiel have known twenty-five centuries ago that the development of modern weapons such as bombs, airplanes and missiles, would have made walls and gates irrelevant for defensive purposes in the last days? Even army bases and Israel's settlements in the West Bank and Gaza have no walls today.

Israel's Plans to Rebuild the Temple

The Bible contains numerous prophecies that tell us that Israel will rebuild the Temple in the last days. The prophet Isaiah wrote, "And it shall come to pass in the last days, that the mountain of the Lord's house shall be established in the top of the mountains, and shall be exalted above the hills; and all nations shall flow unto it" (Isaiah 2:2). In the Book of Revelation (11:1,2) John tells us that the angel took him into the future to measure the Temple that will exist during the seven-year tribulation period. The apostle Paul confirms this in his prophecy about the Antichrist occupying the future Temple. "Let no man deceive you by any means: for that day shall not come, except there come a falling away first, and that man of sin be revealed, the son of perdition; Who opposeth and exalteth himself above all that is called God, or that is worshiped; so that he as God sitteth in the temple of God, showing himself that he is God" (2 Thessalonians 2:3,4). The prophet Ezekiel described his vision of the future Temple with Levites and priests worshiping God: "And thou shalt give to the priests the Levites that be of the seed of Zadok, which approach unto me, to minister unto me, saith the Lord God, a young bullock for a sin offering" (Ezekiel 43:19).

The Oil of Anointing

One of the most unusual aspects of the ancient Tabernacle and Temple was the oil of anointing that was specially prepared with five specific ingredients to anoint the Temple and the High Priests. Moses described God's command to Israel: "And thou shalt make it an oil of holy ointment, an ointment compound after the art of the apothecary: it shall be an holy anointing oil. And thou shalt anoint the tabernacle of the congregation therewith, and the ark of the testimony" (Exodus 30:25,26). One of the five ingredients needed to make the oil was afars'mon. However, the oil and its ingredients were lost, seemingly forever, when the Romans destroyed the Temple in A.D. 70 and burned the only two groves where afars'mon trees grew. Without this special ingredient, they could never obey God's command to anoint the rebuilt Temple.

In addition, the prophet Daniel foretold that, when the Messiah returns, He will be anointed with this oil of anointing. "Seventy weeks are determined upon thy people and upon thy holy city, to finish the transgression, and to make an end of sins, and to make reconciliation for iniquity, and to bring in everlasting righteousness, and to seal up the vision and prophecy, and *to anoint the most Holy*" (Daniel 9:24). How could these prophecies be fulfilled when some of the key ingredients were lost forever. Incredibly, Dr. Joseph Patrich of Hebrew University found a clay flask buried near the Dead Sea caves filled with the ancient oil of anointing. Scientists confirmed that the oil is two thousand years old and is composed of the precise ingredients described in Exodus 30:25,26. (Associated Press, February 16, 1989.)

Vessels For the Future Temple Worship

Ezekiel foretold that the sacred vessels and linen robes will be prepared for use in the Temple in the Millennium. "They shall enter into my sanctuary, and they shall come near to my table, to minister unto me, and they shall keep my charge. And it shall come to pass, that when they enter in at the gates of the inner court, they shall be clothed with linen garments; and no wool shall come upon them, while they minister in the gates of the inner court, and within" (Ezekiel 44:16,17). It is significant that the Temple Institute in the Old City of Jerusalem has prepared over seventy-five of the objects, vessels, and linen priestly garments required for future Temple services. The yeshivas, or Jewish Bible colleges in Jerusalem have trained over five hundred young men from the tribe of Levi to correctly fulfill their future duties of Temple worship and sacrifice. The prophecies describe the resumption of the sacrifice of the Ashes of the Red Heifer to produce the waters of purification (Numbers 19) needed to cleanse the defiled Temple objects, the priests, and the stones on the Temple Mount. The prophet Ezekiel confirmed that the waters of purification will be used to cleanse the future Temple and the Jewish people. "Then will I sprinkle clean water upon you, and ye shall be clean: from all your filthiness, and from all your idols, will I cleanse you"" (Ezekiel 36:25).

The Revival of the Roman Empire

The Bible foretold the revival of the Roman Empire in the final generation when the Messiah will return to establish His eternal kingdom: "And the fourth kingdom shall be strong as iron: forasmuch as iron breaketh in pieces and subdueth all things: and as iron that breaketh all these, shall it break in pieces and bruise. And whereas thou sawest the feet and toes, part of potter's clay, and part of iron, the kingdom shall be divided; but there shall be in it of the strength of the iron, forasmuch as thou sawest the iron mixed with miry clay. And as the toes of the feet were part of iron, and part of clay, so the kingdom shall be partly strong, and partly broken. And whereas thou sawest iron mixed with miry clay, they shall mingle themselves with the seed of men: but they shall not cleave one to another, even as iron is not mixed with clay. And in the days of these kings shall the God of heaven set up a kingdom, which shall never be destroyed: and the kingdom shall not be left to other people, but it shall break in pieces and consume all these kingdoms, and it shall stand for ever" (Daniel 2:40–44). Other prophecies in Daniel 7 and Revelation 13 and 17 confirm the revival of the Roman Empire in the last days in the unique form of a ten-nation superstate. Following the devastation of two world wars the leadership of Europe came together after World War II to plan the creation of a confederate form of superstate bringing the major nations of Europe together for the first time since the days of Rome. In 1957, six countries signed the Treaty of Rome laying the foundation for the future United States of Europe. Henri Spaak, the former secretary-general of NATO admitted in a BBC documentary on the European Union that "we felt like Romans on that day. . . .We were consciously re-creating the Roman Empire once more." Since then, the Maastricht Treaty consolidated the fifteen nations of the European Union into the world's first superstate. It is now an economic, political, and potentially, a military colossus that will dominate world events in the near future.

The Rebuilding of Babylon

One of the most unusual of the Bible's prophecies reveals that the city of Babylon will be rebuilt and later destroyed by God at Armageddon by supernatural fire from heaven like Sodom and Gomorrah. The prophet Isaiah foretold this destruction as follows: "Howl ye; for the day of the Lord is at hand; it shall come as a destruction from the Almighty. . . . And Babylon, the glory of kingdoms, the beauty of the Chaldees' excellency, shall be as when God overthrew Sodom and Gomorrah" (Isaiah 13:6,19). In this remarkable prediction the prophet declared that Babylon will not only exist again but it will be destroyed on the Great Day of the Lord. As unlikely as it seems, the Iraqi government of Saddam Hussein has spent over one billion dollars rebuilding the ancient city of Babylon and intends that it will become the center of their future renewed Babylonian Empire. Interestingly, the whole city of Babylon was built over an underground lake of asphalt and oil. God has already provided the fuel for its final destruction. In another prophecy, God foretold that the wicked city will burn forever. "For it is the day of the Lord's vengeance, and the year of recompenses for the controversy of Zion. And the streams thereof shall be turned into pitch, and the dust thereof into brimstone, and the land thereof shall become burning pitch. It shall not be quenched night nor day; the smoke thereof shall go up for ever: from generation to generation it shall lie waste; none shall pass through it for ever and ever" (Isaiah 34:8–10). Several years ago during the Gulf War we had a foretaste of this burning of Babylon when Saddam Hussein set hundreds of Kuwaiti oil wells on fire and covered the desert with smoke and fire.

One World Government

Over two thousand years ago the prophets Daniel and John described that there would be a global, world government led by the coming dictator, the Antichrist in the last days (Daniel 7:14). "And it was given unto him to make war with the saints, and to overcome them: and power was given him over all kindreds, and tongues, and nations. And all that dwell upon the earth shall worship him" (Revelation 13:7,8). There has never been a world government during thousands of years of human history. However, as I outlined in my last book, *Final Warning*, the elite are moving behind the scenes to produce a world government as quickly as possible. The rising power of the United Nations, the World Trade Organization, and World Court are moving us quickly beyond the days of national sovereignty and individual nations.

Deadly Pestilence

The Bible describes terrible plagues and horrible sores occurring throughout the world's population in the Great Tribulation. The plagues that will destroy hundreds of millions in the last days may include the effects of biological and chemical weapons. Zechariah also described the terrible plagues at the Battle of Armageddon: "And this shall be the plague wherewith the Lord will smite all the people that have fought against Jerusalem; Their flesh shall consume away while they stand upon their feet, and their eyes shall consume away in their holes, and their tongue shall consume away in their mouth" (Zechariah 14:12).

"So I looked, and behold an ashy pale horse, . . . and its rider's name was Death, and Hades . . . followed him closely; and they were given authority and power over a fourth part of the earth, to kill with the sword and with famine and with plague (pestilence, disease) and with wild beasts of the earth" (Revelation 6:8, *[Amplified Bible Version]*). The prophecy of the Four Horsemen of the Apocalypse warned that a fourth of humanity will be killed by plague and pestilence symbolized by the fourth horseman during the Tribulation. How could this prophecy be fulfilled literally? Tragically, the AIDS epidemic throughout Africa, South America, and Asia is demonstrating how this prophecy may be fulfilled in our generation. The AIDS plague is now poised to destroy a large portion of mankind in the worst epidemic in history. Thus far it appears that almost no one has survived AIDS for more than twelve years. Jesus warned His disciples about plagues in the last days, "For nation shall rise against nation, and kingdom against kingdom: and there shall be famines, and pestilences, and earthquakes, in divers places" (Matthew 24:7).

In North America and Europe the AIDS virus is still primarily infecting people within the homosexual community and those who share illegal drugs through needles. However, in the Third World huge numbers of heterosexuals in Africa, South America, and Asia are now infected with AIDS. Scientists have determined that unprotected promiscuous sexual activity between males and females facilitates the rapid transmission of the AIDS virus throughout the sexually active population in the Third World. The combination of high levels of promiscuity, an absence of sanitation, minimal AIDS education, and a lack of antibiotics or protection has produced an epidemic of sexually transmitted diseases, including AIDS. The only real solution to the AIDS crisis is to return to God's laws regarding a monogamous marriage relationship between a faithful husband and wife. This is the only true "safe sex" that exists in a world of promiscuous behavior and sexually transmitted disease. In the fall of 1991, the Central Intelligence Agency produced a report on the AIDS epidemic in Africa that was staggering in its conclusions. The evidence pointed to the greatest epidemic and loss of life in human history. The CIA report concluded that up to 75 percent of the population of Africa living in the area south of the Sahara Desert may become infected with AIDS over the next twelve years. This will mean the death by AIDS of over three hundred million people in Africa alone. We are now witnessing the greatest tragedy in history in the death of a whole continent. The mind can scarcely imagine death on this massive scale. The *South African Medical Journal* in July 1991, reported that a staggering 47 percent of black male and female blood donors tested positive for AIDS during 1989. The prognosis for Asia and parts of South America is tragically similar. One study showed that almost every soldier in the armies of several East

African nations that could be tested were found to have been infected by the AIDS virus.

Worldwide Famine

The apostle John described his vision of the horrible famine in the last days. "And I looked, and behold, a black horse, and he who sat on it had a pair of scales in his hand" (Revelation 6:5). The scales represent famine, and the prophet explains that a day's wages at that time will only buy enough wheat or barley to feed the workman, not his family. The United Nations claims that over thirty million in Africa are now at risk of dying from the most devastating famine in this century. Despite the great advances in food production and food storage techniques more people are starving today than at any other time in history. The UN estimates that one billion people are in danger of starvation while another billion people lack proper nutrition. North American food reserves (grain and corn) are at the lowest level in sixty years. Wheat reserves worldwide are at the lowest level in this century as our government sends its surplus food to Russia, Bosnia, and Africa. In light of the massive changes in world weather patterns we may witness devastating famine in the future in countries that felt themselves immune to hunger.

The Rise in Major "Killer" Earthquakes

Jesus prophesied that the last generation of this age would witness the greatest earthquakes in history. Other prophets, including Ezekiel, Zechariah, Haggai, and John predicted awesome earthquakes that would precede Christ's return. Jesus said these earthquakes will occur in "diverse places" (strange places). Massive earthquakes are now occurring worldwide in "diverse places." Enormous forces are accumulating far beneath the massive tectonic plates supporting the continents. Scientists warn that the major earthquakes felt recently in California, Japan, and other parts of the Pacific Rim are only a foretaste of the coming "Big One," the most massive earthquake in human history. Major "killer" quakes (7.2 or greater on the Richter Scale) occurred only once per decade throughout history until our century. However, since A.D. 1900, the growth in major earthquakes has been relentless. From 1900 to 1949 it averaged three major quakes per decade. From 1949 the increase became awesome with 9 killer quakes in the 1950s; 13 in the 1960s; 56 in the 1970s and an amazing 74 major quakes in the 1980s. Finally, in the 1990s, at the present rate, we will experience 125 major killer quakes in this decade (Source: *U.S. Geological Survey Earthquake Report*, Boulder, Colorado). The prophets warned that the planet will be shaken in the last days as never before. The judgment of God will finally unleash the greatest earthquake in history as part of a series of enormous earthquakes. "There were noises and thunderings and lightnings; and there was a great earthquake, such a mighty and great earthquake as had not occurred since men were on the earth" (Revelation 16:18).

Preparations for the Mark of the Beast

The Book of Revelation describes the end of cash and the creation of a cashless society in the last days where the possession of a certain number, "666," will be essential to enable you to "buy or sell." This was an astonishing prophecy when John proclaimed it in the first century: "And he causeth all, both small and great, rich and poor, free and bond, to receive a mark in their right hand, or in their foreheads: And that no man might buy or sell, save he that had the mark, or the name of the beast, or the number of his name. Here is wisdom. Let him that hath understanding count the number of the beast: for it is the number of a man; and his number is Six hundred threescore and six" (Revelation 13:16–18). However, we are already 95 percent cashless in America today. Studies reveal that less than 5 percent of the total money in our society exists as paper currency or coins. Revelation describes a time when the number 666 will be placed beneath the skin on the right hand or forehead to control people in the Antichrist's empire. For the first time in history we are developing technology which would allow tiny computer chips holding your complete medical and financial records to be placed beneath the skin of the right hand or forehead. Recently, scientists developed a miniature computer chip so powerful that it will hold up to five gigabytes of information in a chip the size of a dime. This tiny chip will hold as much information as contained in thirty complete sets of the *Encyclopædia Britannica*. This chip could also be configured in a shape the size of two grains of rice that could be injected beneath the skin. Your complete financial life records could be held by such a chip which could be read from a distance by electronic scanners. *Business Week* magazine reported on June 3, 1996, p.123, that MasterCard International is testing a "smart card" computer chip that includes information about your fingerprint and identity that can be embedded in a credit/debit card. Card scanners in stores and banks will scan your fingerprint and compare it to the information on the card to verify your identity. How could the apostle John have known that the future would hold such incredible technology unless God inspired him to write the words recorded in Revelation 13:16–18.

Worldwide Television Communications

Another incredible prophecy relating to our era is found in the Book of Revelation that describes worldwide television communications. The prophet John prophesied that in the future tribulation the Antichrist will kill two of God's witnesses who will stop the rain for three-and-a-half years. The prophet declared that the people living around the world will see their deaths and observe their bodies lying unburied for three-and-a-half days in Jerusalem. The whole world will hold a party, exchanging gifts in their relief that their tormentors are dead. Then these people will watch astonished as God resurrects His two witnesses to heaven (Revelation 11:9,10). How could the news that these men were killed travel instantaneously around the world in only three-and-a-half days in any other generation than today? Only seventy years ago it would have taken a week for the news to travel from Israel to Japan or New York. However, today CNN instantly transmits pictures and sound about any important event worldwide. Over a billion people around the world can simultaneously watch the Olympic events every four years. For the first time in history, this prophecy about the whole world watching an event in Jerusalem can be literally fulfilled in this last decade.

Gospel of the Kingdom Shall Be Preached in all the World

One of the most wonderful of the prophecies concerns the prediction of Jesus Christ that: "And this gospel of the kingdom shall be preached in all the world for a witness unto all nations; and then shall the end come" (Matthew 24:14). The Bible has now been translated in more than 3,850 languages in every nation, tribe and dialect on this planet. Electronic communication transmits the message of hope in Jesus Christ through the air waves worldwide. According to researchers on evangelism, over eighty-five thousand people accept Jesus as their personal Savior every day. We have never witnessed such an explosion of the Gospel from the first days following the Feast of Pentecost in Jerusalem until today. There were only one million Christians in China in 1949 after a century of faithful missionary work. However, the Church in China has grown astronomically despite tremendous persecution and the killing of untold millions of believers in concentration camps. Today, the lowest estimates calculate that there are more than one hundred million true followers of Christ in communist China.

Knowledge and Travel Shall Increase in the Last Days

Twenty-five centuries ago the Book of Daniel predicted that there would be an explosion of knowledge and a huge increase in travel in the last days. Daniel wrote these words: "But thou, O Daniel, shut up the words, and seal the book, even to the time of the end: many shall run to and fro, and knowledge shall be increased" (Daniel 12:4). Throughout thousands of years of history the level of knowledge only increased incrementally. In some generations the level of general knowledge actually decreased. Yet, in the last century and a half, there has been an explosion of knowledge beyond anything ever experienced in human history. There are more scientists alive today than have lived in all of the rest of history. Recently it was calculated that the total level of human knowledge is growing so quickly that it literally doubles every twenty-four months. This is staggering in light of Daniel's inspired prediction from the ancient past. In addition, Daniel stated that a characteristic of the last days would be an awesome increase in mobility as "many shall run to and fro." The speed of transportation has also exploded in the last century. Throughout history most people have never traveled faster than a galloping horse. Today men travel at over eighteen thousand miles an hour in the U.S. space shuttle Discovery. In addition, while most people in past centuries never traveled more than twenty miles from the place they were born, millions of people now travel the globe as part of their normal course of daily business or annual vacation.

Preparations for the Battle of Armageddon

Numerous prophecies deal with the climactic battle at the end of this age that will bring about the defeat of the Antichrist's armies and the ultimate victory of Jesus Christ to establish His kingdom on earth for a thousand years. The prophet John named the place of the final battle in this war between the Antichrist and the armies of the Kings of the East. "And he gathered them together into a place called in the Hebrew tongue Armageddon" (Revelation 16:16). John also stated that the army of the eastern nations from the "kings of the east", would consist of an astonishing two hundred million soldiers. This statement was almost impossible in light of the fact that the population of the entire Roman Empire in the days of John was only two hundred million people. "And the four angels were loosed, which were prepared for an hour, and a day, and a month, and a year, for to slay the third part of men. And the number of the army of the horsemen were two hundred thousand thousand: and I heard the number of them" (Revelation 9:15–16).

However, the population of the nations of Asia are growing so quickly that they could field an army in the next few years containing almost two hundred million soldiers. As a result of the cruel and evil One Child Policy, Chinese couples routinely abort any unborn baby that tests indicate will be female. They keep aborting fetuses until the tests reveal that the woman has a male fetus. Then they allow the male child to be born. Numerous reports by human rights organizations reveal that China, India, and North Korea are involved in the selective abortion of female unborn infants. In addition, many in these nations kill young girls who are not wanted by their parents. As a result, the *Toronto Star* newspaper reported in 1995 that Chinese officials admitted that they have a staggering imbalance between boys and girls. This sexual imbalance will result in an excess of over seventy million young men in China by the year 2000 with no women for them to marry. This growing imbalance of sexes throughout Asia will produce up to two hundred million excess young men of military age in the next decade. This situation could fulfill the prophecy of John about the two-hundred-million-man army from the East that will fight in the Battle of Armageddon.

A Military Highway Across Asia and the Drying Up of the Euphrates River

Another prophecy in Revelation declares that the Euphrates River will be dried up to allow this enormous army of two hundred million soldiers to cross from Asia to invade Israel: "And the sixth angel poured out his vial upon the great river Euphrates; and the water thereof was dried up, that the way of the kings of the east might be prepared" (Revelation 16:12). Throughout history the Euphrates River has been an impenetrable military barrier between East and West. However, the government of Turkey recently constructed the huge Ataturk Dam that can now dam up the waters of the Euphrates for the first time in history. The prophet John foretold a future military highway across Asia that would allow this astonishing army to march toward the final battle in Israel. John describes the building of this highway in these words: "The way of the kings of the east might be prepared" (Revelation 16:12). The Chinese government has spent enormous sums and expended the lives of hundreds of thousands of construction workers building a military super-highway across Asia heading directly toward Israel. This highway has no economic purpose and no foreigners are allowed anywhere near this road. The highway has been completed through the south of China, Tibet, Afghanistan, and Pakistan. This curious prophecy about "the way of the kings of the east" is being fulfilled in the 1990s setting the stage for the final battle of this age.

The Staggering Odds Against These Prophecies Being Fulfilled in Our Lifetime

In this chapter we have examined a number of significant prophecies fulfilled in our lifetime that point to the Lord's return in this generation. Almost two thousand years have passed from the time of Christ until our generation. At its simplest level we can ask: What are the odds that even ten of these specific prophecies would be fulfilled by chance during our lifetime? If these prophecies could not have occurred by random chance, then their fulfillment is proof that God inspired the writers of the Bible to correctly predict these future events! In the Bible there are several types of generations. One generation is defined as the length of life of the average person — seventy or eighty years. However, a generation of governing is usually defined as forty years, as indicated in the forty-year reigns of Gideon, King David, King Solomon, et cetera. During the last two thousand years since the days of Christ, there were fifty such forty-year generations. Therefore, the odds are one chance in fifty that any one of these specific prophecies happened by chance in our generation rather than some other generation. Examine the prediction about the rebirth of Israel, as prophesied by Matthew 24:32, as an example. There was only one chance in fifty that Israel would become a nation in our lifetime, rather than in some other generation such as A.D. 350, or A.D. 1600.

According to the laws of combined probability the chance that two or more events will occur in a given time period is equal to the chance that one event will occur multiplied by the chance that the second event would occur. If the odds are fifty to one against Israel being reborn in our lifetime by chance and the odds are also fifty to one against the revival of the Roman Empire in our generation; then the combined probability is fifty times fifty which equals one chance in twenty-five hundred. To calculate the probability of these prophecies occurring by chance:

What are the Odds That These Prophecies Were Fulfilled by Chance?

There are 40 years to a generation.
There are 50 generations from Christ till today.
Therefore:
The odds are 1 in 50 of any of these prophecies occurring in our lifetime
The odds are:

1 event = 1 × 50	1 in 50
2 events = 50 × 50	1 in 2,500
3 events = 50 × 50 (3 times)	1 in 125,000
4 events = 50 × 50 (4 times)	1 in 6.25 million
5 events = 50 × 50 (5 times)	1 in 312.5 million
6 events = 50 × 50 (6 times)	1 in 15.6 billion
7 events = 50 × 50 (7 times)	1 in 780 billion
8 events = 50 × 50 (8 times)	1 in 39 trillion
9 events = 50 × 50 (9 times)	1 in 1,950 trillion
10 events = 50 × 50 (10 times)	1 in 97,500 billion

Obviously, the odds against even ten prophecies occurring by random chance alone in one generation are simply staggering. The above calculation suggests that there is only one chance in 97,500 Trillion that these particular predictions from the Bible could be fulfilled by chance in our lifetime. Another way of looking at this is that the chance that the prophets of the Bible correctly guessed these prophecies is also one chance in 97,500 Trillion. If we calculated the odds against all twenty of these prophecies occurring by chance, the numbers would be beyond our ability to comprehend. In other words, it is simply impossible that men alone could have written the Bible without the supernatural assistance and inspiration of God.

This analysis demonstrates the truly incredible odds against even ten specific prophecies being fulfilled by chance in our generation. The odds against only ten prophecies occurring by random chance was $50 \times 50 \times 50 \times 50 \times 50 \times 50 \times 50 \times 50 \times 50 \times 50 =$ one chance in 97,500 Trillion!! This number is so large that it is hard to conceive of it. However, to illustrate these incredible odds; consider this. The odds of 97,500 Trillion to one are equal to the estimated number of grains of sand that would fill our entire planet. Imagine that we were to take a single grain of sand out of this staggering number of grains of sand and paint it blue. Then we blindfold you and let you search the planet for this buried grain of sand as long as you wish. Remember the entire globe consists of grains of sand and you would need to consider the possibility that the blue painted grain of sand was buried ten miles or, possibly, a thousand miles deep beneath the planet's surface. When you think you have found the right place, stop and pick up a random grain of sand. If you were lucky enough to pick up the only grain of sand painted blue by pure chance, you would have equalled the odds of one chance in 97,500 Trillion against even these ten prophecies being fulfilled by chance in our generation. Frankly, I don't think you would find that grain of sand. Likewise, it is simply impossible that these twenty prophecies were fulfilled by random chance.

The Scriptures teach that the final generation of this age will witness the fulfillment of a staggering number of prophecies pointing to the soon return of the promised Messiah. The evidence presented in this chapter also provides astonishing evidence that proves that only God could have inspired the writers of the Scriptures to accurately predict the startling number of predictions already fulfilled in our lifetime. The words of Jesus speak especially to our generation, "Now when these things begin to happen, look up and lift up your heads, because your redemption draws near" (Luke 21:28).

10

The Mysterious Hebrew Codes

"It is the glory of God to conceal a matter, but the glory of kings is to search out a matter."

Proverbs 25:2

Recently, researchers in Israel discovered a staggering phenomenon of hidden codes beneath the Hebrew text of the Old Testament that reveal an astonishing knowledge of future events and personalities that cannot be explained unless God inspired the writers to record His precise words. The material in this chapter is possibly the most important evidence I will present in this book that will prove to any unprejudiced observer that the Scriptures are truly inspired by God.

Rabbi Michael Dov Weissmandl, a brilliant Czechoslovakian Jewish scholar in astronomy, mathematics, and Judaic studies, found an obscure reference in a book by a fourteenth-century rabbi known as Rabbeynu Bachayah that described a pattern of letters encoded within the Torah. This discovery during the years before World War I inspired Rabbi Weissmandl to begin exploring for other examples of codes hidden within the Torah. During the war years he found that he could locate certain meaningful words or phrases, such as "hammer" and "anvil," if he examined the letters at sequences that were equally spaced in the Hebrew text. In other words, if he found the first letter of a significant word such as *Torah*, and then, by skipping forward seven letters he found the second letter of the word *Torah*, he continued to skip forward the same number of letters to see whether or not the complete word *Torah* was spelled out in the text at equally spaced intervals. Rabbi Weissmandl' described this phenomenon as "equidistant letter sequences" (ELS). The rabbi was astonished to find that an incredible number of significant words were hidden in code within the text of the Torah at equally spaced intervals. These spaced intervals between significant letters varied from every five letters, every seven letters, and numerous other intervals. However, once they found a particular word spelled out at, say every 22nd letter, the balance of the letters from the words in this group were also spaced at an interval of every 22nd letter.

Initially, Rabbi Weissmandl could not be certain if this phenomenon was truly significant or whether it was simply due to the great number of possible combinations of words and phrases that could occur by chance arrangement by skipping forward various intervals of letters in the Hebrew text. The proof that this phenomenon was evidence of a supernatural intelligence and design was confirmed almost forty years later in Israel. The invention of sophisticated computers and statistical analysis was finally able to analyze the text of the Bible to prove that these codes could not have been produced by random chance. Although Rabbi Weissmandl found many coded names by simply manually counting the letters in the text, he did not record his discoveries in writing. Fortunately, some of his students did record several examples of his code discoveries. Over the following decades, students in Israel who had heard about his research began searching the Torah for themselves to ascertain whether or not such codes actually existed. Their discoveries ultimately resulted in the research studies at Hebrew University that have proven the validity of this research. The introduction of sophisticated high-speed computers allowed Jewish scholars at Hebrew University to explore the text of the Torah in ways that previous generations could only dream about.

Equidistant Letter Sequences

A group of dedicated Jewish scholars in Israel, following up on Rabbi Weissmandl's research, found many additional hidden codes embedded within the text of the Torah. A paper called *Equidistant Letter Sequences in the Book of Genesis*, was published in 1988 in the scholarly *Journal of the Royal Statistical* Society. This academic magazine is one of the most prominent mathematical and scientific journals in the world. The study was completed by Doron Witztum, Yoav Rosenberg, and Eliyahu Rips at Hebrew University and the Jerusalem College of Technology. This study has been republished in several other respected scholarly journals recently, including *Bible Review,* October 1995, and on the Internet. Their discoveries of complex Hebrew codes that reveal supernatural and prophetic knowledge about the future is causing tremendous consternation in the academic community because it challenges the long-held beliefs of liberal scholars who generally reject verbal inspiration of the Bible.

This scientific discovery is earth-shaking in its consequences because it reveals a staggering level of mathematical design and intelligence which could only have been produced by a supernatural mind, providing unshakable mathematical proof that the Bible was truly inspired by God. The incredible data demolishes forever the false claim by liberal scholars and skeptics that the Bible was written and edited by uninspired men and that it is full of errors and contradictions. Despite the fact that numerous scholars and scientists have attempted to challenge the validity of this Torah research, the evidence has not been refuted.

Every Jot and Tittle

Jesus Christ, Himself, affirmed that the actual letters composing the Scriptures were directly inspired by God and were preserved in their precise order throughout eternity. "For verily I say unto you, till heaven and earth pass, one jot or one tittle shall in no wise pass from the law, till all be fulfilled" (Matthew 5:18). The English word jot is our translation of the Greek word *iota*, the Greek letter *i*. This *iota* is the Greek equivalent of the Hebrew letter *yod*, which is the smallest letter in the Hebrew alphabet. The word *tittle* is the Greek word *keraia*, derived from the smallest Hebrew grammatical symbol. Jesus Christ stated that even the smallest of the letters and grammatical marks in the original text of the Bible were directly inspired by God.

This intriguing statement by Jesus about the Scriptures has been confirmed two thousand years later by means of an intricate analysis of the Hebrew text of the Bible by mathematicians and computer scientists in Israel. To their total surprise, these researchers discovered that every single letter of the Torah fits into a complicated tapestry of staggering mathematical precision. In this regard we should remember the provocative words found in Proverbs 25:2, "It is the glory of God to conceal matter, but the glory of kings is to search out a matter."

This phenomenon of Hebrew codes was placed beneath the text of the Bible thousands of years ago. However, it has been hidden successfully by God until our generation. Many of these codes could not have been discovered by manual examination of the text. The invention of high-speed computers, developed in the last twenty years, enabled the researchers to examine every possible combination occurring in any of hundreds of possible intervals (from every second letter to every 500th letter, for example) throughout the millions of Hebrew letters in the Old Testament. However, once detected by the computer program, anyone can personally verify the existence of the code by manually counting out the letters to see that a particular name is spelled out by skipping the appropriate number of letters.

The Process of Analyzing the Torah

Using the ancient Hebrew received text (the Masoretic text) of the Torah, the scientists began by eliminating the spaces between the Hebrew letters, words, and sentences throughout the first five books of the Bible. The traditional Orthodox text was written in this manner — without punctuation marks or spaces between letters, words, grammatical marks, or sentences. To demonstrate what this would look like, let us take a sentence in English and write it out as it would appear in an ancient Hebrew manuscript.

THEBIBLEWASWRITTENINHEBREWWITHOUTPUNCTUATIONMARKS

To understand this sentence, we break it up with appropriate spaces:

THE BIBLE WAS WRITTEN IN HEBREW WITHOUT PUNCTUATION MARKS

There is a curious tradition in the writings of the ancient Jewish sages who claim that Moses first saw the Hebrew letters of the Torah revealed in his vision on Mount Sinai as a continuous sequence, without spaces between letters, composed of letters of black fire appearing upon a background of white fire. The sages wrote that Moses wrote these divinely revealed letters one-by-one in the five books of the Law, the Torah, as he recorded God's commands to Israel.

In their initial experiment, reported in their 1988 paper, the scientists arbitrarily chose three hundred Hebrew word-pairs that were logically related in meaning, such as "hammer" and "anvil," or tree and leaf, or man and woman. They asked the computer program to locate any such word pairs in the Genesis text. Once the computer found the first letter in Hebrew of "hammer," it would look for the second letter at various intervals or spaces between letters. If the program couldn't locate the second letter of the target word "hammer" following the first letter at a two-space interval, it would then search at a three-space interval, then a four-space interval, etc. Once it located the second letter at, say, the twelve-space interval, it would then look for the third letter at the same twelve-space interval, and so on through the entire 78,064 Hebrew letters in Genesis. The computer also looked for coded words by checking in reverse order. Since the computer can compute millions of calculations every second, the scientists could quickly examine every 4th, 5th, 6th, 7th letter, for example. The sophisticated computers could examine every one of millions of possible combinations to discover encoded words that no human could ever have found manually, including such words as Hitler, Berlin and Sadat.

After the program had examined the text for each of the three hundred word-pairs, the researchers were astonished to realize that every single word-pair had been located in Genesis in close proximity to each other. As mathematical statisticians, they were naturally astounded because they knew it was humanly impossible to construct such an intricate and complicated pattern beneath a surface text, such as Genesis, which told the history of the Jewish people. After calculating the probabilities of this phenomenon occurring randomly by chance alone, they published their calculations in their scientific journal. The odds against the three hundred word pairs occurring by chance in the text of Genesis are less than one chance in fifty quadrillion. To express this number another way, it would look like this: one chance in 50,000,000,000,000,000! Another way to express this probability is that the odds against this phenomenon occurring by chance are equal to one chance in fifty thousand trillion. Most scientific journals consider an experimental result significant if it exceeds the probability of one chance in one hundred. The bottom line is that only a supernatural intelligence, far beyond our human capacity, could have produced the pattern of secretly coded words found in the Bible.

More Surprises

As they studied this pattern the scientists discovered that many of the coded words described future events and personalities in human history, from ancient times until today. When they looked at the string of Hebrew letters in Genesis 1:1, they counted forward forty-nine letters from the letter ת, the first letter *(tav)* of the Hebrew word *Torah* and found the second letter in the word. Skipping forward another forty-nine letters they found the third letter of the word *Torah*. Incredibly, the Hebrew word *Torah* was spelled out using every fiftieth letter of the text.

To their surprise they found that the opening verse of Exodus, the second book in the Bible, contained the same word *Torah*, once again spelled out at the same fifty-letter intervals beginning with the first appearance of the letter ת. However, when they examined the opening verses of the third book of the Bible, Leviticus, they did not find *Torah* encoded. However, they did discover the word *God* was spelled out when they skipped forward every eighth letter from the first letter י *yod* that appeared in the book.

Upon examining the initial verses of Numbers and Deuteronomy, the fourth and fifth books of the Bible, the scientists again found that the word *Torah* was encoded. In the Book of Numbers, the word *Torah* is spelled out in reverse at a fifty-letter interval. However, to their surprise, while the word *Torah* was also found to be spelled out in reverse order in the Book of Deuteronomy, it appeared at a forty-nine-letter interval beginning with the fifth verse of the book.

Mathematicians calculated that the odds were more than three million to one against the word *Torah* being encoded by chance alone within the opening verses in the first five books of the Bible. Bible students know that the number fifty is very significant in Scripture. For example, God commanded Israel to free their slaves and return family lands that had been pledged to a lender on the fiftieth Year of

Jubilee. In addition, the Bible reveals that Law itself, the *Torah*, was presented to the Jewish people at Mount Sinai by God precisely fifty days after their miraculous Exodus from Egypt.

These coded words are interlaced in intricate patterns at evenly spaced intervals in the text reading both forward and backward. The scientists realized that these coded letters formed words and associations of such complexity and design that it is absolutely impossible that the patterns could have occurred by chance.

It is fascinating to observe that the key word "Eden" is encoded repeatedly sixteen times within the relatively short Genesis 2:4–10 passage of only 379 Hebrew letters dealing with the Garden of Eden. The odds against sixteen "Edens" occurring by chance in such a short passage is one chance in ten thousand. Another fascinating feature of this phenomenon was found, in Genesis 2, which deals with the Garden of Eden. Scientists found twenty-five different Hebrew names of trees encoded within the text of this one chapter. The laws of probability indicate that the odds against this occurring are one hundred thousand to one (Professor Daniel Michelson, *Codes in the Torah*).

Thousands of detailed and precise patterns and codes such as these were discovered hidden in the Hebrew text of the ancient Scriptures. Mathematical and computer statisticians, after exhaustive statistical analysis, concluded that this pattern of coded words could not have occurred by chance nor could a human writer have purposely produced this phenomenon. Their conclusion is that only a divine intelligence could have directed Moses to record this precise text containing such complex codes thousands of years ago.

Other Mysterious Codes Reveal God's Prophetic Foreknowledge

The scientists discovered that some of the words coded in the text of the Torah concerned events and personalities that occurred thousands of years after Moses wrote the text. Naturally, many academics rejected out of hand the possibility that this phenomenon could be real. However, despite many attempts, no one could refute the data. They recently discovered a pair of words — "Zedekiah," the last king of Judah in 587 B.C., when Jeremiah was a prophet, and "Matanya," which was King Zedekiah's original name before he ascended the throne (2 Kings 24:17). Incredibly, they also found the word "Hanukkah," which refers to the festival of lighting the Menorah that commemorates the rededication of the Temple after it was recaptured from Antiochus IV Epiphanes in 165 B.C. The word "Hanukkah" appears near the word "'Hasmoneans" which is the famous name of the family of warriors led by Judas Maccabee, the Jewish general who defeated the Syrian armies of King Antiochus IV Epiphanes. How could the writer of Genesis have known about King Zedekiah and the Festival of Hanukkah when the Book of Genesis was written centuries before they occurred?

Egyptian President Anwar Sadat

Possibly the most astonishing of the phenomena recently discovered involves codes that reveal events that occurred in our generation. As one example, the name of the late Egyptian President Anwar Sadat occurred together with the name of the leader of the Moslem Brotherhood assassination team that killed him. The same code sequence also contained the year of his assassination, 1981, and the words "president," "gunfire," "shot," and "murder." Incredibly, even the Hebrew word for "parade" appears in this coded sequence. President Sadat was assassinated during the president's review of a military parade in 1981.

Adolph Hitler, the Nazis, and the Death Camps Were Prophesied in the Bible

Truly one of the most incredible of the hidden codes is their discovery of the words "Hitler," "Nazis" and names of several of the actual death camps embedded within this text of the Book of Deuteronomy: "For the Lord your God is God of gods, and Lord of lords, a great God, a mighty, and a terrible, which regardeth not persons, nor taketh reward: He doth execute the judgment of the fatherless and widow, and loveth the stranger, in giving him food and raiment. Love ye therefore the stranger: for ye were strangers in the land of Egypt. Thou shalt fear the Lord thy God; him shalt thou serve, and to him shalt thou cleave, and swear by his name. He is thy praise, and he is thy God, that hath done for thee these great and terrible things, which thine eyes have seen. Thy fathers went down into Egypt with threescore and ten persons; and now the Lord thy God hath made thee as the stars of heaven for multitude" (Deuteronomy 10:17–22).

The Hebrew text of this Deuteronomy 10:17–22 passage reads as follows. The word "Hitler" in Hebrew (היטלר) is spelled out at a twenty-two-letter interval.

17כי י_וה א_היכם הוא א_הי הא_הים וא_ני הא_נים
א_ הגדל הגבר והנורא אשר לא-■שא פנים ולא יקח
שחד: 18ועשה משפ■ יתום ואלמנה ואהב גר לתת לו
■חם ושמלה: 19ואהבתם את-הגר כי-ג■■ם הייתם בארץ
מצרים: 20את-י_וה א_היך תירא אתו תעבד ובו תדבק
ובשמו תשבע: 21הוא תהלתך והוא א_היך אשר-עשה
אתך את-הגדלת ואת-הנוראת האלה אשר ראו עיניך:
22בשבעים נפש ירדו אבתיך מצרימה ועתה שמך י_וה
א_היך ככוכבי השמים לרב:

Hebrew text of Deuteronomy 10:17–22 Passage

Hitler – היטלר

Beginning with the second last appearance of the Hebrew letter *bet* ב in this passage, researchers counted every thirteenth letter from left to right. To their amazement they discovered that the coded letters spelled out the phrase, "b'yam marah Auschwitz," which means, "in the bitter sea of Auschwitz." As they carried the counting forward another thirteen letters they came to the letter *resh* ר. From this resh, they counted every twenty-second letter from left to right. To their amazement they found the word היטלר, "Hitler," the name of the greatest enemy of the Jews in history, the one who almost conquered the Western World in World War II. It was Hitler's satanic obsession against the Chosen People that motivated him to create the Final Solution which ultimately slaughtered over six-million Jews and another six-million Poles and Russians in the murderous death camps in Eastern Europe, such as Auschwitz. Amazingly, the actual names of the Nazi concentration camps, "Auschwitz" and "Belsen," were also encoded close to the word "Hitler" and "Berlin" in a cluster of letters hidden within the text of this passage in Deuteronomy.

Scientists found that Deuteronomy 33:16 also contained a hidden message about the Nazi Holocaust. Beginning with the first Hebrew letter *mem* מ, they counted every two hundred and forty-sixth letter from left to right and found that the coded letters spelled out the phrase, "Melek Natzim," which translates as the "King of the Nazis." Another group of nearby letters spelled out the phrase, "laiv m'Laivi" which means, "the heart from Levi," referring to the Levites, one of the twelve tribes of the Jews. Incredibly, this same passage yielded another hidden code about the rise of Nazi Germany; the phrase "kemi bait rah," "an evil house rose up. "

One of the most fascinating of these Nazi codes appeared in Deuteronomy 32:52. Beginning with the appearance of the first letter *aleph* א, the researchers counted from left to right every six hundred and seventy letters throughout the passage, and discovered the name "Aik'man," which is a Hebrew form of the name "Eichmann." Adolph Eichmann was a Nazi official who designed the Final Solution, the evil system of concentration camps used in the Holocaust. Eichmann and Hitler were among the greatest killers in history.

This whole series of hidden codes dealing with Nazi Germany ended in Deuteronomy 33:21 with a final astonishing code. Beginning with the letter *resh* ר that appeared in the word "Yisrael," researchers counted every twenty-second letter from left to right and found the tragic phrase "re'tzach alm" describing the terrible sufferings of the Jews during the Holocaust, which translated as "a people cry murder, slaughter." I have often been asked by Jews about why the Bible's prophecies do not say anything about the Holocaust, the worst event in the history of God's Chosen People. Now we can see that God included these coded words beneath the text of the Bible describing this terrible time of persecution.

The French Revolution in the Torah

Another passage in the Book of Genesis revealed a cluster of encoded words that deals with the French Revolution. The following words are clustered together: "Mapecha HaSarfatit" (which spells "the French Revolution" in Hebrew), "Louis," the name of the French king, and the word "Beit [house of] Bourbon," his royal dynasty. In the same cluster were the following words: "Hamarseilles" (the name of the French national anthem) and the word "Bastillia" (the infamous French prison for political prisoners that was stormed by revolutionaries). Interestingly, this cluster dealing with the French Revolution appears embedded in Genesis, chapters 39 to 41, which describe Joseph's imprisonment in Egypt. The Hebrew word for "Bastillia" is found encoded within the sentence in Genesis 39:20 that describes "the prison in which the king keeps his prisoners."

It is fascinating that these messages and data have been hidden secretly within the text of the Torah for thirty-five centuries until today. However, a skeptical and scientifically minded generation in our lifetime has generally rejected the authority and inspiration of the Bible. There is a greater need for our generation to see evidence and proof that the Bible is the true Word of God. In the sovereign plan of God, it is only in this generation of sophisticated high-speed computers and new techniques of statistical analysis, that men could both discover and fully appreciate this divine message from the past that introduces our skeptical generation to the God of their future.

Dr. David Kazhdan, chairman of the mathematics department at Harvard University, warned those who would casually reject this evidence of Torah codes: "The phenomenon is real. What conclusion you reach from this is up to the individual."

The Scientists Prove Their Findings

The Israeli scientists wrote a follow-up paper for submission to *Statistical Science,* a scientific journal that insisted that a group of opposing scholars review and challenge their data and examine their computer program before publication, Despite the fact that all of the reviewers held previous beliefs against the inspiration of the Scriptures, the overwhelming evidence and the integrity of the data forced the editors to approve the study's scientific accuracy and reluctantly publish the article. Robert Kass, the editor of *Statistical Science,* wrote this comment about the study: "Our referees were baffled: their prior beliefs made them think the Book of Genesis could not possibly contain meaningful references to modern day individuals, yet when the authors carried out additional analyses and checks the effect persisted. The paper is thus offered to *Statistical Science* readers as a challenging puzzle." ("Equidistant Letter Sequences in the Book of Genesis," *Statistical Science,* August 1994). The study concluded that the peculiar sequences of Hebrew letters at equal spaces from each other that formed significant words could not possibly have occurred by simple coincidence.

The Response From Recognized Experts

I realize that this information will sound almost unbelievable to many readers. However, the well-respected mathematician, Professor Kazhdan of Harvard University, and his fellow scientists from other universities including Yale and Hebrew University in Jerusalem, have confirmed that this is "serious research carried out by serious investigators." These recognized experts in mathematics wrote a letter confirming the value of this research in the introduction to a recent Israeli book about this phenomenon called *Maymad HaNosaf* (The Added Dimension), written by Professor Doron Witztum of the Jerusalem College of Technology. Professor Witztum is the leading researcher on these Torah codes. Realizing that this discovery is extremely controversial in today's academic world, these scientists encouraged additional research on the phenomenon and declared that "the results are sufficiently striking to deserve a wide audience." In light of their known attitude of rejection of the Bible's inspiration and the supernatural, their statement is a powerful endorsement that the phenomenon is legitimate.

One of the most interesting of the experiments examined the text of Genesis 38, which describes the history of Judah and his daughter-in-law Tamar, who gave birth to two sons, Pharez and Zerah. The Book of Ruth tells us that King David, the greatest king of Israel, was descended from Pharez in this manner: Pharez was the ancestor of Boaz, who married Ruth and gave birth to Obed, the father of Jesse, who was the father of King David. Every one of the five Hebrew names of these ancestors of King David were found encoded at forty-nine-letter intervals, hidden within the text of Genesis 38. Incredibly, these five names also appeared in the correct chronological order as recorded in the Bible. The statisticians calculated that the odds against these five names occurring in this passage in the exact, chronological order they lived, are more than eight hundred thousand to one against this happening by chance.

They also examined the text of Genesis 28 dealing with Jacob's vision of the ladder to heaven, which he received at Mount Moriah, the "place of God." The scientists found the key words "Temple" and "Torah" encoded at twenty-six-letter intervals in a continuous sequence of nine Hebrew letters. The occurrence of these two significant words occurring together in sequence in a biblical passage declaring that '"this is none other but the house of God, and this is the gate of heaven" is extraordinary. The researchers calculated the probability of these key words occurring by chance in this passage dealing with the "place of God" was less than one chance in seventeen billion.

In another analysis, they examined the first chapter of Leviticus, which records God's laws concerning the priesthood of Aaron, the High Priest of Israel. They found the Hebrew name "Aaron" encoded twenty-five times in this one chapter, not counting the four times the word Aaron appears in the normal surface text. The odds against this occurring by chance are more than four hundred thousand to one.

Scientists who have studied these results state no human could create such a Hebrew document containing hundreds of encoded, significant words hidden within this text. They concluded that it would be impossible to reproduce this phenomenon in a Hebrew text even if they had the help of a group of brilliant language geniuses, or the assistance of the world's most sophisticated supercomputers. In addition, it is impossible to account for the prophetic knowledge of future personalities and events found in these codes. The inescapable, logical conclusion is that God inspired Moses to record the precise Hebrew words in the words of the Torah. In addition to demonstrating that the text of the Torah was dictated by God, this evidence of this marvelous design destroys the false theory of the skeptics that the Book of Genesis was created by different "editors" who interwove several different texts centuries after the life of Moses. Only one supernatural mind could have imposed this marvelously complex design upon these five books of the Law. Only God could have designed the text of the Torah. Recently, the researchers discovered similar codes throughout the Old Testament. As I will reveal in a later chapter, God has provided equally compelling evidence in the text of the New Testament proving that He also inspired the writers to record His precise words to His Church.

More Astonishing Discoveries

In a 1994 follow-up paper, the team of researchers recorded the results of their search for pairs of encoded words that relate to events which occurred during the period long after the time when Moses wrote the Torah. They selected the names of thirty-four of the most prominent rabbis and Jewish sages during the thousand years leading up to A.D. 1900. Interestingly, the researchers simply selected the thirty-four sages with the longest biographies in the *Encyclopædia of Great Men in Israel,* a well-respected Hebrew reference book. They asked the computer program to search the text of the Torah for close word pairs coded at equally spaced intervals that contained the name of the famous rabbis paired with their date of birth or death (using the Hebrew month and day). The Jewish people celebrate the memory of their famous sages by commemorating their date of death. Incredibly, the computer program found every single one of the thirty-four names of these famous rabbis embedded in the text of Genesis paired at significantly close proximity with their actual date of birth or their date of death. The odds against these particular names and dates occurring by random chance were calculated by the mathematicians as only one chance in 775 million.

Scholars at the *Statistical Science Journal* who reviewed this experimental data were naturally astonished. They demanded that the scientists run the computer test program again on a second sample searching for the next thirty-two most prominent Jewish sages listed in the encyclopædia. To the astonishment of the skeptical reviewers, the results on the second set of famous sages were equally successful. The staggering result of the combined test revealed that the names and dates of their birth or death of every one of the sixty-six most famous Jewish sages were coded in close proximity within the text of Genesis.

An article in *Bible Review* magazine by Dr. Jeffrey Satinover, in October 1995, reported that the mathematical probability of these sixty-six names of Jewish sages and their dates of birth or death occurring by chance in an ancient text like Genesis was less than one chance in two and a half billion! Interestingly, the researchers attempted to reproduce these results by running the computer program on other religious Hebrew texts outside the Bible, including the Samaritan Pentateuch. The Samaritans developed their own variant text of the five books of Moses, called the Samaritan Pentateuch, which differs in many very small textual changes from the Hebrew Bible, which is the basis of our modern Authorized King James Version. Despite the surface similarity of the two texts to the normal reader, the researchers could not detect word pairs in the Samaritan Pentateuch or any other Hebrew text outside the Bible.

When you carefully think about the phenomenon you can see that even a minor change of spelling or choice of words would totally destroy the precise sequence of Hebrew letters that reveals these hidden words coded at evenly spaced distances throughout the text of the Torah. A reviewer insisted they attempt to find codes in a Hebrew translation of Tolstoy's famous novel *War and Peace*, because it was the same length as the Book of Genesis. However, the phenomenon was not present in *War and Peace*, nor any other modern Hebrew writing. In fact, an exhaustive analysis reveals that no other Hebrew text outside the Old Testament contains these mysterious codes, not even the Hebrew apocryphal books written during the four hundred years before the birth of Christ.

Naturally, following the appearance of this article on divine authority in *Bible Review,* there was a virtual onslaught of letters to the editor in the following monthly issues attacking the article in the strongest terms. Most of the critical letters dismissed the phenomenon out-of-hand without seriously considering the scientific data that was presented. Several critics attacked the author's argument and data in ways that revealed they either failed to grasp the actual statistical method used to detect the Hebrew codes or they didn't understand the rigorous methodology that eliminated the possibility that this phenomenon had occurred by pure random chance.

After his research was published *in Bible Review in* November 1995, the original researcher, Dr. Jeffrey Satinover, responded to his critics who had challenged his assertion that a pattern of elaborate and significant words was encoded within the text of the Torah. Dr. Satinover replied to his critics as follows: "The robustness of the Torah codes findings derives from the rigor of the research. To be published in a journal such as *Statistical Science,* it had to run, without stumbling, an unusually long gauntlet manned by some of the world's most eminent statisticians. The results were thus triply unusual: in the extraordinariness of what was found; in the strict scrutiny the findings had to hold up under; and in the unusually small odds (less than 1 in 62,500) that they were due to chance. Other amazing claims about the Bible, Shakespeare, etc., have never even remotely approached this kind of rigor, and have therefore never come at all close to publication in a peer-reviewed, hard-science venue. The editor of *Statistical Science,* himself a skeptic, has challenged readers to find a flaw: though many have tried, none has succeeded. All the "First Crack' questions asked by *Bible Review* readers — and many more sophisticated ones — have therefore already been asked by professional critics and exhaustively answered by the research. Complete and convincing responses to even these initial criticisms can get fairly technical" (*Bible Review,* November 1995).

Some critics have suggested that the Israeli scientists simply played with the computer program long enough, that by chance alone, "they got lucky." This objection raises the relevant objection that there might be numerous unreported "hidden failures," a common problem in most scientific research today. To prevent this from occurring, editorial observers from the *Statistical Journal* demanded that the scientists analyze their data by examining a completely new group of personalities that were chosen solely by the *Statistical Journal's* editorial judges, namely the sixty-six most famous Jewish sages. The results I quoted earlier in this chapter were based on this group of individuals chosen by these judges. In addition, the judges appointed by the *Statistical Journal* analyzed the computer programs to determine that they were both valid and neutral in their design.

We need to keep in mind that the standard text of the five books of the Torah was published years ago in widely available computer programs and printed texts. These texts cannot be modified. In fact, as a result of the production and sale of fascinating "Torah Codes" computer programs that are now available in North America, anyone with a computer and lots of time can personally verify the existence of these codes beneath the text of the Scriptures. I have personally verified the presence of these fascinating patterns of hidden codes during long hours of examination using the computer programs I acquired several years ago in Jerusalem when this research was just beginning.

Professor Harold Gans, a senior researcher who examined sophisticated foreign government intelligence codes for the U.S. Army, has publicly confirmed the existence of these codes as reported in *Statistical Journal* through the use of advanced analytic techniques and his own sophisticated computer program. Dr. Gans is a brilliant mathematician who has published one hundred and eighty technical papers. Gans learned of this discovery by Professor Witztum of coded words hidden within the Torah. However, as a skeptic, he initially believed that the claims were "ridiculous." Unlike many readers, as an intelligence specialist dealing with complex codes and computers, Gans had the technical ability to test the claims and data for himself. In 1989 he created a complex and original computer program on his computer to check Witztum's data. For nineteen straight days and nights, Gans let his program examine all possible variations and combinations in the 78,064 Hebrew letters in the Book of Genesis. Dr. Gans computer program checked through hundreds of thousands of possible letter combinations at many different spaced intervals. Finally, Gans concluded that these Torah codes actually existed and that they could not have occurred by chance or by human design. He had confirmed the absolute accuracy of Professor Witztum's conclusions. As a result of his discoveries, Professor Gans now teaches classes in synagogues throughout the world about the incredible evidence proving divine authorship of the Bible.

A follow-up study examined the data on the sixty-six Hebrew sages in the last two thousand years. Incredibly, Dr. Harold Gans's study found that the text of Genesis also revealed the encoded names of the actual cities where each of these sixty-six sages was born. Professor Witztum produced a new scientific paper, on this new set of data about the cities of the sages, which proved that the odds against this occurring by chance was one chance in two hundred and fifty million.

In response to the claim that this phenomenon is a result of simple chance, the scientific team determined that the odds against even the simplest codes occurring by chance is only one chance in 62,500. However, when we examine the most complex patterns mentioned in this chapter, the odds are far in excess of billions to one against the possibility that this phenomenon has occurred by random chance. I can assure you that there are many additional examples of this phenomenon that have been discovered recently that will be revealed in the future. Careful investigations are now being conducted by many scientists from other universities and laboratories that confirm the supernatural nature of the phenomenon.

A Caution Regarding This Phenomenon of Hebrew Codes

There is an important caution we need to keep in mind regarding this phenomenal discovery. Remember that no one can search the Torah using these codes to foretell future events. The reason is that it is impossible to extract the encoded information unless you already know what the future facts are. The information about a future event cannot be pulled out of the text in code in advance of the event because you wouldn't know what to tell the computer to look for. It is only after the event has occurred that you could have the program look for the name of the person or event and check to see if the codes contained the information confirming the event. In other words, this method confirms that the Torah has encoded data about events that occurred centuries after it was written. However, the method cannot be used to foretell the future. The Bible prohibits us from engaging in foretelling the future.

The ability to prophesy future events is left to God alone. The Bible clearly forbids fortune telling. The prophet Isaiah warned against false prophets and declared that only God can prophesy future events accurately (Isaiah 46:9, 10). When an event has occurred and we can verify that the codes within the text of the Bible accurately described it thousands of years ago, then God will receive the glory, not man. Although this discovery proves that some future events were encoded by God within the text of the Torah, we must wait until the future becomes the past before we can find it. It is also important to remember that, although the phenomenon of hidden codes is statistically powerful, it is still relatively weak. The proximity of the word-pairs in the Hebrew text is defined only statistically. In addition, the phenomenon of word-pairs appears only when we examine a large number of examples that reveal a much closer proximity than would be expected by chance occurrence alone.

Another important point to note is that these Hebrew codes do not contain any hidden theological or doctrinal messages. This phenomenon has nothing to do with numerology. There are no secret messages or theology. God's message to mankind is only found in the open words of the Scriptures. However, the discovery in our lifetime of these incredible codes reveals names and events that provide a wonderful proof to a skeptical humanity that God truly inspired the writers of the Bible to record His message to mankind.

The phenomenon of Torah codes is now being presented to Jewish groups and synagogues throughout North America and Israel by a group called the "Discovery Seminar," sponsored by the Aish HaTorah College of Jewish Studies. This group was created in Israel by a number of scientists, mathematicians, and Judaic scholars. In addition to presentations in Israel, Aish HaTorah have adapted the material to English enabling their teams to share this fascinating information with Jewish audiences throughout the world showing the divine inspiration and authority of the Torah. Many people have told me that numerous agnostic Jews have returned to their religious roots in Orthodox Judaism as a result of their exposure to this incredible evidence of God's inspiration of the Scriptures as discussed in this chapter.

The Implications

Even those scholars who are philosophically opposed to God and the inspiration of the Bible are stunned by this research. Despite many arguments and challenges the data still stand uncontested. Secular scientific journals have declared that the phenomenon is real and not a result of fraud or computer error. The simple truth is that this phenomenon could not have occurred by chance alone. Nor could any group of brilliant human beings, even with super-computers at their disposal, produce this awesome result of encoding a huge number of significant names beneath the surface text of the Torah. The odds against these biblical codes occurring by random chance are one chance in several billion.

To those who would casually ignore these odds and suggest that they are not that impressive, consider this equivalent scenario. Imagine that someone blindfolded you and laid out before you a mountain of one billion pills loaded with cyanide. In the whole pile of pills there is only one pill that contains sugar. Would you blindly swallow one of these pills by chance if you knew that only one of the billion pills was sugar while all of the rest would result in instant death by cyanide poisoning? Obviously, no one in their right mind would casually accept the odds of one billion to one against you, that the one pill they chose would result in instant death. However, every day millions of men and women risk their eternal souls as they reject this overwhelming evidence that the Bible is true and that we must either accept Christ as our Savior or face an eternity in hell.

It would surpass the skills of any group of human writers to encode these complex and prophetic messages within the text of the Torah. Since the evidence is overwhelming that the five books of Moses were written over three-and-a-half thousand years ago we are left with the undeniable conclusion that this phenomenon is another clearly authenticated signature of God upon the pages of His message to mankind. The evidence in the next chapter will reveal that God has encoded information throughout the text of the Bible, not just the five books of the Torah. As you will discover in this fascinating chapter, God has also encoded a special message to mankind hidden in the Messianic passages of the Old Testament. The Lord has encoded the name of His Son, the Messiah, *Yeshua*, throughout the Hebrew text of the Old Testament.

Special Addition:
Recent Discoveries in the Hidden Hebrew Codes

Researchers have found additional astonishing codes that refer to the War in the Gulf and the tragic assassination of Yitzchak Rabin. I have spent countless hours exploring the Bible using the Torah Codes computer program. This computer program allows you to personally examine the Hebrew text from Genesis to Deuteronomy to search for targeted words. The Torah Codes program is available in both IBM-compatible and Macintosh format from Frontier Research Publications, Inc.

The War in the Gulf

The researchers were amazed to find the following names that refer to the War in the Gulf in Genesis. I personally verified these discoveries with my computer and my Hebrew-English Interlinear Bible. First they found the name "Saddam" at a 6-letter interval in Genesis 8:12. In Genesis 19:1,2 they found '"Scud-B" and "Russian" clearly identifying the missiles Iraq fired at Israel. In Chapter 19 they discovered the phrase "They shut the door" which may refer to the sealing of rooms by Israelis to protect against chemical weapons. Genesis 19:29 contained the phrase "the missile will terrify" spelled out every second letter followed by "the 3rd of Shevat," the actual day in the Hebrew calendar the first missiles hit Israel. Incredibly, the Hebrew name "America – אמריקה" occurred every 100 letters starting with the letter aleph א in Genesis 29:2. The phrase "in Iraq" and "in Saudi Arabia" appeared at equal spaced intervals in the same chapter. Possibly the most amazing codes reveal the names of the allied leaders "Schwarzkopf" and "George Bush." The researchers found the name "CNN" spelled out in Numbers together with the name of Peter Arnet, the famous CNN reporter who broadcast from Bagdad throughout the Gulf War. The name "Peter – פיטר" was spelled out every fourth letter left to right while his last name "Arnet – ארנט" was spelled out right to left in Hebrew every second letter in Numbers 36:5.

The Tragic Assassination of Yitzchak Rabin

The world has been fascinated by the momentous Middle East Peace Talks. Millions watched Yassir Arafat reach out to shake the hand of a reluctant Yitzchak Rabin during the signing of the Declaration of Principles on the White House lawn several years ago. Incredibly, this dramatic event was hidden in code in the Torah written by Moses 3500 years ago. Dr. Moshe Katz, one of the Israeli Hebrew Codes scholars, reported in his book, *Computorah – Hidden Codes in the Torah,* that they discovered the names of Arafat and Rabin in Genesis 32:23–26. They were astonished to find the coded words spelled out "Arafat – shook the hand – of Rabin." The word

"Arafat – ערפאת" was spelled out every twelve letters in reverse in Genesis 3 2:26 together with the phrase "shook the hand". The words "of Rabin – לרבין" appear in Genesis 32:23 counting every eighth letter. It is intriguing to note that the phrase "not a real peace" is spelled out in the same chapter every 196 letters beginning in Genesis 32:19. The name "Rabin" is found in another passage of the Torah spelling out "first-born son" together with "head" and "Israel." Yitzchak Rabin was the first prime minister who was born in Israel. The most startling of all the coded words refers to Yitzchak Rabin's tragic assassination. Following his assassination the scientists searched the Bible's text to see if there were any coded words hidden near the place where Rabin's name occurred. The computer found the eight Hebrew letters of "Yitzchak Rabin – יצחק רבין" spelled out beginning in Deuteronomy 2:33 at an interval of every 4,772 letters. The researchers were shocked to discover the four letter Hebrew word ירצח that spells "will be assassinated" actually incorporates the צ letter, the second letter in Yitzchak Rabin's Hebrew name. These codes displaying prophetic knowledge of events thousands of years in advance of their writing provide irrefutable evidence of the supernatural inspiration of the Bible.

New codes are being discovered every day by researchers in Israel and around the world. However, the next chapter will introduce you to the greatest code discovery yet – the name of God's Messiah Yeshua – ישוע – Jesus, revealed throughout the Old Testament passages written more than a thousand years before He was born in Bethlehem.

11

The Name of Jesus Encoded in the Old Testament

Yeshua Is My Name

ישוע שמי

Of all the discoveries and information that I have researched for *The Signature of God*, the following material is the most thrilling revelation that I could share with my readers. Not only has God included thousands of hidden coded messages within the text of the Bible but He has actually hidden the name *Yeshua* which means Jesus in numerous passages from Genesis to Malachi throughout the Old Testament. Especially within the great Messianic prophetic passages God has hidden at equally spaced intervals in the Hebrew text the incredible message that "Yeshua is My Name." This is one of the most astonishing and tremendous biblical discoveries in the last two thousand years.

The research on the phenomenon of Hebrew codes hidden within the text of the Torah during the last several years has given us one of the strongest possible proofs that the Bible was truly inspired by God. Naturally, as a committed Christian, I realized that Jesus Christ appeared numerous times in the Old Testament narrative. However, as I pointed out in the previous chapter, once I fully appreciated that the hidden codes revealed an awesome amount of information about events such as Hitler's death camps and the French Revolution, I naturally wondered if God had secretly encoded the name of Jesus Christ in the text of the Old Testament. Providentially, a while ago I received a request from Yacov Rambsel, a Jewish student of the Scriptures asking if he could quote from the research material I had written on the Laws of Probability regarding the prophecies fulfilled in the life, death and resurrection of Jesus from my earlier book *Armageddon – Appointment With Destiny*. In discussing this material with Yacov I realized that he had a real passion for the study of the Scriptures and for Jesus Christ as his Messiah. After I completed my writing of the chapter on the "Mysterious Hebrew Codes" in April 1996, I asked Yacov to review it for accuracy because he had spent years studying the Hebrew Scriptures.

In the providence of God, I then learned that Yacov had just completed his own book that focused on a series of extraordinary discoveries which he had made independently, that complimented my research. In addition, Yacov's research provided the answer to my question about whether God had placed the name of Jesus in code within the Hebrew Scriptures. With Yacov Rambsel's permission I want to share a small part of the phenomenal research that he had completed through thousands of hours of painstaking analysis of the hidden codes. As I mentioned earlier, the Israeli researchers used complex computer programs to explore these codes and I purchased three computer programs in Jerusalem several years ago that I used on my Power Macintosh computer to verify the research at Hebrew University. However, Yacov completed his detailed analysis by patiently examining the text of the Old Testament and individually counting the equally spaced intervals between the letters. The amount of work and dedication involved to complete this analysis is staggering. I highly recommend to anyone who is fascinated by this research that they acquire a copy of Yacov Rambsel's new book, *Yeshua – The Hebrew Factor*. His book is available directly from our ministry through the order form at the back of the book, or you can purchase it in Christian bookstores.

Incredibly, the original Hebrew name of Jesus, *Yeshua* – ישוע was found encoded in the Book of Genesis beginning with the very first verse Genesis 1:1, "In the beginning God created the heaven and the earth." Starting with the very first word in the Bible, *B'raisheet* בראשית "In the beginning" the name of Jesus *Yeshua* – ישוע is found encoded beginning with the fifth letter in the word בראשית, the Hebrew letter yod י. Counting forward every 521st letter we can read the letters of the words *Yeshua* Yakhol which translates as "Jesus is able."

One of the most astonishing features is that the clearly Messianic passages of the Old Testament often contain the name *Yeshua* – Jesus – encoded beneath the text of the words of the prophecy about the coming of the Messiah Jesus. As an example, Yacov found the name *Yeshua* embedded in the text of Isaiah 53:10 that prophesied about the grief of our Lord and the atoning sacrifice that Christ made for our sins when He was offered as the Lamb of God, a perfect sacrifice, on the cross two thousand years ago. "Yet it pleased the Lord to bruise him; he hath put him to grief: when thou shalt make his soul an offering for sin, he shall see his seed, he shall prolong his days, and the pleasure of the Lord shall prosper in his hand" (Isaiah 53:10). Beginning with the second Hebrew letter yod י that appears in the phrase "He shall prolong," ya'arik יאריך, Yacov counted forward every 20th letter and discovered that the phrase "ישוע שמי – *Yeshua* – *Shmi*" which means "Yeshua [Jesus] is My Name" was encoded in this verse that teaches us about the suffering Messiah who died to atone for our sins. Mathematical experts that have calculated the probability of this astonishing combination "Yeshua [Jesus] is My Name" would occur by random chance in this Messianic prophecy in Isaiah is only one chance in 50 quadrillion, an inconceivable number!

A passage in the Book of Genesis declared that the Lord provided "coats of skin" for Adam and Eve to cover their nakedness after they sinned: "And Adam called his wife's name Eve; because she was the mother of all living. Unto Adam also and to his wife did the Lord God make coats of skins, and clothed them" (Genesis 3:20,21). God was forced to kill the first animal as a sin sacrifice to provide their covering. This was a prophetic sign of the perfect sacrifice of the Lamb of God to cover the sins of all those who would confess and ask Christ to forgive them. However, this important passage also contains a hidden message about Jesus. Beginning with the last Hebrew letter heh ה in Genesis 3:20 and counting forward every ninth letter we find the word "Yoshiah" meaning "He will save." The word

Yoshiah is a Hebrew equivalent name for *Yeshua* (Jesus). This encoded name *Yoshiah*, meaning "He will save," found in the first few verses of the Old Testament reminds us of the parallel message given to the young virgin Mary by the angel that "thou shalt call his name Jesus: for he shall save his people from their sins" (Matthew 1:21) as recorded in the first few verses of the New Testament in Matthew 1:21. The sacred message in Genesis 3:20,21 containing a reference to Jesus is confirmed by the fact that another code revealing the name *Yeshua* is also hidden in this passage. Beginning with the letter ayin ע in the Hebrew the word for "coats of skin" and counting forward every seventh letter spells out another form of the word *Yeshua* – ישע, which is spelt without using the letter vav ו.

One of the most well known of the Messianic prophecies in the Old Testament describes the exact price of Christ's betrayal, namely 30 pieces of silver. Over five hundred years before the birth of Jesus the prophet Zechariah gave this prediction: "And I said unto them, If ye think good, give me my price; and if not, forbear. So they weighed for my price thirty pieces of silver" (Zechariah 11:12). The phrase in the verse that reads "My price" is *se'kari*. Beginning with the letter yod י Yacov counted forward every 24th letter and found the word *Yeshua* ישוע. In this astonishing hidden message, as He did throughout the Scriptures, the Lord inspired the writers of the Old Testament to choose specific Hebrew words and precise spelling to create this phenomenon. Here in the exact prophecy that five hundred years earlier, described the precise price of our Lord's betrayal, God chose to include a hidden encoded message to His chosen people that identified forever the name of the promised Messiah –"*Yeshua* – Jesus." In the prophetic passage that followed this first prediction of Christ's first coming, the prophet Zechariah looked forward over twenty-five centuries to describe the incredible emotional upheaval and mourning that will occur when the Jewish people have their spiritual eyes opened to see that the Messiah that they have longed for many centuries, is in fact, the Messiah *Yeshua* – Jesus Christ who was crucified two thousand years ago. Zechariah looks forward to His second coming to save Israel following Armageddon: "And I will pour upon the house of David, and upon the inhabitants of Jerusalem, the spirit of grace and of supplications: and they shall look upon me whom they have pierced, and they shall mourn for him, as one mourneth for his only son, and shall be in bitterness for him, as one that is in bitterness for his firstborn" (Zechariah 12:10). Beginning with the letter chet ח found in the phrase, "an only son" *ha'yachid*, Yacov discovered that the word *Mashiach*, which is "Messiah" was encoded by counting forward every 38th letter.

The Book of Leviticus reveals an astonishing hidden coded message about the blood of Jesus Christ being shed for our sins. In this passage Moses gave God's detailed instructions regarding the rules of the holy priesthood and the sacrifices for the sins of the chosen people. "And he that is the high priest among his brethren, upon whose head the anointing oil was poured, and that is consecrated to put on the garments, shall not uncover his head, nor rend his clothes; Neither shall he go into any dead body, nor defile himself for his father, or for his mother; Neither shall he go out of the sanctuary, nor profane the sanctuary of his God; for the crown of the anointing oil of his God is upon him: I Am the Lord" (Leviticus 21:10–12). Yacov examined this passage and found that, beginning with the first heh ה in Leviticus 21:10 and counting forward every third letter, it spelled out the phrase *hain dam Yeshua*, which means "Behold! The blood of Yeshua." It is awesome to realize that God has secretly encoded these profound messages regarding His Son Jesus in these significant passages throughout the Old Testament.

One of the most startling of all the Messianic messages was found hidden within the passage in Psalm 41:7–10 which predicted the betrayal of Jesus by His disciple Judas Iscariot: "All My haters whisper together against Me; they plot evil against Me; saying, A thing of ruin is poured out on Him; and He Who lies down shall not rise again. Even My own familiar friend, in whom I trusted, who did eat of My bread, has lifted up his heel against Me. But Thou, o Lord, be merciful unto Me, and raise Me up, that I may repay them" (Psalm 41:7–10). Yacov noted that verse 8 contained the phrase "they plot evil," *yach' shvu rah'ah*. However, he noticed that beginning with the letter yod י, when he counted forward every second letter he found it spelled out the word *Yeshua*.

The Book of Ruth contains a wonderful love story that reveals the ancestry of King David. It is fascinating to note that the name *Yeshua* – ישוע is encoded in the very first verse, Ruth 1:1. Counting every fifth letter from right to left from the letter י spells out the name *of Yeshua* – ישוע.

The prophet Isaiah announced centuries before the birth of Christ that He would come as the great liberator to mankind. This prophecy of the Great Jubilee at the end of this age reminded Israel that their Messiah would finally cancel all their debts and proclaim liberty to all of those who were captives to sin. "The Spirit of the Lord God is on Me, because The Lord has anointed Me to preach the Good News to the meek. He has sent Me to bind up the broken-hearted, to proclaim liberty to the captives, and complete opening to the bound ones; to proclaim the acceptable year of the Lord, and the day of vengeance of our God; to comfort all who mourn" (Isaiah 61:1,2). Starting with the yod י in the phrase, The Spirit of the Lord God, *Ruach Adonai Yehovah,* counting nine letters from left to right spells *Yeshua.* In addition, Yacov discovered that the word Oshiyah אושיע, was also encoded beginning with the last letter aleph א in the second verse and counting every 36th letter from left to right. This word *Oshiyah* means, "I will Save" and is a variation on the word *Yeshua* – "Jesus" as we saw earlier in Genesis 3:20.

Of the many incredible discoveries made by Yacov Rambsel, one of my favorites concerns the great prophecy of the Seventy Weeks given by the prophet Daniel in Daniel 9:25–27. "Know therefore and understand, that from the going forth of the commandment to re-store and to build Jerusalem unto the Messiah the Prince shall be seven weeks, and threescore and two weeks: the street shall be built again, and the wall, even in troublous times. And after threescore and two weeks shall Messiah be cut off, but not for himself: and the people of the prince that shall come shall destroy the city and the sanctuary; and the end thereof shall be with a flood, and unto the end of the war desolations are determined. And he shall confirm the covenant with many for one week: and in the midst of the week he shall cause the sacrifice and the oblation to cease, and for the overspreading of abominations he shall make it desolate, even until the consummation, and that determined shall be poured upon the desolate" (Daniel 9:25–27). Students of the Bible are familiar with the controversy over the last century about the correct identity of the "Messiah the Prince" that Daniel referred to in verse 25. Those who deny that the prophecy teaches about Jesus Christ's first coming have usually claimed that "Messiah the Prince" was Hezekiah or some other individual. However, Yacov made a wonderful discov-ery when he found that the name *Yeshua* was embedded in Daniel

9:26 starting with the letter yod ' in the phrase "the city," *v'ha'iry,* by counting left to right every 26th letter.

The significance of Yacov Rambsel's discovery is overwhelming. When added to the awesome research in Israel on the hidden codes of the Torah we can see the sovereign hand of God bringing about an incredible proclamation of His inspiration of the Word of God. Hundreds of thousands of people around the world, mostly Jews, have heard about the secret Torah codes. These people, who have reaffirmed their belief in God's inspiration of the Old Testament because of this phenomenon, will now learn that God has secretly encoded the actual name of His Son, the Messiah, *Yeshua,* within these numerous Messianic texts. For anyone who ever wondered about whether or not the Old and New Testaments were equally inspired, the overwhelming evidence now available proves the unity of both the message of redemption through God's Messiah and that *Yeshua* – Jesus is the central figure of both testaments that make up our Holy Scriptures.

This revelation of God's matchless wisdom and inspiration in this decade as we rapidly approach the new millennium reminds me of the angel's prophecy to Daniel: "But you, Daniel, shut up the words, and seal the book until the time of the end; many shall run to and fro, and knowledge shall increase. . . . Many shall be purified, made white, and refined, but the wicked shall do wickedly; and none of the wicked shall understand, but the wise shall understand" (Daniel 12:4,10). Truly, the discovery of these codes revealing the name of God's Son *Yeshua,* that were hidden within the text of the Bible for over three thousand years, is a fulfillment of the angel's prophecy to Daniel. Our knowledge of the Bible, its hidden code, and its divine prophecies is truly increasing at a phenomenal rate in these exciting last days as we approach the time of the Messiah's return to set up His kingdom on earth.

Over the course of my research on The Signature of God, Yacov Rambsel and I have had many conversations about the tremendous significance of his discovery of the Yeshua codes. There is much more exciting material in Yacov's book than I could cover in this chapter. As a result of these discussions, our ministry will be publishing Yacov's fascinating book Yeshua ישוע – The Name of Jesus Revealed in The Old Testament. If any reader is interested in studying this phenomenon and documentation in greater detail, they can order the book from any Christian bookstore or directly from our ministry, Frontier Research Publications, Inc. As Yacov wrote in his book, "Without a doubt, the Messiah's Name is Yeshua – ישוע, but in English, His Name is Jesus."

> *Illustrations of these Yeshua codes can be found at the*
> *end of the book.*

12

The Mathematical Signature of God in the Words of Scripture

The Scriptures reveal God as the great mathematician who knows the smallest detail of His creation, and measures and numbers all things. This character of God is consistent with the revealed phenomenon of staggering complexity involving mathematical patterns within the text of the Scriptures. The Bible declares that God is so concerned with the details of His children's lives that He has numbered the hairs on our head. "But the very hairs of your head are all numbered" (Matthew 10:30). The prophet Isaiah speaks of His majesty and His concern for numbering and measuring all things: "Who has measured the waters in the hollow of his hand, measured heaven with a span and calculated the dust of the earth in a measure? Weighed the mountains in scales and the hills in a balance?" (Isaiah 40:12). When you consider the Bible's declaration that God "measured the waters," "measured heaven with a span," and "calculated the dust of the earth in a measure" it does not seem unusual or out of character that this same Almighty God would inspire His writers to record His precise message to mankind in the Scriptures with a mathematical precision within the original text that surpasses our ability to fully understand.

Evidence of Divine Authorship of the Old Testament

Ivan Panin was one of the most remarkable Christians to live in this century. Almost one hundred years ago this fascinating and famous mathematician left Russia to eventually settle in Canada in the town of Aldershot, Ontario, not far from where I live. Although he was a committed atheist in his early years he discovered the reality of Jesus Christ in his early life. In 1890, Panin embarked on an exciting journey of scientific exploration of the text of the Bible that would prove that the Bible is truly the inspired Word of God. This century has witnessed a progressive abandonment of the doctrine of verbal inspiration of the Scriptures by many biblical scholars and religious leaders. As the leaders of many mainline churches succumbed to the continuous assaults on fundamental doctrines and the authority of Scripture, many Christian laymen began to lose their confidence that they could absolutely trust that the Bible was truly the inspired Word of God. As Ivan Panin wrote, "In the early centuries Christianity suffered most from its avowed enemies; in the last, from its professed friends."

Panin completed an astonishing study during the course of fifty years that revealed the most amazing mathematical pattern beneath the surface layer of the text of the Bible. He worked diligently up to eighteen hours a day for half a century to illustrate the divine inspiration and authority of Scripture. As one small example, Panin discovered that the first verse of the Book of Genesis contains an astonishing number of mathematical patterns that illustrate divine inspiration, "In the beginning God created the heaven and the earth" (Genesis 1:1).

The phenomenon of these mathematical patterns cannot be understood until we realize that the Bible was composed in alphanumeric languages — Hebrew and Greek. These ancient languages did not possess Arabic numbers to express numeric data. Therefore, these languages used various letters of their alphabet to express numbers such as "1, 2, 3," etc. In addition, a small portion of the Bible was written in Aramaic, which is also alpha-numeric. Each letter in these languages stood for a number. In other words, each of the letters expressed both a letter and a number. When they wished to express a number such as 22 they would choose two Hebrew letters — one letter כ stood for 20 and the second letter ב stood for 2.

The first letter of the Hebrew alphabet stood for 1, the second for 2, the third for 3, etc. When we come to the eleventh letter, it represented 20, the twelfth stood for 30, etc., all the way through to 800. Because each letter had a numeric value, every word can be given a *Numeric* value by adding up the total value of each of the individual letters. In addition, every one of the Hebrew and Greek letters was given a *Place* value as well. To help illustrate this phenomenon let's apply this system to the English language. It would look like this:

An Example Illustrated in the English Language
PLACE VALUE

1	2	3	4	5	6	7	8	9	10	11	12	13	14	15
A	B	C	D	E	F	G	H	I	J	K	L	M	N	O
1	2	3	4	5	6	7	8	9	10	20	30	40	50	60

NUMERIC VALUE

The Hebrew Language
PLACE VALUE

1	2	3	4	5	6	7	8	9	10	11	12	13	14	15
א	ב	ג	ד	ה	ו	ז	ח	ט	י	כ	ל	מ	נ	ס
1	2	3	4	5	6	7	8	9	10	20	30	40	50	60

NUMERIC VALUE

Note that in the above example using the English alphabet the first ten letters have the same *Place* values and *Numeric* values. However, when we get to the eleventh letter K, the numeric value begins to increase by ten with each additional letter until we reach the value of 100. From that point in the alphabet forward the Numeric value of each letter will increase by 100.

Every single word in Hebrew contains a series of letters with individual numeric values. For example, the word *Brayshith*, "beginning" is expressed in Genesis 1:1 in Hebrew as בראשית. If you add up the total value of the individual letters in *Brayshith* the numeric value of the word is 913. Since each word has a numeric value we can add up the value of each of the words in a biblical verse to determine the numerical value of the sentence.

The Astonishing Pattern of SEVENS in Genesis 1:1

Let us begin by examining the first verse of the Bible to explore Panin's discovery.

"In the beginning God created the heaven and the earth"

(Genesis 1:1)

בראשית ברא אלהיס את השמיס ואת הארץ:

(Genesis 1:1)

Ivan Panin carefully examined the Hebrew text of Genesis 1:1 and discovered an incredible phenomenon of multiples of 7 that could not be explained by chance. Genesis 1:1 was composed of seven Hebrew words containing a total of 28 letters. Throughout the Bible the number seven appears repeatedly as a symbol of divine perfection — the 7 days of creation, God rested on the 7th day, the 7 churches, the 7 seals, the 7 trumpets, etc. In total, Panin discovered 30 separate codes involving the number 7 in this first verse of the Bible.

A Listing of the Phenomenal Features
of Sevens Found in Genesis 1:

1. The number of Hebrew words	Seven
2. The number of letters equals 28 ($28 \div 4 = 7$)	Seven
3. The first three Hebrew words translated "In the beginning God created" contain 14 letters ($14 \div 2 = 7$)	Seven
4. The last four Hebrew words "the heavens and the earth" have 14 letters ($14 \div 2 = 7$)	Seven
5. The fourth and fifth words have 7 letters	Seven
6. The sixth and seventh words have 7 letters	Seven
7. The three key words: God; heaven and earth have 14 letters ($14 \div 2 = 7$)	Seven
8. The number of letters in the four remaining words is also 14 ($14 \div 2 = 7$)	Seven
9. The middle word is the shortest with 2 letters. However, in combination with the word to the right or left it totals 7 letters	Seven
10. The numeric value of the first, middle and last letters is 133 ($133 \div 19 = 7$)	Seven
11. The numeric value of the first and last letters of all seven words is 1393 ($1393 \div 199 = 7$)	Seven

When professors on the mathematics faculty at Harvard University were presented with this biblical phenomenon they naturally attempted to disprove its significance as a proof of divine authorship. However, after valiant efforts these professors were unable to duplicate this incredible mathematical phenomenon. The Harvard scientists used the English language and artificially assigned numeric values to the English alphabet. They had a potential vocabulary of over 400,000 available English words to choose from to construct a sentence about any topic they chose. Compare this to the limitations of word choices in the biblical Hebrew language which has only forty-five hundred available word choices that the writers of the Old Testament could use. Despite their advanced mathematical abilities and access to computers the mathematicians were unable to come close to incorporating 30 mathematical multiples of 7 as found in the Hebrew words of Genesis 1:1.

If any one doubts the difficulty of producing a passage following such an intricate pattern of sevens, I challenge you to try it yourself. I have tried, and it is impossible to complete a paragraph on any topic and remain true to the system of interlocking sevens. I doubt that anyone could complete a paragraph of over one hundred and fifty words following such a pattern of sevens, as found in Genesis 1:1 and Matthew, chapter 1, even if they were to devote several years to the effort. The problem is that with the addition of every single word and sentence the magnitude of the challenge to integrate the new phrase into the existing pattern grows geometrically. Each word and sentence must fit into the pattern existing within the preceding sentences. In light of this virtual impossibility we need to remember that the writers of the Bible were forty-four mostly common men who wrote their individual texts separated from each other over a period of sixteen centuries. How could these ordinary men contribute to this hidden pattern without consultation when most of them never met their fellow authors? The only logical explanation is that God directed their minds through supernatural inspiration to write His precise inspired words.

The number "seven" permeates the totality of Scripture because the number speaks of God's divine perfection and perfect order. The actual number 7 appears 287 times in the Old Testament ($287 \div 41 = 7$) while the word "seventh" occurs 98 times ($98 \div 14 = 7$). The word "seven-fold" appears seven times. In addition, the word "seventy" is used 56 times ($56 \div 8 = 7$).

Ivan Panin discovered literally thousands of such mathematical patterns underlying all of the books of the Old Testament before his death in 1942. I refer the interested reader to Panin's book, *The Inspiration of the Scriptures Scientifically Demonstrated*, which discusses these phenomena extensively. Panin and others have examined other Hebrew literature and have attempted to find such mathematical patterns, but they are not found anywhere outside the Bible.

Matthew 1:1–17 – Evidence of Divine Authorship of the New Testament

Panin also examined the New Testament to discover whether or not the pattern continued. There were four hundred years of silence between the completion of the Old Testament around 396 B.C. and the writing of the New Testament following the resurrection of Jesus Christ. However, when God inspired the New Testament authors, including Matthew, to begin writing the Gospels, He again manifested His signature on the pages of Scripture by creating a marvelously complex pattern of sevens beneath the text of Matthew's Gospel.

The first section in Matthew's account consists of seventeen verses from Matthew 1:1 to 1:17 that describe in detail one particular subject, the genealogy of Jesus Christ. This seventeen-verse text contains 72 Greek Vocabulary words. A Vocabulary word is a particular and different word from any other word that was used in a passage. In other words, a Greek word that appears 6 times in the passage would only be counted as 1 Vocabulary word. Obviously, the number of Vocabulary words will differ from the number of total words appearing in the passage. The same system of Numeric and Place values for letters exists in the Greek language used in the New Testament as we found in Hebrew of the Old Testament.

A Listing of the Phenomenal Features of Sevens Found in Matthew 1:1–17

1. The total numeric value of the 72 vocabulary
   words is 43,364 (42,364 ÷ 6,052 = 7)   Seven
2. The number of Greek nouns in the passage is
   56. (56 ÷ 8 = 7)   Seven
3. The Greek article for "the" occurs 56 times
   (56 ÷ 8 = 7)   Seven

In the first eleven verses of Matthew 1:1–11 we
find these additional features:

4. The number of Greek vocabulary words is 49
   (49 ÷ 7 = 7)   Seven
5. Of these 49 words, 28 words begin with a vowel
   (28 ÷ 4 = 7)   Seven

6. Of these 49 words, 21 begin with a consonant
   $(21 \div 3 = 7)$ Seven

7. The number of letters in these 49 words equals
   266 $(266 \div 38 = 7)$ Seven

8. Of these 49 words, 35 words occur more than one
   time $(35 \div 5 = 7)$ Seven

9. Of these 49 words, 14 words occur only one time
   $(14 \div 2 = 7)$ Seven

10. The number of proper names is 35 $(35 \div 5 = 7)$ Seven

11. The number of times these proper names occur
    is 63 $(63 \div 9 = 7)$ Seven

12. Of the 35 proper names, the number of male
    names is 28 $(28 \div 4 = 7)$ Seven

13. Three women, Tamar, Rahab and Ruth, are
    named in this section. The number of Greek letters
    in these three names is 7 $(14 \div 2 = 7)$ Seven

Only a few of the numerical features that are found in this passage are listed in this analysis by Ivan Panin. However, these features reveal an underlying profound mathematical design that reveals the signature of the true author of both the New Testament and the Old Testament-God Himself. However, to illustrate that this is not an unusual phenomenon occurring only in this one isolated passage, I will list some additional mathematical features that occur in the balance of Matthew 1:18–25 that describe the birth of Jesus Christ. In this seven-verse section God has placed an astonishing pattern of SEVENS that verify the signature of the original author.

The Pattern of SEVENS in Matthew 1:18–25 — The History of Christ's Birth

1. The number of letters in the seven word passage
   is 161 $(161 \div 23 = 7)$ Seven

2. The number of Vocabulary words is 77 $(77 \div 11 = 7)$ Seven

3. Six Greek words occur only in this passage and
   never again in Matthew. These six Greek words
   contain precisely 56 letters $(56 \div 8 = 7)$ Seven

4. The number of distinct proper names in the
   passage is 7   Seven

5. The number of Greek letters in these seven proper
   names is 42 $(42 \div 6 = 7)$ Seven

6. The number of words spoken by the angel to
   Joseph is 28 (28 ÷ 4 = 7)   Seven
7. The number of Greek forms of words used in this
   passage is 161 (161 ÷ 23 = 7)   Seven
8. The number of Greek forms of words in the angel's
   speech is 35 (35 ÷ 5 = 7)   Seven
9. The number of letters in the angel's 35 forms of
   words is 168 (168 ÷ 24 = 7)   Seven

This phenomenal discovery by Panin has been examined by numerous authorities and the figures have been verified. In total, Panin accumulated over forty thousand pages of detailed calculations covering most of the text of the Bible before his death. These incredible, mathematical patterns are not limited to the number seven. There are numerous other patterns. These amazing patterns appear in the vocabulary, grammatical forms, parts of speech, and particular forms of words. They occur throughout the whole text of the Bible containing 31,173 verses. When you consider the amazing details of this mathematical phenomenon you realize that the change of a single letter or word in the original languages of Hebrew or Greek would destroy the pattern. Now we can understand why Jesus Christ declared that the smallest letter and grammatical mark of the Scriptures was preserved by God's Hand: "For verily I say unto you, Till heaven and earth pass, one jot or one tittle shall in no wise pass from the law, till all be fulfilled" (Matthew 5:18).

Naturally, the religious skeptics did not abandon their atheism in response to these incredible discoveries by Ivan Panin that revealed a staggering pattern of complexity hidden beneath the text of Scripture. After many skeptics had dismissed his research, Ivan Panin issued a public challenge through one of the major newspapers of the day, *The New York Sun,* in a letter to the editor on November 20, 1899, offering his detractors an opportunity to prove his research wrong if they could. Panin issued his public challenge to some of the greatest atheist scholars of the day. "I herewith respectfully invite any or all of the following to prove that my facts are not facts: namely Messrs. Lyman Abbott, Washington Gladden, Herber Newton, Minot J. Savage, Presidents Eliot of Harvard, White of Cornell, and Harper of the University of Chicago, Professor J. Henry Thayer of Harvard, and Dr. Briggs, and any other prominent higher critic so called. They may associate with themselves, if they choose, all the contributors to the ninth edition of the *Encyclopædia Britannica*, who wrote its articles on Biblical subjects, together with a dozen mathematicians of the calibre of Professor Simon Newcomb. The heavier the calibre of either scholar or mathematician, the more satisfactory to me. They will find that my facts are facts. And since they are facts, I am ready to take them to any three prominent lawyers, or, better still, to any judge of the superior or supreme court, and abide by his decision as to whether the conclusion is not necessary that Inspiration alone can account for the facts, if they are facts. All I should ask would be that the judge treat the case as he would any other case that comes before him."

Despite his public challenge in the *The New York Sun*, not one of these prominent men attempted to refute Mr. Panin's undeniable facts or to deal with the unavoidable conclusion that the evidence produced by Panin proved that the Bible was truly inspired by a divine intelligence. The critics could not refute these facts. The only thing they could do was to ignore them. Were Mr. Panin's research and calculations wrong? If so, where? If they were correct, and they are, then the evidence exists for all to see that God did truly inspire the words of Scripture. One of Panin's last challenges consisted of this argument. He wrote to his detractors: "Lastly, my argument can also be refuted by showing that even though my facts be true, my arithmetic faultless, and my collocation of numerics honest, that men could have written thus without inspiration from above." However, any honest attempt to create a paragraph on any subject that will contain this astonishing pattern of mathematical features within the surface text will utterly fail. I doubt that even a modern Cray super-computer could produce a passage containing the "wheels within wheels" pattern of sevens as revealed in Genesis 1:1 or Matthew 1:1–25. To date, no one has succeeded in duplicating the phenomenon produced by the biblical writers in ancient times.

What was Panin's own view of the Scriptures after a lifetime of diligent study? He wrote the following statement in one of his essays after warning of the limitations of wisdom found in secular philosophy. "Not so, however, with The Book. For it tells of One who spake as men never spake, who was the true bread of life, that which cometh down from the heavens, of which if a man eat he shall never hunger." Ivan Panin's conclusion of the matter was the following challenge. "My friend of the world, whoso you are: Either Jesus Christ is mistaken or you are. The answer that neither might be is only evading the issue, not settling it. But the ages have decided that Jesus Christ was not mistaken. It is for you to decide whether you shall continue to be."

Why Did God Hide This Information Until This Century?

Possibly, the Lord hid this incredible revelation of His divine authority and authorship of the Scriptures until a generation would arise in the last days that would be primarily a generation of skeptics and unbelievers who would require such scientifically, verifiable evidence to convince men that the Bible is true. In addition, the prophet Daniel foretold that "knowledge shall be increased" in the last days and that the secrets of God would finally be unsealed. Daniel was told to "seal the vision until the end." As we approach the apocalyptic days when all of these prophecies will be fulfilled it is consistent that God would allow His servants to lift the veil and share His secrets to this final generation.

A careful examination of the evidence for divine inspiration demonstrated in the mathematical patterns and the words hidden beneath the text of Scriptures in this chapter reveal the true author of the Holy Scriptures. When comparing two documents or two devices a judge will look for similarities of design and pattern to determine if one creator is responsible for the creation of the two items. In a similar manner, the same mathematical patterns revealed in the Scriptures are also found in the rest of the physical creation proving that God is the author of both. The prophet Daniel reveals that one of the angelic messengers sent to him to prophesy about coming events of the last days is called "Palmoni" in the original Hebrew text, which means "the numberer of secrets" or "the wonderful numberer." In the English translation of Daniel 8:13 we find the angel's name was translated as "that certain saint." We are informed that Palmoni told Daniel the precise time of the duration of the defilement of the Temple sanctuary. "How long shall be the vision concerning daily sacrifice, and the transgression of desolation, to give both the sanctuary and the host to be trodden under foot? And he said unto me, Unto two thousand and three hundred days; then shall the sanctuary be cleansed." As I showed in my earlier book *Armageddon — Appointment With Destiny*, this prophecy points to the final cleansing of the Temple sanctuary in our generation. This same angel Palmoni, the "numberer of secrets" declares to the prophet Daniel, "For at the time appointed the end shall be" (Daniel 8:19).

Just as the number seven is found repeatedly hidden beneath the text of Scripture we find the same number used repeatedly by the Creator in His physical creation of the universe and its inhabitants. There are precisely seven colors in the light spectrum that merge together to form light. The study of music again reveals that there are exactly seven musically whole tones in the scale. Every eighth musical note creates a new higher octave repeating the pattern of seven tones. The seven colors correspond to the seven musical notes. In another manifestation of design, the whole human body is effectively renewed at the cellular level every seven years. By the end of seven years almost every single cell of our flesh, organs and bones will be replaced with new cells manufactured according to an incredibly complex genetic program in our DNA. Our blood pulse rate slows down noticeably every seven days throughout our life. The gestation cycle to produce a baby takes 280 days (7 x 40). Our lives are marked with the number seven as God commanded us to rest every seventh day and noted that our life expectancy is seventy years (7 × 10). Almost all of the animals have gestation periods that are multiples of seven: lion = 98 days; sheep = 147 days; hens = 21 days; ducks = 28 days; cats = 56 days; dogs = 63 days.

The number "seven" in Hebrew is derived from the root word שבע meaning "to be full, satisfied, or have enough of" while another meaning of the root is "to swear", or "to make an oath." We find "seven" appearing on the surface of the biblical text as well as in prominent places, including the seven spirits or manifestations of God (Isaiah 11:2); the seven-fold blessing of Abraham (Genesis 12:2,3); God's seven-fold covenant with Israel (Exodus 6:6–8); and the marvelous design of sevens found in the Book of Revelation. John describes seven groups of seven in his Apocalypse including: 7 churches, 7 seals, 7 trumpets, 7 vials, 7 personages, 7 dooms and 7 new things. A profound and mysterious pattern of sevens runs through the Scriptures from Genesis to Revelation both on its surface text as well as hidden deep beneath the Hebrew and Greek letters. The consistency of these remarkable patterns reveal the common authorship behind all sixty-six books of Holy Scripture.

Just as an expert's examination of a disputed document can reveal the unmistakable signature and character of the original writer, the mathematical and textual phenomenon explored in this chapter prove conclusively to any open-minded reader that the text of Scripture contains the genuine signature of its author — God. Four thousand years ago, Moses wrote these words under the inspiration of God's Holy Spirit: "The secret things belong unto the Lord our God, but those things which are revealed belong unto us and to our children forever, that we may do all the words of this law" (Deuteronomy 29:29). The evidence in this chapter reveals once more the signature of God revealed in the pages of the Scriptures.

13

The Phenomenon of "Undesigned Coincidences"

One of the strongest proofs that the Scriptures are absolutely reliable and inspired by God is revealed in the phenomenon called "undesigned coincidences" found in the Bible which cannot be explained unless these writings are absolutely true. The evidence of undesigned coincidences was first noted in 1738 by Dr. Philip Doddridge in his *Introduction to the First Epistle to the Thessalonians*. Doddridge wrote, "Whoever reads over St. Paul's epistles with attention . . . will discern such intrinsic characters of their genuineness, and the divine authority of the doctrines they contain, as will perhaps produce in him a stronger conviction than all the external evidence with which they are attended. To which we may add, that the exact coincidence observable between the many allusions to particular facts, in this as well as in other epistles, and the account of the facts themselves, as they are recorded in the history of the Acts, is a remarkable confirmation of the truth of each."

Dr. Paley in his noteworthy book *Horæ Paulinæ* was the first writer to develop this evidence regarding these coincidences in great detail as proof that no man could have created these Epistles of Paul without the divine aid of God Himself. However, the greatest evidence of this type was researched by Rev. J. J. Blunt as detailed in his book, *Undesigned Coincidences in the Writings of the Old and New Testament*. As Rev. Blunt declared in his fascinating manuscript, the evidence from "instances of coincidence without design" provide an incredibly strong proof that the Scriptures were inspired by God (Rev. J. J. Blunt, *Undesigned Coincidences in the Writings of the Old and New Testament* [London: John Murray, 1847]). The evidence from co-incidence is so strong in the mind of the average person that juries have often convicted people to the death penalty upon this kind of evidence. The value of this evidence is that it establishes a strong proof that the individual authors of the books of the Bible acted as independent witnesses to the facts that they observed and recorded in the Scriptures. Furthermore, these coincidences are such as could not possibly have arisen as a result of mutual understanding among the biblical writers or artificial arrangement. Often the facts and ev-idence that coincidentally prove the accuracy of the Bible's narrative are found in obscure passages unconnected with the main passage describing the story.

The Rebellion of Absalom Against King David

One of the saddest and most tragic stories found in the pages of the Scriptures concerns the revolt of David's son Prince Absalom to-ward the end of David's reign and the agony experienced by the king when his beloved and rebellious son was killed. Absalom was the third son born to David as a result of his marriage with Maacah the daughter of Talmai, the king of Geshur. This story has often been preached from the pulpit to remind us of the consequences of pride and blind ambition in the inevitable judgment of God upon Absa-lom's rebellion and his ultimate death. Many preachers have re-minded parents about David's complacency in failing to discipline his favorite son as he grew to manhood, full of pride and arrogance. The Scriptures record that "Absalom prepared him chariots and horses, and fifty men to run before him" (2 Samuel 15:1) and stirred rebellion against his father by promising the people that he would rule in their favor when he became king of Israel. David's unwilling-ness to deal with the growing rebellion of his son ultimately set the stage for Absalom's revolt against his father's throne, David's flight from Jerusalem, and the bitter war against the rebels. Finally, the tragic moment came when David heard of his loyal army's victory over the rebels. He cried out in anguish, "Is the young man Absalom safe?" (2 Samuel 18:29). When the servants of the king finally had the courage to tell the truth they admitted that Absalom was dead. King David wept bitterly for the loss of his beloved son, crying out, "O my son Absalom, my son, my son Absalom! Would God I had died for thee, O Absalom, my son, my son!"

In the midst of the rebellion the Bible records that, "Absalom sent for Ahithophel the Gilonite, David's counsellor, from his city, even from Giloh, while he offered sacrifices. And the conspiracy was strong; for the people increased continually with Absalom." Ahithophel had been King David's faithful counsellor or prime minister for many decades giving the king the benefit of his great wisdom. The Book of Samuel tells us that Ahithophel was considered a brilliant counselor. "And the counsel of Ahithophel, which he counselled in those days, was as if a man had inquired at the oracle of God: so was all the counsel of Ahithophel both with David and with Absalom" (2 Samuel 16:23). In fact, when David learned that his trusted friend and counselor had betrayed him, he was so afraid of the danger from Ahithophel that he prayed, "O Lord, I pray thee, turn the counsel of Ahithophel into foolishness" (2 Samuel 15:31). Years earlier King David had prophesied a double prophecy in his Book of Psalms that foresaw the betrayal by his friend Ahithophel. However, David's words also predicted the ultimate betrayal a thousand years later of Jesus of Nazareth by His friend and disciple Judas Iscariot. "Yea, mine own familiar friend, in whom I trusted, which did eat of my bread, hath lifted up his heel against me" (Psalm 41:9).

The question that has troubled many Bible students and writers of commentaries is this. Why did Ahithophel, David's trusted counselor, immediately join Absalom's rebellion against his father's throne after a lifetime of faithful service? Furthermore, why would Ahithophel ask the young prince to allow him to personally lead the army of rebels to immediately attack and kill King David before the king could escape? "Moreover Ahithophel said unto Absalom, 'Let me now choose out twelve thousand men, and I will arise and pursue after David this night . . . and I will smite the king only'" (2 Samuel 17:1,2). Finally, why would Ahithophel advise Absalom to openly have sexual relations with his father's wives on the roof of the palace? "And Ahithophel said unto Absalom, 'Go in unto thy father's concubines, which he hath left to keep the house; and all Israel shall hear that thou art abhorred of thy father: then shall the hands of all that are with thee be strong.' So they spread Absalom a tent upon the top of the house; and Absalom went in unto his father's concubines in the sight of all Israel" (2 Samuel 16:21,22). The Bible does not openly record the motivation for this incredible betrayal of King David as if the reason was so obvious to people living in that day that there was no need to comment on it.

The answer to this great mystery is found in several of the passages in the Old Testament that often cause readers to skip forward because the list of names recorded in the chapter seems to have little relevance to us. However, the solution to this puzzle about Ahithophel's motive does exist in the Word of God and it reveals a very important lesson that every single follower of Christ needs to learn. To find the solution to the mystery of the betrayal surrounding Absalom's rebellion, we need to go back almost thirty years to the incident when David committed adultery with Bathsheba, the beautiful wife of Uriah the Hittite. Most commentators and preachers have discussed the sin of David as if it was the result of a momentary weakness when he happened to observe the woman Bathsheba bathing. The truth is somewhat different. When David was supposed to be at war leading his troops against the enemy, the Scriptures record that he had stayed home in his palace in Jerusalem. "And it came to pass, after the year was expired, at the time when kings go forth to battle, that David sent Joab, and his servants with him, and all Israel; and they destroyed the children of Ammon, and besieged Rabbah. But David tarried still at Jerusalem" (2 Samuel 11:1). David's first mistake was that he was not in the place God had called him to be, leading his nation against their enemies as their king. As the evidence unfolds about this biblical mystery we will also find that Bathsheba was no stranger to the king.

When you read the Scriptures carefully you will note that the passage describing Bathsheba tells us that she was the "daughter of Eliam" and "the wife of Uriah the Hittite" (2 Samuel 11:3). Another significant passage in the Book of Samuel lists the great military heroes that guarded King David throughout his many battles against Saul, the Philistines, and many enemy nations. This list of the thirty-seven "mighty men" of David records that "Uriah the Hittite" and "Eliam, the son of Ahithophel the Gilonite" were part of this elite force that fought for the king (2 Samuel 23:34,39). Now we can begin to understand what was occurring behind the scenes in this famous biblical story. Uriah the Hittite, the husband of Bathsheba, and Eliam, the father of Bathsheba, are not strangers to David. They are friends who had fought back-to-back against their enemies over many years. They had sat together around the campfire at night during many military campaigns. Bathsheba is the wife of Uriah, David's loyal bodyguard, and the daughter of Eliam, another faithful bodyguard. David viewed Bathsheba while she was bathing because Uriah and his wife had a house close to King David's palace as a probable reward for his years of loyal service. It is very likely that Bathsheba, Uriah, and her father Eliam had attended royal banquets in David's palace.

The story of David's sin with Bathsheba takes on a very different complexion in light of these Scriptural facts that have been unnoticed for centuries. When David committed adultery with Bathsheba he took the wife of Uriah, a loyal friend and the daughter of another friend. Then when she becomes pregnant David tried to get Uriah to visit his wife to provide confusion about when and how she became pregnant. When Uriah refused to visit his wife, David conspired with his general Joab to murder Uriah to cover up his shameful betrayal and adultery. Later, the prophet Nathan came to David and proclaimed God's anger against David's sins of adultery and the murder of Uriah. Nathan warned that David would be afflicted by warfare the rest of his life in punishment for his sins. Furthermore the prophet foretold that "by this deed thou hast given great occasion to the enemies of the Lord to blaspheme, the child also that is born unto thee shall surely die" (2 Samuel 12:14). Throughout history this prophecy was fulfilled as the skeptics and critics attacked the Bible and King David's character by referring to his great sin with Bathsheba.

Yet, there is still more to the story. Note carefully that 2 Samuel 23:34 told us that Eliam, the father of Bathsheba, was also the son of Ahithophel, David's counselor. Therefore, Ahithophel, David's prime minister, was the grandfather of Bathsheba. After David sinned with Bathsheba and killed Uriah, many people in the palace and the army would have realized that David was the father of the child born to Bathsheba after the death of her husband. People living at that time knew the length of a woman's pregnancy was nine months and therefore knew that the king must be the father of the widow Bathsheba, whom he later married. As David's counselor in the palace, Ahithophel must have burned with rage to know his king had betrayed his granddaughter's honor and killed Uriah, her husband, who was a fellow soldier with his son Eliam, Bathsheba's father. However, there was nothing he could do at that time to exact his revenge. If he had risen in anger against the king he would have lost his life. So he remained silent, keeping his thoughts of revenge secretly to himself all of the years that followed until he saw an opportunity to destroy King David. The Arabs have an expression, "That a man who seeks his revenge before forty years has past, has moved in haste."

Finally, after decades of waiting, King David's rebellious son Absalom revolted against his aged father. This was Ahithophel's chance to get revenge for the wrongs committed years earlier against his family. He joined Absalom's conspiracy and offered to kill David personally. Finally, we can understand Ahithophel's strange advice to Absalom to have sexual relations with David's wives "in the sight of all Israel." He was attempting to get his revenge by encouraging Absalom to do the same thing to David's wives as the king had done to his granddaughter. Significantly, as David fled from Jerusalem, a man named Shimei cursed the king and cast stones at him saying, "Behold, thou art taken in thy mischief, because thou art a bloody man" (2 Samuel 16:8). When David's men wanted to kill this man, the king stopped them, and stated that the man was right and that God had told him to curse the king. Obviously, King David knew very well, as did the people around him, why Ahithophel had joined Absalom's revolt.

These verses provided clues and evidence that finally allowed us to solve the mystery of Ahithophel's betrayal of David. More importantly, these clues scattered in passages throughout the Old Testament provide an overwhelming evidence for the truthfulness of the Bible's report about the life of King David. No one writing a story like this as fiction would hide the clues so well that the mystery of Ahithophel's motive for betrayal could not be discovered for thousands of years. However, someone truthfully recording a contemporary series of events will often pass over in silence the motive for a person's actions because that motive is so obvious and well known to the writer and those who were living at the time of the events. The presence of coincidental evidence such as we find in this analysis provides very strong proof that the biblical record is a faithful and reliable account of the events in question. As Paul Harvey often says when he completes his fascinating radio program, "Now you know the rest of the story!"

There is one further detail that should not be overlooked. Consider how David responded to his sin and God's punishment in the death of his child born to Bathsheba. While the baby was sick, King David fasted and prayed that God would allow the child to live. However, after his child died, David stopped fasting and said, "But now he is dead, wherefore should I fast? Can I bring him back again? I shall go to him, but he shall not return to me" (2 Samuel 12:23). In this touching scene, where the Bible assures us that children who die will go to heaven, we can see the difference between the way a man thinks about his sin and the way God deals with our sins. King David had sinned in his weakness. He sincerely repented of his sins as witnessed by his touching words of deep repentance in his Psalms. His son had died as God warned through his prophet Nathan's words. David stopped fasting and prepared to carry on with the rest of his life, believing that his sin and its consequences were over forever.

This is the way most Christians think about their sins. When convicted of our sin, we sincerely repent and ask God to forgive us. The Lord forgives our sin and we believe, like King David, that the consequences of our sins are removed. We believe that it's all over. However, although God truly forgives our sins, it's not over. God will not stop the natural consequences of our sin from affecting our lives and the lives of those around us. When we sin, it is similar to throwing a pebble on a pond. The ripples on the pond are like the effects of our sinful actions that will affect many things in our lives and those we know. Often the consequences will cause great problems many years later. King David thought his sin with Bathsheba was dealt with forever, but the tragic consequences caught up with him years later and almost caused him to lose his life and throne. At a time in his life when David should have been enjoying his victories and honors, the consequences of his sin from years before almost destroyed him. David was forced to flee from his royal city, up the side of the Mount of Olives in fear after the betrayal of his son and his closest counselor. It was the worst moment in his long life.

The true and lasting consequences of our sins are often underestimated by Christians. Sometimes Christians, when they are tempted to sin, begin to think like King David. They feel that they can sin, then ask God to forgive their sin and that He will make everything perfect as if their sin had never occurred. But our sins have consequences that will continue to destroy our body, our friendships, our families, and our career, years after God has forgiven us if we truly repent of our rebellion. We need to realize that, when we choose to sin against God, the effects of our choice will continue to affect our life as long as we live. While God does forgive He does not change the law of cause and effect that will inevitably produce the consequences of our sins.

David and Goliath

The story of David and Goliath is one of the most well known of the Bible stories. During that time the Jews were under the brutal domination of the Philistines. Finally, the Lord raised up a hero to stand against the Philistines and defeat their great champion, Goliath, The army of Israel faced the army of the Philistines but King Saul could not find an Israelite brave enough to engage the Philistine's giant warrior in hand-to-hand combat that would determine who would dominate the land. There are a number of small details or coincidences in this biblical story that provide very strong proof that it is a genuine account. Consider that the Bible mentions that Goliath comes from the village of Gath. "And there went out a champion out of the camp of the Philistines, named Goliath, of Gath, whose height was six cubits and a span" (1 Samuel 17:4). This is significant because Gath was one of the villages where the giant race of Anakims lived. When the twelve spies entered Canaan they were fearful of the giant races that lived in the land. "And they brought up an evil report of the land which they had searched unto the children of Israel, saying, 'The land, through which we have gone to search it, is a land that eateth up the inhabitants thereof; and all the people that we saw in it are men of a great stature'" (Numbers 13:32).

Another passage in the Book of Joshua tells us that Gath was one of the few places where the giant race of Anakim still survived. "And at that time came Joshua, and cut off the Anakims from the mountains, from Hebron, from Debir, from Anab, and from all the mountains of Judah, and from all the mountains of Israel: Joshua destroyed them utterly with their cities. There was none of the Anakims left in the land of the children of Israel: only in Gaza, in *Gath*, and in Ashdod, there remained" (Joshua 11:21,22). There were only three cities in Israel where the remnants of the giants survived. This coincidence that, four hundred years after the conquest of

Canaan, we find Goliath living in Gath, one of those three villages, is a marvelous confirmation of the truthfulness of the biblical record about David and Goliath. In this coincidence we find that three separate biblical books, Numbers, Joshua, and Samuel, confirm the accuracy of one of the elements in this famous biblical account.

One other feature in the story of David and Goliath always fascinated me as a young boy. Why did David pick up five smooth stones for his sling when he knew that God would guide his aim to kill the Philistine giant with only one stone? Did David lack faith in God's supernatural power to destroy Israel's great enemy? The answer to this mystery appeared to me one night when I was reading the Book of 2 Samuel, chapter 21. To my surprise I found that Goliath was not the only giant in his family. The father of Goliath was a giant who had five sons, all of whom fought for the Philistines. Every one of these four brothers were also giants who ultimately died in combat with the brave soldiers of David. Summarizing the story of their death in combat with David's men, the prophet Samuel recorded: "These four were born to the giant in Gath, and fell by the hand of David, and by the hand of his servants" (2 Samuel 21:22). When David picked up five smooth stones for his sling he was simply being prudent in preparing for the possibility that Goliath's four brothers might have joined the battle when Goliath was killed. He might have needed the additional four stones to defeat the four other giants.

Why Did Israel Not Use Horses?

I believe the horse is the most noble and beautiful animal on earth. As a young boy I grew up on a ranch in Canada where my family ran a western-style Christian summer camp for young people, Frontier Ranch, where we raised over a hundred quarter horses. Some of my fondest memories are those when I would ride my horse along old abandoned logging trails and camp out overnight in the forest. As one who loves horses I always thought it strange that the Israelites never used horses in their many battles against the pagan armies in their conquest of the Holy Land prior to the reign of King Solomon.

Why did Israel never use horses to defend themselves against the cavalry and war-horses of their enemies? There are one hundred and eighty-eight references to horses throughout the Old Testament proving that the horse was well known to the Jews. The Book of Job describes the glory and bravery of the horse in the following passages: "Hast thou given the horse strength? hast thou clothed his neck with thunder? Canst thou make him afraid as a grasshopper? The glory of his nostrils is terrible. He paweth in the valley, and rejoiceth in his strength: he goeth on to meet the armed men. He mocketh at fear, and is not affrighted; neither turneth he back from the sword. The quiver rattleth against him, the glittering spear and the shield. He swalloweth the ground with fierceness and rage: neither believeth he that it is the sound of the trumpet" (Job 39:19–24).

Archeology has revealed that horses were commonly used in the armies and societies of all of the ancient nations of the Middle East, with the exception of Israel, until the reign of King Solomon approximately 970 B.C. For example, the Ten Commandments prohibited the Jews from coveting an ox or ass, but there was no mention of horses. "Thou shalt not covet thy neighbour's house, thou shalt not covet thy neighbour's wife, nor his manservant, nor his maidservant, nor his ox, nor his ass, nor any thing that is thy neighbour's" (Exodus 20:17). In the Book of Judges we find evidence that donkeys were the normal mode of transportation for Israel rather than horses. As an example, according to Joshua 15:18, when the daughter of Caleb, a leader of Israel, came to visit Othniel she used an ass, or donkey, not a horse. The Book of Judges revealed that the governors of Israel rode upon white asses. Later, we read of Saul searching for the lost asses of his father. In the passages of the Old Testament dealing with this period before the reign of King Solomon, although the Jewish state trained very effective armies and won numerous wars in their conquest of Canaan, they never used horses for cavalry nor for their war chariots. The only horses mentioned were those of the enemies of Israel such as the nine hundred chariots of the cavalry of King Jabin of Canaan. In the Bible's description of the battle with the Philistines, when they seized the Ark of God, Israel lost thirty thousand infantry, but there was no mention of horsemen, proving they had no cavalry. The Scriptures describe the battle against King David, when his son Absalom was killed by riding his mule under the branches of a tree, proving that even royal princes did not ride horses in that time.

Why did Israel refuse to use horses for their cavalry when the foreign armies had the advantage of horses in their cavalry and war chariots? The answer is found in a single command of God forbidding the use of horses as recorded in Deuteronomy 17:16. "But he shall not multiply horses to himself, nor cause the people to return to Egypt, to the end that he should multiply horses: forasmuch as the Lord hath said unto you, 'Ye shall henceforth return no more that way.'"

The primary reason for God's prohibition of horses for Israel was the fact that Egypt was the world's premier source of breeding farms to produce war-horses. God knew that Israel would be tempted to enter into alliances with Egypt to acquire horses for their army. Therefore, the Lord gave a prohibition against the use of horses to ensure that Israel would not depend on an alliance with Egypt to obtain war-horses. Egypt used its virtual monopoly on war-horses to enforce a series of alliances. Just as America and Russian use the supply of advanced weapons they offer to client states to lock them into defensive treaties, nations could only purchase Egyptian war-horses if they entered into defensive treaties with Egypt. Therefore, if Israel had acquired horses from Egypt, she would have been entangled in foreign alliances rather than trust in the power of God to save her.

However, there is another reason. Israel was a nation of valiant soldiers who won astonishing battles against the overwhelming armies of her pagan enemies through the supernatural power of God. When they won such battles against the more powerful armies of her pagan enemies they knew that it was only through the supernatural power of their God. When they acknowledged that they won such battles through God's miraculous intervention, the Lord received the glory. War chariots with horses and cavalry were the equivalent of modern tanks in terms of warfare. By forbidding the Jewish state to acquire horses, God assured that the Israelites would be forced to fight defensive battles to protect the territory of the Holy Land that the Lord had given to them. If the aggressive armies of Israel had access to highly mobile horses, they would have been tempted to use their increased mobility with horses and war chariots to conquer foreign lands and nations far beyond the borders of the Promised Land. The coincidence that Israel never used horses in its many battles until the apostasy that followed King Solomon's reign, without the writers ever explaining their motive, provides a strong indication that the narrative is genuine and accurate.

The coincidences discussed in this chapter form a subtle kind of proof for the inspiration of the Scriptures. I have just touched the tip of the iceberg of those that we could examine. However, if you think about this evidence carefully, you will appreciate that these undesigned coincidences are absolutely consistent with God's direct inspiration of the Bible.

14

The Evidence of the Men who Wrote the New Testament

"The Bible itself is a standing and an astonishing miracle. Written, fragment by fragment, throughout the course of fifteen centuries, under all different states of society, and in different languages, by persons of the most opposite tempers, talents, and conditions, learned and unlearned, prince and peasant, bond and free: cast into every form of instructive composition and good writing, history, prophecy, poetry, allegory, emblematic representation, Judicious interpretation, literal statement, precept, example, proverbs, disquisition, epistle, sermon, prayer — in short all rational shapes of human discourse; and treating, moreover, of subjects not obvious, but most difficult — its authors are not found, like other writers, contradicting one another upon the most ordinary matters of fact and opinion, but are at harmony upon the whole of their sublime and momentous scheme" (Professor Maclagan).

Aside from the pages of the Scriptures we know almost nothing about the lives of the Jewish patriarchs, priests and prophets who were chosen by God to record His revelations to mankind in the Old Testament. However, one of the unusual features of the Scriptures that proves it was inspired by God is that the writers of the Bible wrote as no men have ever written, before or since. The normal tendency of writers in literature is to protect their reputations by disguising or minimizing their weaknesses and failures. In total contrast to normal human motivations, the writers of the Bible reveal themselves "warts and all" throughout their manuscripts. Rather than minimize their mistakes and weaknesses, these writers revealed their total character; both weaknesses and strengths. This is one of the strongest proofs that these men were inspired by God to record these words for eternity in the Word of God. The apostles who wrote the Gospels admit that they hid in fear when their leader was arrested and crucified. They admit to many human weaknesses and failures, yet they changed their world through the supernatural power of God's Holy Spirit.

The Lives of the Apostles

On the other hand, when we examine the lives of the writers of the New Testament, we find that there is a considerable amount of historical evidence about the lives of the disciples and apostles revealed within the writings of the early Church. Jesus Christ chose the twelve apostles whose role was to confirm by their words and their lives the reality of the life, death, and resurrection of Jesus Christ. As a new faith, Christianity needed reliable eyewitness accounts who would personally verify the facts regarding the life of Jesus of Nazareth. He commanded these fishermen and tax collectors to abandon their previous lives and follow Him to a destiny beyond that of any other men in the history of mankind. To this day, two thousand years later, millions of parents still name their sons by the names of the apostles who followed Jesus Christ and turned their world upside down. Certainly, Christ's choice of disciples was not based on their previous character or accomplishments because none of them had risen to prominence in the society of Israel in the first century. It is interesting to note that Jesus did not choose the type of men most modern leaders would choose for such an overwhelming task of preaching a revolutionary message to the world. None of the twelve disciples were religious scholars or professional men of distinction before Christ chose them. None of the disciples were wealthy; none were professionals or natural leaders within the Jewish society during that first century. None of the revealed personal qualities of the disciples at the time Jesus chose them suggested that they would ultimately prove to be great men of faith who would stand the test of time. However, after only three-and-a-half years in the daily presence of Jesus, these men were transformed into great men of God who would stand unflinching against the imperial power of Rome, the greatest power on earth in their lifetime.

Jesus apparently chose His disciples — in the same manner that the sculpture Michelangelo chose the rough marble for His projects, because he saw the possibilities hidden within the uncut stone. A story about Michelangelo tells about a young girl who watched the sculptor as he produced his masterpiece in his workshop in Rome. As she watched him chisel into the huge block of marble she asked Michelangelo how he knew that the figure of David lay hidden within the huge block of uncut marble. The answer, of course, was that Michelangelo, the master sculptor, saw in his imagination the possibility of what the marble could reveal if he removed the unnecessary material that surrounded and hid the potentially beautiful sculpture from the eyes of anyone but the master sculptor. Jesus Christ chose His band of disciples, not for what they were in themselves before He met them, but for what they could become after the touch of the Master's Hand. The truth of this statement is found in the Gospel of John which recorded Christ's words: "And when Jesus beheld him, he said, *Thou art Simon* the son of Jona: *thou shalt be called* Cephas, which is by interpretation, A stone" (John 1:42). The transformation of the character of the apostles was possibly the greatest miracle performed by Jesus Christ during his years of ministry. These simple disciples, after living in the presence of Jesus Christ, turned the world upside down. The result of their teaching the words of Jesus Christ was to turn their world right side up.

When Jesus entered history two thousand years ago, the Roman Empire held over half of the population of the known world as slaves, subject to the vilest abuse of their masters. Most of humanity lived as slaves or serfs under the cruel brutality of Rome's mighty legions. Yet the life and teaching of Jesus, as expressed in the lives of these twelve men and those who took up the cross to follow Him, would ultimately transform this wicked Roman Empire into the first society in history that would proclaim and uphold the rights of men and women to live in freedom and liberty. In a similar manner, Jesus is still transforming the lives and characters of countless men and women who are still turning their world right side up. When we encounter Jesus Christ, the most important thing is not our previous personal history of sinful rebellion, but the transformation that Jesus Christ will produce in us when we surrender our lives to His power and authority. Through His grace and power He can transform every one of us into someone who can make a true difference in our world as witnesses of His power to save and transform the lives of His followers.

One of the criteria by which we can judge the trustworthiness of the testimony of the apostles is whether or not they held firmly and consistently throughout their lives to their testimony about Christ's miracles, His claims to be God, and His death and resurrection. The combined testimony of their teachings, the history of their lives, and their martyrdom provides the strongest witness to the truthfulness of their story. After the arrest, trial, and death of Jesus, these men initially fled in fear. However, these same men were totally transformed in their characters by the power of the Holy Spirit in the days following the resurrection of Christ. The historical records of the first century clearly prove that every one of these men later faced a martyr's death without denying their faith in Jesus Christ as their Savior. What could possibly account for their transformation from defeated cowards to mighty men of God within a few days of the death of their leader? Obviously, the only answer that makes sense is that these men were transformed in their character and motivation by their personal knowledge of the facts surrounding the resurrection of Jesus Christ.

Some atheists have suggested that the disciples, during the decades following His death, simply invented their accounts of Jesus. These Bible critics say that the disciples, in an attempt to enhance His authority, then published the story that Jesus claimed to be God and was resurrected. Any fair-minded reader should consider the historical evidence. First, the apostles were continually threatened and pressured to deny their Lord during their ministry; especially as they faced torture and martyrdom. However, none of these men who spent time with Jesus chose to save their lives by denying their faith in Him. Consider this hypothetical situation: Suppose these men had conspired to form a new religion based on their imagination. How long would anyone continue to proclaim something they knew was a lie when faced with lengthy torture and an inescapable, painful death? All they had to do to escape martyrdom was to admit they had concocted a lie and simply deny their faith and claims about Jesus as God. It defies both common sense and the evidence of history that anyone, let alone a group of twelve men, would persist in proclaiming a lie when they could walk away by admitting that it was a fraud.

Yet, history reveals that not one of these men, who knew Jesus personally, ever denied their testimony about Him despite the threat and reality of imminent death. This proves to any fair-minded observer that these men possessed an absolute, unshakable personal knowledge about the truth of the life, death, and resurrection of Jesus. Each of the apostles was called upon to pay the ultimate price to prove their faith in Jesus, affirming with their life's blood that Jesus was the true Messiah, the Son of God, and the only hope of salvation for a sinful humanity.

The Martyrdom of the Apostles

Most of our information about the deaths of the apostles is derived from early church traditions. While tradition is unreliable as to small details, it very seldom contains outright inventions. Eusebius, the most important of the early church historians wrote his history of the early church in A.D. 325. He wrote, "The apostles and disciples of the Savior scattered over the whole world, preached the Gospel everywhere." The Church historian Schumacher researched the lives of the apostles and recounted the history of their martyrdoms.

Matthew suffered martyrdom in Ethiopia, killed by a sword wound.

Mark died in Alexandria, Egypt, after being dragged by horses through the streets until he was dead.

Luke was hanged in Greece as a result of his tremendous preaching to the lost.

John faced martyrdom when he was boiled in a huge basin of boiling oil during a wave of persecution in Rome. However, he was miraculously delivered from death. John was then sentenced to the mines on the prison island of Patmos. He wrote his prophetic Book of Revelation on Patmos. The apostle John was later freed and returned to serve as Bishop of Edessa in modern Turkey. He died as an old man, the only apostle to die peacefully.

Peter was crucified upside down on an x-shaped cross, according to church tradition because he told his tormentors that he felt unworthy to die in the same way that Jesus Christ had died.

James the Just, the leader of the church in Jerusalem, was thrown over a hundred feet down from the southeast pinnacle of the Temple when he refused to deny his faith in Christ. When they discovered that he survived the fall, his enemies beat James to death with a fuller's club. This was the same pinnacle where Satan had taken Jesus during the Temptation.

James the Greater, a son of Zebedee, was a fisherman by trade when Jesus called him to a lifetime of ministry. As a strong leader of the church, James was ultimately beheaded at Jerusalem. The Roman officer who guarded James watched amazed as James defended his faith at his trial. Later, the officer walked beside James to the place of execution. Overcome by conviction, he declared his new faith to the judge and knelt beside James to accept beheading as a Christian.

Bartholomew, also known as Nathanael, was a missionary to Asia. He witnessed to our Lord in present day Turkey. Bartholomew was martyred for his preaching in Armenia when he was flayed to death by a whip.

Andrew was crucified on an x-shaped cross in Patras, Greece. After being whipped severely by seven soldiers they tied his body to the cross with cords to prolong his agony. His followers reported that, when he was led toward the cross, Andrew saluted it in these words: "I have long desired and expected this happy hour. The cross has been consecrated by the body of Christ hanging on it." He continued to preach to his tormentors for two days until he expired.

The apostle Thomas was stabbed with a spear in India during one of his missionary trips to establish the church in the subcontinent.

Jude, the brother of Jesus, was killed with arrows when he refused to deny his faith in Christ.

Matthias, the apostle chosen to replace the traitor Judas Iscariot, was stoned and then beheaded.

Barnabas, one of the group of seventy disciples, wrote the *Epistle of Barnabas*. He preached throughout Italy and Cyprus. Barnabas was stoned to death at Salonica.

The apostle Paul was tortured and then beheaded by the evil Emperor Nero at Rome in A.D. 67. Paul endured a lengthy imprisonment which allowed him to write his many epistles to the churches he had formed throughout the Roman Empire. These letters, which taught many of the foundational doctrines of Christianity, form a large portion of the New Testament.

The details of the martyrdoms of the disciples and apostles are found in traditional early church sources. These traditions were recounted in the writings of the church fathers and the first official church history written by the historian Eusebius in A.D. 325. Although we can not at this time verify every detail historically, the universal belief of the early Christian writers was that each of the apostles had faced martyrdom faithfully without denying their faith in the resurrection of Jesus Christ.

The Transformed Lives of Men and Women

"The study of God's Word for the purpose of discovering God's will, is the secret discipline which has formed the greatest characters" (J. W. Alexander, quoted in *Leaves of Gold*).

One of the greatest and most convincing body of evidence proving the truth of the Bible is found in the transformed lives of men and women who placed their faith and trust in Jesus Christ. An abiding faith in the revealed truth of God in the Scriptures strengthens people to rely on God in the face of the greatest trials and tribulations of their life. An unshakable faith in the Bible's revelation will enable us to stand against the greatest persecutions as Hebrews 11 records how great heroes of the Bible stood against the opposition of Satan.

The Scriptures have fascinated and held the undying attention of the most brilliant men of each age. An anonymous writer once wrote, "He who teaches the Bible is never a scholar; he is always a student." An early church father living in the second century, Tertullian, devoted his life to the study of Scripture each day and night. By the end of his life Tertullian had memorized most of the Bible by heart, including the punctuation! A profound love of the Scriptures motivated the Christians in those early centuries of persecution to walk in obedience to their Savior, Jesus Christ. Eusebius, the greatest historian of the early church, wrote about one persecuted Christian whose eyes were burned out during one of the ten great waves of persecution against the early church. Despite the loss of his eyes, this Christian saint could repeat to assembled Christians large portions of the Bible from memory. Thomas Beza, the brilliant translator of the Scriptures in A.D. 1585, had such a profound love of the words of his Savior that, at the age of eighty, he could still repeat from memory in the Greek language all of the New Testament Epistles. Two of the leading reformers during the Protestant Reformation, Cranmer and Ridley, found their faith immeasurably strengthened as both memorized the entire New Testament during the time of their persecution. Those who love the Bible will never find themselves without a faithful friend, a wholesome and wise counselor, the most cheerful companion, and the most effectual comforter of their soul.

Dr. A. T. Pierson suggested in one of his books about the Scriptures, that we should approach spiritual discovery much as the ancient Jews approached the Temple in Jerusalem. The outer Court of the Gentiles is analogous to the letter of Scripture. The Inner Court of the Israelites, a much holier place, is similar to the inner truth of Scripture; the Holy of Holies, the most holy place in the Temple is equivalent to the person of Jesus Christ Himself. It is only when we pass through the veil into the innermost Holy of Holies that we come to meet Him face to face.

The great men who founded the United States of America, including George Washington, were strongly influenced by their faith in the Word of God. President Washington once declared, "It is impossible to rightly govern the world without God and the Bible." The great writer, Charles Dickens, stated that the Bible is the Word of God. "The New Testament is the very best book that ever was or ever will be known in the world." Another great writer, Lord Francis Bacon, was the finest scientist in England in the sixteenth century and contributed much to the scientific study of nature. Bacon wrote a pivotal book, *The Advancement of Learning*, in which he called for a study to be made of Bible prophecy to systematically show how God had precisely fulfilled the predictions made over thousands of years. Filled with wonder at the creation of the world, Francis Bacon wrote: "Thy creatures, O Lord, have been my books, but thy Holy Scriptures much more. I have sought thee in the courts, fields and gardens; but I have found thee, O God, in thy sanctuary, thy temples." Although Bacon acknowledged the awesome evidence about God revealed by science and nature, he discovered that the most profound knowledge of God was found in his detailed study of the inspired Word of God.

Many Christians have personally studied the Scofield Reference Bible. However, very few are aware of the spiritual motivation that encouraged C. I. Scofield to embark upon the production of a study Bible complete with cross references and study notes to help the student explore the biblical text. When he was a young Christian, Scofield met a friend, C.E. Paxson, in his office and noted that his friend had marked his Bible with notes and underlined related passages. Scofield was initially angry at the idea that his friend had defaced his Bible with these personal markings. However, he soon realized that these markings were extremely helpful to his friend and assisted in his understanding of the relation between various passages. In his later life Scofield would declare that the inspiration of his friend's Bible markings would lead him to prepare the exhaustive study notes and research presented in the now-famous Scofield Reference Bible with its helpful footnotes, maps and cross-references. Truly, the Bible is a deep well that can never be exhausted by a student of the Scriptures. Those who preach constantly from the depths of God's Word will always have something fresh and meaningful to say to their hearers.

The Seven Wonders of the Word of God

We have all heard of the Seven Wonders of the World that have fascinated mankind throughout history. Yet, for those who will examine the evidence, the Scriptures should hold an equal fascination. The Bible also manifests Seven Wonders of the Word of God.

1. The wonder of its formation.

The marvelous manner in which the Scriptures grew from the first five books of Moses to include all thirty-nine books of the Old Testament and, then, the addition of the twenty-seven books of the New Testament in the first century of our era, is one of the greatest mysteries of the ages.

2. The wonder of its unity.

The Bible is a complete library composed of sixty-six books written by forty-four different authors over a period of sixteen hundred years. The authors came from different backgrounds — including kings of Israel, warriors, shepherds, poets, a physician and fishermen. However, the Bible is the most unified book in the world, containing a progressive revelation of the message of God without any real contradictions.

3. The wonder of its age.

The Bible is without doubt the oldest and most ancient book in the world, beginning with its first section of five books written by

Moses thirty-five centuries ago. What other ancient writing is read daily by hundreds of millions of people who find answers to their most immediate problems and concerns?

4. The wonder of its sales.

Despite the fact that it is the oldest and most popular book in the world, its continuing sales year after year are the greatest wonder in the field of book publishing. Scholars have estimated that there are far more than two billion Bibles published throughout the globe. Incredibly, the American Bible Society printed its two billionth Bible in 1976 and presented it to President Ford. Despite the phenomenal number of Bibles that exist, it continues to outsell every other book with several hundred million in annual sales worldwide.

5. The wonder of its popularity.

Despite the fact that the Bible was written over two thousand years ago by ancient inhabitants of the Middle East in an oriental form of literature, the Bible remains the most fascinating and intriguing book on earth. Every year the Bible is read by over a billion adults and young people representing every nation and class of people on the planet.

6. The wonder of its language.

The Scriptures were written in three languages, Hebrew, Aramaic and Greek, by forty-four writers. Most of these writers were not well educated, nor did most of them know each other. Yet the wisest men of every age have acknowledged the Bible as the world's greatest literary masterpiece.

7. The wonder of its preservation.

There is no other book in history which has suffered more opposition, hatred, persecution and outright burning. Yet, after thousands of years of opposition, the Bible has not only survived, it has triumphed over emperors, kings and dictators who sought to silence its message of salvation through the blood of Jesus Christ.

The Bible's Transformation of Society

Did the Bible actually change society? The answer is *Yes!* The early Christians startled the pagan world of Rome by their altruism and unselfish care for the poor, the sick, and the dispossessed. Despite the overwhelming wealth of the powerful Roman Empire and other pagan empires of Egypt, Babylon and Assyria, there is no evidence from inscriptions or archeology that these societies ever developed hospitals, housing for the poor, or any other provision for the unfortunate people in great need. However, early Christians manifested the love of Christ by caring for both the sick and the needy out of a pure altruism that shocked the jaded Romans.

Let us examine the social situation in England before the Evangelical Revival led by John and Charles Wesley that saved England from a moral abyss. The situation faced by England in the early 1700s was virtually the same as the current moral collapse we see in North America every day. Bishop George Berkeley wrote in his 1738 book, *Discourse Addressed to Magistrates and Men in Authority,* that the level of public morality and religion had collapsed in Britain "to a degree that has never been known in any Christian country. . . .Our prospect is very terrible and the symptoms grow worse from day to day." Berkeley spoke of a torrent of evil in the land "which threatens a general inundation and destruction of these realms. . . .The youth born and brought up in wicked times without any bias to good from early principle, or instilled opinion, when they grow ripe, must be monsters indeed. And it is to be feared that the age of monsters is not far off." Many different writers and observers, including Daniel Defoe, Alexander Pope and Samuel Johnson confirm that England was on the point of moral collapse in the early part of the 1700s. In the previous century the official Church of England had severely suppressed other Christians through strict laws, such as the Act of Conformity, forbidding Nonconformist (independent pastors who were not endorsed by the Church of England) from teaching or preaching. Many of the greatest preachers in England were driven out of their churches for refusing to accept these laws.

When the Great Plague of 1665 killed one in every five people in London, everyone who could, fled London, including most of the leaders of the official Church of England and the government. Many of the Nonconformist pastors ignored the laws and returned to help their dying congregations by preaching that the only hope for mankind was by trusting in Jesus Christ. Then the apostate government of England passed the infamous Five Mile Act which prohibited any of the expelled clergy from approaching within five miles of their former church. As a result of this continuing persecution, the Puritans and other nonconforming pastors were driven from their churches and from society. Over four thousand pastors were thrown into prison. Finally, in 1714, the Schism Act prohibited anyone from teaching anywhere without a special license from his bishop. The result of the suppression of the free preaching of the Word of God was the descent of England into a morass of immorality, perversion, and a widespread moral collapse. The writer Thomas Carlyle wrote his verdict on this society which could easily fit the condition of North America today, "Stomach well alive, soul extinct." The writer Mark Pattison wrote about the state of morals in this period as follows, "Decay of religion, licentiousness of morals, public corruption, profaneness of language — a day of rebuke and blasphemy." As the moral code broke down, with the teaching of the Gospel repressed, and the crime rate rising, the ruling classes naturally responded by fearfully demanding severe laws to restrain criminals. The moral debasement of England in this century can be illustrated by its savage laws which showed no mercy to those who violated them.

At a time when the writer William E. Blackstone was proudly writing about the glory of England's "unmatched Constitution" both adults and children were subject to one hundred and sixty different laws that resulted in hanging. If anyone shoplifted more than one shilling, stole one sheep, harmed a tree, gathered fruit from someone's property, or snared a rabbit on someone's estate, they would be hanged until dead. The evangelist Charles Wesley reported in his *Journal* that he preached in one jail to fifty-two people on death row including one child of ten years. Public drunkenness was so widespread that many adults and children died as alcoholics. Millions of children and women were working in appalling conditions in factories and mines with unbelievably low wages and no safety rules whatsoever. In other words, England was a moral and spiritual wasteland. Truly, the name *Ichabod*, "the glory of the Lord hath departed," was the epitaph that should be written over this tragic and most shameful century of England's history.

Yet, into this cesspool, God sent the only hope for England; His Holy Scriptures as preached by the greatest evangelists of that age, John and Charles Wesley. In 1769 John Wesley began the Sunday School movement that ultimately flourished throughout England teaching the Bible to millions of young English children. The preaching of the Wesley brothers brought about a spiritual revolution in England and the return to a true faith in the Word of God and its laws. John Wesley's preaching of the whole Bible transformed an immoral state into a reformed nation based to a great extent on the Word of God. As Wesley addressed three thousand people on one occasion, he declared these words from the prophet Isaiah 61:1–2: "The spirit of the Lord is upon me, because he hath appointed me to preach the Gospel to the poor; he hath sent me to heal the broken-hearted; to preach deliverance to the captive, and recovery of sight to the blind; to set at liberty them that are bruised, to proclaim the acceptable year of the Lord" (Wesley's *Journal*, March 31, 1739).

The incredible spiritual energy of this renewed preaching of the Gospel of Christ produced a remarkable series of Christians including John Milton and John Bunyan who collectively transformed the soul of that nation. Their faithful preaching of the Word of God produced a marvelous passion for righteousness and freedom that became the central principle of the Evangelical Renewal that saved England from moral corruption. John Wesley preached, "We know no Gospel without salvation from sin. . . .Christianity is essentially a social religion; to turn it into a solitary religion is indeed to destroy it." The revival of Christianity under the Wesleys and other great preachers of the Gospel produced a practical religion that transformed every aspect of their world. Wesley declared that "a doctrine to save sinning men, with no aim to transform them into crusaders against social sin, was equally unthinkable" (Henry Carter, *The Methodist*, p. 174). The Christian revival in England spread across the English speaking world causing innumerable souls to turn to personal faith in Jesus Christ. The brilliant writer, Thomas Macaulay, wrote about the Scriptures in the *Edinburgh Review* (January 1828), "The English Bible, a book which, if everything else in our language should perish, would alone suffice to show the whole extent of its beauty and power."

In addition to the personal transformations, this evangelical revival based on the Word of God transformed all of society. Many features of modern western society that we take for granted today, were the result of the great move of God produced by the Wesleyan Revival. The imprisonment of debtors and children was made illegal. Schools were opened to every child who wanted to learn in every parish in the nation. Harsh penal laws and child labor in mines and factories ended as a result of new laws based on the Scriptures. The evangelical movement created the first hope for prosperity and self-respect that the forgotten masses of England had ever known. Finally, the return to the Bible brought about the greatest religious transformation known to mankind. England was restored to greatness. Universal free schools, charities and free hospitals were formed by Christians who found their motivation in following the Savior, who said, "And ye shall know the truth, and the truth shall make you free" (John 8:32).

Bishop Davidson declared that Wesley was "one of the greatest Englishmen who ever lived" and stated that "Wesley practically changed the outlook and even the character of the English nation." In truth, it was the return to the Bible, the Word of God, that transformed England from a moral wasteland into a land based on the Bible and the faith of Jesus Christ. The only hope for North America today is a similar spiritual revival based on a return to the unchanging Word of God.

15

The Decision Is Yours

In the final analysis the evidence presented in this book regarding the authority and inspiration of Scripture should prove to any fair-minded reader that there is overwhelming proof that the Bible was truly inspired by God. This fact brings us to the place where there is one basic choice that each of us must make. For those who still reject the Bible, there are only two possibilities: either Jesus Christ is wrong or you are. The suggestion that neither is wrong or that it doesn't really matter is untenable because you are simply avoiding the real issue. The evidence presented in this book and the history of the last two thousand years proves that Jesus Christ is not mistaken about the truths He articulated. Each of us must decide if we will personally accept or reject the truth about Jesus Christ expressed in the inspired Word of God. Our answer to this question will determine our happiness in this life and our eternal destiny in either heaven or hell in the next life.

Our personal determination about whether or not the Bible is the inspired Word of God will depend on our evaluation of the Scriptures and the evidence we have explored in this book *The Signature of God*. However, God never told us, "Believe in the Bible and you shall be saved." The demons of hell know that the Scriptures are true, but this knowledge does not save them. It is significant that the Bible tells us: "Believe on the Lord Jesus Christ, and thou shall be saved, and thy house" (Acts 16:31). The clear message of the Scriptures is that our personal relationship to Jesus Christ will determine our eternal destiny — heaven or hell.

The Coming Kingdom of God

The ancient Scriptures tell us that there will be a generation of men at the end of this age living in the tribulation period who will endure the greatest evil ever unleashed by Satan. The wrath of God will be poured out on unrepentant sinners during that unprecedented seven-year period. Satan himself will be unleashed to attempt his final rebellion against Almighty God in his relentless campaign to establish his satanic kingdom throughout the earth under the rule of his personal representative, the Antichrist. However, these same Scriptures assure us that Jesus Christ will return from heaven at the moment the earth faces its final crisis to defeat the armies of the Antichrist and save mankind from certain destruction. The Lord will defeat Satan after a terrible seven-year period of trial known as the Tribulation. The prophets reveal that two-thirds of mankind will die in horrific judgments, wars, famines, and plagues during this terrible seven-year period. However, this final trial of mankind in this age will end triumphantly with the glorious return of Jesus Christ from heaven with an army of powerful angels and the saints of all the ages. When Christ finally defeats the evil leaders of the world, He will establish His righteous government throughout the world from His throne in Jerusalem. Ultimately, the sound of gunfire will be silenced forever, the terror of torture chambers will be destroyed, the horror of starvation and plague will be removed, the fear of violence and abuse will be lifted from the hearts of men and women. Mankind will finally experience true peace under the kingdom of the Messiah, Jesus Christ.

The Nature of God

What is the nature of God who inspired the writers of the Bible? For thousands of years men have attempted in every culture and society to imagine the nature of God. They have created God in their own image, in the image of the sun, moon, stars, the earth and a hundred other objects. Regardless of their philosophical speculations about the divine intelligence that created our universe, man will never be able to find the truth about God unless he is willing to accept God's written revelation regarding His nature and commands to mankind. The Bible, from Genesis to Revelation, reveals the nature of God as a loving, holy, powerful personality who is vitally interested in the lives and destiny of men.

Years ago, philosophers assigned the name *First Cause* to describe the intelligent supernatural power that must have created our universe. Someone once analyzed the nature of the First Cause by comparing the nature of the First Cause, the Creator, and the nature of the universe.

> The First Cause of limitless Space must be infinite in extent.
> The First Cause of endless Time must be eternal in duration.
> The First Cause of perpetual Motion must be omnipotent in power.
> The First Cause of unbounded Variety must be omnipresent in phenomena.
> The First Cause of infinite Complexity must be omniscient in intelligence.
> The First Cause of Consciousness must be personal.
> The First Cause of Feeling must be emotional.
> The First Cause of Will must be volitional.
> The First Cause of Ethical values must be moral.
> The First Cause of Religious values must be spiritual.
> The First Cause of Beauty values must be aesthetic.
> The First Cause of Righteousness must be holy.
> The First Cause of Justice must be just.
> The First Cause of Love must be loving.
> The First Cause of Life must be alive.

This analysis reveals that the First Cause of all things, the Creator, must be infinite, eternal, omnipotent, omnipresent, omniscient, personal, emotional, volitional, moral, spiritual, aesthetic, holy, just, loving, and alive. However, when we examine the nature of God as revealed throughout the Holy Scriptures we discover that the Holy nature of God is precisely that as described above.

Your Final Decision

The decision as to whether or not the Bible is truly the inspired Word of God is vital for every person because it will affect every other area of their lives. If the Bible is true then we are accountable to Jesus Christ who will judge each of us at the end of our life. However, if the Bible is not the inspired Word of God, we can safely ignore its commands and warnings about heaven and hell. In the absence of the Word of God those who search for ultimate truth are like a man searching in a strange country for a hidden treasure without the assistance of a map or a guide.

In light of the overwhelming evidence presented in this book for the inspiration and authority of the Bible any fair-minded reader can see that only a supernatural intelligence could have produced the Scriptures. *The Signature of God* proves that the Bible contains scientific, archeological and historical information that could not have been produced by human beings unless God directed their writing. However, there are many people, including some readers of this book, who will still claim they can't accept that the Bible is the inspired Word of God. The problem with those readers who still refuse to acknowledge the evidence for inspiration is not a problem of belief, rather it is their lack of willingness to accept information that challenges long-held positions. While such people can see the strong evidence supporting the Bible, they cannot bring themselves to accept the inevitable conclusion because they would have to abandon their previously held agnostic position to which they are emotionally and intellectually committed. In other words, the problem is not that they *can not* believe the evidence before their eyes; the problem is that they *will not* believe the evidence pointing to the Bible's divine inspiration, no matter how powerfully the evidence points to the authorship of the Scriptures by God Himself.

Many individuals who have rejected God and the Bible have a huge "investment" in their declared position of rejection of the Scriptures. When they are faced with the evidence that proves the Bible is inspired by God, they are threatened by this information because it requires them to think seriously about God and their responsibility to Him. Many people have avoided thinking seriously about Jesus Christ and eternity by hiding behind their denials of the authority of the Bible and its demands for a decision about Jesus Christ. However, in light of the fascinating evidence provided in this book, every one of us needs to carefully consider the implications. If the Bible is truly the Word of God, then every one of us will stand before Jesus Christ at the end of our life to answer for our sins. On that day, Christians, who accepted Christ's payment of our debt to God through His sacrifice on the cross, will know that their sins have been forgiven by God. Their destiny will be to live with God forever in heaven. However, those who rejected Christ's salvation and the hope of heaven as presented in the Scriptures will have to bear their own punishment for their sinful rebellion when they are exiled to hell forever.

The powerful evidence in this book that proves the Bible is truly the Word of God provides us with a confidence that we can believe the words of the apostle Peter when he spoke about the necessity of faith in Jesus Christ: "Neither is there salvation in any other: for there is none other name under heaven given among men, whereby we must be saved" (Acts 4:12). This declaration of Paul runs counter to the natural inclination of mankind to believe that all religions are equally true and that all roads lead to Rome. Many in our society today believe that, if a person is sincere, God will allow them to enter heaven. However, the Word of God declares that sincerity is not enough. If you are sincere in your faith, but have chosen to place your faith in a false religion, then you are sincerely wrong.

There is only one way to reconcile ourselves as sinners to a holy God. The true path to salvation according to the Bible is through personal repentance of our sins, and placing our total faith in Christ's sacrificial death on the cross. Every one of us has rebelled against God through our personal sins: "For all have sinned, and come short of the glory of God" (Romans 3:23). The Scriptures declare that our sinful rebellion has alienated each of us from the holiness of God and prevents us from ever entering heaven unless our sins are forgiven by God. "For the wages of sin is death; but the gift of God is eternal life through Jesus Christ our Lord" (Romans 6:23). The death of Jesus Christ on the cross is the key to bringing us to a place of true peace in our heart. The death of our old nature when we identify with Christ's death is the key to finding true peace with God. The only way we can be filled with the grace of God is to approach Him as we would bring a container to a well. It must be empty. It is only then that God can begin to fill us with His grace and spirit.

God cannot simply ignore our sin and allow an unrepentant sinner into heaven despite their rejection of God. God's absolute justice makes it impossible for Him to ignore our sins. God's holiness demands that "death," as the "wages of sin," must be paid for our sins in order for His justice to be satisfied (Romans 6:23). If unrepentant sinners actually entered heaven without repenting of their sins, their presence in the Holy New Jerusalem would actually turn that portion of heaven into hell. If you think carefully about it, sinners who reject the forgiveness and worship of Christ would not want to live in heaven. They would despise the holy living and glorious worship of God. The sacred nature of a holy heaven and the evil nature of sin make it absolutely impossible for God to forgive men's sins unless they wholeheartedly repent and turn from them. Only then can God forgive and transform us into sinners saved by the grace of Jesus Christ who cleanses us from our sinful rebellion against His laws. Although we can cleanse our bodies with water, the cleansing of our souls requires the spiritual application of the blood of Christ to our heart.

The Gospel of John records the answers Jesus gave to Nicodemus, one of the religious leaders of Israel, who asked Him about salvation. He told him that, "Ye must be born again" (John 3:7). Jesus explained to Nicodemus, "Whosoever believeth in him should not perish, but have eternal life. For God so loved the world, that he gave his only begotten Son, that whosoever believeth in him should not perish, but have everlasting life" (John 3:15,16). Every sinner stands condemned by God because of our sinful rebellion against His commandments as revealed in the Scriptures. Jesus said, "He that believeth on him is not condemned: but he that believeth not is condemned already, because he hath not believed in the name of the only begotten Son of God" (John 3:18).

The decision to accept Christ as your personal Savior is the most important one you will ever make. It will cost you a great deal to live as a committed Christian today. Many people will challenge your new faith in the Bible and in Christ, The British writer John Stuart Mill wrote about the importance of our belief in Christ: "One person with a belief is equal to ninety-nine people who only have opinions." However, the Lord Jesus Christ asks His disciples to "follow Me." That decision and commitment will change your life forever. Your commitment to Christ will unleash His supernatural grace and power to transform your life into one of joy and peace beyond anything you have ever experienced. While the commitment to follow Christ will cost a lot, it will cost you everything if you are not a Christian at the moment when you die. Jesus challenges us with these words, "For what shall it profit a man, if he shall gain the whole world, and lose his own soul?" (Mark 8:36).

If you are a Christian, I challenge you to use the evidence in this book when you witness to your friends about your faith in Christ. The proof that the Bible is inspired by God will not convince anyone to place their faith in Jesus Christ. Nevertheless, this evidence proving the Bible's inspiration may remove the intellectual barriers that many people in modern society have raised against seriously considering the claims of Jesus Christ. Once they acknowledge the Scripture's authority, they can begin to consider whether or not they want to accept Christ as their Savior.

If you have never accepted Christ as your Savior, the evidence in *The Signature of God* provides proof that God inspired the writers of the Bible to record His message to mankind. The Scriptures reveal that every one of us will be judged by God as to what we have done with His Son, Jesus Christ. Will you accept Him as your personal Savior and find peace with God throughout eternity; or will you reject Him forever?

You have seen the evidence. The decision is yours.

Yeshua Coded in the Old
Testament Prophecies

יֵשׁוּעַ

גִּילִי מְאֹד בַּת־צִיּוֹן הָרִיעִי בַּת יְרוּשָׁלַ͏ִם
הִנֵּה מַלְכֵּךְ יָבוֹא לָךְ צַדִּיק וְנוֹשָׁע הוּא
עָנִי וְרֹכֵב עַל־חֲמוֹר וְעַל־עַיִר בֶּן־אֲתֹנוֹת:

Rejoice greatly, O daughter of Zion; shout, O daughter of Jerusalem

Behold, thy King cometh unto thee: he is just, and having salvation;

lowly, and riding upon an ass, and upon a colt the foal of an ass.　　Zechariah 9:9

יֵשׁוּעַ

כַּמַּיִם נִשְׁפַּכְתִּי וְהִתְפָּרְדוּ כָּל־עַצְמוֹתָי
הָיָה לִבִּי כַּדּוֹנָג נָמֵס בְּתוֹךְ מֵעָי
יָבֵשׁ כַּחֶרֶשׂ כֹּחִי וּלְשׁוֹנִי מֻדְבָּק מַלְקוֹחָי
וְלַעֲפַר־מָוֶת תִּשְׁפְּתֵנִי כִּי סְבָבוּנִי כְּלָבִים
עֲדַת מְרֵעִים הִקִּיפוּנִי כָּאֲרִי יָדַי וְרַגְלָי:

My strength is dried up like a potsherd; and my tongue cleaveth

to my jaws; and thou hast brought me into the dust of death.

For dogs have compassed me: the assembly of the wicked have

enclosed me: they pierced my hands and my feet.

I may tell all my bones: they look and stare upon me.　　Psalms 22:15-17

יֵשׁוּעַ

וְתֵדַע וְתַשְׂכֵּל מִן־מֹצָא דָבָר לְהָשִׁיב וְלִבְנוֹת יְרוּשָׁלַ͏ִם
עַד־מָשִׁיחַ נָגִיד שָׁבֻעִים שִׁבְעָה וְשָׁבֻעִים שִׁשִּׁים וּשְׁנַיִם
תָּשׁוּב וְנִבְנְתָה רְחוֹב וְחָרוּץ וּבְצוֹק הָעִתִּים וְאַחֲרֵי
הַשָּׁבֻעִים שִׁשִּׁים וּשְׁנַיִם יִכָּרֵת מָשִׁיחַ וְאֵין לוֹ וְהָעִיר
וְהַקֹּדֶשׁ יַשְׁחִית עַם נָגִיד הַבָּא וְקִצּוֹ בַשֶּׁטֶף וְעַד
קֵץ מִלְחָמָה נֶחֱרֶצֶת שֹׁמֵמוֹת:

Know therefore and understand, that from the going forth of the commandment to

restore and to build Jerusalem unto the Messiah the Prince shall be seven weeks,

and threescore and two weeks: the street shall be built again, and the wall, even

in troublous times. And after threescore and two weeks shall Messiah be cut off,

but not for himself: and the people of the prince that shall come shall destroy the

city and the sanctuary.　　Daniel 9:25,26

Yeshua Coded in the Old Testament Prophecies

ישוע

מֵעֹצֶר וּמִמִּשְׁפָּט לֻקָּח וְאֶת־דּוֹרוֹ מִי יְשׂוֹחֵחַ כִּי נִגְזַר
מֵאֶרֶץ חַיִּים מִפֶּשַׁע עַמִּי נֶגַע לָמוֹ: וַיִּתֵּן אֶת־רְשָׁעִים
קִבְרוֹ וְאֶת־עָשִׁיר בְּמֹתָיו עַל לֹא־חָמָס עָשָׂה וְלֹא מִרְמָה
בְּפִיו וַיהוָה חָפֵץ דַּכְּאוֹ הֶחֱלִי אִם־תָּשִׂים אָשָׁם נַפְשׁוֹ
יִרְאֶה זֶרַע יַאֲרִיךְ יָמִים וְחֵפֶץ יְהוָה בְּיָדוֹ יִצְלָח:

He was taken from prison and from judgment: and who shall declare his generation?

for he was cut off out of the land of the living: for the transgression of my people was

he stricken. And he made his grave with the wicked, and with the rich in his death

because he had done no violence, neither was any deceit in his mouth.

Yet it pleased the Lord to bruise him; he hath put him to grief: when thou shalt make

his soul an offering for sin, he shall see his seed, he shall prolong his days, and the

pleasure of the Lord shall prosper in his hand.   Isaiah 53:8-10

ישוע

לָכֵן יִתֵּן אֲדֹנָי הוּא לָכֶם אוֹת הִנֵּה הָעַלְמָה   7:14

הָרָה וְיֹלֶדֶת בֵּן וְקָרָאת שְׁמוֹ עִמָּנוּ אֵל:

חֶמְאָה וּדְבַשׁ יֹאכֵל לְדַעְתּוֹ מָאֹס בָּרָע וּבָחוֹר בַּטּוֹב: 7:15

Therefore the Lord himself shall give you a sign;

Behold, a virgin shall conceive, and bear a son,

and shall call his name Immanuel.

Butter and honey shall he eat, that he may know

to refuse the evil, and choose the good.   Isaiah 7:14, 15

ישוע

יַחַד עָלַי יִתְלַחֲשׁוּ כָּל־שֹׂנְאָי עָלַי וּ חָשְׁבוּ רָעָה לִי: 41:8

דְּבַר־בְּלִיַּעַל יָצוּק בּוֹ וַאֲשֶׁר שָׁכַב לֹא־יוֹסִיף לָקוּם: 41:9

An evil disease, say they, cleaveth fast unto him:

and now that he lieth he shall rise up no more.

Yea, mine own familiar friend, in whom I trusted,

which did eat of my bread, hath lifted up his heel against me   Psalms 41:8, 9

The
Handwriting
of God

Sacred Mysteries of
the Bible

Grant R. Jeffrey

Acknowledgements

The Handwriting of God is the result of countless hours of research involving thousands of books, articles, and commentaries, plus countless hours of Bible study over the last thirty-five years. Although almost one hundred volumes are referred to in the footnotes and selected bibliography, these books represent a fraction of the authors who have influenced and challenged my thinking. However, the inspired Word of God is the major source and continual guide to my studies.

The Bible is under relentless attack today in the universities, the seminaries, and the media. Yet everything we believe as Christians, our hope for salvation and heaven itself, depends upon the total truthfulness and trustworthiness of the sacred Scriptures. I believe it is time for Christians to stand up and launch a vigorous defence of the inspiration and authority of the Word of God. *The Handwriting of God* is a small contribution to that defence of the authority of Scripture. This book continues the theme established in my last book, *The Signature of God,* that the Lord has clearly placed within the sacred pages of the Holy Bible evidence that should convince any inquiring mind that the Bible is the true and inspired Word of God.

My parents, Lyle and Florence Jeffrey, have inspired within me a profound love for Jesus Christ and His holy Word. Their encouragement over the years means so much to me.

A very special thanks to Adrienne Jeffrey, my niece, who has worked very closely with me through this entire project in the research and editing.

My heartfelt appreciation to Nancy Phillips, whose superb editorial skills have made this manuscript complete.

I dedicate *The Handwriting of God* to my lovely wife, Kaye, who is my inspiration, my faithful partner in ministry, and the manager of our publishing company.

I trust that the information revealed in the following pages will encourage you to personally study the Word of God and come to know Jesus of Nazareth in a deeper way.

Grant R. Jeffrey,
Toronto, Ontario

Table of Contents

Introduction

Can we trust the Bible? Does Scripture present the truth about God, mankind, and eternity? Is Christianity credible? Can we rationally believe that Jesus of Nazareth actually rose from the dead two thousand years ago? Is Jesus Christ truly the only way of salvation for mankind? Is it possible, as we approach the year 2000, for an intelligent person to still believe that the ancient Scriptures are truly the inspired Word of God? Is the Bible truly "without error" and trustworthy, despite the growing attacks on its authority in our generation? The answers to these questions are vital if we are to arrive at any meaningful conclusions about the Bible's claim that it alone is the genuine written revelation of God.

The Bible is certainly the most fascinating and controversial book ever written. The Word of God is unique among religious and philosophical literature. No other book in history has boldly and repeatedly made the absolute claim that it alone is the unique and authoritative revelation of God to humanity. The Bible declares in over three thousand verses that it is the Word of God. Both the Old and New Testaments abound with statements such as "saith the Lord." (Exodus 4:22; Hebrews 8:8).

The Bible is under relentless attack today both in the universities, the seminaries, and the media. Yet everything we believe as Christians, our hope for salvation and heaven itself depends upon the total truthfulness and trustworthiness of the sacred Scriptures.

In the first few centuries of this era Christianity suffered greatly from its outward enemy, pagan Rome. However, in the final generation as we look for Christ's return the greatest attacks on the fundamental beliefs of the Church come from those who profess to be Christians while abandoning every one of the tenets of the orthodox faith that have been defended by believers for two thousand years. I believe it is time for orthodox Christians to stand up and launch a vigorous defence of the inspiration and authority of the Word of God. *The Handwriting of God* is a small contribution to that defence of the authority of Scripture. This book continues the theme established in my last book *The Signature of God* that the Lord has clearly placed within the sacred pages of the holy Bible evidence that should convince any inquiring mind that the Bible is the true and inspired Word of God. I hope to provide you with the evidence from the words of Scripture together with the evidence from science, history, and the Bible Codes that proves that the Bible is truly the Word of God.

The issue that must be addressed by every inquirer is the question of the literal truthfulness and spiritual authority of the written revelation of God as it appears in the Bible. Is every passage in the Bible equally inspired, or are there statements that are purely human or passages that reflect an inaccurate knowledge of science? This is a fundamental question. Its resolution is vital for every human who desires to know the truth about God and eternity. For two thousand years, hundreds of millions of Christians have accepted without question that the Bible is an absolute "rule of faith."

In the strongest terms the apostle Paul declared that the Scriptures were written under the direction and authority of Almighty God. Paul wrote the following words to his disciple Timothy: "All scripture is given by inspiration of God, and is profitable for doctrine, for reproof, for correction, for instruction in righteousness" (2 Timothy 3:16). It is clear that the doctrine of the infallible Scripture is directly related to the divine sovereignty of God. If God is truly the supernatural Creator of the universe, then His written revelation would display the same characteristics of His sovereign, supernatural nature. The sovereignty of God's nature guarantees the accuracy of His written record.

Both Christianity and Judaism are historical religions whose faith and doctrines are based directly on historical events that were recorded by human authors in the Holy Scriptures. Christianity is based directly on the facts of the death and resurrection of Jesus of Nazareth, as prophesied in the Old Testament and fulfilled in the historical accounts of the Gospels. These remarkable events were observed by hundreds of living witnesses who were still alive when the written accounts were first distributed throughout the Roman Empire. This fact alone establishes their truthfulness to anyone who carefully considers the issue. Christianity would have died stillborn had the eyewitnesses to the miracles of Jesus and the events of his crucifixion and resurrection denied the accuracy of these supernatural accounts in the written Gospel accounts. Christianity could never have survived, let alone have flourished, in the first century if the Gospel accounts had been untrue.

The Bible declares that the whole of God's creation reveals His majesty and glory. The Psalmist David wrote these words three thousand years ago: "The heavens declare the glory of God; and the firmament showeth his handiwork. Day unto day uttereth speech, and night unto night showeth knowledge. There is no speech nor language, where their voice is not heard. Their line is gone out through all the earth, and their words to the end of the world. In them hath he set a tabernacle for the sun" (Psalms 19:1–4). However, while the glory of creation reveals, to any unbiased observer, that there must be a supernatural Creator, humanity needed a written revelation from God to confirm our relationship to Him and His plan to redeem us.

Despite the overwhelming evidence of God displayed by the wonders of creation, there are many people in our generation who still reject His existence and deny His divine revelation, the Bible. In this book we will explore astonishing scientific discoveries that provide overwhelming evidence that the Bible could not have been written by men alone. We will also examine fascinating new discoveries that will convince any impartial reader that the Scriptures were created thousands of years ago under the direction of a supernatural mind.

Despite the claims of the critics that the Scriptures are not historically accurate, the science of archeology discovers new evidence every month throughout the Middle East that establishes the absolute trustworthiness of scriptural accounts. We are living in the first time of human history that archeology is fulfilling the age-old prophecy of Habakkuk — the stones are speaking and revealing the knowledge of the Lord. This prophecy of Habakkuk was made over twenty-seven centuries ago. "For the stone shall cry out of the wall, and the beam out of the timber shall answer it. . . . For the earth shall be filled with the knowledge of the glory of the Lord, as the waters cover the sea" (Habakkuk 2:11, 14).

Some have responded that they personally feel no need to examine proof of the authority of the Scriptures. However, there are millions of people in our society that have heard so many attacks on the credibility of the Bible that they find it hard to believe any statements found in the Word of God. Those in honest pursuit of truth deserve to have their questions answered. As Christians, we are commanded by God to be able to give people a reason for our faith in Jesus Christ. The apostle Peter advised us as follows: "But sanctify the Lord God in your hearts: and be ready always to give an answer to every man that asketh you a reason of the hope that is in you with meekness and fear" (1 Peter 3:15).

The Bible declares that every one of its words is inspired by Almighty God. The word "inspired" means that God over-shadowed the mind and spirit of the human writers of the Scriptures, motivating them to write the precise words as recorded in the Word of God. The apostle Paul declared that all of the Scriptures, from Genesis to Revelation, was inspired by God: "All scripture is given by inspiration of God, and is profitable for doctrine, for reproof, for correction, for instruction in righteousness" (2 Timothy 3:16). Jesus Christ declared that this inspiration included much more than simply the thoughts of the sentences or even the words used to express those thoughts. He boldly affirmed that the very grammar and the spelling of the words found in the original biblical manuscripts as written by its human authors were under the control of the supernatural inspiration of the Holy Spirit of God. The gospel writer Matthew recorded His declaration about the inspiration of the Word of God: "For verily I say unto you, Till heaven and earth pass, one jot or one tittle shall in no wise pass from the law, till all be fulfilled" (Matthew 5:18).

The Handwriting of God will examine a number of the sacred mysteries of the Bible, including the astonishing Bible Codes. It will provide fascinating insights into the nature of God's revelation to humanity. It is significant that the apostle Paul wrote, "Behold, I show you a mystery . . ." as he introduced the wonderful doctrine of the future resurrection of our bodies from the dead, when each Christian will receive a new body like the body Jesus Christ had after He arose from the grave. Part of the mystery surrounding the Holy Scriptures arises from the great chasm that stands between the time of its composition and the modern generation in which we now live. The huge gulf between the world of the human writers of the Bible and our world consists of two thousand years of time, language, history, and culture. Although the Scriptures were written thousands of years ago, they still communicate to us the timeless wisdom of God with fresh truth regarding our life and purpose as God's precious creation.

The Bible has often been referred to as "the greatest book ever written." It has captured the imagination and love of countless generations of readers who have found within its pages the truth about God and a hope of resurrection from death that awaits us all. The Scriptures have captivated people throughout the centuries with its fascinating stories about biblical heros and heroines who have succeeded against great odds through the supernatural power of God.

Naturally, the other major world religions reverence various written books that also claim to be the revelation of God. The religious books of other religions include the Koran of the Islamic peoples, the Veda and Upanishads of the Hindus, the Tripitaka, acknowledged by the Buddists, and the Zend-Avesta of Zoroastrianism. It is fascinating to note that none of these other religious books claim divine inspiration (except for the Koran, as written by Mohammed). Interestingly, Mohammed acknowledged that the Bible is inspired by God. He called both Jews and Christians the "people of the Book," referring to our acceptance of the authority of the Bible as the written revelation of God. John Calvin, one of the greatest of the reformers leading the Protestant Reformation in Europe, spoke of the unique ability of this ancient Book to speak to Christians with the living voice of God. Calvin wrote, "It is only in the Scriptures that the Lord hath been pleased to preserve his truth in perpetual remembrance; it obtains the same complete credit and authority with believers, where they are satisfied of its divine origin, as if they heard the very words pronounced by God Himself" (John Calvin, *Institutes*, Vol. 1, 1536).

The word "Bible" is derived from the Greek word *biblios*,

meaning "book," which comes from the word *byblos*, referring to the papyrus reeds used to make the paper upon which the original words of Scriptures were written by the biblical authors. From the time of Christ until the fifth century of our era, the Scriptures were usually known by the name *biblia*, meaning "the books" of the Bible. However, from the fifth century on, the complete collection of sixty-six books composing the Old and New Testaments became known as *biblos*, or the "Bible."

The overwhelming value of the Bible, in comparison with all other writings that fill the libraries of nations, was illustrated quite well by an experiment conducted by a London newspaper several years ago. The editor of this well-known London newspaper sent a letter to one hundred of the most important leaders in a variety of fields throughout the United Kingdom. These leaders included powerful members of the House of Lords, members of parliament, respected university professors, well-known authors, and wealthy businessmen — a list that included a representative sample of those who lead British society. The question asked by the editor in his letter was this: "Suppose you were sent to prison for three years and you could only take three books with you. Which three would you choose? Please state them in order of their importance." The replies were fascinating. Ninety-eight of these leaders choose the same book as the first choice on their list — the Bible. More surprising than their choice of reading was the fact that very few of these men were religious. Most of them did not even attend church regularly, and others were open agnostics or atheists. However, these men knew in their heart, that there was no other book in existence that could give them hope, joy, and peace in the midst of the fear and loneliness they would feel, surrounded by those hypothetical prison walls.

The German writer Heinrich Heine wrote about the marvellous and universal nature of the Bible: "What a book great and wide as the world, rooted in the abysmal depths of creation and rising aloft into the blue mysteries of heaven. . . . Sunrise and sunset, promise and fulfillment, birth and death, the whole human drama, everything is in this book. . . . It is the book of books, the Bible" (*Ludwig Boerne*, 1840).

There are a number of unique features of the Bible that provide overwhelming evidence that the Scriptures are truly inspired by God. The Word of God is unique among all other religious writings of man, as indicated by the features discussed below.

The Authority of the Bible

Moses and the prophets of the Old Testament repeatedly affirmed that they wrote the Bible under the direction of the Holy Spirit of God. More than 2500 times throughout the Old Testament the writers used expressions such as "This is what the Lord says," or "The word of the Lord came to . . ." to affirm the divine authority for their inspired statements. In addition, the New Testament continually declares that both it and the Old Testament were inspired by God. The apostle Paul wrote, "All scripture is given by inspiration of God, and is profitable for doctrine, for reproof, for correction, for instruction in righteousness" (2 Timothy 3:16). It is significant that the last book of the New Testament, the book of Revelation, confirms the inspiration of the Bible in its condemnation of anyone who would eliminate or change the words of Scripture. The apostle John warned, "And if any man shall take away from the words of the book of this prophecy, God shall take away his part out of the book of life, and out of the holy city, and from the things which are written in this book" (Revelation 22:19).

The Remarkable Unity of the Bible

The process by which the Bible was actually created is one of the greatest mysteries of the ages. The Bible contains sixty-six books written by forty-four men using three languages —- Hebrew, Aramaic, and Greek — over a period of sixteen centuries. No other book in history was written over such an extended period of time. Thirty-five centuries ago, Moses wrote the first five books of the Law, beginning with Genesis, which describes the creation of the whole universe, including mankind. Over the next millennium thirty-four other books were written by a diverse group of men as they were inspired by God to record a series of histories, laws, poetry, and prophecy. Finally a great man of God, Ezra, rose to unite the Jews into a renewed nation, following their return from seventy years of captivity in Babylon. In addition, Ezra was inspired by God to collect together all of the thirty-nine inspired books and to publish this as one collection called the Scriptures. Finally, at the end of the first century of the Christian era, the apostle John completed his astonishing prophecy, called the Revelation, which completed the canon of the New Testament. The Bible was written by men from widely different backgrounds including kings, generals, shepherds, prophets, tax collectors, and fishermen. Some of these writers were highly educated, such as Luke the physician and the brilliant Jewish teacher Paul. Other books of the Bible were written by uneducated men, including the shepherd Amos and Peter, a fisherman. Despite the radically different backgrounds of the writers who composed the message of the Bible over a period of sixteen hundred years, the Scriptures speak with one voice in its presentation of God's progressive revelation of His plan to redeem us from the consequences of our sinful rebellion.

There is no question that the Bible is the oldest book in the world with the most ancient portions written by Moses and Job approximately thirty-five hundred years ago. It is truly marvellous that this ancient writing is read by hundreds of millions of people every day in their search for the truths of God in the pages of the Scriptures. Another mystery is that although the Bible is the oldest book in the world and far and away the most published book in history with billions of copies in print, the sales of Bibles throughout the world in vast numbers of translations and versions is unprecedented. Despite the billions of copies of the Scripture in print, hundreds of millions of new Bibles are purchased throughout the world every year. Scholars estimate that over a billion people representing every nation and class of people on the planet call themselves Christians. Despite the diversity of writers and themes, the most brilliant men throughout history have reverently acknowledged that this book is the greatest literary masterpiece ever penned by man. Lastly, the very survival of the Bible in the face of the greatest persecution and censorship over thousands of years is inexplicable unless God preserved this book as His inspired gospel of salvation through the blood of Jesus Christ. The powerful, life-changing spiritual impact of the Bible on the lives of billions of readers is unprecedented in history.

1

Can We Trust the Bible As the Inspired Word of God?

During numerous conversations over the last few years, I have often been asked why I believe that the Bible can be trusted as the authoritative Word of God. These questions are legitimate and deserve to be answered. Fortunately, answers to these questions are available. *The Handwriting of God* will attempt to provide intelligent answers to the many questions raised by individuals who are honestly seeking the truth about God and those who want to know whether or not they can trust the Bible. Some of the questions addressed include the following:

Why should we believe that the Bible is the only genuine revelation of God when the world is full of hundreds of religious books that claim to reveal the wisdom of God to mankind?

Does the Bible bear any peculiar characteristics that uniquely identify the Scriptures as the only genuine revelation of God?

In what way is the Bible unique from all other religious books that claim our attention?

The Bible's claim to be the true Word of God has been widely rejected by philosophers, theologians, academic scholars, and millions of laymen in our generation. Why then should we pay attention to the message of this ancient book?

The Denial of the Verbal Inspiration of Scripture

The Bible claims that the very words of Scripture were inspired by God as His authoritative revelation to humanity. "The grass withereth, the flower fadeth: but the word of our God shall stand for ever" (Isaiah 40:8). However, it is very common today to find liberal theologians, mainline pastors, and the secular media expressing a complete denial of the verbal inspiration of the Scriptures. Tragically, there are some who belong to conservative denominations, which have historically upheld the doctrine of verbal and plenary inspiration of the Scriptures, who are beginning to experience doubts about the fundamental doctrines of the Christian faith and the inspiration of the Scriptures. Those who have retreated from the ancient doctrine and inspiration of Scripture suggest that there may be some inaccuracy in the words that have been transmitted down through the centuries. Logically, however, any inaccuracy in the text of the Bible would naturally involve inaccuracy in the statements of the Bible. These doubters even suggest the possibility of errors in the doctrines of the Bible's written revelation. This suggestion of inaccuracy is simply wrong.

The denial of verbal and plenary inspiration is also a denial of the supernatural power of God to both inspire the original writers and to preserve His message through the ages to communicate His doctrines to mankind. Logically, if the Bible contains inaccurate language, then it naturally follows that the text contains inaccurate statements, and therefore, we cannot have confidence in the authority of any scriptural doctrine. Such reasoning would replace the Bible's authoritative declarations such as "Thus saith the Lord," that have guided Christians for two thousand years with vague and tentative notions, such as "this biblical statement may (or may not) contain the words of God." This liberal approach of denying the accuracy of the Scriptures strips the Bible of its authority and weakens its usefulness as a rule of life for those who seek to follow God's will for their lives.

Sometimes people's motive for the denial of verbal inspiration is the desire to evade the clear teaching of the Scriptures in some area that restricts their immorality or freedom of action. This approach to the Bible is ultimately founded on an assumption of inaccuracy in both the words and the specific teachings of the Scriptures. In the end, this position will inevitably lead to a denial of the Bible itself, and finally, a denial of the supernatural claims of Jesus Christ as God, who is the One who reveals His will to us through the pages of Scripture.

Consider the implications of the position held by those who deny the verbal inspiration of the Bible. If God is truly a supernatural being who has caused these forty-four men to write His message, then what are we to make of the proposition that He was either unwilling or unable to cause these men to accurately record His revelation to humanity? If God is truly God then it is obvious that He could both accurately inspire the human authors to precisely record His message to humanity, as well as supernaturally preserve these precious words of spiritual wisdom through the centuries by ensuring the careful copying of the Scriptures by both the Jewish scribes and later the Christian scholars.

I cannot image a God who desired to convey His instructions for life, salvation, and eternity to a lost humanity who would be unwilling or unable to preserve His written revelation so that each generation would receive the genuine Word of God. The question of the trustworthiness of the Bible is one that is fundamental to all those who take the Scriptures seriously. The issue of our personal salvation is at stake. If the Bible is truly the inspired Word of God then we can have confidence as Christians in our eternal salvation. If the Bible is partially the Word of God and partially filled with human speculation, contradictions, scientific and historical errors, then it is a totally different Bible than the book that has been read reverently by Christians for the last two thousand years. If we cannot trust the Bible to tell us the truth on every page than we are left without any reason for confidence in our salvation. Therefore, the question of whether or not we can trust the Bible as the inspired and authoritative Word of God is one that everyone of us needs to determine for ourselves.

One of the glories of true science is that discoveries are as true today as they were when the first researcher made the original discovery. Statements that are true do not change as a result of the passage of time. When we proclaim the biblically demonstrated truth about God and salvation as found in the pages of the Bible, we are dealing with true statements inspired by God thousands of years ago. His words are as true today as they were when the Holy Spirit of God first inspired His prophets to record His unchanging revelation to those who seek the truth of God. While we constantly seek to expand our knowledge of science, history, et cetera, we do not progress by abandoning those things from our past that have been proven to be true. Rather, we build on the truth of past understanding and seek further understanding of God's revelation by continued study of His inspired Word.

Consider the attitude displayed by those who deny the inspiration of the Word of God. If these scholars truly loved the doctrines of God, but were forced by their textual and scientific discoveries to reluctantly abandon the doctrine of inspiration of Scripture, you would expect that they would announce with sorrow in their hearts that Christians could no longer be confident that the Bible was absolutely accurate and divinely inspired. However, after three decades of reading numerous articles and books written by those who deny the inspiration of the Bible, I believe the evidence is overwhelming that those who attack the verbal inspiration of the Scriptures do so with great fervor and enthusiasm. Rather than sadly express a reluctant conclusion that they no longer believe that the Bible contains the true words of God, these liberal religious writers almost invariably denigrate the so-called "ignorant" and "unlearned" views of those Christians who defend the orthodox belief that the Bible contains the true Word of God.

Truth is unchangeable. Truth and scientific knowledge advance as new discoveries are added to our store of knowledge. While researchers constantly add to their knowledge, those scientific discoveries that were true a century ago remain true today. When we expand our understanding of an area of study, we add additional facts without abandoning true statements discovered in the past. The only way modern theology can legitimately abandon past biblical doctrines is on the basis that they are now found to be false, not simply that they are old. The attempt to repudiate orthodox Christian beliefs based on the Bible on the basis that they are "obsolete" is simply a manifestation of cultural bias or the modern infatuation for that which is new or novel, at the expense of timeless and fundamental truth. When modern theologians claim that fundamental Christian doctrines are "not suited to our generation," they are actually condemning the attitudes of this generation. However, the unshakable truths of the Word of God remain true long after these theologians are forgotten. Just as genuine science can only progress on the basis of its continuing adherence to the fundamental principles discovered in the past, it is equally true that genuine progress in our understanding of theology will come from our continuing adherence to the fundamental principles of biblical doctrine discovered through the ages by men of God who faithfully searched the Scriptures to discover the doctrines of God.

Many people in our modern society cannot accept the reality of the miracles and the supernatural events described in the pages of the Bible. However, if there is a God, by definition, He is supernatural and is therefore capable of both creating this universe and producing the miracles described in the Scriptures. A mother recently sent her son to a local Sunday School in the hope that he would learn some values from the teaching of the Bible. When he returned home she asked her son what his Sunday School teacher had taught that morning. He replied, "Well, they told us that the general Moses led his people to freedom from slavery in Egypt. She told us how Moses used his radio to call in an air-to-ground attack with advanced fighter planes and powerful tanks to defeat the armies of the Egyptian pharaoh at the Red Sea." His shocked mother questioned him further. "That isn't how I remember my teachers telling me the story" she said. "Well," said her son, "if I told you what the teacher actually said you wouldn't believe me!"

This humorous account illustrates part of the problem modern readers of the Bible have with the miracles and supernatural elements of scriptural history. Yet, we cannot remove one part of the supernatural element of the Bible without destroying its integrity as the authoritative and inspired Word of God. The Bible does not give its readers the option to pick and choose what parts of the Bible appeal to us and to reject whatever we dislike. If the Bible is what it claims to be, the inspired Word of God, then we are faced with a fundamental choice: accept its authority or reject its authority. However, many in our western society claim they are Christians who love the Bible but yet reject large portions of its testimony on the basis that they think that the Bible is out of date, insensitive to modern social issues, and judgmental on certain sexual behavior. They have set themselves up as judges of what portions of the Bible pass their personal test of acceptability. How can the Bible speak to them with authority regarding the eternal issues of salvation, heaven, and hell when they are unsure whether any particular passage of the Bible is actually inspired by God? Abandonment of any one issue in the Bible is an abandonment of the Bible in its entirety.

Those who denigrate the inspiration of Scripture often strongly assert that they have abandoned an outdated and ignorant view of the Bible. They claim they have replaced the outdated historic faith of the last two thousand years with a new sophisticated understanding that ignores the clear statements of Scripture and attempts to find the so-called "deeper meaning" of a "New Christianity" that has superseded the Gospel's literal statements about the historic Jesus of Nazareth. In the end liberal theologians abandon the very biblical principles that made Christianity powerful and capable of transforming the lives of men and women. These skeptics have replaced the living Christ with a New Age "Christianity." However, thousands of years ago, Jesus Christ Himself warned His disciples: "Ye are the salt of the earth: but if the salt have lost his savour, wherewith shall it be salted? It is thence forth good for nothing, but to be cast out, and to be trodden under foot of men" (Matthew 5:13). It is difficult for these people to worship fully the Jesus Christ that is revealed in the pages of the Scriptures when, in their minds, they have reduced the Scriptures to a collection of fallible opinions of human writers, who they believe were often mistaken in their statements.

However, a careful examination of the evidence will establish to the satisfaction of all unbiased readers that the Bible is truly the authoritative and inspired Word of God. In this controversy we should remember the inspired words of the apostle Peter: "For all flesh is as grass, and all the glory of man as the flower of grass. The grass withereth, and the flower thereof falleth away: But the word of the Lord endureth for ever. And this is the word which by the gospel is preached unto you" (1 Peter 1:24–25). The Jewish historian Flavius Josephus, who lived as a contemporary of the apostle Paul, wrote the following statement in his defense of the authority of the Word of God in his debate with Apion. In his description of the sacred books of the Old Testament, the historian Josephus declared that they wrote "according to the *pneustia* (inspiration) that comes from God." In another passage Josephus wrote, "After the lapse of so many centuries, no one among the Jews has dared to add or to take away, or to transpose any thing in the sacred Scriptures." Significantly, the Jewish scholar Philo, who lived from approximately 20 B.C. to A.D. 50, wrote about the authority of the Bible in his personal representation to the Roman Emperor Caligula. Philo stated that the oracles of the Old Testament Scriptures were *"theochrest oracles,"* which means that he declared that these Scriptures were produced under the authority and power of God Himself.

Does the Bible actually claim that it is truly inspired by God? Consider the scriptural evidence found in the words of the apostle Paul, who wrote the following declaration in his epistle to the Church in Rome: "What advantage then hath the Jew? Or what profit is there of circumcision? Much every way: chiefly, because that unto them were committed the oracles of God" (Romans 3:1–2). This statement by Paul affirms that the words of the Bible were not simply the words of men but that they were truly the inspired "oracles of God."

A Remarkable Description of How God Inspired the Scriptures

Throughout recorded history the proclamation of the message of the Bible has resulted in a response whose pattern appears predictable. First, the vast majority of the people reject the call of God to obedience and holiness in the Scriptures. Secondly, the elite religious, political, and business leaders almost invariably join this widespread rejection to the revelation of God's Word. Finally, a small minority of the people become believers in the Word of God and respond to the written revelation of God in personal repentance, obedience, and a genuine desire to see the will of God manifested in their lives and in the lives of their families. An example of the biblical record of this response is found in the words of Jeremiah the prophet, who was commanded to write his prophecies and deliver them to King Jehoiakim, the evil king of Judah. The nation of Judah was experiencing a period of total apostasy, under the leadership of King Jehoiakim, an evil king who hated God and His prophets. During these years of apostasy the Lord inspired His prophet Jeremiah to record His prophetic instructions to His Chosen People. While the leaders and the general population rejected God's written revelation, a small group of righteous individuals responded to the inspired Word of God with reverence and devotion.

This remarkable passage in the book of Jeremiah provides a unique insight into the process of how God actually inspired one of His prophets to record the direct words of God. It is fascinating to note that, even though the initial inspired words of God were physically destroyed by the actions of the evil king, God inspired His prophet Jeremiah to re-record these exact inspired words to preserve forever the declaration of God in the pages of the Bible. The prophet Jeremiah describes this event as follows:

> And it came to pass, that when Jehudi had read three or four leaves, he cut it with the penknife, and cast it into the fire that was on the hearth, until all the roll was consumed in the fire that was on the hearth. Yet they were not afraid, nor rent their garments, neither the king, nor any of his servants that heard all these words. Nevertheless Elnathan and Delaiah and Gemariah had made intercession to the king that he would not burn the roll: but he would not hear them. But the king commanded Jerahmeel the son of Hammelech, and Seraiah the son of Azriel, and Shelemiah the son of Abdeel, to take Baruch the scribe and Jeremiah the prophet: but the Lord hid them. Then the word of the Lord came to Jeremiah, after that the king had burned the roll, and the words which Baruch wrote at the mouth of Jeremiah, saying, *Take thee again another roll, and write in it all the former words that were in the first roll, which Jehoiakim the king of Judah hath burned.*
>
> (Jeremiah 36:23–28)

In this fascinating passage, the evil king of Judah actually burned in the fire the inspired written words of God recorded by Baruch, the scribe of Jeremiah the prophet, that warned of the coming judgment of God upon the wicked nation of Judah. Rather then repent of his sins, the wicked king Jehoiakim responded to the delivery of the written prophecy of Jeremiah by destroying the scroll. This destruction of the physical Bible has been attempted countless times throughout history, but the enemies of God have always failed to destroy His written message in the Scriptures. Just as King Jehoiakim tried to destroy the Scriptures, the evil Syrian king Antiochus Epiphanes attempted to eliminate the Bible when he ordered the burning of all of the religious scrolls in the Temple in 168 B.C. However, God overthrew the wicked king in

165 B.C. when the victorious family known as the Maccabees led the Jewish rebel soldiers to a miraculous victory over their pagan enemies. The Jews restored the system of sacrifice in the Temple, and the surviving Old Testament Scripture provided the inspired instruction that allowed the Jews to follow the Word of God.

Four and a half centuries later, the evil Roman emperor Diocletian ordered the destruction of the Scriptures throughout the Roman Empire in 303 A.D. However, to the amazement of the Christians, within a few years the miraculous conversion to faith in Christ by the Emperor Constantine ended three centuries of persecution against the Christians and their Holy Scriptures. In A.D. 325 Constantine, the emperor of Rome, sat down with the bishops of the Christian Church to affirm the essential beliefs of the faith based on the eternal Word of God. This remarkable history reveals that, despite great opposition to the Bible, the message of Jesus Christ continues to prosper. The history of this world shows that the Bible has triumphed over the violent opposition and indifference of evil men.

However, another key element in the revelation recorded in Jeremiah 36:23–28 is the precise record of how God inspired Jeremiah to create this inspired portion of the Word of God. Even though the king had physically burnt the original scroll in a fire, God commanded Jeremiah and his scribe to carefully re-create the scroll — word for word — exactly as the Lord dictated: "Take thee again another roll, and write in it all the former words that were in the first roll, which Jehoiakim the king of Judah hath burned" (Jeremiah 36:28).

The Original Manuscripts of the Scriptures

The above account is perhaps the most direct written record found in the Bible of how God actually inspired the human writer to record His precise revelation. This unusual biblical account described the destruction and replacement of the actual original manuscript on which the inspired prophet Jeremiah wrote the words of God. This account raises an interesting question regarding the original manuscripts of the Old and New Testament. When orthodox Christians affirm that the Bible is inspired and without error, they are referring to the original autographs or manuscripts, as written by biblical writers such as King David and the apostle Paul. Each translation in a modern language should attempt to reverently reproduce the inspired words of God in its own language. It is obvious that none of these original manuscripts are in our possession. Over the last several thousand years, these original manuscripts have been lost. As a result of the absence of these original manuscripts, some scholars have suggested that the claims that the original manuscripts are inspired and without error is meaningless. They are wrong. The claim that the original manuscripts are inspired and without error is fundamental and is supported by numerous statements from the Bible itself. Furthermore, the claim for inspiration of the original manuscripts protects us from the totally subjective interpretations of those who would deny the accuracy of the Word of God.

The tremendous scholarly work accomplished by the textual critics in the last century is supported by the exegesis or study of the historical background and grammar. The result of this scholarly work is that we have a high degree of confidence that the surviving manuscript copies of the Hebrew Old Testament and the Greek New Testament manuscripts are correct and accurate copies of the original manuscripts written by the biblical authors. The important point to note is that, as long as the words of the original manuscript were correctly and perfectly copied over the centuries, we still possess the precise inspired words of God.

As we will see in a later chapter that explores the astonishing phenomenon of the Bible Codes, recent discoveries by computer analysis of the Hebrew text of the Old Testament provide remarkable evidence that God has preserved the integrity of His Holy Scriptures from the time of their writing until today. Sometimes people have come to an incorrect assumption that there is major confusion as to the correct text of the Hebrew and Greek manuscripts that are translated into our present Old and New Testaments. However, the reality is that there is a tremendous degree of agreement between both liberal and conservative scholars as to the best text of the Bible in the original languages. Therefore, we have tremendous confidence that the Bible in our hands is an accurate transmission in our modern language of the inspired words of God, as delivered to the biblical authors thousands of years ago.

Does the Bible Claim That It Is Inspired and Infallible?

The Bible repeatedly declares that it is inspired directly by God Himself and that it is free from error. Several examples will prove this point. The Torah reveals that God actually wrote a portion of the Scriptures — the Ten Commandments — on tablets of stone with His finger. Moses recorded this event as follows: "And he gave unto Moses, when he had made an end of communing with him upon mount Sinai, two tables of testimony, tables of stone, written with the finger of God" (Exodus 31:18). King David confirmed the absolute accuracy and authority of the testimony of God recorded in the Bible in the following passage: "The law of the Lord is perfect, converting the soul: the testimony of the Lord is sure, making wise the simple" (Psalms 19:7). "For ever, O Lord, thy word is settled in heaven" (Psalms 119:89). Centuries later, the Gospel writer Matthew, who ministered for several years with Jesus of Nazareth, wrote, "For verily I say unto you, Till heaven and earth pass, one jot or one tittle shall in no wise pass from the law, till all be fulfilled" (Matthew 5:18). This statement declares that the very words and the spelling of words in the original Hebrew and Greek languages were inspired by God. The discovery of the phenomenal Bible Codes in the last ten years strongly suggests that Jesus was telling the precise truth when He declared that the exact spelling of the words found in the Bible was inspired by God thousands of years ago.

Years later, the Gospel writer John, the beloved disciple of our Lord, wrote, "For had ye believed Moses, ye would have believed me: for he wrote of me. But if ye believe not his writings, how shall ye believe my words?" (John 5:46–47). It is fascinating to note that Jesus compares the ancient words of Moses with His own words and declares that both statements are equally inspired and authoritative. Finally, the apostle Peter declared the authority and inspiration of the written Scriptures: "Knowing this first, that no prophecy of the scripture is of any private interpretation. For the prophecy came not in old time by the will of man: but holy men of God spake as they were moved by the Holy Ghost" (2 Peter 1:20–21). In this passage, the apostle Peter confirms that the authors of the Bible were directed by the power of God's Holy Spirit. This epistle of Peter describes the inspiration of Scripture in his statement that "holy men of God spoke as they were borne along by the Holy Spirit."

Some critics of the Bible's inspiration have tried to differentiate between the inspiration that is affirmed for the writings in the Old Testament from the writings found in the New Testament. These critics have wondered if the Bible's own declarations regarding its authenticity in the Old Testament is equivalent to the twenty-seven books found in the New Testament. However, a careful evaluation of the doctrines taught throughout the entire Word of God reveals that the whole Bible continuously declares that every passage from Genesis to Revelation is truly inspired of God; it is therefore without error. As evidence for this conclusion, we note that the apostle Peter wrote that the epistles of the apostle Paul were being twisted by the unlearned and the unstable "as they do the other Scriptures" (2 Peter 1:21; 3:16). In this letter, the apostle Peter clearly affirmed that all of Paul's writings were truly Scripture in the same manner that the whole of the Old Testament was Scripture. The twenty-one epistles of the apostle Paul comprise a majority of the twenty-seven books found in the New Testament. In another New Testament passage, Paul wrote, "The scripture saith, Thou shalt not muzzle the ox that treadeth out the corn. And, The laborer is worthy of his reward: (I Timothy 5:18). We should note that Paul's first quotation occurs in the Old Testament, in Deuteronomy 25:4. His second quotation can be found in Luke 10:7. It is fascinating to note that the apostle Paul connects these two quotations together and affirms that both statements are Scripture without qualification. This statement of Paul provides powerful evidence for the inspiration of the whole of the Bible, both the Old and New Testaments.

Even modern liberal New Testament scholars, including F. C. Grant and John Knox, admit that Jesus accepted the absolute infallibility of the Scriptures, as did the Jewish rabbis and Temple priests during Jesus' lifetime. Since Jesus and His disciples accepted the truthfulness of the Scriptures, those who follow Christ can be confident that the Bible is truly the Word of God.

2

The Bible's Astonishing Influence on the West

Western civilization is founded upon the Bible; our ideas, our wisdom, our philosophy, our literature, our art, our ideals come more from the Bible than from all other books put together. It is a revelation of divinity and of humanity.
William Lyon Phelps (*Human Nature in the Bible* [1922])

The British and Foreign Bible Society was created in the last century for the express purpose of providing the Holy Scriptures in every language to every individual and every nation throughout the world. This project's purpose was to achieve the universal distribution of the Scriptures throughout the globe. It received the support of virtually all levels of British society, from the aristocracy and royalty to the poorest subjects in the land. In addition, other Bible distribution societies were created throughout the British Empire to facilitate this goal. The virtually universal approval by British society of the Word of God was such that a well-known pastor, Reverend Benson, could write the following words in the introduction to *Benson's Bible Commentary*: "In such an age and nation, to say any thing in commendation of the Scriptures seems perfectly unnecessary; their truth, excellence, and utility being acknowledged by high and low, rich and poor, from one end of the land to the other. Who, indeed, that believes and considers the testimony which the Holy Ghost, speaking by the inspired writers, has given to the excellence of the Scriptures, can call their excellence in question?"

Another indication of the estimation of the importance of the Bible is found in the words of the brilliant writer Charles Dickens. He wrote, "The New Testament is the very best book that ever was or ever will be known in the world." When we compare the attitude of that society of two centuries ago to the contemporary attitudes of indifference or opposition to the Bible, we can recognize the vast changes that have occurred as a result of the continuing attack on the authority of the Word of God in this century.

Changing Attitudes about the Authority of the Bible

Charles Dickens' ringing endorsement of the obvious value of the Bible from 1815 illustrates the tragic transformation that has occurred in western society in the last 175 years. Today, the Bible, the greatest book ever written, has been almost exiled from our Congress and Parliaments, the courts of the land, and our schools. The result of this exile of the Scriptures is apparent to all who have eyes to see. The moral breakdown in modern society has produced an appalling situation in which America has a higher percentage of its population in prison than any other nation on earth. The level of crime and violence is frightening. The problem is that unless people are ruled by their own personal moral code, self-governed by absolutes of right and wrong, there will never be enough policemen or prisons to make our streets safe.

The beloved apostle Paul wrote about the great privilege that God had granted his Chosen People, the Jews. The chief advantage and responsibility they acquired from God was that "unto them were committed the oracles of God" (Romans 3:2). The apostle John revealed the overwhelming value of the written revelation of God to the Church in these inspired words: "Howbeit when he, the Spirit of truth, is come, he will guide you into all truth: for he shall not speak of himself; but whatsoever he shall hear, that shall he speak: and he will show you things to come (John 16:13)." The psalmist David declared that the wisdom and power of God was demonstrated by the fact that "He showeth his word unto Jacob, his statutes and his judgments unto Israel"

(Psalms 147:19). David concluded his praise to God for providing Israel with this written revelation in these words: "He hath not dealt so with any nation: and as for his judgments, they have not known them. Praise ye the Lord" (Psalm 147:20). It was Jesus Christ Himself who commanded His disciples as to "Search the Scriptures; for in them ye think [or rather, are assured] ye have eternal life: and they are they which testify of me" (John 5:39).

It is fascinating to note that after our Lord Jesus Christ rose from the dead and began to display His divine power in both heaven and earth, He appeared to his beloved disciples and enlightened their knowledge and understanding of the sacred Scriptures. Luke records these words of Jesus to His disciples about the revelation of God in the Scriptures: "And he said unto them, These are the words which I spake unto you, while I was yet with you, that all things must be fulfilled, which were written in the law of Moses, and in the prophets, and in the psalms, concerning me. Then opened he their understanding, that they might understand the Scriptures, And said unto them, Thus it is written, and thus it behoved Christ to suffer, and to rise from the dead the third day: And that repentance and remission of sins should be preached in his name among all nations, beginning at Jerusalem. And ye are witnesses of these things" (Luke 24:44—48).

These affirmations by Jesus Christ of the value of the Old Testament Scriptures, as well as the New Testament Scriptures, are as true for Christians today as they were during the life of Jesus. Unfortunately, a number of Christians today believe that the Old Testament is primarily, or only, a message to the Jewish people and that it has limited spiritual value for modern followers of Christ. Nothing could be further from the truth. The entire Word of God from the first word of the book of Genesis to the last word of the book of Revelation is equally valuable and precious for all those who claim to follow Jesus Christ as their Savior.

Unfortunately many believers neglect reading the Old Testament in the mistaken notion that God intended these Scriptures solely for the Jews. They have wrongly assumed that the Old Testament is of little use to Christians in our modern world. However, many of the greatest truths of God are revealed in the pages of the Old Testament. A careful evaluation of the New Testament reveals that both Jesus and the apostles continuously appealed to the authority of the Old Testament to support their doctrines and teachings.

For example, the apostle Paul wrote, " For whatsoever things were written aforetime were written for our learning, that we through patience and comfort of the Scriptures might have hope" (Romans 15:4). Later Paul declared, "Now all these things happened unto them for ensamples: and they are written for our admonition, upon whom the ends of the world are come" (1 Corinthians 10:11). Again and again Paul reminds his readers that the Old Testament is the bedrock of the revelation of God's great truths that form the foundation of the doctrines of the true Christian Church. He wrote to his beloved disciple Timothy to remind him of the foundation of his faith: "And that from a child thou hast known the holy Scriptures, which are able to make thee wise unto salvation through faith which is in Christ Jesus" (2 Timothy 3:15). The apostle Paul's most ringing endorsement of the inspiration and authority of the Scriptures is found in these words: "All scripture is given by inspiration of God, and is profitable for doctrine, for reproof, for correction, for instruction in righteousness. That the man of God may be perfect, thoroughly furnished unto all good works." (2 Timothy 3:16–17). In these words, from what many scholars believe is the last of the apostle's epistles, Paul confirms a fundamental truth: our Christian walk before God depends ultimately upon our conforming our life to the sacred words of the divinely inspired Scriptures.

The apostle Peter also declared the essential role of the inspired Word of God in the life of the individual believer in these words: "We have also a more sure word of prophecy; whereunto ye do well that ye take heed, as unto a light that shineth in a dark place, until the day dawn, and the day star arise in your hearts: Knowing this first, that no prophecy of the scripture is of any private interpretation. For the prophecy came not in old time by the will of man: but holy men of God spake as they were moved by the Holy Ghost" (2 Peter 1:19–21).

The reality is clear from direct biblical statements by both Jesus and the apostles that the New Testament doctrines are built upon the firm foundation of biblical revelation, as given in the Old Testament. This affirmation is proven by the frequent quotations by Christ and his apostles from the Old Testament — from the historical portions of Genesis to 2 Chronicles, the Psalms, and the great prophetic passages found in the later portions of the Old Testament.

It is fascinating to note the inspired words of Jesus Christ, following His resurrection from the grave, when He met two of His disciples on the road to Emmaus. After first reproaching them for not understanding the clear prophetic teachings found in the writings of the Old Testament, Christ teaches them: "And beginning at Moses and all the prophets, he expounded unto them in all the Scriptures the things concerning himself" (Luke 24:27). Later when Christ appeared to His disciples in the same Upper Room where they had celebrated the Last Supper, He announced, "These are the words which I spake unto you, while I was yet with you, that all things must be fulfilled, which were written in the law of Moses, and in the prophets, and in the psalms, concerning me. Then opened he their understanding, that they might understand the Scriptures" (Luke 24:44–45). Our understanding of the doctrines of Christianity depends to a great degree upon our understanding of the foundational truths found in the Old Testament.

When we fully understand the Old Testament revelation, we will begin to understand that Jesus Christ truly came to fulfill the law of God and to reconcile a lost humanity to God through His perfect sacrifice on the Cross for our sins. Then we can appreciate that all of the details of the Israelite worship in the Tabernacle and, later, in the Temple were a shadow of the ultimate fulfillment of God's plan to reconcile sinners to Himself through the shed blood of Jesus Christ at Calvary. Jesus of Nazareth, the Lamb of God, was prefigured in the ancient Temple sacrificial system.

Many of the New Testament books are unfathomable to Christians unless they understand the teaching of the Old Testament. In addition, the tremendous prophecies of the Old Testament enable us to grasp the marvellous sovereignty of God, as we witness the unfolding of these prophecies in the life, death, and resurrection of Jesus Christ. As we examine the forty-eight specific prophecies about the life of Jesus found in the passages of the Old Testament, written more than five hundred years before He was born, we marvel at the power of God to both foresee and to bring to pass His divine will in history. The pages of the Bible reveal astonishing details about the rise and fall of Assyria, Egypt, and Babylon. Although these powerful empires ruled the known world in their days of glory, the ancient Scriptures foretold that each in their turn would be destroyed and fall into ruin. Yet the Jewish people, one of the most insignificant of all of the many races inhabiting the ancient Middle East, were prophesied by God to continue to flourish to the end of time because they were God's Chosen People. Today, we look in vain for the Nabateans, the Moabites, the Edomites, or the Chaldeans — all powerful nations that fought against Israel long ago. The Jewish people still exert an incredibly positive influence throughout our world. Their influence is evident in medicine, science, literature, and many other fields. In a later chapter we will explore the mystery of the Jews' survival and their vital role in God's plan to redeem and reconcile humanity to Himself.

In the New Testament we find the revelation of the true character of God, as Jesus reveals Himself as the God of mercy and love, our gracious Redeemer, and the Savior of a sinful, lost humanity. The New Testament reveals the incredible sacrifice of Jesus Christ to reconcile mankind to God forever through His shed blood on Calvary.

The writings in the New Testament reveal the glorious nature and offices of Jesus of Nazareth, the Son of God who came to earth to suffer and die for our sins as God's perfect substitutionary sacrifice. The Gospels and Epistles reveal the true nature of the spiritual warfare that surrounds us in our Christian walk, as well as God's supernatural provision for our protection through our putting on "the whole armour of God." Paul commanded believers to "put on the whole armour of God, that ye may be able to stand against the wiles of the devil" (Ephesians 6:11).

The New Testament reveals our glorious privileges as Christians — most importantly, that the curse of death will be removed as the power of the grave is broken forever by Christ's resurrection power. The Gospels declare the resurrection glory that will be revealed in all who will freely accept the salvation offered through Christ's blood. The biblical writers tell us that our life here on earth is no more than a journey toward the Promised Land of heaven itself, where all who name the name of Christ will enjoy an eternal life of blessed immortality forever. An examination of the empty lives and dim spiritual expectations of those races that have never heard the Gospel of Christ reveals that the people in all ages and nations where the light of Jesus has not shined have lived in abject spiritual darkness without hope for eternal peace after death.

The Gospel of Luke recounts the wonderful promise that was announced by the priest Zacharias when he was filled with the Holy Ghost and prophesied in the Temple of the coming glory to be revealed in the birth of Jesus of Nazareth: "And thou, child, shalt be called the prophet of the Highest: for thou shalt go before the face of the Lord to prepare his ways; To give knowledge of salvation unto his people by the remission of their sins, Through the tender mercy of our God; whereby the day spring from on high hath visited us, To give light to them that sit in darkness and in the shadow of death, to guide our feet into the way of peace" (Luke 1:76–79). The history of the vast expansion of Christian missions throughout the nations of the world during the last two hundred years has fulfilled this Gospel promise, as the glorious spiritual light of Christ has been shed upon the lives of untold millions in virtually every nation on earth.

The Power of the Bible to Transform Lives

The transforming power of the Gospel of Jesus Christ is illustrated by an examination of the nations of central Africa that British and American missionaries explored during the last century in their desire to bring these tribes the saving message of the love of Christ. According to the writings of the explorers and missionaries Dr. David Livingstone and Henry M. Stanley, over half of all of the tribes they encountered during thousands of miles of exploration through eighteen-century Africa practiced cannibalism and other unspeakable pagan practices prior to the introduction of the saving Gospel of Christ. Truly, these peoples had sat "in darkness and in the shadow of death" until the glorious light of Jesus entered their lives. From 1800 on, thousands of faithful European and North American Christians gave up their family ties, their promising careers, and worldly success to travel halfway around the world as missionaries to share the wonderful truth that Jesus Christ died for our sins to set every one of us free if we would follow Him. As a result of their faithful efforts to share their faith, hundreds of thousands of African pastors and workers are now completing the Great Commission of Jesus Christ throughout the vast continent of Africa, where more than five hundred million people now live. Mission organizations estimate that over one thousand new churches are built every week in Africa today. Some studies indicate that up to half of Africa's population will be followers of Jesus Christ by the year 2000.

As an example of the marvellous power of the Word of God to spiritually transform both individuals and whole societies, we should consider the well-documented story of the events on Pitcairn Island. The true story of *Mutiny on the Bounty* has been retold numerous times in print, as well as in several famous movies. The fugitives from the mutiny on the British ship known as the *Bounty* took refuge on Pitcairn Island. They were hoping to escape the vengeance of the British navy. The following account was found in a quotation from the *Gospel Herald* (*7700 Illustrations*): "One part that deserves retelling was the transformation wrought by one book. Nine mutineers with six native men and twelve native (Tahitian) women put ashore on Pitcairn Island in 1790. One sailor soon began distilling alcohol. And the little colony was plunged into debauchery and vice. Ten years later, only one white man survived, surrounded by native women and half-breed children. In an old chest from the Bounty, this sailor one day found a Bible. He began to read it and then to teach it to the others. The result was that his own life and ultimately the lives of all those in the colony were changed. Discovered in 1808 by the USS *Topas*, Pitcairn had become a prosperous community with no jail, no whisky, no crime, and no laziness."[1]

Years ago an anonymous writer wrote a profound comment on the unique quality of the Bible: "Other books were given for our information, the Bible was given for our transformation." Throughout the centuries, those who have lived under the darkness of paganism and those who dwell today in spiritual darkness remain in the hopelessness of a closed grave, without purpose or meaning in life. To these people without hope, the universe is simply the accidental result of random chance. They dwell in a spiritual darkness of their own making, and, as a consequence, they live without hope or purpose in their lives. This bleak existential philosophy, which is widely taught throughout our world today, reduces life to meaninglessness. Relationships become mere accidental encounters. One cynical and ironic existentialist characterized his grim and pessimistic view of life as follows: "We are born naked, wet and hungry. From then on things get worse!" If we truly lived in a world without purpose or meaning then the ancient philosophy of the Epicureans — "Eat, drink, for tomorrow we die"— is a rational response.

Fortunately, there is an alternative view of life. Its meaningful purpose is revealed by the inspired Word of God and reverberates with hope, joy, and purpose. If we are living in a world of purpose and meaning, created by a supernatural God who is vitally interested in our lives, then we need to know the truth about our situation. Some who do not know the truth about the complete message of the Bible imagine that God wishes to curtail their joy and withhold from them the good things of life. Nothing could be further from the truth. Jesus Christ declared His purpose for humanity: "The thief cometh not, but for to steal, and to kill, and to destroy: I am come that they might have life, and that they might have it more abundantly" (John 10:10). The promise of faith in Christ gives us purpose, meaning, and an eternity with God.

In this day of government-mandated warning labels that must be affixed to packages of ant poisons and cigarettes, someone has ironically suggested that we might place a warning label on the covers of our Bibles — Warning: This Book is habit-forming. Regular use causes loss of anxiety, decreased appetite for lying, cheating, stealing, hating. Symptoms: increased sensations of love, peace, joy, compassion.

Testimonies about the Influence of the Bible

Some of the critics of Christianity denigrate the reverence that orthodox believers give to the precious Word of God. These modern critics suggest that the Bible is out of date and irrelevant to our sophisticated and highly technological world. Yet the enduring value of the Bible to provide an unchanging but totally relevant guide to the problems and challenges of human life has been affirmed by countless Christians throughout the last two thousand years.

In my earlier book, *The Signature of God*, I mentioned the remarkable study of American life conducted in 1830 on behalf of the French government by the brilliant writer and judge Alexis de Tocqueville. Alexis de Tocqueville was sent to America to study American society, its beliefs, and its prisons to discover the reason there was so little crime and so few prisoners in jail. America seemed a veritable paradise in comparison to the corruption and criminality that swept France during the period following the

French Revolution, a period in history in which the church and religion in general were totally repudiated by the French. After travelling across the nation for several years, Alexis de Tocqueville completed his study and wrote a fascinating book in 1840 entitled *Democracy in America*. He wrote about the true source of America's greatness as a nation and the real reason for her extremely low crime rate at that time.

> I sought for the greatness of the United States in her commodious harbors, her ample rivers, her fertile fields, and boundless forests-and it was not there. I sought for it in her rich mines, her vast world commerce, her public schools system and in her institutions of higher learning-and it was not there. I looked for it in her democratic Congress and her matchless Constitution-and it was not there. Not until I went into the churches of America and heard her pulpits flame with righteousness did I understand the secret of her genius and power. America is great because America is good, and if America ever ceases to be good, America will cease to be great![2]

Tragically, his analysis and prediction has proven to be correct. As America has progressively abandoned her rich spiritual heritage, based on the public and private reverence and teaching of the Bible, we have witnessed growing violence and crime from the lowest levels of society to the highest. Scandal and corruption in the highest political offices are now so commonplace that they seldom merit mention on the front pages of our newspapers. Our society has become so disillusioned by immorality and greed among business, military, religious, and political leaders that we are almost shell-shocked. Stories of sexual abuse of children and acceptance of bribes are so common that we rarely stop to register how far we have fallen from the high standards of public and private morality that existed in North America until the 1950s.

Can you imagine the shock of someone living in America in 1957 who had fallen into a coma that lasted for forty years, only to awake in 1997 to observe what has happened to our nation over the last four decades. He would be astonished. If he should ask the reason for this sorry state of affairs, the only rational answer would be to point to our society's public and private abandonment of the Bible during this same period. During the last forty years, the Bible has been relegated to the dusty bookshelves of our homes and libraries. The Bible is no longer considered relevant or authoritative by many in our modern educational establishments, government, courts, and even some churches. We have sown a wind of secularism, modernism, and flexible moral values. As a direct result, we are now reaping a whirlwind of immorality, sexually transmitted disease, corruption, and violent crime. The only hope for our national, spiritual, and institutional recovery is to return to the spiritual values based upon the unchanging Word of God that originally formed the foundation of our national life.

In light of the growing battle by secularist groups, such as the American Civil Liberties Union and People For the American Way, to banish the Bible from the courts, the schools, and any public places in our society, it might be enlightening to examine the attitude displayed towards the Word of God by the great leaders of the past who served as presidents of the United States. A small sampling of their publicly expressed views on the supreme value of the Bible is quite instructive.

The first president of the United States of America, George Washington, wrote, "It is impossible to rightly govern the world without God and the Bible." John Quincy Adams, the sixth president of the United States wrote, "So great is my veneration of the Bible, that the earlier my children begin to read it the more confident will be my hope that they will prove useful citizens of their country and respectable members of society." Adams also declared, "I have for many years made it a practice to read through the Bible once a year. My custom is to read four or five chapters every morning immediately after rising from my bed. It employs about an hour of my time, and seems to me the most suitable manner of beginning the day. In what light soever we regard the Bible, whether with reference to revelation, to history, or to morality, it is an invaluable and inexhaustible mine of knowledge and virtue." President Andrew Jackson referred to the Bible as the foundation of the nation: "That book, sir, is the rock on which our republic rests."

In a letter to his friend Mr. Speed, written during the tragic years of the Civil War, President Abraham Lincoln wrote, "I believe the Bible is the best gift God has ever given to man. All the good from the Saviour of the world is communicated to us through this book." Lincoln also gave this suggestion to those who wondered how they should approach the Word of God: "Take all this book upon reason that you can, and the balance on faith, and you will live and die a happier and better man."

In this century, President Woodrow Wilson declared in a speech he gave on May 7, 1911, "A man has found himself when he has found his relation to the rest of the universe, and here is the Book in which those relations are set forth." President Wilson was so committed to the importance of the Bible to the life of this republic that he called for daily Bible reading by all citizens to strengthen the moral fiber and destiny of the American nation: "I ask every man and woman in this audience that from this day on they will realize that part of the destiny of America lies in their daily perusal of this great Book." President Herbert Hoover suggested that the key to the unique strengths of American democracy and her stable institutions is to be found in the pages of the Holy Scriptures. Hoover wrote, "The whole of the inspiration of our civilization springs from the teachings of Christ and the lessons of the Prophets. To read the Bible for these fundamentals is a necessity of American life." Another president, the beloved Dwight D. Eisenhower, indicated his own profound love for reading the pages of the Scriptures: "To read the Bible is to take a trip to a fair land where the spirit is strengthened and faith renewed." Many more examples could be given but these quotations reveal the profound understanding of these great military and political leaders of the United States. This nation was founded upon the principles of the Word of God.

Those who love Jesus Christ as their Lord and Savior need to reawaken their passion for daily reading of the Bible. It is truly the source of our spiritual food and sustenance. I read a fascinating account of the profound love for the Scriptures that was experienced by a village in eastern Poland in the years before World War II, when the Bible was virtually unavailable to the average citizen. A few years before the war, a colporteur named Michael Billester visited this small village near the Russian border. A colporteur was a travelling missionary whose mission was to place Bibles in the hands of those who had never possessed the Word of God. When Bellester passed through this Polish hamlet, he gave a humble villager a Bible. The man read the Scriptures avidly and was converted. He then shared this precious Bible with others.

Ultimately, through that one Bible, more than two hundred villagers and farmers in the area became followers of Christ.

When Michael Billester revisited the village a few years later in the summer of 1940, hundreds of these new converts gathered to worship God and hear Billester preach the Gospel. Usually he would ask new Christians to share their testimony, but this time Billester suggested that each believer recite their favorite verse of Scripture. At this suggestion, one of the new Christians stood up and asked, "Perhaps we have misunderstood. Did you mean verses or chapters?" In astonishment Mr. Billester asked, "Do you mean to say there are people here who can recite chapters of the Bible?" It turned out that these new Christians so loved their precious Bible that each of them had memorized, not only chapters, but whole books of the Bible. Thirteen of them could recite the Gospel of Matthew and Luke and half of Genesis. One man had committed all the Psalms to memory. All together, the two hundred converts had memorized almost the entire Bible. The Bible had been passed around from family to family and read in their meetings every Sunday. The old Book had become so worn with use that its pages were hardly legible (taken from an article in the *Sunday School Times* quoted from *7700 Illustrations*)[3]. If every Christian today had an equally strong passion to read and memorize the precious Word of God, we would witness a spiritual revival and transformation of our families and nation.

The apostle Paul raised a profound question about our responsibilities as Christians to our neighbors and to those in other lands who have never heard the Gospel. Paul asks, "How then shall they call on him in whom they have not believed? And how shall they believe in him of whom they have not heard? And how shall they hear without a preacher?" (Romans 10:14).

The real question is, how can we who are Christians, in possession of the Good News revealed through the inspired Old and New Testament, fail to take every opportunity to share this incredible revelation of divine truth with those in our western society, as well as those in the rest of the world who have not yet encountered the reality of Jesus Christ? How can we who have received the unsearchable riches of God's grace and the glorious hope of redemption for mankind, as declared to us through the Scriptures, stand aside with indifference in light of the coming judgment on mankind if they choose to reject the only way of salvation promised by God.

The Bible's Influence on the West

When we examine the social situation in England in the years before the Evangelical Revival of the Wesleys, we find a moral abyss without hope. The Bible was not preached in the churches, and it was virtually unread by millions of citizens in their homes. Before the Evangelical Revival, led by John and Charles Wesley, public morality and spiritual values had collapsed in England "to a degree that has never been known in any Christian country."[4] A number of contemporary writers such as Pope and Samuel Johnson provided striking evidence that the nation was at the point of moral collapse in the early 1700s. However, into this great spiritual darkness, God mercifully sent the light of His written revelation of truth, the Bible.

Two centuries ago the Lord sent the written Word of God as the only hope for revival. Two great evangelists, John and Charles Wesley, preached their biblically based message of salvation throughout the nation. In 1769, John Wesley created the incredibly successful Sunday school movement, with the goal of teaching the Bible to millions of young children. Sunday schools prospered throughout the British Empire and produced a marvellous increase in understanding of the Bible in the hearts of millions. The Bible-based preaching of the Wesley brothers was used by God to give birth to a spiritual revolution in England that created a reformed nation based on the principles of the Word of God.

It is important to note that John Wesley declared that the Gospel was meant to transform both the individual as well as society: "We know no Gospel without salvation from sin. . . . Christianity is essentially a social religion; to turn it into a solitary religion is indeed to destroy it." Our Christian faith, if it is real, must reveal itself in our treatment of those around us. As a result of this revival, Christianity transformed every aspect of the society. John Wesley declared that "a doctrine to save sinning men, with no aim to transform them into crusaders against social sin, was equally unthinkable."[5] The Christian revival that began in England ultimately spread throughout the world, bringing millions to a personal faith in Jesus Christ.

Many people in our society imagine that many of the positive distinguishing characteristics of Western culture are the results of political democracy. However, I would challenge my readers to consider the features and institutions of our modern society: universal, free education for every child, regardless of wealth; virtually universal health care; massive charities; anti-slavery and child labor laws; women's rights; and basic human-rights laws. What is the true origin of these beneficial institutions that we all take for granted as the fruits of our democratic government? The answer will surprise many people, including Christians. These institutions and laws are the result of a "back to the Bible" movement led by the powerful Evangelical Revival in England and North America that began with the Weslyian spiritual revival movement in the 1800s. It is the application of the principles of the Word of God that produced the wonderful institutions of Western society that are the glory of our modern world. The Bible is the source of the greatest benefit that God has provided to mankind.

The return to biblical values by the evangelical Christian movement in the 1700s created the first real hope for the people of England to improve their lives since the first introduction of Christianity to the British Isles more than a thousand years earlier. The widespread reading of the Bible in the common language of the people produced the greatest religious revival in history. England was raised from moral destitution to greatness, as the biblical principles were practically applied to the challenges and issues of society. Free universal education, charity hospitals, anti-slavery and child labor laws, together with hostels for the poor, were created by Christians who were motivated by their love of Jesus to help their weaker brothers and sisters. It is no exaggeration to declare that the return to the Bible transformed the character of England. In truth, it was the distribution of the Bible throughout the Western world that transformed England from a moral wasteland into a country that was proud to send the Bible to every nation on earth. Our only hope for our nation's spiritual health today is a similar revival based on a return to the unchanging Word of God.

Notes

1. *Gospel Herald (7700 Illustrations).*

2. Alexis de Tocqueville, *The Democracy in America* (1840).

3. *Sunday School Times (7700 Illustrations).*

4. Bishop George Berkeley, *Discourse Addressed to Magistrates and Men in Authority* (1738).

5. Henry Carter, *The Methodist.* 174.

3

The Impact of Jesus on the World

The evidence is overwhelming that Jesus of Nazareth made a greater impact on the culture, history, religion, attitudes, and laws of the Western world than any other person or group of men. Unlocking the mystery of the awesome influence of the life of Jesus of Nazareth will enable us to understand who Jesus really is. The evidence that will be examined throughout this book reveals overwhelming proof that both the Old and New Testaments declare that Jesus is God. The acceptance of the deity of Jesus of Nazareth brings us to that point where we must choose to accept or reject Jesus Christ's claims on our life and soul.

An examination of the writings of many modern liberal theologians reveals that they have concluded that Jesus of Nazareth was simply a prophet, a man of God who was a great teacher and moral leader. However, they reject out of hand the orthodox biblical teaching of the Scriptures that Jesus is God. Consequently, liberal theologians and preachers usually reject the supernatural elements in the Bible that surround the life of Jesus, including His virgin birth, His miracles, and His physical resurrection from the dead. There are a number of logical contradictions in this widely held theory. This view of Christ completely ignores the tremendous historical evidence from the Gospels, as well as independent historical records that confirm the historical reality of the life, death, and resurrection of Jesus Christ. This historical evidence is explored in detail in my earlier book, *The Signature of God*.

As one confirmation of the historical truth of the crucifixion of Jesus, consider that the supernatural darkness that covered the earth while Jesus hung on the Cross was recorded by several pagan historians. Matthew recorded this event: "Now from the sixth hour there was darkness over all the land unto the ninth hour" (Matthew 27:45). However, a contemporary pagan historian named Thallus also wrote about this astonishing event in A.D. 52, only twenty years after the resurrection of Christ. Thallus wrote that the darkness totally covered the face of the earth at the time of the Passover in A.D. 32. The writer Julius Africanus, writing in approximately A.D. 220, records, "This darkness, Thallus, in the third book of his *History*, calls, as appears to me without reason, an eclipse of the sun."[1] Julius explained that Thallus' theory was unreasonable because an eclipse of the sun cannot occur at the same time there is a full moon. The moon is almost diametrically opposite the sun during full moon making a solar eclipse impossible. The priests of Israel carefully calculated the time of the full moon to set the date of the Passover Feast. The Gospels record that it was at the season of the Passover full moon that Christ died.

There are two important points here. First, a pagan historian who was alive at the time Jesus' death occurred has confirmed that darkness covered the earth at the very time recorded in the Gospels. Secondly, the fact that there was a full moon present makes it certain that this darkness was not an eclipse but that it was a supernatural event. Another remarkable historical reference to this darkness is found in the writings of Phlegon. He noted the seemingly impossible fact that this "eclipse" occurred at the time of the full moon during the reign of Tiberius Caesar as emperor of Rome. Further, Phlegon wrote that the darkness covered the earth for precisely three hours, from the sixth to the ninth hour, precisely the time period that is recorded in the Gospels.

One of the problems with this liberal view of Jesus as a mere man is the logical necessity that either Jesus or the Gospel writers must have totally fabricated the supernatural events of His life and resurrection. How can Jesus or His followers be credited with launching the greatest moral revival in the history of mankind if they lied about the events, miracles, and resurrection of Jesus?

How could Jesus be called a wise and moral teacher of ethics if He or His disciples engaged in the greatest deception in history — claiming that He was God and that He could forgive sins — if He was only a man according to their view.

In addition to these problems, there is an incredible and arrogant assumption in this viewpoint that suggests that the people living in Judea and throughout the Roman Empire in the first century were ignorant fools who believed stories about supernatural miracles without any logical evaluation or historical evidence. However, this view of the population of the first century as simple-minded is totally contradicted by the letters, speeches, and historical documents from that era which have survived the centuries. Both the Jewish people and the Romans were as intelligent as our population today.

One factor in considering just how improbable the liberal theory of Jesus as a mere man truly is the history of the growth of Christianity in the first century. If the liberal theologians are correct, then Jesus performed no miracles, died on the cross as a criminal, and was never seen again. However, the history of the period reveals that His disciples quickly recovered from their shock at His death and that, within fifty days, they met to launch the most powerful spiritual movement in history, which has impacted literally billions of lives. Furthermore, during the seventy years following Christ's death, hundreds of thousands of Christians endured the most horrible persecution, torture, and martyrdom rather than deny their faith in the risen Lord. Remember that these Christians refused to save their lives by denying Jesus' resurrection at a time when thousands of believers who were eyewitnesses to the events of Christ's life were still alive.

Another factor to consider is the transformation in the behavior of the disciples. What could possibly account for the sudden transformation from an attitude of helplessness, fear, and despair among the eleven disciples at the Cross to an attitude of joy and bold confidence in declaring the Good News of the risen Savior that these men demonstrated to the whole of the known world? The only rational answer is that they personally witnessed the resurrected Jesus of Nazareth with their own eyes and personally experienced His supernatural empowerment through the Holy Spirit. It is noteworthy that the writers of the New Testament repeatedly affirm that they were eyewitnesses of these events. For example, Luke the physician tells us that his written account is based on eyewitness reports. "Even as they delivered them unto us, which from the beginning were eyewitnesses, and ministers of the word" (Luke 1:2). The apostle Peter confirmed that he personally witnessed the glory and majesty of Jesus in His resurrection body. "For we have not followed cunningly devised fables, when we made known unto you the power and coming of our Lord Jesus Christ, but were eyewitnesses of his majesty" (2 Peter 1:16).

The history of this persecution, which began during the reign of Emperor Nero within thirty years of the Cross, reveals that these followers of Jesus were noteworthy for going to their painful deaths with hymns and prayers. Is it probable — is it even possible to imagine that hundreds of thousands of intelligent people would endure torture and martyrdom rather than deny their faith in the risen Jesus if they had the slightest doubt that He was truly God and that His resurrection, attested to by eyewitnesses, was the guarantee that they too would arise one day through His victory over death and sin? The only logical explanation is that these people were absolutely convinced that Jesus was the Son of God because they personally were eyewitnesses or they had heard from other eyewitnesses trustworthy accounts of the death and resurrection of Jesus. The staggering growth of the Christian faith, despite the most horrendous persecution, provides powerful evidence that these people were supernaturally motivated to reach the world with the good news of Jesus Christ. It is estimated that up to one-half of the population of the Roman Empire were followers of Jesus within one hundred years of His resurrection.

Does It Really Matter If Jesus Actually Rose from the Grave?

Some religious writers have questioned if it really matters whether or not the resurrection of Jesus actually occurred as an historical event. The answer: Absolutely! The historical truth of the Gospel account of the life, teachings, death, and resurrection of Jesus of Nazareth is of supreme importance to Christians today, as well as to all believers throughout the last two thousand years. If Jesus of Nazareth never died and rose from the dead on that first Easter Sunday, Christians are fools to follow Him. However, the overwhelming historical evidence proves that we are not fools. Those who follow Jesus Christ as their Lord and Savior are basing their life and their hope for eternity on the historical reality of the greatest fact and miracle in human history — the physical resurrection of Jesus of Nazareth. The apostle Paul declared openly that the historical truthfulness of the physical resurrection of Jesus was the foundation and most essential truth of Christianity: "And if Christ be not risen, then is our preaching vain, and your faith is also vain" (1 Corinthians 15:14). Paul correctly announced that our faith in Christ would be in vain and a useless lie if Jesus' body was still in the ground. Furthermore, he logically pointed out that the forgiveness of our sins and, consequently, our reconciliation with God in heaven are totally dependent upon the fact that Jesus, as the Son of God, paid the price of our sins on the Cross and rose victorious over death and sin. Paul wrote, "And if Christ be not raised, your faith is vain; ye are yet in your sins" (1 Corinthians 15:17).

It is interesting to note that the doctrine of physical resurrection from the dead was held by many Jews during the time of Christ, as well as in later centuries. Paul appealed to this faith in the resurrection, held by the Pharisees, during his trial. The Jewish Talmud that records in great detail the theology and doctrines of the ancient Jewish faith makes this statement about the resurrection: "He who maintains that the resurrection is not a biblical doctrine has no share in the world to come" (*Mishneh Sanhedrin* 10.1. c. 200). From Genesis to Revelation, the Bible teaches us that the purpose of the life, death, and resurrection of Jesus is to reconcile a lost and sinful humanity to our holy God through His perfect sacrifice of His innocent blood in full payment of the price of our sins. The Word of God teaches us that Jesus, the Son of God, demonstrated His power to defeat sin and death forever through His resurrection

Some liberal and agnostic scholars argue that the examination of the validity of the historical evidence about Jesus of Nazareth is a waste of time. While many scholars concede that the archeological and manuscript evidence confirms the historical reality of the life and death of Jesus Christ as Christians affirm, they claim that this has little, if any, religious importance today. Some liberal theologians argue, "What difference does it ultimately make whether or not Jesus was actually born in Bethlehem as the son of Mary and lived with his family in Nazareth?" These liberals ask, "What is the relevance of the fact that Jesus taught for three and one-half years and was crucified by Rome on a charge of sedition, as long as we can spiritually experience the inner Christ and live our lives in the light of His inspired teachings?" They believe they can escape from guilt for sin and find meaning for their lives through the mere idea of Christ's atonement of our sins as portrayed by the symbolic "myth" of the death of Jesus on the Cross. Modern liberal theologians argue that, if Jesus the Christ, "God incarnated in man," lives within our spirits, it matters very little whether or not the historic Jesus, the physical son of Mary, actually lived and died in Israel two thousand years ago. However, they are absolutely wrong!

It matters very much whether or not Jesus of Nazareth actually lived, died, and rose from the dead two thousand years ago. If the critics are correct and the Gospels are merely myths, then we are still trapped in our guilt and sins. The forgiveness of our sins and our hope for redemption and an eternity in heaven with God depend on the historical reality of the actual sacrifice of the blood of the Lamb of God to atone for our sins on the Cross. If Jesus never lived, died, and rose from the dead as the Gospels record, the symbol of "Christ" would lose all of its relevance and meaning. The word "Christ" would simply become an imaginary religious concept that would be divested of all objective reality. Divorced from the historical Jesus of Nazareth, as taught in the inspired Scriptures, this subjective "Christ" can mean anything one chooses it to mean.

However, there is another matter to consider. If the liberal theologians are correct in their belief that Jesus was basically a myth, it is virtually impossible to understand how the dynamic Christian faith could have come into existence among a group of intensely persecuted people who chose to die in martyrdom for their faith in the reality of the resurrected Jesus and His divinity. How could the concept of "Christ" have incarnated itself in the hearts of hundreds of millions of people throughout the Roman Empire if there was no actual historical Jesus of Nazareth who rose from the grave to inspire this extraordinary religion? The only reasonable answer is that this extraordinary religion of Christianity could not have occurred unless Jesus of Nazareth actually lived, died, and rose from the dead, as the Gospels affirm.

The Bible's Progressive Revelation of God

In Genesis, we witness the God of power in His marvellous powers of creation. In the Torah, we find the record of the history of the Patriarchs, their Exodus from Egypt, and the giving of the Law. We witness the God of justice and mercy revealed in the pages of the Scriptures. In the balance of the Old Testament, especially the Psalms, Proverbs, and Ecclesiastes, we see the God of wisdom. However, in the Gospels, we finally receive the revelation of the God of love and mercy revealed in Jesus Christ.

The Gospel of John records that three women each named Mary, were present at the crucifixion of Jesus. "Now there stood by the cross of Jesus His mother, and His mother's sister, Mary the wife of Cleophas, and Mary Magdalene. When Jesus therefore saw His mother, and the disciple [John] standing by, whom He loved, He saith unto His mother, Woman, behold thy son! Then saith He to the disciple [John], Behold thy mother! And from that hour that disciple took her unto his own home" (John 19:25–27). This moving passage reveals the profound love of Jesus for His mother, Mary, and His loyal friend John. In the primitive attitudes of the ancient Middle East, it was common for a rabbi to comment "Thank God that I was not born a woman" as part of his customary morning prayers. Some of the peoples in the ancient Middle East denied that women even possessed souls. The status of women in the time preceding the life of Jesus was very restricted in comparison to that of men. In contrast to this ancient attitude that tended to minimize the role of women, Jesus surrounded Himself with women disciples who were often the first to recognize Him as their Messiah and respond to His message about the need for personal repentance. In this way, Jesus elevated forever the role of women by treating them as equal in spiritual and social value to men. Edith Hamilton wrote that "the Bible is the only literature in the world up to our century which looks at women as human beings, no better and no worse than men."[2]

Despite the constant attacks in our generation on the biblical doctrine that Jesus is the Son of God, the world's fascination with the character and teachings of Jesus continue to grow with each generation. Sometimes it seems as though the critics are winning, but the truth is that the Christian faith has triumphed throughout the globe to the point that more than a billion people today acknowledge Jesus of Nazareth as the Son of God. The spiritual history of the last two thousand years reveals an astonishing increase in the numbers who follow Christ over the centuries. The profound and lasting spiritual influence of the teachings of Jesus and the significance of His death and resurrection are beyond calculation. Jesus personally transformed the formal, ceremonial, and external religion of Temple worship into a powerful and spiritually dynamic experience with God for each individual believer. He introduced humanity to a universal faith that united all men and women as the children of God under the providence of our heavenly Father. Thus, Jesus Christ made possible a previously unknown brotherhood of man that transcended race and ethnic backgrounds. Jesus changed our age-old fear of death into a glorious anticipation of being reunited with Him in a heaven of indescribable splendor. Further, He guaranteed our own immortality through His glorious victory over death and the grave.

Jesus introduced humanity to a new revelation of the fundamental law and command of God — that we should love God with our whole mind, body, and soul. In addition, Jesus taught us to love our neighbour as ourselves. He went further and taught us the revolutionary concept that we should love our enemies and care for those who hurt us. By working as a carpenter in Joseph's business for many years, Jesus honored physical labor and acknowledged the value of those who toil. This was a radical change in attitude because the aristocracy and priesthood of the ancient world usually looked with contempt upon those who toiled for a living. The Lord also changed forever the way adults would look at children by surrounding Himself with young people and declaring "of such is the kingdom of God." This was a revolutionary change in attitude from the prevailing ancient cultural attitude that held children to be of little value. Jesus elevated forever the precious value of every single person regardless of their position, capabilities, age, sex, or race because each of us is made in the image of God. These principles taught by Jesus motivated the reformers during the past several centuries to finally put an end to slavery. The prominent position of women as followers of Jesus and His dignified treatment of women ultimately led to a transformation of the rights and roles for women in Western society. If we will examine the lives and attitudes of the great reformers of the past and present, we will often find that the wellspring of their motivation to improve their society is their love of Jesus Christ and the inspiration they derive from the contemplation of His life and teachings, as found in the Word of God.

The writer Madonna Kolbenschlag wrote a fascinating book in 1988, called *Lost In the Land of Oz*, in which she describe the central role of Jesus Christ to the essence of Christianity: "For the Christian, Jesus is the Way. All things are measured by his Way: by his healing grace, his call to forgiveness and purity of heart, nonviolence and a concern for justice; by his relinquishment of earthly power and dominance; affection of agape (sacrificial Love) as a new basis for kinship, of change of heart as the requirement for righteousness, and of the transcendent power of suffering."[3]

One Solitary Life

Years ago an anonymous writer summed up the extraordinary influence and impact of human life of the one solitary life of Jesus of Nazareth. While many of us have read this beloved passage it is worthy of repetition because these words reveal the awesome influence of the life of Jesus as the Son of God.

He was born in an obscure village, the child of a peasant woman. Until He was thirty, He worked in a carpenter shop and then for three years He was an itinerant preacher. He wrote no books. He held no office. He never owned a home. He was never in a big city. He never travelled two hundred miles from the place He was born. He never did any of the things that usually accompany greatness. The authorities condemned His teachings. His friends deserted Him. One betrayed Him to His enemies for a paltry sum. One denied Him. He went through the mockery of a trial. He was nailed upon a cross between two thieves. While He was dying, His executioners gambled for the only piece of property He owned on earth: His coat. When He was dead He was taken down and laid in a borrowed grave.

Nineteen centuries have come and gone, yet today He is the crowning glory of the human race, the adored leader of hundreds of millions of the earth's inhabitants. All the armies that ever marched and all the navies that were ever built and all the parliaments that ever sat and all the rulers that ever reigned — put together — have not affected the life of man upon this earth so profoundly as that One Solitary Life.[4]

Notes

1. Julius Africanus. *Ante Nicene Fathers.* 200.

2. Spokesmen For God: The Great Teachers of the Old Testament. 1948.

3. Madonna Kolbenschlag. *Lost in the Land of Oz.* 1988.

4. Anonymous writer.

4

The Incredible History of The Bible

The remarkable history of the writing, the preservation, and the profound influence of the Bible on the Western world is an extraordinary story that will help us to understand our Western culture and history.

How Did We Get Our Present Bible?

King David was a man greatly beloved by God. David was a very passionate man who loved God and His Scriptures with all of his heart, mind, and soul. In addition to his diligent study of the Bible, God inspired David to record His inspired words for the instruction of future generations. The psalmist wrote these words, "Thy word is a lamp unto my feet, and a light unto my path" (Psalms 119:105). However, David knew that a mere reading of the Word of God would not transform our lives. Rather, he taught us that those who desire to know God must study the Scriptures with the assistance of the Holy Spirit to gain a deeper understanding of the great truths that will change our lives. David wrote, "I am thy servant; give me understanding, that I may know thy testimonies" (Psalms 119:125). It is vital that Christians understand the history of both the creation of the Bible and how the Word of God was supernaturally preserved and translated through the ages. Unfortunately, few people today know the remarkable history of how the Bible was created and preserved. This study will produce a greater confidence in God's miraculous preservation of His inspired Scriptures from the ancient times, when the biblical writer recorded the inspired words of God, down through the centuries until these words were printed recently in your personal Bible.

The Canon of the Old Testament

Both Jewish and Christian scholars generally agree that Ezra, the great leader of the Jewish captives who returned to Israel from Babylon in 536 B.C., collected all of the sacred scrolls of the Hebrews and published them as the Scriptures (our Old Testament). During the earlier reign of King Josiah, a priest by the name of Hilkiah found a scroll in the Temple that contained the written law of God. The righteous king commanded that the people join him in the Temple to hear his reading of the Scriptures (2 Kings 22). King Josiah led his people in a genuine revival of worship, based on the laws of God as revealed in the Torah. However, this history of King Josiah's revival explains that the Scriptures were suppressed for many years by the previous wicked kings of Judah and Israel, including the evil King Manasseh. This spiritual revival under the leadership of King Josiah led to a renewal of the reading of the scrolls of the Scriptures, which the Jews ultimately carried to Babylon during their seventy years of captivity.

When the Jewish exiles returned to the Promised Land God raised up Ezra as their spiritual and political leader to restore both the nation and their religious worship. Ezra gathered together all of the available scrolls, including the five books of the Law, the historical records, the prophetic writings, the Psalms, and all the other scrolls. Under the supernatural inspiration of God, Ezra prepared a complete edition of these sacred writings and thus established the canon of the Old Testament Scriptures. The word *Canon* is derived from a Hebrew and Greek source meaning a type of cane or measuring rod. The word canon was first used as a reference to the approved, authoritative, and inspired books of the Bible by bishops of the Christian Church during the fourth century after Christ.

Ezra divided these sacred scrolls into three sections: (1) The Torah (the Law or Pentateuch); (2) Nevi'im (the Prophets); (3) The

Ketuvim, or Hagiographa (the Holy Writings). The Jewish historian Josephus, who lived at the time of the apostle Paul, mentions
this threefold division of the Hebrew Scriptures in his history of
the Jewish people: "We have only twenty-two books which we
believe to be of divine authority, of which five are the books of
Moses. From the death of Moses to the reign of Artaxerxes, the son
of Xerxes king of Persia, the prophets who succeeded Moses have
written in thirteen books. The remaining four books contain
hymns to God, and moral precepts for the conduct of life." It is
likely that the books of Chronicles, Ezra, Nehemiah, Esther, and
Malachi were placed in the canon of Holy Scripture during the
lifetime of Simon the Just, the last of the great religious leaders of
the Great Synagogue.

The Jews refer to the Hebrew Bible (the Old Testament) as the
"Tanakh." This word is derived phonetically as an acronym from
the Hebrew words for the three divisions: Torah — Nevi'im —
Ketuvim = TaNaKh. Naturally many Jews resent the Christian
identification of their sacred books of Tanakh as the Old Testament because they reject the concept that God has added twenty-
seven additional, inspired books of Scripture to the Bible in the
form of the New Testament. However, God Himself chose to refer
to this new revelation of His covenant as His "new covenant" in
the words of the prophet Jeremiah: "Behold, the days come, saith
the Lord, that I will make a new covenant with the house of Israel,
and with the house of Judah" (Jeremiah 31:31). The word
"testament" that is universally used by Christians to refer to both
sections of the Bible is derived from the words of Jesus Christ in
the Gospel account of the Last Supper with His disciples: "For this
is my blood of the new testament, which is shed for many for the
remission of sins" (Matthew 26:28). The word "testament" is
related to a will or a covenant that disposes of one's estate after
their death. The expressions "Old Covenant" and "New Covenant" would be equally accurate names for the Old and New
Testaments.

The first section of the Hebrew Bible, the Torah or Law, con-
tains five books: Genesis, Exodus, Leviticus, Numbers, and
Deuteronomy. The second section, The Prophets, contains Joshua,
Judges-Ruth, Samuel, Kings, Isaiah, Jeremiah-Lamentations,
Ezekiel, Daniel, a scroll with the twelve Minor Prophets, Job, Ezra,
Nehemiah, and the book of Esther. The third section, the

Hagiographa (the Writings) include the Psalms, Proverbs, Ecclesiastes, and Song of Solomon.

It is interesting to note that the number of books or scrolls in the Old Testament has changed from ancient times, but the total inspired text of the Scriptures was preserved faultlessly by God's providence. While the arrangement of the Scriptures changed, the inspired text of the Bible was not altered in the slightest. The Jews joined together several related books such as 1 and 2 Samuel into one book called Samuel. The following sets of books were joined together: Judges and Ruth, 1 and 2 Samuel, 1 and 2 Kings, 1 and 2 Chronicles, Ezra and Nehemiah, Jeremiah and Lamentations, and the twelve Miinor Prophets. Apparently, the Jews combined these thematically linked books to reduce the number of the sacred scrolls in the Hebrew Scriptures to twenty-two, the precise number of letters in the Hebrew alphabet. Numerous early writers, including Josephus and Jerome refer to the ancient Jewish canon containing just twenty-two books, allowing one volume for Ezra-Nehemiah. In the Latin Vulgate (common language) translation of the Bible, the book Ezra-Nehemiah was divided into 1 Ezra and 2 Ezra (Nehemiah) around A.D. 400. However, it is worthwhile to note that these changes and combinations of books into larger scrolls did not add or subtract a single letter or word from the Hebrew Bible.

The Jews divided the text of the first five books of the Bible, the Torah, into fifty-four sections. This division may date back to the days of Moses, but it is more likely that these sections were established during the lifetime of Ezra, when the canon of Old Testament was established. In addition, these sections of the Torah were divided into verses for the first time at this point. Every Sabbath day throughout the year, each one of these fifty-four sections would be read in turn in the synagogue. The ancient Hebrew calendar had an extra intercalary (leap) month that they added to the end of the year approximately every third year to adjust their 360-day calendar to the solar calendar of 365.25 days. In these intercalated (leap) years, there were thirteen months that produced, as a consequence, fifty-four weekly Sabbaths. Thus the Jews would read each of the fifty-four sections in the course of that year. In the other years without the leap month, which had only fifty-two Sabbaths, the leaders of the synagogue would combine together two short sections on two particular Sabbaths to enable them to cover the whole of the Torah in a yearly reading.

However, during the terrible persecution by the evil Syrian king Antiochus Epiphanes who conquered Israel for three years between 168 B.C. and 165 B.C., the reading of the Torah was forbidden under severe punishment. Instead, the Jewish priests substituted the reading of Torah portion with the reading of one of fifty-four sections from the writings of the prophets every Sabbath day. When the Jewish people succeeded in defeating the Syrian army in 165 B.C. the reading of the sections from the Torah was restored. However, the Jewish priests chose to continue to read the sections of the Prophets as a second lesson every Sabbath day after reading the Torah section.

The Targums, or Paraphrases of the Hebrew Bible

When the Jewish exiles returned from the seventy years of captivity in Babylon, most of the people had lost their understanding and use of the Hebrew language. Naturally, during the seventy years of captivity, they had learned to speak the Chaldean (Babylonian) language as their common tongue. Consequently, after the return from Babylon, the priest would first read the Torah portion in the original Hebrew and then he would interpret the Hebrew portion to the people using the Chaldee language that they understood. The division of the fifty-four sections of the Torah into verses made it more convenient to read both the Hebrew Scriptures and the *Targums* which were written paraphrases or commentaries on the relevant Scripture written in the Chaldee language.

This practice apparently began in the days of Ezra, as his book describes his reading the Torah to the people in the rebuilt Temple. The leaders then explained the text in the common Chaldee language to allow the people to understand the Scriptures. The book of Nehemiah records this practice as follows: "The Levites, caused the people to understand the law: and the people stood in their place. So they read in the book in the law of God distinctly, and gave the sense, and caused them to understand the reading" (Nehemiah 8:7–8). The two major *Targums* (paraphrases) were the *Targum of Jonathan* and the *Targum of Onkelos*. Although spoken commentary on the Scriptures in the Chaldee language was common for centuries, the Jews did not possess written paraphrases before the time of Onkelos and Jonathan, both of whom lived just before the birth of Jesus. These written commentaries or paraphrases of the Bible in the Chaldean language became known as *Targums*, which contained paraphrases combined with commentary on the Scriptures by the Targum interpreters. The *Targum of Jonathan* was written by Jonathan ben Uziel, a famous scholar who was himself taught by the brilliant sage Hillel the Great during the reign of King Herod the Great. The date of the writing of the *Targum of Onkelos*, who commented only on the five books of Moses, is not certain, but likely it preceded the time of Jesus as well. Onkelos the Proselyte likely was descended from Gentile converts to Judaism. His Targum was considered so valuable that it was almost treated as inspired literature in the synagogue.

The *Targums* are valuable in helping us to understand both the Old Testament as well as the New. They provide tremendous evidence that the present Hebrew text is genuine because the detailed commentaries confirm that the original Hebrew text is identical to our present Hebrew text. In the Targums we find the explanation of many difficult words, phrases, and customs found in the Hebrew Bible. In addition, some of the idioms, phrases, and unusual forms of speech found in the New Testament can be better understood through studying these Targums. Lastly, these Jewish commentaries reveal clearly that the ancient Jewish sages interpreted the Old Testament prophecies about the Messiah precisely as we Christians understand them today. This will be dealt with in a future chapter on the prophecy of Isaiah 53 about the suffering Messiah.

The Division of the Bible into Chapters and Verses

The Scriptures were not divided into the chapters we find in our modern Bible until approximately 1240. Hugo de Sancto Caro, more commonly known as Hugo Cardinalis, after he became a cardinal in the church, created the division of the Bible into its present form of chapters to facilitate the reader's ability to find any particular portion of Scripture. Hugo wrote a Bible commentary entitled *Comment on the Scriptures* and created a valuable concordance based on the Vulgate Latin Bible, which enabled a reader to find any passage in which a particular word or phrase occurs from Genesis to Revelation. Hugo realized that it would improve immensely the usefulness of his concordance if he divided the Bible's text into sections (chapters), which were then numbered. Until Hugo's time, the books of the Bible had no divisions at all which made it very difficult to find a particular passage. Imagine the difficulty you would have in finding a favorite passage, such as "For God so loved the world," if the whole book of John had written out as one paragraph with no divisions, chapters, or verses. Hugo's division of the Bible into sections has now become the chapter divisions universally used in the billions of Bibles printed in the last seven centuries. However, Hugo did not subdivide the chapters into the numbered verses found in our present-day Bibles. Interestingly, Hugo placed the letters of the alphabet, A, B, C, D, et cetera in the margins of the Bible at an equal distance from each other. This helped identify the approximate position in the chapter where a particular passage was located.

Over two centuries later, in A.D. 1445, a famous Jewish rabbi, Mordecai Nathan, subdivided the chapters created by Cardinal Hugo into the individually numbered verses we find in our modern Bibles. Rabbi Nathan created a *Concordance to the Hebrew Bible* to assist Jews in their study of the Word of God. While he used the same chapter divisions created by Hugo several centuries earlier, Rabbi Nathan further subdivided the chapters into individually numbered verses. Once Rabbi Nathan's Bible was published, this division of the Scriptures into chapters and verses became so popular and useful that every Bible printed since that day has followed this same method. It is ironic and quite fitting that the Jews borrowed the Christian Hugo's division of the Bible into chapters, while the Christians borrowed the division of the sacred Scriptures into verses created by the Jewish Rabbi Nathan. For the last five centuries, all students of the Scriptures, both Christians and Jews, have benefited immensely from these inventions.

A number of scholars, including Dr. H. Prideaux, have suggested that Ezra was inspired by God to make several editorial additions to some of the books of the Bible in order to connect several sections of the Bible together or to complete the final pages of a particular book. If this suggestion is correct, then we would have a logical explanation for a number of problems and puzzles in the Bible that have been used by atheists to attack the inspiration and authority of the Scriptures. A multitude of biblical statements affirm the total inspiration of the Bible, including Paul's declaration that "all Scripture is given by inspiration" (2 Timothy 3:16). These scriptural declarations provide a strong witness to the fact that any such editing by Ezra would have been as equally inspired by God as the writing of the original author.

There are a number of puzzling verses in the Bible which can be explained on the basis of this principle. For example, the final chapter of Deuteronomy records the details of the death and burial of Moses, as well as the commencement of the leadership of Joshua. Since the five books of the Law, including Deuteronomy, are ascribed in the Bible to Moses, a number of critics have pointed to these verses as an obvious error because Moses could not have recorded his own death and burial. However, it would be very natural and necessary for the inspired writer Ezra, who was inspired by God to write his own book as well as to gather together the books of the Old Testament, to add the final details of the death and burial of Moses to the final chapters of Deuteronomy under the same inspiration of God as moved Moses to record the pages of the Torah.

My friend Yacov Rambsel is the author of two best-selling books on the phenomenal Bible Codes that reveal that the name *Yeshua* (Jesus) is encoded at equally spaced intervals in every major messianic prophecy. His books are entitled *Yeshua: The Name of Jesus Revealed in the Old Testament* and his latest release *His Name Is Jesus*. Recently I asked Yacov to research the Hebrew text of the last chapter of Deuteronomy to discover if anything significant was encoded in this passage at equal letter sequences. The fascinating story of the phenomenal Bible Codes is revealed in a later chapter of this book. To my amazement, Yacov found that the name "Ezra" was actually encoded in this passage regarding the death and burial of Moses, a passage that many scholars believe was actually written by Ezra the scribe. The first verse of the last chapter of Deuteronomy reads, "And Moses went up from the plains of Moab unto the mountain of Nebo, to the top of Pisgah, that is over against Jericho. And the Lord showed him all the land of Gilead, unto Dan" (Deuteronomy 34:1). Beginning at the very first verse of Deuteronomy 34, describing the death and burial of Moses, we find the name of the scribe Ezra is encoded at an interval of every forty-seventh letter left to right, beginning with the third letter in the first word of the verse. In addition, the name "Ezra" also occurs in the encoded phrase "I pray Ezra" in Deuteronomy 34:4, beginning with the third letter of the thirteenth word of this verse at an interval of every second letter spelled left to right.

There are many other difficult passages in the Bible that are used to support objections to the doctrine of the inspiration and authenticity of the Scriptures. Another example is Genesis 22:14 where the verse reads "As it is said to this day, In the mount of the Lord it shall be seen." The problem is that Mount Moriah, where Abraham offered Isaac, was not called "the mount of the Lord" until King Solomon built the Temple almost a thousand years after the life of Abraham. Therefore, it is likely that another person (probably Ezra) added this statement to the original words of Moses to explain the passage.

In Genesis 36:3, we find this passage: "And these are the kings that reigned in the land of Edom, before there reigned any king over the children of Israel." This statement would not make sense until centuries later, when Israel began to be ruled by kings, beginning with Saul and David. While it is certainly possible that God inspired Moses to record the details of his death and burial and the future monarchy of Israel, these particular passages do not appear to be written in the normal language of direct prophecies as we find throughout the Scriptures. It is probable that Ezra added these finishing comments under the inspiration of God to complete the Divine revelation.

Another example is found in Exodus 16:35: "And the children of Israel did eat manna forty years, until they came to a land inhabited; they did eat manna, until they came unto the borders of the land of Canaan." However, the death of Moses (Deuteronomy 34) had occurred before the Jews crossed the Jordan River at the time of Passover and began to eat the new corn of the Promised Land after the manna had ceased to fall from heaven. Therefore, it is more probable that Ezra added this inspired explanatory verse rather than Moses.

Apparently, Ezra also changed the names of several cities that were no longer known in his time by their ancient names. For example, the book of Genesis records the fact that Abraham's small armed force fought against the five Canaanite kings "unto Dan." The passage reads, "And when Abram heard that his brother was taken captive, he armed his trained servants, born in his own house, three hundred and eighteen, and pursued them unto Dan" (Genesis 14:14). Since the name of Dan as a city or territory was unknown at the time when Abraham lived, it is possible that Ezra was inspired by God to change the name of the city, which was known as Laish in the days of Moses, to the name Dan, the new name given to the city by the Danites who conquered it centuries after the days of Moses.

Pharoah Ptolemy Philadelphus was the king of Egypt in 285 B.C. Philadelphus was known as a great scholar and lover of knowledge. He created the largest library in the ancient world at Alexandria, Egypt. His wealth and power enabled him to acquire volumes from many nations throughout the known world. The Jewish tradition is that the king of Egypt sent representatives to Israel to gather the greatest Jewish sages for the purpose of translating the ancient Hebrew Scriptures into the Greek language. Greek was the common language of the known world following the conquest of the Middle East by Alexander the Great in 330 B.C. These Jewish scholars reportedly produced a Greek version of the five books of the Torah in the Old Testament, called the Septuagint, or "version of the Seventy." The word Septuagint was based on an ancient tradition that the king of Egypt employed seventy or seventy-two interpreters to produce this invaluable translation. It is probable that a small group of scholars produced the Greek translation which was later approved as a correct and authoritative version of the Jewish Bible by the seventy members of the Sanhedrin of Alexandria, the highest Jewish court of law in Egypt. The remaining books of the Old Testament were translated into the Greek language by scholars in later years and added to the Septuagint version over a period of years until it ultimately contained all of the books of the Old Testament. The Hellenist or Greek speaking Jews used the Septuagint version for several centuries before the birth of Jesus to approximately A.D. 128.

The Jewish people gradually abandoned the Greek Septuagint version and created another Greek language version because the Christians constantly quoted from the Septuagint version, especially the messianic prophecies, to prove that Jesus of Nazareth had fulfilled these predictions. A Jewish convert by the name Aguila, from the city of Sinope in the province of Pontus joined Rabbi Akiba, the most famous Jewish teacher of his day, and was given the responsibility of creating a new Greek translation of the Old

Testament in A.D. 128. It is interesting to note that Jesus and His disciples, as well as the early Church writers, almost invariably quoted from the Septuagint Greek version rather than from the Hebrew original, indicating the great respect Christians held for this version.

Curiosities About the Bible

Over the last thirty-five years of Bible study I discovered numerous curious details regarding the publication of the Bible that I found fascinating. When I first began to consider publishing my first book *Armageddon — Appointment With Destiny* I decided to create a publishing company to publish my books in order to maintain control over the process and enable us to offer the books to various ministries and mission groups throughout the world. Today these books are published in numerous foreign languages including French, Spanish, Portuguese, Korean, Japanese, Mandarin, Cantonese, Russian, Polish, Ukrainian and Romanian. My interest in publishing naturally led me to examine the history of the printing of the Bible over the centuries. Centuries ago the printing of a Bible was a time consuming and very exacting process. Naturally, any publisher is mortified when he finds that a book contains typographical errors and he does his best to immediately correct such errors in his next printing. However, in past centuries it was much more difficult to produce a perfect printed text because each letter of type was set by hand. In my research I found that several of the most notorious cases of typographical errors resulted in the particular editions of these Bibles being rejected by the printer and destroyed.

Printing Errors in Past Bibles

The So-called "Wicked" Bible

In 1631 a wealthy religious businessman commissioned a printer in England to publish ten thousand copies of the Bible, an enormous sized printing for that time period. However, one of the printer's apprentices made a tragic error during the process of manually typesetting the passage containing the Ten Commandments. While typesetting the verse Exodus 20:14, the apprentice inadvertently dropped the word "not" from the commandment, "Thou shalt not commit adultery." The buyer indignantly demanded that the entire ten thousand misprinted "Wicked"

Bibles must be destroyed and replaced with a corrected edition. In addition, the court fined the printer three hundred pounds, a considerable sum in those days. That unfortunate result must have made subsequent printers of Bibles much more careful in their typesetting.

The "Printers" Bible

However, in 1702 another printer's apprentice was typesetting the Book of Psalms. When he came to Psalm 119:161 which reads, "Princes have persecuted me without a cause," for some unknown reason, he carelessly typeset the verse as follows: "Printers have persecuted me without cause." Perhaps this was an unconscious complaint about his employer.

The "Bugs" Bible

In 1551 a translator inadvertently mistranslated Psalm 91:5. In the original Scriptures it reads, "Thou shalt not be afraid of the terror by night." However, when he completed his translation, the printer rendered the verse as follows: "Thou shalt not be afraid of the bugs by night." Unknowingly, the printer printed the translated Bible with the error. Thereafter this edition became known as "the Bugs Bible."

Lest you think that such notorious errors in typesetting a Bible cannot happen anymore as a result of modern spell checkers and word processors, think again. A very large Bible publisher in the United States, which shall remain nameless, produced a new Bible several years ago in the familiar Red Letter Edition which prints the actual words of Jesus in red ink to differentiate them from the rest of the biblical text. Since the color of text is different for that particular verse the printers use a separate film that solely contains the particular red letter verse containing Christ's words. The rest of the black text that appears on that page is produced from a separate film plate. The printers had carefully used both the red letter and black letter film together to produce the four Gospels. However, when they began to print the New Testament book — Timothy — the printer was not used to using the red letter film and when he printed that particular page he used only the black letter film leaving a blank space on the page where the particular verse with Jesus' words should have appeared in red ink. When they discovered the error it was too late because thousands of these Bibles had been printed and bound in leather. The publisher knew that people would not accept a Bible with a missing verse, especially the words of Jesus. The only thing they could do was to destroy the misprinted Bibles at great cost.

The Lost Books Mentioned in the Bible

While God has preserved the totality of His inspired Scriptures in the present Old and New Testaments, the Bible refers to at least fourteen ancient books that are no longer in existence. These curious texts are referred to in a number of biblical passages as the official royal historical records of the kings of Israel and Judah plus numerous other texts containing the prophecies of various seers such as the prophet Nathan. While these particular books are lost to history there is no reason to believe that they were inspired by God. It is obvious that a person may be used of God in one instance to write a divinely inspired book of Scripture while other examples of their writing would not be inspired but the result of his normal intellect. God is capable of sovereignly preserving His holy Scriptures as demonstrated by our present complete Bible.

In the Old Testament, the book of Numbers 21:14 refers to *The Book of the Wars of the Lord*, while Joshua 10:13 describes *The Book of Jasher*. In 2 Kings 11:41 we find a reference to *The Book of the Words of the Days of Solomon*, and *The Book of the Chronicles of the Kings of Judah* is referred to six times in 1 and 2 Kings, including 1 Kings 14:29: "Now the rest of the acts of Rehoboam, and all that he did, are they not written in the book of the chronicles of the kings of Judah?"

There are nineteen references throughout the historical books of the Old Testament to the lost *Book of the Chronicles of the Kings of Israel*, which was certainly the royal historical chronicle of the nation that would be updated to record the history of each succeeding king. Three additional missing books with the titles *The Book of Samuel the Seer, the Book of Nathan the Prophet*, and *The Book of Gad the Seer* are referred to in 1 Chronicles: "Now the acts of David the king, first and last, behold, they are written in the book of Samuel the seer, and in the book of Nathan the prophet, and in the book of Gad the seer, with all his reign and his might, and the times that went over him, and over Israel, and over all the kingdoms of the countries" (1 Chronicles 29:29–30).

Two other lost books, *The Prophecy of Ahijah the Shilonite*, and *The Visions of Iddo the Seer*, along with *The Book of Nathan the Prophet*, are referred to in 2 Chronicles 9:29: "Now the rest of the acts of Solomon, first and last, are they not written in the book of Nathan the prophet, and in the prophecy of Ahijah the Shilonite, and in the visions of Iddo the seer against Jeroboam the son of Nebat?" There is a reference to *The Book of Shemaiah the Prophet* and *The Book of Iddo the Seer* in 2 Chronicles 12:15: "Now the acts of Rehoboam, first and last, are they not written in the book of Shemaiah the prophet, and of Iddo the seer concerning genealogies?" The missing *Book of Jehu* is referred to in 2 Chronicles 20:34. In 2 Chronicles 33:19 we find a reference to *The Sayings of the Seers*, which may be a separate book or may be a reference to one of above books.

A tantalizing reference to a book written by the prophet Isaiah is found in 2 Chronicles 26:22: "Now the rest of the acts of Uzziah, first and last, did Isaiah the prophet, the son of Amoz, write." There is a reference to three thousand parables of King Solomon together with his songs, that may refer to a missing book of Solomon that appears in 1 Kings 4:32: "And he spake three thousand proverbs: and his songs were a thousand and five."

5

The Reason Many Reject The Bible

Why have so many individuals in our generation rejected the teachings of the Bible and the claims of Jesus Christ to be the Son of God? Throughout the greater part of the last two thousand years, the vast majority of all classes within the nations of Western Europe and North America have willingly accepted that the Bible is the true Word of God and that Jesus Christ was sent by God to bring salvation to mankind. However, approximately a century ago, a strong attack on Christianity and the Holy Scriptures began in European universities among the academic community. During the following decades, a large majority of the scholars in the universities, the mainline Protestant churches, and the secular media began to openly reject the claims of Christianity and deny the accuracy of the historical statements found in the Bible regarding Jesus' miracles, His virgin birth, and His resurrection.

As a result of a century of growing attacks on the Bible most North Americans and Europeans believe today that the Scriptures contain scientific, historical, and archeological errors that prove that the Bible is simply a work produced by less advanced and, perhaps, ignorant authors thousands of years ago, who wrote from a perspective of limited human knowledge. The negative spiritual consequences of this widespread belief that the Bible is not the accurate and inspired Word of God is incalculable.

Attacks on the Accuracy of the Bible

As a result of the relentless attack on the truthfulness of the Scriptures by the academic community, the educational establishment, the secular media, and liberal clergy, the majority of people in our culture are convinced that the Bible is simply compiled of stories by ancient men writing to the best of their natural ability thousands of years ago. This widespread rejection of the supernatural origin of the Scriptures has caused many liberal theologians, pastors, and rabbis to abandon their confidence in the Scriptures as the inspired Word of God. A theological statement made at the Central Conference of American Rabbis (1985) is just one example that demonstrates this loss of faith in the clear assertions of the Bible: "We reject as ideas not rooted in Judaism, the beliefs both in bodily resurrection and in Gehenna and Eden."

The consequence of this widespread rejection in our culture of the supernatural claims of the Bible has been profound. The Ten Commandments, which were accepted for thousands of years as the bedrock of divine law, have now been rejected by our courts of law, the Congress, and our schools. The repudiation of these divinely inspired Ten Commandments has set our legal-justice system adrift on an ocean without a moral anchor or a compass to direct our justice system. If there is no reliable revelation from God of absolute right and wrong, then mankind is free to choose its own standards of right and wrong without any reference.

If there is no absolute right and wrong — good and evil — as revealed for all time by an Almighty and holy God, then man is free to set his own standards, based on constantly changing cultural opinions expressed by votes, polls, referendums, and laws. This shift in the basis of moral values is reflected in our current laws on abortion. According to modern values, if the mother would rather not have the responsibility of bearing a particular child at a particular time, she can terminate her inconvenient pregnancy. Currently, a mother can choose to abort her unborn child in the last day of the ninth month of her pregnancy. According to this "new morality," a doctor can now legally plunge a pair of scissors into the skull of a child just a few minutes before this child would naturally enter the world as a healthy baby. He can legally use a suction device to suck the brains out, facilitating the crushing of the skull of the baby. Then he is able to withdraw the now lifeless body, and refer to the child as an aborted "piece of flesh." The incredible justification for this morally repugnant procedure is that the mother's health must be protected. However, the law does not define the "health of the mother" in any meaningful way. If the mother decides that she does not want to give birth to a live child for any reason whatsoever, the doctor can lawfully destroy the child's life by this horrendous torture called "partial birth abortion."

Many of those working in the abortion industry admit that the "health justification" for most abortions is motivated by a simple desire to escape the economic inconvenience or emotional embarrassment of a child's birth. Furthermore, an overwhelming majority of obstetricians agree that even when the physical health of a woman is serously compromised by her pregnancy, there is no circumstance in which this barbaric technique is medically necessary. It's sole purpose is to provide a means for abortion at the end of a pregnancy that will ensure that the mother and doctor will escape charges of murder. After the U.S. government hearings on the "partial birth abortion" were over, a pro-abortion witness admitted that this disgusting procedure was not nearly as rare as the testimony had suggested.

We have arrived at a time when, every year, over one and one-half million North American women decide to kill their unborn children to avoid the social or economic inconvenience of an unwanted child. Remember that at the same time as these abortions occur, millions of North American couples are desperately seeking to adopt newborns. Despite this overwhelming demand for new babies for adoption, the "family planning" network almost always suggests to the pregnant woman that she abort rather than give birth and place her child in a loving home with parents willing to raise it properly.

Modern philosophers and liberal theologians have contemptuously rejected the literal truth of the Bible. In its place, they have attempted to create a new "Christian" religion that would be unrecognizable to the early Church or to the hundreds of millions who have experienced faith in Jesus Christ, as revealed in Scripture over the last two thousand years. These modernists and rationalists have rejected altogether the supernatural element in the Bible, along with the accounts of miracles, prophecies, the virgin birth, and the resurrection of Jesus from the tomb. However, true Christianity cannot be divorced from the physical resurrection of Jesus of Nazareth without losing its very reason for being. If Jesus' body still lies moldering in some unknown grave in Israel, then the billions of Christians over the last two thousand years are fools. As Clement C. J. Webb wrote in his 1935 book *The Historical Element in Religion*, "A Christianity without the belief in the resurrection of Christ as an historical event would be another Christianity than that which the world has hitherto known."[1]

Modern liberals have rejected the supernatural elements in the Bible, yet they attempt to call themselves "Christians" while repudiating the defining elements of the orthodox Christian faith. For example, the liberal theologian Emil Brunner wrote that the orthodox belief of Christians since the time of Christ has "killed" what he terms the true conception of revelation as "personal encounter" with Christ. Incredibly, Brunner claims that orthodox belief in the literal truth of the Bible's accounts has created virtually irreparable damage to the concept of "faith" as he holds it. In his book *Revelation and Reason* (p. 168), Emil Brunner condemned the orthodox Christian belief in the literal truth of Scripture:

> All Christian faith is based, according to this theory, upon faith in the trust-worthiness of the Biblical writers. The whole edifice of faith is built upon them, upon their absolute and complete inspiration. What a fearful caricature of what the Bible itself means by faith. And on what a quaking ground has the Church of the Reformation, in its (orthodox) perversion, placed both itself and its message! We owe a profound debt of gratitude to the historical criticism that has made it quite impossible to maintain this position. This mistaken faith in the Bible has turned everything topsy-turvy. It bases our faith-relation to Jesus Christ upon our faith in the Apostles. It is impossible to describe the amount of harm and confusion that has been caused by this fatal perversion of the foundations of faith; both in the Church as a whole and in the hearts of individuals.[2]

Emil Brunner also wrote that "revelational events must be

separated from anything like propositional revelation." By this statement, Brunner declares that his subjective experience of the revelation of Christ is not related to or dependent upon the written statements about the life, teaching, death, or resurrection of Jesus found in the Bible. Obviously, such a personal "revelational event" is totally subjective and therefore cannot be tested or measured against anything as objective as the doctrines or testimony of Scripture. This kind of subjective faith or "Christianity" is grounded solely within the internal beliefs or assumptions of the individual and is, therefore, unrelated to historic Christian faith. In this subjective approach, people are free to create their own "Christ" in their imagination without reference to any historical record of Jesus, His teachings, or His actions. The problem is that such a "Christianity" has nothing to do with Jesus Christ.

However, orthodox Christians throughout the ages simply believed that the supernatural God who created this universe also possesses the ability to inspire the human writers to accurately record His revelation to humanity, as affirmed by the clear statements of the Bible. Logically, if a supernatural God exists who truly cares for His creatures, there is no difficulty in concluding that He could have supernaturally inspired these writers to record His precise words. Furthermore, such a supernatural God could have preserved His divine written revelation down through the centuries in order to continue to communicate His genuine revelation to all generations of mankind. The underlying assumption of the majority of those who contemptuously reject the inspiration of the Scriptures is that a supernatural God with miraculous powers does not exist.

The theologian Emil Brunner expressed his totally subjective experience of "Christ" in contrast to the literal, orthodox Christian faith based on the teachings of the Bible. Brunner wrote the following statements expressing his views of the essentials of Christianity:

> Substituting the idea of revelation as personal encounter
> for the orthodox one of system I may as a believer become
> as contemporary with Christ as was Peter . . . No longer
> must I first of all ask the Apostle whether Jesus is really
> Lord. I know it as well as the Apostle himself, and indeed
> I know it exactly as the Apostle knew it; namely, from the

Lord Himself, who reveals it to me . . . Being thus contemporaneous with Christ the believer now shares in the grace and glory of God. Being face to face with Christ as his contemporary also means having the true content of revelation . . . We must say quite clearly Christ is the Truth. He is the content; He is the "point" of all preaching of the Church; but He is also really its content.[3]

A careful examination of these statements reveals that these modern liberal theologians have created a new religion that bears no resemblance to the orthodox Christian faith. Rather, these modern theologians have created a new "Christianity" that can be infinitly adjusted to suit their own desires because they deny the fundamental doctrines of historic orthodox Christianity and they reject the truthfulness of the Gospel account about Jesus. The criteria for accepting or rejecting a particular statement of the Scriptures seems to be whether or not it agrees with their personal religious preferences.

If these critics were honest, they would admit they are no longer Christians because they vehemently and contemptuously reject every major doctrine of the apostolic Christian faith. Meanwhile, they reject the literal truth of biblical statements while suggesting that they have discovered some deeper, subjective truth behind these scriptural statements. They often claim to have a profound experience of "Christ" while they denigrate the historical reality of the biblical accounts of the life, death, and resurrection of Jesus Christ.

The "Christ" and the "Christianity" of the modernist liberal theologians has become an extremely flexible philosophical creation of their own making, absent of any of the supernatural elements or the objective historical facts recorded in the Bible that they find so objectionable. They reject as embarrassing the Bible's teaching of the historical reality of the virgin birth of Jesus, His identity as the Son of God, the accuracy of His words as recorded in the Gospels, His supernatural miracles, His resurrection, and His ascension. Having stripped away any historical or supernatural reality from Jesus of Nazareth, they are then free to create a new "Christ" limited only by their own imagination. The word "Christ" has become an empty vessel for the liberal theologians into which they can pour whatever New Age philosophical or religious concepts they imagine. If these liberal theologians were to physically take a pair of scissors and cut out from the sacred pages of the Scriptures every verse referring to the supernatural, the prophecies, the miracles, and the statements of Jesus that they reject, the Bible that remained in their hands would be a mere fraction of the one that Christians have treasured for thousands of years. If they doubt this truth, I would challenge them to take a highlighter and highlight the few verses in the Bible that they still accept unreservedly to be literally true. This experiment would reveal to many liberals, who reject the literal statements of the Scripture, that their "acceptable" Bible has been reduced to a shadow of the inspired volume that has profoundly affected billions of lives over the last two thousand years.

Bishop John Spong's Attack on Fundamental Biblical Beliefs

The controversial Episcopalian Bishop John Spong is known for his prominent attacks on Christians who believe the fundamental doctrines of the Word of God. Bishop Spong claims that there are three main paths for Christians to take in addressing the words of the Bible. These alternatives are described in his words as "ignorant fundamentalism," "vapid liberalism," and his own unique path. However, Spong's path is merely another example of a modernist liberalism that results in a wholesale rejection of the orthodox doctrines of Christianity. The bishop claims he wants to free Christians and Jesus from "2000 years of misunderstanding." Spong declares that the Gospel writers and Paul never intended their "stories" to be taken literally. As a result of his denial of the reality of the New Testament accounts Bishop Spong openly admits his rejection of the foundational doctrines of the orthodox Christian faith. He denies the reality of the virgin birth, the reality of the miracles and prophecies, details of the crucifixion, and the resurrection of Jesus. As a result of his rejection of the literal meaning of Scripture, Spong logically feels no need to submit morally to the Bible's condemnation of homosexuality. Therefore, the bishop proudly proclaims his endorsement of homosexuality and the fact that he oversees twenty-three openly homosexual priests in his Newark, New Jersey Episcopalian diocese.

While Spong despises fundamentalist, orthodox Christians (like myself) as "uniformed, unquestioning, and ignorant," he is forced to admit that the fundamentalist churches are rapidly growing because biblical literalism appeals to people's need for certainty. Spong rejects the Genesis account of the beginning of man's sinful disobedience and states that "the fall of man . . . no longer makes sense." He then dismisses as "no longer believable" the Bible's revelation, in which "Christ has been portrayed as the divine rescuer — sent to save the fallen human creature from sin and to restore that creature to the goodness of his or her pre-fall creation."[4] Together with many liberal theologians and modern religious writers, Bishop Spong condemns as "ignorant" those who uphold the orthodox Christian, biblically based beliefs that have sustained billions of believers for two thousand years.

However, anyone who observes the religious attitudes exhibited today in America and Europe recognizes the utter failure of this liberal, anti-literal, anti-Bible, and anti-Christian religious viewpoint to motivate people to join the shrinking congregations of liberal mainline denominations. Spong admits that the fundamentalist, Bible-believing churches are growing at an unprecedented rate, while the liberal mainline churches that reject the Bible's teaching "shrink every day in membership." He complains, "The only churches that grow today are those that do not, in fact, understand the issues and can therefore traffic in certainty. They represent both the fundamentalistic Protestant groups and the rigidly controlled conservative Catholic traditions." In other words, Spong believes the successful and growing Bible-believing churches "do not, in fact, understand the issues," primarily because they still espouse traditional, orthodox Christian beliefs.

Bishop Spong admits, "The churches that do attempt to interact with the emerging world (rejecting historic orthodox Christian beliefs) are for the most part the liberal Protestant mainline churches that shrink every day in membership and the silent liberal Catholic minority that attracts very few adherents. Both are, almost by definition, fuzzy, imprecise, and relatively unappealing. They might claim to be honest, but for the most part they have no real message." Incredibly, although Spong himself admits the liberal mainline Protestant position is "fuzzy, imprecise, and relatively unappealing," he presents his own slight variation of that same "fuzzy" liberal position that also rejects the orthodox, literal view of the Bible. Spong wants to create a new "Christianity" that is stripped of the following doctrines that have been fundamental to the orthodox faith for centuries: the reality of the historical Jesus Christ as described in the Gospels, His status as the Son of God, His role as the Savior for our sins, and the truth of His physical resurrection from the dead.

However, once someone divorces their "Christianity" from the statements about the Jesus of the Bible, they have, in reality, created a new religion or myth that has nothing to do with Jesus of Nazareth or with God's biblical revelation of salvation, heaven, or hell. In other words, Bishop Spong's new "Christianity" is a new religion that, apart from the name "Christian," would be unrecognizable to the disciples of Christ or to the vast majority of followers of Jesus of Nazareth over the last two thousand years. When Christianity is divorced from the historic written documents of revelation that guided it for centuries, theologians and religious leaders are free to create whatever doctrines or myths they desire because there is no longer any agreed standard against which their statements can be measured. However, their new "faith" is no longer Christian in any meaningful sense of the word. If the words of the Bible are no longer meaningful according to their normal grammatical-historical usage, then liberal religious leaders are free to re-create their "mythical" Jesus, and Christianity itself, into any shape or teaching that appears popular at the moment. However, this divorce from historic and biblical Christian faith should be obvious to anyone who compares these beliefs against the unchangeable Word of God.

Sincere, long-suffering Christians who have sat in the pews of these "fuzzy, imprecise and relatively unappealing" liberal churches are finally leaving in sadness and frustration because the preaching from the pulpit no longer provides spiritual sustenance or meaningful guidance for their lives. Sitting in church Sunday after Sunday, they have heard a vague message that denies that the Bible truly means what it says when it promises forgiveness for sins and guilt or when it offers a real heavenly home. Their liberal "ship of faith" has lost its anchor and is now drifting hopelessly on the ocean of ever-changing theological opinion. It is no wonder that millions in recent years have abandoned liberal churches in their earnest search for an orthodox, biblically-based Christian church that confidently bases its faith and teaching on the unchanging, inspired Word of God.

A fascinating Gallop Poll completed several years ago

examined the attitudes of many people by asking this question: "What is your number one personal goal for the next year?" It was fascinating and encouraging for Christians to note that 57 percent of the respondents declared that their number one personal goal was to find a strong personal relationship with God. This outcome suggests that millions of our fellow citizens are longing for a more meaningful relationship with God. The conservative, orthodox, Bible-believing churches are growing at an unprecedented rate worldwide because hundreds of millions are seeking a spiritual meaning and certainty in their life that can only be found in a reliance in the unshakable truths expressed in the Word of God. Many people are seeking a biblically based faith that produces the spiritual confidence to affirm the historic Christian statement: "I know in whom I have believed, and am persuaded that he is able to keep that which I have committed unto him against that day" (2 Timothy 1:12).

Notes

1. Clement C. J. Webb, *The Historical Element in Religion* (1935).

2. Emil Brunner, *Revelation and Reason* (Philadelphia: 1946) 168.

3. Emil Brunner, *Revelation and Reason* (Philadelphia: 1946) 98–171.

4. John Shelby Spong, *Rescuing the Bible from Fundamentalism* (San Francisco: Harper Collins, 1991) 35.

6

The Sacred Mystery of the Trinity

"Hear, O Israel: The Lord our God is one Lord."

Deuteronomy 6:4

Many Christians and virtually all non-Christians acknowledge that the mystery of the Trinity is the most profound and difficult of all biblical doctrines to understand. During my years at Bible college in Philadelphia, I can remember many late-night conversations with my fellow students as we vainly attempted to come to terms with this difficult concept. As a result of numerous conversations over thirty-five years with both pastors and laymen, I have come to believe that many Christians do not have a clear understanding of the great scriptural truths about the triune nature of God. Unfortunately, many pastors and Bible teachers in our generation have failed to teach this vital doctrine, perhaps because of its obvious difficulty. However, the sad result of this failure is that many Christians are unable to express clearly in either thought or word their understanding of the true nature of God as revealed in the Bible. Surely, we who love God with all our heart and have dedicated our lives to His service need to come to a full, mature understanding of the great biblical truths regarding the nature of God. It is obvious that the only source of true knowledge about God's nature must be found in the genuine written revelation of God, as found in the Holy Scriptures. However, in this study we will also examine the writings of the Early Church about the nature of God. Finally, I will share some fascinating research that will reveal an extraordinary discovery — the greatest of the Jewish rabbis in the years before Jesus was born taught, in the clearest language possible, about the sacred mystery of the Trinity.

When we examine the pages of the Bible, we find that there is a deep mystery concerning the nature of God, beginning with the opening verses of the Scriptures. From the initial verses in the book of Genesis through to the closing promises found in the book of Revelation, we discover numerous inspired statements that affirm that there is only one God. However, it is equally clear that the Word of God constantly affirms, often in the very same verses, that this same God, is revealed in three persons or three manifestations. This seeming contradiction has puzzled millions of thoughtful believers over the centuries. The infinite and omnipresent nature of God is far beyond the power of our finite minds to understand perfectly. However, while we still struggle to appreciate the inner mystery of His triune nature, the truth of the Trinity has been taught throughout the Scriptures from Genesis to Revelation.

One of my favorite biblical commentators is the brilliant Russian writer Ivan Panin, who completed an exhaustive study of the Word of God to discover its marvellous doctrines and the phenomenal textual features within the Scriptures. He once wrote, "I used to doubt God. Now I only doubt my knowledge of Him."[1] While the doctrine of the Trinity is beyond our ability to fully appreciate, it is not fundamentally contrary to reason. This is a study that needs to be approached with a holy reverence, an open heart, and an obedient spirit that will examine the inspired statements of the Scriptures to learn from its sacred pages what our Lord reveals regarding His divine nature.

What does the Bible actually teach about the Trinity, the triune nature of God? The scriptural revelation of the nature of God can be succinctly described in one sentence.

The Bible declares that there is one God who is revealed to us as Father, Son, and Holy Spirit, each of whom has distinct personal attributes; however, there is no division regarding nature, essence, or being.

This statement sums up every significant point that the Scriptures teach us about the doctrine of the Trinity, as held by orthodox Christian believers in all denominations during the last two thousand years. While the Bible clearly describes this triune or threefold nature in its constant use of the words *Father, Son,* and *Holy Spirit,* the Scriptures also declare authoritatively that there is only one God. As we consider these passages that describe God, we need to fix our mind on the truth that God is one God, not three. Because of the lack of biblical teaching about this important doctrine of the Trinity, some believers who are young in their faith have misunderstood the true nature of God. Some immature believers unfortunately imagine that they will see three individual Gods — the Father, Son, and Holy Spirit — sitting on three separate thrones when they arrive in heaven. This is a profound misunderstanding of the true doctrine of the Trinity.

Let us examine the teaching of the Bible itself to learn what these inspired passages can teach us about the nature of God. First, the Bible repeatedly and emphatically rejects the pagan idea of polytheism (the view that there are many gods). In ancient times polytheism was virtually universal, with the exception of the Jews and Christians. The Hindus of India believe that there are millions of gods. The various ethnic groups making up the vast Roman Empire acknowledged thousands of different gods. However, the teaching of the Bible, from the first pages of Genesis to the last verses of Revelation, has declared that there is only one God.

Jesus Taught the Trinity

Consider the profound words of Jesus Christ that reveal His authoritative teaching about the triune nature of God, or the Trinity: "Believe me that I am in the Father, and the Father in me: or else believe me for the very works' sake . . . And I will pray the Father, and he shall give you another Comforter, that he may abide with you for ever" (John 14:11,16). In this one verse Jesus affirmed that He and the Father were one. At the same time, He identified himself and the Father as two distinct persons under the titles of His own name and that of "the Father." Then Jesus promised His Church that the Father would answer the prayer of Jesus and send "another Comforter," referring to the Holy Spirit, as the third person in the Triune God. A careful examination of these words of Jesus reveal clearly that He taught the unity of God expressed in three distinct persons: the Father, the Son, and the Comforter (the Holy Spirit).

The word "Trinity" comes from the Latin word *trinitas*, or the word *trinitus*, which means "three in one" or "threefold." This word expresses the clear teaching of the Church on the profound biblical doctrine of the nature of God, as revealed in the Scriptures, as a Trinity in unity.

The Unity and Attributes of God

The Bible teaches repeatedly that there is only one God. Numerous examples from the Scriptures could be sighted, but these few verses will suffice to prove the truth of this important doctrine. Moses, the great lawgiver of the Jews, declared, "Thou shalt have no other gods before me" (Exodus 20:3). Moses also declared the unity of God in the famous words of the "Shema," the daily affirmation of righteous Jews throughout the world for thousands of years: "Hear, O Israel: The Lord our God is one Lord" (Deuteronomy 6:4). However, there is a mystery found in the Hebrew words of this declaration that we will study more deeply later in this chapter. The prophet Isaiah also declared the unity of God in his prophetic words, "I am the Lord: that is my name: and my glory will I not give to another, neither my praise to graven images" (Isaiah 42:8). Isaiah also wrote of God in the following words: "To whom will ye liken me, and make me equal, and compare me, that we may be like?" (Isaiah 46:5). The prophet Malachi wrote of one God when he said, "Have we not all one father? hath not one God created us?" (Malachi 2:10).

One of the most important attributes of God is that He is both eternal and uncreated. In other words, there was never a time when God did not exist. Therefore, God has no beginning and no ending. The Scriptures reveal the eternal nature of God in numerous passages, including the words of King David in the Psalms: "Before the mountains were brought forth, or ever thou hadst formed the earth and the world, even from everlasting to everlasting, thou art God" (Psalms 90:2). Jesus Christ confirmed His eternal nature in these words: "Verily, verily, I say unto you,

Before Abraham was, I am" (John 8:58). Furthermore, the Bible teaches us that God is omnipresent, which means that He is simultaneously everywhere throughout His creation, not only in awareness but in His actual divine presence. This omnipresence of God was alluded to by King Solomon, as recorded in the book of Kings at the building of the Temple: "But will God indeed dwell on the earth? Behold, the heaven and heaven of heavens cannot contain thee; how much less this house that I have builded?" (1 Kings 8:27). The Scriptures also declare that God is unchangeable, that His nature will remain the same forever. The prophet Malachi wrote, "For I am the Lord, I change not" (Malachi 3:6). This inspired declaration by Malachi confirms that God's nature, as expressed in the Trinity in unity, did not change when the Son incarnated in the body of the Christ child, Jesus of Nazareth, 2000 years ago. In other words, the Father, the Son, and the Holy Spirit have always existed as the Trinity.

The Father, the Son, and the Holy Spirit Are Called God

Now that we have examined the passages that affirm there is only one God, we need to explore the other passages of Scripture that also teach us clearly that God the Father, God the Son, Jesus, and God the Holy Spirit are all identified and named as God. Paul wrote the following letter referring to both the Father and Jesus as God: "To Timothy, my dearly beloved son: Grace, mercy, and peace, from God the Father and Christ Jesus our Lord" (2 Timothy 1:2). Paul again affirms that both are God in his letter to the Church at Philippi: "And that every tongue should confess that Jesus Christ is Lord, to the glory of God the Father" (Philippians 2:11). In the Gospel of John we find a clear declaration by the beloved disciple, John, that both Jesus and the Father are God. "No man hath seen God at any time; the only begotten Son, which is in the bosom of the Father, he hath declared him" (John 1:18).

Jesus, the Son of God, Created the Universe

However, while John reveals that Jesus and the Father are both God, he also reveals that it was Jesus, the Son of God, as the Word (Logos) of God, who created the entire universe and everything within it. I am constantly surprised to find that many Christians have assumed that God the Father created everything. However, a careful examination of the Scriptures reveals that the act of creation was committed to Jesus, the Son of God. "In the beginning was the Word, and the Word was with God, and the Word was God. The same was in the beginning with God. All things were made by him; and without him was not any thing made that was made" (John 1:1–3). This teaching is confirmed by the letter Paul wrote to the Ephesians Church: "And to make all men see what is the fellowship of the mystery, which from the beginning of the world hath been hid in God, who created all things by Jesus Christ" (Ephesians 3:9). The Psalmist David alludes to the fact that the Son is the One who created all things by identifying the Creator as "the Word of the Lord." Later in this chapter we will examine the scriptural evidence that "the Word of the Lord" is often used as an Old Testament title for the Son of God, the second person of the Trinity. David declares, "By the word of the Lord were the heavens made; and all the host of them by the breath of his mouth" (Psalms 33:6).

The Bible continually refers to the Holy Spirit as a distinct person of the Godhead who teaches, acts, witnesses about Christ, and dwells within the spirit of the believer as the Spirit of God. At the end of His earthly ministry, Jesus Christ promised His disciples that He would send them "a Comforter" to guide and direct them after He ascended to heaven. "And I will pray the Father, and he shall give you another Comforter, that he may abide with you for ever; Even the Spirit of truth; whom the world cannot receive, because it seeth him not, neither knoweth him: but ye know him; for he dwelleth with you, and shall be in you" (John 14:16–17). This passage reveals the three divine persons of the Trinity. However, this verse also clearly identifies the Holy Spirit as the person of God the Comforter, who will indwell the believers. King David also wrote about the divine Holy Spirit as a separate person of the Trinity when he appealed to God (the Father) in the following words: "Cast me not away from thy presence; and take not thy holy spirit from me" (Psalms 51:11). Additionally, in the New Testament, Jesus identified the Holy Spirit as both God and as a distinct person of the Trinity. Jesus taught about the Holy Spirit as God in His conclusion to the Lords Prayer, which was addressed to "Our Father." Jesus taught, "If ye then, being evil, know how to give good gifts unto your children: how much more shall your heavenly Father give the Holy Spirit to them that ask him?" (Luke 11:13). These Scriptures obviously teach the threefold nature of God as we describe it under the word "Trinity."

The Bible Teaches the Trinity

We have examined the scriptural teaching that there is only one God. In addition, we have examined the Scriptures that teach that the Father, the Son, and the Holy Spirit are three distinct persons of the Godhead. We now need to look at the Scriptures that reveal the three persons as one God. One of the most significant passages revealing this teaching about the Trinity is found at the beginning of the ministry of Jesus when John baptized our Lord. The Gospel of Matthew records, "And Jesus, when he was baptized, went up straightway out of the water: and, lo, the heavens were opened unto him, and he saw the Spirit of God descending like a dove, and lighting upon him: And lo a voice from heaven, saying, This is my beloved Son, in whom I am well pleased" (Matthew 3:16–17). In this well-loved passage we observe Jesus, the Son of God, being baptized by John and the Holy Spirit of God descending upon Him. Simultaneously, God the Father speaks from heaven saying, "This is my beloved Son."

This critical passage clearly reveals the three distinct persons of the Trinity acting as individual persons, yet in perfect harmony as the Trinity of God. It is significant that at the end of His ministry on earth, Jesus Christ instructed His disciples by giving them His Great Commission: "Go ye therefore, and teach all nations, baptizing them in the name of the Father, and of the Son, and of the Holy Ghost" (Matthew 28:19). Since baptism is the most profound profession of faith, devotion, and worship, which is due only to God, the words of Jesus confirm that "the Father, the Son, and the Holy Ghost" are equally God, as taught in the biblical doctrine of the Trinity. This teaching of the Trinity also appears in the final benediction, in which the apostle Paul concludes his second inspired letter to the church at Corinth. Paul gave them his blessings in the names of the three persons of God, as revealed in the Trinity, "The grace of the Lord Jesus Christ, and the love of God, and the communion of the Holy Ghost, be with you all. Amen" (2 Corinthians 13:14).

The Trinity As Taught in the Old Testament

The unusual language used by Moses in the first verses of the book of Genesis presents a great mystery regarding the nature of God and His creation of this universe and mankind. The first verse of the Bible records the creation of the heavens and the earth by God. However, the inspired writer used the word *Elohim* אלהים "Gods," which is the plural name for God, rather than the singular name *Jehovah* יהוה "God." It is fascinating to note that Moses uses this plural name for "God" *Elohim* אלהים more than five hundred times in the first five books of the Bible. The mystery is that the plural name of God *Elohim* appears with a singular verb each time. The normal laws of grammar demand that the plural form of the noun must agree with the plural form of the verb. However, throughout the Scriptures, we find that the plural noun for God *Elohim* appears invariably with the singular form of the verb, such as we find in the first verse of Genesis. Here the singular verb "created" ברא *bara* occurs with the plural noun *Elohim* אלהים in Genesis 1:1: "In the beginning God created the heaven and the earth." The Hebrew Scriptures record this passage as follows [reading from right to left in the Hebrew]:

"the heavens and the earth." "*Elohim* (Gods)" "created" "In the beginning"

בראשית   ברא   אלהים   את השמים ואת הארץ
[plural noun for Gods] [singular verb]

There is only one logical solution to this problem. If there is no grammatical agreement between the plural noun *Elohim* and the singular verb "created," then there must be an overriding logical agreement that demands the unusual grammatical construction found in these sentences. The logical agreement is that the word *Elohim* clearly reveals the sacred mystery of the nature of God as a Trinity. In other words, Genesis 1:1 reveals this declaration: "In the beginning the Trinity (the Father, Son, and Holy Spirit) created the heavens and the earth."

The Teaching of the Early Church on the Trinity

The early Church upheld the biblical doctrine of the Trinity universally from the Day of Pentecost in A.D. 32 throughout the last two thousand years. An examination of the early Church writings will verify their unwavering support for this teaching found in the writings of both the Old and New Testament. The real value of these ancient Christian writings is that they are the best interpreters of the doctrine of the Trinity as it was preached by Jesus and the apostles. As some of these early Christians were taught by those who personally knew the apostles, they would have been in an excellent position to understand the true meaning of the New Testament teachings. Some critics of the doctrine of the Trinity have complained that the word "Trinity" cannot be found in the actual Hebrew or Greek words of the Scriptures. However, the truth of this doctrine is taught clearly from Genesis to Revelation. Many scholars believe that the word "Trinity" was used for the first time in reference to this biblical doctrine during a church council held at Alexandria, Egypt in A.D. 317. However, the history of the early Church reveals that this doctrine of the Trinity was taught by Jesus Christ, His disciples, and the apostles. The Trinity of God was the universal belief of the church from the very beginning of the Christian era. For example, the secular Greek writer Lucian, in his book *Philopatris*, written in A.D. 160, confirmed the well-known belief of the Christians in the Trinity. Lucian described the first generations of Christians confessing their faith in God in the following words: "The exalted God . . . Son of the Father, Spirit proceeding from the Father, One of Three, and Three of One."[2]

Some critics and theologians have claimed that the doctrine of the Trinity was unknown until the Council of Nicca in A.D. 325, where they claim it was invented by the unanimous collusion of the Church fathers in that council. However, this claim is totally contradicted by the many writings of the early Church from Christ to A.D. 325. I will share some passages from several of these writers to establish this fact. In addition, the orthodox Christian faith has continued to teach the Trinity for two thousand years, from the resurrection of Jesus Christ until today.

One of the earliest of the manuscripts written by Church leaders is the *Shepherd of Hermas*. He was a brother of Pius, the bishop of Rome. Some scholars believe Hermas is the person mentioned in the apostle Paul's epistle to the Romans (16:14). Hermas wrote, "The Son of God is more ancient than any created thing, so that He was present in council with His Father at the creation."[3]

Justin Martyr was a great leader and writer in the early

Church in A.D. 150. His writing declares that the doctrine of the Trinity was proclaimed with great clarity from the earliest ages of the Church. Justin and many of the early Church fathers wrote that it was Jesus Christ who appeared as God to Moses in the burning bush. He criticized the Jews for confusing the roles of God the Father with that of His Son in the passages of the Old Testament. Justin Martyr wrote,

> The Jews, who think that it was always God the Father who spoke to Moses, (whereas He who spoke to him was the Son of God, who is also called an Angel, and an Apostle) are justly convicted both by the prophetical spirit, and by Christ himself, for knowing neither the Father nor the Son. For they, who say that the Son is the Father, are convicted of neither knowing the Father, nor of under-standing that the God of the universe has a Son: who, being the first-born Word of God, is also God.[4]

Justin Martyr also wrote the following statement in his *Dialogue With Trypho*. He establishes a general rule that wherever God appears or converses with any man in the Old Testament, as in Genesis 17:22, we should understand that the passage is refer-ring to Jesus as God the Son.

> Now that Christ is Lord, and substantially God the Son of God, and in times past appeared potentially as a man and an angel, and in fiery glory as He appeared in the bush. and at the judgment of Sodom, has been proved by many arguments."[5]

The Council of Sirmium was held in A.D. 351 to deal with a number of heresies that were beginning to plague the Church. This council established a creed as a clear statement of the teach-ing of the Church regarding the Trinity. In one of its comments on this subject we find the following words: "If any one say that the Father did not speak the words, 'Let us make man,' to His Son, but that he spoke them to Himself, let him be anathema."[6] The declaration "Let him be anathema" means "Let him be accursed or cut off from the Church." This statement shows how strongly the Trinity was held to be an essential doctrine of the faith by the early Church.

The Mystery of the Trinity Revealed in Ancient Jewish Writings

A few years ago I made a fascinating discovery in the ancient writings of the Jewish sages that were recorded thousands of years ago during the centuries surrounding the life of Jesus Christ and the destruction of the Second Temple in A.D. 70. This discovery suggests that the mystery of the Trinity was understood by some of the greatest of the ancient Jewish sages and writers. Furthermore, this doctrine of the Trinity was recorded in the writings of these great Jewish teachers and sages in their *Targums* (paraphrases of Scripture) and their commentaries (including the *Zohar*).

Both Christians from Gentile backgrounds and Jewish Messianic believers accepted the teaching of the Bible from Genesis to Revelation that shows that God has revealed Himself throughout the Scriptures in the form of the three persons of the Godhead, or as the Jewish sages wrote, "three manifestations" or "three emanations."

Many students of the Bible will be as astonished as I was when I first discovered these provocative ancient Jewish theological writings. They helped me understand why so many of the Jews in Israel and throughout the Roman Empire rapidly accepted the claims of Jesus of Nazareth to be both the Messiah and the true Son of God. Any student of the history of religion knows that the Jewish people, together with the Muslims, have historically rejected the truth of Christianity, primarily because they reject the claims that Jesus is the Son of God. The Jews and Muslims generally reject Christ because they believe that Christianity teaches polytheism, that we believe there are three Gods, not one. They generally fail to understand that Christians believe and uphold the biblical teaching that there is only one God. Both Jews and Muslims understand the truth that is clearly expressed numerous times in the Old Testament that there is only one God, but because they misunderstand the biblical teaching about the Trinity, they reject Christianity without examining the claims of Christ.

The question that occurred to me several years ago was this: Why did hundreds of thousands of Jews accept the claims of Jesus to be the Son of God? We know from early Church history that many of those who first accepted the Gospel throughout the Roman Empire were Jews. The apostle Paul and other Jewish Christian missionaries were accepted as teachers and worshippers in the Jewish synagogues throughout the empire for one hundred years, from the resurrection of Jesus in A.D. 32 until the rebellion against Rome in A.D. 135. During the three years of battle for Jewish independence led by the general Simeon Bar Kochba, many of his followers (including the famous Rabbi Akiba) declared that Bar Kochba was Israel's true messiah.

Naturally the Jewish Christian believers were forced to withdraw from the Jewish forces fighting against Rome because, as followers of Jesus Christ as the true Messiah, they could not acknowledge the false claims of Simeon Bar Kochba. Unfortunately, this rejection was treated as treason by the Jews who were involved in a life and death struggle with six legions of the cruel Emperor Hadrian. The war for Jewish independence ended in A.D. 135 with the massacre of one and a half million men, women, and children in the Jewish army and their civilian followers. From A.D. 135, the Jews that were believers in Jesus were no longer welcome in the Jewish synagogues. The great schism began between Jews and Christians that has tragically continued for the last two thousand years.

However, to return to my question: Why did many Jews in the first century of this era accept the claim that Jesus is God, while most Jews in later centuries have rejected this claim out of hand? I believe the answer can be found in these ancient Jewish *Targums* and the *Zohar*, which we will examine in this chapter. These writings clearly reveal that the Jews in the centuries surrounding the life of Jesus Christ understood that the sacred Scriptures taught that there was a profound mystery regarding the triune nature of God. That mystery is revealed in the *Targums* and the *Zohar*. There is One God, who is revealed in three persons — the Trinity. Since these *Targums* were read in the synagogue every Sabbath day, these concepts would have been widely known to religious Jews in that day. I believe that the evidence we will examine will prove that these writings prepared many Jews to accept the claim of Jesus to be the Son of God because their greatest religious teachers, including Rabbi Simon ben Jochai and Rabbi Eliezer, writers of the *Zohar*, and the writers of the *Targums*,

Jonathan ben Uziel and Onkelos the Proselyte, all taught the mystery of God expressed as "Three in One."

In the remaining pages of this chapter, I will share a number of fascinating ancient Hebrew writings from the distant past that reveal that these brilliant Jewish writers anticipated the New Testament's revelation that Jesus was truly the Son of God. It was natural that the Jews in the first century found it difficult to accept the claims of Jesus of Nazareth to be the Son of God and to be "equal with the Father." The obvious problem faced by Jewish religious scholars when they encountered the unusual name *Elohim* אלהים, the plural name for God, repeatedly in the Bible was the question, Why would God identify Himself in the plural form? One of the ways these Jewish scholars escaped the clear suggestion of the plurality of persons in the Godhead, as found in the word *Elohim*, was to claim that this expression was simply an example of the "royal plural form" used by kings and queens to express their royal nature. The famous Rabbi Aben Ezra, writing around A.D. 1100, suggested this as a solution. The "royal plural" is an unusual plural form of speech used by such royalty as Queen Victoria when she uttered her famous line, "We are not amused."

While this evasion regarding "Elohim" as a "royal plural" appears in numerous Jewish commentaries on the Scriptures, it does not solve the problem. There is no evidence that this royal plural form of speaking was ever used in ancient biblical days. The kings and leaders of Israel and the leaders of surrounding pagan nations, such as King Nebuchadnezzar or King Cyrus, never used this form of speech. In fact, it is a comparatively modern invention that was created by medieval monarchs to emphasize their elevated status to rule their kingdoms in accordance with the theory of the "divine right of kings." However, all of the leaders and kings in the Scriptures speak in the singular form, never in the plural form of address. The normal mode of royal speech in biblical times was always the same singular form used by King Nebuchadnezzar in the book of Daniel: "Therefore I make a decree . . ." (Daniel 3:29). Therefore, the plural name for God *Elohim* אלהים must refer to the mystery of the plurality and unity of God in the Trinity.

The *Zohar*

The *Zohar* is a fascinating book written by Rabbi Simon ben Jochai and his son Rabbi Eliezer in the years following the Roman army's tragic destruction of the Temple in Jerusalem in A.D. 70. For many years father and son were forced to hide from the troops of the Roman emperor who had passed the death sentence on them both. The *Zohar* is held in great reverence by Jewish scholars, and has also been of great interest to many Christian scholars in past centuries, beginning with Pico della Mirandola (a medieval scholar), who wrote Latin summaries of its teachings. Pico della Mirandola was the first Christian writer to conclude that significant parallels existed between some of the deeper doctrines of Christianity and Judaism, as found in the writings of the *Zohar*. He believed that the doctrines of the Trinity, the doctrine of original sin, and the mystery of the incarnation of Christ were referred to in the ancient *Zohar*.

The Christian writer Petrius Galatinus published his book, *De Arcanis Catholicae Veritatis*, which illustrated his research into the ancient Jewish teachings of the *Zohar* which paralleled several of the major doctrines of the Church. Other Christian researchers on the *Zohar's* teaching include the writer Gasparellus, Kircher, and Knorr von Rosenroth. The fascinating book *Kabbalah Denudata* by Knorr von Rosenroth was published in 1677 and later translated into English almost two centuries later. His book is valuable for Christian scholars unfamiliar with the Hebrew and Aramaic languages who wish to examine the teachings of the *Zohar*.

Many of the most difficult areas of the Scriptures are discussed and debated in the pages of the *Zohar*. The primary value for Christians is the deeper understanding we can gain as to what the Jewish religious leaders truly thought about the teachings of the Old Testament, including the mystery of the Trinity. I was amazed when I first read the English translations of this book because I discovered that these brilliant Jewish sages had come to a clear understanding of the mystery of the Trinity two thousand years ago. This important discovery of the teaching of the Trinity by the ancient Jewish sages helps us to understand why many Jews accepted the teaching of John the Baptist and Jesus of Nazareth during the first century of this era. Although many Jews naturally rejected Jesus' claims to be the Messiah and the Son of

God, many Jews accepted that Jesus was the fulfillment of the ancient prophecies of the Old Testament. In addition, the fact that the ancient Jewish sages spoke of the mystery of the plural nature of God prepared many in the Jewish nation to accept Jesus' claims that "I and my Father are one" (John 10:30).

The Trinity As Taught by the Ancient Jewish Sages

Do the ancient Jewish books such as the *Zohar* and the *Targums* actually refer to the Trinity and clearly describe the plural nature of God? Let me present the evidence, and you will be able to judge for yourself. Consider the following statements:

"How can they (the three) be One? Are they verily One, because we call them One ?

How Three can be One, can only be known through the revelation of the Holy Spirit."[7]

According to the *Zohar*, one day Rabbi Simeon ben Jochai was teaching his son Rabbi Eliezer about the mystery of the triune nature of God. He instructed his pupil by saying, "Come and see the mystery of the word יהוה, Jehova: there are three steps, each existing by itself; nevertheless they are One, and so united that one cannot be separated from the other."[8]

Rabbi Simeon ben Jochai indicates in another passage of the *Zohar* that these three steps as revealed in *Elohim* אלהים (God) are three substantive beings or three divine persons united in one.

The Ancient Holy One is revealed with three Heads, which are united in One, and that Head is thrice exalted. The Ancient Holy one is described as being Three; it is because the other Lights emanating from Him are included in the Three. Yet the Ancient One is described as being two. The Ancient One includes these two. He is the Crown of all that is exalted; the Chief of the chief, so exalted, that He cannot be known to perfection. Thus the other lights are two complete ones, yet is the Ancient Holy One described complete as one, and He is one, positively one; thus are the other lights united and glorified in because they are one.[9]

Rabbi Simeon ben Jochai wrote a fascinating passage recorded in the *Zohar* that is as clear a discussion of the mystery of the

Trinity as you could find in any Christian theology text. Rabbi Simeon comments on the text found in Deuteronomy 32:39: "See now that I, I am he, and Elohim is not with me."[10]

> He said: "Friends, here are some profound mysteries which I desire to reveal to you now that permission has been given to utter them. Who is it that says, 'See now that I, I am He?' This is the Cause which is above all those on high, that which is called *the Cause of causes*. It is above those other causes, since none of those causes does anything till it obtains permission from that which is above it, as we pointed out above in respect to the expression, 'Let us make man.' 'Us' certainly refers to two, of which one said to the other above it, 'Let us make,' nor did it do anything save with the permission and direction of the one above it, while the one above did nothing without consulting its colleague. But that which is called 'the Cause above all causes,' which has no superior or even equal, as it is written, 'To whom shall ye liken me, that I should be equal?' (referring to Isaiah 40:25), said, 'See now that I, I am he, and Elohim is not with me,' from whom he should take counsel, like that of which it is written, 'and God said, Let us make man.'"

Another book written by Rabbi Simeon ben Jochai, known as *The Propositions of the Zohar*, records the mystery of the Shechinah glory of God in these words.

> . . . the exalted Shechinah comprehends the Three highest Sephiroth; of Him (God) it is said, (Ps. lxii. 12), "God hath spoken once; twice have I heard this." Once and twice means the Three exalted Sephiroth, of whom it is said: Once, once, and once; that is, Three united in One. This is the mystery.[11]

Another famous Jewish scholar, Rabbi Eliezer Hakkalir, who lived at the time of Rabbi Simeon ben Jochai, also taught the scriptural doctrine that there were three distinct Beings revealed in the one unified Godhead. In his commentary on Genesis 1:1, Rabbi Hakkalir wrote the following:

> When God created the world, He created it through the

Three Sephiroth, namely, through Sepher, Sapher and Vesaphur, by which the Three הויות (Beings) are meant . . . The Rabbi, my Lord Teacher of blessed memory, explained Sepher, Sapher, and Sippur, to be synonymous to Ja, Jehovah, and Elohim meaning to say, that the world was created by these three names.[12]

Rabbi Bechai, in his commentary on Genesis 1:1 (p. 1, col. 2) explained that the word Elohim אלהים is compounded of two words, הם and אל, that is, "These are God." The plural is expressed by the letter jod (י).

Another extraordinary reference to the Trinity is found in the *Zohar* :

> Here is the secret of two names combined which are completed by a third and become one again. "And God said Let us make Man." It is written, "The secret of the Lord is to them that fear him" (Psalm 25:34). That most reverend Elder opened an exposition of this verse by saying "Simeon Simeon, who is it that said: 'Let us make man?' Who is this Elohim?" With these words the most reverend Elder vanished before anyone saw him . . . Truly now is the time to expound this mystery, because certainly there is here a mystery which hitherto it was not permitted to divulge, but now we perceive that permission is given." He then proceeded: "We must picture a king who wanted several buildings to be erected, and who had an architect in his service who did nothing save with his consent. The king is the supernal wisdom above, the Central Column being the king below: Elohim is the architect above . . . and Elohim is also the architect below, being as such the Divine Presence (Shekinah) of the lower world.[13]

The Shema: "Hear O Israel, the Lord Our God Is One Lord."

Every religiously observant Jew makes a daily affirmation of his faith in speaking the Shema, the inspired words of Scripture, as recorded in Deuteronomy 6:4: "Hear O Israel, the Lord our God is one Lord." In these sacred words, the speaker first uses the singular name of God, יהוה "Jehovah," then the plural name, אלהים "our God" (strictly, "Gods"), and then again the singular name, יהוה "Jehovah," and concluded with אחד "One." Most people hearing this affirmation would assume that the simple meaning is a direct declaration that "there is only one God." This biblical statement does declare that there is only one God — a statement accepted whole heartedly by both Jews and Christians. However, as pointed out earlier in this chapter, the mysterious use of the plural name for God, *Elohim* אלהים, suggests that this passage also contains God's revelation of His mysterious nature as Three in One and One in Three. When I searched the ancient Jewish books that were written during the period from the return from the captivity in Babylon in 536 B.C. to the destruction of the Second Temple in A.D. 70 I was amazed to find that many prominent Jewish sages taught the mystery of the Trinity based on this very passage in Deuteronomy 6:4.

We need to carefully read the words of this ancient teaching found in the *Zohar* regarding the deeper meaning and mystery of God found in Deuteronomy 6:4: "Hear, O Israel: The Lord our God is one Lord." Although the language is awkward, it clearly teaches the Trinity.

> We have said in many places, that this daily form of prayer is one of those passages concerning the Unity, which is taught in the Scriptures. In Deut. vi. 4, we read first יהוה "Jehovah", then, אלהים "our God," and again, יהוה "Jehovah," which together make one Unity. But how can three Names [three beings] be one? Are they verily one, because we call them one? How three can be one can only be known through the revelation of the Holy Spirit, and, in fact, with closed eyes. This is also the mystery of the voice. The voice is heard only as one sound, yet it consists of three substances, fire, wind, and water, but all three are one, as indicated through the mystery of the voice. Thus are (Deut. 6:4) "The Lord, our God, the Lord," but One Unity, three Substantive Beings which are One; and this is indicated by the voice which are One; and this is indicated by the voice which a person uses in reading the words, "Hear, O Israel," thereby comprehending with the understanding the most perfect Unity of Him who is infinite; because all three (Jehovah, Elohim, Jehovah) are read with one voice, which indicates a Trinity.[14]

374

This statement from the *Zohar* is an incredible acknowledgment of the nature of God, as revealed in the Scriptures, as a Trinity. Rabbi Menachem of Recanati, writing in his *Commentary on the Pentateuch* about the Deuteronomy 6:4 passage, also clearly describes the mystery of the Trinity, the threefold Unity of the Godhead. Rabbi Menachem wrote about these mysteries and concluded, "These are secrets which are revealed only to those who are reaping upon the holy field, as it is written 'The secret of the Lord is with them that fear Him'" (Psalms 25:14). Rabbi Menachem wrote the following on the Trinity:

> "Hear, O Israel, the Lord our god is one Lord." This verse is the root of our faith, therefore Moses records it after the ten commandments. The reason (that there is said יהוה, Lord, אלהים, our God, and יהוה, Lord) is, because the word שמע does not here signify "Hear;" but "to gather together, to unite," as in 1 Samuel 15:4, "Saul gathered together the people." The meaning implied is The Inherent-Ones are so united together, one in the other without end, they being the exalted God. He mentions the three names mystically to indicate the three exalted original Ones.[15]

Let Us Make Man in Our Image

Moses recorded God's creation of man in the first chapter of Genesis. The inspired account read, "And God said, 'Let us make man in our image.'" The question that has been asked by many Christian and Jewish commentators is this: Who did God refer to as "us" when he stated "Let *us* make man in our image?" The answer is this: God referred to the other members of the Trinity when He said "Let us. . . ." This statement clearly refers to the Trinity.

In Genesis 1:26 God says, "Let us make man in our image." In this passage we find God definitely speaking of the Godhead in the plural form using the word "us." Then, we find a sentence in which the word "God" is written in the singular tense (Genesis 1:27). Therefore, this passage suggests that God as revealed in plurality is yet One God. In Genesis 11:5, Moses speaks of God using the singular noun, "And the Lord came down to see the city." However, in the seventh verse of this passage God Himself speaks in the plural form "us": "Go to, let us go down, and we will confound their language." This transformation from the singular form of God to the plural reveals the mystery of the Trinitarian nature of God as declared in the doctrine of the Trinity.

In the prologue to the *Zohar* we find the following statement that suggests the clear knowledge of the Jewish sages about the plurality of the One God.

> The fourth precept is to acknowledge that the Lord is God, as we read: 'Know this day, and lay it to thy heart that the Lord, he is God' (Deuteronomy 4:39); namely, to combine the name *Elohim* "God" with the name *Jehovah* "Lord" in the consciousness that they form an indivisible unity.[16]

The latest English translation of the *Zohar* also contains fascinating passages revealing the knowledge of the ancient Jews about the Trinity.

> All those supernal lights exist in their image below — some of them in their image below upon the earth; but in themselves they are all suspended in the "firmament of the heaven." Here is the secret of two names combined which are completed by a third and become one again. "And God said, Let us make Man. . . ."[17]

In the second Psalm, we read, "Thou art My Son; this day have I begotten Thee." It is interesting that Rabbi Simeon ben Jochai comments in *The Propositions of the Zohar* on this passage:

> There is a perfect Man, who is an Angel. This Angel is Metatron, the Keeper of Israel; He is a man in the image of the Holy One, blessed be He, who is an Emanation from Him; yea, He is Jehovah; of Him cannot be said, He is created, formed or made; but He is the Emanation from God. This agrees exactly with what is written, Jeremiah 23:5, of צמח דוד, David's Branch, that though He shall be a perfect man, yet He is "The Lord our Righteousness.[18]

In this incredible passage from *The Propositions of the Zohar* we can see the ancient Jewish sages understood the mystery of the Trinity and the realization that the "Son of God" is truly the Holy One of God.

The Trinity Was Also Taught in the Ancient Jewish Targums

As I mentioned in an earlier chapter, the *Targums* were a series of paraphrases and commentaries on the Jewish Bible written in the Chaldean language that were read in the synagogue every Sabbath day. The two major commentaries were written by Jonathan and Onkelos. *The Targum of Jonathan* was written by Jonathan ben Uziel, a famous scholar who was a student of the great Jewish scholar Hillel the Great during the decades before the birth of Christ. *The Targum of Onkelos*, which contained commentary on the five books of Torah, was written around the same time period. Jewish scholars believe that Onkelos the Proselyte was probably descended from Gentiles who had converted to Judaism. Both *Targums* were considered virtually as inspired as the Bible itself and were read in the synagogue after the reading of the Torah in Hebrew.

These *Targums* are valuable because they allow us to understand exactly how the ancient Jewish sages interpreted these important biblical passages that deal with the mystery of the nature of God. While only the words of Scripture itself are authoritative in teaching us the true doctrines of God, we can learn a great deal from examining the writings of the ancient Jewish scholars who understood the nuances of the Hebrew text. Furthermore, these *Targums* provide a precious insight into the true understanding of the Trinity by the Jewish sages who lived before the birth of Jesus. Let's examine these *Targums* to understand exactly what they taught about the nature of God.

In the so-called *Jerusalem Targum*, written by Jonathon ben Uziel, we find a commentary on the passage in Genesis that describes God's destruction of Sodom and Gomorrah: "Then the Lord rained upon Sodom and upon Gomorrah brimstone and fire from the Lord out of heaven" (Genesis 19:24). The Targum describes the Lord (יהוה) in this passage as "the Word of the Lord," which is a title for Jehovah suggesting the second person of the Trinity that appears often throughout these paraphrases: "And the Word of the Lord caused to descend upon the people of Sodom and Gomorrah, brimstone and fire from the Lord from heaven."[19]

The Targum on Exodus 3:14 reveals God's declaration of His eternal identity using the same title of "the Word of the Lord" to describe God. "And God said unto Moses, I AM THAT I AM: and he said, Thus shalt thou say unto the children of Israel, I AM hath sent me unto you" (Exodus 3:14). The *Jerusalem Targum* on Exodus 3:14 reads as follows: "And the Word of the Lord said unto Moses: I am He who said unto the world, Be! and it was: and who in the future shall say to it, Be! and it shall be. And He said Thus thou shalt say to the Children of Israel: I Am hath sent me unto you."[20]

The Angel of the Lord and the Angel of the Covenant

The ancient Jewish commentary by Rabbi Bechai (col. 1, p. 35) that describes Abraham's obedience to God's call for him to sacrifice Isaac provides an extraordinary insight into the writer's appreciation of the Trinity. Moses records in Genesis 22:11 that "the angel of the Lord" was the person of the Trinity that intervened to prevent the sacrifice of Isaac. "And the angel of the Lord called unto him out of heaven, and said, Abraham, Abraham: and he said, Here am I."[21] This portion of the deepest teaching of the great sages of Israel provides powerful evidence for the fact that some of the Jewish writers in ancient times understood the mystery of the Trinity:

> It is necessary that thou shouldest understand what in this section (Abraham's sacrifice) is related; namely, that He who is tempting is God, and He who is restraining is the *Angel* of the blessed God. . . . The eyes of Abraham's understanding were opened, that this *Angel* was not one of the intelligences, but one of the Inherent Ones, which cannot be separated, nor cut off one from the other. If this *Angel* had been one of the intelligences, Abraham would not have obeyed his voice, when restraining him to do what God had commanded him; yea, an *Angel* would have no authority to say, "Thou hast not with holden thy son from *Me*, but would have said, from Him." But this *Angel* was one of the Inherent Ones, the great *Angel* . . . and in fact it was that *Angel* of whom it is said, "for my name is in Him."

Another famous sage, Rabbi Moses ben Nachman, wrote about this mysterious Angel of the Lord, the great Lawgiver, that appeared to Moses in the flames of the burning bush. Rabbi Nachman points out that the Bible refers to this appearance of God to Moses as the Angel of the Lord in Exodus 3:2: "And the angel of the Lord appeared unto him in a flame of fire out of the midst of a bush." However, only two verses later Moses declared that it was the Lord God who was speaking to him from the burning bush: "And when the Lord saw that he turned aside to see, God called unto him out of the midst of the bush, and said, Moses, Moses. And he said, Here am I" (Exodus 3:4). These Jewish sages obviously understood that the Scriptures taught that the Angel of the Lord was truly God. Rabbi Nachman commented as follows:

> It is said: "An Angel of the Lord appeared unto him in a flame of fire," and *(Elohim)* אלהים, "God called unto him." This is all one, namely, whether he saith "The *Angel,* or *(Elohim)* אלהים, "God spake to him out of the midst of the bush". . . Therefore be not astonished that Moses hid his face before this *Angel*; because this *Angel* mentioned here is the *Angel, the Redeemer,* concerning whom it is written; "I am the God of Bethel;" and here, "I am the God of thy father, the God of Abraham, the God of Isaac, and the God of Jacob." It is the same of whom it is said, "My name is in Him."[22]

The significance of this study of the Trinity is that it will enable us to appreciate the biblical revelation of the mysterious nature of God who is revealed to us as the Father, the Son, and the Holy Spirit. As we grow and mature as Christians we need to come to a fuller understanding of the deeper truths taught to us by the beloved Scriptures. The apostle Paul shared this wonderful blessing with the Church at Ephesus that I would like to use to conclude this chapter. "Blessed be the God and Father of our Lord Jesus Christ, who hath blessed us with all spiritual blessings in heavenly places in Christ" (Ephesians 1:3).

Notes

1. Ivan Panin.

2. Lucian, *Philopatris* (A.D. 160).

3. *Shepherd of Hermas*, 1, III, Similitude 9, 12, 118.

4. Edward Burton, *Testimonies of the Ante-Nicene Fathers to the Divinity of Christ* (1829).

5. Edward Burton, *Testimonies of the Ante-Nicene Fathers to the Divinity of Christ* (1829).

6. The Council of Sirmium, *Ath. de Synodis,* vol. 1 (A.D. 351) 743.

7. *Zohar*, vol. ii. p. 43, versa., 22.

8. *Zohar*, vol. iii. Amsterdam edition. 65.

9. *Zohar*, vol. iii. Amsterdam edition. 288.

10. Rabbi Simeon ben Jochai, *Zohar.*

11. Rabbi Simeon ben Jochai, *The Propositions of the Zohar*, cap. 38, Amsterdam edition. 113.

12. Rabbi Eliezer Hakkalir, *The Book of Creation.* 28–29.

13. *Zohar*, vol. 1, Soncino Press edition. 90–91.

14. *Zohar.*

15. Rabbi Menachem, *Commentary on the Pentateuch,* Venice edition. 267.

16. *Zohar*, vol. 1, Soncino Press edition. 51.

17. *Zohar*, vol. 1, Soncino Press edition. 90–91.

18. Rabbi Simeon ben Jochai, *The Propositions of the Zohar.*

19. Jonathon ben Uziel, *Jerusalem Targum.*

20. Jonathon ben Uziel, *Jersualem Targum.*

21. Rabbi Bechai, col. 1, 35.

22. Rabbi Moses ben Nachman.

7

The Incredible Bible Codes

Several years ago computer scientists in Israel discovered a staggering phenomenon — encoded words hidden within the text of the Bible. Within the Hebrew text of the Old Testament they found hidden codes that revealed an astonishing knowledge of future events and personalities. The existence of these codes can only be explained if God inspired the writers to record His precise words.

An Astonishing Discovery

Rabbi Michael Dov Weissmandl, a brilliant Czechoslovakian Jewish scholar in astronomy, mathematics, and Judaic studies, found an obscure reference to these codes in a book written by a fourteenth-century rabbi, Rabbeynu Bachayah. This reference described a pattern of letters encoded within the Torah, the first five books of the Bible. This discovery during the years before World War I inspired Rabbi Weissmandl to search for other examples of codes hidden within the Torah. During the war years, he found that he could locate certain meaningful words, phrases, and word pairs, such as "hammer" and "anvil," if he found the first letter and then skipped forward a certain number of letters to find the second one, and the same number again to find the third one, and so on. As an example, he found the letter tav (ת), the first letter of the word *Torah* תורה, the Hebrew word for "law," within

381

the first word of Genesis 1:1, "Beginnings" *Bereishis* בראשית.
Then, by skipping forward fifty letters, he found the second letter
vav ו. He continued to skip forward fifty letters and found reysh ר
and finally the last letter hey ה, completing the spelling of the
word *Torah* תורה. The rabbi was astonished to find that many
significant words were hidden within the text of the Torah at
equally spaced intervals. These intervals varied from every two
letters up to hundreds of letters apart.

Although Rabbi Weissmandl found many encoded names by
manually counting the letters in the text, he did not record his
code discoveries in writing. Fortunately, some of his students did.
Over the following decades, students in Israel who had heard
about his research began searching the Torah for themselves to
ascertain whether or not such codes actually existed. Their discoveries ultimately resulted in research studies at Hebrew University
that have proven the validity of the codes, now known as Equidistant Letter Sequence (ESL) codes. In the last decade, the introduction of sophisticated high-speed computers has allowed
Jewish scholars at Hebrew University to explore the text of the
Torah in ways that were unavailable to previous generations.

In 1988 three mathematics and computer experts at Hebrew
University and the Jerusalem College of Technology (Doron Witztum, Yoav Rosenberg, and Eliyahu Rips) completed an astonishing research project that followed up Rabbi Weismandl's original
research. As a result, they published a paper in August 1994 called
"Equidistant Letter Sequences in the Book of Genesis" in one of
the most prominent mathematical and scientific journals in the
world, the American mathematics journal *Statistical Science*.

In one experiment, the scientists arbitrarily chose three hundred Hebrew word-pairs that were logically related in meaning,
such as "hammer" and "anvil," or "tree" and "leaf," or "man" and
"woman." They asked the computer program to locate any such
word pairs anywhere in the Genesis text. Once the computer
found the first letter in the Hebrew word for "hammer," it would
look for the second letter at various intervals or spaces between
letters. If the program could not locate the second letter of the
target word "hammer" following the first letter at a two-letter
interval, it would search at a three-letter interval, then a four-letter
interval, and so forth. Once it located the second letter at, say, the
twelve-letter interval, it would then skip forward at the same

twelve-letter interval looking for the third letter, and so on through all 78,064 Hebrew letters in the book of Genesis. The computer also looked for coded words by checking in reverse order.

After the program had examined the text for each of the three hundred word pairs, the researchers were astonished to find that every single word-pair had been located in Genesis in close proximity to each other. As mathematicians and statisticians, they were naturally astounded because they knew it was impossible for humans to construct such an intricate and complicated pattern beneath a surface text, such as Genesis, which tells the history of the beginnings of the Jewish people. The odds against the three hundred word pairs occurring by random chance in the text of Genesis was staggering! The bottom line is that only a supernatural intelligence, far beyond our human ability, could have produced the intricate pattern of secretly coded words found in the Bible.

The Bible Codes Speak of Future Events

That was only the beginning of the story. In a 1994 follow-up paper, the team of researchers recorded the results of a new experiment involving their search for pairs of encoded words that related to events that occurred thousands of years after Moses wrote the Torah. They selected the names of thirty-four of the most prominent rabbis and Jewish sages who lived from the beginning of the ninth to the end of the eighteenth century. These Jewish sages had the longest biographies found in the *Encyclopedia of Great Men in Israel*[1], a well-respected Jewish reference book. They asked the computer program to search the text of the Torah for close word pairs coded at equally spaced intervals that contained the names of the famous rabbis, paired with their dates of birth or death (using the Hebrew month and day). The Jewish people celebrate the memory of their famous sages by commemorating the dates of their deaths. Incredibly, the computer program found every single one of the thirty-four names of these famous rabbis embedded in the text of Genesis. Each name of a rabbi was paired in significantly close proximity to the actual date of his birth or the date of his death. The odds against this occurring by chance were calculated by the Israeli mathematicians to be only one chance in 775,000,000!

The scientists and editors at the *Statistical Science* journal who reviewed the experimental data were naturally amazed. They demanded that the Israeli scientists run the computer test program again on a second sample group. This time they searched for the names of a second group of thirty-two prominent Jewish sages listed in the encyclopedia. To the astonishment of the skeptical reviewers, the results were equally successful with the second set of famous sages. The combined test revealed that the names and dates of the births or deaths of every one of the sixty-six most famous Jewish sages were encoded in close proximity within the text of Genesis.

Despite the fact that all of the science journal reviewers previously denied the inspiration of the Scriptures, the overwhelming evidence from the data was so strong that the journal editors reluctantly agreed to publish the article in its August 1994 issue under the title "Equidistant Letter Sequences in the Book of Genesis." Robert Kass, the editor of *Statistical Science*, wrote this comment about the study: "Our referees were baffled: their prior beliefs made them think the Book of Genesis could not possibly contain meaningful references to modern day individuals, yet when the authors carried out additional analyses and checks the effect persisted. The paper is thus offered to *Statistical Science* readers as a challenging puzzle." After three years of careful analysis by many scholars throughout the world, the experiment remains credible.

In October 1995, an article in *Bible Review* magazine by Dr. Jeffrey Satinover, reported that the mathematical probability that these sixty-six names of Jewish sages paired with their dates of birth or death occur by chance in an ancient text like Genesis is less than 1 chance in 2.5 billion! Interestingly, the researchers attempted to discover codes by running the computer program to test other religious Hebrew texts other than the Bible, such as the Samaritan Pentateuch. The Samaritans developed their own variant text of the five books of Moses, called the Samaritan Pentateuch, which differs in numerous small textual details from the standard Masoretic text of the Hebrew Bible. Despite the surface similarity of the two texts, the researchers could not detect significant numbers of word pairs in the Samaritan Pentateuch or any other Hebrew text. Similar tests were run on other Hebrew literature including the Jewish *Talmud* and a Hebrew translation of Tolstoy's novel *War and Peace*. The researchers also analyzed the Jewish Apocryphal books including *Tobit* and *Maccabees*. No significant codes were found in any of these non-biblical texts. Similar experiments were used to analyze sample texts written in other languages, such as English and German, but the tests failed to discover significant ELS codes in any other text.

The *Bible Review* article provoked an onslaught of letters (mostly critical) to the editor. Dr. Satinover responded to his critics as follows: "The robustness of the Torah codes findings derives from the rigor of the research. To be published in a journal such as *Statistical Science*, it had to run, without stumbling, an unusually long gauntlet manned by some of the world's most eminent statisticians. The results were thus triply unusual: in the extraordinariness of what was found; in the strict scrutiny the findings had to hold up under; and in the unusually small odds (less than 1 in 62,500) that they were due to chance. Other amazing claims about the Bible, Shakespeare, and so forth, have never even remotely approached this kind of rigor, and have therefore never come at all close to publication in a peer-reviewed, hardscience venue. The editor of *Statistical Science*, himself a skeptic, has challenged readers to find a flaw; though many have tried, none has succeeded. All the [basic] questions asked by *Bible Review* readers — and many more sophisticated ones — have therefore already been asked by professional critics and exhaustively answered by the research. Complete and convincing responses to even these initial criticisms can get fairly technical" (*Bible Review*, November 1995).

The Incredible Hitler and Holocaust Codes

The Israeli Jewish code researchers naturally wondered if these incredible Bible Codes might reveal anything about the Holocaust, the greatest tragedy in the history of the Jewish people. When they asked the computer program to search for the target words *Hitler*, *Nazis*, and *Holocaust*, the computer found that each of these target names were encoded in a cluster of codes within a passage in Deuteronomy 10:17–22. The word *Hitler* in Hebrew, היטלר, is spelled out at a 22-letter interval. Several of the names of concentration death camps were found embedded within this text, beginning with the second to last appearance of the Hebrew letter bet ב in this passage. The researchers counted every 13th letter from left to right and discovered that the coded letters spelled out the phrase *b'yam marah Auschwitz,* which means "in the bitter sea of Auschwitz." As they carried the counting forward another thirteen letters, they came to the letter resh ר. From the resh, they counted every 22nd letter from left to right and connected to the word היטלר *Hitler,* the greatest enemy of the Jews. The actual names of two of the Nazi concentration camps, *Auschwitz* and *Belsen,* were also encoded close to *Hitler* and *Berlin* in a cluster of encoded words hidden within the text of Deuteronomy. In addition, the researchers found the words *Germany, Poland, genocide, plagues, cremetoria, Fuhrer,* and *Mein Kampf.*

The researchers found that Deuteronomy 33:16 also contained a hidden message about the Nazi Holocaust. Beginning with the first Hebrew letter mem מ, they counted every 246th letter from left to right and found the encoded word *Melek Natzim,* which means as the "King of the Nazis." This passage revealed another fascinating code found in Deuteronomy 32:52. Beginning with the letter aleph א and counting from left to right every 670 letters spells the name *Aik'man,* a Hebrew variant of the name "Eichmann." Adolph Eichmann was the wicked Nazi official who designed the Final Solution, the evil system of concentration death camps used in the Holocaust. The series of hidden codes dealing with the Holocaust concluded in Deuteronomy 33:21. Many Jews have asked why the prophecies of the Bible say nothing about the Holocaust, the worst tragedy in the history of God's Chosen People. The discovery of the Bible Codes in the closing years of this century reveal that God encoded prophetic words about the Holocaust within the text of the Bible.

Note: The word "interval" indicates the number of Hebrew letters that are skipped in the orginal biblical passage to spell out the encoded word in equally spaced intervals (ELS). If the interval number in brackets is positive (22) then the encoded word begins at the indicated passage and reads right to left, skipping the indicated number of Hebrew letters. However, if the interval number in brackets is preceded by a minus sign (–13), the encoded word begins at the indicated passage and reads left to right, skipping the indicated number of Hebrew letters.

The Holocaust Codes

Encoded Name	Hebrew	Interval	Begins at:
Hitler	היטלר	(22)	Deut. 10:17
Auschwitz	אושויץ	(−13)	Deut. 10:21
Holocaust	שואה	(13)	Deut. 10:20
Germany	גרמניה	(−933)	Deut. 33:28
Crematorium for my sons	כבשן לבני	(134)	Deut. 31:28
The Holocaust	השואה	(50)	Deut. 31:16
Plagues	מגפות	(−134)	Deut. 32:32
Eichmann	אייכמן	(9670)	Deut. 32:52
Hitler	היטלר	(−3)	Num. 19:13
Mein Kampf	מין קאמפ	(9832)	Num. 22:1
Auschwitz	אושויץ	(−536)	Deut. 33:24
In Poland	בפולין	(−107)	Deut. 32:22
King of the Nazis	מלך נאצים	(−246)	Deut. 33:16
Genocide	רצח עם	(−22)	Deut. 33:21
The Fuhrer	הפירר	(5)	Deut. 32:50

The discovery of complex Hebrew codes that reveal supernatural and prophetic knowledge about the future has caused tremendous consternation in the academic community. The Bible Code phenomena challenges the long-held beliefs of liberal scholars, who generally reject the supernatural origin, as well as the verbal inspiration, of the Bible. In 1996, I published my book *The Signature of God*, which analyzed the archeological and scientific evidence that supported the inspiration and authority of the Scriptures. In this book, I presented numerous Bible Code discoveries, as well as those discovered by my friend Yacov Rambsel that reveal the name of Jesus encoded in the messianic passages of the Old Testament. Many Christians throughout the world viewed these code discoveries as powerful new evidence of the inspiration of the Word of God. Yacov and I have independently researched the phenomenon of the Bible Codes for the last six years. In the past twelve months, we have worked together to carefully examine a number of significant codes that will be fascinating to all those who love Jesus Christ as their Savior and Lord. These code discoveries will be revealed in the next two chapters.

A Word of Caution about the Bible Codes

Bible Codes are found only in the orthodox Hebrew text of the Old Testament

No one has been able to locate detailed, meaningful Bible codes in any other Hebrew literature outside the Bible. Experimenters have carefully examined other Hebrew writings for the existence of codes including the Jewish *Talmud*, the *Mishneh*, the Apocryphal writings of *Tobit* and *Maccabees*. They even examined modern Hebrew literature such as translations of *War and Peace*. However, the scientists found no significant pattern of codes in any other Hebrew literature outside the Old Testament. Several researchers have told me they found indications of codes in the Greek of the New Testament but no detailed research has been published to date.

Bible Codes cannot be used to accurately foretell future events.

One cannot discover meaningful encoded information about a future event until the event occurs. Otherwise, it is impossible to know what target word to ask the program to search for. However, once an event occurs, such as the War in the Gulf, we can ask the computer to look in the Bible text for such target words as "Saddam Hussein" or "General Schwarzkopf." The encoded information about a future event cannot be discovered in the biblical text in advance of the event because you wouldn't know what to ask the computer to look for. In other words, the Bible Codes can confirm that the Scriptures contain encoded data about historical events that occurred centuries after the Scriptures were written. However, the codes cannot be used to foretell future events. Even if you correctly guessed at the right target words for a future event, such as the assassination of a prominent politician, and you found the name of the person and the word "killed," you would still not know anything certain about the future. Until the event occurs, any suggestion that the occurrence of these two code words means that the politician would be killed would be merely a guess.

The Bible prohibits us from engaging in foretelling the future. A recent book called *The Bible Code*, by agnostic writer Michael Drosnin, claims that he, himself, discovered codes that allowed him to predict future events. However, a careful examination of his claims reveals that the encoded information he discovered is insufficient to allow anyone to confidently predict any future event. Michael Drosnin may have made a guess about a particular, tragic future event based on his discovery of the encoded name "Yitzchak Rabin." However, it was simply a guess. There was not enough information in the code he discovered to allow him to confidently affirm that a particular future event, namely the assassination of Yitzchak Rabin, would actually occur. Michael Drosnin claims that he warned the Prime Minister of Israel about the danger of assassination based on the fact that he found that one of the eight letters of the encoded words "Yitzchak Rabin" happened to appear in the surface text of Deuteronomy 4:42, which reads in Hebrew "assassin that will assassinate."

However, it was impossible to know in advance of the event what this particular combination actually meant. It could easily have meant that Prime Minister Rabin might order the assassination of some terrorist in the future, or it could easily have meant nothing at all. The point is that the limited information from the encoded words can only be accurately interpreted after the fulfillment of an historical event, such as the Holocaust, the Gulf War, or the crucifixion of Jesus Christ. The Lord did not place these codes within the Bible to enable men to play at becoming prophets of future events. The Bible repeatedly forbids fortune telling.

Both the major Israeli code researchers, including Professor Eli Rips, and all of the Christian researchers, including Yacov Rambsel and myself, deny that the Bible Codes can be used to accurately predict future events. The information encoded in the Bible can only be accurately interpreted after a historical event has actually occurred. Then, we can compare the details of the historical event with the encoded information in the Bible to determine whether or not God had encoded these prophetic details centuries before the events occurred. In this manner, the Bible Codes give God the glory, not the human researcher. The prophet Isaiah declared these words of God, "I will not give my glory unto another" (Isaiah 48:11).

Bible Codes do not reveal any hidden theological sentences, teachings, or doctrines.

There are no secret sentences, detailed messages, or theological statements in the encoded words. God's message of salvation and His commandments for holy living are only found in the normal, surface text of the Scriptures. The Bible Codes can only reveal key words, such as people's names, places, and occasionally, dates (using the Hebrew calendar), which provide confirmation of the supernatural inspiration and origin of the Scriptures.

The Bible Codes have nothing to do with numerology.

The phenomenon of the Bible Codes has nothing to do with numerology. Numerology is defined by the authoritative Webster's *Dictionary* as "the study of the occult significance of numbers." Numerology is connected with divination or foretelling the future and is clearly forbidden by the Bible. There is nothing occult or secret about the codes. This phenomenon was openly published in scientific and mathematical journals, taught, and broadcast since it was first discovered twelve years ago.

The particular interval between the Hebrew letters, the actual number of letters to be skipped, has no importance or significance. The codes have nothing to do with "the occult significance of numbers." Obviously, the coded words are found at various intervals (i.e., by skipping 2, 7, 61, or more letters). However, the significance or meaning of the encoded word does not relate to the particular interval (the number of letters skipped). Either a particular word is spelled out in Hebrew letters at equal intervals or it is not. Anyone can examine a particular encoded word and verify for themselves that these words are truly spelled out at ELS intervals. Computer programs such as Torah Codes and Bible Scholar are publically available to allow anyone to verify these codes for themselves. These programs can be ordered from our company if you wish to personally research the Bible Codes.

Why Did God Place These Hidden Bible Codes in the Bible?

For almost seventeen centuries, from the time of Emperor Constantine's conversion in A.D. 300 until the beginning of our century, the Bible was generally accepted by the majority of Western culture as the inspired and authoritative Word of God. However, we have witnessed an unrelenting assault on the authority of the Bible by the intellectual elite, the academic community, liberal theologians, and the media during the last hundred years. Most people in our culture have been exposed to countless attacks on the authority and accuracy of the Scriptures throughout high school, university, and from the mass media. I believe that God has provided this extraordinary new evidence in the form of the Bible Codes to prove to this generation of skeptics that the Bible is truly the Word of God. The complex nature of these codes means that the phenomenal discovery of these encoded words could not have occurred until the development of high-speed computers during the last fifteen years. In a sense, God secretly hid these incredible codes within the text of the Bible thousands of years ago with a time lock that could not be opened until the arrival of our generation and the development of sophisticated computers. In His prophetic foreknowledge, God knew that our generation would be characterized by an unrelenting attack on the authority of the Scriptures. No previous generation needed the additional scientific evidence provided by the discovery of these codes as much as our present skeptical generation.

The discovery of these incredible Bible Codes provides powerful evidence to our skeptical generation that God truly inspired the writers of the Bible to record His message to mankind. These encoded words describing the names of people, places, and dates provide powerful evidence to any unbiased inquirer that they can trust the supernatural message of the Bible.

Hundreds of years ago a famous rabbi, known as the Vilna Gaon, lived and taught in the city of Vilna, Latvia, near the Baltic Sea in northern Europe. This brilliant and mystical Jewish sage taught his students that God had hidden a vast amount of information secretly encoded within the Hebrew letters of the Torah. Consider the fascinating and suggestive statement about the hidden codes by this famous Jewish sage.

> The rule is that all that was, is, and will be unto the end of time is included in Torah from first word to the last word. And not merely in a general sense, but including the details of every species and of each person individually, and the most minute details of everything that happened to him from the day of his birth until his death; likewise of every kind of animal and beast and living thing that exists, and of herbage, and of all that grows or is inert. (Vilna Gaon, Introduction to *Sifra Ditzniut*)

There is a tradition that a number of codes were discovered in past centuries by various Jewish sages, including Rabbeinu Bachya, Moses Maimonides, and the Vilna Gaon. Since World War II Rabbi Michael Weissmandl and others have taught about these codes. There is an interesting statement suggesting knowledge of the codes in the Jewish mystical writing known as the *Zohar*. "The entire Torah is replete with Divine Names. Divine Names run through every single word in the Torah" (*Zohar* II, 87a). In approximately A.D. 1200, the brilliant Jewish sage Moses Maimonides, known as Ramban, made a curious comment about this statement in the *Zohar* that indicated he understood that there were complex codes hidden in the Torah. He said that the hidden codes provided another reason why a Torah scroll should be considered as unfit for use if even one single letter was missing from the text. The removal or addition of a single letter from the Hebrew text would eliminate the codes found hidden within that section of text. Also, there is a suggestive statement in the *Talmud* that refers to the codes: "Everything is alluded to in the Torah" (*Talmud Tan'anis* 9a). Other references to the existence of the Bible Codes are found in the following passages: *Zohar* II, 161a; *B'reishis Rabah* 1:1; *Tanchuma* 1:1; *Raya M'hemna*; and *B'reishis* 23a.

ELS Bible Code Analysis Using Computer Programs

The primary method used by researchers to find the coded words is called *equidistant-letter sequence* (ELS). During the last six years I have analyzed the Hebrew Scriptures using this method with several computer programs I obtained in Jerusalem during the 1991 War in the Gulf. These computer programs enable a researcher to discover various Bible Codes for themselves through the examination of particular Hebrew letters that are distributed at equal intervals, (i.e., fifth, tenth, seventeenth letter, throughout the text). I use the Torah Codes computer program that allows a researcher to personally search for any encoded word within the first five books of the Old Testament. In addition, the Bible Scholar computer program will print out the text of any passage of the Old Testament in Hebrew or English from Genesis to Malachi. This will allow a researcher with a MacIntosh or IBM-compatible computer to verify a particular code discovery reported by any other researcher. These computer programs are allowing thousands of Bible students to begin searching the biblical text to both verify the code discoveries of others and to conduct independent research on their own. Anyone familiar with computers who is fascinated by this research project can personally participate by acquiring such a computer program. In addition, they will find that a Hebrew-English Interlinear Bible and a Hebrew-English dictionary are helpful in their research.

The Bible Codes: Equidistant-Letter Sequence

The Hebrew word for "equidistant sequence" is *shalav* שלב, which means either "equally spaced rungs on a ladder" or "several objects equally spaced from one another," such as letters in a text.

I invited my friend Yacov Rambsel to a scholarly Bible conference in January 1997 held at Tyndale Theological Seminary in Dallas, Texas. I presented the phenomenon of the Bible Codes to this group of academics and Hebrew scholars. I illustrated numerous encoded words, as shown in my book *The Signature of God*, including a number of Yacov's discoveries of the name of Jesus *Yeshua* encoded in the Old Testament. After discussing numerous codes found in the Hebrew text, I introduced Yacov to the group for an in depth discussion about the method of analysis used in our research. One of the scholars asked if we had discovered any direct reference to the Bible code phenomenon encoded in the Scriptures itself.

The Encoded Phrase "Equidistant-Letter Sequence"
Shalav A'ot

Immediately, Yacov and I entered the Hebrew word *shalav* שלב, which means "equidistant," into the Torah Codes computer program on my Powerbook 1400 laptop computer to search the Scriptures for this target word. In just a few minutes, we were able to report to this group that we had discovered the encoded words "equidistant" *shalav* שלב in every one of the five books of the Torah. The full phrase, "equidistant-letter sequence" *shalav a'ot*, was found in the Hebrew text at equal intervals in Genesis through Deuteronomy. One example of this insight is found in Genesis 20:2, at equal intervals of every 5th letter from right to left. This example from Genesis 20:2 that we presented to the scholars at the Dallas conference is illustrated below.

Genesis *Bereishis* בראשית 20:2 says, "And Abraham said of Sarah, his wife, She is my sister: and Abimelech king of Gerar sent, and took Sarah." The Hebrew text for this verse, according to the Masoretic text, is given below. I have removed the spaces between each word and enlarged every fifth letter to emphasize the Hebrew letters that spell out the words "the lattice work of the equidistant-letter sequence."

וייאמראבּרהמסאלשׁרהאשׁתואחתיהוא
וישׁלחאבימלךמלדגררויקחאתשׁרה

Starting with the enlarged heh (ה) on the second line to the far left and counting every fifth letter from left to right, we find the encoded words *hacharak oht shalav* החרך אות שלב, which means, "the latticework of the equidistant-letter sequence." It was fascinating to discover that God had encoded in every one of the five books of the Torah the Hebrew letters of the words "equidistant-letter sequence" *shalav a'ot* אות שלב, the actual words used by the modern Israeli researchers to describe the Bible Codes phenomenon. This phrase was encoded in the following passages: Genesis 20:2, every fifth letter from left to right; Exodus 35:21–24, every 38th letter from left to right; Leviticus 10:10, every 78th letter from left to right; Numbers 1:45, every 89th letter from left to right; Deuteronomy 13:19, every 61st letter from left to right.

Answers to Criticism and Questions about the Codes

Michael Drosnin's book, *The Bible Code*, published in the late spring of 1997, caused a great sensation in the secular community and the Christian community. Although this book appeared almost one year after my book, *The Signature of God,* and the books of several Israelis about the codes, *The Bible Code* was extensively promoted by its publisher in virtually every major media outlet from CNN, to *TIME* magazine, to "The Oprah Winfrey Show." The result is that the whole world is now talking about the phenomenal Bible Codes. On balance, I believe this publicity will prove positive in that it will create a curiosity about the phenomenon in the minds of tens of millions of readers who would otherwise never read about the codes in a Christian book like this. Perhaps God will use this secular approach to the Bible Codes to draw many people into a closer examination of the Bible with the result that many will be introduced to Jesus Christ. Naturally, I have received many letters and questions on radio talk shows about my response to Drosnin's book *The Bible Code.*

Firstly, I believe the book is fascinating in its reporting of many additional code discoveries by Israeli code researchers. Unfortunately, the author Michael Drosnin reveals that he is somewhere between an atheist and an agnostic in his rejection of the existence of God, despite the overwhelming evidence of the supernatural origin of the Bible that is obvious to any unbiased reader of the incredible code discoveries. While he admits that only a supernatural being could have produced the Bible Codes three and a half thousand years ago, Drosnin firmly rejects the conclusion that the author of the codes is God.

Can the Bible Codes Allow Us To Correctly Predict the Future?

Many readers have written to ask if we could use the Bible Codes to discover the name of the Antichrist or tell of any other future events. The answer is "no." A much greater objection to Drosnin's book is his false claim that the Bible Codes can be used to accurately predict future events. As mentioned earlier in this chapter, one of his major claims is that he personally discovered the coded word "Yitzchak Rabin," the first letter of his name, beginning in Deuteronomy 2:33 and the second letter 4772 letters forward, in the text of Deuteronomy 4:42 where the letter appears in the Hebrew surface text which reads "will be assassinated." In the King James Bible this phrase is translated "kill his neighbour unawares." Drosnin makes an extraordinary declaration. He claims that he flew to Israel and warned Prime Minister Rabin of imminent danger based on this code discovery. Although I read Israeli newspapers regularly and follow Israeli events daily on the Internet, I have not yet seen any of the prime minister's staff confirm that this warning was actually given to Rabin. Therefore it is difficult to evaluate his claim.

Nevertheless, if Drosnin actually flew to Israel to warn the prime minister, based solely on the fact that he found the second letter of Rabin's name in the phrase "will be assassinated" in Deuteronomy 4:42, he simply made an astonishing guess. How could Drosnin "know" that this code actually meant that Rabin would be assassinated in advance of the event? I don't deny that the code is significant. That is why I wrote about the "Rabin" code in my earlier book. However, in advance of the tragic event, it was impossible to know that the encoded word meant that the assassination would definitely occur. The most Drosnin could do was make a guess. He was certainly aware of the growing public threats to Rabin's life that appeared in letters to newspapers and on signs held up at political rallies in the year proceeding the assassination.

Why would Drosnin become convinced to the point of flying to Israel to warn Rabin simply because one of the eight letters of Rabin's name occurred in the surface text in the phrase "will be assassinated"? How could anyone *know*, in advance of the assassination, that the particular phrase "will be assassinated" was significant as opposed to the other phrases containing the other letters of Rabin's name stretched out every 4772 letters throughout the book of Deuteronomy. For example, the first letter of "Yitzchak Rabin" name in code is spelled out in Hebrew beginning in the first word of Deuteronomy 2:33 which reads: "And the Lord our God delivered him." The second last letter of Rabin's name, the letter yud, ׳ appears in the words "sons of Levi." Before the assassination, how could Drosnin or anyone else know absolutely which of these phrases, if any, related to Rabin's future: "And the Lord our God delivered him," or "will be assassinated," or the words "sons of Levi?" Logically, at best Drosnin could only guess which, if any, of these phrases would turn out to be significant. Drosnin has already been proven wrong in his book's false prophecy that there would be a world war in 1996.

In his press release criticizing Drosnin's attempts to prophesy future events, Eli Rips, one of the major Israeli code researchers, pointed out a place in the Bible where you can find the words "Winston Churchill" encoded close to the phrase "will be murdered." If Drosnin had found this code years earlier when Churchill was still alive, would he have flown to Britain to warn Winston that his life was in imminent danger? However, this guess would have proven to be mistaken because Winston Churchill died peacefully. Therefore, the placement of Winston Churchill's name close to the phrase "will be murdered" was not a code foretelling the future. This illustrates the truth that we cannot and should not attempt to use the Bible Codes to predict future events. Significantly, the Israeli researchers, especially Eli Rips, who Drosnin quotes extensively, have publically repudiated Drosnin's sensational conclusions that the codes can be used to predict future events such as earthquakes or the next world war.

God forbids fortune telling and divination of any kind. The point is that the Bible Codes can only be interpreted accurately and confidently after an event has occurred to determine if the Bible contained encoded words that reveal God's supernatural prophetic knowledge thousands of years in advance. When the codes are interpreted after an event, we can verify that the codes are prophetically accurate. These discoveries support the Bible's claim to be supernatural in its origin, and God receives the glory, not the researcher. We need to remember the words of the prophet Isaiah: "For mine own sake, even for mine own sake, will I do it: for how should my name be polluted? and I will not give my glory unto another" (Isaiah 48:1).

An article recently appeared on the Internet, entitled *A Caution Concerning the Torah Codes,* that raises several concerns about the discovery of the Bible Codes. In the article, the writer found it surprising that the particular study of Genesis discovered the names and dates of death of numerous prominent Jewish rabbis and sages over the last two thousand years. Some critics have asked why God would encode within the Bible the names of rabbis who rejected the revelation Jesus Christ in the New Testament. We need to understand that the presence of a particular name in the Bible Codes, such as Anwar Sadat, Rabin, or the rabbis, does not imply an endorsement of their lives and teachings. It simply indicates that God must be the true author of the Bible because no one else could have encoded these names of people centuries before they were born. However, the presence of a particular name or group of names in the codes does not imply God's stamp of approval on their lives or teachings. Obviously, the discovery of the Holocaust codes, including the names *Hitler, Eichmann, Fuehrer, Genocide, Holocaust, Mein Kampf, Auschwitz, Belsen,* and *King of the Nazis* within Deuteronomy 10:17–22 and the surrounding verses does not suggest God's approval of the evil deeds associated with the tragedy of the Holocaust. Both the Bible surface text and the embedded codes contain the names and descriptions of many people, from the most noble to the most evil.

The critical article asked, "Why not [discover the encoded] apostles, or at least the prophets?" However, Yacov Rambsel and I independently discovered a series of fascinating ELS codes revealing the names of Jesus, His disciples, Passover, the Naza-rene, and much more that will be discussed in the next chapter. Surely, the discovery of the name of Jesus *Yeshua* in dozens of messianic passages throughout the Old Testament provides powerful evidence to any unbiased reader that Jesus of Nazareth is the promised Messiah of God. I personally believe that the Yeshua codes glorifying Jesus Christ provide strong evidence that the Bible Codes are genuine and that they were created by God to speak to this skeptical generation.

The Yeshua codes examined in *The Signature of God* and *Yeshua* glorify Jesus and reveal His divine nature as our Lord and Savior. These codes (especially the Messiah codes in the next chapter) reveal that it is Jesus of Nazareth who came in the flesh to fulfill the messianic prophecies. The apostle John wrote, "Hereby know ye the Spirit of God: Every spirit that confesseth that Jesus Christ is come in the flesh is of God: And every spirit that confesseth not that Jesus Christ is come in the flesh is not of God: and this is that spirit of antichrist, whereof ye have heard that it should come; and even now already is it in the world" (1 John 4:2–3). Both Yacov and I feel that the hundreds of coded words that glorify Jesus Christ as the Messiah and the Son of God are the Lord's seal of approval on the code phenomenon. These codes were placed in the text of the Hebrew Scriptures by the Lord Himself thousands of years ago to provide evidence of the supernatural origin of the Bible to this generation of skeptics.

Some critics point out that these codes are used by the ortho-dox Jewish community in seminars as evidence to convince assimilated and agnostic Jews that the Bible is authentic. How-ever, the critics complain that these seminars try to convince participants through the use of the codes that the Jewish rabbinic authorities hold a monopoly on unlocking the hidden truths of the Bible. While it is true to some extent that they use these codes for these purposes, it does not change the fact that the Bible Codes were created by God. No human could have created such an incredibly complex series of coded words as we have reported in *The Signature of God* and *Yeshua*. In effect, some critics suggest that the phenomenon of the codes (even though it is genuine) should be rejected simply because the orthodox rabbis use it for their purposes. However, this is foolish because the same argument would demand that Christians refuse to teach from Old

Testament passages because the rabbis use the Hebrew Bible to teach against Christian beliefs.

Some have suggested that Christians should reject the Bible Codes because some orthodox rabbis relate these codes to their teaching of Kabbalah, Jewish mysticism, and gematria. Some rabbis use the Kabbalah to find guidance, uncover secrets, and attempt to foretell the future. This is fallacious reasoning. The fact that the some people misuse the Bible Codes as other groups misuse the Scriptures to teach false doctrines does not provide a valid reason to reject either the codes or the Bible.

The Bible Codes Do Not Allow Anyone To Predict the Future

The codes do not permit anyone to become a prophet and predict future events accurately. In my earlier book I reminded readers that God forbids fortune telling. The Bible warns, "For there shall be no more any vain vision nor flattering divination within the house of Israel" (Ezekiel 12:24). I have received more written questions and radio call-in questions asking whether we can use the codes to foretell the future than any other question asked. Let me explain why you cannot use the codes to accurately predict future events.

How Do We Actually Find Bible Codes?

First of all you need to understand how we actually use the computer program to discover a particular code. A researcher such as myself will ask the program to search the text of the Hebrew Bible to find a target word, such as "Hitler." The computer then begins with the first letter of the Hebrew word "Hitler" היטלר, which is the letter heh ה (Hebrew reads right to left). Then the program will search forward by skipping 2 letters, 3 letters, 4 letters, et cetera, (skipping up to 500 letters forward, for example) searching for the second letter in Hitler's name, the letter yud י. When the computer finds the second letter י in the target word "Hitler," after skipping, for example, 22 letters, the program will automatically skip forward an equal number of letters (22), looking for the third, fourth, and fifth letters. When the program fails to find the next letter in the target word at an equal spaced interval, it abandons that search and examines the next occurrence of the letter heh ה in the text and begins the process again.

There are more than 45,000 Hebrew heh ה letters in the first five books of the Bible alone and the program will search up to 500 letters forward and 500 letters in reverse from each of the 45,000 heh ה letters. in the experiment. That means the computer will compete 45 million calculations or searches just to find if the word "Hitler" is encoded anywhere in the Torah. This is why serious research could only be done after scientists had created high speed computers in the last two decades.

To return to the question of predicting future events with the codes, the answer is that it is simply impossible. Until a historical event occurs, such as Anwar Sadat's assassination, you would not know what target words to ask the computer program to search for. It is only after an event has occurred that you can ask the computer program to search a given area of the Hebrew text and determine if a target word such as "Sadat" exists at any particular interval (such as every 5th, 20th letter, etc.). To illustrate this: imagine that you know about the Bible Codes and that you had a computer with this program back in 1920. Could you have used the codes back in 1920 to find "Adolph Hitler"? The answer is clearly no! Adolph Hitler's real family name was Schicklgruber until they changed it. He was an obscure demobilized Austrian army soldier, a failed painter who lived in flop houses in Vienna. Could you have found "Auschwitz" in 1920? No. Auschwitz was an equally obscure Polish village with no importance at that time. It is only after the evil historical events of the Holocaust had occurred that you could ask the computer program to search for a particular target word that may or may not be encoded.

No one can use the Bible Codes to discover the name of Antichrist or anything else about the future. Even if a researcher found a particular name of a current public person, the presence of their name or other words would not tell you anything meaningful. The only prophecies that reveal anything meaningful about future end-time events are found in the surface text of the Bible, such as the Matthew 24 predictions of the signs of the Second Coming of the Messiah.

Some critics ask whether the discovery of the encoded name "Rabin" in the Bible means that God ordered the assassination? Absolutely not! As I mentioned earlier, the fact that a name or event is encoded does not mean that God is thereby endorsing that person or event. The Bible records many events, good and bad, in both the codes and the surface text. Secondly, the cowardly assassin Yigal Amir was tragically and sinfully motivated by his irrational hatred of the prime minister's peace policies. The Bible Codes had nothing to do with his motivation for his despicable act. The discovery of these fascinating Bible Codes has caused many people to accept the supernatural origin of the Bible as the Word of God. It is illogical and ill-conceived to condemn the codes on the grounds that someone discovered that one of the letters of the encoded name "Rabin" appeared in a surface text of the Bible in the phrase "will be assassinated."

Let's examine the real issue. Are the Bible Codes valid? The answer is *yes*. Do these coded words appear in the biblical text in a manner that is beyond the statistical possibility that this is simply a random-chance occurrence? Anyone who spends a few hours studying the scholarly articles in *Statistical Science* journal (Aug. 1994), and *Bible Review* magazine (Nov. 1995), will conclude that the phenomenon is real. Dr. David Kazhdan, head of the mathematics department of Harvard University confirmed, "This is serious research carried out by serious investigators."

Answering Claims That the Codes Reveal That Yeshua Is A False Messiah

Some of the critics of the Yeshua codes discovered by Yacov Rambsel have claimed that they have discovered a hidden code in a messianic prophecy that spelled *yeshua mashiach sheker* "Jesus is a false messiah." First of all, we need to recognize that the name *Yeshua*, as the name of God's Messiah, naturally appears many times throughout the Old Testament. Therefore, the name *Yeshua* will inevitably be found in texts close to many other words. The claim that someone has found a text where the encoded word *Yeshua* occasionally appears within a few verses of the word *sheker* "false messiah" does not mean that the codes teach that Jesus is the false messiah, as some anti-Christians would like to suggest.

In conclusion, I have studied the phenomenon of the Bible Codes for the last ten years. In the last six years, I have used the computer programs to find new codes as well as to verify the discoveries by the scientists at Hebrew University and my friend Yacov Rambsel. I believe that the Bible contains a number of significant proofs that it is inspired by God. The Bible Codes are simply one additional proof that is especially meaningful to our generation in that they could not have been discovered or analyzed until the development of high-speed computers in our lifetime.

Why would God have placed hidden codes in the Bible that would not be discovered until the final generation of this millennium? Only God knows. However, I would suggest that God knew that our generation would be filled with skepticism and doubt more than any other generation in history. The Bible has suffered relentless attacks in the last eighty years that have caused many pastors and laymen to abandon their confidence in the authority and inspiration of the Scriptures. If these codes are genuine, and I believe they are, they were placed there by God to speak to this generation, to those who deny the supernatural inspiration of the Scriptures.

No human could have produced these incredibly complex codes. In addition, they glorify and lift up the name of Jesus Christ. Therefore, I conclude that they are powerful evidence of the inspiration and authority of the Bible. Together with the standard apologetic evidences, including the archeological and historical evidence, the advanced scientific and medical statements in the Bible, and the evidence from fulfilled prophecy, the Bible Codes will motivate many in our generation to consider the claims of the Bible about Jesus Christ. If we use this material wisely and carefully, in conjunction with these other evidences, we will fulfill God's command to us as revealed in 1 Peter 3:15: "But sanctify the Lord God in your hearts: and be ready always to give an answer to every man that asketh you a reason of the hope that is in you with meekness and fear."

In the following chapters we will examine the most fascinating codes I have ever seen — the Messiah Codes. These codes reveal the names of "Jesus," the "Nazarene," and the names of Christ's disciples encoded 740 years before the birth of Jesus.

Note

1. M. Margalioth, ed., *Encylclopedia of Great Men in Israel* (Tel Aviv: Joshua Chachik, 1961).

8

New Bible Code Discoveries

Since the publication of my book *The Signature of God*, numerous new Bible Codes have been discovered by various researchers in Israel and North America. In this chapter, I will share a number of the most fascinating codes that provide evidence of the supernatural origin of the Bible as the Word of God.

The Peace Process Between Israel and the PLO

For the last few years the eyes of the world have watched the dangerous peace negotiations between the PLO and Israel and their desperate search for an elusive peace in the Middle East. It is fascinating to discover that a series of encoded words in Deuteronomy, written by Moses over three and a half thousand years ago, reveal the names of the major participants in these negotiations. In a passage of only thirteen verses, beginning at Deuteronomy 8:16 through to 9:8, we find the following key words encoded: Israel ישׂראל; Arafat ערפאת; PLO אשׁפ; Peace Treaty חוזה שׁלום; and the names of both of Israel's former prime ministers who were intensely involved in the peace process, Yitzchak יצחק (Rabin), and Shimon Peres שׁמעון פרס. These words are encoded as follows:

Word	Hebrew	Interval	Reference begins at
Israel	ישראל	(1)	Deut. 9:1
Arafat	ערפאת	(1)	Deut. 9:6
PLO	אשף	(–15)	Deut. 9:4
Teaty	חוזה	(32)	Deut. 9:7
Peace	שלום	(–14)	Deut. 9:4
Yitzchak	יצחק	(1)	Deut. 9:5
Shimon	שמערנ	(92)	Deut. 8:20
Peres	פרס	(–283)	Deut. 8:16

It is interesting that these coded words appear in a passage of the Word of God that deals with Israel's rebellion against God in provoking Him to wrath because they did not trust that He would enable them to possess the whole of the Promised Land. Perhaps significantly, the name of *Arafat* appears encoded in the surface text in Deuteronomy 8:6: "For thou art a stiff necked people." It is very hard to understand the decision of the political leaders of Israel to enter into negotiations to surrender portions of the Promised Land to the enemies of Israel, who have dedicated themselves, in their proclamations in the PLO Covenant, to destroying the Jewish people. At the time of the beginning of the Madrid peace negotiations, the PLO was at the weakest point they had ever been, yet Prime Minister Rabin surrendered vital areas of Israel to this fierce enemy when the PLO was on its last legs. Even Senator Jesse Helms, the Chairman of the United States Committee on Foreign Relations, was profoundly disturbed by Israel's surrender of land to her deadliest enemies. Senator Helms wrote at the time, "I mistrust Arafat profoundly. . . . "I will never completely understand how the leaders of Israel reached the decision to enter into negotiations with Yasser Arafat. . . ." (A letter to Alice Novick dated March 12, 1996).

The Assassination of Prime Minister Yitzchak Rabin

The tragic assassination of Yitzchak Rabin stunned the people of Israel and millions of Christians and Jews throughout the world who love the Promised Land and her people. In the days after the assassination code researchers in Israel and North America naturally checked with their computer code search programs to examine every instance where the name of the late prime minister appeared at ELS intervals in the biblical text. In an earlier chapter of this book I examine the claim of the author Michael Drosnin, who states that he sent a warning to the prime minister based on the occurrence of the coded words "Yitzchak Rabin" and a phrase in Deuteronomy 4:42 that suggested the possibility of assassination.

However, another passage of the Torah contains encoded information about the assassination that is even more extensive. When we examine the passage Genesis 48:13 through 48:19 we find the encoded names of Yitzchak Rabin, Israel, the day and year of Rabin's birth, the month and year of his tragic assassination, the name of his assassin, Yigal Amir, the phrase "will be murdered," and the word "Oslo." It is incredible to see that these eleven significant words are encoded together in only eight verses of the book of Genesis. The year 5682 in the Hebrew calendar corresponds to 1922, the year Yitzchak Rabin was born, while the first day of the Jewish month Adar occurred on our March 1. The month Heshvan in the Hebrew calendar year 5682 corresponds to November, 1995.

Prime Minister Yitzchak Rabin's Assassination

Word	Hebrew	Interval	Reference begins at
Yitzchak	יצחק	(1)	Gen. 48:15
Rabin	רבין	(138)	Gen. 48:15
Will be murdered	ירצח	(85)	Gen. 48:13
Yigal	יגאל	(−241)	Gen. 48:16
Amir	עמיר	(15)	Gen. 48:15
Israel	ישראל	(1)	Gen. 48:14
5682 — Year of Rabin's Birth	התרפב	(−225)	Gen. 48:14
1st Adar — Rabin's Birthday	אאדר	(−177)	Gen. 48:15
5756 — Year of Rabin's Death	תשנו	(118)	Gen. 48:19
Heshvan — Month of Rabin's Death	חשון	(−285)	Gen. 48:13
Oslo	אוסלו	(182)	Gen. 49:3

Bible Codes Relating to The War in the Gulf

It is astonishing to find codes in the Bible that reveal the names of the major participants in the War in the Gulf. During that war President Saddam Hussein of Iraq attempted to destroy many of the Jews living in Israel through his unprovoked missile attack on Israeli cities. The codes reveal an astonishing series of encoded words that reveal the names of key players in that recent conflict in which God manifested His power to save both the Jews of Israel and the Christian soldiers of America and its allies fighting against the armies of Iraq. The eleven encoded words located by computer programs in the Bible include the following key words: President Saddam Hussein of Iraq: *Saddam* סאראם; *in Iraq* בעירק; the name of the thirty-nine Russian missiles fired against Israel: *Russian* רוסי; *Scud-B* סקאר בי; a description of the effect of the Scud-B missiles on those attacked:*the missile will terrify* יבהל טיל. In addition, an astonishing code actually named the day in the Israeli Hebrew calendar when Iraq's first missile attack began: *the 3rd of Shevat,* which fell on January 18, 1991. In Genesis 19:10 they discovered the phrase *they shut the door,* which may refer to the sealing of rooms by Israelis to protect against chemical weapons.

Within the same biblical passage, we find significant additional encoded names describing America's involvement in that conflict against Saddam Hussein: *George Bush* גורג בוש; *America* אמריקה; *and also in Iraq* והנ בעירק; and the name of the general who led the allied armies: *Schwarzkopf* שׁורצקופ.

The Gulf War Codes

Word	Hebrew	Interval	Reference begins at
Saddam (Hussein)	סאראם	(6)	Gen. 8:12
And also in Iraq	והנ בעירק	(6)	Gen. 29:9
America	אמריקה	(100)	Gen. 29:2
George Bush	גורג בוש	(–3129)	Gen. 33:8
Schwarzkopf	שׁורצקופ	(6777)	Gen. 29:24
the Missile will terrify	יבהל טיל	(2)	Gen. 19:29
They shut the door	ואת הדלת סגרו	(1)	Gen. 19:10
Russian	רוסי	(–1)	Gen. 19:2
Scud-B	סקאר בי	(15)	Gen. 19:1
the 3rd of Shevat	בני בשבט	(–258)	Gen. 20:14

One of the greatest miracles during the War in the Gulf occurred when thirty-nine Russian designed Scud-B missiles rained down on Tel Aviv, the largest populated area of Israel, where the vast majority of the Jewish state's five million citizens live. Although the American Patriot anti-missile system proved of some use in destroying Iraq's Scud-B missiles launched against U.S. troops in Saudi Arabia, the same anti-missile system did nothing to protect the Jews against these thirty-nine missiles. Several times the Patriot managed to break up the incoming Scud-B missile in the air, but it did not destroy the weapon as hoped. The huge destructive explosives in the warheads of each of these thirty-nine missiles destroyed over 15,000 Israeli apartments and homes. However, not one single Jew was killed by this devastating attack! The odds against this miracle of protection occurring by chance are astronomical. Surely this was a demonstration of the supernatural protection of God to preserve His Chosen People from their enemies.

However, another miracle also occurred during those terrifying missile attacks that went almost unreported in the Western news. One of the powerful Scud-B missiles managed to hit its intended target precisely. Although launched from more than five hundred miles away, the Iraqi missile made a direct hit with its warhead on the Gush Dan main gas-line terminal in Tel Aviv that supplied hundreds of thousands of homes and apartments with gas. These gas lines, which connected every home in the area to the main terminal, would normally be filled with extremely flammable and explosive gas. Normally, a missile explosion on a main gas terminal would have created a chain reaction of exploding gas below every street in Tel Aviv, creating a fire storm holocaust that would have killed tens of thousands of innocent Israeli citizens or more.

However, to the astonishment of the Israeli military, there was no secondary explosion when the missile warhead detonated. The fires were immediately extinguished with no loss of life whatsoever and no chain reaction of exploding gas lines. Just days before the missile attack, technicians working for the utility detected a minor malfunction in the gas lines that forced the management to shut off and empty the entire gas-line system by draining off all of the gas to allow for a safe inspection and repairs. This miracle reminds me of the tremendous promises of God to protect His people so they can dwell in safety: "But when ye go over Jordan, and dwell in the land which the Lord your God giveth you to inherit, and when he giveth you rest from all your enemies round about, so that ye dwell in safety" (Deuteronomy 12:10).

Dr. Moshe Katz has reported in his excellent book, *Compu-Torah*, that another group of encoded words relate to the War in the Gulf was found in the book of Numbers. The worldwide television network CNN and its star reporter Peter Arnet were watched virtually every day of the conflict by millions around the world. In the book of Numbers, researchers in Israel found the names of CNN and Peter Arnet encoded. Interestingly, the reporter Peter Arnet's full name appeared in code in one single verse of Numbers. The name "Peter" פיטר was encoded left to right every four letters while his last name "Arnet" ארנט was encoded right to left every two letters in Numbers 36:5.

War in the Gulf — CNN Codes

Encoded Name	Hebrew	Interval	Begins at
CNN	סי-אנ-אנ	(–780)	Num. 33:28
Peter	פיטר	(–4)	Num. 36:5
Arnet	ארנט	(2)	Num. 36:5

The Oklahoma City Bombing

On April 19, 1995, the worst terrorist attack in the history of North America destroyed the U. S. federal Murrah Building and killed 169 innocent people. For the first time, the heartland of America felt itself to be vulnerable to the terrorism and madness that has afflicted so many other countries of the world during the last few decades. This tragic event destroyed forever the feeling of security that had been known by generations of Americans who felt they were immune from the random terrorist violence experienced by other nations throughout the modern world. The trial of the accused bomber has concluded with the conviction and death sentence of Timothy McVeigh who was found guilty by a jury for intentionally killing these innocent civilians who happened to work in a federal government building. The evidence put forward at the trial suggests that Timothy McVeigh was motivated by an intense hatred of the U. S. government as a result of the disastrous attack two years earlier on the Waco, Texas compound of the Branch Davidians, a strange messianic cult led by David Koresh, that led to the tragic death of many innocent lives, the greatest massacre of civilians in U. S. history.

Apparently, according to testimony given at his trial, Timothy McVeigh was filled with hatred against the American government as a result of his view of the injustice of the FBI attack on the Branch Davidians in Waco, Texas. As a result, McVeigh decided to exact his revenge against the government on the second anniversary of the April 19th, 1993 destruction of the Branch Davidian compound by the FBI, and U. S. military support units. Tragically, McVeigh was successful in destroying the building and hundreds of citizens. Serious questions remain unanswered as to possible foreknowledge of this terrorist event by agencies of the U. S. government who may have infiltrated the group but somehow failed to stop the attack in time to avert disaster. This event remains the single most destructive terrorist attack to date in the history of North America.

It is fascinating to discover encoded words that describe detailed aspects of this frightening event described in the pages of the Scriptures that were written three and a half thousand years ago by the prophet Moses. An extensive examination of the Bible Codes that relate to this tragic event reveals that there are ten specific codes that describe the tragic events that occurred on April 19, 1995 in Oklahoma City in precise detail. The codes discovered in the book of Genesis record the following words that appear to relate to the tragic Oklahoma bombing: *Oklahoma* אוקלהומה; *terror* חתת; *Murrah* מרה; *desolated, slaughtered* שממזבח; *death* מורת; *his name is Timothy* שמו טימותי; *McVeigh* מקוויי; *Day 19* יומיט; *on the 9th hour* שעהטם; *in the morning* בבקר. This is an incredible listing of key words describing a tragic event that will effect the world for many years. The following list includes the information revealing where these ten encoded words are found within the text of the Hebrew Bible. Anyone with a Hebrew-English Interlinear Bible or the Torah Codes software program (available from our company through the order form at the end of the book) will be able to verify these encoded words in the text of the book of Genesis.

The presence of these codes in the text of the Holy Scriptures written by Moses more than thirty-five centuries ago is powerful evidence to all who will examine the data that the Bible is truly inspired by a supernatural God. There is no natural explanation to explain the existence of these encoded words describing detailed events in our generation found in the pages of the Bible, written by Moses thousands of years before the event occurred.

The Oklahoma City Bombing

Encoded Name	Hebrew	Interval	Begins at
Oklahoma	אוקלהומה	(–1445)	Gen. 35:5
Terror	חתת	(1)	Gen. 35:5
Murrah	מורה	(–5)	Gen. 36:8
Building	ביריג	(96)	Gen. 36:24
desolated,			
slaughtered	שממזבח	(1)	Gen. 35:7
death	מורת	(19)	Gen. 35:7
His Name is			
Timothy	שמו טימותי	(–377)	Gen.44:4
McVeigh	מקורייי	(389)	Gen. 34:21
Day 19	יומיט	(191)	Gen. 32:13
On the 9th hour	שעהט	(–126)	Gen. 34:18
In the morning	בבקר	(47)	Gen. 36:10

The Terrorist Assassination of the Israeli Policeman Nissim Toledano

One of the most extraordinary of the Bible Codes relates to a relatively little-known event that occurred in Israel several years ago involving the terrorist assassination of an Israeli border policeman, First Sergeant Nissim Toledano. He was assassinated by Arab terrorists from the Hamas Islamic organization that refuses to accept the existence of the state of Israel. At the end of 1992 the Israeli government exiled four hundred notorious Hamas terrorists to the northern Lebanese border who were previously convicted of various terrorist crimes against Israeli citizens.While the United Nations condemned Israel's mild actions against her worst enemies, the Hamas organization decided to launch a retaliatory attack against Israel. The leadership of Hamas sent a three-man team of Palestinian Arabs into Israel with the goal of assassinating an Israeli soldier or police officer. Three Arab terrorists infiltrated into Israel, stole a car, and searched for a target of opportunity. As the three-man terrorist team approached the Ben Guerion airport outside the city of Lod, they drove by an Israeli border policeman, First Sergeant Nissan Toledano, who was waiting for a bus.

The terrorists decided to kill their innocent target by running him down with their stolen car. However, after hitting him, they noticed he was still alive. They backed up and pulled their victim into their car and sped away. Some Israelis who were approaching the bus stop saw the kidnapping and alerted the authorities. After the reports of the kidnapping became public knowledge on the Israeli radio network that night, the whole nation realized the extreme threat to the Jewish population from random terrorist attacks. Dr. Moshe Katz, one of the most brilliant of the Israeli Bible Code researchers who has examined the code phenomenon for a decade, immediately went to his computer and asked the program to search for the name of the kidnapped victim, border policeman First Sergeant Nissim Toledano. Immediately, Dr. Katz found that names of the victim, *Toledano*, together with the words *captivity*, *Lod*, *First Sergent*, and *Border Policeman*. His incredible code discovery is described in his book *Compu Torah*.

The Captivity of Toledano

Encoded Name	Hebrew	Interval	Begins at
the captivity of Toledano	לשביית טולינו	(3191)	Gen. 21:23
first sergeant	רב סמל	(5)	Gen. 48:8
border police	מג״ב	(2)	Gen. 31:39
Lod	לוד	(−1)	Gen. 39:14

Immediately after the kidnapping, the terrorists had an argument in the car regarding what they should do with their captive. One argued for his immediate murder with a dagger, while two of his companions suggested that Toledano be kept alive as a ransom for their imprisoned terrorist comrades. Finally, the three terrorists decided to kill their captive, but they disagreed as to whether they should kill him with a knife or smother him. One terrorist suggested that they should "shed no blood." Another suggested that they smother him to death. Finally, after failing to smother Todedano, one said, "Lets kill him." The terrorists used a knife to kill their victim and cast his body into a pit in the desert. Three days later, the body of Toledano was found in a pit, and the Israeli security forces succeeded in capturing the three terrorists.

Following the capture of the terrorists, the captured men recounted to the police their assassination plans and the argument they had in the car about how to kill their victim. Incredibly, the reported conversations of the terrorists corresponded to the information revealed in the encoded words, as discovered by the Israeli researcher Dr. Moshe Katz, who used the minimal interval code technique on the night of the kidnapping. Incredibly, the surface text of the Genesis passage, approxiamately where the encoded words "Lod," and "border police" appeared is the story of Joseph being thrown into a pit in the desert by his brothers. In this Genesis account, we find these phrases that were uttered thousands of years ago by Joseph's brothers and were also uttered by the three terrorists during this kidnapping and assassination: "lets kill him"; "shed no blood"; "cast him"; "in the desert"; "lay no hand upon him"; "cried in a loud voice."

"lets kill him"	Gen. 37:21
"shed no blood"	Gen. 37:22
"cast him"	Gen. 37:22
"in the desert"	Gen. 37:22
"lay no hand upon him"	Gen. 37:22
"cried in a loud voice"	Gen. 39:14
"he will die"	Gen. 32:14

After the Israeli security forces captured the three terrorists their names were published in the Israeli newspapers, allowing Dr. Katz to confirm that the actual statements of the murderers were exactly as found in the text in Genesis. However, Dr. Katz went back to his computer and input the names of the three terrorists: *Atun; Abu Katish; and Isa.* To his amazement, all three of their names were found encoded at minimal ELS intervals in the surrounding biblical text.

The Names of the Three Terrorists Who Killed Toledano

Encoded Name	Hebrew	Interval	Begins at
Atun	עטון	(19)	Gen. 41:45
Abu Katish	אבו קתיש	(–1584)	Gen. 37:22
Isa	עיסא	(2)	Gen. 41:16

The Hebron Massacre

The discovery of the precise details of the death of Nissim Toledano encoded in the text of Genesis is very thought provoking. If the history of this private man is encoded, it is possible that the Bible Codes may contain information of an astonishing number of topics. It is important to remember that this research of the Bible Codes has only begun in the last few years. Much more remains to be discovered. One of the saddest events in the history of modern Israel occurred when an American-born Jewish doctor, Baruch Goldstein, went insane and mercilessly attacked a group of Moslem worshipers who were peaceably worshipping within the ancient Cave of the Patriarchs in Hebron. This ancient building was built by Herod the Great two thousand years ago to surround the cave containing the revered tombs of Abraham, Sarah, and other patriarchs who are honored ancestors to both the Muslims, Christians, and Jews. This site is sacred to both the Jews and Muslims containing both a synagogue and a mosque. Both groups accept the ancient tradition that this site is the ancient burial place of the patriarchs of both the ancient Israelis as well as the Arab Muslims.

Baruch Goldstein was descended from a Jewish family who had lived through a brutal Arab massacre and riot that killed most of the Jews living in Hebron in 1929 during the British Mandate. He came to the Hebron area to help the Jewish nation rebuild in the Promised Land. However, as a doctor, he was constantly dealing with the violent results of Arab PLO terrorism against both innocent Jews and Palestians. When one of his friends was killed, he became insane. Goldstein took an assault rifle and attacked a group of Muslim worshippers, killing and wounding many in a mad act of revenge. Significantly, the last letter in the encoded word *Goldstein* forms the first letter of the word *revenge*. The following encoded words appear to relate to this tragic event.

The Hebron Massacre

Encoded Name	Hebrew	Interval	Begins at
Cave of the Patriarchs	מערת המכפלה	(1)	Gen. 25:9
Baruch	ברוך	(-1)	Ex. 13:15
Goldstein	גלדרשטין	(9193)	Ex. 31:10

415

Revenge	נקמה	(-1)	Lev. 25:16
Year 5689 = 1929	ה"תרפט	(18)	Lev. 19:21
Al Fatah			
(Arafat's PLO)	אל-כתח	(1)	Lev. 19:21

Twenty-five Trees Encoded in Genesis 2

In my book *The Signature of God* I pointed out that the Israeli code researchers had discovered the encoded names of twenty-five trees within the Hebrew text of Genesis 2, which contains the story of God's creation of Adam and Eve as well as the plants and animals in the Garden of Eden. Every one of the twenty-five trees that are mentioned by name in the rest of the Old Testament appear encoded within this short chapter (635 words in English). Obviously, this encoding of the Hebrew names of the trees is not prophetic. However, it is an incredibly complicated thing for any human to attempt to write a short story about any topic while, at the same time, encoding twenty-five names of trees at ELS intervals within the text. My estimate is that it would take the better part of one year for someone to accomplish this in Hebrew or English. In addition, the researchers found that the name of the garden "Eden" was also encoded sixteen times in this same chapter.

The Names of Twenty-five Trees Encoded in Genesis 2

Encoded Name	Hebrew
vine	גפן
grape	ענב
chestnut	ערמן
dense forest	עבת
date	תמר
accacia	שטה
bramble	אטר
cedar	ארז
nut	בטן
fig	תאנה
willow	ערבה
pomegranate	רמון
aloe	אהלים
tamarisk	אשל
oak	אלון

poplar	לבנה
cassia	קדה
almond	שקד
mastic	אלה
thorn bush	סנה
hazel	לוז
olive	זית
citron	הדר
fir	גפר
wheat (related to	חטה
tree of knowledge)	חטה

In my own recent computer code research on this fascinating portion of the Bible, I found that God had also encoded in this same chapter, Genesis 2, the Hebrew names of seventeen animals that are named throughout the balance of the Old Testament. Furthermore, the name *Torah* is encoded five times, and the name *Yeshua* is found ten times in this same chapter. These incredibly complex codes appear embedded in a text that flows quite naturally in the Hebrew and English language. In other words, there appears to be nothing artificial or contrived in the choice of words that the author has used to express the story of God's creation of mankind in the Garden of Eden. I believe that it would be virtually impossible for a human or a computer program to produce a short passage such as Genesis 2 and place as many encoded words hidden at ELS intervals within the text.

Among the most fascinating code discoveries made in recent years is the discovery that God has encoded the names of Jesus and His disciples, together with numerous other individuals involved in the life and ministry of our Lord, in two different portions of the Old Testament. In the following chapter that deals with the Messiah Codes, you will find overwhelming evidence that these codes describe virtually every significant person in the life of Christ in the Old Testament, written many centuries before Jesus of Nazareth was born. The following chapter will reveal Bible Code discoveries about Jesus Christ that will provide powerful evidence of the supernatural origin of the Scriptures as well as the identification of Jesus as the true Messiah.

The Hebrew Aleph-bet
Sefardi Pronunciation

Numerical Value	Phonetics	Letters Form	Final Form
1	aleph	א	
2	bet, vet	ב	ב
3	gimmel	ג	
4	dalet	ד	
5	hey	ה	
6	vav	ו	
7	zayin	ז	
8	chet	ח	
9	tet	ט	
10	yod	י	
20	kaf	כ	ך
30	lamed	ל	
40	mem	מ	ם
50	nun	נ	ן
60	samek	ס	
70	ayin	ע	
80	pey, feh	פ	ף
90	tzadi	צ	ץ
100	qof	ק	
200	resh	ר	
300	shin, sin	שׁ	שׁ
400	tav	ת	

Note: Hebrew is written and read from right to left.

9

The Messiah Codes

The Names of Jesus the Nazarene and His Disciples
Encoded in Isaiah 53

The central theme of the prophecies of both the Old Testament and the New Testament is God's inspired revelation of Jesus of Nazareth as the Messiah and the Son of God.

Special Note

While we cannot use the codes to predict future events, once a historical event such as the life, death, or resurrection of Jesus has occurred, we can examine the text of the Bible to see whether or not there are ELS-encoded words that reveal God's foreknowledge of that event. In this manner, only God receives the glory from our examination of these fascinating codes.

A powerful indication of the validity of these encoded insights is found in the fact that these codes truly glorify Jesus of Nazareth in His divine roles as the Messiah, Adonai, Jehovah, and Lord. The First Epistle of John teaches us that one important spiritual test is that those who declare that Jesus Christ has come in the flesh are speaking in the Spirit of God: "Hereby know ye the Spirit of God: Every spirit that confesseth that Jesus Christ is come in the flesh is of God" (1 John 4:2). I believe that the fact that these coded words glorify Jesus Christ as the Son of God who came in the flesh to die for our sins on the Cross, provides irrefutable evidence that God placed these codes into the ancient scriptural text to glorify Jesus Christ.

After my book *The Signature of God* and Yacov Rambsel's book *YESHUA* were released last year, they quickly became international bestsellers. However, some scholars challenged the significance of Yacov's discovery of the name *Yeshua* encoded in virtually every major messianic prophecy in the Old Testament, as presented in our books. Some critics claimed that since the name "Jesus" *Yeshua* יׁשוע was a relatively short name with only four Hebrew letters, it could be found by random chance almost anywhere in Hebrew literature. However, they could not explain why the name *Yeshua* would appear encoded at small ELS intervals within so many major messianic prophecies throughout the Old Testament. We have not found any other significant names of historical individuals appearing repeatedly in small ELS intervals within these major messianic passages. These particular messianic prophecies where we found the name Yeshua encoded are considered significant messianic prophetic passages by most Christian students of the Bible. In addition, many of these same prophecies are identified as messianic by the Jewish sages in their writings.

Do the Yeshua Codes Point to Jesus of Nazareth?

However, the skeptics dismissed Yacov's discovery of the Yeshua Codes and declared that the encoded word *Yeshua* did not refer to Jesus of Nazareth. While they acknowledge that the word *Yeshua* appears repeatedly within these messianic passages, as our books claimed, they reject our claim that these codes are significant and meaningful. The skeptics claim that you can find *Yeshua* encoded in ELS intervals in almost any Hebrew literature, including the Israeli phone book or Woody Allens's writings translated into the Hebrew language. While you can find random or accidental ELS letters showing the name *Yeshua* and other names in Hebrew literature, the skeptics have not explained why the name Yeshua appears repeatedly in virtually every significant messianic prophecy. Our research indicates that no other name of any other historical personality turns up repeatedly in these messianic verses. However, the real question to be determined is this: Do the ELS codes showing the name *Yeshua* in messianic passages actually refer to the historic Jesus of Nazareth, or is this just a coincidence as the skeptics suggest? After thinking about this question for a while, I thought of an experiment that should settle the issue.

A few months ago I asked Yacov to complete an exhaustive analysis of the famous "Suffering Servant" messianic prophecy in Isaiah 52:13 through Isaiah 53 to search for other codes that would identify Jesus of Nazareth. This well-known messianic prophecy predicts many incredible details about Jesus Christ's death on the Cross that were precisely fulfilled seven centuries later. If there was any particular passage in the Old Testament that one might anticipate that God would place ELS codes about Jesus Christ and His disciples, most Christians would assume that Isaiah 53 would be the logical place to look.

Yacov made an astonishing discovery that God has encoded the names of Jesus Christ and virtually everyone that was involved in His tragic crucifixion two thousand years ago. He found the encoded names of Jesus, the Nazarene, Messiah, the three Marys, the two High Priests, Herod, Pilate, and many of Christ's disciples in one prophetic passage — Isaiah 53. Furthermore, these names were encoded in Isaiah's prophecy written in 740 B.C., more than seven centuries before Jesus was born. Can any unbiased observer of this evidence honestly claim that these codes refer to anyone other than Jesus of Nazareth?

The prophet Isaiah wrote a powerful passage known as the "Suffering Servant" prophecy that depicts Israel's Messiah suffering and dying for our sins. This famous passage is found in the messianic chapters of Isaiah — Isaiah 52–53. Isaiah 52 reveals God's promise of blessing. Isaiah 53 depicts the sacrificial price of the blessing. These two chapters in Isaiah should be read together as a complete passage. Beginning with Isaiah 52:13 and continuing through Isaiah 53:12, the prophet Isaiah provides a powerful description of the Messiah as the Lamb of God, as prophesied by His death, His burial, and His resurrection to life.

Throughout these vital chapters, God has hidden many astonishing ELS codes that reveal historic events and names of key individuals. Every one of these events and the role of the named people were fulfilled in the life of Jesus as recorded in the New Testament precisely seven centuries after the prophecy of Isaiah was written. Within these prophetic Scriptures, God encoded the name of His Messiah, Jesus *Yeshua*, together with the names of almost every single person involved in the crucifixion of Jesus the Messiah. In addition, Isaiah 53 reveals the names of both of the chief priests at the time of the crucifixion, as well as the names of Herod, Caesar, and many others involved in the crucifixion of Jesus of Nazareth.

God is perfect in all of His works. The Lord has meticulously placed every single word and letter in the whole Bible in its proper location. Jesus Christ affirmed the unerring accuracy of the Scriptures in these inspired words: "For verily I say unto you, Till heaven and earth pass, one jot or one tittle shall in no wise pass from the law, till all be fulfilled" (Matthew 5:18). The Lord declared that not "one jot or tittle" (the smallest letter and grammatical mark) is out of place. God has inspired every word of the Scriptures, allowing us to believe that every part of His revelation will be fulfilled to the letter.

First Thessalonians 5:21 declares, "Prove all things; hold fast that which is good," while 1 Peter 3:15 affirms, "But sanctify the Lord God in your hearts: and be ready always to give an answer to every man that asketh you a reason of the hope that is in you with meekness and fear." After the crucifixion, Thomas the disciple required more proof of Jesus' resurrection. Despite the fact that Jesus had been predicting His crucifixion and resurrection on the third day for three and one half years, Thomas would not believe the reports of the women that Jesus had indeed risen from the dead. However, the Lord personally appeared to Thomas in the Upper Room to give him the visual proof he needed. Many people today are like Thomas; they require additional verification of the truth of the Bible and the deeper things of God. In our generation, I believe God is using the discovery of the Bible Codes, including the astonishing insights recorded in this book about Jesus, to provide overwhelming scientific proof of the claims of Jesus Christ to be the Son of God. In addition, these Bible Codes provide a unique proof of the authority and inspiration of the infallible Word of God to our skeptical generation.

"Yeshua is My Name" ישוע שמי

One of the most astonishing discoveries mentioned in my book *The Signature of God* was the fact that the name of Jesus *Yeshua* was found encoded within the Hebrew text of the messianic passages of the Old Testament. Yacov Rambsel wrote an extraordinary book, *YESHUA*, that documented his incredible discovery of the name of *Yeshua* Jesus encoded in the major messianic prophetic passages throughout the Old Testament from Genesis to Malachi. The name "Jesus" in Hebrew is *Yeshua* יֵשׁוּעַ. *Yeshua* is spelled with four Hebrew letters (right to left) as follows: yod (י); shin (שׁ); vav (ו) and ayin (ע). I was delighted when I verified by computer and through manual examination of my Hebrew-English Interlinear Bible that my friend Yacov Rambsel had found the name *Yeshua* encoded in Isaiah 53:10. This famous prophecy foretold the grief of the suffering Messiah and His atoning sacrifice when He offered Himself as the Lamb of God, a perfect sacrifice for our sins by His death on the Cross: "Yet it pleased the Lord to bruise him; he hath put him to grief: when thou shalt make his soul an offering for sin, he shall see his seed, he shall prolong his days, and the pleasure of the Lord shall prosper in his hand" (Isaiah 53:10).

The words *Yeshua Shmi* "Yeshua [Jesus] is My Name" יֵשׁוּעַ שְׁמִי are encoded in this messianic verse beginning with the second Hebrew letter yod (י) in the phrase "He shall prolong" *ya'arik* יַאֲרִיךְ and counting every 20th letter left to right. Yacov's discovery of the name *Yeshua* encoded in Isaiah 53 and in dozens of other well-known messianic prophecies has thrilled hundreds of thousands of readers of the books *The Signature of God* and *YESHUA*.

However, I challenged Yacov to continue his research and complete an in-depth investigation of additional codes related to the life of Jesus of Nazareth in Isaiah 53. As a result of hundreds of hours of detailed research, I would like to share Yacov's incredible new discovery. Over forty names of individuals and places associated with the crucifixion of Jesus of Nazareth are encoded in Isaiah's Suffering Servant passage, which was written seven centuries before the birth of Jesus. I hope that you will be as thrilled with this astonishing discovery as I am. Yacov's complete research on this project is documented in his latest book entitled *His Name Is Jesus*, published recently by our ministry, Frontier Research Publications, Inc. I highly recommend his book to anyone who is fascinated by the phenomenon of the Bible Codes. With Yacov's permission, I will share a portion of his research on the incredible codes found in Isaiah 53 together with my own discovery of a similar code in Exodus 30:16.

The Names of Jesus and His Disciples

Within these key chapters of Isaiah, God has secretly encoded the names of the people, the actual locations, and events in the life of Jesus Christ that are recorded in the New Testament. Incredibly, the precise details of the people, the places, and the precise history of Christ's crucifixion were encoded in the Old Testament Scriptures seven centuries before the events took place. God clearly is in charge of human history. The Lord has revealed His supernatural prophetic knowledge of future events to our generation through the extraordinary discovery of the Bible Codes. This unprecedented phenomenon is a forceful reminder of the words recorded by Moses thousands of years ago: "The secret things belong unto the Lord our God: but those things which are revealed belong unto us and to our children for ever, that we may do all the words of this law" (Deuteronomy 29:29). Let us examine the details of this remarkable series of Bible Codes about Jesus Christ and His crucifixion.

First, we need to review the words of Isaiah's remarkable prophecy about the Messiah who would suffer for the sins of mankind. The full passage from Isaiah 52:13 through chapter 53 reads as follows:

Isaiah's Suffering Servant Prophecy
Isaiah 52:13–53:12

Behold, My Servant shall deal prudently, He shall be exalted and extolled, and be very high. As many were astonied at Thee; His visage was so marred more than any man, and His form more than the sons of men: So shall He sprinkle many nations; the kings shall shut their mouths at Him: for that which had not been told them shall they see; and that which they had not heard shall they consider.

(Isaiah 52:13–15)

Who hath believed our report? and to whom is the arm of the Lord revealed? For he shall grow up before him as a tender plant, and as a root out of a dry ground: he hath no form nor comeliness; and when we shall see him, there is no beauty that we should desire him. He is despised and rejected of men; a man of sorrows, and acquainted with grief: and we hid as it were our faces from him; he was despised, and we esteemed him not. Surely he hath borne our griefs, and carried our sorrows: yet we did esteem him stricken, smitten of God, and afflicted. But he was wounded for our transgressions, he was bruised for our iniquities: the chastisement of our peace was upon him; and with his stripes we are healed. All we like sheep have gone astray; we have turned every one to his own way; and the Lord hath laid on him the iniquity of us all. He was oppressed, and he was afflicted, yet he opened not his mouth: he is brought as a lamb to the slaughter, and as a sheep before her shearers is dumb, so he openeth not his mouth. He was taken from prison and from judgment: and who shall declare his generation? for he was cut off out of the land of the living: for the transgression of my people was he stricken. And he made his grave with the wicked, and with the rich in his death; because he had done no violence, neither was any deceit in his mouth. Yet it pleased the Lord to bruise him; he hath put him to grief: when thou shalt make his soul an offering for sin, he shall see his seed, he shall prolong his days, and the pleasure of the Lord shall prosper in his hand. He shall see of the travail of his soul, and shall be satisfied: by his knowledge shall my righteous servant justify many; for he shall bear their iniquites. Therefore will I divide him a portion with the great, and he shall divide the spoil with the strong; because he hath poured out his soul unto death: and he was numbered with the transgressors; and he bare the sin of many, and made intercession for the transgressors.

(Isaiah 53:1–12)

Isaiah 52:13–15

13. הנה ישׂכיל עבדי ירום ונשׂא וגבה מאד.

14. כאשר שׁממו עליך רבים כן-משׁחת
מאישׁ מראהו ותארו מבני אדם:

15. כן יזה גוים רבים עליו יקפצו מלכים פיהם כי אשׁר
לא-ספר להם ראו ואשׁר לא-שׁמעו התבוננו.

Isaiah 53:1–12

1. מי האמין לשמעתנו וזרוע יהוה על-מי נגלתה.

2. כיונק לפניו וכשרש מארץ ציה לא-תאר
ויעל לו ולא הדר ונראהו ולא-מראה ונחמדהו.

3. נבזה וחדל אישים איש מכאבות וידוע
חלי וכמסתר פנים ממנו נבזה ולא חשבנהו.

4. אכן חלינו הוא נשא ומכאבינו סבלם
ואנחנו חשבנהו נגוע מכה אלהים ומענה.

5. והוא מחלל מפשעינו מדכא מעונתינו
מוסר שלומנו עליו ובחברתו נרפא-לנו.

6. כלנו כצאן תעינו איש לדרכו
פנינו ויהוה הפגיע בו את עון כלנו.

7. נגש והוא נענה ולא יפתח-פיו כשה לטבח
יובל וכרחל לפני גזזיה נאלמה ולא יפתח פיו.

8. מעצר וממשפט לקח ואת-דורו מי ישוחח
כי נגזר מארץ חיים מפשע עמי נגע למו.

9. ויתן את-רשעים קברו ואת-עשיר במתיו
על לא-חמס עשה ולא מרמה בפיו.

10. ויהוה חפץ דכאו החלי אם-תשים אשם נפשו
יראה זרע יאריך ימים וחפץ יהוה בידו יצלח.

11. מעמל נפשו יראה ישבע בדעתו יצדיק
צדיק עבדי לרבים ועונתם הו יסבל.

12. לכן אחלק-לו ברבים ואת-עצומים יחלק
שלל תחת אשר הערה למות נפשו ואת-
פשעים נמנה והוא חטא-רבים נשא ולפשעים יפגיע.

Jesus of Nazareth

Christ was called Jesus of Nazareth because He was raised in the city of Nazareth with His family until commencing His public ministry when He was thirty years of age: "And He [Jesus] came and dwelt in a city called Nazareth: that it might be fulfilled which was spoken by the prophets, He shall be called a Nazarene" (Matthew 2:23). Some of the critics of the Yeshua Codes have challenged our conclusion that the name *Yeshua* found encoded in

Isaiah 53 and other passages actually refers to the historical Jesus of Nazareth. However, if the critics examine the encoded words we have discovered in this messianic prophecy, they will find over forty encoded names identifying virtually everyone who was present at the crucifixion of Jesus Christ. The odds against finding these precise words naming each of these important people, places, and events in the life of Jesus of Nazareth by random chance in a similar sized non-biblical Hebrew text are simply astronomical.

Yeshua The Nazarene

In Isaiah 53:6, starting with the third letter in the eleventh word and counting every forty-seventh letter from right to left, we find the word *Nazarene* נזיר. Throughout Isaiah's messianic passage, the word Nazarene is encoded several times. This discovery of the encoded name *Nazarene* נזיר near the name *Yeshua* ישוע in the same messianic prophecy, together with the names of many of His disciples, is overwhelming evidence that these Bible codes refer to the historical Jesus of Nazareth. This identification was primarily based on the fact that Jesus lived with his family for most of His life in the town of Nazareth in northern Galilee where Joseph, the husband of Jesus' mother Mary, pursued the occupation of a carpenter. The word "Nazarene" was also used to describe a special person who was chosen for a sacred purpose and dedicated to the service of God. A Nazarite was totally dedicated to the worship of the Lord and was willing to take the serious vow of the Nazarene. Jesus is often called the Nazarene because of His total commitment to His sacred calling to fulfill the will of God to redeem mankind from the curse of sin. The prophet Samuel was dedicated to the Lord by his mother Hanna when she pledged her unborn son to the service of the Tabernacle under the terms of the vow of the Nazarene. The book of Samuel states, "And she vowed a vow, and said, O Lord of hosts, if Thou wilt indeed look on the affliction of thine handmaid, and remember me, and not forget Thine handmaid, but wilt give unto Thine handmaid a man child, then I will give him unto the Lord all the days of his life, and there shall no razor come upon his head" (I Samuel 1:11). Another identification with the Nazarene name in the life of Jesus, the Messiah, as described in the Gospel of Matthew: "And [Jesus] came and dwelt in a city called Nazareth:

that it might be fulfilled which was spoken by the prophets, He
shall be called a Nazarene נזיר" (Matthew 2:23).

The Nazarene

Nazarene נזיר   (every 47 letters forward) ⬡

6.   כלנו כצאן תעינו איש לדרכו

פנינו ויהוה הפגיע בו את עו**ן** כלנו.

7.   נגש והוא נענה ולא יפתח-פיו כשה לטבח

יובל וכרחל לפני ג**ז**יה נאלמה ולא יפתח פיו.

8.   מעצר וממשפט לקח ואת-דורו מי ישוחח

כל נגזר מארץ חיים מפשע עמי נגע למו.

9.   ויתן את-רשעים קברו ואת-עשי**ר** במתיו

על לא-חמס עשה ולא מרמה בפיו.

Isaiah 53:6-9

Galilee

In addition, the codes reveal the place where Jesus lived for
most of his life — Galilee. In Isaiah 53:7, starting with the second
letter in the first word and counting every thirty-second letter
from left to right spells "Galilee" גליל. There are two ways in
Hebrew to spell "Galilee." The first is with the hen ה at the end of
the word, and the second is without the hen letter. Jesus was
raised in Nazareth, in a region of northern Israel called Galilee, as
confirmed in Matthew 21:11: "And the multitude said, this is Jesus
[Yeshua] the prophet of Nazareth of Galilee." In addition, much of
His ministry was conducted at various locations surrounding the
beautiful Sea of Galilee.

The Three Marys Who Witnessed the Crucifixion

The Gospel of John records that three women named Mary *Miryam* מרים were present at the crucifixion of Jesus, together with His beloved disciple, John *Yochanan* יוחנן. John 19:25–27 says, "Now there stood by the cross of Jesus His mother, and His mother's sister, Mary the wife of Cleophas, and Mary Magdalene. When Jesus therefore saw His mother, and the disciple [John] standing by, whom He loved, He saith unto His mother, Woman, behold thy son! Then saith He to the disciple [John], Behold thy mother! And from that hour that disciple took her unto his own home." This moving passage reveals the profound love of Jesus for His mother Mary and His loyal friend John.

Three Marys and the Disciple John at the Cross

When we analyse this prophecy in the Hebrew text, we find that the names of the three Marys and the disciple John are also encoded beside the name "Jesus" *Yeshua* ישוע, which is spelled out at a twenty letter interval reading left to right beginning in Isaiah 53:10. These phenomenal codes were fulfilled precisely over seven hundred years after Isaiah recorded his prophecy.

In Isaiah 53:11, starting with the fifth letter in the ninth word and counting every twentieth letter from left to right spells *Ma 'al Yeshua Shmee ohz* מעל ישוע שמי עז, which means "exceedingly high, Yeshua is my strong name." From the yod (י) in Yeshua's name, counting in reverse every twenty-eighth letter spells "John" יוחנן. Isaiah 52:13 says, "Behold, my Servant [Yeshua] shall deal prudently, He shall be exalted and extolled, and be very high." In Isaiah 53:11, starting with the first letter in the first word and counting every forty-second letter from left to right spells "Messiah" *Mashiach* משיח. From the mem (מ) in the word "Messiah," counting every twenty-third letter from left to right spells "Mary" מרים.

In Isaiah 53:10, all three of the names of Mary use the letter yod (י) in the word, *ya'arik* יאריך. This is the same letter yod (י) that forms the first letter in the encoded names "Yeshua" and "John." In Isaiah 53:10, starting with the third letter in the seventh word and counting every sixth letter from right to left spells "Mary" *Miryam* מרים. In Isaiah 53:12, starting with the fifth letter in the fourth word and counting every forty-fourth letter from left to right again spells "Mary" *Miryam* מרים. It is incredible to find the names of three Marys encoded in these verses beside the encoded names "Yeshua" and "John" when we remember that John's Gospel records that these four individuals were present at the crucifixion of Jesus Christ. In addition to naming Mary, the mother of Jesus, we find in Isaiah 53:2, starting with the second letter in the first word and counting every 210th letter from right to left spells "Joseph" *Yoseph* יוסף, the name of Mary's husband.

In the following illustration, we show the text of Isaiah's prophecy that reveals three encoded words: the name of the disciple John *Yochanan* יוחנן and two appearances of the name "Mary" *Miryam* מרים. To simplify the illustration, I have included only two of the three occurrences of the name "Mary."

The Name of the Disciple John and Two of the Marys

John   יוחנן   (every 28 letters in reverse)

[note: the final two letters נן both represent the letter N]

Two Marys   מרים   (every 6th letter in reverse and every 44th letter forward)

8. מעצר וממשפט לקח ואת-דורו מי ישוחח
כי נגזר מארץ חיים מפשע עמי נגע למו.

9. ויתן את-רשעים קברו ואת-עשיר במתיו
על לא-חמס עשה ולא מרמה בפיו.

10. ויהוה חפץ דכאו החלי אם-תשים אשם נפשו
יראה זרע יאריך ימים וחפץ יהוה בידו יצלח.

11. מעמל נפשו יראה ישבע בדעתו רצדיק
צדיק עבדי לרבים ועונתם הוא יסבל.

12. לכן אחלק-לו ברבים ואת- עצומים יחלק
שלל תחת אשר הערה למות נפשו ואת-פשעים
נמנה והוא חטא-רבים נשא ולפשעים יפגיע.

Isaiah 53:9-12

The Name "Disciples" Found in Isaiah 53

In Isaiah 53:12, starting with the third letter of the second word and counting every fifty-fifth letter from left to right spells *limmudim ahnan* אנן למדים, which means "the disciples mourn." Sometimes, the letter tav (ת) precedes this word. In this same count of fifty-five, but adjacent to "disciples," we find the word "priest." In Isaiah 53:5, starting with the second letter in the first word and counting every fifty-fifth letter from left to right spells "the Kohanim" (the priestly tribe) *ha'kohain* הכהן. It is astonishing to discover that the names of almost every one of Jesus' disciples (Judas Iscariot is excluded, for example) are encoded within this famous messianic prophecy of Isaiah, written seven centuries before Jesus was born.

The Names of the Disciples Encoded before Jesus was Born

The disciple's names are encoded as follows:
1. *PETER. Kepha* כפה.

In Isaiah 53:3, we find the name "Simon Peter," starting with the second letter in the fifth word and counting every nineteenth letter from right to left, the code spells "Peter" *Kepha* כפה.

2. *JAMES*, the son of Zabbadai. *Ya'akov* יעקב.

In Isaiah 52:2, starting with the third letter in the ninth word and counting every thirty-fourth letter from left to right, the code spells "James" *Ya'akov* יעקב.

3. *JOHN*. The brother of the disciple James is known as "John" *Yochanan* יוחנן.

In Isaiah 53:10, starting with the fourth letter in the eleventh word and counting every twenty-eighth letter from left to right, the code spells "John" *Yochanan* יוחנן.

4. *ANDREW. And'drai* אנדרי.

In Isaiah 53:4, starting with the first letter in the eleventh word, which is "God" *Elohim* אלהים, and counting every forty-eighth letter from left to right, we find the encoded word "Andrew" *And'drai* אנדרי.

5. *PHILIP. Pilip* פילף.

In Isaiah 53:5, starting with the third letter in the tenth word and counting every 133rd letter from left to right spells "Philip" *Pilip* פילף.

6. *THOMAS. Toma* תומא.

In Isaiah 53:2, starting with the first letter in the eighth word and counting every thirty-fifth letter from right to left the encoded word spells "Thomas" *Toma* תומא.

7. *MATTHEW.* There are three ways to spell the name of the disciple Matthew: *Mati* מתי, *Mattai* מתתי, *Mattiyahu* מתתיהו. The encoded word *Mattai* מתתי is an accepted abbreviated form of Mattiyahu מתתיהו. In Isaiah 53:8, starting with the first letter in the twelfth word and counting every 295th letter from left to right we find the encoded word "Matthew" *Mattai* מתתי.

8. *JAMES,* son of Alphaeus. *Ben Chalipi Ya'akov* בן חלפי יעקב.

In Isaiah 52:2, starting with the fourth letter in the third word and counting every twentieth letter from left to right the encoded word spells the word *Ya'akov* יעקב. Two of Christ's disciples were known by the name "James" *Ya'akov* יעקב. It is fascinating that we have found the name "James" *Ya'akov* יעקב encoded twice within Isaiah 53, in recognition that there were two disciples of Christ who were named James.

9. *SIMON,* (Zelotes) the Canaanite. *Shimon hakanai* שמעון הקני.

In Isaiah 52:14, starting with the first letter in the second word and counting every forty-seventh letter from right to left we find the encoded word "Simon" *Shimon* שמעון.

10. *THADDAEUS. Taddai* תדי.

In Isaiah 53:12, starting with the first letter of the eighth word and counting every fiftieth letter from left to right the encoded word spells the name "Thaddaeus" *Taddai* תדי.

11. *MATTHIAS. Mattiyah* מתיה.

In Isaiah 53:5, starting with the fourth letter in the seventh word and counting every eleventh letter from left to right spells "Matthias" *Mattiyah* מתיה. It is fascinating to note that this name "Matthias" is the name of the last disciple who was chosen by lot by the elders of the early Church to replace the dead traitor Judas Iscariot, whose guilt in betraying Jesus Christ caused him to commit suicide. Luke, the writer of the book of Acts, records how Matthias, the replacement disciple, was actually chosen: "And they gave forth their lots; and the lot fell upon Matthias מתיה; and he was numbered with the eleven apostles" (Acts 1:26). It is noteworthy that in the early Church an essential qualification for choosing a disciple to replace the deceased Judas Iscariot was that he had to have personally witnessed the three and one half year ministry of Jesus Christ and His supernatural resurrection (Acts 1:21–26). This eyewitness requirement was established so that Matthias could also personally testify to everyone about his personal, eyewitness experience of the life of Christ from His baptism to His death and resurrection from the dead, and finally, His ascension to heaven. It is fascinating to note that the names of virtually all of Christ's disciples are encoded near the name *Yeshua* within Isaiah's prophecy. However, the name of Judas Iscariot, the Lord's betrayer, is not found encoded in this passage.

The Names of Three of Christ's Disciples
Thomas, Peter and Andrew

Thomas *Toma* תומא (every 35 letters in reverse)

Peter *Kepha* כפה (every 19 letters)

Andrew And'drahi אנדרי (every 48 letters)

1. מן האמין לשמעתנו וזרוע יהוה על-מי נגלתה.

2. ויעל כיונק לפניו וכשרש מארץ ציה לא-תאר

לו ולא הדר ונראהו ולא-מראה ונחמדהו.

3. נבזה וחדל אישים איש מכאבות וידוע

חלי וכמסתר פנים ממנו נבזה ולא חשבנהו.

4. אכן חלינו הוא נשא ומכאבינו סבלם

ואנחנו חשבנהו נגוע מכה אלהים ומענה.

Isaiah 53:1-4

Jesus' Trial and the Names of the Two High Priests

When we examine the encoded information about those in power at the time of the crucifixion, we discover the names of the key participants. The codes reveal the names of Israel's two high priests at that time. Starting with the third letter in the seventh word in Isaiah 52:15, and counting every forty-first letter from right to left spells "Caiaphas" *Kayafa* כיפה, the name of the high priest of Israel named in the Gospel account of the trial of Jesus. In 1991, Israeli archeologists discovered the tomb of Caiaphas the High Priest. In Isaiah 53:3, starting with the fifth letter in the sixth word and counting every forty-fifth letter from right to left spells "Annas" *Ahnan* ענן, who was the former high priest and the uncle of Caiaphas. The New Testament reveals the names of these high priests in Luke 3:2: "Annas and Caiaphas being the high priests, the word of God came unto John the son of Zacharias in the wilderness." The high (chief) priests were leaders in the Sanhedrin trial in the Temple that lead to the crucifixion, according to John 19:15: "But they cried out, Away with Him, away with Him, crucify Him. Pilate saith unto them, Shall I crucify your King? The chief priests answered, We have no king but Caesar [the Roman]."

The Names of Israel's Two High Priests

The Names of Israel's Two High Priests

Caiaphas *Kayafa* כיפה **(every 41 letters forward)**

Annas *Ahnan* ענן **(every 42 letters forward)**

15. כן יזה גוים רבים עליו יקפצו מלכים פיהם כי אשר

לא־ספר להם ראו ואשר לא־שמעו התבוננו.

1. מי האמין לשמעתנו וזרוע יהוה על־מי נגלתה.

2. ויעל כיונק לפניו וכשרש מארץ ציה לא־תאר

לו ולא הדר ונראהו ולא־מראה ונחמדהו.

3. נבזה וחדל אישים איש מכאבות וידוע

חלי וכמסתר פנים ממנו נבזה ולא חשבנהו.

4. אכן חלינו הוא נשא ומכאבינו סבלם

ואנחנו חשבנהו נגוע מכה אלהים ומענה.

Isaiah 52:15 to 53:4

The Pharasees, the Levites, King Herod, Rome, and Caesar

The Pharisees and King Herod were also involved in the crucifixion, and we see their names encoded in Isaiah 53. In verse 9, starting with the second letter in the fourteenth word and counting every sixty-fourth letter from left to right we find the word "Pharisee" *pahrush* פרוש. These Jewish religious leaders were a strong force in both the Temple and in the broader Israeli society. They encouraged people to follow the strict religious laws of the Scriptures and the written and oral traditions based on the teachings of their rabbis over the centuries. It is amazing to note that in Isaiah 53:6, starting with the first letter in the fourth word and counting every twenty-ninth letter from left to right, we find the encoded words "the man Herod" *ish Herod* איש הורד. The fact that both the names "Pharisees" and "Herod" are encoded in this messianic prophecy in Isaiah is remarkable.

In Isaiah 53:11, starting with the first letter of the second word and counting every fourteenth letter from left to right spells the Hebrew word "Levis" *Levim* לוים, clearly identifying the Temple priests, chosen from the Jewish tribe of Levi, who joined in the attack on Jesus. In addition, starting with the second letter in the thirteenth word, in Isaiah 53:9, and counting every seventh letter from left to right the encoded letters spell "the evil Roman city" *rah eer Romi* רע עיר רומי, which identifies the Roman Empire, the political power ruling the known world at that time that actually ordered the death of Jesus. The Jewish authorities did not possess the legal power to inflict a death sentence upon any offender found guilty in their Sanhedrin Court in the Temple. The only way a death sentence could be carried out in Judea at that time was to find a Roman law that the prisoner had also broken and to then appeal to the Roman governor to sentence the person to death under the laws of Rome.

The Gentile soldiers of the Roman Empire who were present at the crucifixion clearly represented the Roman Emperor Caesar and the entire Gentile world who rejected the claims of Jesus as the Son of God and thus spiritually joined in the execution of God's Messiah. In this sense, all of humanity was represented at the crucifixion of the Lamb of God, Jesus Christ. In Isaiah 53:11, starting with the fourth letter in the seventh word and counting every 194th letter from left to right, we find the encoded words

Kaisar ahmail ovaid קיסר עמל אבר, which means "wicked, Caesar wretched (perish)," or alternatively phrased as "wicked Caesar, to perish." It is interesting to note that the Roman emperor Tiberius died within five years following the death of Jesus Christ.

Jesus Christ — The Atonement Lamb and the Light of the World

The gospel of John records that John the Baptist received a profound revelation of Christ as the Atonement Lamb of God when Jesus came to be baptized in the Jordan River. "The next day John seeth Jesus coming unto him, and saith, Behold the Lamb of God, which taketh away the sin of the world" (John 1:29). In Isaiah 52:12, starting with the second letter in the twelfth word and counting every nineteenth letter from left to right spells "from the Atonement Lamb" *me'kippur tela* מכפר טלא.

In Isaiah 53:5, starting with the seventh letter in the fifth word and counting every twentieth letter from right to left, "lamp of the Lord" *ner Adonai* נר יהוה is spelled out. This encoded word is adjacent to *Yeshua* ישוע at a twenty-letter interval. The gospel of John affirms repeatedly that Jesus Christ is the true light of the world. This is confirmed in the following quotation from John's gospel: "Then spake Jesus again unto them, saying, I am the Light of the world: he that followeth Me shall not walk in darkness, but shall have the Light of life" (John 8:12).

The Messianic Title "Shiloh"

In Isaiah 53:9, starting with the second letter in the eleventh word and counting every fifty-fourth letter from right to left spells *Shiloh* שילה. Both Jewish and Christian scholars acknowledge that the word *Shiloh* is a clear prophetic title of the coming Messiah. In Genesis 49:10, Moses recorded the deathbed prophecy of the patriarch Jacob: "The sceptre shall not depart from Judah, nor a lawgiver from between his feet, until Shiloh come; and unto Him [Yeshua] shall the gathering of the people be." This famous prophecy clearly identified the coming Messiah as "Shiloh." The discovery of the word *Shiloh* encoded beside the name *Yeshua* in the powerful messianic prophecy of Isaiah 53 provides powerful evidence of the identity of Jesus of Nazareth in this passage.

The Name of Jesus and His Messianic Title — Shiloh

Jesus - Yeshua ישרע (every 20 letters in reverse)

Shiloh שילה (every 54 letters forward)

9. ויתן את-רשעים קברו ואת-עשיר במתיו

על לא-חמס עשה ולא מרמה בפיו.

10. ויהוה חפץ דכאו החלי אם-תשים אשם נפשו

יראה זרע יאריך ימים וחפץ יהוה בידו יצלח.

11. מעמל נפשו יראה ישבע בדעתו יצדיק

צדיק עבדי לרבים ועונתם הוא יסבל.

12. לכן אחלק-לו ברבים ואת- עצומים יחלק

שלל תחת אשר הערה למות נפשו ואת-פשעים

נמנה והוא חטא-רבים נשא ולפשעים יפגיע.

Isaiah 53:9-12

In addition we have found the word *Yeshua* together with the word *Messiah* encoded in this key passage. In Isaiah 53:8, starting with the third letter in the second word and counting every sixty-fifth letter from left to right spells "Messiah" *Mashiach* משיח. In this same count, but starting with the third letter in the tenth word of verse 10, which is the ayin (ע), and counting every sixty-fifth letter from left to right spells *Yeshua* ישרע. It is fascinating that the words "Jesus" and "Messiah" are both encoded in this prophecy of Isaiah sharing the same 65-letter ELS interval. Also, the word "Passover" was found encoded in Isaiah 53:10. Beginning at the third letter of the thirteenth word at an interval of every sixty-two letters in reverse spells "Passover" *Peh'sakh* פסח.

Jesus the Messiah and the Feast of Passover

JESUS THE MESSIAH CRUCIFIED ON PASSOVER

Jesus   Yeshua   ישוע   (in reverse every 20 letters)

Passover   *Peh'sakh*   פסח   (In reverse every 62 letters)

Messiah   *Mashiach*   משיח   (In reverse every 42 letters)

8.   מעצר וממשפט לקח ואת-דורו מי ישוחח

כי נגזר מארץ חיים מפשע עמי נגע למו.

9.   ויתן את-רשעים קברו ואת-עשיר במתיו

על לא-חמס עשה ולא מרמה בפיו.

10.   ויהוה חפץ דכאו החלי אם-תשים אשם נפשו

יראה זרע יאריך ימים וחפץ יהוה בידו יצלח.

11.   מעמל נפשו יראה ישבע בדעתו יצדיק

צדיק עבדי לרבים ועונתם הוא יסבל.

Isaiah 53:8-11

The Prophetic Symbols at the Passover Supper
The Bread and Wine

In Isaiah 53:1, starting with the fifth letter in the eighth word and counting every 210th letter from right to left spells "the bread" *ha'lachem* הלחם, which may refer to the powerful symbol of bread that Jesus used at the Last Supper to refer to His body, which was broken for our sins. Another group of Hebrew letters at the same 210-letter interval spells the word "wine" *yeyin* יין, which was the other symbol used by Jesus at His last Passover Supper in the Upper Room to symbolize His blood, which was shed for our sins. The word "wine" is spelled out in reverse at a 210-letter interval beginning with the second letter in the eleventh word and counting from right to left. The words "wine" and "bread" clearly represent the body and blood of Jesus, as revealed by Jesus to His disciples in the Upper Room.

It is interesting to find the names "Jonah" and "water"

encoded close together in this passage. In Isaiah 52:4, starting with the fourth letter in the sixth word and counting every nineteenth letter from left to right spells "Jonah" יונה. A few verses later, in Isaiah 52:7, starting with the first letter in the ninth word and counting every nineteenth letter from left to right spells "water" מים. The prophet Jonah was placed in the water to awaken him to God's command to preach to his enemies, the Ninevites. These codes revealing "Jonah" and "water" remind us of the history of the prophet Jonah, who was "three days and three nights in the whale's belly." Jesus used Jonah's experience as a prophetic symbol of His own death and resurrection.

Those Who Watched the Crucifixion from Afar

Mark 15:40 says, "There were also women looking on afar off: among whom was Mary Magdalene, and Mary the mother of James the less and of Joses, and Salome." In Isaiah 52:15, starting with the third letter in the sixteenth word and counting every 113th letter from right to left spells "Salome" *Shalomit* שלמית. In verse 13, starting with the fourth letter in the second word and counting every 149th letter from right to left spells "Joses" *Yosai* יוסי. The man Joses was apparently a son of Jesus' mother Mary, and therefore His half-brother. According to Mark 15:40, both Marys were weeping at the crucifixion of Jesus. Encoded in Isaiah 52:15, starting with the fifth letter in the eighteenth word and counting every thirteenth letter from left to right spells the words "the Marys weep bitterly" *na'ar Miryam be'ku abhor* נאר מרים בכו. In Isaiah 53:9, starting with the first letter in the third word and counting every twenty-eighth letter from right to left spells "tremble Mary" *rahal Miryam* רעל מרים. The letters adjacent to the above spell "the blessed" *habarucha* הברוכה. Mary, the mother of Jesus, was called blessed in the Gospel of Luke: "And the angel came in unto her [Mary], and said, Hail, thou that art highly favoured, the Lord is with thee: blessed (ברוכה) art thou among women" (Luke 1:28).

Thus far, we have found encoded words naming virtually every one of the people involved with the crucifixion of Jesus, in addition to many others who were present during His remarkable life of ministry.

The Cross and the Passover Feast

In Isaiah 53:10, starting with the third letter in the second word and counting every fifty-second letter from right to left spells "cross" צלב. From the same word, taking the first letter and counting every 104th letter from right to left spells "Passover" פסח, as mentioned earlier. In Isaiah 52:14, starting with the third letter in the sixth word and counting every twenty-sixth letter from left to right spells "My Feast (my sacrifice)" *Chaggai* חגי. After sharing His last Passover Supper with His disciples in the Upper Room, Jesus was betrayed by Judas, and taken to a series of trials. His crucifixion took place the next afternoon on the day of the Passover Feast, known as *Chaggai* חגי.

The Ancestors of King David

The gospel of Luke records the genealogy of Jesus, proving that He was descended from the royal line of King David and therefore has the right to be called king. Luke 3:32 records a significant part of the royal lineage of Jesus, beginning with King David: "Which was the son of Jesse, which was the son of Obed, which was the son of Booz [Boaz]" It is intriguing to find these names encoded in Isaiah 53:7. Starting with the second letter in the third word for "was afflicted" נענה, and counting every nineteenth letter from left to right spells "Obed" *Ohved* עבד. The name Obed means "servant." It is significant that Obed was the son of Ruth and Boaz, the grandfather of King David. Jesus is called both "the Son of David" and "the suffering Servant [Obed]." In Isaiah 52:9, beginning with the first letter in the third word, which is "together" יחדו, and counting every nineteenth letter from left to right spells "Jesse" *Yishai* ישי, the son of Obed and the father of King David. The name Jesse means "wealthy" or "gift." Incredibly, these key ancestors of King David and Jesus of Nazareth are encoded in this messianic prophecy of Isaiah.

The Time and Place of Christ's Crucifixion

Jesus was crucified on the day of the Passover Feast, which took place annually on the 15th of the Jewish month Nisan (also known as the month of Aviv). Mount Moriah, the Temple Mount, is the place where God provided a ram as a substitute sacrifice in the place of Abraham's son Isaac. This was also the place where

God commanded King David to prepare for the building of the Temple, which was built by his son Solomon. However, Mount Moriah is a long mountain ridge that begins in the south of Jerusalem and continues northward past the northern city walls to the site of Golgotha, where Jesus was crucified outside the city walls, just north of the Damascus Gate. The book of Hebrews confirms the Gospel account that Christ's death took place outside the city walls: "Wherefore Jesus also, that he might sanctify the people with his own blood, suffered without the gate" (Hebrews 13:12). In Isaiah 52:1, starting with the third letter in the eighth word and counting every twenty-seventh letter from right to left spells *aviv ve'moriah* אביב ומריה, which means "Aviv of Mount Moriah." This is an astonishing code discovery naming the actual month, Aviv, and the place of Christ's sacrifice for our sins written by Isaiah centuries before the event. The adjacent letters spell *rosh* ראש, which means "the first" or "the head of the year" (the first month of the religious year was the month Nisan-Aviv, the month of Passover), when Jesus was crucified.

"Let Him Be Crucified"

Two thousand years ago, the Romans and the Jewish leaders joined together to crucify Jesus of Nazareth. Every human being on earth was morally represented by the Romans and the Jewish leadership because Jesus died on the cross for our sins. The gospel of Matthew records the terrible moment when the Roman governor decided on Christ's death. "Pilate saith unto them, What shall I do then with Jesus which is called Christ? They all say unto him, Let him be crucified" (Matthew 27:22). The prophet Isaiah foretold this tragic series of events seven centuries before they occurred. "He was taken from prison and from judgment: and who shall declare his generation? for he was cut off out of the land of the living: for the transgression of my people was he stricken" (Isaiah 53:8). Perhaps the most astonishing code discovery in this passage is the fact that this exact phrase was encoded in Isaiah's prophecy. Starting with the second letter in the sixth word of Isaiah 53:8 and counting every fifteenth letter right to left spells "let Him be crucified" *yitz'tzahlaiv* יצלב.

"LET HIM BE CRUCIFIED"

Jesus Is My Name Yeshua Shmi ישוע שמי (every 20 letters in reverse)

Let Him Be Crucified Yitz'tzah'laiv יצלב (every 15 letters forward)

8. מעצר וממשפט לקח ואת-דורו מ●ישוחח
    כי נגזר מארץ חיים מפשע עמי נגע למו.

9. ויתן את-רש●עים קברו ואת-עשיר במתיו
    על לא-חמס עשה ולא מרמה בפיו.

10. ויהוה חפץ דכאו החלי אם-תשים אשם נפשו
    יראה זרע יארך ימים וחפץ יהוה בידו יצלח.

Isaiah 53:8-10

Over one thousand years before the birth of Jesus, the psalmist David wrote his prophetic Psalm that foretold the tragic crucifixion of Christ. David wrote of the future death of the Messiah: "The assembly of the wicked have enclosed me: they pierced my hands and my feet" (Psalm 22:16). Incredibly in Isaiah 52:10, we find the word "pierce" encoded. Starting with the third letter in the fifteenth word, which is "in His hands" בידו, and counting every ninety-two letters from left to right spells "pierce" *dahkar* דקר in reverse.

Can any unbiased reader have any remaining doubt that the Bible Codes identify Jesus of Nazareth as the Messiah who died for our sins as the Son of God?

The Signature of God

Last year, I wrote a book entitled *The Signature of God*, which explored the fascinating evidence from archeology, scientific and medical discoveries, fulfilled prophecy, and the incredible Bible Codes that prove the supernatural origin of the Bible. My thesis was that God had, in effect, written His authenticating signature on the inspired pages of His Holy Word through this supernatural evidence in the text, which no unaided human could have created. I was amazed when Yacov recently sent me a fax showing his latest discovery — a code that contained the words *me'chatimo* מחתימו, which means "His Signature." In Isaiah 52:7, starting with the fourth letter, the final mem ם, in the Hebrew word *shalom* שלום, the eighth word, and counting every forty-ninth letter from right to left spells "His Signature" *me'chatimo* מחתימו. The Hebrew letters ם and מ are variations of the same letter. These astonishing codes surely are the signature of God on the pages of the His word.

The final pages of this chapter contain a detailed summary of the major codes in Isaiah's prophecy that name virtually everyone associated with the crucifixion of Jesus. This list should be a convenience for the reader and an aid for those students of the Bible who wish to check out these Bible Codes for themselves.

A Challenge to the Critics of the Yeshua Code

When my book *The Signature of God* and Yacov Rambsel's book *Yeshua* were published in 1997, hundreds of thousands of readers rejoiced in this discovery about the Bible Codes. Many students of the Scriptures were especially fascinated with Yacov's research that revealed the encoded name of Jesus in well-known messianic prophecies. However, a number of Bible Code researchers in Israel and North America, as well as orthodox Jewish rabbis, have disputed the significance of this discovery of Yeshua's name. They have pointed out that the name *Yeshua* ישוע is a relatively small word with only four letters and two common vowels. Some of these critics have contemptuously challenged the significance of the Yeshua Codes and declared that one could find the name *Yeshua* ישוע in virtually any passage in Hebrew literature (from a novel to the Israeli phone book). However, the critics ignore the fact that the name *Yeshua* appears at very small ELS intervals (i.e., every 5th, 9th, or 20th letter, etc.) in dozens of familiar messianic prophecies. We have not found significant names of any other historic personalities encoded at small ELS intervals in dozens of messianic prophecies.

One critic claimed on the Internet that the name of the false messiah Rev. Sung Yung Moon appears frequently in these same messianic prophecies. However, this is false. While the short three letter Hebrew word for "moon" does appear frequently including some places near some of these messianic passages, the word "moon" does not identify the Rev. Sung Young Moon of South Korea, who formed the Unification Church. The encoded words do not reveal "Rev. Sung Young Moon" as the critics falsely imply; it is only the three letter word "moon" that appears frequently. This criticism is without merit.

Yacov's astonishing discovery of over forty names of individuals and places associated with the crucifixion of Jesus of Nazareth in this Isaiah Suffering Servant messianic passage is unprecedented. I would like to issue a challenge to the critics who reject the Yeshua Codes to find any other passage of similar length (fifteen sentences) in Hebrew literature outside the Bible that contains forty ELS codes, including the names of Jesus, the Nazarene, Messiah, Passover, Herod, Mary, and the names of Christ's disciples. A partial list of Yacov's code discoveries found in this prophecy from Isaiah 52:13 through Isaiah 53 is provided at the end of this chapter to help the reader realize the astonishing amount of detailed information encoded in this remarkable prophecy. The critics claim that these codes about *Yeshua* can be found by random chance in any Hebrew literature, and, therefore they reject the significance of this discovery.

Here is a challenge from Yacov and myself to the critics. Let them produce any other Hebrew literature of the same length as or shorter than this Isaiah passage that also contains all of the encoded names listed in the summary that follows. If they cannot discover these names encoded in any passage outside the Bible, and we believe it will be impossible, we will have additional evidence that these codes about *Yeshua* the Nazarene, and His disciples, are truly unprecedented.

Jesus and His Disciples Found Encoded in Isaiah 53

Name	Begins	Word	Letter	Interval
Yeshua Shmi	Isa. 53:10	11	4	(−20)
Nazarene	Isa. 53:6	11	3	(47)
Messiah	Isa. 53:11	1	1	(−42)
Shiloh	Isa. 53:12	21	4	(19)
Passover	Isa. 53:10	13	3	(−62)
Galilee	Isa. 53:7	1	2	(−32)

Herod	Isa. 53:6	4	1	(−29)
Caesar	Isa. 53:11	7	4	(−194)
The evil Roman city	Isa. 53:9	13	2	(−7)
Caiaphas — High Priest	Isa. 52:15	7	3	(41)
Annas — High Priest	Isa. 53:3	6	5	(−45)
Mary	Isa. 53:11	1	1	(−23)
Mary	Isa. 53:10	7	3	(6)
Mary	Isa. 53:9	13	3	(44)
The Disciples	Isa. 53:12	2	3	(−55)
Peter	Isa. 53:10	11	5	(−14)
Matthew	Isa. 53:8	12	1	(−295)
John	Isa. 53:10	11	4	(−28)
Andrew	Isa. 53:4	11	1	(−48)
Philip	Isa. 53:5	10	3	(−133)
Thomas	Isa. 53:2	8	1	(35)
James	Isa. 52:2	9	3	(−34)
James	Isa. 52:2	3	4	(−20)
Simon	Isa. 52:14	2	1	(47)
Thaddaeus	Isa. 53:12	9	1	(−50)
Matthias	Isa. 53:5	7	4	(−11)
Let Him Be Crucified	Isa. 53:8	6	2	(15)
His Cross	Isa. 53:6	2	2	(−8)
Pierce	Isa. 52:10	15	3	(−92)
Lamp of the Lord	Isa. 53:5	5	7	(20)
His Signature	Isa. 52:7	8	4	(49)
Bread	Isa. 53:12	2	3	(26)
Wine	Isa. 53:5	11	2	(210)
From Zion	Isa. 52:14	6	1	(45)
Moriah	Isa. 52:7	4	5	(153)
Obed	Isa. 53:7	3	2	(−19)
Jesse	Isa. 52:9	3	1	(−19)
Seed	Isa. 52:15	2	2	(−19)
Water	Isa. 52:7	9	1	(−19)
Levites	Isa. 54:3	3	6	(19)
From the Atonement Lamb	Isa. 52:12	12	2	(−19)
Joseph	Isa. 53:2	1	2	(210)

New Code Discoveries Revealing Jesus of Nazareth in the Torah
Exodus 30:16

After the astonishing code discovery by Yacov Rambsel of the forty-one names related to the ministry and crucifixion of Jesus of Nazareth in Isaiah 53, I wondered if God had encoded this prophetic information confirming the identity of Jesus as His Messiah in any other place in the Bible. Using my Torah Codes computer program, I began a systematic search through the Hebrew Bible, focusing especially on the Torah to see if this information was encoded there as well. To my amazement, I found the following series of codes naming everyone who was significant in the ministry of Jesus Christ, including the three Marys, the names of every disciple, including the replacement for Judas Iscariot, the disciple Matthias, and much more. The following list of codes will enable anyone with a Hebrew-English Interlinear Bible to confirm my discovery.

Significantly, phenomenal codes were found in Exodus 30:16 that deal with God's commands to Moses regarding the atonement price for Israel's sins.

> And thou shalt take the atonement money of the children of Israel, and shalt appoint it for the service of the tabernacle of the congregation; that it may be a memorial unto the children of Israel before the Lord, to make an atonement for your souls.   (Exodus 30:16)

Jesus of Nazareth and His Disciples in Exodus 30

Name	Begins	Word	Ltr	Interval	Ends	Word	Ltr
Yeshua	Ex. 30:16	19	1	(12)	Ex. 30:18	1	2
Nazarene	Ex. 30:16	15	3	(8)	Ex. 30:16	20	4
Messiah	Ex. 30:13	12	3	(60)	Ex. 30:18	3	2
Shiloh	Ex. 30:14	7	1	(40)	Ex. 30:16	12	2
Passover	Ex. 30:9	7	4	(-9)	Ex. 30:10	1	3
Galilee	Ex. 29:19	7	3	(-39)	Ex. 29:21	8	3
Mary	Ex. 30:15	7	2	(60)	Ex. 30:18	11	1
Mary	Ex. 30:16	13	1	(61)	Ex. 30:20	8	2
Mary	Ex. 30:17	5	3	(92)	Ex. 30:23	14	2
Peter	Ex. 30:16	2	2	(32)	Ex. 30:17	1	2

Matthew	Ex. 30:20	8	2	(20)	Ex. 30:21	6	2
John	Ex. 29:19	9	1	(14)	Ex. 29:20	12	2
Andrew	Ex. 29:27	15	4	(115)	Ex. 29:36	7	4
Philip	Ex. 29:24	9	4	(50)	Ex. 29:27	4	5
Thomas	Ex. 30:18	14	4	(11)	Ex. 30:19	7	2
James	Ex. 30:7	6	2	(−59)	Ex. 30:10	14	5
Simon	Ex. 29:19	7	3	(−39)	Ex. 29:21	8	3
Nathanael	Ex. 30:4	8	2	(−100)	Ex. 30:12	8	2
Judas	Ex. 29:13	9	2	(24)	Ex. 29:15	2	1
Thaddaeus	Ex. 30:16	2	2	(32)	Ex. 30:17	1	2
Matthias	Ex. 30:20	8	2	(20)	Ex. 30:21	6	2
Let Him Be							
Crucified	Ex. 30:20	1	1	(8)	Ex. 30:20	8	1

In this passage, we find twenty-one signficant codes naming virtually every significant person in the minstry of Jesus of Nazareth. The fact that these codes were found in the Torah is especially important. The Bible established the principle that the truth was confirmed in the word of two witnesses. Moses wrote, "At the mouth of two witnesses, or at the mouth of three witnesses, shall the matter be established" (Deuteronomy 19:15). Therefore, it is extremely significant that this complex series of codes revealing the identity of Jesus of Nazareth as the Messiah has been located in two separate portions of the Bible by two independent researchers using two different search methods. I believe that these Messiah codes are the most important code discoveries that have been found to date.

10

The Heavenly Prince Melchisedec Scroll

In 1947, through the providence of God, an Arab shepherd boy discovered the greatest treasury of ancient Jewish manuscripts the world has ever seen. In one moment of time the world's confidence in the total accuracy of the transmission of the Old Testament by the Jewish scribes through the last two thousand years sky rocketed. The scholars were delighted to find that every one of the thirty-nine books of the Old Testament were hidden in these caves with the sole exception of the book of Esther. However, the discovery contained a manuscript that includes a commentary on the book of Esther. This precious library was owned by the Essenes, a somewhat monastic Jewish group that longed for the coming Messiah. This group of religious Jews had left the Temple in rejection of the increasing corruption in the religious life and practices of the Temple priesthood. They established their own religious center, Qumran, in the desert beside the Dead Sea. The Jewish historian Flavius Josephus wrote that the Essenes were the third largest sect practicing ancient Judaism during the time of Christ. With four thousand members, the Essenes were smaller than only the Pharisees and Sadducees.

When the scholars compared these two-thousand-year-old biblical texts against the oldest biblical manuscripts in the libraries of Europe, they were astonished to discover that there were almost no significant textual changes in any of the books of the Old Testament. The Jewish Masoretic scholars had carefully preserved the accuracy of the biblical text to such a remarkable degree that when the scholars examined the Torah, from Genesis to Deuteronomy, there were only 169 Hebrew letters that differed in the Dead Sea Scrolls text from the biblical texts that were used by the King James Bible translators in 1611. Significantly, none of these 169 letter variations changed the meaning of a single word. In other words, 99.94% of the letters of the Torah were identical with the texts that had been copied over the centuries.

For thousands of years, God had preserved the accuracy of His Holy Scriptures through the careful reproduction of the manuscripts by these extraordinarily dedicated Jewish Masoretic scribes. When the scribe copied the manuscript of Genesis (which contains 76,064 Hebrew letters), he would literally count out the precise number of times each of the twenty-two letters in the Hebrew alphabet occurred in the text. He would also make notations on the margin of the page to assure that no letters were added or taken away. If even one letter was missed or added improperly, the master scribe would destroy the imperfect copy, lest an error creep into the holy text of the Word of God.

These Masoretic notes were originally placed in a separate text, but eventually they were added to the margins of the medieval Jewish Bibles. They included notes identifying the middle clause in each book of the Bible, together with notations of the exact number of times each of the twenty-two Hebrew letters appeared in that particular book of the whole of the Scriptures. As an example, the scribes calculated that there were 1534 verses or sentences in Genesis and that the middle clause was found in Genesis 27:40, "By thy sword shalt thou live." A researcher named Walton completed an exhaustive analysis of the Masoretic notes in the last century and produced the following table that illustrates the incredible precision of the dedicated labor involved in order to preserve the accuracy of the Bible.

The Masoretic Counting of the 815,140 Letters of the Hebrew Bible

Hebrew Letter		Times Found in the Bible	Hebrew Letter		Times Found in the Bible
א	Aleph	42,377	ל	Lamed	41,517
ב	Beth	38,218	מ	Mem	77,778
ג	Gimel	29,537	נ	Nun	41,696
ד	Daleth	32,530	ס	Samech	13,580
ה	He	47,554	ע	Ain	20,175
ו	Vau	76,922	פ	Pe	22,725
ז	Zain	22,867	צ	Tsaddi	21,882
ח	Cheth	23,447	ק	Koph	22,972
ט	Teth	11,052	ר	Resh	22,147
י	Yod	66,420	ש	Shin	32,148
כ	Caph	48,253	ת	Tau	59,343

Source: *A General and Critical Introduction to the Study of Holy Scripture* by A. E. Breen

One of the most incredible of the valuable scrolls found in the caves of Qumran was a little known scroll called *The Heavenly Prince Melchizedek*. This fascinating manuscript was found in thirteen fragments in the floor of Cave 11 near the village of Qumran by the Dead Sea. It was first published in Stduien, Leiden by A. S. Van der Woude under the title *Melchizedek als himmlishce Erlosergestalt. . . . 'Oudtestamentishche* (p. 354–73) as an Essene example of an eschatological Midrash, a Jewish prophetic commentary on a passage of the Old Testament. It also appeared in an article entitled "11Q Melchizedek and the New Testament" in *New Testament Studies* (p. 301–26), published in 1966.

This scroll includes an astonishing teaching of the ancient Jewish sages about the role of the most mysterious person in the Bible — Melchizedek. The Genesis account hints that Melchizedek is a theophany, a mysterious appearance of the second person of the Godhead on earth. Melchizedek appears in the biblical record as the king of Salem (Jerusalem) who encounters Abraham. This event followed Abraham's great victory over five kings of this region who had conquered Sodom and Gomorrah and had taken his nephew Lot and his property in their conquest. Before examining this remarkable scroll a review of the Bible's own teaching about the nature of the mysterious king of Salem will be helpful.

The Biblical Record of Melchizedek, King of Salem

And Melchizedek king of Salem brought forth bread and wine: and he was the priest of the most high God. And he blessed him, and said, Blessed be Abram of the most high God, possessor of heaven and earth: And blessed be the most high God, which hath delivered thine enemies into thy hand. And he gave him tithes of all.

(Genesis 14:18–20)

There is clearly a mystery about the nature of Melchizedek. Abraham receives the priestly blessing from the king of Salem, who is called "the priest of the most high God." Furthermore, Abraham gives "tithes of all" to Melchizedek as a sign of worship. Note that Melchizedek offers Abraham bread and wine, exactly as did Jesus to His disciples at the Last Supper at Passover.

The Psalmist David records the following significant declaration about who Melchizedek really is:

The Lord said unto my Lord, Sit thou at my right hand, until I make thine enemies thy footstool. The Lord shall send the rod of thy strength out of Zion: rule thou in the midst of thine enemies. Thy people shall be willing in the day of thy power, in the beauties of holiness from the womb of the morning: thou hast the dew of thy youth. The Lord hath sworn, and will not repent, Thou art a priest for ever after the order of Melchizedek. The Lord at thy right hand shall strike through kings in the day of his wrath. He shall judge among the heathen, he shall fill the places with the dead bodies; he shall wound the heads over many countries. He shall drink of the brook in the way: therefore shall he lift up the head. (Psalms 110:1–7)

This remarkable prophecy of King David reveals the future victory of Jesus the Messiah who is called David's Lord. When David wrote, "The Lord said unto my Lord, Sit thou at my right hand, until I make thine enemies thy footstool," he clearly referred to the mystery of the Trinity. However, while prophesying of the Messiah's final victory, David identifies Jesus the Messiah, our High Priest and Son of God, with Melchizedek: "Thou art a priest for ever after the order of Melchizedek." Therefore, the Bible teaches that God appeared to Abraham as a theophany in the person of Melchizedek.

In the book of Hebrews, the apostle Paul also wrote about the mysterious Melchizedek. Referring to Jesus of Nazareth, Paul declared, "As he saith also in another place, Thou art a priest for ever after the order of Melchisedec. . . . Called of God an high priest after the order of Melchizedek" (Hebrews 5:6, 10). Again, Paul affirms the connection between Melchizedek and Christ in these words, "Whither the forerunner is for us entered, even Jesus, made an high priest for ever after the order of Melchizedek" (Hebrews 6:20). The final New Testament passage about this subject is found in the book of Hebrews:

> For this Melchisedec, king of Salem, priest of the most high God, who met Abraham returning from the slaughter of the kings, and blessed him . . . For he was yet in the loins of his father, when Melchisedec met him. If therefore per-fection were by the Levitical priesthood, (for under it the people received the law,) what further need was there that another priest should rise after the order of Melchisedec, and not be called after the order of Aaron? (Hebrews 7:1, 10–11).

> And it is yet far more evident: for that after the similitude of Melchisedec there ariseth another priest, . . . For he testifieth, Thou art a priest for ever after the order of Melchisedec. . . For those priests were made without an oath; but this with an oath by him that said unto him, The Lord sware and will not repent, Thou art a priest for ever after the order of Melchisedec (Hebrews 7:15, 17, 21).

The Heavenly Prince Melchizedek Scroll

The Melchizedek scroll, found in 1947 by the scholars who first examined the Dead Sea caves surrounding Qumran, has received little attention in the last fifty years since its discovery. However, I believe that this scroll reveals an astonishing teaching about Melchizedek that parallels exactly the teaching of the New Testament, in which the king of Salem is identified with the Messiah, the Son of God. We know that to this day Judaism has continued to vehemently reject the Christian teaching that Jesus is the true Messiah and that He is also the Son of God, equal with the Father and Holy Spirit. However, as I discussed earlier in the chapter on the mystery of the Trinity, remarkable Jewish teachings about the Trinity existed during the time of Christ in the first century. The existence of these amazing Jewish texts detailing the nature of the triune God — One in Three and Three in One — helps answer the question of how someone like the apostle Paul and many other Jews, including rabbis, could accept the claims of Jesus to be the true Son of God, while still remaining true to their monotheistic Jewish teaching that there is only one God.

This Heavenly Prince Melchizedek scroll provides us with fascinating insights into the beliefs of at least some of the Jewish Essenes living during the first century. I believe that these teachings prepared some of the Essenes to accept the claims that Jesus of Nazareth was the Son of God. In my last book, *The Signature of God*, I quoted from a number of scrolls found in the Qumran caves that refer to the Messiah as the Son of God. One five-line scroll identifies the Messiah as the leader of the community who was "pierced" and "wounded" (crucified) for the sins of the people, as the prophet Isaiah had predicted in the Old Testament. This scroll must refer to Jesus because He is the only person who claimed to be the Messiah who was crucified. Although these scrolls were discovered fifty years ago, they were not well known outside the small circle of scroll scholars until today. During the last half century, the liberal scroll scholars denied that any of the scrolls found in the Dead Sea caves referred to Jesus or to Christianity. Now that the scrolls are more widely available, evidence exists to prove that, not only do these manuscripts refer to Jesus, they even contain remarkable quotations from portions of the New Testament. These facts suggest that some members of the Essenes, a group strongly committed to holiness and the Jewish Scriptures, might have responded positively to the message of John the Baptist and the teachings of Jesus of Nazareth.

The following excerpts are from the English translation of *The Heavenly Prince Melchizadek* scroll. Note the incredible parallels between the nature, titles, and actions of Melchizedek and Jesus Christ. I have included in brackets the biblical references for Scriptures that the writer of this scroll refers to in his manuscript.

The Heavenly Prince Melchizedek

And concerning that which He said, In this year of Jubilee each of you shall return to his property (Leviticus 25:13) and likewise, And this is the manner of release: every creditor shall release that which he has lent to his neighbour. He shall not exact it of his neighbour and his brother, for God's release has been proclaimed (Deuteronomy 15:2) And it will be proclaimed at the end of days concerning the captives as He said: To proclaim liberty to the captives (Isaiah 61:1). Its interpretation is that He will assign them to the Sons of Heaven and to the inheritance of Melchizedek; for He will cast their lot amid the portions of Melchizedek who will return them there and will proclaim to them liberty, forgiving them the wrongdoings of all their iniquities.

And this thing will occur in the first week of the Jubilee that follows the nine Jubilees. And the Day of Atonement is the end of the tenth Jubilee, when all the Sons of Light and the men of the lot of Melchizedek will be atoned for. And a statute concerns them to provide them with their rewards. For this is the moment of the Year of Grace for Melchizedek. And he will, by his strength, judge the holy ones of God, executing judgment as it is written concerning him in the songs of David, who said Elohim has taken his place in the divine council; in the midst of the gods he holds judgment (Psalms 82:1). And it was concerning him that he said; Let the assembly of the peoples return to the height above them; El (God) will judge the peoples (Psalms 7:7–8). As for that which he said How long will you judge unjustly and show partiality to the wicked? Selah (Psalms 82:2). Its interpretation concerns Satan and the spirits of his lot who rebelled by turning away from the precepts of God to . . .

And Melchizedek will avenge the vengeance of the judgments of God . . . and he will drag them from the hand of Satan and from the hand of all the spirits of his lot. And all the gods of Justice will come to his aid to attend to the destruction of Satan. And the height is all the sons of God

... this ... This is the day of Peace/Salvation concerning which God spoke through Isaiah the prophet, who said, How beautiful upon the mountains are the feet of the messenger who proclaims peace, who brings good news, who proclaims salvation, who says to Zion: Your Elohim reigns (Isaiah 52:7).

Its interpretation; the mountains are the prophets ... and the messenger is the Anointed one of the spirit, concerning whom Daniel said, Until an anointed one, a prince (Daniel 9:25) ... And he who brings good news, who proclaims salvation: it is concerning him that it is written ... To comfort all who mourn, to grant to those who mourn in Zion (Isaiah 61:2–3). To comfort those who mourn; its interpretation, to make them understand all the ages of time ... In truth ... will turn away from Satan ... by the judgment(s) of God, as it is written concerning him, (who says to Zion); your Elohim reigns. Zion is ..., those who uphold the Covenant, who turn from walking in the way of the people. And your Elohim is Melchizedek, who will save them from the hand of Satan.

As for that which He said, Then you shall send abroad the loud trumpets in the seventh month.   (Leviticus 25:9)

The Parallel Views of Melchizedec Prefiguring Jesus Christ

1. *Timing*: This fascinating text, describing Melchizedek as the key figure in the final judgment of mankind and the angels, uses a number of phrases that remind us clearly of Old and New Testament prophecies about the return of Jesus Christ. These phrases include "the end of days," "the year of Jubilee," "the Day of Trumpets in 7th month," "the Day of Atonement," "the Year of Grace," "the Day of Vengeance," "the day of Peace/Salvation," and "the day when Elohim reigns."

2. *Jubilee*: The scroll refers repeatedly to the "redemption of the land" and "redemption of the captives," reminding us of the New Testament teaching of Christ's role as our Redeemer. "And grieve not the holy Spirit of God, whereby ye are sealed unto the day of redemption" (Ephesians 4:30).

3. *Judgment*: We read in the scroll about Melchizedek

"executing judgment." Further, he will judge the "Sons of Heaven" and "the Holy Ones" and give "vengeance," exactly as the Bible teaches that all judgment is in the hands of Jesus Christ. In the book of Jude we read, "And Enoch also, the seventh from Adam, prophesied of these, saying, Behold, the Lord cometh with ten thousands of his saints, To execute judgment upon all" (Jude 14–15).

4. *Forgiveness of sins*: It is astonishing to discover that the scroll teaches of Melchizedek "forgiving them the wrongdoings of all their iniquities," exactly as Christ forgives our sins if we repent. The writer also describes Melchizedek's role in atonement for the righteous: "Sons of Light and the men of the lot of Melchizedek will be atoned for." The New Testament teaches us that Christ atones for our sins. We know that only God can forgive sin. Therefore, the scroll's author is declaring the divinity of Melchizedek.

5. *Divinity*: Although most ancient Jewish writings describe the Messiah as a man with a divine mission, this Melchizedek scroll, as well as the *Targums*, describes the Messiah as God. The scroll says that "He takes His place in the Divine Council." The scroll also declares that Melchizedek will judge Satan and destroy him. In addition, the author of this scroll calls Melchizedek "Elohim" (the plural name for God), four times in this manuscript.

6. *Melchizedek's Identification*: A careful reading of this scroll reveals that the author identified Melchizedek as both the Messiah and as Elohim (God) in several passages. This is a remarkable indication that some of the Jews truly understood the mystery of the divine nature of God's Messiah. Consider the following titles that the author of the scroll ascribes to the Heavenly Prince Melchizedek:

The Messiah, the Prince

The Anointed One who proclaims salvation

The Prince

The Judge

The Avenger

Elohim

The High Priest of the Year of Jubilee

The Messenger of God

This extraordinary scroll, hidden in a cave for two thousand years, throws an entirely new light on the religious views of some of the Jewish people during the critical years of the first century, when the new Christian faith was presented to Israel in the life, death, and resurrection of Jesus Christ. It appears that at least some of the Jews were prepared to accept the claims of Jesus to be the Son of God, due to the teachings they received from these texts.

11

The Mystery of the Jews: God's Hand in Human History

But, whether you abandon it or whether you follow it, Israel will journey on to the end of days.

> Edmond Fleg, *Why I Am A Jew*

And I will make my covenant between me and thee, and will multiply thee exceedingly. And Abram fell on his face: and God talked with him, saying, As for me, behold, my covenant is with thee, and thou shalt be a father of many nations. Neither shall thy name any more be called Abram, but thy name shall be Abraham; for a father of many nations have I made thee.   (Genesis 17:2–5)

As the host of heaven cannot be numbered, neither the sand of the sea measured: so will I multiply the seed of David my servant, and the Levites that minister unto me.

> (Jeremiah 33:22)

Centuries ago a skeptical and agnostic king of France was discussing philosophy and religion with his royal court counsellor. After numerous arguments were presented by the Christian advisor in favor of the position that God had revealed Himself in the Holy Scriptures, the king finally demanded that his counsellor prove to him that God existed in an argument using only two words. After careful deliberation the counsellor replied, "The Jews!" In those two words the counsellor summed up one of the most miraculous demonstations of God's supernatural intervention in the history of humanity. The survival and prospering of the Jewish people during thousands of years of brutal persecution, pogroms, and the tragedy of five and one-half million Jews massacred in Hitler's Holocaust is a mysterious miracle unparalled in the history of the human race.

Each of the mighty empires of the past — Assyria, Egypt, Babylon, Media-Persia, Greece, and Rome — who conquered Israel and carried her Jewish citizens into slavery have themselves turned to dust. Their powerful armies and huge treasuries did not stop the relentless march of history. Their time of power and grandeur came and went, leaving their great cities and monuments in ruins to be covered by the sands of the deserts. Where is mighty Rome or Babylon today? Yet the Jewish people, the least among the ancient nations of the Middle East, have survived throughout centuries, despite the overwhelming persecution and opposition against them. No other people in history have ever lost their national homeland for thousands of years, survived dispersed in over seventy different nations for twenty centuries, and then returned to their ancient homeland to rebuild their national life atop the desolate ruins of the cities and fortifications of its many conquerors.

What other nation lost its national language for twenty centuries, only to recover it and teach its ancient language to millions of its returning exiles? Today, five million Jews in Israel speak Hebrew, the language of her ancient prophets and kings. The miracle of the survival of the Jewish people is unprecedented. In fact, throughout the world, the only peoples who can claim to trace their continued existence as a race as far back as the Jews are the Chinese people. The Bible's declaration that God made an eternal, unbreakable covenant with the Jews, through their father Abraham, has remained the guiding principle and focus of the Jewish people's survival against overwhelming odds for the last thirty-five hundred years. God's covenant with Israel was the motivating force behind the Jews remarkable survival as a distinct people, even when surrounded by Gentile cultures.

In addition to the miracle of Israel's survival in a cruel world, we must add the remarkable history of the astonishing Jewish contribution to the arts, philosophy, writing, science, and medicine. Consider the difficulty placed in the paths of most Jews in a world of Gentiles throughout most of the last two thousand years. While the influence of ancient Rome and Greece on Western society is as great as that of the Jewish people, these nations were much more powerful and conquered huge areas of the ancient world for many centuries. Despite the small size of the Jewish population, the Jewish contribution to Western and Eastern society is unparalled by any other comparably sized group. There are approximately six billion people alive in the world today. Of these, only eighteen million (less than one-half of 1 percent of the world's population) are Jews. There are hundreds of equally small population groups throughout the planet that are absolutely unknown to anyone but their closest neighbours.

However, the contributions of the Jewish people to modern culture is overwhelming. A recent estimate calculated that more than 12 percent of the Nobel prizes have been awarded to Jews in the fields of medicine, mathematics, chemistry, and physics. The contribution of the Jewish people to the fields of arts, music, literature, and religious writing is outstanding in its quality and quantity. The influence of Jews on the history and the thinking of the Western world, as represented by the communist Karl Marx, the mathematician Albert Einstein, the psychologist Sigmund Freud, and the philosopher Baruch Spinoza, is staggering. The success of the Jewish people in the areas of business and finance is far beyond what one would expect, considering their small numbers and the opposition they face from people with anti-Semitic attitudes. However, the greatest Jewish influence on the history of mankind came from the lives, teachings, and actions of two Jews — Moses and Jesus of Nazareth. The Jews are finally looking at the life and teachings of Jesus and acknowledging that His influence on the nations has been both powerful and beneficial. They realize that the terrible atrocities and persecutions of the medieval period and the Holocaust were not based on genuine Christianity but were a perversion of evil produced by sinful men who, by their evil actions, rejected the teachings of Jesus.

In light of the great tragedy to the Jews, few people realize that the Nazi Holocaust was an attack on Christianity just as much as it was an attempt to annihilate the Jewish people. While five and one-half million Jews were savagely killed in the evil Nazi concentration camps, the Nazis also murdered seven million Europeans of the Christian faith in those same death camps. Captives from thirty European nations were taken in trains to those terrible death camps to be worked to death or immediately executed. A fascinating book by the brilliant author Max I. Dimont, entitled *Jews, God, and History* reveals startling information that most Christians have never been told:

> We must recognize the fact that Nazism was not anti-Semitic but anti-human. Because Nazi beliefs of racial superiority had no basis in fact, Nazism was like a nightmare, unfolding without a past or future in an ever-moving present. Because none but German Aryans were qualified to live in the Nazi view, it stood to reason that everyone else would be exterminated. The chilling reality is that when the Russians overran the concentration camps in Poland they found enough Zyklon B crystals to kill 20 million people. Yet there were no more than 3 million Jews left in Europe. The ratio of contemplated mass killing was no longer 1.4 Christians for every Jew, but 5.3 Christians for every Jew. Nazi future plans called for the killing of ten million non-German people every year.

> If the Christian reader dismisses what happened in Germany as something which affected a few million Jews only, he has not merely shown his contempt for the seven million Christians murdered by the Nazis but has betrayed his Christian heritage as well. And, if the Jewish reader forgets the seven million Christians murdered by the Nazis, then he has not merely let five million Jews die in vain but has betrayed his Jewish heritage of passion and justice. It is no longer a question of the survival of the Jews only. It is the question of the survival of man.

The greatest evidence of the influence and importance of the Jewish people is the fact that God chose the Jews to receive and carefully preserve His written commandments to man in the inspired Holy Scriptures. Both the Old and New Testaments were written by Jews who were obeying the command of God to record His words for all of mankind. The Bible is the inspired and authoritative record of God's progressive revelation of Jesus Christ, His divine and human nature, His marvellous character, and His perfect revealed will for our lives. The Scriptures are a special revelation given to a distinct people, the Jews, who were chosen by God to be both the guardians of this precious treasure and the sharers of this divine revelation with the rest of humanity. The Lord commanded the Jewish people to communicate this written revelation of the will of God to all mankind. It is significant that God's blueprint for the Temple included a Court of the Gentiles. However, the Jewish people, by and large, chose to hold this revelation as their national possession. With very few exceptions, including the prophet Jonah's reluctant mission of prophetic warning to the Assyrian capital of Nineveh, the Jews generally did not preach the revealed message of God to the nations.

The Scriptures contain a written revelation of God's plan to redeem all who repent that was ultimately consummated in the unique person, life, and message of Jesus Christ. Despite the fact that the Jewish race has never constituted more than a small fraction of 1 percent of the world's population, the profound religious influence of the Jews upon the rest of mankind over the last four thousand years is incalculable. Today, almost one third of the six billion humans throughout the planet acknowledge that God revealed Himself in an astonishing and unique way to the prophets and patriarchs of the ancient Jews. Today almost two billion people, including Jews, Muslims, and Christians, have accepted that portions of the Jewish Bible are a sure guide through time to eternity. The Bible deserves constant and careful study. This study will be richly repaid by an ever-growing appreciation in the spirit of the follower of Jesus Christ who will see Him afresh in every page.

The Phenomenon of Biblical Anniversaries

When we examine the biblical and historical records concerning the nation of Israel we encounter a phenomenon that is unprecedented in the history of the nations. I refer to my discovery that God has displayed His sovereign control over the destiny of the Jewish people by His influence over the events surrounding the nation of Israel. God has caused an incredible series of eight major historical events to occur on a single day in the ancient Jewish calendar. If we closely examine the history of the nations of Europe or Asia, we discover that these nations have experienced their victories, defeats, and natural disasters on random days that occur on various days of the calendar. Since there are 365 days in the solar calendar, the odds are obviously 365 to 1 against any nation experiencing two defeats or two victories in war on the exact same day of the calendar. This is why so few nations in history have ever experienced parallel events occurring on the very same day of the year as an earlier victory or defeat.

However, when I began to examine the remarkable history of the Jewish people, I discovered an extraordinary phenomenon of biblical anniversaries in which every one of over forty major events in the history of the nation of Israel had occurred on one of the major feast or fast days of the biblical calendar. This calendar of religious feasts and fast days was established thirty-five hundred years ago by God when the Jews where still wandering in the Sinai during the forty-year Exodus from their slavery in Egypt. A detailed study of these amazing anniversaries can be found in my book *Armageddon — Appointment With Destiny*. However, in this book I would like to explore eight major events in the history of Israel that have occurred on one single day in the ancient Hebrew calendar. This will illustrate the awesome pattern of God's sovereign control of the destiny of the nations. In the following pages we will witness the unprecedented phenomenon in which Israel experienced a series of eight national disasters — the most devastating in her history — every one of which occurred on the same day of the calendar. The odds against these eight disasters occurring on the same day is staggering. At the conclusion of this section, I will share with you the awesome mathematical odds against any nation experiencing these eight disasters on one single day of the calendar.

The Appointed Feast Days: "A Shadow of Things to Come"

The apostle Paul spoke of the importance of these special feast days in his epistle to the church at Colosse. "Let no man therefore judge you in meat, or in drink, or in respect of an holy day, or of the new moon, or of the sabbath days: Which are a shadow of things to come; but the body is of Christ" (Colossians 2:16–17). In these verses, Paul was primarily admonishing the church to free itself of legalisms. However, he also clearly revealed that the holy-day feast, the new moon celebration, and the Sabbath day were intended by the Lord as prophetic signs of future events.

As we contemplate the sovereignty of God revealed in this precise alignment of feast days and significant anniversary events in Israel's history and future, we should feel a profound sense of wonder. God is truly in charge of the events in the lives of individuals as well as nations, such as Israel. God knows the end from the beginning, and He is concerned that we seek to understand His will as He unfolds His plan of redemption in human history.

The Ninth Day of Av: A Fast of Mourning

The prophet Zechariah referred to this fast day as follows: "When ye fasted and mourned in the fifth [Av] and seventh month" (Zechariah 7:5). This day of fasting, known to the Jewish people as Tisha Be-Av, became a day of national mourning and remembrance of Israel's loss of both of their sacred Temples. It is one of the most historically significant anniversaries in the life of their nation and is commemorated by Jews throughout the world as the tragic day when God withdrew His Presence and divine protection. The children of Israel wept as their precious Temple burned to the ground on the ninth day of Av, not once but twice in history. The Jewish historian, an eyewitness to the Roman destruction of the Temple, in A.D. 70, pointed to the burning of both Temples on the same day as proof of the Hand of God in these tragic events.

Tisha Be-Av, Israel's fast of mourning, which occurs on the ninth of the month of Av (our month of August), has witnessed eight of the greatest disasters in Israel's history. In fact, this date has seen more national disasters than any other date in world history. The ninth of Av has become a day when Jews not only mourn their loss but also look forward to that great day when their Messiah will finally appear to end their centuries of suffering. The prophet Zechariah declared that when the Messiah and the long promised Kingdom comes, all of their fasts, including this one, "shall be to the house of Judah joy and gladness, and cheerful feasts" (Zechariah 8:19). Let us examine the biblical and secular history of the Jewish people which contains the record of the tragic events which occurred on this day.

Eight National Disasters that Fell on the Ninth of Av

1. *The Twelve Spies Return with their Evil Report*

Moses sent out the twelve tribal leaders to spy out the Promised Land for forty days prior to entering the Promised Land of Canaan. However, due to their unbelief, ten of the twelve spies returned with pessimistic reports about how impossible it would be to conquer the inhabitants of the land, even though God had promised them victory. The ancient Jewish commentary, the *Mishna*, records that the people believed the evil report and mourned all night in fear. They turned against Moses and the two faithful spies (Joshua and Caleb) on the ninth day of the month Av *(Ta'anit* 29a). The result, according to Numbers 14:1–10, was a mutiny and led to an attempt to stone Moses. The rebels planned a return to the bondage of Egypt on the ninth of Av, 1490 B.C.

If this rebellion had been successful, this violation of God's covenant with Abraham would have led to the death and final assimilation of the Jewish people in Egypt. God destroyed the rebel leaders and warned Israel that their sinful rebellion would result in the death of that whole generation of Jews while wandering in the wilderness of Sinai over the next forty years, even as the spies had searched out the land for forty days. The result of this awful rebellion and their lack of belief in God's promises was the loss of the Promised Land for that entire generation, save for the two faithful spies, Joshua and Caleb. The Bible records that "Moses told these sayings unto all the children of Israel: and the people mourned greatly" (Numbers 14: 39).

Thus, from the time of this rebellion on the ninth of Av, this day became a fast of mourning as Israel wept over their lack of obedience to God and the tragedies that followed repeatedly during the next thirty-five centuries.

2. *The Destruction of Solomon's Temple by the Babylonian Army*

The Babylonian army under Nebuchadnezzar besieged Jerusalem in 589 B.C. After a two-year siege, on the seventeenth of Tammuz, they breached the walls and forced the ending of the daily sacrifice in the Temple. Twenty-one days later, on the ninth of Av, 587 B.C., the Babylonian army broke through the walls of

Jerusalem to directly attack the Jews' final defenses on the massive Temple Mount.

According to the Jewish commentary, *Me'am Lo'ez,* by Rabbi Yaakov Culi and Rabbi Aguiti, and other historical sources, including *Ta'anit* 29a from the *Jerusalem Talmud,* the Babylonian army fought their way into the Temple courtyard on the seventh day of Av. "His men ate, drank and caroused there until the ninth of Av. Toward evening, they set the Temple on fire. It burned all night and through the next day, the tenth day of Av." The prophet Jeremiah, who was an eyewitness to the terrible destruction of Jerusalem, recorded that the Babylonian captain of the guard, Nebuzaradan, conquered the city, captured King Zedekiah, and burned the Temple. With no one attempting to fight the enormous fire, the huge Temple complex burned throughout the next day as well, the tenth of Av (Jeremiah 52:5–14).

This tragedy of the loss of their beloved Temple has been commemorated by the Jews ever since. This commemoration has been held on the solemn fast on the ninth of Av, known as Tisha Be Av. For twenty-five hundred years, on this day, the Jews have read the book of Lamentations in which Jeremiah laments the Babylonian destruction of Jerusalem and the great Temple of Solomon. "The Lord hath cast off His altar, He hath abhorred His sanctuary, He hath given up into the hand of the enemy the walls of the palaces; they have made a noise in the House of the Lord, as in the day of a solemn feast" (Lamentations 2:7; Zechariah 8:9).

3. *The Destruction of the Second Temple by the Roman Legions*

The Roman Empire had been at war with the Jews for three and one-half years since their initial revolt in A.D. 66. The Roman legions were finally ready to crush the Jewish revolt by destroying their capital, Jerusalem, in A.D. 70. Over 1,250,000 people were surrounded inside the city by the encircling wall built by the Roman legions to prevent escape or supplies reaching the city. The original Roman attack occurred on the Feast of Passover. A huge number of Jewish pilgrims had arrived in Jerusalem to celebrate the Passover Feast and were trapped there, along with the rest of the population. Since the Passover Feast attracted up to five times the normal population of the city, the Romans were glad to seize the opportunity to seal off the city in hopes of starving the rebels into submission.

The daily sacrifice in the Temple ceased again on the same day, the seventeenth of Tammuz, due to the Roman attacks. Twenty-one days later, on the ninth day of the month of Av, the Roman army reached the edge of the Temple compound. The Roman general, Titus, gave strict orders that the beautiful Temple, the most magnificent building in the whole Roman Empire, should not be destroyed. He implored the Jewish defenders to surrender, so that their city and their beloved Temple would not have to be destroyed. However, the judgment of God had been delivered almost forty years earlier by Jesus Christ. Jesus had warned the population of Jerusalem what awaited her because they had chosen to reject God's Messiah:

> And when he was come near, he beheld the city, and wept over it, Saying, If thou hadst known, even thou, at least in this thy day, the things which belong unto thy peace! but now they are hid from thine eyes. For the days shall come upon thee, that thine enemies shall cast a trench about thee, and compass thee round, and keep thee in on every side, And shall lay thee even with the ground, and thy children within thee; and they shall not leave in thee one stone upon another; because thou knewest not the time of thy visitation. (Luke 19:41–44).

This terrible appointment with destiny could not be avoided. The Jewish rebel leaders rejected the offers of General Titus. The last desparate pitched battle for the Temple Mount began.

Despite his firm orders to the Roman centurions to preserve the Temple intact, the enraged soldiers, who had endured two years of Jewish attacks from the Temple walls, threw torches into the Temple. Within minutes, the holy Temple became an inferno. An eyewitness, Flavius Josephus, reported that General Titus stood in the great entrance to the Holy Place of the burning Temple and beat back his soldiers with his sword in a vain attempt to save at least the Inner Temple from their cruel act of destruction. It is also reported that when Titus saw that the flames had reached the inner sanctuary, he fell to his knees and cried out, "As God is my witness, this was not done by my order."

Neither General Titus nor his soldiers realized that they were unconsciously fulfilling two very specific scriptural prophecies. First, the prophet Daniel, more than six hundred years earlier, had predicted in his great prophecy of the Seventy Weeks that "after threescore and two weeks shall Messiah be cut off, but not for himself: and the people of the prince that shall come shall destroy the city and the sanctuary; and the end thereof shall be with a flood, and unto the end of the war desolations are determined" (Daniel 9:26).

This strange phrase reveals two facts: (1) the people (the Roman soldiers), would be responsible for the destruction, not their leader, "the prince"; and (2) "the prince that shall come" refers to the "prince" of the Roman Empire. When General Titus initially began the Jewish War, he was not of royal blood. However, his father, the General Vespasian (a commoner), became Emperor of Rome in A.D. 69. When the final siege was undertaken in A.D. 70, Titus, Vespasian's son, had, therefore, become the "prince," and thus initially fulfilled the ancient prophecy. The final fulfillment of Daniel's prophecy of the "prince that shall come" will occur in the rise of the future Antichrist, when the Antichrist and his revived Roman Empire again attack the city of Jerusalem and the rebuilt Temple during the last days.

The second major prophecy regarding the destruction of the Temple was given by Jesus Christ in Luke 19:41–44. After the Pharisees had told Jesus to restrain His disciples from their joyful praise of God, "He answered and said unto them, I tell you that, if these should hold their peace, the stones would immediately cry out" (Luke 19:40). As the crowd drew near to Jerusalem, Jesus looked at the city and its Temple and wept over it. He warned them in these words: "For the days shall come upon thee, that shine enemies shall cast a trench about thee, and compass thee round, and keep thee in on every side, and shall lay thee even with the ground, and thy children within thee; and they shall not leave in thee one stone upon another; because thou knewest not the time of thy visitation" (verses 43–44).

This prophecy was fulfilled to the smallest detail in A.D. 70. As the Romans burned the Temple to the ground, the tremendous heat of the fire melted the sheets of gold that covered much of the Temple building. The molten gold ran down into every crack between the foundation stones. When the fire finally died down, the Roman soldiers used wedges and crowbars to overturn every stone to search for this gold, thus fulfilling Christ's words.

4. *The Romans Plowed Jerusalem and the Temple with Salt in* A.D. *71*

In A.D. 71, one year after the destruction of the city of Jerusalem and the burning of the Temple, on the ninth of Av, the Roman army plowed the Temple Mount and the city of Jerusalem with salt to destroy any vegetation necessary to support a population. This was a complete fulfillment of the prophecy of Micah: "Therefore shall Zion for your sakes be plowed as a field, and Jerusalem shall become heaps, and the mountain of the house as the high places of the forest" (Micah 3:12). A rabbinical source, *Ta'anit* 26b, records that this was done to turn the city into a Roman colony totally dependent on Rome for survival.

5. *The Destruction of Bar Kochba's Army in* A.D. *135*

After the fall of Jerusalem in A.D. 70, there was a period of enforced peace for six decades. In Matthew 24, Jesus spoke about Daniel's prophecy of the destruction of the Temple: "If any man shall say unto you, Lo, here is Christ, or there; believe it not. For there shall arise false Christs, and false prophets, and shall shew great signs and wonders; insomuch that, if it were possible, they shall deceive the very elect" (Matthew 24: 23–24). There were no false messiahs before the life of Jesus of Nazareth. Following His death and resurrection, a number of false messiahs arose to bring religious confusion to the Jewish people.

Among those false prophets was a dynamic Jewish leader named Simon Bar Kochba. As Jesus had predicted, many people, including the famous Jewish scholar Rabbi Akiba, proclaimed Simon Bar Kochba as the Messiah. Jesus had prophesied this event before His rejection: "I am come in my Father's name, and ye receive me not; if another shall come in his own name, him ye will receive" (John 5:43). How sad that after rejecting the true Messiah the Jewish people would now accept a counterfeit messiah who led them to national disaster.

For two years, despite overwhelming odds against them, Simon Bar Kochba and his followers succeeded in defeating the Roman legions. Finally, Emperor Hadrian and his enormous Roman army with six legions attacked and destroyed the Jewish rebels at Beitar, a few miles southwest of Jerusalem. On that tragic ninth of Av, A.D. 135, the last great army of an independent Israel was slaughtered without mercy.

Dio Cassius, the Roman historian, says that 580,000 Jewish soldiers fell by the sword alone, not counting those who fell by fire and famine. The horses of the Romans, he says, were wading in blood up to their girths in the mud and mire of the valley battleground. Sixty-five years to the day after the city of Jerusalem and the Temple were destroyed in A.D. 70, this final rebellion against Rome ended in terrible tragedy for the Jews with the destruction of Israel's army in A.D. 135, the ninth day of Av.

The prophet Isaiah may have referred to this event when he prophesied, "For the head of Syria is Damascus, and the head of Damascus is Rezin; and within threescore and five years shall Ephraim [Israel] be broken, that it be not a people" (Isaiah 7:8). In 721 B.C., sixty-five years after Isaiah spoke these words, the Assyrian exile of the northern tribes of Israel fulfilled Isaiah's prophecy. However, it appears that the prophet Isaiah may also have been alluding to the final shattering of the nation of Israel in 135 A.D., which also occurred on the sixty-fifth anniversary of the Roman burning of the Temple, the ninth of Av.

6. *England Expelled All Jews in A.D. 1290*

On July 18, 1290, the ninth of Av in the Jewish calendar, King Edward I ordered the expulsion of all Jews from England. For the next four centuries, England did not prosper as a nation beyond her own small island. Almost four hundred years later, Oliver Cromwell, Lord Protector of England, a strong Bible believing Christian, granted the Jews the legal right of settlement throughout England in 1657. It is interesting to note that the British Empire's prosperity and world power can be traced to its beginnings during the reign of Lord Cromwell. The Jews returned and prospered in England and in all her colonies throughout the British Empire. The history of England's rise and fall can be traced to this ancient prophecy in the book of Genesis: "And I will bless them that bless thee, and curse him that curseth thee: and in thee shall all the families of the earth be blessed" (Genesis 12:3). As England blessed the Jews, God blessed the British Empire until it ruled one-quarter of the globe.

On November 2, 1917, Lord Balfour, the British Foreign Secretary, wrote his historic declaration endorsing the setting up of a national homeland for the Jews in Palestine. This was partly in response to the tremendous scientific contribution by Chaim

Weizmann (who later became Israel's first president), a Jew who produced explosives to aid England's war effort. At the end of World War I, a victorious England held power through its British Empire over one-quarter of the world. Tragically, at the very same time as England was promising the Jews a national homeland in Palestine, Lawrence of Arabia was promising the Arabs that England would give them the lands that were occupied by the Turkish Empire in return for their help in defeating Germany and Turkey in the war. However, in these intense negotiations, the territory of Israel itself was never demanded by the Arabs. The reason for this lack of interest was that few Arabs lived in the barren and empty land of Palestine. Ultimately, the Arabs received five hundred times as much territory as Israel, over five million square miles of land which now comprise twenty-one Arab countries. Meanwhile, the Jews received only eight thousand square miles of land in a strip along the Mediterranean Sea (less than one-fifth of 1 percent of what the Arabs received).

In the 1920s and throughout the period until 1948, England repeatedly reversed its promises to the League of Nations to facilitate Jewish immigration and failed to provide the promised national homeland for the Jews. Israel ultimately received only 17.5 percent of the territory promised her by the Balfour Declaration and the British Mandate, as endorsed by the League of Nations (the predecessor to the United Nations). Britain prevented most Jewish immigration from Europe to Palestine throughout that thirty-year period. This illegal and immoral reversal of her solemn obligation to allow the Jews to return to the Promised Land contributed tragically and immeasurably to the magnitude of the Holocaust. The Jews of Europe had no homeland to flee to when the savage persecution of Adolf Hitler began. The five and one-half million Jews who died in the Nazi death camps might have fled to Palestine if the British had not broken their word and stopped Jewish immigration to Palestine.

It is not improbable that the decline of Britain from its exalted status as the preeminent superpower that "ruled the seas" to the position of a second-level power is connected to her betrayal of the Jews and her opposition to a Jewish national homeland in Israel. In this same period, 1917–1948, England lost her vast empire, spanning one-quarter of the globe, including the southern part of Ireland. Over four thousand years ago, God gave us a profound insight into the reasons behind the history of the rise and fall of many nations and His divine intervention in history: "I will bless them that bless thee, and curse him that curseth thee" (Genesis 12:3). This lesson of history from both the Bible and the events of this century should stand as a severe warning to our national leaders to stand with the Jewish people in their right to live in Israel in peace with secure borders.

7. *Spain Expelled All Jews in* A.D. *1492*

On August 2, 1492, the ninth of Av, the Spanish government ordered the expulsion of 800,000 Jews, despite the fact that these Jews had lived in Spain for more than fifteen hundred years. The New Testament records that the apostle Paul travelled to Spain to preach to the Jews and Gentiles in that country. This tragic expulsion of the Jews marked a watershed in the rise of the Spanish Empire. From that point on, the Spanish Empire's fortunes began to decrease, in fulfillment of God's promise to Abraham that "I will bless them that bless thee, and curse him that curseth thee" (Genesis 12:3).

It is interesting also to note that the ninth of Av, 1492 was the very same day that the Italian explorer Christopher Columbus left Spain to discover the New World. This pivotal event was of tremendous importance to the Jews because America ultimately became a place of refuge for the Jewish people. In addition, there is some evidence to suggest that Columbus may have been of Jewish ancestry. Therefore, the ninth of Av, 1492 was a propitious day for him to leave Spain to avoid the persecution. Significantly, when the new nation of Israel was reborn in 1948, the United States of America became Israel's strongest protector and supporter.

8. *Russia Mobilized for World War I and Launched Persecutions against the Jews*

On the ninth of Av, August 1, 1914, as the Jews fasted and mourned, Russia and Germany declared war, beginning World War I, one of the major disasters in human history. This four-year war involved the greatest military struggle in history to that point, in fulfillment of Christ's prophecy that in the last days, "nation shall rise against nation and kingdom against kingdom" (Matthew 24:7). As Russia mobilized its huge army on the ninth day of Av, the local governors triggered persecutions and attacks against the Jews in the Pale of Settlement in eastern Russia including Poland (then part of Russia), killing as many as one hundred thousand Jews. These persecutions forced many Jews to emigrate to either America or the Holy Land. These Russian and eastern European Jewish immigrants joined the native-born Jewish "Sabras" in building the agricultural settlements and infrastructure of the embryonic Jewish state. This wave of Jewish immigration set the stage for the dramatic events leading to the creation of Israel in 1948.

As mentioned earlier, the phenomenon of eight major historical disasters affecting one nation over a period of thirty-five centuries occurring on a single day of the year is unprecedented in human history. As a student of history over the last thirty-five years, I can assure you that no other nation has experienced any such pattern of historical anniversaries or "coincidences."

In fact, if any of my readers are mathematically inclined, I would suggest that they check the probability that these eight historical tragedies could have occurred by random chance rather than by God's foreknowledge and sovereignty. Because there are 365 days in a year, the chance that even a second significant historical tragedy would occur by chance alone on the anniversary date of a previous tragedy on a given day, say, the ninth day of Av (August), is only one chance in 365. The odds against a third similar event occurring on exactly the same day, the ninth day of Av, can be calculated as follows:

$$1 \times 365 \times 365 = \text{one chance in } 133,225$$

In other words, the odds against even three national disasters occurring by chance alone on a particular anniversary day, such as the ninth day of Av, is only 1 chance in 133,225!

This mathematical reality is why the historical records of the nations do not reveal any other nation, except for Israel, that has sustained repeated victories or defeats on particular anniversary dates of the calendar.

The odds that all eight disastrous events for Israel would occur by chance alone on the ninth day of Av, rather than by God's design, is equal to:

$$1 \times 365 \times 365 \times 365 \times 365 \times 365 \times 365 \times 365 \times 365 =$$
$$\text{Only 1 chance in } 863,078,009,300,000,000$$

or

1 chance in 863 Million Times a Billion!

It is important to remember that the above probability analysis only considers eight of Israel's anniversary events, only those that occurred on the ninth day of the biblical month Av.

In all, there are more than forty major anniversary events that have occurred throughout Israel's history. I examine these events in my book *Armageddon — Appointment With Destiny*. If we were to add these additional thirty-two anniversary dates to our probability figures, the numbers would be so astronomically high that no rational person could conclude that these events had happened on their respective dates by chance alone.

The consideration of these astonishing historical records will lead many to believe, along with this author, that the only rational explanation for this phenomenon is that God has had His hand upon the Jewish people and the nation of Israel. Furthermore, this evidence provides strong proof that the Bible, which reveals these staggering, historically verified events, is truly the inspired Word of God.

12

The Rocks Cry Out: The Historical Evidence For the Bible

The last one hundred and fifty years of archeological exploration in the Middle East has provided students of the Bible with an
unparalleled abundance of evidence confirming thousands of
detailed historical statements found in both the Old and New
Testaments. In this chapter, we will explore a small fraction of the
powerful historical and archeological evidence that has been discovered in Israel and throughout the Middle East that throws new
light on the pivotal events that have shaped our modern Western
culture. It is important that we place this evidence in its proper
context. Archeology and historical documents can never prove
that the Bible is inspired. Rather, the confirmation of the statements of the Bible through archeological and historical investigations provides us with powerful evidence of the historical truthfulness of the Word of God and indicates that its statements were
accurately transmitted over thousands of years.

One of the greatest of these pioneer archeologists is the Jewish
scholar Dr. Nelson Glueck, considered by many to be the greatest
Jewish archeologist in history. Professor Glueck has written, "It is

worth emphasizing that in all this work no archaeological discovery has ever controverted a single, properly understood biblical statement."[1] Professor Glueck's statement is a powerful antidote to the pervasive skepticism and unbelief of so many of the liberal theologians who inhabit the seminaries and universities of the West. Despite the cynicism and skepticism of many liberal theologians to the accuracy of the biblical account the scientific evidence of archeology continues to confirm the accuracy of the Bible's statements. Meanwhile, liberal theologians continue to ignore this overwhelming evidence in favor of their presuppositions and strongly held prejudice against the authority, inspiration, and accuracy of the Word of God.

Dr. Glueck wrote about the wonder of exploring the ancient ruins of the Promised Land and finding confirmation after confirmation of the truthfulness of this incomparable book, the Holy Scriptures.

> Acquaint yourself with the needs and fears, the moods and manners, of the broken array of peoples and civilizations that appeared at intervals along the horizon of time and, in a general way, you will know in advance where to look for the clues they left behind in the course of their passage.... And above all, read the Bible, morning, noon and night, with a positive attitude, reading to accept its historical references.... And then go forth into the wilderness of the Negev and discover, trite as it may sound, that everything you touch turns into the gold of history, and that it is almost impossible not to stumble across the treasures of a robust past, whose existence becomes as real and as full of content and color and sound and fury and the thrill of progress and the pity of failure as the transient present, which is always ticking away so furiously to join the throng of those that need no longer hurry.[2]

Jerusalem, The City of David

Modern liberal scholars who reject the biblical evidence about the monarchies of King David and his son Solomon in the tenth century before Christ also dismiss the Bible's claims about Jerusalem being the capital city of a united Israel. Many of these biblically minimalist scholars, including Professor Thomas

Thompson of the University of Copenhagen, totally reject the Bible's description of Jerusalem as Israel's capital city during the reigns of King David and Solomon in the period 1000 B.C. to 930 B.C. In an article in *Biblical Archeological Review*, Thompson stated, "We don't have a tenth-century Jerusalem ... The last point is that Jerusalem becomes a really major town only after the destruction of Lachish in 701 B.C. . . . Its very difficult to talk about a united monarchy [under David and Solomon] in the tenth century B.C.E."[3] [*Note*: academic scholars use B.C.E. (before common era) rather than the normal designation B.C. (before Christ) for fairly obvious reasons].

In other words, Professor Thompson and his many liberal colleagues totally deny the detailed biblical record of the reigns of Israel's greatest kings and Solomon's Temple. From their skeptical standpoint, they automatically reject every biblical statement unless it is verified by multiple pagan historical or archeological sources. However, a logical question arises. How could such a detailed historical tradition and national memory of King David's and King Solomon's deeds, their conquests, and their Temple have arisen in Israel if these events never occurred?

Modern anthropologists admit that nearly always there is some historical event behind every tradition. The biblical minimalist scholars reject the historical and archeological evidence, as well as the biblical evidence, that attests to Jerusalem's existence as a significant city in Palestine during the time of Israel's conquest of Canaan, which occurred several centuries before the rise of King Saul and then King David to rule Jerusalem as Israel's capital. A fascinating article entitled "Cow Town or Royal Capital" by Nadav Na'aman appeared in the July/August 1997 issue of the respected *Biblical Archeological Review* magazine. This article contained interesting archeological evidence about ancient Jerusalem including a reference to the Tell el Amarna Letters. Although I had read a summary of these letters years ago, I was delighted to acquire an excellent copy and translation of these vital ancient documents from a rare-book dealer several weeks ago. It was fascinating to read these letters by the pagan king of Jerusalem during the time of the conquest of the Promised Land.

Evidence about Jerusalem From the Tell el-Amarna Tablets

The famous Amarna letters were discovered at Tell el-Amarna in Egypt more than a century ago. These thirty-five hundred-year-old clay tablets included diplomatic letters that were written in the 14th century B.C. in Akkadian cuneiform characters, the common official language at the time. This valuable library of government documents includes more than three hundred diplomatic letters written by the governors or kings of Canaan to the Egyptian pharaoh who ruled Canaan as a province of the Egyptian-controlled territory in Palestine and Syria. This extensive correspondence includes hundreds of letters written by two well-known Egyptian pharaohs (Amenophis III [1391–1353 B.C.] and Amenophis IV, popularly known as Akhenaten [1353–1337 B.C.]). The dates when these Egyptian pharaohs ruled are widely accepted.

The most important portion of the letters for biblical scholars include six diplomatic messages sent from the King of Jerusalem, who ruled Canaan (present-day Israel and the West Bank). These letters are incredibly valuable for the detailed historical evidence they provide about the situation in Canaan at the approximate time of the conquest of the Promised Land under the leadership of Joshua and Gideon, according to the biblical record found in Joshua and Judges. The Tell el-Amarna Tablets provide invaluable independent information about historical conditions in Canaan. Written by several kings who ruled their provinces and cities under the rule of Egypt, these letters are of vital importance to scholars because they describe conditions in Canaan only one or two generations after the Exodus at the very time the Bible tells us the conquest of the Promised Land was occurred.

All serious scholars who have examined the Tell el-Amarna letters agree that the name "Urusalim" found in the letters clearly refer to the city of Jerusalem, according to the detailed geographical descriptions about its location. The Amarna letters mention the city of "Urusalim" (Jerusalem) which appears repeatedly in this fascinating correspondence. At the time of this correspondence, Jerusalem and other cities of Canaan were ruled by local kings under ultimate Egyptian control. Jerusalem itself was ruled by a local dynasty which passed the crown from father to son. Other sources refer to these local rulers of city-states as kings. In most of these letters, the king of Jerusalem appeals desperately, and without success, for troops and archers from his overlord, the pharaoh of Egypt. Apparently at this time, the pharaoh ruling Egypt was distracted from defending his province of Canaan against the invaders who were attacking the cities under the control of the king of Jerusalem. This invasion of the foreign "Habiru" occurred during the reign of Pharaoh Amenophis IV, often called Akhenaten (1353–1337 B.C.). Apparently Akhenaten ignored military defense because he was focussed solely on creating a new religion in Egypt to worship the sun god.

Consider the powerful historical evidence provided in these six letters from the king of Jerusalem to his overlord, the king of Egypt, that prove Jerusalem existed as a capital city during this critical historical period. In addition, these letters provide evidence that the Promised Land was being invaded at this time by a victorious army of foreign people called "Habiru." Many scholars admit that the "Habiru" were most likely the conquering Israelites, who called themselves "Hebrews." For example, Abdi-Hiba, the king of Jerusalem, wrote to the pharaoh in desperation requesting Egyptian troops to defend his territory.

Letters From The Tell el-Amarna Tablets[4]

There is no garrison here.
So let the king care for his land.
Let the king care for his land.
The lands of the king, the lord,
have all deserted.
Ilimilku has devastated the whole land of the king.
(Letter of Abdi-Hiba, King of Jerusalem to
the Pharaoh —Tell el Amarna Letter — Number 2)

No lands of the king remain.
The Habiru plunder all lands of the king.
If archers are here this year, then the lands of the king,
the lord, will remain; but if archers are not here,
then the lands of the king, my lord, are lost.
(Letter of Abdi-Hiba, King of Jerusalem to
the Pharaoh — Tell el Amarna Letter — Number 3)

Verily, the king has set his name
upon the land of Urusalim for ever.
Therefore he cannot abandon
the lands of Urusalim.
(Letter of Abdi-Hiba, King of Jerusalem
to the Pharaoh — Tell el Amarna Letter — Number 3)

In his letters the king protested that the pharaoh's indifference to his desperate military request for additional troops indicated that he didn't want to fight the "Habiru."

As long as the king, my lord, lives
I will say to the deputy of the king, my lord:
"Why do you love the Habiru, and hate the regents ?"
(Letter of Abdi-Hiba, King of Jerusalem to
the Pharaoh — Tell el Amarna Letter — Number 2)

But if there are no archers
the land of the king will desert to the Hiabiru.
This will be the fate of the land.
(Letter of Abdi-Hiba, King of Jerusalem
to the Pharaoh — Tell el Amarna Letter — Number 6)

Could the reluctance to fight this group of invaders stem from the historical memory of the Egyptians' of God's supernatural deliverance of the Israelites and the destruction of Egypt's army at the Red Sea during the Exodus?

Abdi-Hiba, the king of Jerusalem, indicated the significance of his kingdom and capital in his description of his gift of over five thousand slaves to his Egyptian overlord. If Jerusalem was a small, insignificant town, its king would not have had a military victory that afforded him the opportunity to send a gift of five thousand prisoners captured from his enemies. The biblical minimalist scholars assert that during this period (three centuries before King David and Solomon), Jerusalem was only a tiny, insignificant town, but their assertions have been proven to be false by the Amarna Letters of the Egyptian government.

___ I have sent to the king, [my] lor[d]
___ prisoners, five thousand _ __ _ _ ,
[three hundr]ed and eigh[teen] bearers for
the caravans of the king;

they were taken in the fields (iati) near [Ialuna.
(Letter of Abdi-Hiba, King of Jerusalem to
    the Pharaoh — Tell el Amarna Letter — Number 3)

Finally, Abdi-Hiba reveals his personal fear of imminent defeat by these conquering "Habiru" (Hebrews), who are taking city after city throughout his weakly defended territory. The king of Jerusalem warns the pharaoh that his fellow regents (local kings under Egypt's rule) are succumbing to the Habiru attack. Lastly, he admits that because Egypt is indifferent ("yet the king holds himself back") that the soldiers of another Canaanite king, "Zimrida of Lakisi," have deserted to join the victorious Habiru army.

But now the Habiru are taking
the cities of the king.
No regent is (left)
to the king, my lord; all are lost.

Behold, Turbazu has been killed
in the gate of Zilu, yet the king holds himself back.
Behold, Zimrida of Lakisi — servants,
who have joined with the Habiru, have smitten him.
(Letter of Abdi-Hiba, King of Jerusalem to
    the Pharaoh — Tell el Amarna Letter — Number 4)

Other correspondence in the series of Tell el Amarna Letters indicates that the territory ruled by the king of Jerusalem at that time (during the days of Joshua and Gideon) included land extending from Hebron in the south to the town of Bethel in the north. In addition, these letters indicate that the territory of the king of Jerusalem extended from the midpoint of present-day West Bank to the Jordan River.

In conclusion, an analysis of the Tell el Amarna Letters clearly confirms that, in the 14th century B.C., the city of Jerusalem was a capital city ruling over a considerable amount of territory in Canaan under the oversight of the Egyptian pharaohs. The area encompassed a significant portion of the current West Bank as well as the areas to the west of Jerusalem. The letters confirm that the king of Jerusalem lived in a palace with a pagan temple and a full court of officials. Most importantly, these records confirm that Jerusalem was sophisticated enough to possess court scribes who carried on a continuing diplomatic correspondence with neighboring states, including its overlord, Egypt. In addition, the letters confirm that couriers from Egypt carried on regular correspondence with the court of Jerusalem.

In conclusion, the powerful historical evidence from these ancient Egyptian Tell el Amarna documents provides one more strong link in the chain of evidence from sources outside the Bible that tends to confirm the historical accuracy of these biblical accounts.

King Hezekiah's Tunnel Inscription

The ancient king of Judea, King Hezekiah ordered his workmen to carve a long tunnel through 1,749 feet of hard bedrock to bring in a safe supply of water from a spring that was located outside the walls of the City of David, ancient Jerusalem. This undertaking was a truly phenomenal engineering task, especially when we consider the limited mining and surveying knowledge as well as the primitive tools, available to Jewish engineers in the 8th century B.C. An inscription describing this undertaking reveals that the leader of the project ordered two groups of miners to begin digging toward each other from opposite ends of the tunnel. The reason for attempting the very difficult task of trying to bore through so much solid rock in the hope of meeting in the center rather than simply working from one end only, must have been the fear of an impending invasion of Jerusalem. Tourists visiting Jerusalem can now safely wade through the shallow waters of Hezekiah's Tunnel that lead to the Gihon Spring. Kaye and I have walked underground in this engineering marvel, and have witnessed proof of the incredible accuracy of the historical accounts recorded in the Holy Scriptures.

The tunnel inscription was written in ancient classical Hebrew on a plaque located near the pool. The inscription described the construction of this unusual tunnel: "Behold the tunnel. This is the story of its cutting. While the miners swung their picks, one towards the other, and when there remained only 3 cubits to cut, the voice of one calling his fellow was heard — for there was a resonance in the rock coming from both north and south . . . and the water flowed from the spring towards the pool, 1200 cubits. The height of the rock above the head of the miners was 100 cubits." This engraved inscription is enormously important to archeologists because it clearly confirms a very specific and unusual biblical account. The engraving was carved out of the base rock that formed the side of the ancient excavated tunnel. After its discovery, it was removed by the Turkish authorities to their capital of Istanbul in 1880. It was forgotten and laid aside as an unknown inscription until an Israeli archeologist visited the museum and recognized that the engraved stone was incredibly valuable, the long-forgotten Hezekiah Tunnel inscription. He alerted the museum curator to the fact. This priceless inscription from the past can now be seen in an exhibit in an archeological museum in Istanbul, Turkey.

It is interesting to look back in Church history to view the attitudes toward the authority of the Bible expressed by the great men of faith in past generations. In the fourth-century book *The City of God*, Saint Augustine declared, "Scripture, which proves the truth of its historical statements by the accomplishment of its prophecies, gives no false information.

Can We Trust the Historical Statements of the Bible?
The Testimony of Archaeologists and Classical Scholars

Professor Millar Burrows of Yale University discussed the findings of recent archeological digs and their impact on the views of the critics of biblical historical accuracy: "Archaeology has in many cases refuted the views of modern critics. It has shown in a number of instances that these views rest on false assumptions and unreal, artificial schemes of historical development"[5] Dr. Burrows explained the underlying assumptions that creates this climate of rejection of the Scriptures: "The excessive skepticism of many liberal theologians stems not from a careful evaluation of the available data, but from an enormous predisposition against the supernatural." His comments underline the fundamental role of presuppositions in the minds of all intellectuals as they approach any area of study. If you approach the Bible determined to reject any of the statements that reveal the prophetic and supernatural nature of God's revelation to man, then you have determined your negative conclusions before commencing your study.

As a leading archaeologist in the field of biblical Middle Eastern studies Burrows revealed that the results of modern archeological research have provided powerful new evidence in favor of the historical accuracy of the statements found in the Scriptures: "On the whole, however, archaeological work has unquestionably strengthened confidence in the reliability of the scriptural record. More than one archaeologist has found his respect for the Bible increased by the experience of excavation in Palestine"[6] In conclusion Burrows affirmed that the net result of the recent discoveries has actually increased our ability to categorize the Bible's statements as solid evidence by eyewitnesses to these ancient events: "Such evidence as archaeology has afforded thus far, especially by providing additional and older manuscripts of the books of the Bible, strengthens our confidence in the accuracy with which the text has been transmitted through the centuries."[7]

Sir Frederic Kenyon, a well-known archeologist in the earlier part of this century, has written that the results of modern research has profoundly increased our knowledge and understanding of the biblical world. Professor Kenyon wrote that Christians can welcome the results of continued archeological research because the continuing evidence produced from the digs in the Middle East has strengthened our confidence in the total accuracy of the Word of God.

> It is therefore legitimate to say that, in respect of that part of the Old Testament against which the disintegrating criticism of the last half of the nineteenth century was chiefly directed, the evidence of archaeology has been to re-establish its authority, and likewise to augment its value by rendering it more intelligible through a fuller knowledge of its background and setting. Archaeology has not yet said its last word; but the results already achieved confirm what faith would suggest, that the Bible can do nothing but gain from an increase of knowledge.[8]

F. F. Bruce is a leading researcher in the area of biblical studies. He has stated that, far from disproving the Bible, recent archeological finds have proven the truthfulness of the scriptural account: "Where Luke has been suspected of inaccuracy, and accuracy has been vindicated by some inscriptional evidence, it may be legitimate to say that archaeology has confirmed the New Testament record."[9] Professor Merrill Unger, the editor of the well respected *Unger Bible Dictionary* has pointed out the incomparable value from the results of modern archeology in enabling us to understand the ancient world of the kings and prophets of Israel: "Old Testament archaeology has rediscovered whole nations, resurrected important peoples, and in a most astonishing manner filled in historical gaps, adding immeasurably to the knowledge of biblical backgrounds."

The dismissive attitude toward the literal truth of the historical accounts in the Bible as displayed by liberal theologians such as Bishop Spong, the author of *Rescuing the Bible From Fundamentalism*, is in direct contradiction to the powerful evidence confirming the reliability of the Bible's history from the actual archeological digs. An underlying attitude and prejudice of the liberals is that they deny that the four Gospels were written by Matthew, Mark, Luke, and John, all eyewitnesses and contemporaries of Jesus and the people who were present during the life, death, and resurrection of Jesus of Nazareth. This attitude is displayed in the Jesus Seminar and its negative conclusions that any statement of Jesus that displays evidence of the supernatural, prophecy or His claim to be the Messiah and the Son of God, is "inauthentic." These liberals declare that the four Gospels were created by editors or redactors at least a century after the events they record. In denying the claims of the New Testament writers that they were actually recording events in which they participated, these liberal scholars suggest that the claims of the New Testament regarding the virgin birth, and the resurrection of Jesus, as well as His teachings and miracles, can be dismissed as imaginary creations of editors far removed from the historical events they describe.

The underlying assumption of the liberal scholars who reject the historicity of the Gospels is their belief that these documents were composed over one hundred years after the events of Jesus' life and death. The scholars call the period between the death of Christ and the writing of the Gospels the formative period. The popular German Tubingen school of thought or theory is that the Gospels were edited by unknown Christian redactors to create new theological statements that Jesus never uttered. They suggest that these Gospel accounts were mainly myths or religious legends that developed during the lengthy interval between the lifetime of Jesus and the time these accounts were set down in writing. While this attitude is extremely widespread in liberal universities and seminaries, the evidence produced in the last fifty years provides powerful proof that the Gospel writers were eyewitnesses and contemporaries of Jesus of Nazareth.

The continuing historical research provides overwhelming proof that the three Gospels of Matthew, Mark, and Luke were written within forty years of the Cross. The importance of this fact cannot be overestimated. Archeologists had discovered numerous early papyri manuscript portions of the four Gospels in Egypt and Syria that were written between A.D. 32 and the beginning of the second century. These early manuscripts closed the gap between the time of the Cross and the previously known Gospel manuscripts from the second century. Professor William F. Albright, an outstanding biblical archaeologist, concluded in 1955, "We can already say emphatically that there is no longer any solid basis for dating any book of the New Testament after circa A.D. 80, two full generations before the date between 130 and 150 given by the more radical New Testament critics of today."[10] Dr. Albright's personal assessment of the conclusions of the liberal critics who deny the authenticity of the New Testament is informative: "Only modern scholars who lack both historical method and perspective can spin such a web of speculation as that with which critics have surrounded the Gospel tradition."

Concerning the Old Testament, Professor William F. Albright has written, "There can be no doubt that archaeology has confirmed the substantial historicity of Old Testament tradition." In response to the question of widespread skepticism and outright contempt for the authority of the historical statements of the Bible Dr. Albright wrote the following:

> The excessive skepticism shown toward the Bible by important historical schools of the eighteenth and nineteenth centuries, certain phases of which still appear periodically, has been progressively discredited. Discovery after discovery has established the accuracy of innumerable details and has brought increased recognition to the value of the Bible as a source of history . . . As critical study of the Bible is more and more influenced by the rich new material from the ancient Near East we shall see a steady rise in respect for the historical significance of now

neglected or despised passages and details in the Old and New Testament.[11]

The importance of this proof of the early composition of the Gospel records cannot be overestimated. If the Gospels were written and widely distributed within the lifetime of thousands of people who personally saw the miracles of the feeding of the five thousand and the resurrected Jesus then they must be true historical accounts. In another interview with *Christianity Today* magazine in January 1963, Dr. Albright announced his professional conclusion that every one of the books of the New Testament were written "probably sometime between circa A.D. 50 and 75." Professor Albright correctly noted that this twenty-to forty-five-year interval between the actual historical event and the subsequent writing of the Gospels is "too slight to permit any appreciable corruption of the essential center and even of the specific wording of the sayings of Jesus." Many modern scholars suggest the hypothetical existence of a "Q" source manuscript, containing numerous traditions about Jesus's life and ministry, that they believe was used by Matthew and Mark. However, even these liberal scholars usually suggest this hypothetical (nonexistent) "Q document" was written by some follower of Jesus before A.D. 50. Therefore, even if this theory were correct, the Gospel tradition was still written by eyewitnesses and immediately read by people who personally knew Jesus and the apostles.

If the Gospels contained imaginary or false information then Christianity would never have prevailed in light of the massive persecution of its followers. Why would hundreds of thousands of Christians allow themselves and their beloved family members to die horribly in the Roman Coliseum when all they had to do to escape was to deny their faith that Jesus was God? It is inconceivable that these martyrs would die for their Christian faith if they held the slightest doubt as to the historical accuracy of the Gospel accounts that Jesus was the Son of God who had risen from the dead. The only possible way to explain the steadfast faith of these first-century believers is to acknowledge that they were totally persuaded of the truth of the Gospel account about Jesus of Nazareth.

Consider the confident faith represented by the apostle Paul in his inspired letter to the church at Rome, to people who lived in constant expectation of martyrdom.

> Who shall separate us from the love of Christ? shall tribulation, or distress, or persecution, or famine, or nakedness, or peril, or sword? As it is written, For thy sake we are killed all the day long; we are accounted as sheep for the slaughter. Nay, in all these things we are more than conquerors through him that loved us. For I am persuaded, that neither death, nor life, nor angels, nor principalities, nor powers, nor things present, nor things to come, Nor height, nor depth, nor any other creature, shall be able to separate us from the love of God, which is in Christ Jesus our Lord. I say the truth in Christ, I lie not, my conscience also bearing me witness in the Holy Ghost (Romans 8:35 –9:1).

During the last year, I completed a detailed study of the research on the dating of New Testament documents in *Redating the New Testament*, written by Dr. John A. T. Robinson, the well respected lecturer at Trinity College, Cambridge. Dr. Robinson is an eminent critic of the New Testament period. He concluded that the New Testament is the work of the actual disciples of Jesus and their contemporaries who worked in the early Church, and that, furthermore, every one of the New Testament books, including John, must have been written before A.D. 64.[12] Robinson also wrote about the reliability and early dating of the Gospel of Luke in his book *Luke the Historian in the Light of Research*. He concluded that both Luke and Mark were written at some point before A.D. 59 by the named authors. Furthermore, he wrote, "The early date of both Gospel and Acts gives a strong presumption in favor of the historical value of the books. There was less time for legends to grow. The author was nearer to his sources of information . . . But at any rate, since Luke the physician, the friend of Paul, wrote the two books, they cannot be thrown aside as second-century romances written to deify Jesus and to idealize Peter and Paul. The writer is so close to the facts of which he writes that he has to receive serious consideration to see if, after all, he has not drawn his characters to the life."[13]

Saint Peter's Fish

Some of my favorite passages in the Gospels tell us about the life, teachings, and miracles of Jesus that occurred during His ministry in His home region surrounding the Sea of Galilee. When my wife, Kaye, and I travel to Tiberias on the Sea of Galilee, we always stop at St. Peter's Restaurant to enjoy their main course of St. Peter's Fish, while watching the fishing boats on the usually quiet sea. This species of fish belongs to the Cichlidae family and flourishes in this warm freshwater sea. St. Peter's Fish is occasionally called the "mouth breeder." It is found naturally in only three places, all of which lie along the geological zone extending from the Sea of Galilee thousands of miles to the south in Lake Victoria, Uganda. This species of fish is found only in the Nile River, in Lake Victoria, and in the Sea of Galilee. The Gospel account recorded in Matthew 17:24–27 describes the disciple Peter catching a fish with a shekel coin in its mouth to provide the tribute money that the government officials demanded of Peter and Jesus of Nazareth. Jesus told Peter, "Notwithstanding, lest we should offend them, go thou to the sea, and cast an hook, and take up the fish that first cometh up; and when thou hast opened his mouth, thou shalt find a piece of money: that take, and give unto them for me and thee" (Matthew 17:27)

Dr. Jim Fleming, a professor of archaeology and historical geography at Hebrew University in Jerusalem, has taught about the unusual nature of this fish in connection with Matthew 17:24–27. The female St. Peter's Fish carries her eggs in her mouth to protect them against predators until they hatch. As the brood of minnows begins to grow, she opens her mouth to let them out to swim around her from time to time. However, the mother fish opens her mouth again and quickly scoops them up whenever danger is present. The mother will fast almost to the point of starvation to avoid the danger of inadvertently swallowing her young offspring. On account of her well-known maternal habits, the fishermen of Galilee call the female St. Peter's fish by the Hebrew name "The Mother-Fish." After the young mature to the point where they can survive independently, they swim away. However, the mother fish often keeps a substitute in her mouth to perpetuate her habit of carrying her young. St. Peter's Fish are sometimes caught by fishermen and when they examine their mouths they find pebbles or coke bottle caps inside. The popular name for the fish is "St. Peter's fish" because of the account in Matthew 17:24–27 about Peter catching a fish that carried a shekel coin in its mouth. This habit of the fish to pick up items from the lake bottom in no way minimizes the miracle of our Lord. Only the Son of God could have known that this particular fish would be carrying a shekel coin in its mouth.

In the last century, the writer H. L. Hastings wrote about the astonishing survival and success of the Bible, despite centuries of attacks on its authority and accuracy. The Scriptures have withstood the blistering attacks of skepticism. Hastings wrote, "Infidels of eighteen hundred years have been refuting and over-throwing this book, and yet it stands today as solid rock. Its circulation increases, and it is more loved and cherished and read today than ever before. Infidels, with all their assaults, make about as much impression on this book as a man with a tack hammer would on the Pyramids of Egypt."

Notes

1. John W. Montgomery, *Christianity for the Tough Minded* (Minneapolis: Bethany Fellowship Inc., 1973) 6.

2. Dr. Nelson Glueck, *Exploring Southern Palestine — The Negev* (1959).

3. *Biblical Archeological Review* July/August, 1997.

4. *The Tell el-Amarna Tablets.*

5. Millar Burrows, *What Mean These Stones?* (New York: Meridian Books, 1956) 29.

6. Millar Burrows, *What Mean These Stones?* (New York: Meridian Books, 1956) 1.

7. Millar Burrows, *What Mean These Stones?* (New York: Meridian Books, 1956) 42.

8. Sir Frederic Kenyon, *The Bible and Archeology* (New York: Harper & Row Publishers, 1940) 27.

9. F. F. Bruce, *Revelation and the Bible* (Grand Rapids: Baker Book House, 1969) 33.

10. Howard Frederick Vos, *Can I Trust My Bible?* (Chicago: Moody Press, 1963) 136.

11. William Albright, *The Archaeology of Palestine* (Middlesex: Pelican Books, 1960) 127–128.

12. John A. T. Robinson, *Redating the New Testament* (Philadelphia: Westminster Press, 1976) 351-353.

13. John A. T. Robinson, *Luke the Historian in the Light of Research* (New York: Charles Scribner's Sons, 1923) 39–40.

13

New Scientific Discoveries and the Scriptures

The Marvel of the Human Eye

Three thousand years ago, the wisest man in the world, King Solomon, wrote, "The hearing ear, and the seeing eye, the Lord hath made even both of them" (Proverbs 20:12).

The human eye is a marvel of God's creation. It astonishes the mind of anyone who begins to contemplate the scientific research that has been conducted on its amazing construction and activity. The degree of complexity displayed in the wondrous construction of the various parts of the eye make the theory that it "evolved over millions of years by tiny random-chance mutations" an absolute impossibility. The naturalist creator of the theory of evolution, Charles Darwin, actually admitted that the engineering of the human eye was so specialized and complex that he could not begin to image how it might have developed through the evolutionary processes of random mutation and natural selection.

> To suppose that the eye with all its inimitable contrivances for adjusting the focus to different distances, for admitting different amounts of light, and for the correction of spherical and chromatic aberration, could have been formed by

495

natural selection, seems, I freely confess, absurd in the highest degree.[1]

Another evolutionary scientist, Dr. Ernst Mayer, admitted the difficulty in imagining how the complex human eye could possibly form through chance mutations. It is a considerable strain on one's credulity to assume that finely balanced systems such as certain sense organs (the eye of vertebrates or the feathers of birds) could be improved by random mutations[2]. One of the great problems facing those who deny a Creator is to explain how natural selection or random mutation could evolve such a phenomenally complex organ as the human eye when none of the hundreds of thousands of imagined intermediate mutations could have any value until the entire system was in place to allow vision to take place. The only rational conclusion is that God created the fully developed human eye when He created Adam and Eve.

The eye is engineered far more precisely than a modern, sophisticated camera. However, recent research into its functions reveals that the human eye is vastly more complex and sophisticated than any camera ever made by man. In a manner similar to advanced cameras in the last decade, the human eye displays advanced auto-focus features with a remarkable ability to adjust the diaphragm of the iris automatically and at a phenomenal speed. The lens of your eye modifies its shape through tiny muscles that allow the eye to correctly focus on an object that is moving toward you or away from you. This act is not unlike the workings of a sophisticated, computer-controlled modern camera when it calculates distances and automatically adjusts to bring the object into focus. The lens of your eye is constructed of microscopic and transparent living cells. These cells allow light photons to enter through the cornea, pass through the fluid, and be analyzed by the phenomenal organ known as the retina.

To understand the complexity and sophistication of the engineering of the eye, we need to appreciate the retina. The retina lines the back of your eye and acts as a form of film which receives the actual image composed of light photons passing through the iris, cornea, and eye fluid. Your retina is thinner than paper yet its tiny surface (one inch square) contains 137 million light-sensitive cells. Approximately 95 percent of these cells are rods that can analyse black and white images, while the balance of approximately seven million cone cells are used to analyze color images. Each of these millions of cells are separately connected to the optic nerve that transmits the signal to your brain at approximately three hundred miles per hour. The millions of specialized cells in your eye can analyze more than one million messages a second.

The retina in your eye is the most light-sensitive object in the universe. It is so much more sophisticated in its design than even the most powerful electron microscope or spy camera. For example, the most advanced film available today can differentiate between a range of one thousand to one. However, recent experiments have confirmed that the retina of the human eye can easily differentiate and analyze a range of ten billion to one. Experiments have revealed that the retina can actually detect one single photon of light in a dark room, something beyond the range of engineering instruments. Recently, scientists have determined that the specialized cells in the retina actually partially analyze the image in the eye before it is ever transmitted through the optic nerve to the brain. These retina cells perform up to ten billion calculations per second in determining the nature of the image transmitted to the eye by light photons. No computers on earth are capable of matching these virtually instantaneous calculations.

In an article in *Byte* computer magazine in April 1985, Dr. John Stevens made the following comparison:

> To simulate 10 milliseconds of the complete processing of even a single nerve cell from the retina would require the solution of about 500 simultaneous non-linear differential equations one hundred times and would take at least several minutes of processing time on a Cray super computer. Keeping in mind that there are 10 million or more such cells interacting with each other in complex ways it would take a minimum of a hundred years of Cray time to simulate what takes place in your eye many times every second.

In the article, Dr. Stevens wrote that if we were to attempt to duplicate the computing power of the human eye, we would have to build the world's most advanced computer with a single silicon chip (normally the size of a dime) that would cover 10,000 cubic inches and contain billions of transistors and hundreds of miles of circuit traces. The retina is so small that it fills only 0.0003 inches of space. If we could ever build the advanced device to mimic the human eye, the single computer chip would weigh at least 100 pounds, in comparison to the human retina that weighs less than a gram. The retina operates with less than 0.0001 watts of electrical charge. To duplicate the retina's abilities, the computer would need to consume 300 watts of power. In other words, the retina is 3,000,000 times more efficient in its power consumption.

When we consider the marvellous design of the smallest parts of our body, we are filled with wonder at the glory of God's creation. Anyone who suggests that these phenomenally complex and sophisticated organs have evolved without a designer, by random-chance mutations, is a fool or a liar. The Bible has only one answer to those who would deny the Creator: "The fool hath said in his heart, There is no God" (Psalms 14:1). The Psalmist David acknowledged the truth that we are created by God. "Know ye that the Lord he is God: it is he that hath made us, and not we ourselves; we are his people, and the sheep of his pasture" (Psalms 100:3).

The Function of the Eye

The light of the body is the eye: if therefore thine eye be single, thy whole body shall be full of light. But if thine eye be evil, thy whole body shall be full of darkness. If therefore the light that is in thee be darkness, how great is that darkness! (Matthew 6:22–23)

As mentioned above, the human eye functions like a modern camera. The light enters the eye through the iris — the "lamp of the body." The "light" we allow to enter into our eye affects our soul and our spirit. The cornea of the eye can become very painful if it is hurt or scratched. The prophet Zechariah warned those who would attack God's Chosen People: "For thus saith the Lord of hosts; After the glory hath He sent me unto the nations which spoiled you: for he that toucheth you toucheth the apple of his eye" (Zechariah 2:8). In other words, when men hurt the Jewish people, it is as if they have inflicted the same pain to God as we feel when our eye is injured.

A fascinating insight into the physiology of the human eye is demonstrated in the book of Judges. The passage describes the Israeli army's attack on their enemies. Led by their brilliant general, Gideon, the Jewish army waited to attack until the change of the guard, when "they had but newly set the watch," meaning that the general in charge of the enemy army had just placed newly awakened troops on watch to perform sentry duty. The book of Judges declares, "So Gideon, and the hundred men that were with him, came unto the outside of the camp in the beginning of the middle watch; and they had but newly set the watch: and they blew the trumpets, and brake the pitchers that were in their hands" (Judges 7:19). In other words, Gideon, as a wise general, delayed his attack until the moment the enemy soldiers, who had just awakened from sleep, were placed on guard duty. This meant that the pupils of their eyes would not yet have fully adapted to the darkness and would have had difficulty in seeing their enemy approaching in the dark.

The Seed of the Father Determines the Sex of the Child

"For the man is not of the woman; but the woman of the man." (1 Corinthians 11:8)

This verse in the New Testament may refer to the fact that Genesis declares that God formed the woman Eve from the rib of the man Adam. However, another, more subtle scientific truth is revealed in this inspired statement by the apostle Paul. The apostle's statement "the woman of the man" reveals the scientific truth that "the woman comes out of the man." In other words, the determination that the child will be born female is dependent solely upon the genetic information contained in the sperm of the man. The sex of the child is not determined by genetic information from the ova from the woman's body. In a similar manner, Paul affirms "for the man is not of the woman." His statement confirms that the sex of the male child is not determined by the mother. In fact, the sex of the child is dependent solely on the sperm of the father. It is the father's sperm containing either the X or the Y chromosome that will determine the sex of the baby. Tragically, throughout history, many wives have been unjustly repudiated by their aristocratic or royal husbands because they bore female offspring rather than male children. However, science now knows that the sex of the baby is entirely determined by the sperm of the father, exactly as indicated by the Scriptures two thousand years ago.

The Virgin Birth of Jesus of Nazareth

Both the Old Testament prophecies and the New Testament histories agree in affirming the virgin birth of Jesus of Nazareth. Significantly, the first prophecy in the Bible predicted the miraculous virgin birth of the promised Messiah. The prophetic words of God revealed that the Messiah would be of the "seed" of the woman. Since all children are produced naturally by the "seed" of the man, this curious prophecy revealed the mystery of the virgin birth of our Lord. This unique expression "her seed" has no parallel in the rest of Hebrew literature, within or outside of the pages of the Bible. Since all of Hebrew literature and common sense affirm that a child is born of "his seed," the sperm of a man, it was unusual and unprecedented for the Bible to declare that the future Messiah, the victor over Satan, would be born supernaturally from a virgin as "her seed." "And I will put enmity between thee and the woman, and between thy seed and her seed; it shall bruise thy head, and thou shalt bruise his heel" (Genesis 3:15).

The prophet Isaiah also predicted the supernatural nature of the birth of Jesus 740 years before the event in the following verse, "Therefore the Lord himself shall give you a sign; Behold, a virgin shall conceive, and bear a son, and shall call his name Immanuel" (Isaiah 7:14). Some scholars have disputed this prophecy of the virgin birth of Christ. They have rejected the King James translators' choice of the word "virgin" to translate the Hebrew word העלמה *almah* that is used by Isaiah in this verse. However, the Hebrew word *almah* is normally translated as an "unmarried young woman." The question is this: Does העלמה *almah* refer to a young, moral, virginal, unmarried woman, or does the word refer to an immoral, sexually experienced, young, unmarried woman. As far as I can determine, the word *almah* always refers to a "an unmarried young woman" who is a virgin, as indicated in Strong's Concordance reference to a "damsel, maid, virgin."

Only an immoral society would suggest that "an unmarried young woman" does not refer to a virgin. Furthermore, the prophet Isaiah refers to the fact that this "almah" would "conceive, and bear a son" as a prophetic "sign" given by the Lord to the nation. If the skeptics were correct in their assertion that the word *almah* does not denote that the woman was a virgin when she gave birth to the son, then we must ask the question: Where is the prophetic "sign"? According to the critics, the prophet Isaiah simply predicted that an "almah," an "unmarried young woman," would have sexual relations with a man and give birth to an illegitimate son. If this was correct, where is the prophetic "sign?" Immoral young women give birth to sons everyday worldwide. There is nothing unusual about this that would qualify this event as a prophetic "sign" to Israel of the coming of their Messiah. Obviously, this refusal to accept the normal meaning of the word "almah" as a "young unmarried, virgin woman" is a vain attempt to evade the clear prophecy of Scripture that foretold the miracle of the virgin birth of the coming Messiah.

Finally, the Gospel records the historical fact that Jesus of Nazareth was supernaturally born to the virgin Mary (Matthew 1:23). This "virgin birth" of Jesus was essential to fulfill the ancient prophecies of the coming Messiah. If Jesus had been born as the result of the union of the natural seed of a man and woman, He would not have qualified as the perfectly innocent and sinless Son of Man. However, in addition to separating Jesus of Nazareth from all other humans born of a mother, the virgin birth of Christ ensured that His blood would be unique from all other human blood. He would therefore be the perfect sacrifice for the sins of mankind. The genetic information that produces the blood in the body of the unborn baby is produced solely from the genetic information in the sperm of the father. That is why there are paternity blood tests (as opposed to maternity blood tests) to determine the father of a child. Every person's blood is determined by the father. As a result of the virgin birth, Jesus of Nazareth was the first person in history who did not have within Him the sin-tainted blood of Adam that has been passed down to every human through every generation from Adam until today. Since Jesus had no biological father, it was essential for God to create His blood by means of a special miracle.

Jesus Was Supernaturally Conceived in the Womb of Mary

The New Testament writers referred clearly to the virgin birth of the Messiah. The Gospel writer Luke recorded the inspired message of the angel Gabriel to Mary, the mother of Jesus: "And, behold, thou shalt conceive in thy womb, and bring forth a son, and shalt call his name Jesus" (Luke 1:31).

The Holy Scriptures proclaim that Jesus was supernaturally

conceived by God within the womb of Mary (without the necessity of a male sperm) as God's true Messiah. Modern medicine reveals that normal human conception (the union of the male sperm and the female ova) takes place within the female body as the sperm meets the ova in the fallopian tubes of a woman. However, the Holy Scriptures declared that God caused the conception of Jesus to supernaturally occur within the womb of Mary, the chosen vessel to be the mother of our Lord. This biblical statement confirms the true supernatural nature of the conception and birth of Jesus.

The Value of PI Revealed in the Bible

An astonishing discovery was made by Shlomo Edward G. Belaga that appeared in Boaz Tsaban's Rabbinical Math section on the Internet. In addition, a number of other sources have recently examined this interesting subject. The discovery indicates that the scientific value of PI, which enables us to accurately calculate the precise circumference of a circle, is contained in the Bible.

The Bronze Laver in Solomon's Temple

And he made a molten sea, ten cubits from the one brim to the other: it was round all about, and his height was five cubits: and a line of thirty cubits did compass it round about. And under the brim of it round about there were knops compassing it, ten in a cubit, compassing the sea round about: the knops were cast in two rows, when it was cast. It stood upon twelve oxen, three looking toward the north, and three looking toward the west, and three looking toward the south, and three looking toward the east: and the sea was set above upon them, and all their hinder parts were inward. And it was an hand breadth thick, and the brim thereof was wrought like the brim of a cup, with flowers of lilies: it contained two thousand baths. (1 Kings 7:23–26)

This huge bronze laver was used by the priests to wash themselves and the rest of the Temple worship objects connected with the Temple sacrifices.

A paraphrase of the key passage would read as follows:

"He [King Solomon] made the Sea of cast metal, circular in shape, measuring ten cubits from rim to rim [the diameter was 10 cubits] and five cubits high. It took a line of thirty cubits to measure around it. [The circumference was equal to 30 cubits]."

Everyone of us can remember our geometry classes in high school in which we learned that the formula to calculate the precise value of a circumference was the value of PI times the diameter of the object to be measured. The precise value of PI was extremely difficult to calculate until fairly recently.

The Declared Scientific Value of PI = 3.1415926

A casual reading of 1 Kings 7:23 appears to suggest that the Scriptures declared that the value of PI was only 3. The text says the huge cast metal basin was ten cubits wide (18 feet) and that its circumference was precisely thirty cubits around. In other words, it looks as though the biblical writer was mistaken and gave only a rough approximation of the value of PI as being equal to 3 by mistakenly stating that the circumference of the basin was only ten cubits.

However, a careful analysis of this passage by some Israeli scientists and rabbis has revealed a mysterious feature in the language of this Hebrew text that provides a startling revelation of the wisdom of God regarding the true scientific value of PI.

The normal Hebrew word for "line" or "circumference" קו is spelled with two letters: qof ק and vav ו.

But, in this particular verse, 1 Kings 7:23, the word for "circumference" is spelled with an extra letter heh ה. This unusual spelling of circumference with the additional letter is קוה.

The ancient Jews did not have Arabic numerals so they used each of the 22 letters of their alphabet to stand for numbers. Thus they spelled out their numbers, such as the number 5, using the Hebrew letter heh ה. Similarly, the number 100 is indicated by the Hebrew letter qof ק, and the number 6 is indicated by the Hebrew letter vav ו.

Since the unusual spelling of "circumference" in 1 Kings 7:23 is קוה the Israeli rabbis noted that this indicated a formula. The numerical value of קוה is 111:

Qof ק = 100 + Vav ו = 6 + He ה = 5, which total 111.

However, the usual spelling of circumference is קו, whose whole letters add up to 106:

Qof ק = 100 + Vav ו = 6, which total 106.

Expressed as a mathematical formula, the unusual spelling of "circumference" would read as follows:

$(111/106) = (3.14150943 \ldots /3)$

Remember, that the real scientific value of PI = 3.1415926 . . .

The difference between $3 \times 111/106$ [3.14150943 . . .] and the true value of pi (3.1415926 . . .) is only 0.0000832, which is only an error of 0.00026%.

Due to the inherent limitations of expressing numbers in the form of Hebrew letters, this revelation of the value of PI in 1 Kings 7:23 is as close as the biblical Hebrew language could come to expressing this extremely precise number.

This calculation indicates that the ancient Scriptures included this astonishingly accurate calculation of the value of PI indicating the tremendous engineering knowledge available to King Solomon, the wisest man in history according to the Scriptures.

Notes

1. Charles Darwin. *The Origin of Species*. (London: J.M. Dent & Sons Ltd., 1971) 167.

2. E. Mayer. *Systematics and the Origin of Species*. (Columbia: University Press, 1942) 296.

14

The Coming Collapse of Evolution

The main philosophical position that underlies much of the attack on the authority of the Bible as the inspired Word of God is based on an almost universal acceptance of the theory of evolution. This widely held evolutionary theory itself is based on an assumption of atheism — that there is no God and that everything in this universe, including mankind, has accidentally evolved from dead, inanimate matter by random chance over billions of years. This fundamental rejection of the existence of God and His role as the Designer of Creation provides the intellectual climate within which the educational and scientific communities espouse the theory of evolution. Moreover, the theory of evolution provides the only other possible alternative to Creation that can explain the amazing complexity of biological life on this planet.

I will not attempt an exhaustive refutation of the theory of evolution in this chapter. However, the fundamental importance of this topic demands that we examine the mounting evidence that evolution is about to collapse of its own weight. This topic is vital to all who wish to come to terms with the authority of the Bible because the Scriptures clearly teach us that God created the heavens and the earth by His marvellous design with a purpose to create man in His own image. This biblical doctrine that is taught from Genesis to Revelation is fundamentally contradicted by the theory of evolution which denies the existence of God and proclaims that man lives in an accidental universe without purpose, plan, or design. If evolution is true, then the Bible and the words of Jesus Christ are false. It is as clear as that. When the world abandoned the biblical teaching that God created the heavens and the earth, they substituted a theory of evolution that made man nothing more than a random accident in a meaningless universe with no absolutes of good or evil.

The reason this subject is so important is the powerful contradiction that exists between the paradigm of Christianity and the world view of evolution. They are so fundamentally opposite that there is no possibility that both can be true. Therefore, this inherent conflict produces a dangerous double-mindedness in the minds of millions of Christians who have been educated from elementary school to the university in the theory of evolution as if it was an absolute truth. At some point in their lives Christians enter into a personal relationship with Jesus Christ as their Lord and Savior, based on their acceptance of the teaching of the Bible about the nature of Jesus, His sacrifice on the Cross, and their hope for salvation and heaven. If they never receive adequate information that proves to them that evolution is flawed, they continue to hold within their mind the unchallenged teachings about evolution taught to them through their schools and television. On the one hand, they hold the belief, based on their education, that evolution is true and that logically the Bible's account of God's special creation of the universe must be false. On the other hand, they are trusting for their salvation, their peace of mind and their hope of heaven based on their belief that the Bible is absolutely true in all of its statements regarding the nature of Jesus Christ, salvation, and heaven.

Do you see the problem? If evolution is true then logically the Bible is fundamentally false in its teachings about the creation in its first book, Genesis. If evolution is true, then Jesus Christ would have to be mistaken when He spoke approvingly of the biblical account of the creation of the universe and Adam. If evolution is true, then it would be illogical to trust your very soul on the belief that the Scriptures are wrong about Creation but are absolutely trustworthy regarding the rest of the Bible's doctrines including salvation and hell. If the Bible is false about Creation, how can we know that it is true in its other doctrines. In other words, if a Christian simultaneously holds to a belief in evolution and his belief in the truthfulness of the Bible, then he is in serious danger of being a "double minded man." The apostle James wrote, "A double minded man is unstable in all his ways" (James 1:8).

I believe that a major reason for the weakness of the Church today, as well as the weakness of many Christians in their daily walk and in witnessing to others about their faith, is the fact that they have accepted the truthfulness of the theory of evolution without examination. As a result, they have a profound but often unrecognized weakness in their faith in Christ and in the teachings of the Bible because they have never come to terms with the contradictions between their biblically based faith and their acceptance of the theory of evolution. This contradiction is seldom thought about consciously, but it is so profound that it can not help but affect their general confidence in the truth of the Scriptures and, thus, weaken their daily faith.

When we examine the lives, deaths, and statements of faith of Christians in past centuries, we find evidence of an unshakable faith in Jesus and the truthfulness of the Scripture. This confidence motivated millions of believers to face torture and bloody martyrdom rather than deny their faith in Jesus Christ. Where did this faith come from? What motivated these believers to count their lives as insignificant in comparison to their utter confidence in the Lord Jesus Christ as taught in the beloved pages of Scripture? The evidence of history is overwhelming that Christians in past centuries were motivated by a profound love and trust in the absolute authority and inspiration in the Word of God. This faith in the trustworthiness of the Bible motivated the reformer Martin Luther to stand before the German authorities who held his life in their hands and say to them, "Here I stand. I can do no other." It was the firm confidence of the Reformers in the truth of the Holy Scriptures that motivated their rallying cry "Sola Scripture," an affirmation that their faith and doctrine were based solely on the divine revelation in the pages of the Bible.

The Theory of Evolution

The theory of evolution suggests that all living things on earth have come into being through accidental, natural processes that began with a primeval mass of subatomic particles and radiation billions of years ago. Evolution is taught as if it is a fact, not a theory, in the universities and schools throughout the world. Although the theory was popularized by Charles Darwin almost one hundred and fifty years ago, it remains just that — a theory — because the evidence to prove it has not been found.

In fact, the scientific problems and inconsistencies of evolution are so overwhelmingly obvious that it faces collapse on all fronts. The only thing holding the tattered theory of evolution together is the overwhelming desire of millions of people to hold on to evolution regardless of its weakness because the alternative is "unthinkable" to its practitioners. The only logical alternative to evolution to any thinking person is obviously the theory that a supernatural being — God — actually created the universe and man. The idea of God as Creator ruled Western society for almost nineteen hundred years. However, during the last one hundred years, the widespread rejection of the Bible's authority and its claim for God's special creation of life has produced a virtual monopoly for the evolutionary theory in our lifetime.

A fascinating book, entitled *The Intellectuals Speak Out About God*, was published a few years ago that astonished many readers with its revelations about the recent scientific discoveries that disprove evolution. These scientists discuss numerous scientific discoveries that support both special creation and the existence of God as the great Designer.

Professor Stephen D. Schwarz explained that many of the latest discoveries of science have illustrated the impossibility that this complex universe and life itself could have formed by random chance, no matter how old we assume the universe is.

> Until recently it was thought by many people that science supports atheism, that science is even the rational alternative to theism. It is now clear that science not only does not support atheism, but even lends rational support for theism. There is strong scientific evidence for God. Scientists, without presupposing God or creation, without trying to prove them, have come up with findings that strongly support God, His creation of the universe and man, and a supernatural purpose for the world we live in.[1]

Where Did the Universe Originate?

There are four fundamental scientific reasons why the universe and life itself could never have come into existence without a supernatural Creator. One of the most fundamental of all scientific observations is known as the Second Law of Thermodynamics. This law of science states that the total amount of usable energy throughout the universe is constantly decreasing. In other words the universe is running down, the constant loss of its original usable energy, which means the universe is ultimately running out of usable energy. This law is fundamental in science because scientists have never found a single exception to this observation. The obvious conclusion is that the universe must have been created at some point in time and has been running down ever since. This means the theory of some early evolutionary scientists that the universe has always existed is false.

In addition, since the universe is running down there must have been some point in the past when it began with the original totality of energy available — the moment of its beginning or creation. However, the question that must be faced is this: Where did the universe and its massive energy come from and when did it begin? It is illogical to believe that the universe came into existence out of nowhere accidentally, by random chance, without a designer or creator. The only logical conclusion is that the universe was created out of nothing by a Creator with an intelligent design and supernatural power. That Creator is God.

The Impossibility That a Prebiotic Soup Ever Existed on Earth

The second fundamental problem faced by evolutionary theory is the absolute impossibility that life was spontaneously generated from inanimate or nonliving elements. The evolutionist accounts for the chance development of life from nonliving matter by imagining that the earth's oceans in the distant past (in a universe without life) were an unusual chemical mixture they call "prebiotic soup." In other words they suppose that the oceans were accidently filled with all of the essential chemicals and that some energy source, possibly lightning, somehow stimulated these chemicals to bond together over billions of years by purely random chance to spontaneously generate life from nonliving material. Although it seems improbable that this spontaneous generation of life could occur by chance without a designer or purpose, the evolutionist is forced to imagine this actually occurred. Since he rejects the possibility of a supernatural God, he is forced to accept the only other rational alternative — random chance.

Professor Chandra Wickramasinghe, an eminent British scientist, describes the absolute impossibility of this prebiotic soup ever forming in the oceans of earth by random chance to create even the possibility of life being spontaneously generated over billions of years. The professor concluded:

> One of the earliest questions that was raised in connection with the primordial soup was deciding whether at any early stage in the earth's history, if there was a situation when the earth's atmosphere was not of its present character, that is, it was reducing rather than oxidizing. We looked at this rather carefully, and we decided that the earth's atmosphere was never of the right character to form an organic soup . . . we published this in a book under the title of *Lifecloud* . . . Geochemists and geologists have now come round; they now go on to say that the primordial soup had to be imported from outside . . . There's no way it could have developed upon the Earth . . . The organic soup itself is not such a marvellous thing. It is a prerequisite for any biological activity to start; that's certainly true. But it doesn't follow that if you have an organic soup it could get life started . . . And when we looked at the probabilities of the assembly of organic materials into a living system, it turns out that the improbabilities are really horrendous, horrific in extent and I concluded along with my colleague that (this) could not have happened spontaneously on the earth . . . There's not enough time, there's not enough resources and there's no way in which that could have happened on the earth.[2]

The Impossibility of Spontaneously Generating Life From Non-Life

Let's, for the sake of argument, imagine that the impossible occurred by chance, producing this prebiotic soup. But, then what are the actual odds against the spontaneous generation of life from this "prebiotic soup." Biologists have calculated that the odds against these chemicals spontaneously generating life by random chance are one chance in $10^{40,000}$. This number is 10 to the 40,000 power. The odds are equal to 10 followed by 40,000 zeros! It is a number so large that the human mind can scarcely conceive of it. To put this in perspective, scientists have calculated that the total number of atoms existing throughout the known universe of 50 billion galaxies (each containing 100 million stars like our Milky Way) is only 10^{74}. That is 10 followed by 74 zeros. However, the odds against life being generated by random chance from dead matter are inconceivably less than your chance of locating one single target atom in a whole universe of atoms by travelling blindfolded through the universe in a spaceship aimlessly hoping to find a particular target atom by chance. Theorizing how an incredibly complex biological system could evolve by random chance from these processes belongs in the realm of pure fantasy, not science.

The truth is that biologists know that the probability of life being generated by chance out of nonliving chemicals is a virtual impossibility. However, many evolutionary scientists argue that, no matter how statistically impossible it is, life must have formed from dead matter by chance. Given billions of years, they argue that even the most statistically unlikely event might have occurred. This is pure blind faith in the religion of evolution! The truth is that the odds against life occurring spontaneously by random chance are so large that it is more probable that you would win the one million dollar grand prize in the Lottery every single night for the next ten thousand years in a row!

Some of the evolutionary scientists who admit that life could never have spontaneously evolved on earth have made a novel suggestion that either the prebiotic soup or life itself was brought to earth from another universe! They call this novel and totally bizarre theory "Panspermia," as noted in a February 1992 article in the *Scientific American* magazine. This is not science; it is science fiction! If the mathematical odds make evolution impossible on earth then the same odds make evolution impossible anywhere else. This desperation of the scientists reveals two things. Evolution is finally collapsing due to the total absence of evidence in its favor and the insurmountable problems with the theory that life evolved by chance. Secondly, their desperation reveals their real motive for holding to this discredited theory — their desire to escape the consequences of the existence of God. A British academic journal made an interesting admission regarding creation. "By spreading out creation in time and space, there is no reduction in the mystery" (*The British Journal for the Philosophy of Science,* 1954).

What About Natural Selection?

The evolutionary scientists argue that natural selection provides the answer as to why random chance would result in the progressive evolution of life. Natural selection requires continuous progressive development at every successive step. However, random evolution cannot possess understanding and planning and thus produce a half-formed heart as a transition in order to ultimately form a final heart. How could the heart have been produced by evolution in stages as natural selection demands it to have been formed by step by step mutations in gradual stages? Obviously, until the heart was fully formed and functional it was of no use whatsoever. "It seems that evolutionists, whether consciously or unconsciously, have regarded the blind and inanimate forces of the environment, or nature, as having the ability to create and think."[3]

How Could the Hemoglobin in our Blood be Produced by Chance?

Dr. David Humphreys of McMaster University recently gave a speech called "Evidence for a Creator" in which he suggested that conventional science has produced substantial evidence that the universe, and hence life on Earth, was created by an intelligent rational being (a speech at the University of Waterloo, Canada on July 12, 1997). Dealing primarily with the evidence from chemistry and biology, Dr. Humphreys compared the theory of evolution which suggests everything was produced by random chance, against the theory that an intelligent being, namely God the Creator, created the universe.

Dr. Humphreys suggests that it is statistically improbable and unreasonable to assume that the universe was created by pure chance, given the statistical improbability of life occurring on earth, the complexity and diversity of biological life forms, and the current estimated age of the universe. For Humphreys, it is more logical and more consistent with current scientific evidence to conclude that the universe and life were produced as a result of intelligent design. Dr. Humphreys noted that hemoglobin molecules in our blood are composed of twenty amino acids that occur in nature. These twenty amino acids could be arranged by random chance into a total of 10^{650} possible chemical combinations. However, only one of those nearly infinite combination would produce the correct complex hemoglobin molecule that is essential for the blood system of billions of animals and human beings. "The simultaneous formation of two or more molecules of this complexity is so improbable as to be inconceivable . . . Some people argue that given enough time the improbable may become probable. Although five billion years for the age of the earth sounds like a long time, it is actually less than 10^{18} seconds. If the sequence of each protein molecule could be changed a thousand times per second, there could be only a total of 10^{67} sequences in five billion years."[4] In other words, even five billion years would not be enough time for evolution to form the haemoglobin in our blood by random chance.

Professor Chandra Wickramasinghe discussed his conclusions from his years of research on the possibility of life forming in this prebiotic soup in the earth's oceans by random chance.

And from the point of view of geo-chemistry and terrestrial experiments, if you look at the early earth as a possible site for manufacturing life, it turns out that the case is non-existent, I would say, for such a thing happening on the earth . . . All that I am sure about is that life could not have happened on the earth spontaneously.[5]

Professor Chandra Wickramasinghe has written that years of laboratory research has provided powerful evidence that the evolutionary theory of the development of biological life on earth is simply impossible. The scientist concluded that complex biological life could not have formed by chance even if we supposed that the prebiotic soup existed on earth (the evidence shows that the prebiotic soup could not have formed on earth). Furthermore, even if we suppose that a simple form of micro-organism life actually formed by chance (which has been proven to be impossible) the evolution of that simple life into the complex forms as witnessed in millions of insect species, etc. is still impossible.

These scientists have shown that every one of the essential steps required by the evolutionary theory is fatally flawed.

Furthermore, even if every one of the these essential steps to evolve life by chance was possible (and they are not possible), the evolution of increasingly complex life forms from simple one-celled biological life forms by random mutations is still impossible. Professor Wickramasinghe summarizes the absurdity of this theory.

> If you start with a simple micro-organism no matter how it arose on the earth, primordial soup or otherwise, then if you just have that single organizational, informational unit and you said that you copied this sequentially time and time again, the question is does that accumulate enough copying errors, enough mistakes in copying, and do these accumulations of copying errors lead to the diversity of living forms that one sees on the earth. That's the general usual formulation of the Theory of Evolution . . . It's been claimed that the combination of the mistakes and the selection leads to the steady evolution of life. We looked at this quite systematically, quite carefully, in numerical terms. Checking all the numbers, rates of mutation and so on, we decided that there is no way in which that could even marginally approach the truth. On the contrary, any organized living system that developed or emerged say in the form of a microbe, 4 billion years ago, if it was allowed to copy itself time and time again, it would have destroyed itself essentially . . . For every favorable mutation there will be hundreds of unfavorable mutations.[6]

Aside from the obvious impossible odds against a particular species of life developing by random chance without design, we need to keep in mind that there are more than three million existing species of insects, together with thousands of species of mammals, reptiles, and birds. Remember, for evolution to be true, every one of these millions of individual species would have needed to beat the unimaginably large odds against the accidental evolution of its own species. To anyone who is willing to look at these odds, it is obvious that the origin of millions of separate species cannot be explained by the theory of evolution.

The Evidence of Design

The huge advances in genetic research in the last four decades have enabled scientists to unlock some of the vast mysteries of the DNA genetic code which determines the formation of every organ in your body, the color of your eyes and whether or not you will have black hair or blonde. The recent science called *Information Theory* allows us to analyse mathematically the information patterns of a written language such as English. Recently researchers studied the information patterns encoded in the double helix DNA of simple, one-celled bacteria. Incredibly, the scientists discovered that identical mathematical information patterns exist in human language as exists in DNA. The information patterns in a language such as English can be mathematically analyzed because the information forms a purposeful pattern. Obviously, by definition, information in a language is purposeful, not random. If words were thrown together by random chance, they would not convey information. When we find words in patterns of sentences expressing meaningful information, we naturally conclude that this information was created by an intelligent mind like our own.

All living biological organisms are incredibly complex. When we examine the simplest one-celled bacterial organism, we discover an almost unbelievable complexity of miniaturized design that make the technical specifications for a modern automobile look relatively simple. Biologists realize that the simplest cell is not simple at all. A cell is an enormously complex structure that is far more complicated than a computer. The smallest of cells is composed of over fifty billion atoms arranged into one hundred different proteins, together with the staggering amount of information encoded in the DNA and RNA that govern its activities, nutrition, repair, and replication. The problem for evolution is that it takes all of the above to function at all. You can't start with part of this material because everything is necessary to function as a whole.

Dr. A. E. Wilder-Smith wrote about the awesome complexity of the biological cells:

> When one considers that the entire chemical information
> to construct a man, elephant, frog, or an orchid was
> compressed into two minuscule reproductive cells [sperm

and egg nuclei], one can only be astounded. In addition to this, all the information is available on the genes to repair the body (not only to construct it) when it is injured. If one were to request an engineer to accomplish this feat of information miniaturization, one would be considered fit for the psychiatric clinic.[7]

Logically, the discovery of incredibly complex information patterns encoded within the double helix DNA genetic code governing all biological life provides overwhelming evidence that an intelligent designer must have created this DNA. Professor Geisler wrote about the significance of the DNA information patterns, "It is scientifically necessary to point to intelligence as the cause of the first living cell." The Bible reveals that this supernatural intelligence is God: "In the beginning God created the heaven and the earth" (Genesis 1:1).

When the evolutionary scientist examines fossils, he finds that very complex entities appear quite suddenly in the fossil record without any evidence of simpler forms existing before them. For example, the trilobites, which supposedly evolved in the far-distant past, are found with incredibly complex compound lens in their eyes. The only answer that fits the evidence is that each of these marvelously designed species was created in perfection by a supernatural designer.

However, when we consider the design of the human brain, we are filled with absolute awe. The human brain weighs only three pounds but this small organ is now known to be the most complicated and masterfully designed machine in the universe. The complex design of the brain is far in advance of the greatest computers ever designed or that man could ever design. Each of our brains contains up to fifty billion neurons, special communication cells, as well as an additional three hundred billion glial cells. Incredibly every one of the fifty billion neuron cells is connected with every other neuron cell. Each microscopically small neuron cell has thousands of slender dendrites which interconnect with other dendrites from other neurons. The point of connection between these dendrites is called a synapse. Some researches calculate that your brain contains up to a thousand trillion synapses. Astonishingly, recent research confirms that some neurons are communicating information to as many as

50,000 other neurons. This phenomenally complex design makes it possible for the brain to communicate amongst its billions of neurons instantaneously. As a result of this awesome design, our human brain can store and manipulate almost infinite amounts of data. The capabilities of the brain are staggering. Anyone who can declare that the marvelously complex brain evolved from a simple one-celled organism through random chance mutation is kidding.

The brilliant English astronomer Sir Fred Hoyle, the Professor of Astronomy at Cambridge University, wrote that it was virtually impossible that life has formed through evolutionary means. Professor Hoyle wrote this memorable phrase to describe the likelihood of evolution as a solution to the question of the origin of animals and man. "The chance that higher life forms might have emerged in this way is comparable with the chance that 'a tornado sweeping through a junk-yard might assemble a Boeing 747 from the materials therein.'"[8]

What About the Fossil Evidence — the Missing Links?

The theory of evolution declares that simple forms of life gradually mutated over long periods of time to produce successive and gradual changes in a species until it actually formed a new species. Charles Darwin was troubled by the fact that the new science of paleontology had failed to find a single fossil that provided any evidence of these transitional forms or "missing links." Darwin wrote, "I have asked myself whether I may not have devoted my life to a fantasy . . . I . . . am ready to cry with vexation at my blindness and presumption."[9] He also admitted, "If it could be demonstrated that any complex organism existed which could not possibly have been formed by numerous, successive, slight modifications, my theory would absolutely break down."

However, writing in 1850, Darwin optimistically predicted that, as more scientists joined the search, it was certain that thousands of these missing link fossils would show up in the fossil record and thereby prove the truth of his evolutionary theory.

Why then is not every geological formation and every stratum full of such intermediate links? Geology assuredly does not reveal any such finely graduated organic chain; and this, perhaps, is the most obvious and serious objection which can be urged against the theory. The explanation lies, as I believe, in the extreme imperfection of the geological record.[10]

In other words, Charles Darwin explained the total lack of missing links as a result of the fact that they had only begun in the 1850s to search for these transitional forms. These transitional forms are intermediate forms of life appearing in the fossils that would provide evidence of a stage between existing organisms and ones from the past. However, Charles Darwin was honest enough to admit that the absence of transitional forms or missing links would prove that his theory was false. Darwin wrote, "Why, if species have descended from other species by insensibly fine gradations, do we not everywhere see innumerable transitional forms? Why is not all nature in confusion instead of the species being, as we see them, well defined?" The obvious answer is that the well defined species found everywhere in the fossil record is precisely what you would expect to find if the theory of special creation of the universe and life by God's supernatural action is true. The Bible declares that God created each of the many species "after his kind" which is exactly what the fossil record confirms (Genesis 1:24, 25).

The evolutionists in desperation point to one single fossil, discovered in Austria, which is known as archaeopteryx. They boldly claim that this archaeopteryx fossil provides the absolute evidence of a "missing link" or transitional form between primitive dinosaurs and birds. However, despite the fact that this fossil displays a set of unusual teeth, everything else about the fossil reveals that it is a true bird, complete with fully developed wings, feathers, and warm blood. Although the presence of teeth is unusual, this in no way proves that this fossil was partly a bird and partly a dinosaur as the evolutionary textbooks proudly affirm. God has produced some very strange creatures on this planet, including the duck-billed platapus that has the duck of a bird but the other characteristics of a mammal. There is still no conclusive evidence of a single missing link, let alone the millions that must exist if the theory of evolution was true.

One hundred and fifty years after the death of Charles Darwin most evolutionary scientists are deeply embarrassed by the *total absence* of transitional forms in the fossil record. If evolution truly developed over millions of years, the planet would be filled with missing link fossils that would demonstrate the gradual series of mutations representing a continuum of change in the fossil record. However, biologists know that mutations are random, very small, and almost always harmful to the organism. This reality about the nature of mutations makes it impossible to believe that random mutations could account for the constant improvements in organisms that evolutionary theory demands. Virtually all mutations that have been observed in the laboratory have proven to be harmful, or even fatal, to the organism. Evolutionary scientists admit that more than 999 mutations in a thousand proved to be harmful or fatal.[11]

Despite the fact that tens of thousands of scientists and millions of dedicated amateurs have been searching worldwide for these missing link fossils for a century and a half they have never found a single example. Therefore, the evidence is clear that there is no evolutionary continuum. When the fossil record is carefully examined we find that it reveals both extinct species and existing organisms with clearly defined gaps between them with no transitional forms. This fossil record is precisely what you would expect to find if the Bible's account of special creation is true.

Does the Fossil Record Support the Theory of Evolution?

Dr. Stephen Jay Gold, the Professor of Geology and Paleontology at Harvard University, is a strong and eloquent supporter of evolution but he is honest enough to admit that the evidence from the fossil record does not support evolution. Dr. Gold admits that the number of transitional forms is extremely rare! How rare? The answer is Zero! They have never found one. Dr. Gold actually admits that the illustrations in the evolutionary science textbooks and documentaries are total inventions of creative artists because they do not represent scientific facts. Dr. Stephen Gold wrote the following statement in an article for *Natural History* magazine:

> The extreme rarity of transitional forms in the fossil record persists as the trade secret of paleontology. The evolutionary trees that adorn our textbooks have data only at the

tips and nodes of their branches; the rest is inference, however reasonable, not the evidence of fossils. Yet Darwin was so wedded to gradualism that he wagered his entire theory on a denial of this literal record: The geological record is extremely imperfect and this fact will to a large extent explain why we do not find interminable varieties, connecting together all the extinct and existing forms of life by the finest graduated steps. He who rejects these views on the nature of the geological record, will rightly reject my whole theory.[12]

Incredibly, Professor Gold admits that the claims of science textbooks that the fossil record supports evolution is false. "I wish only to point out that it was never 'seen' in the rocks . . . we view our data as so bad that we never see the very process we profess to study." In other words, he admits that the fossil record does not support the theory of evolution. Since special creation is the only logical alternative to the theory of evolution, the fossil record that only reveals distinct species actually supports the theory of special creation.

The Latest Evolutionary Retreat — Macroevolution or "Punctuated Evolution"

Many evolutionary scientists have admitted that the fossil record provides no evidence whatsoever of the transitional steps or missing links demanded by the evolutionary theory. However, they are now proposing a new theory of evolution called macroevolution or "punctuated evolution," in which they admit that there is no observed change in a species for millions of years and then, suddenly, these animals change spontaneously to a new species without any gradual or transitional process. This modification of Darwin's theory is, in fact, a total repudiation of his theory of gradual accumulated mutations over millions of years of uniform processes. The real motivation behind their creation of this new theory of "punctuated evolution" is their growing embarrassment that no fossil evidence has been found that shows gradual transitions from simple forms to more complex forms of animals. According to this new theory, this rapid change in one generation accounts for the evolution without any evidence for gradual change remaining in the fossil record. This is not science!

This new theory is a vain attempt to explain the fact that *none* of the data in the fossil record provides evidence for the theory of evolution.

The Fossil Record Does Not Support Evolution

Professor Ronald R. West, Assistant Professor of Paleobiology at Kansas State University confirmed what Dr. Stephen Gold and others have finally admitted — the fossils do not support evolution at all. This fact of course is absolutely the opposite of what virtually every student in the western world was told during his or her science courses. We were constantly told in science and biology courses in high school that the fossil record "proves" the truth of evolution and totally contradicts the Bible's account of special creation. In May 1968 Professor West wrote an article in the scientific journal *Compass* in which he made the following admission:

> Contrary to what most scientists write, the fossil record does not support the Darwinian theory of evolution because it is this theory (there are several) which we use to interpret the fossil record. By doing so we are guilty of circular reasoning if we then say the fossil record supports this theory.[13]

What About the Twelve Fossils of Ape-Men Showing Evolution?

One of the most effective techniques to convince the average person that the evolutionary theory is true is the continual referral to the discovery of a series of twelve hominid fossils that were discovered during the last hundred and fifty years of paleontology. These "missing-link" ape-men creatures supposedly demonstrate the evolution from primitive apes to modern men. The evolutionists have confidently presented each of these discoveries as the promised "missing links," the ape-men which existed as the transition between our ancient ancestors, the apes and the evolution of modern version of homo sapiens. However, a detailed examination of the actual fossil record reveals an astonishing account of fraud, mistaken identification, and outright misrepresentation. Few readers of these "scientific" accounts of evolutionary discoveries of "ape-men" in the popular press know that these so-called hominids often consist of little more than a tooth, a jaw fragment, a portion of an elbow or knee joint. From this sparse material the scientist and their willing accomplices, the evolutionary textbook artists, create an imaginary illustration of a complete human being based on a single bone or tooth!

These evolutionary cavemen illustrations are accepted by the vast majority in our Western culture as overwhelming scientific proof that man developed by gradual transitions through evolutionary processes from an ancient monkey-like ancestor to the introduction of homo sapiens, modern man. However, a careful examination of the actual evidence reveals that this presentation of the evolution of man is a pure fiction based solely upon the underlying evolutionary presuppositions of the scientists. Some of these "discoveries" of small portions of bone and teeth were actually found miles away from the other bone particles that they connect together to form a complete new hominid fossil skeleton.

Other "discoveries" of hominid fossils have proven to be the bones of pigs, donkeys, or apes. Occasionally, these discoveries prove to be a complete hoax, such as the Piltdown Man that was accepted by scientists as legitimate for fifty years. Finally, detailed examination in 1953 proved that someone had placed a modern human skull cap on top of the jaw of an ape in the original site fifty years earlier. Hundreds of researchers and scientists wrote more than 500 treatises about the Piltdown Man as a direct ancestor of modern man during the fifty years that followed the discovery until it was proved that this was a cruel hoax.

Another important hominid fossil discovery is known as Ramapithecus, which was held forth as the primary "missing link" between apes and humans for nearly fifty years. However, few people understood that the whole imaginary skeleton of Ramapithecus was based solely on some teeth. Unfortunately for the evolutionary theory, someone examined the teeth and discovered that they were actually the teeth of a modern orangutan (an ape), not the teeth of an evolutionary ape-man.[14]

The Neanderthal Man convinced many that the scientists had proven the theory of the evolution. However, further research has proved that Neanderthal Man is a fossil of a modern man. The deformed skull was caused by serious damage to his brain. In fact, Neanderthal Man turns out to be a fairly recent human skeleton of a man who suffered from a vitamin D deficiency that produced the disease known as rickets which accounted for the ridges over the eyebrows and his curved leg bones. However, most people who were taught evolution in school still believe that we are descended from cavemen ancestors with heavy ridges on their eyebrows. Not one of the other fossilized skeletons have these raised eyebrows (that resulted from the disease of rickets). "Scientists have concluded that all of the so-called primitive features of Neanderthal people were due to pathological conditions, or diseases."[15]

My personal favorite character in the imaginary evolutionary lineup is the so-called Nebraska Man whose remains were discovered in 1922 in the western portion of the state of Nebraska. The head of the American Museum of History, Dr. Henry F. Osborn, announced that this was evidence of the "missing link" between ancient chimpanzees, Java Man and modern man. Detailed drawings of this illustrious caveman ancestor (and his wife!) with his club were printed in various publications including the *Illustrated London Times* in 1922. However, the artists had to create the entire skeleton, muscles, face, skull, and hair out of their pure imagination because the only thing the scientist actually found was *a single tooth*! The punch line to this sad evolutionary joke is that the single tooth finally turned out to be the tooth of an extinct pig.[16]

The discovery of another missing link, the "Lucy" found in Ethiopia, supposedly provided powerful evidence of another link in the evolution of man. The scientists announced that Lucy was about three and a half feet high, walked erect, and lived over three million years ago. Lucy was described as an early ancestor of modern humans. They catalogued Lucy as *"Australopithecus afaarensis."* However, few people knew that the knee joint used by the scientists to prove that Lucy walked upright as a human rather than an ape was found two miles away from the original discovery of bones. Only a fool would believe that this knee joint was positively related to the rest of her bones which were found two miles away. The scientists wisely refrained from telling the public about this small detail. It is well known in scientific circles that Lucy is another fiction in the ongoing tale of evolution. "Lucy — when they required a knee joint to prove that Lucy walked upright, they used one found more than 200 feet lower in the (earth) and more than two miles away."[17]

Further digging at the "Lucy" site found fossilized bones of extremely ape-like creatures with chimpanzee-sized forearms that made it very likely that these creatures walked on four feet as opposed to the erect walking on two feet by humans (*Nature*, 368:449–451 1994.). One of the most famous of the paleontologists is Richard Leakey, the son of the eminent evolutionary scientists Louis and Mary Leakey. Dr. Richard Leakey identified Lucy as a hominoid, a definite ancestor of mankind. However, Richard Leakey admitted that the paleontologists are often working from their imagination more than from the actual fossil evidence, which is usually so meager. "Our task is not unlike attempting to assemble a 3-dimensional jigsaw puzzle in which most of the pieces are missing, and those few bits which are at hand are broken!" Some of the scientists have candidly admitted that their preconceived opinions in favor of evolution govern to a great degree the conclusions they reach about their fossil evidence. Dr. Gareth Nelson of the American Museum of Natural History admitted this in the following statement. "We've got to have some ancestors. We'll pick those. Why? Because we know they have to be there, and these are the best candidates. That's by and large the way it has worked. I am not exaggerating."[18]

Nine of the Twelve "Missing Links" Have Been Proven to be Apes

An analysis of the so-called "missing link" evidence showing the evolutionary development of man from apes includes twelve supposed hominid fossils presented by evolutionary scientists as evidence of the gradual evolutionary transition from apes to man. However, recent research had proven that nine of these twelve examples of ape-men are actually extinct forms of apes or monkeys and have no relationship to modern humans. Significantly, these nine "missing link" fossil examples that have proven to be extinct apes or monkeys were found in geographic areas where apes and monkeys skeletons are found in abundance. These skeleton fragments are often deformed by the same common diseases experienced by people in past centuries including rickets, starvation, Paget's disease, syphilis, and arthritis. Many of these hominid skulls were believed to be ancient ape-men because the scientists did not know that the normal range of size for modern human skulls included the same small size as found in the skulls of the these so-called ape-men. Scientists have found that modern human skeletons throughout the world differ markedly in the size of the skull and various bones, but they are still modern humans. There is a fairly wide range of skull sizes in modern humans which accounts for the differences discovered in the skull fragments that scientists previously suggested belonged to a previous ape-man.

The nine "missing links" have been found to be fossils of well known representatives of the monkey or ape family of mammals. Each of these fossils were found in areas where monkeys and apes have lived for thousands of years. The nine so-called hominids (as evolutionary scientists call them) are listed as follows: 1. Pliopithecus; 2. Proconsu; 3. Dryopithecus; 4. Oreopithecus; 5. Ramipithecus; 6. Australopithecus Africanus; 7. Australopithecus Robustus; 8. Australopithecus Boisei; 9. Australopithecus Afarensis (Lucy).

The Remaining Three "Missing Links" are Proven to be Modern Humans

The remaining three "missing links" presented by evolutionists have recently been proven to be actual fossil remains of modern humans with no significant differences from our present human skeletons. These three modern human skeletons were found in areas where monkeys and apes never existed. These three fossilized remains that have been proven to belong to modern humans included:

1. *Homo Erectus*: His name refers to the demonstrated fact that he walked erect. The only reason evolutionists suggested he was a sub-human was the fact that this particular specimen had a somewhat smaller brain size than some modern humans. However, it has now been proven that the brain of Homo Erectus was almost the average size of most European men today.

2. *Neanderthal Man*: As mentioned earlier, this fossil was examined by medical experts and found to be a modern human being whose brain was deformed by the disease of arthritis deformans in addition to suffering ridges on the brow plus deformed legs as a result of prolonged vitamin D deficiency or rickets.

3. *Cro Magnon Man*: This fossil is indistinguishable from modern man. The sole reason for supposing that it was that of a

primitive cave man was the fact that it was found near a series of cave drawings that were considered primitive.

The final result of this analysis of the evidence regarding these missing links of evolutionary evidence, for the transition from apes to modern man, is that the evidence for evolution itself is missing. The evolutionary scientists have failed to find a single genuine transitional form between apes and men despite their constant search during the last 150 years.

The Anthropic Principle

In the last few decades scientists have increased their understanding of the known universe through massive additions to our scientific knowledge in a variety of fields including astrophysics, quantum physics, and microbiological genetic research. The sum total of our scientific knowledge is now doubling every twenty-four months — a staggering increase in information unprecedented in human history. We are surely witnessing the fulfillment of the curious prediction of the prophet Daniel made twenty-five centuries ago: "Seal the book, even to the time of the end: many shall run to and fro, and knowledge shall be increased" (Daniel 12:4).

Among the new discoveries made by science recently, one of the most fascinating is called the anthropic principle. This anthropic principle simply concludes that a staggering number of scientific variables such as the composition of our atmosphere, the distance from the sun, the chemical composition of soil are precisely what is necessary for life to exist and prosper.

Recent discoveries in the field of astronomy, for example, prove that human life could not survive if our solar system was even slightly different. An astronomer, Dr. Jastrow, declared that even a small increase in the nuclear forces that hold together all atoms would result in a universe of stars composed primarily of helium instead of the present universe in which stars are made of hydrogen. In a universe with slightly increased nuclear forces the helium stars would have burned up much more quickly than our hydrogen stars. If the nuclear forces were slightly less, the carbon atoms would not have formed. Without carbon atoms, life could not exist.

The same anthropic principle can be seen in the other scientific variables such as the force of gravity which would make life impossible if the force were either much greater or much less. The communication between every one of the trillion cells in our body is based on the earth's magnetic field. Therefore, a reduction of the strength of this magnetic field beyond a certain level would make biological life impossible. Life could not exist if our earth was either too close or too far from the sun which provides the necessities of life through a complete spectrum of radiation including visible light. The twenty-four hour rotation of our planet facilitates life. If the planet did not rotate one half of the globe would be desolate under the constant glare of the sun and the other half would freeze in perpetual darkness. In sum total, the scientists have concluded that there are dozens of these scientific factors that are precisely correct to facilitate life on this planet.

Professor Jastrow suggests that "the universe was constructed within very narrow limits, in such a way that man could dwell in it."[19] In other words, this evidence in support of the anthropic principle strongly argues that our universe and earth were designed for the life of man by an intelligent and supernaturally powerful Creator. The evidence of brilliant design demands that an intelligent Designer must have created that design, namely God. The recent discoveries of science provide overwhelming evidence that the simplistic view of the atheists that our universe and life could have arisen by random chance over billions of years is scientifically false. In summary these scientific discoveries demolish the evolutionary theory of the formation of life by random chance. These discoveries provide incontrovertible evidence that an intelligent Creator purposely designed and created both the universe and life itself.

Dr. Chandra Wickramasinghe suggested that the anthropic principle strongly supported the theory of special creation, as opposed to evolution. When he was asked if his scientific research proved that Charles Darwin's theory of evolution was fatally flawed, he agreed. When asked how he would evaluate the scientific arguments of the Creationists, who suggest that only God could have created the universe and life itself, Dr. Wickramasinghe responded, "You mean the arguments that are justifications of their position? I think they have a very good case by and large."[20]

The Strong Bias of Scientist and Educators
Towards Evolution

In the light of the overwhelming scientific evidence that evolution is not supported by the fossil record and that evolution is mathematically impossible the average reader must wonder why evolution has survived for so long as a universally taught theory. I believe the answer lies in the strong desire by many scientists and educators to escape the consequences of a belief in God and the truth that each of us has an appointment to meet God as our judge following our death. Supporters of evolution understand very clearly that, if evolution is false, then the only possible logical explanation for this universe and the complexity of life is that there is a God who has created us. This alternative conclusion is so unthinkable to many scientists that they will desparately hold onto the faltering theory of evolution to their dying day despite the absence of evidence to support it. Evolutionary scientist Arthur Keith has admitted: "Evolution is unproved and unprovable. We believe it only because the only alternative is special creation which is unthinkable."[21] In reality, these scientists demonstrate a blind faith in their scientific religion of evolution that will ignore all evidence that contradicts their theory. Their realization of the scientific weakness of evolution is the real reason evolutionists are so determined to keep the theory of special creation out of the schools and universites. Evolution can only survive if no one is allowed to challenge it with the facts.

Some evolutionist are honest enough to admit that evolution is a matter of faith as opposed to pure science. Professor G. A. Rerkut of the University of Southampton (London) expressed his conclusion regarding the attitudes of scientists on biogenesis (evolution): "It is therefore a matter of faith on the part of the biologist that biogenesis did occur and he can choose whatever method of biogenesis happens to suit him personally; the evidence for what did happen is not available."[22]

Dr. Henry Morris was a firm believer in evolution until he began to examine the evidence critically for himself. He soon realized that the whole theory was not supported by scientific evidence at all but that evolution had become a new religion for those who wished to escape the consequences of the truth of the Bible about a personal God, salvation, and judgment.

Many . . . believe in evolution for the simple reason that they think science has proven it to be a 'fact' and, therefore, it must be accepted . . . In recent years, a great many people . . . having finally been persuaded to make a real examination of the problem of evolution, have become convinced of its fallacy and are now convinced anti-evolutionists."

In the last decade numerous evolutionists have admitted that the actual scientific evidence in the fossil record does not support the theory of evolution. Some scientists have acknowledged that they have not found any evidence at all in the fossil record of animals with partially developed organs such as legs, brains or eyes. Yet their theory of evolution, if true, demands that the fossil record must contain millions of such examples.

A strong supporter of the theory of evolution, T. L. Moor, wrote, "The more one studies paleontology, the more certain one becomes that evolution is based on faith alone."[23] Another evolutionist, Dr. Miles Eldredge, has written, "We paleontologists have said that the history of life supports (the story of gradual adaptive change), all the while really knowing that it does not."[24] Another evolutionist scientist, Dr. Solly Zuckerman admitted the truth when she wrote, "(the record of reckless speculation of human origins) is so astonishing that it is legitimate to ask whether much science is yet to be found in this field at all."[25]

Dr. Paul Davies wrote about his personal beliefs and his estimate of the views of other physicists in a fascinating article entitled "The Christian Perspective of a Scientist" in the academic magazine *New Scientist*. Dr. Davies wrote, "The temptation to believe that the Universe is the product of some sort of design, a manifestation of subtle aesthetic and mathematical judgement, is overwhelming. The belief that there is 'something behind it all' is one that I personally share with, I suspect, a majority of physicists" (Paul Davies, *New Scientist*, June 1983, p. 638). Another evolutionist, D. M. S. Watson, admitted: "Evolution itself is accepted by zoologists, not because it has been observed to occur or can be proved by logical coherent evidence, but because the only alternative — special creation — is clearly incredible."[26]

The Biblical Flood of Noah

The Bible's account of a worldwide Flood provides an alternative explanation for much of the geological and fossil evidence that has been produced by scientists in support of their theory of evolution. For those who wish to study the geological evidence for the Flood in depth, I strongly recommend Dr. Henry Morris's excellent study *Scientific Creationism* and Dr. John C. Whitcomb's book *The World That Perished*. Naturally, the evolutionary scientists reject out of hand the theory that the biblical account of the Flood is a true description of an historical geological event. However, a worldwide flood would have produced ideal conditions to create massive numbers of fossils in sedimentary rock.

The Evidence For Noah's Flood in the Ancient Traditions

Obviously, if a worldwide flood actually occurred as the Bible affirms, such a devastating event would leave an indelible mark on the historical memory of various races throughout the world. In addition to the written account in the Bible we would expect to find widespread traditions of a flood in many nations. The Scottish geologist Hugh Miller searched the historical records and found an astonishingly number of Flood accounts among widely dispersed nations and tribal groups throughout the world.[27] Evolutionary critics of the Bible's Flood account often suggest that if there is any truth to the Flood story, then it must have been a local flood. However, the Bible's description of the flood reaching to the heights of the highest mountains proves that Moses was recording a worldwide flood. In addition, a local flood would not have justified the building of the Ark. Why not just instruct Noah's family to migrate to the high mountains to escape a local flood? The area of Mesopotamia is quite flat, which means a flood would inevitably cover a vast area.

Some critics suggest that the Bible's account could not be accurate because Mount Everest and other high mountains now reach to a vast height of several miles above sea level. Does this mean the waters reached many miles in depth? The answer is found in the fact that the Bible suggests that massive geological changes took place as a result of the Flood both during and after that event. Therefore, it is entirely possible that the world before the Flood did not possess the massive mile-high mountains that exist today. Marine scientists have confirmed that there is enough water in the oceans of the world to cover the entire globe to a depth exceeding one mile if the earth was smooth with no deep ocean trenches and no high mountains. Therefore there is ample water to accomplish the Bible's account of a worldwide flood. Furthermore, the explorers and sociologists during the last two centuries discovered that virtually every nation and tribe on earth possesses an ancient tradition of a worldwide flood, the survival of a man and his family with animals in a large boat, as well as stories about the replenishing of the human race following the deluge.

The Babylonian Story of the Noah and the Flood

Beyond doubt the most remarkable flood tradition outside the Bible's own account is found in the ancient tablets of Babylon that were miraculously discovered in the last century during excavations in ancient Mesopotamia. Several years ago I was able to examine the copy of the Deluge Tablet on display at the British Museum in London. Many scholars believe that this four thousand year-old Babylonian clay tablet may be one of the most important inscriptions yet discovered. The Deluge Tablet is the eleventh book of the larger Chaldean *Epic of Gilgamesh*. It has been dated approximately 2200 B.C. Gilgamesh is another name for Nimrod, a name that appears in the biblical Genesis account. This Babylonian account of the Flood is found in the eleventh book of the epic poem because the eleventh month of the ancient Babylonian year was known as the "Month of the Curse of Rain." This month was also known as the "Month of Destruction," and corresponds to the eleventh sign in the Babylonian astrology Zodiac, the sign of Aquarius, the sign associated with fish and water. In this epic poem, the story of the Flood is told to Gilgamesh by his ancestor Nuh-Napishtim, also called Atrahasis, "the very wise or pious" (the Chaldean Noah).

This account of the Flood is of tremendous importance because it contains a number of startling parallels to the biblical account of the Flood as found in the book of Genesis. The Flood, with its destruction of virtually the complete animal kingdom and the death of every human on earth except for Noah's family, would obviously have left its mark on the consciousness of mankind. If such a cataclysmic event actually occurred, you would expect to find a universal race memory of the Flood in the ancient histories and literature of the oldest human cultures. In addition to the detailed biblical account recorded by Moses in the book of Genesis, scholars have discovered a surprising number of Flood accounts in the histories of other peoples that display an astonishing number of parallels with the biblical account. While these nonbiblical accounts naturally contain a number of variations from the Genesis account, the discovery of numerous key points in these stories that parallel the Flood story provide strong evidence that this historical event truly occurred as recorded in the Bible.

Parallels Between the Babylonian Deluge Tablet and the Genesis Flood

In the Deluge Tablet in the *Epic of Gilgamesh* the flood is a punishment of the "gods" for man's sin, exactly as described in the Genesis account. Atrahasis (the Chaldean Noah) and his family were worshippers of Ia, the god of deep waters. The "gods" decreed a flood to punish mankind's sins and overwhelming violence ("the city was full of violence"), as also described in Genesis. Significantly, both accounts record these key events occurring in the same geographical area. Atrahasis (Noah) was commanded to build a ship to protect himself, his family, (and the ship builders), as well as a variety of animals. The ship (ark) was built with a deck house or covering and was covered with bitumen (pitch) both inside and outside exactly as Genesis described ("within and without"). The rainfall lasted only six days and nights in the Babylonian epic as opposed to the Bible's account of "forty days and forty nights."

It is fascinating to note that both accounts record that Atrahasis (Noah) sent forth three birds in succession to ascertain the conditions outside the ark. In both accounts three birds were sent forth from the ark, including a raven and a dove. Both stories record that the last bird failed to return, indicating that it had found a safe home. The two flood accounts record that the ark finally rested on a mountain top at which point the survivors come forth from the ark to offer sacrifice to God. Both histories record that God (or the gods) promised to never again punish mankind with a flood. In the conclusion of the Gilgamesh account, Atrahasis (Noah) and his wife begin to rebuild mankind in a renewed land in what is now known as Iraq-Iran. This is paralleled in the Genesis account as Noah and his family begin to replenish the earth following their departure from the ark. Some of the most important confirmations of the statements found in the Genesis account that are also found in the Babylonian Flood account as noted below in italics.

The Deluge Epic of Gilgamesh

(Key Phrases from the 11th Tablet of the Epic of Nimrod)
(Haupt, Nimrod-Efos, No. 70.)

Nuh-napishtim (the Chaldean Noah) saith to him, even to
     Gilgamesh (Nimrod);
Let me unfold to thee, Gilgamesh, a secret story,
And the decree of the gods let me tell thee
Shurippak, a city thou knowest,
On the bank of Euphrates it lieth;
That city was full of violence, and the gods within it,
To make a flood their heart urged them, even the mighty gods.

Man of Shurippak, son of Ubara-Tutu,
Pull down the house, *build a ship.*
Leave goods, seek life.
Property forsake, and life preserve.
Cause seed of life of every sort to go up into the ship.
The ship which thou shalt build . . .

I will [go] down to the Ocean, [and] with my, [Lord] will I dwell
[Upon] you it will rain heavily . . .

I laid down its form, I figured (or fashioned) it:
     I chose a mast (or rudder-pole), and supplied what was necessary:
Six sars of bitumen I poured over the outside,
Three sars of bitumen [I poured over] the inside . . .

With all that I had of seed of life of every sort [I freighted it] . . .
I put on board all my family and my clan;
Cattle of the field, wild beasts of the field,
all the craftsmen, I put on board . . .

When the Lord of Storm at even tide causeth the heavens to rain
    heavily,
"Enter into the ship, and shut thy door." That time came:
The Lord of Storm at even tide caused the heavens to rain heavily.
I dreaded the appearance of day;
I was afraid of beholding day:
I entered the ship and shut me my door . . .

When the seventh day came, storm (and) flood ceased the battle . . .
The sea lulled, the blast fell, the flood ceased.
I looked for the people, with a cry of lamentation;
But all mankind had turned again to clay:
The tilled land was become like the waste.
I opened the window, and daylight fell upon my cheeks . . .
The mountain of the country of Nizir caught the ship . . .
But when the seventh day was come,
I brought out a dove (and) let it go.
The dove went to and fro, but found no foothold, and returned.
Then I brought out a swallow (and) let it go.
The swallow went to and fro, but found no foothold, and returned.
Then I brought out a raven (and) let it go: The raven went off,
noticed the drying of the water, and feeding, wading, croaking, returned
    not.
Then I brought out (everything) to the four winds, offered victims
    (sacrifices)
Made an offering of incense on the mountain top. . .

Nuh-napishtim shall dwell far away, at the mouth of the rivers
Then they took me, and made me dwell far away, at the mouth
    of the rivers
(the site of Paradise at the mouth of the four rivers including
    Euphrates).

Other Historical Traditions of a Worldwide Flood

Numerous additional historical accounts of the Flood are
found in the traditions of every one of the six inhabited continents.
These independent traditions strongly support the truthfulness of
the Bible's account.

The Phrygian Flood Account

For example, one of the most interesting of the Flood traditions is the Phyrgrian flood tradition that tells us that someone named Nannakos (Enoch), who reached the age of 300, predicted the coming Flood and wept tears in anticipation of the coming deluge. This parallels the biblical account in Genesis where the righteous man Enoch, who walked with God, became the father of a son named Methusalah at the age of 65 and lived for 300 more years. whose His son's name "Methusalah" means "After he goes, it happens." The tradition of the Jewish sages is that Methusalah died on the very day the Flood began. However, the most interesting part of the Phrygian flood account is the fact that a Medal of Apamea (A.D. 201-210) was struck in the mint of Phrygia during the reign of the Roman emperor Septimius Severus which illustrates the Flood account in detail.

The Phrygian Medal of Apamea Showing Noah's Ark

This wonderful Medal of Apamea provides powerful historical confirmation of the Flood from ancient times. Several of these fascinating medals have been found that illustrate a rectangular barge-like ark floating in the water. Through a window of the ark we can see the image of two people, a man and woman. It is fascinating to note that a bird is seen resting on the roof of the ark while another bird is seen flying back to the ark with a branch in its feet exactly as described in the biblical account in Genesis 8:11. Another portion of the medal illustrates the same two people leaving the ark to walk on dry land. Incredibly, several of these Phrygian medals bear an additional inscription containing the Greek letters NΩ or NΩE which means "After the Flood" written on the sides of the ark as illustrated in the medal shown above. This two thousand year-old medal provides powerful historical evidence that the biblical account of the Flood is true.

Other examples of flood traditions are found in Greece where the historian Pindar wrote about their memory of the flood around the fifth century before Christ. The Roman writer Ovid confirmed these ancient flood traditions in which the fountains of the deep were opened to unleash the flood waters that drowned almost the whole race of mankind. Aside from the Greeks and Romans we find few ancient European legends of the Flood for the simple reason that the widespread distribution of the Bible's account of Noah's Flood throughout Europe, as a result of the efforts of Christian missionaries in the early centuries of this era, replaced whatever independent ancient traditions remained about the Flood with the true biblical account from Genesis.

Many of these flood traditions were recorded by the eminent sociologist Professor James George Frazer in his fascinating book *Folk-Lore in the Old Testament* [28]. The North American Athapascan Indian tribes that lived on the West Coast tell about an ancient flood in which the rains continued until the earth was totally covered with water. All animals and birds died in the subsequent flood. Another Indian tribe, the Papago Indians of Arizona, have a tradition that God made man from some clay. When the great flood came, a man named Montezuma and a coyote who predicted the flood survived in a large boat which he built on a mountain. When the flood was over, Montezuma sent the coyote to search the land to verify the water had receded. The Mongolian peoples of northern Asia also have a strong flood tradition.

The Sudanese tribes in East Africa believe there was a massive flood in which a leader named Noh survived. The Hawaiian natives have a tradition that after mankind developed from one man the people became evil and disobeyed God. When the flood came, one righteous man named Nu-u survived with his family by building a huge canoe and filling it with plants and animals. The Mexican natives tell the story that a man named Coxcox saved himself, his family, his animals, and grain from the great flood by building a huge boat. When the waters receded, Coxcox sent out a vulture which did not return because it ate the floating carcasses. Then he sent other birds including a hummingbird that returned with a twig with leaves. The Indian tribes of Alaska relate that their tribal father was warned in a dream of the coming flood. He build a large boat in which he saved his family and all of the animals by floating for many moons on the flood waters.

Sociologists have discovered flood traditions involving boats and animals in the South Sea islands, including Polynesia, Tahiti, New Zealand, and New Guinea. The peoples of India possess strong flood traditions in which a righteous man with the name Manu received a warning that a great flood was coming. He was commanded to build a great ship and fill it with foods of all kinds. When the flood waters came, God commanded Manu to embark upon the ship with seven other people together with ample provisions including all seeds. Manu and his seven companions survived the flood and landed on the highest mountain in the Himalayas. Later Manu became the father of the new race of mankind. The startling parallels to the biblical account include the righteousness of the leader, eight survivors, a large boat, a long flood, the landing on a mountain, together with replenishing the human race.

Professor Hugh Miller added a remarkable detail from this Indian flood tradition in the Sanskrit literature that appeared more than six centuries before the birth of Christ. This righteous Manu became drunk after drinking mead wine and fell asleep naked. Charma, one of his three sons, discovering his naked father, called his brothers to witness his father's drunken shame. The Indian tradition records that the two responsible brothers took some clothes and respectfully covered their father's nakedness. When Manu awakened from his drunkenness, he immediately recognized that Charma had despised him. As a result, Manu cursed his sinful son Charma by declaring, "Thou shall be a servant of servants." This astonishing parallel with the details of the biblical account of Noah's Flood is verified by Hugh Miller's detailed research.

In China they tell the story of a universal flood that destroyed all of mankind with the exception of Fah-he and his family who survived in a boat. Furthermore the Chinese record that Fah-he survived with his wife, his three sons and their wives, precisely eight people as found in the Genesis account. The ancient Egyptian historian Manetho recorded the Egyptian flood tradition in his book written in 250 B.C. A worldwide flood destroyed everyone except Toth and his family. It is fascinating that the Egyptian priest celebrated Toth's survival of this flood by launching a sacred ark onto the sea on the 17th day of Athyr, the same day recorded in the Bible.

The discovery in the last two centuries that virtually every nation and tribe on earth have deeply held traditions of a worldwide flood in the ancient past that destroyed most of humanity save a man and his family who were preserved in a large boat filled with animals and food provides a wonderful confirmation of the truthfulness of the biblical account of Noah's Flood. It is impossible to explain why widely dispersed peoples throughout the globe would simultaneously develop such an astonishing story of a worldwide flood with such agreement in the precise details unless a real historical event actually occurred in the distant past.

Ultimately, when we consider the truthfulness of the biblical account of the Flood we need to examine the evidence from both the Bible and from recent discoveries from the scientists that provide fascinating evidence about the earliest ages of mankind. In this connection we should consider this question carefully: "Why not consider the possibility that life is what it so evidently seems to be, the product of creative intelligence? Science would not come to an end, because the task would remain of deciphering the languages in which genetic information is communicated, and in general finding out how the whole system works. What scientists would lose is not an inspiring research program, but the illusion of total mastery of nature. They would have to face the possibility that beyond the natural world there is a further reality which transcends science."[29]

In conclusion, the inspired Word of God commands us to follow the words of our Lord and Saviour who instructs us as follows:

> If any of you lack wisdom, let him ask of God, that giveth to all men liberally, and upbraideth not; and it shall be given him. But let him ask in faith, nothing wavering. For he that wavereth is like a wave of the sea driven with the wind and tossed. For let not that man think that he shall receive any thing of the Lord. A double minded man is unstable in all his ways (James 1:5–8).

Finally, the Bible tells us in the clearest language that God is the Creator of both our universe and mankind. The Scriptures instruct us to consider the inspired words of the Bible that command us to consider these instructions from the Word of God:

> For the wrath of God is revealed from heaven against all ungodliness and unrighteousness of men, who suppress the truth in unrighteousness; because that which may be known of God is manifest in them; for God hath shewed it unto them. For the invisible things of Him from the creation of the world are clearly seen, being understood by the things that are made, even His eternal power and Godhead; so that they are without excuse: because that, when they knew God, they glorified Him not as God, neither were thankful; but became vain in their imaginations, and their foolish heart was darkened. Professing themselves to be wise, they became fools. (Romans, 1:18–22).

Notes

1. Roy Abraham Varghese, ed., *The Intellectuals Speak Out About God* (Chicago: Regnery Gateway, 1984) 100–103.

2. Chandra Wickramasinghe, *The Intellectuals Speak Out About God* (Chicago: Regnery Gateway, 1984) 25–26.

3. B. G. Ranganathan, *Origins?* (Carlisle: The Banner of Truth Trust, 1988) 11.

4. David Humphreys, speech, "Evidence for a Creator," University of Waterloo, Canada, July 12. 1997.

5. Chandra Wickramasinghe, *The Intellectuals Speak Out About God* (Chicago: Regnery Gateway, 1984) 25–29.

6. Chandra Wickramasinghe, The *Intellectuals Speak Out About God* (Chicago: Regnery Gateway, 1984) 29.

7. A. E. Wilder-Smith, *The Illustrated Origins Answer Book* (Gilbert, AZ: Eden Communications, 1995) 25.

8. Fred Hoyle, "Hoyle on Evolution," *Nature*, vol. 294 (12 November 1981) 105.

9. Wendt, Herbert, *From Ape to Man* (New York: The Bubbs Merril Co., 1972) 59.

10. Charles Darwin, *The Origin of Species* (London: J. M. Dent & Sons Ltd., 1971) 292–293.

11. Henry, M. Morris, *Evolution and the Modern Christian* (Phillipsburg, NJ: Presbyterian and Reformed Publishing Co., 1988).

12. Jay Gold Stephen, *Natural History* (May 1977) 14.

13. Ronald R. West, *Compass*, vol. 45 (1968) 216.

14. Duane T. Gish, *Evolution: The Fossils still say No!* (El Cajon, CA.: Institute For Creation Research, 1995) 326.

15. Duane T. Gish, *The Amazing Story of Creation from Science and the Bible* (El Cajon, CA: Institute for Creation Research, 1990) 81.

16. Duane T. Gish, *Evolution: The Fossils still say No!* (El Cajon, CA.: Institute For Creation Research, 1995) 326.

17. Duane T. Gish, *The Amazing Story of Creation from Science and the Bible* (El Cajon, CA: Institute for Creation Research, 1990) 83.

18. Garth Nelson, *Lucy's Child* (New York: William Morrow and Co., 1989) 74.

19. Robert Jastrow, *The Intellectuals Speak Out About God* (Chicago: Regnery Gateway, 1984) 100–103.

20. Chandra Wickramasinghe, *The Intellectuals Speak Out About God* (Chicago: Regnery Gateway, 1984) 36.

21. B. G. Ranganathan, *Origins?* (Carlisle: The Banner of Truth Trust, 1988) 22.

22. G. A. Rerkut, *Implications of Evolution* (London: Pergamon Press, 1960) 150.

23. B. G. Ranganathan, *Origins?* (Carlisle, PA: The Banner of Truth Trust, 1988) 22.

24. Philip Johnson, *Darwin on Trial* (Washington, D.C.: Regnery Gateway, 1991) 59.

25. Philip Johnson, *Darwin on Trial* (Washington, D.C.: Regnery Gateway, 1991) 82.

26. D. M. S. Watson, B. G. Ranganathan, *Origins?* (Carlisle: The Banner of Truth Trust, 1988) 22.

27. Hugh Miller, *The Footprints of the Creator* (New York: Robert Carter and Brothers, 1881).

28. James George Frazer, *Folk-Lore in the Old Testament* (London: MacMillan and Co., Ltd., 1919). ′

29. Phillip Johnson, *Darwin on Trial* (Washington, D.C.: Regnery Gateway, 1991) 110.

15

Who Do You Say That I Am?

When Jesus came into the coasts of Caesarea Philippi, he asked his disciples, saying, Whom do men say that I the Son of man am? And they said, Some say that thou art John the Baptist: some, Elias; and others, Jeremias, or one of the prophets. He saith unto them, But whom say ye that I am? And Simon Peter answered and said, Thou art the Christ, the Son of the living God.   (Matthew 16:13–16)

"Whom say you that I am?" This question by Jesus Christ is the most fundamental and important question you and I will ever answer. Upon our answer to that question lies our present happiness, the forgiveness for our sins, and our eternal reconciliation with God in heaven. If we reject the claims of Jesus as the true Son of God, we will have, in effect, chosen to be our own God — our own supreme being in our life. The eternal consequences of such a choice are beyond the scope of human language to express. If we reject the only salvation that God offers to us, then we will end our lives as unrepentent sinners, and will have chosen to go to our deaths in permanent rebellion against God.

Throughout the pages of the Scriptures, we read the claim that Jesus is the Messiah, the Son of God. Furthermore, the Bible declares that His death on the Cross is the only acceptable sacrifice that will pay the full price of our sins. The apostle Paul warns mankind of this in his epistle to the church at Rome, "For the wages of sin is death; but the gift of God is eternal life through Jesus Christ our Lord" (Romans 6:23). As a result of our sins, each of us has walked away from God in disobedience. The problem is this: How can we ever be reconciled to a holy God when we have been rebelling against God all our lives? Every person who has lived on earth has rebelled against God and lived their life as a sinner. The apostle Paul declared, "For all have sinned, and come short of the glory of God" (Romans 3:23).

There is nothing in our sinful nature that would make it possible for us to totally reform and stop sinning. Even if the impossible occurred, we would still be barred from the gates of heaven because of our past sins. The only way to live with God in heaven after this sinful life is to somehow become holy. But it is impossible for us to accomplish this on our own. Paul declared that the only way we would "see the Lord" was to walk in "holiness." "Follow peace with all men, and holiness, without which no man shall see the Lord" (Hebrews 12:14).

God knew that the only way we could ever be reconciled to Him and become capable of entering heaven forever was to transform those of us willing to repent of our sins. Paul explained God's purpose in bringing salvation to those who would confess their sins in this passage: "To the end he may stablish your hearts unblameable in holiness before God, even our Father, at the coming of our Lord Jesus Christ with all his saints" (1 Thessalonians 3:13).

One of the most important decisions a person must make is what you will do with the written revelation of God found in the Bible. Your decision as to whether or not the Bible is truly the inspired Word of God will profoundly affect every other area of your life. If the Bible is true, then we are accountable to Jesus Christ, and He will judge each of us at the end of our life. However, if the Bible is not the inspired Word of God, one could ignore its commands and warnings about heaven and hell. In the absence of the written revelation found in the Word of God, those who search for ultimate truth are lost and without any hope of finding it.

In light of the overwhelming evidence presented in *The Handwriting of God* regarding the inspiration and authority of the Bible, any unbiased person can conclude that only God could have produced the Bible. The evidence in this book proves that the

Scriptures contain scientific, archeological, and historical information that only God could produce. However, there are many people who will still state that they don't believe the claims of the Bible. The problem with those readers who still refuse to acknowledge the evidence for inspiration is not one of conviction; rather it is their lack of willingness to accept information that challenges their long-held positions. It is extremely difficult for most people to abandon their previously held agnostic positions. After years of defending such a liberal position, it is very hard to admit fallibility and submit to the truth. The problem is not an alternative explanation for creation; rather, it is a fear of how the acceptance of this information will mandate a change in their daily life.

Those who have previously rejected God and the Bible have made a huge emotional and intellectual investment in their declared position of agnosticism or rejection of the Scriptures. When they are faced with the evidence that proves the Bible is inspired by God, they naturally feel threatened because they must think seriously about God and their responsibility to Him. Many people have never seriously considered the claims of the Gospels about Jesus Christ. They have never even thought about the matter. Their denial of the authority of the Bible has shielded them against asking questions such as: What if the Bible is true? What if there truly is a heaven and hell? However, in light of the evidence presented in this book, we need to carefully consider the implications. If the Bible is truly the Word of God, then every one of us will stand before Jesus Christ at the end of our life to answer the question: Who do you say that I am?

On that day, those who have accepted Christ's salvation through His sacrifice on the cross will bow their knees willingly to Jesus knowing that their sins are forgiven by God. Their destiny will be to live joyfully with Christ forever in heaven. However, those who have chosen to reject the Bible and Christ's salvation will be forced by their irrevocable decision to bear punishment in hell forever. Many in our modern society are offended by the fact that the Bible says that there is only one possible way to be saved. However, the apostle Paul spoke about the absolute necessity of faith in Jesus Christ: "Neither is there salvation in any other: for there is none other name under heaven given among men, whereby we must be saved" (Acts 4:12). This declaration of Paul runs counter to the natural inclination of mankind to believe that all religions are equally true and that "all roads lead to Rome."

Many suggest that, as long as one is sincere, they will make it to heaven. This is a lie from the pit of hell. The Word of God declares that sincerity is not enough. If you are sincere in your faith, but have chosen to place your faith in a false religion, then you are sincerely wrong and lost for eternity. Why would Jesus Christ have willingly gone to the Cross for your sins if there were other equally valid ways to be reconciled to God?

One of the religious leaders of Israel named Nicodemus came to Jesus secretly one night to ask Him how he could be assured of salvation. The gospel of John records the answers Jesus gave to Nicodemus. Jesus told him, "Ye must be born again" (John 3:7). He explained to Nicodemus, "Whosoever believeth in him should not perish, but have eternal life. For God so loved the world, that he gave his only begotten Son, that whosoever believeth in him should not perish, but have everlasting life" (John 3:15–16). Every one of us is a sinner who therefore stands condemned by God. Jesus said, "He that believeth on him is not condemned: but he that believeth not is condemned already, because he hath not believed in the name of the only begotten Son of God" (John 3:18).

Your decision to accept Jesus Christ as your personal Savior is the most important decision you will ever make. This commitment will lift the guilt of sin from your heart and give you an abundant new life in Jesus. However, the Lord Jesus Christ asks His disciples to "follow Me." That decision and commitment will change your life forever. Your commitment to Christ will transform your life into one of joy, peace, and spiritual purpose beyond anything you have ever known. Jesus challenges each of us to consider the choices of life in terms of eternity, "For what shall it profit a man, if he shall gain the whole world, and lose his own soul?" (Mark 8:36).

If you are already a follower of Jesus Christ, I would like to encourage you to share this book with your friends and family. It is an effective way to share your faith in Christ. However, we need to remember that the evidence that the Bible is inspired by a supernatural God will not, of itself, lead anyone to a personal faith in Christ. That decision to follow Christ is a fundamental choice of each person to choose spiritual life over spiritual death by responding to Christ's offer of salvation. However, the evidence supporting the supernatural origin of the Bible presented in this book may assist someone in taking the Scriptures seriously and considering the claims of Jesus Christ for the first time.

If you have never accepted Jesus Christ as your personal Savior, I pray that the evidence in *The Handwriting of God* persuades you that God has inspired the writers of the Bible to record His message to mankind. Someday you will meet Jesus Christ. Will you accept Him as your personal Savior and meet Him with open arms? Or will you reject Him and be forced to meet him as your final judge? The decision is yours.

Selected Bibliography

Anderson, Christopher. *The Annals of The English Bible*. Vol. 1 & 2. London: William Pickering, 1845.

Anderson, Sir Robert. *Human Destiny*. London: Pickering & Inglis. 1913.

Aviezer, Nathan. *In The Beginning . . . Biblical Creation and Science*. Hoboken: KTAV Publishing House, Inc., 1990.

Ball, Rev. C. J. *Light From The East*. London: Eyre and Spottiswoode, 1899.

Bentwich, Norman. *Fulfilment in the Promised Land*. London: The Soncino Press, 1938.

Blomberg, Craig. *The Historical Reliability of the Gospels*. Leicester: Inter-Varsity Press, 1987.

Blunt, Rev. J. J. *Undesigned Coincidences in the Old and New Testament*. London: John Murray, 1876.

Bready, J. Wesley. *England: Before and After Wesley*. London: Hodder and Stoughton Ltd., 1939.

Bright, John. *The Authority of the Old Testament*. Grand Rapids: Baker Book House, 1967.

Burrows, Millar. *The Dead Sea Scrolls of St. Marks Monastery*. New Haven: The American Schools of Oriental Research, 1950.

Canton, William. *The Bible and the Anglo-Saxon People*. London: J. M. Dent & Sons, Ltd., 1914.

Cobern, Camden M. *The New Archeological Discoveries*. London: Funk & Wagnalls Co., 1929.

Duncan, J. Garrow. *Digging Up Biblical History*, Vol. I & II. London: Society For Promoting Christian Knowledge, 1931.

De Haan, M. R. *The Chemistry of the Blood*. Grand Rapids: Zondervan Publishing House, 1943.

Ebers, Georg. *Egypt: Descriptive, Historical, and Picturesque*, Vol. I & II. London: Cassell, Petter, Galpin & Co., 1878.

Finegan, Jack. *Light From the Ancient Past*. Princeton: Princeton University Press, 1946.

Finegan, Jack. *Archeological History of the Ancient Middle East*. New York: Dorsett Press, 1979.

Flavius, Josephus. *Antiquities of the Jews*. Grand Rapids: Kregal Publications, 1960.

Forster, Rev. Charles. *Sinai Photographed*. London: Richard Bentley, 1862.

Frazer, Sir James George. *Folk-Lore in the Old Testament*. London: Macmillan and Co., Limited, 1919.

Gaussen, L. *The Divine Inspiration of the Bible*. Grand Rapids: Kregel Publications, 1971.

Geikie, Cunningham. *The Holy Land and the Bible*. New York: James Pott & Co. Publishers, 1891.

Greenblatt, Robert B. *Search The Scriptures*. Toronto: J. B. Lippincott Co., 1968.

Jeffrey, Grant R. *The Signature of God*. Toronto: Frontier Research Publications, Inc., 1996.

Keith, Alexander. *Christian Evidences: Fulfilled Bible Prophecy*. Minneapolis: Klock & Klock Christian Publishers, Inc., 1984.

Keith, Alexander. *Evidence of the Truth of the Christian Religion*. London: T. Nelson and Sons, 1846.

Kenyon, Sir Frederic. *The Bible and Archeology*. London: George G. Harrap & Co. Ltd., 1940.

Kenyon, Sir Frederic. *The Story of the Bible*. London: John Murray, 1936.

Kenyon, Sir Frederic. *Our Bible and the Ancient Manuscripts*. London: Eyre and Spottiswoode, 1948.

Layard, Austen H. *Discoveries Among the Ruins and Nineveh and Babylon*. New York: Harper & Brothers, 1853.

Little, Paul. *Know Why You Believe*. Downers Grove: Inter-Varsity Press, 1988.

Loftus, William Kennett. *Travels and Researches in Chaldea and Susiana*. London: James Nisbet & Co., 1857.

Manniche, Lise. *An Ancient Egyptian Herbal*. London: British Museum Press, 1993.

Maspero, G. *History of Egypt*. London: The Grolier Society, 1900.

McDowell, Josh. *Evidence That Demands a Verdict*. Arrowhead Springs: Campus Crusade For Christ, 1972.

McMillen, S. I. *None of These Diseases*. Grand Rapids: Fleming H. Revell, 1984.

Mercer, S. A. B., ed. *The Tell El-Amarna Tablets*, vol. 1&2. Toronto: The Macmillan Company of Canada Limited, 1939.

Morris, Henry M. *Many Infallible Proofs*. El Cajun: Master Books, 1974.

Morris, Henry M. *Remarkable Record of Job*. Santee: Master Books, 1988.

Morris, Henry M. *The Bible and Modern Science*. Chicago: Moody Press, 1968.

Morris, Henry M. *The Biblical Basis for Modern Science*. Grand Rapids: Baker Book House, 1984.

Morris, Henry M. *Scientific Creationism*. El Cajun: Master Books, 1985.

Morris, Herbert W. *Testimony of the Ages*. St. Louis: William Garretson & Co., 1884.

Panin, Ivan. *The Writings of Ivan Panin*. Agincourt: The Book Society of Canada, Ltd., 1972.

Petrie, Flinders. *Seventy Years in Archeology*. New York: Henry Holt and Co., 1932.

Ragozin, Zenaide A. *Chaldea from the Earliest Times to the Rise of Assyria*. London: T. Fisher Unwin, 1886.

Rambsel, Yacov A. *Yeshu — The Hebrew Factor*. San Antonio: Messianic Ministries, Inc., 1996.

Rambsel, Yacov A. *Yeshua — The Name of Jesus in the Old Testament*. Toronto: Frontier Research Publications, Inc., 1996.

Rambsel, Yacov A. *His Name is Jesus*. Toronto: Frontier Research Publications, Inc., 1997.

Rappaport, S. *History of Egypt*. London: The Grolier Society, 1904.

Rosner, Fred. *Medicine in the Bible and the Talmud*. Hoboken: KTAV Publishing House, Inc., 1995.

Rawlinson, George. *History of Herodutus*, 4 vol. London: John Murray, 1875.

Richards, Lawrence O. *It Couldn't Just Happen*. Fort Worth: Word, Inc., 1989.

Robertson, A. T. *Luke the Historian in the Light of Research*. New York: Charles Scribner's Sons, 1923.

Robinson, John A. T. *Redating the New Testament*. Philadelphia: The Westminster Press, 1976.

Robinson, Gershon. *The Obvious Proof*. London: CIS Publishers, 1993.

Rule, William Harris. *Biblical Monuments*. Croydon: Werteimer, Lea and Co., 1873.

Sayce, A. H. *Records of the Past*, 5 vol. London: Samuel Bagster & Sons, Ltd., 1889.

Sheppard, Lancelot C. *Prophecy Fulfilled — The Old Testament Realized in the New*. New York: David McKay Co. Inc., 1958.

Siculus, Diodorus. *Library of History*. Cambridge: Harvard University Press, 1989.

Smith, George Adam. *The Historical Geography of the Holy Land*. London: Hodder and Stoughton, 1894.

Smith, William. *A Dictionary of the Bible*. Boston: D. Lothrop & Co., 1878.

Stanley, Arthur Penrhyn. *Sinai and Palestine*. London: John Murray, 1905.

Stone, Michael. *The Armenian Inscriptions From the Sinai*. Cambridge: Harvard University Press, 1982.

Stoner, Peter W. *Science Speaks*. Chicago: Moody Books, 1963.

Thompson, J. A. *The Bible and Archeology*. Grand Rapids: Eerdmans Publishing Co., 1972.

Thompson, William M. *The Land and the Book*. Hartford: The S. S. Scranton Co., 1910.

Tiffany, Osmond. *Sacred Biography and History*. Chicago: Hugh Heron, 1874.

Unger, Merrill F. *Archeology and the Old Testament*. Grand Rapids: Zondervan Publishing Co., 1954.

Varghese, Roy Abraham. *The Intellectuals Speak Out About God*. Chicago: Regnery Gateway, 1984.

Vermes, Geza. *The Dead Sea Scrolls In English*. London: Penguin Books, 1988.

Vermes, Geza. *Discovery in the Judean Desert*. New York: Desclee Co., 1956.

Vincent, Rev. J. H. *Curiosities of the Bible*. Chicago: R. C. Treat, 1885.

Vos, Howard. *Can I Trust The Bible?* Chicago: Moody Press, 1963.

Warfield, Benjamin Breckinridge. *The Inspiration and Authority of the Bible*. Philadelphia: The Presbyterian and Reformed Publishing Company, 1970.

Wilson, Bill. *A Ready Defense — The Best of Josh McDowell*. San Bernardino: Here's Life Publishers, Inc., 1990.

Wood, Percival. *Moses — The Founder of Preventative Medicine*. London: Society For Promoting Christian Knowledge, 1920.